Asian-Pacific Rim Logistics

For the next generation of Asian-Pacific Rimmers:
Marina, Joshua, Imogen, Jethro and Griffin

Asian-Pacific Rim Logistics

Global Context and Local Policies

Peter J. Rimmer

Emeritus Professor, School of Culture, History and Language, ANU College of Asia & the Pacific, Australian National University, Canberra, Australia

Edward Elgar

Cheltenham, UK • Northampton, MA, USA

Published by
Edward Elgar Publishing Limited
The Lypiatts
15 Lansdown Road
Cheltenham
Glos GL50 2JA
UK

Edward Elgar Publishing, Inc.
William Pratt House
9 Dewey Court
Northampton
Massachusetts 01060
USA

A catalogue record for this book
is available from the British Library

Library of Congress Control Number: 2014941538

This book is available electronically in the ElgarOnline.com
Economics Subject Collection, E-ISBN 978 1 78347 866 8

FSC
www.fsc.org
MIX
Paper from
responsible sources
FSC® C013056

ISBN 978 1 84720 628 2

Typeset by Servis Filmsetting Ltd, Stockport, Cheshire
Printed and bound in Great Britain by T.J. International Ltd, Padstow

Contents

Preface

This study stems from an opportunity as the Hanjin Shipping Chair Professor of Global Logistics to participate in creating the new Master of Global Logistics Management (MGLM) programme at Inha University, Incheon, Republic of Korea (South Korea). The programme's rationale is to assist the development of a new generation of logistics and supply chain professionals that would be capable of meeting the changing demands and evolving challenges arising from the globalization of logistics and extension of supply chains across national borders. The programme seeks to produce visionary logisticians and supply chain leaders within the Asian-Pacific Rim stretching from the Russian Far East to the Indonesian archipelago and, on occasions, encompassing Australia and extending to India. At a corporate level the programme's focus is to explore ways of enhancing operational excellence in organizations, building strategic leadership capabilities among logisticians and supply chain managers, and deepening the Rim's business network.

The MGLM programme has its origins in the rapid growth of the Asian-Pacific Rim's international trade in manufactured goods and the emergence of urban clusters, variously attributed to globalization, liberalization and deregulation, advanced information and communications technology, and multimodal transportation. These developments have intensified the demand for logistics education to support the Rim's dynamic economies.

This demand has led the students from the Asian-Pacific Rim to seek logistics education in Europe and North America. The highest achievers have been guided by prestige or reputation towards research-oriented universities. Those heading to the United States pore over the *US News and World Report's* (2013) ranking of the best business schools to target institutions with a strong emphasis on supply chain management. Others search the profiles of universities in Canada offering an array of bilingual logistics and supply chain programmes. Apart from similar broad-based programmes offered by the United Kingdom's universities, the country's specialist aviation, and ports and shipping programmes have proved attractive to students. Also appealing in continental Europe are the supply chain and logistics programmes within engineering, economics and management sciences, and the speciality offerings in ports and shipping.

Many of these students return from Europe and North America to work in Asian-Pacific Rim corporations, research institutes and universities. Nevertheless there is an acknowledged shortfall of logistics professionals to meet the increased demand, especially in the People's Republic of China (PRC). As student growth in Europe and North America has slowed, the academic institutions of these regions, with strong logistics and supply chain interests, are actively locating branches within the Rim. This raises the issue as to the relevance of overseas educational experience for the needs of the Rim's vibrant home economies.

In response, economies within the Asian-Pacific Rim, which hitherto have relied upon cross-border logistics education, are now seeking to develop their own capabilities. This has led to the proliferation of logistics courses not only to meet the local demand for knowledge and skills, but also to drive economic and social development. Regional economies want to gain their own share of the 'education industry', particularly as almost 80 per cent of total global demand for international education by 2020 is expected to be from Asia (Böhm et al., 2004).

Different educational models for teaching logistics and supply chain management have been developed within the Asian-Pacific Rim's wider region. These include the 'regional model' followed by Australia's RMIT University, which offers its supply chain and logistics management course from its hub in Melbourne to 'offshore' sites such as Shanghai and Viet Nam; the 'in-house model' providing a Master of Science programme in enterprise management at the Hong Kong University of Science and Technology (HKUST) that stems from collaboration between the School of Engineering and the School of Business and Management; and the 'Singapore model' where the Government has gone beyond attracting specialized logistics activities, developing an integrated regional distribution hub, and creating a supply chain management 'control tower', by recognizing that logistics education has a critical role to play in national competitiveness. Singapore's national approach has resulted in the National University of Singapore (NUS) partnering the Supply Chain & Logistics Institute at Georgia Tech (GT) in the Transport Logistics Institute Asia Pacific (TLI-Asia Pacific), which offers a Double Master Program: MSc in Logistics and Supply Chain Management (NUS) and MSc in Supply Chain Engineering (GT). This arrangement is part of an assemblage of 11 'elite' universities (ten from the USA and one from Germany), which is the basis of the Singapore Government's strategy to become the 'global schoolhouse', drawing students from across the world (Toh, 2012).

The Government of the Republic of Korea (ROK) wanted to devise its own educational model to respond to the logistics challenges and opportunities offered by its 'nutcracker' position, sandwiched between China and Japan, in order to become a hub for both logistics and education in Northeast Asia. Inha University took up the challenge to respond to these needs by seeking to develop new knowledge and viewpoints in logistics education based upon an interdisciplinary approach, which embeds engineering, economics and management science with culture and languages, and combines theory and practice (IUILC, 2012). This led to a 'global network model' that emphasizes the exchange of knowledge and people across national boundaries. Recognition of this need was one of the prime reasons why Inha University pioneered the Global U8 Consortium, and sought to collaborate in logistics education with universities drawn from Asia, Australia, Europe and North America to provide opportunities for staff and student exchanges.

In developing Inha University's Master of Global Logistics Management (MGLM) Program a distinction is made between core courses and two sets of electives (Rimmer et al., 2007). Core courses offer a range of common tools and techniques in logistics such as the design of distribution networks, gravity modelling and non-linear programming, demand forecasting, inventory control, warehousing, transportation, and revenue and pricing management. One elective stream covers aspects of business logistics, notably supply chain planning, design and evaluation, information and communications technology in logistics and supply chain management, innovation and leadership, financial aspects of supply chain management, and purchasing and supply management. The other elective stream focuses upon transport and communications modes, particularly the function of planning, scheduling and controlling activities related to shipping and port management, airlines and airport management, and logistics service management; multimodalism, covering 'the carriage of goods by two or more modes of transport' (for example sea–air combination); and intermodalism, involving 'a system of transport whereby two or more modes of transport are used to transport the same loading unit or truck in an integrated manner, without loading or unloading, in a (door to door) transport chain' (ESCAP, 2004, 1–4).

Given this intersectionist approach, in which business logistics and supply chain management overlap, my responsibility has been to develop the initial core module, entitled 'Global + Local Logistics', to provide a broad course overview by situating the Asian-Pacific Rim within its wider global logistics context, before supplying insights into the logistics policies of particular economies within the Rim (Figure P.1). Over the six years spent in developing and refining this conspectus, groups of postgraduate students at Inha University have canvassed the life histories, main ideas and key publications of a selection of scholars in logistics and supply chain management. Their number and representative publications have

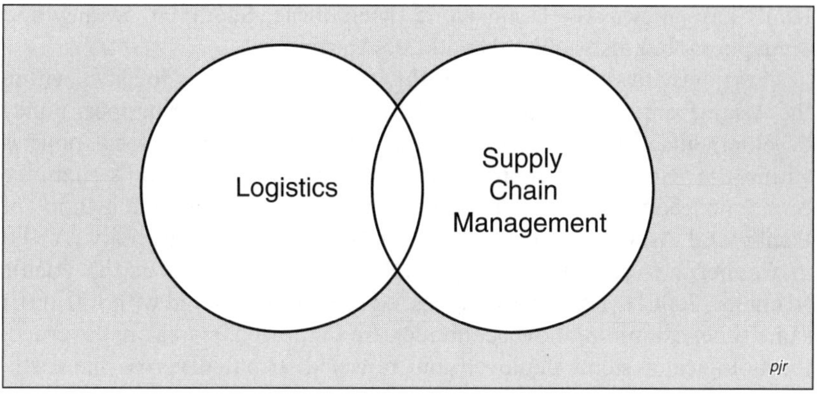

Source: Adapted from Larson and Haldorsson (2004, 19).

Figure P.1 The 'intersectionist' approach

included: Benjamin S. Blanchard (2004), Donald J. Bowersox (Bowersox et al., 2002), Mary R. Brooks (2008), Kenneth Button (Button et al., 1998), Sunil Chopra (Chopra and Meindl, 2013), Martin Christopher (2011), John J. Coyle (Coyle et al., 2011), Richard L. Daft (2008), John Gattorna (2010), Robert A. Handfield (Handfield and McCormack, 2008), Douglas M. Lambert (2008), C. John Langley, Jr (Coyle et al., 2003), Hau L. Lee (2004), John A. Quelch (2005), Yossi Sheffi (2005), David Simchi-Levi (Simchi-Levi et al., 2007), Tage Skjøtt-Larsen (Skjøtt-Larsen et al., 2007), Eiichi Taniguchi (Taniguchi and Nemoto, 2001), Thomas L. Vollman (Vollman et al., 2004), and Richard Wilding (Wilding and Braithwaite, 2004). Recourse has also been made to their websites (e.g. Wilding, 2013).

Conscious of the need to counterbalance the largely North American or European flavour of these logistics and supply chain texts, an attendant emphasis has been on highlighting Asian-Pacific Rim perspectives. Key regional texts on airports (Williams, 2006), air transport (Findlay et al., 1997; Oum and Yu, 1999), ports (Reveley and Tull, 2008), shipping (Hawkins and Gray, 2000) and a framework for studying Asian-Pacific supply chains and logistics operations (Oakden and Leonaite, 2011) have been examined. Insights from reviewing the regional literature have been complemented by class discussions of the context, issues, methodology and implications of specific papers on logistics and supply chain activities within the Rim. Students have undertaken internships with the Rim's global logistics service providers, and multinational manufacturing and retailing firms. Not only have site visits been made to some of the

Rim's key gateways – Hong Kong, Melbourne, Shanghai, Sydney and Singapore – but also to Dubai and Los Angeles.

These activities are reflected in this study, which puts logistics within the Asian-Pacific Rim into a global context before exploring local policy developments with the region itself. The examination of local policies within the Rim draws upon 50 years of studying the region's changing economic geographies while based in the former Research School of Pacific and Asian Studies at the Australian National University (ANU) in Canberra, Australia, now the ANU College of Asia & the Pacific (Rimmer, 2006a). These geographies 'cannot be considered without, at the same time, examining how economies are organized, states are governed, technological systems deployed and power distributed across the earth' (Toal, 2009, 51).

This exploration of global patterns and local policies within the Asian-Pacific Rim draws upon a wide range of case studies and statistical sources. As some statistical sources on logistics are tardy in publishing their annual reports, a 2010 baseline has been used for creating global patterns. The impact of major events that have occurred since that date, notably the Great East Japan Earthquake of 11 March 2011, tsunami and nuclear meltdown, and the Great Thailand Flood of late 2011, have been accommodated in the text.

A feature of this study is the emphasis on mapping global patterns and local logistics configurations to add an economic geographer's perspective to those of engineers, economists and management scientists that populate the emerging disciplinary field of logistics (Klaus and Müller, 2012; Maltz, 2012). Even in a mobile world, location is still of prime importance. Attention is paid to mapping both global and the Asian-Pacific Rim networks and flows. Geographical coverage is provided of the activities of key global logistics service providers and multinational manufacturers and retailers. The resultant maps were designed originally to communicate with students in cross-cultural exchanges. International border markings on these maps are for indicative purposes only, and may not be representative of actual international borders as recognized by sovereign nations. Given the old adage that a picture is worth a thousand words, it follows that a map must be worth a thousand pictures!

Acknowledgements

In undertaking this study I have received assistance from a wide range of people and organizations both within and beyond the Asian-Pacific Rim. In the Republic of Korea (South Korea) I have had the strong support of Dr Seoung-Yong Hong, both the 10th & 11th President of Inha University, and colleagues in its Asia-Pacific School of Logistics (APSL) and the Graduate School of Logistics (GSL), notably Professors Young-Tae Chang, Hun-Koo Ha, Hwa Jung Kim, Minsung Kim, Oh Kyoung Kwon, Sang-Yoon Lee, Jung Un Min, Kichan Park, Min-gyu Park, Yongwha Park and Jose Tongzon, and a legion of students on the Masters of Global Logistics Management (MGLM) course, technical officers, Wooyoung Jeong and Sung Hee Won, and an array of university administrators. Also the Graduate School provided opportunities for site visits to Hanjin Shipping, Hyundai Motor, Hyundai Shipping, Incheon International Airport, Samsung, LG and the ports of Busan, Gunsan and Incheon. Special mention must also be made of a former student, Jin-Hwan (Jennings) Bae, who has assisted my research endeavours in South Korea over more than eight years.

While in Korea I learned much from the international visiting faculty on the Masters of Global Logistics Management (MGLM) course during my period as the Inaugural Director, especially from Professors Jess H. Browning, Rommert Dekker, Charles Henri Fredouet, Thomas A. Grigalunas, Mary A. Hamilton, Booi H. Kam, Hirohito Kuse, Jang-hyuk Lee, Gerhardt G. Muller, Tae Hoon Oum, Edouard Reppert, Chris Whitaker and Anming Zhang.

Elsewhere in Korea I have had links with the Graduate School of Logistics in Northeast Asia at neighbouring Incheon University through Professor Hong-Seop Kim, and its inaugural chair, the late Professor Jun-il Soo, and with Professor Jin-hwan Kim from the Department of International Trade at Korea National Open University. Also I have enjoyed contacts with the Directors and staff of the Korea Maritime Institute (KMI) and the Korea Transport Institute (KOTI), particularly their respective librarians Mi-Gyeong Kim and Su-jin Kim. The Korean Port Economic Association invited me to their conferences, as did the Incheon International Airport Corporation.

In Japan I am indebted to the Asian Development Bank Institute, the Japan Transport Economics Research Center, the International Association of Ports and Harbours, particularly the late Rinnosuke Kondoh and the late Kimiko Takeda, the Japan International Freight Forwarders Association, especially Nobuyuki Kumazawa, the Institute of Supply Network Management and Strategy at Tama University, Professor Eiichi Taniguchi at Kyoto University, Hideo Yamada of the Japan Shipping Research Center, and representatives of Nippon Express, NYK Line and Nissin Corporation.

Within the People's Republic of China I have had many opportunities to observe logistics first hand in working on consultancies for the Asian Development Bank and the World Bank. More recently, I have worked with the Director and Staff of the Transport Research Planning Institute in Beijing, particularly Ran Fang, Li Xu, Jianguo Yang, Meizhen Gao, Xingyuan Yu, Xinoxia Yao and Jiaqiang Wang. Helpful advice was also received from Naijie Liu, Director-General of the *Journal of China Logistics and Purchasing*, Chaohe Rong from Beijing Jiatong University, and Wang Yankun from the Comprehensive Transport Research Institute, National Development Reform Commission. My thanks are also extended to provincial officials, transport and terminal operators, and manufacturers from Anhui, Hunan and Sichuan provinces.

Beyond the Asian-Pacific Rim I have had the opportunity to visit India to extend my interaction with Dr Prabir De and his colleagues at Research and Information System for Developing Countries (RIS). In the United States Amy St Peter at Armstrong & Associates at Madison, Debra Hofman formerly AMR Research, now at Gartner Inc., and Andrew Hok Fan Sze from the Fastraxx Group have provided responses to specific queries. In Dubai Alexander Borg, Consultant for the Middle-East Region, the Chartered Institute of Logistics and Transport, has also assisted.

In Australia I am grateful to colleagues in the Division of Culture, History and Language, College of Asia and the Pacific (CAP) at the Australian National University (ANU). Particular mention must be made of the camaraderie of Professors Kent Anderson (now University of Adelaide), Prem-Chandra Athukorala, James Fox, Stuart Harris, Hal Hill, Terry Hull, Igor de Rachewiltz, Gavan McCormack, Tessa Morris-Suzuki and the late Darrell Tryon.

Throughout my 47-year career at the University I have been indebted to the Cartographic Office of the then Research School of Pacific and Asian Studies (RSPAS), particularly the work of Ian Heyward and Keith Mitchell. On this occasion I have decided to draw my own figures, but I have benefitted immensely from the tutelage, advice and tweaking of Kay

Dancey, Jennifer Sheehan and Karina Pelling from CAP's Multimedia group. Sandie Walters from CAP's Information Technology Services, Tristan Peemoeller from MAC1 ANU Pty Ltd and Joe Rimmer have helped with specific computing matters.

My thanks are also due to the staff of the Asian Collections, National Library of Australia (NLA), Canberra: Amelia McKenzie (Assistant Director General); Alexander Philip (Director, Overseas Collections Management); Di Ouyang, Irina Chou, Jie Chen and Maihua Qi (China Unit), Tieke Atikah (Indonesian Unit); Mayumi Shinozaki, Rika Wright and Sumiko Kanazawa (Japan Unit); Jung-Ok Park and Jee-Young Lee (Korean Unit); and Sophie Virayong, Jane Hopkins and Lek McFadden (Thai Unit). Brendan Whyte from the NLA's Map Collection has assisted greatly with the location of railways in Asia prior to the Second World War. I have also received invaluable assistance from Yasna Palaysa and Anna-Maria Sviatko, the librarians of the Australian Government's former Department of Broadband, Communications and the Digital Economy (now the Department of Communications).

Elsewhere in Australia the late Peter Gilmour of the Graduate School of Management at Macquarie University provided me with an introduction to physical distribution management in the early 1970s. Since then I have been appreciative of the spirited interchanges with Howard Dick, my long-term collaborator from the University of Melbourne, on transport, and urban and regional development matters. He has learnt over the years that the most favourable response to his queries follows a Liverpool Football Club victory!

Professors Jin-bang Kim, Jong-kil Kim and Young-il Park from Inha University have made comments on specific chapters, as have Booi Kam from the Royal Melbourne Institute of Technology (RMIT) University and Matthew Rimmer from the Australian National University. Responsibilities for any errors and omissions remain with the author.

In producing this book my appreciation is due to Dr Sue Rimmer for her meticulous editing. Edward Elgar, Alex Pettifer and Alexandra O'Connell of Edward Elgar Publishing have been patient in awaiting its completion. Thanks are also due to Edward Elgar Publishing's production staff, notably Jennifer Stanley, Sue Sharp, Rebecca Hastie and Cathrin Vaughan.

On a more personal note, thanks are due to the extended Rimmer family in England, especially my late brother Dr Ralph W. Rimmer and his wife Mair, and the extended Ford family in Australia and its matriarch, Joane Ford. My children and their partners, Joseph and Belinda, Matthew and Susan, and Rachel and Arunas, and five grandchildren, Marina, Joshua,

Imogen, Jethro and Griffin, have brought me much pleasure. Above all, I am indebted to my wife, Sue, for her love and unstinting encouragement over the past 47 years.

Peter J. Rimmer
Canberra
2 March 2014

Permissions

The author and publisher wish to thank the following for permission to reproduce material:

- Figure 1.1: DHL Global Insight (Deutschland) GmbH for allowing data be drawn from a copyright figure.
- Table 1.1: Armstrong & Associates Inc. for approving its reproduction.
- Figure 1.4: Pearson Education Limited for consenting to the use and adaptation of Figure 2.3 in *Living Supply Chains: How to Mobilize the Enterprises Around Delivering What Your Customers Want* by John Gattorna (ISBN 9780273706144), p.43, and Figure 2.4 in *Dynamic Supply Chains: Delivering Value through People* (2nd edn) by John Gattorna (ISBN 978-0-273-73040-8), p.50, with the author's approval.
- Figure 1.5: Fukunari Kimura of both Keio University, Tokyo, and Economic Research Institute for ASEAN and East Asia (ERIA), Jakarta, for countenancing the copying of the diagram on the fragmentation of production.
- Figure 1.6: Pearson Education Limited for agreeing to the reproduction of Figure 9.1 in the fourth edition of *Logistics and Supply Chain Management: Creating Value-Adding Networks* (4th edn), by Martin Christopher (ISBN 9780273731122), p.172, with the author's approval.
- Figure 2.6: Gartner Inc. for sanctioning the publication of the original version of the diagram copyrighted by AMR Research in 2004.
- Table 2.6: Gartner Inc. for consenting to the abstraction of material from http://www.gartner.com/technology/supply-chain/top25.jsp.
- Figures 2.7 and 2.8: TNT Express N.V. for agreeing to the reproduction of two diagrams with small amendments.
- Tables 2.8. 2.9 and 2.11: Armstrong & Associates Inc. for approving their reproduction.
- Figure 3.3: Charles McMillan, York University, Toronto, for allowing his diagram to be reproduced.

- Figure 3.5: Theo Notteboom, Institute of Transport and Maritime Management, University of Antwerp, for permitting an amended version of his figure.
- Figures 3.7 and 3.12: Jean-Paul Rodrigue, Hofstra University, New York, for allowing an amended version of the Evolution of a Port (The Anyport Model) and the reproduction of silhouettes showing the evolution of container ships from the website of 'The Geography of Transport Systems'.
- Figure 4.11: John Kasarda, University of North Carolina, Chapel Hill, for allowing the transformation of his original aerotropolis diagram.
- Figures 5.5 and 5.13: Her Majesty the Queen in Right of Canada, Department of Transport for allowing the use and adaptation of the original diagrams from 'Canada's Gateway Update: Connecting Canada to Global Opportunities', Asia Pacific Gateway and Corridor Initiative Workshop, Toronto, CA, 18 June 2010, available at http://www.gateway-corridor.com/torontoworkshop/presentations.htm.
- Figure II.2: Dr Sangbeom Seo, Korea Transport Institute, for allowing an amended version of a block diagram outlining the directions for a nation-state to develop strategies and actions.
- Figure 11.1: Ian Clarke, University of Edinburgh, for approving an amendment of a diagram that appeared in *The Spatial Organisation of Multinational Corporations* published by Croom Helm.
- Figure E.1: Asian Development Bank for consenting to the reproduction of a figure showing the major transit directions in Eurasia.

Abbreviations

1PL	first-party logistics
2PL	second-party logistics
3/11	3 March 2011 (Great East Japan Earthquake, tsunami and nuclear meltdown)
3D	three-dimensional
3PL	third-party logistics
4PL	fourth-party logistics
ACCC	Australian Competition and Consumer Commission
ADB	Asian Development Bank
AFCN	Australian Freight Councils Network
AH	Asian Highway
AIF	Asian Infrastructure Fund
AIIB	Asian Infrastructure Investment Bank
ALC	Australian Logistics Council
ALIS	Australian Logistics Industry Strategy
ANA	All Nippon Airlines
ANU	Australian National University
APEC	Asia-Pacific Economic Cooperation
APEX	Sinotrans A-Plus Express
APMT	APM Terminals
APMM	A.P. Møller-Maersk Group
APROC	Asia-Pacific Regional Operations Centre (Taiwan)
APSL	Asia-Pacific School of Logistics
ARTC	Australian Rail Track Corporation
ASEAN	Association of Southeast Asian Nations
ASEAN + 3	ASEAN + China, Japan and South Korea
ASEAN + 6	ASEAN + China, Japan, South Korea, Australia, India and New Zealand
ATC	Australian Transport Council
AWB	Australian Wheat Board
B2B	business-to-business
B2C	business-to-consumer
BaU	business as usual
BESOTO	Beijing–Seoul–Tokyo

BESOTOSHAOS	Beijing–Seoul–Tokyo–Shanghai–Osaka
BIMP-EAGA	Brunei Darussalam–Indonesia–Malaysia–Philippines East ASEAN Growth Area
BIMSTEC	Bay of Bengal Initiative Multi-Sectoral Technical and Economic Cooperation
BOO	build, own, operate
BOT	build, own, transfer
BRICS	Brazil, Russia, India, China, South Africa
BT	biotechnology
Bujin	Busan-Jinhae (South Korea)
C2B	consumer-to-business
C2C	consumer-to-consumer
C-4	proportion container shipping slot capacity held by the four largest container shipping companies
CADP	Comprehensive Asia Development Plan
CAGI	Council for Asian Gateway Initiative
CAGTC	Coalition for America's Gateways and Trade Corridors
CAP	College of Asia and the Pacific
CAREC	Central Asia Regional Economic Cooperation
CBTA	Cross Border Transport Agreement (Greater Mekong Subregion)
CEAC	Council on East Asian Community
CEO	chief executive officer
CEPA	Closer Economic Partnership Agreement (China and Hong Kong)
CFLP	China Federation of Logistics and Purchasing
CIS	Commonwealth of Independent States
CJK FTA	China–Japan–South Korea Free Trade Agreement
CKD	completely knocked down
CKHY	COSCO Container Lines (China), K-Line (Japan), Hanjin Shipping (South Korea) and Yangming Line (Taiwan)
CKHYE	COSCON (China), K-Line (Japan), Hanjin Shipping (South Korea), Yangming Line (Taiwan) and Evergreen Line (Taiwan) shipping alliance
CKS	Chiang Kai Shek International Airport
CLM	Council of Logistics Management
COAG	Council of Australian Governments
COSCO	China Ocean Shipping (Group) Company
CSCL	China Shipping Container Line
CSCMP	Council of Supply Chain Management Professionals

DFCCIL	Dedicated Freight Corridor Corporation of India Limited
DP	Deutsche Post
DPDHL	Deutsche Post DHL
DPJ	Democratic Party of Japan
DPWN	Deutsche Post World Net
DTW	Tianjin Datian W. (Group Ltd)
ECFA	Economic Cooperation Framework Agreement (People's Republic of China and Republic of China)
EDI	electronic data interchange
EMS	Express Mail Service (China)
ERIA	Economic Research Institute for ASEAN and East Asia
ERTMS	European Rail Transport Management System
ESCAP	Economic Commission for Asia and the Pacific (United Nations)
ETC	electronic toll collect
EU	European Union
FBIC	Fung Business Intelligence Centre
FDI	foreign direct investment
FedEx	Federal Express
FEU	forty-foot equivalent unit
FEZ	Free Economic Zone (South Korea)
FMCG	fast-moving consumer goods
FT	financial technology
FTC	Fair Trade Commission (South Korea)
FTK	freight tonne-kilometres
FY	financial year
GATT	General Agreement on Tariffs and Trade
GaWC	Globalization and World Cities
Gbps	gigabits per second
GCI	Global Cities Index
GDP	gross domestic product
GIS	geographical information system
GKN	Guest Keen & Nettlefolds
GLCs	global logistic corporations
GM	General Motors
GMS	Greater Mekong Subregion
GNI	gross national income
GPCI	Global Power Cities Index
GPS	global positioning system
GRDP	gross regional domestic product

GSL	Graduate School of Logistics
GT	Georgia Tech (Georgia Institute of Technology)
HACTL	Hong Kong Air Cargo Terminal Limited
HHIC	Hanjin Heavy Industry and Construction
HIST	Hanjin Information Systems and Telecommunications Co. Ltd
HJS	Hanjin Shipping
HKIA	Hong Kong International Airport
HKIT	Hong Kong International Terminals
HKUST	Hong Kong University of Science and Technology
HKWDC	Hong Kong & Whampoa Dock Company
HPH	Hutchison Port Holdings
IATA	International Air Transport Association
ICAO	International Civil Aviation Organization
ICD	inland container depot
ICT	information and communications technology
IDB	Inter-American Development Bank
IEAT	Industrial Estate Authority of Thailand
IFT	integrated freight terminal
IIRSA	Initiative for the Integration of the Regional Infrastructure of South America
ILB	inland logistics base (South Korea)
ILO	International Labour Organization
IMF	International Monetary Fund
IMO	International Maritime Organization
IMT-GT	Indonesia–Malaysia–Thailand Growth Triangle
IMV	Innovative International Multipurpose Vehicle
IoT	Internet of Things
ISPRE	Institute for Spatial Planning and Regional Economy (China)
IT	information technology
ITS	intelligent transport systems
ITU	International Telecommunications Union
JETRO	Japan External Trade Organization
JIFFA	Japan International Freight Forwarders Association
JILS	Japan Institute of Logistics Systems
JIT	just-in-time
KAL	Korea Air Lines
KCCI	Korea Chamber of Commerce and Industry
KRIHS	Korea Research Institute for Human Settlements
KLN	Kerry Logistics Network
KOTI	Korea Transport Institute

KPN	Koninklijke PTT Nederland
Lao PDR	Lao People's Democratic Republic (Laos)
LCC	low-cost carrier
LCD	liquid-crystal display
LDP	Liberal Democratic Party (Japan)
LFRC	Li and Fung Research Centre
lo-lo	lift on/lift off
LPI	Logistics Performance Index
LSI	local state institution
LT	logistics technology
LTL	less-than-truckload
M&A	merger and acquisition
MGLM	Master of Global Logistics Management
MICs	multinational industrial corporations
MLIT	Ministry of Land, Infrastructure and Transport (Tourism added after 8 January 2008) (Japan)
MLTM	Ministry of Land, Transport and Maritime Affairs (South Korea)
MMF	Mori Memorial Foundation
MOC	Ministry of Commerce (China)
MOCT	Ministry of Construction and Transportation (South Korea)
MPA	Maritime and Port Authority (Singapore)
MSC	Mediterranean Shipping Company
MSc	Master of Science
NAFTA	North American Free Trade Agreement
NCPDM	National Council of Physical Distribution Management
NDRC	National Development and Reform Commission (China)
NEAL-NET	Northeast Asia Logistics Information Service Network
NEAT	Network of Northeast Asian Think Tanks
NIEs	newly industrializing economies
NIRA	National Institute for Research Advancement (Japan)
NLA	National Library of Australia
NPC	National People's Congress (Communist Party of China)
NRTC	National Road Transport Commission (Australia)
NT	nanotechnology
NTC	National Transport Commission (Australia)

NUS	National University of Singapore
NYK	Nippon Yusen Kabushiki Kaisha
OEM	original equipment manufacturer
OM	operations management
OOCL	Oriental Overseas Container Line
OSRA	Ocean Shipping Reform Act, 1998 (USA)
P4	Trans-Pacific Strategic Economic Partnership Agreement
P&O	Peninsular and Oriental Steam Navigation Company
PAIF	Pan-Asia Infrastructure Forum
PC	personal computer
PCNACI	Presidential Committee on the Northeast Asian Cooperation Initiative (South Korea)
PCRD	Presidential Commission on Regional Development (South Korea)
PDM	physical distribution management
PIL	Pacific International Lines
PPP	purchasing power parity
PRC	People's Republic of China
PRIDe	Peninsular Region Industrial Development Corridor (India)
PSA	Port of Singapore Authority
PSC	Port State Control
R&D	research and development
RCEP	Regional Comprehensive Economic Partnership
RCL	Regional Container Lines
RFID	radio frequency identification
RIS	Research and Information System for Developing Countries
RMIT	Royal Melbourne Institute of Technology
ROC	Republic of China
ROK	Republic of Korea
ro-ro	roll on/roll off
RPK	revenue passenger kilometre
RSPAS	Research School of Pacific and Asian Studies
RTK	revenue tonne-kilometre
SAARC	South Asian Association for Regional Cooperation
SAIC	Shanghai Automotive Industry Corporation
SAR	Special Administrative Region
SARS	Severe Acute Respiratory Syndrome
SCM	supply chain management

SCOT	Standing Committee on Transport (Australia)
SCOTI	Standing Council on Transport and Infrastructure (Australia)
SEZ	special economic zone (China)
SF Express	Shenzhen Shun Feng Express Group Co. Ltd
SI	system integration
SIA	Singapore Airlines
SICC	standard industrial classification code
Sijori	Singapore–Johor–Riau
SKRL	Singapore–Kunming Rail Link
STOM	Senior Transport Officials Meeting (ASEAN)
SUV	sports utility vehicle
SWOT	strengths, weaknesses, opportunities, threats
SYCG	Shanghai Yuan Cheng Group
TALC	Transport and Logistics Centre (Australia)
TAR	Trans-Asian Railway
TCR	Trans-China Railway
TEN-T	Trans European Transport Network
TENs	Trans-European Networks
TEU	twenty-foot equivalent unit
TISOC	Transport and Infrastructure Senior Officials' Committee (Australia)
TLI-Asia Pacific	Transport Logistics Institute Asia Pacific
TMG	Tokyo Metropolitan Government
TMR	Trans-Manchurian Railway
TNT	Thomas Nationwide Transport
TPP	Trans-Pacific Partnership
TPRI	Transport Planning Research Institute (China)
TSR	Trans-Siberian Railway
TUDB	Tokyo Urban Development Bureau
TV	television
TWA	Trans World Airlines
UK	United Kingdom of Great Britain and Northern Ireland
UNASUR	Unión de Naciones Suramericanas (Union of South American Nations)
UNCLOS	United Nations Convention on the Law of the Sea
UPS	United Parcel Service
USA	United States of America
USPS	United States Postal Service
VICS	Vehicle Information and Communications System
VMI	vendor managed inventory

WACC	weighted average cost of capital
WATS	World Air Transport Statistics
WTO	World Trade Organization
YRC	Yellow Roadway Corporation

1. Global + local logistics: Asian-Pacific Rim perspectives

The 'seven Rs' (of logistics) stand for having the right product, in the right quantity, in the right condition, at the right place, at the right time, for the right customer, at the right cost (Wisner et al., 2008, 358).

In 1950 the impoverished and economically stagnating coastal arena stretching from Russia to the Indonesian archipelago was not designated as the 'Asian-Pacific Rim' but subsumed under the British term 'the Far East', an expression covering the lands beyond India, but excluding Australasia or Oceania. Despite the Far East's historical importance in international trade during both the pre-colonial and the colonial eras, there was no pressing need for perspectives on logistics. At that time logistics was still a branch of military science, having to do with procuring, maintaining and transporting material, personnel and facilities. There was no formal or integrated concept linking highly fragmented logistics activities with manufacturing and marketing. The terms 'global logistics' and 'local logistics' were not in fashion, nor were container shipping, jumbo jets and the Internet in operation.

Fast-forwarding 60 years to the second decade of the new millennium, the situation has changed dramatically. The Asian-Pacific Rim, covering the archipelago between the Russian Far East and Indonesia and, on occasions, extended to include Oceania, is now a defined area for academic study (Le Heron and Park, 1995). Accounting for two-thirds of the tonnage of international trade and more than half of the total intra-regional tonnage, the Rim is now the world's prime economic growth centre (Figure 1.1). Over the intervening period since 1950 logistics itself has been transformed into an activity for studying business organizations, because many of the early operations management (OM) researchers left the military for business, and used their quantitative methods to improve the efficiency of transporting materials and finished products. Global, if not local, logistics has become a prominent topic of study, buoyed by the triple revolution involving container shipping, jumbo jets, and information and communications technology (ICT).

This chapter reviews global logistics patterns to highlight the nature and extent of the Asian-Pacific Rim's involvement in different spheres of

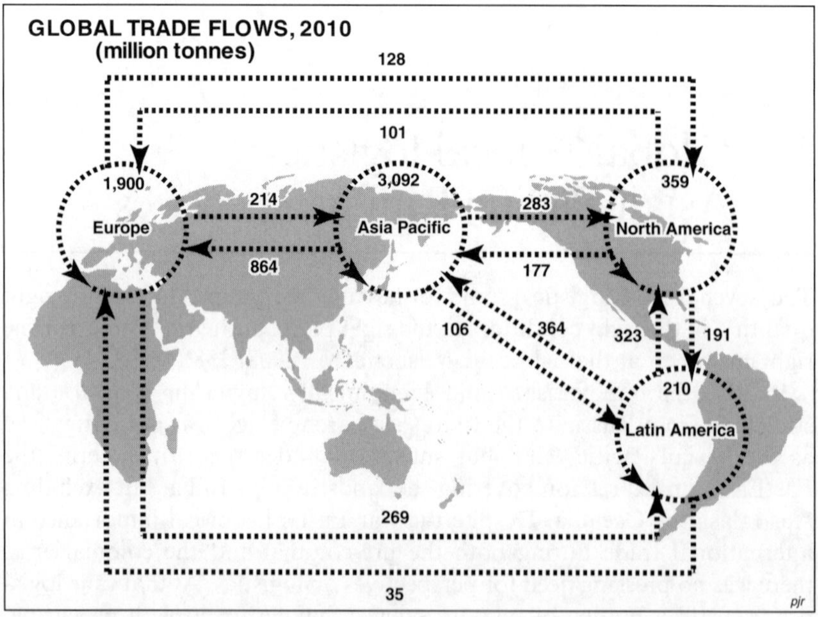

Note: The original diagram has been reorganized to centre on the Asia Pacific region.

Source: Data from DPDHL (2011, 30).

Figure 1.1 Major trade flows between the world's supra-regions, 2010

activity – manufacturing and retailing, shipping, air transport and telecommunications – before appraising a range of local logistics policies. The chapter's purpose is to provide a context within which to explore links between global and local logistics by identifying key issues and suggesting appropriate methodologies for exploring them. Insights drawn from the Rim may assist in making comparisons with logistics in the world's other key economic regions, notably Europe and North America. The Rim's logistics arena warrants detailed attention, because the sector's logistics costs as percentage of gross domestic product (GDP) exceed those of both Europe and North America; there is also scope for greater outsourcing because the Rim's revenue from this activity as a proportion of logistics costs is lower than its counterparts (Table 1.1). Before outlining the book's framework for examining the implications of these trends, the broad changes that have occurred in analysing logistics since the 1950s are reviewed; the essential character of global logistics is outlined; the term 'local logistics' is coined; and key features of the Asian-Pacific Rim are highlighted.

Table 1.1 Estimates of the global logistics market's size, 2012

Region	Gross domestic product	Logistics/ GDP	Logistics cost	Outsourced revenue/ Logistics cost	Outsourced revenue
	US$ bn	%	US$ bn	%	US$ bn
Asian-Pacific Rim	21 881.9	12.8	2809.8	8.6	242.7
Europe	16 394.9	9.2	1504.8	10.5	158.0
North America	18 676.0	8.8	1639.6	10.5	171.2
Other	14 877.2	16.1	2396.4	4.7	113.2
	71 830.0	11.4	8350.6	8.2	685.1

Note: Australia and India are included in Asia-Pacific.

Source: Armstrong & Associates (2013a).

LOGISTICS

During the 1950s the term 'logistics' was 'borrowed' from military practice to address the neglected issue of getting products promptly to where customers resided. Since then the civilian expression of 'logistics' has been progressively redefined as physical distribution, business logistics, and supply chain logistics, before social logistics was added to the mix.

Physical distribution was invoked to enhance cost economies in marketing that top management had already achieved in production and finance (Drucker, 1962). The task involved integrating seven hitherto separate and independent activities – transport, inventory control, warehousing, packaging, materials handling, order processing and consumer service – into an organized framework with the intention of balancing costs and service in moving goods to maximize customer satisfaction (Smykay et al., 1961). As defined by the National Council of Physical Distribution Management (NCPDM), formed in 1963, the purpose of the physical distribution management (PDM) system was to get the product to the right place at the right time (the first two of the seven Rs of logistics), particularly as the concept of safety stock had been neglected (LaLonde and Dawson, 1969; Glencowets, 1979).

Once this integration had been achieved through the spatial arrangement of plant capacity and warehouse facilities, and the connecting transport linkages, the components could be combined into a simulation model aimed at minimizing costs while satisfying marketing requirements (Gilmour, 1974). Adoption and modelling of the combined components of transport and warehousing promised a large-scale cost reduction, and then, when the central management of physical distribution was firmly established and consolidated, the enhanced arrangement provided a competitive advantage to distributors because they were able to offer a superior cost-efficient service. Although the importance of distribution was elevated in strategic decision-making within the firm, attention was concentrated upon the movement of material from the manufacturer to the user, usually finished goods or service parts; there was no coverage of the flow of raw materials and semi-finished components into the vertical manufacturing production process (that is, materials management).

Business logistics was mooted in the 1960s prompted by the need to broaden the activities under discussion and create value for the customer (Plowman, 1964, vii–viii). By the mid-1970s the process involved integrating the multiple sub-functions covered in materials management and physical distribution management under a single umbrella to integrate inbound and outbound flows (Buytenen et al., 1976). This development sought to accommodate increased acceptance of the systems approach, customer demands, multinational distribution, and government influence over distribution policy and practice (LaLonde and Zinszer, 1976).

Operations management had come to the fore in the planning, scheduling and control of activities that transformed inputs into finished goods and services. This led Martin Christopher (1974) to outline a systems engineering approach to resolving logistics issues, and to stress the connection between marketing and distribution. In 1985 these developments, designed to improve a company's overall performance and competitiveness, led to the business logistics process being defined by the Council of Logistics Management (CLM) as 'planning, implementing and controlling the efficient flow and storage of raw materials, in-process inventory, finished goods, services and related information from point of origin to point of consumption (including inbound, outbound, internal and external movements) for the purpose of conforming to customer requirements' (Mentzer et al., 2001, 16). This definition suggests that logistics is focused on optimizing processes within the firm, from development through procurement, production and transport to selling. The network of inter-company relationships involving multiple tiers of suppliers, distributors and customers, which comprise the supply chain, are considered external to the firm and, at best, a subset of logistics. Thus customer satisfaction and value beyond the efficient movement and storage of materials are not prioritized.

Supply chain logistics sought to redress this oversight by focusing upon

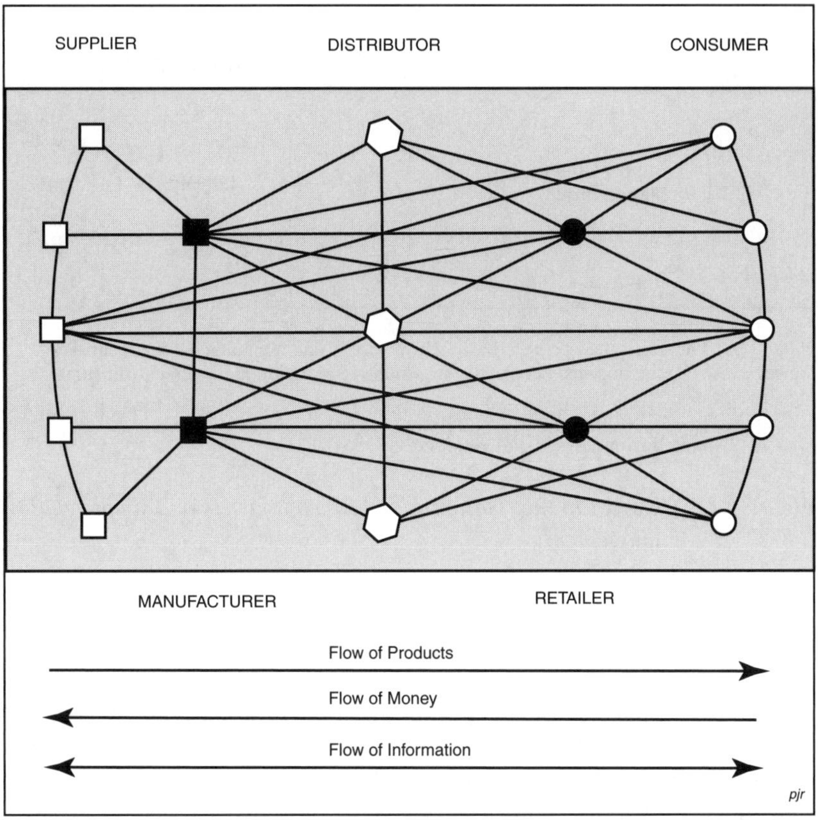

Note: Three core activities are involved in attaining the efficiency of transport activities in moving goods and creating added value: (i) the coordination of the physical flow of products through the supply chain, including waste disposal and repairs; (ii) the organization of financial flows; and (iii) the management of information flows between key players involving the transfer of intellectual property, and managerial and marketing knowledge (i.e. strategic requirements).

Figure 1.2 The extended supply chain

optimizing the efficiency of all stages involved, directly or indirectly, in fulfilling a customer's request (Figure 1.2). Linking the supplier, manufacturer, wholesaler (distributor), retailer and customer together to accommodate customer service, time compression, the globalizing of industry, and organizational integration prompted Martin Christopher (1992) to declare that supply chains, not companies, are in competition. Functions, involved in the upstream and downstream linkages between organizations

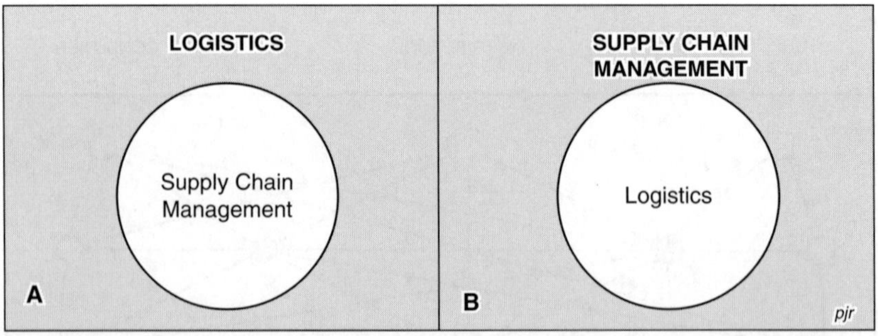

Note: (A) The traditional perspective in which supply chain management is a subset of logistics; and (B) the unionist perspective in which supply chain management subsumes logistics.

Source: Adapted from Larson and Haldorsson (2004).

Figure 1.3 Changes in the relationship between logistics and supply chain management

in the supply chain network, range from new product development through marketing and operations, to finance and customer service (Lambert et al., 1998).

The prime objective of integrating different processes, which produce financial gain through the efficient provision of products and services for the satisfaction of the ultimate customer, is to maximize the overall value created in the supply chain network. This objective has led to logistics being recast as a subset of supply chain management (SCM) that plans, sources, makes, delivers and returns commodities (Figure 1.3). In 2004 the Council of Logistics Management was renamed the Council of Supply Chain Management Professionals (CSCMP) to incorporate 'not only logistics, but also procurement, manufacturing operations, and sales/marketing functions' (MH&L, 2004, 1). CSCMP (2012) provides a working definition of supply chain management as the process that 'plans, implements, and controls the efficient, effective forward and reverse flow and storage of goods, services and related information between the point of origin and the point of consumption in order to meet customer's requirements'.

Over time different configurations of supply chains have evolved. Looking at supply chain design and operation from the point of view of a customer's dominant buying behaviour, John Gattorna (2006, 2009) identifies four discrete configurations: (1) 'continuous replenishment', for loyal customers with a strong emphasis on long-term supplier relationships; (2) 'lean', for customers focusing on efficiency and lowest cost

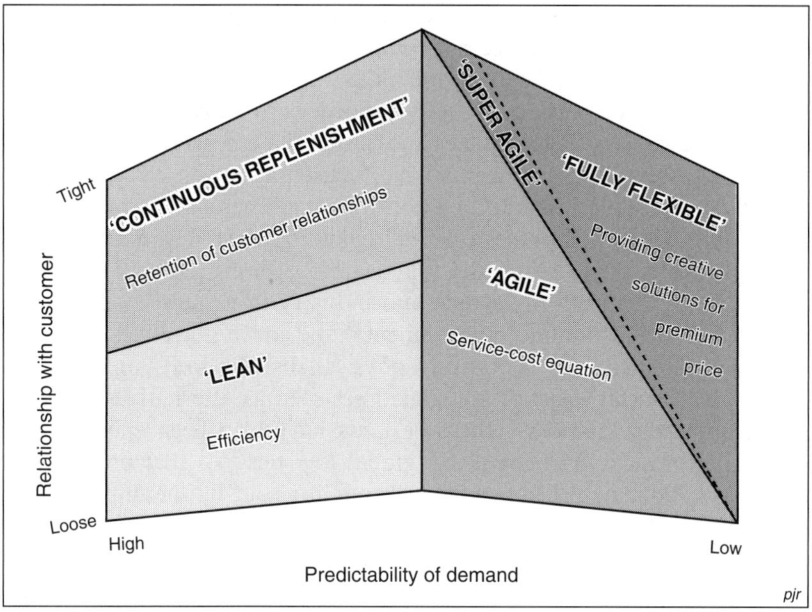

Note: 'Super-agile' has been added to cover events such as 9/11 and natural disasters.

Source: Abstracted from Gattorna (2006: 43). © Pearson Education Limited.

Figure 1.4 Simplified version of John Gattorna's four generic supply chain types

per serve; (3) 'agile', for customers where a quick response is paramount; and (4) 'fully flexible', for customers requiring a quick-change innovative solution (Figure 1.4). The continuous replenishment and lean strategies were fashioned during a period of relative economic stability in the 1980s and 1990s. Agility and flexibility strategies have become more prized than cost efficiency in the more turbulent environment experienced during the new millennium marked by volatility and uncertainty in demand and transport costs that peaked during the Global Financial Crisis (2008–09) (Christopher and Holweg, 2011). To ensure that the four different supply chain configurations harmonize with the environment, governments have injected social needs into the equation.

Social logistics is a hybrid concept aimed at reducing energy requirements and the external effects of logistics operations on the environment arising from climate change, air quality and noise (Tanimoto, 2000). Not only does the concept cover reverse logistics, identified in the earlier definition of supply chain management that incorporates recycling and energy savings from the reuse of products, but it also covers green logistics, that deals with air pollution, and industrial and packaging waste. Also involved are the inspection of goods at border crossings, confirmation of regulatory compliance, tolls, taxes and duties and emergency responses to natural disasters. These concerns have focused attention on 'the setting, maintenance, regulation, and taxation by governments of the infrastructure within which companies operate' (Baudin, 2004, 17). Such matters of public policy cover managing the location of logistics facilities, information flows, institutions, people and industry to achieve a sustainable balance between economic, environmental and social objectives.

Business logistics (incorporating physical distribution), supply chain logistics and social logistics are sometimes seen as alternatives (Baudin, 2004). Since the mid-1980s these variants have also been encompassed within the broader framework of 'global logistics', so that both operational and wider public policy issues brought about by the unpacking of factories and offices to locate production tasks within industrial agglomerations in different countries can be discussed together. To distinguish this finer level of disintegration from the 'first great unbundling' that occurred between 1850 and 1914, when the railways and steamships first enabled production to be separated from consumption by cutting shipping costs, Richard Baldwin (2006) refers to the period since the mid-1980s as the 'second great unbundling'.

Global Logistics

Global logistics came into vogue from the late 1980s to cover the increased international movement of raw materials, components and finished goods associated with the 'second great unbundling' (Waters, 1988 [2003]). Soon after logistics management in a global setting was given a fillip by new political and technological realities. Key among the political actualities was the fall of the Berlin Wall on 11 November 1989 that boosted world trade, and opened up new markets and sources of raw materials. These new political realities included the increased mobility of capital that followed the liberalization of financial markets and the reduction of trade barriers after the General Agreement on Tariffs and Trade (GATT) in 1994.

Most prominent among the new technological realities have been an expanded set of transport and ICT connections that have brought people and places closer together through infrastructural developments in airports, seaports, railroads, highways and telecommunications. The personal computer, the Internet, the World Wide Web, workflow software with standardized protocols to coordinate a dispersed workforce, and personal and wireless technologies have been particularly significant in reducing international communication and coordination tasks (Friedman, 2008). This technological progress, coupled with the deregulation of transport and communications services, has boosted world trade because instead of following South Korea and Taiwan in building a domestic supply chain, economies such as China have industrialized by joining supply chains that have been built across borders (Baldwin, 2011). As industrial activities are divided between countries, a distinction can be made between the headquarter economy, typified by Japan, South Korea or Taiwan, and factory economies, represented by China and Thailand.

The dynamics of international fragmentation has allowed industrial corporations to fragment their entire production process into several blocs and service links and relocate them to capitalize on the locational advantages of different economies in capital or labour-intensive activities to reduce total production cost (Jones and Kierzkowski, 1990). This strategy has permitted vertical command-and-control systems to be moved horizontally offshore to facilitate the development and extension of production networks or supply chains to serve emerging markets across the world (Figure 1.5). As exemplified by the offshoring of contract manufacturing to China and the migration of business functions to India, the practice is most advanced in Asia.

Fragmentation is designed to reduce the cost of materials and production and, more or less, break-even on inventory (Figure 1.6). In moving away from a localized production site to multinational operations, transport costs have increased. This has led the management of some complex supply chains, comprising suppliers, retailers and customers, to complement the offshoring process by outsourcing their logistics activities. The logistics provider's task is to ensure that the costs involved in moving items between the production blocs are both low enough not to discourage the fragmentation process and of sufficient quality to meet the service needs of the market. Where these needs are not met, multinational corporations may return to locations closer to home (that is, near-sourcing) when the proposition that '"low cost country advantage" offsets the transportation cost in supply chains' is no longer sustainable (Christopher and Holweg, 2011, 80). These developments in 'global logistics' ('global supply chains' or 'global value chains') have been captured in both single texts (Gourdin, 2001; Voortman, 2004; Mangan et al., 2008 [2012]; Gereffi and Lee, 2012; Cattaneo et al., 2013) and collections of essays (Waters, 1988 [2003], 2007; Bookbinder, 2005, 2013; Elms and Low, 2013).

Adding the word 'global' to logistics does not have any profound effect upon the subject's content other than to emphasize the importance

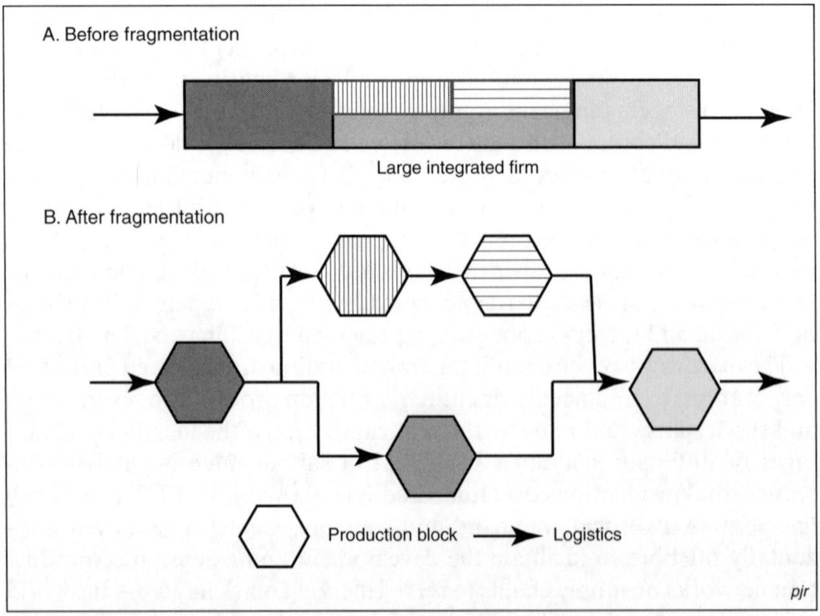

Note: (A) An industrial corporation builds an entire product within a factory. (B) The industrial corporation reduces production costs by unbundling some of its production processes and logistics service tasks according to their labour or capital-intensive characteristics.

Source: Based on Kimura and Umezaki (2011, 5).

Figure 1.5 The fragmentation theory: production blocks and links provided by logistics service providers

of connectedness. An obvious drawback to any uncritical adoption of this title is the underlying assumption that globalization explains almost everything by downplaying or disregarding the role and power of the local nation-state (Bookbinder and Matuk, 2009). Multinational manufacturing and retailing corporations, and increasing international trade, are widely accepted as explanatory variables of current economic trends, but globalization is still a contentious proposition.

There are arguments that globalization is not a new phenomenon, but the continuation of processes whose antecedents can be traced at least to the nineteenth century, if not back to the fifteenth. The drive towards free trade since the 1990s has echoes of the period prior to the First World War, dating from 1870, although international integration was still limited. Even if 'global' is used explicitly to describe the period in logistics

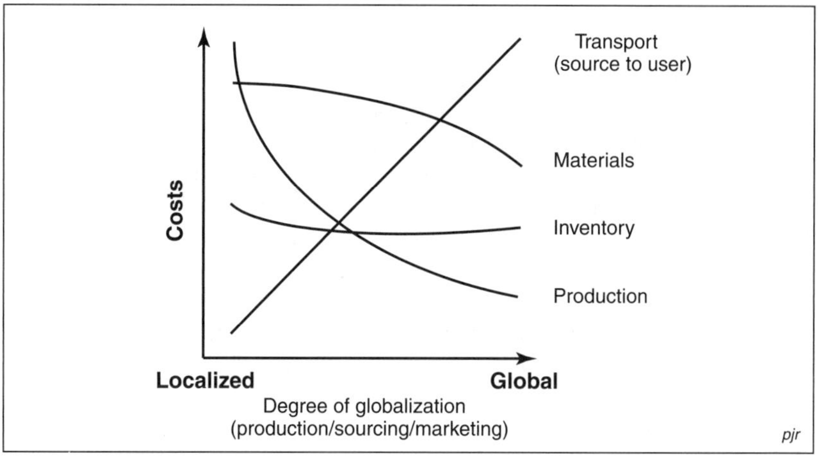

Source: Christopher (2011, 172). © Pearson Education Limited.

Figure 1.6 Trade-offs involved in switching from a localized towards a global sphere of operation

of deeper international economic integration since the 1990s, it should not be taken as a given. Different logistics patterns have to be tested to determine the extent to which they represent full, partial or semi-globalization (Ghemawat, 2007).

Also there is often the implicit supposition in using the term 'globalization' that economic geography is no longer relevant in a business world, where the distinction between a corporation's domestic and international markets is fading. Logistics issues within large countries such as China or India are claimed to be almost identical to those experienced by selling internationally in Europe and North America. Eye-catching, but extravagant, propositions have arisen to describe the competitive business landscape, notably: 'the world is flat', 'the end of geography' and 'distance is dead'. Even in a global virtual world, place still matters because cyberspace markets, exemplified by Google's confrontation with the People's Republic of China, are still governed by political boundaries and state laws (Quelch and Jocz, 2012, 8). As a counter to globalization 'steamrolling' all other arguments, the term 'local logistics' is coined to suggest that even in a flattening and shrinking world, location is of prime importance, and distance still remains to be modified, conquered and subjugated.

Local Logistics

This book evokes the term 'local logistics' to discuss significant developments in high-speed rail, trucking and inland waterways within the Asian-Pacific Rim that otherwise would be glossed over when examining global patterns. Already the term 'city logistics' exists to cover the logistics and transport activities of private companies within urban areas (ICL, 2013). The broader concept proposed here also encompasses logistics at other local levels such as the region, nation, province and firm. Thus, logistics in the Asian-Pacific Rim, Europe and North America, South Korea, Zhejiang Province in China, Tokyo and Chengdu Xindu Logistics Centre would all come under the same 'local' umbrella. On this reckoning many of the articles that appear in collections of essays on 'global logistics' would be classed as 'local logistics'. Even 'the global supply chain', as observed by Richard Baldwin (2013, 20), 'is not very global – it's regional'; an observation confirmed by Olivier Cattaneo et al. (2013, 3).

Integrating interactions between logistics within specified local areas and the global level provides an opportunity to develop a more embracive analytical framework. This framework is important because local logistics networks have become increasingly significant under a newly emerging set of competitive economic and social conditions pertaining in the world's major economic regions. Manufacturing and retailing in an increasingly interdependent world are knitted together by horizontal international linkages arising from lower freight costs, and the cutting of tariffs and quotas on trade in goods and services. A reduction in the cost of these items does not automatically result in the dispersal of economic activities (Figure 1.7). Both spatial concentration and redispersion processes can stem from the non-linear impact of transport and communications on development.

Economic activities, given limited and imperfect information, are not spread evenly, but attracted to an increasing number of urban platforms or gateways that are expanding their areas of influence by offering innovation, entrepreneurship, and an educated and skilled workforce. Capitalizing on linkages between clustered firms in the same industry within these spatial agglomerations can save transaction costs incurred when buying or selling, especially through a reduction in search and information costs. Even where redispersion occurs from agglomerations to the peripheries, it involves, as exemplified in Greater Bangkok, the deconcentration of activities within the immediate hinterland rather than decentralization to remote areas. Within the urban agglomerations and their immediate hinterlands, attention is being focused upon the adequacy of logistics and the supporting institutional infrastructure because of

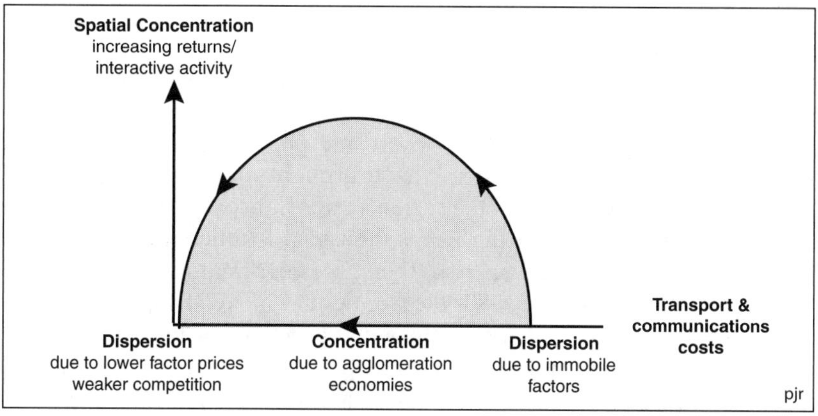

Note: The shaded area represents the degree of spatial concentration. Dispersion occurs when capital and labour, owing to lack of information, cannot respond to changes in rewards and job opportunities. Concentration stems from economies of scale, proximity to market and easy access to capital that attracts economic activities into clusters (i.e. agglomeration economies). Re-dispersion arises from congestion, reflected in wage rises, land prices, traffic jams and pollution, and the attraction of lower labour costs, that encourages some economic activities to deconcentrate to peripheral metropolitan sites or decentralize to rural locations.

Source: Based on Fujita (1999).

Figure 1.7 The spatial economy is shaped by tensions between dispersive and agglomerative forces

their significant effect upon costs, productivity and efficiency. Thus the logical outcome of the fragmentation of production on local logistics is an increasingly 'uneven', 'tilted' or 'spiky' world between and within the richest and poorest regions, nations, provinces and cities stemming from differences in infrastructure, education and governance.

Local logistics is not intended to be an end in itself. There is a need for more than a series of assertions about the nature and significance of logistics in different localities as an antidote to pronouncements by management leaders and commentators concerning the global nature of logistics. The alternative is to develop a 'third way' that integrates both global and local elements in a bid to come closer to seeing 'the world as it really is'. This third way is sought by providing a more flexible analytical framework for studying logistics that explores relationships between the global and the local, illustrated here by reference to the economic integration of the Asian-Pacific Rim. However, before developing the 'global + local' perspective, the features of the Rim's distinctive economic geography must be outlined.

THE ASIAN-PACIFIC RIM

The Asian-Pacific Rim came to the fore after the Pacific War (1941–45) when cross-border trade, capital flows, logistics developments, and other economic and social interactions overcame political barriers. Different economic and regulatory systems have brought about closer economic integration and resurgence in the region's importance. Over time there has been a progressive shift in the Rim's industrial frontier, which has been likened by Japanese observers to a 'flying geese' formation (Kuroiwa and Kumagai, 2011). Since the 1980s the frontier has moved from the immediate post-war leadership of Japan, through the Asian newly industrializing economies (NIEs) of Hong Kong, Singapore, South Korea and Taiwan to the second-tier of Indonesia, Malaysia and Thailand. Now China is the prime focus of the 'world factory', while the frontier is shifting further west to Viet Nam, Laos, Cambodia and Myanmar, and to Bangladesh in South Asia.

Economic integration of the Asian-Pacific Rim has been facilitated by the establishment of special economic zones (SEZs) in coastal locations, together with the appreciation of Japanese currency against the United States dollar following the Plaza Accord in 1985, which prompted multinational manufacturers and retailers based in Japan to invest in facilities, training, technology and long-term business relationships within other economies within the Asian-Pacific Rim. Over time intra-regional trade has shifted from agricultural to manufactured goods, buoyed by the incorporation of the Rim's economies in expanding multinational production networks, particularly those in the motor vehicle, electrical machinery and electronics industries.

This process of fragmenting production has occurred in tandem with the Rim becoming a multi-core economy stretching through a string of mega-city platforms and industrial belts from Sapporo to Surabaya that offer agglomeration economies to multinational industrial corporations (Figure 1.8). The straight-line distance between Tokyo and Singapore (5310 km) is greater than that between New York and San Francisco (4140 km), while the Rim's geographical area, excluding Oceania (11.8 million km^2), is larger than that of the United States (9.8 million km^2). As instanced by the Asian Financial Crisis (1997–98), the Rim's multi-core economies experienced similar instabilities to those experienced in the development of the United States' 'frontier economy' during the late nineteenth and twentieth centuries, and the earlier European frontier economy in the mid-nineteenth century when the centre of manufacturing moved progressively from the United Kingdom to Germany and France (Fujita, 1999). As the latest in the line of 'frontier economies' the

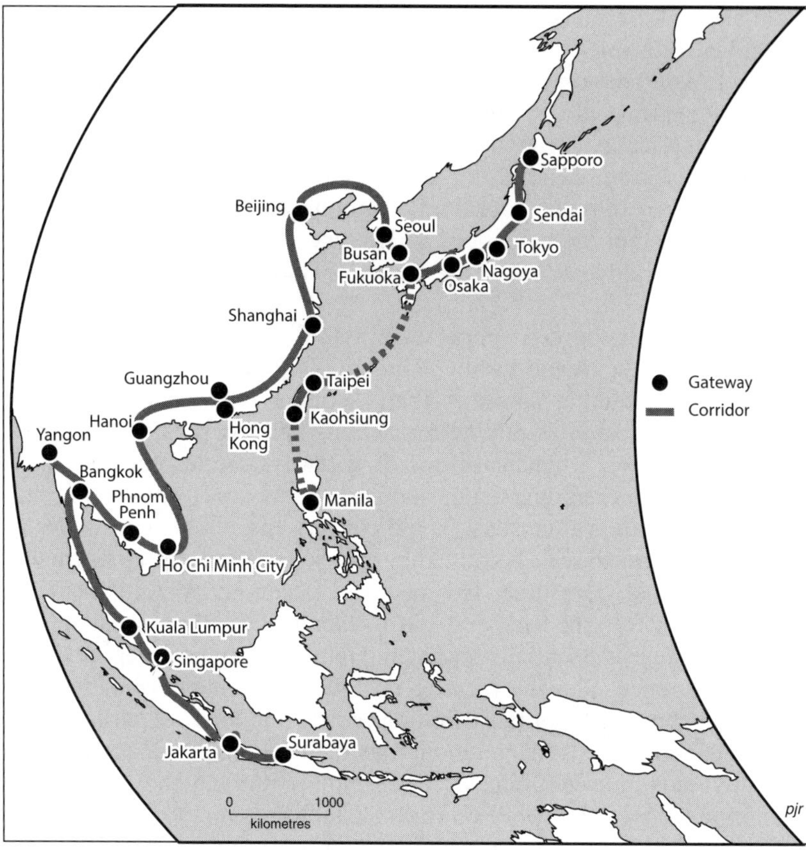

Source: Developed from Fujita (1999).

Figure 1.8 The Asian-Pacific Rim's multi-core economy

Asian-Pacific Rim does not enjoy the same level of institutional, physical and people-to-people connectivity as its mature counterparts in Europe and North America (APEC PSU, 2013a).

A 'seamless' Asian-Pacific Rim is still a long way from reality (ADB and ADBI, 2009). There is great diversity in supply chains and logistics within and between economies within the region, ranging from Singapore to Myanmar. Shortcomings are encapsulated in Peter Backhouse's (2006) catalogue of inadequacies highlighting that: (1) supply chains are increasingly influenced by the impact of lower-cost manufacturing belts due to highly fragmented, unsophisticated material flow infrastructure; (2) supply chain principles, including just-in-time, are being eroded by extended and unreliable lead times, and increasing inventory levels; and (3) land, sea and air freight lane capacities are being stretched to their limits. Besides inadequate infrastructure and logistics capacity, the 'across-the-border' issues of physical connectivity and the 'behind-the-border' issues arising from the inefficient clearance of goods and burdensome documentation procedures, lack of policy coordination among government agencies, variability of cross-border regulations and absence of custom-transit arrangements have an adverse effect on supply chains (APEC PSU, 2013b, 3; Goh, 2013).

The 'behind-the border' supply chain issues are compounded by some mega-cities in the Asian-Pacific Rim, notably Bangkok, Jakarta and Manila, still retaining some of their 'frontier' characteristics associated with the evasion of zoning restrictions and lax pollution controls. Nevertheless these urban platforms or gateways are leading the Rim's growth by agglomerating major industries and service functions into localized geographical clusters. These clusters enjoy scale economies or increasing returns to scale because they offer innovation, entrepreneurship and an educated workforce. This pattern of economic development has become locked into the Rim, and 'path-dependent', in the sense that technological change is essentially 'local', and reinforces and privileges existing urban economies, allowing them to stay at the cutting edge of regional progress by hosting freight distribution centres and logistics parks.

The Asian-Pacific Rim's boundary, as defined here, does not coincide with any economic grouping or trade bloc. Although the Asia-Pacific Economic Cooperation (APEC) forum established in 1989 encompasses the area and highlights the critical importance of connectivity and supply chain performance in its policy studies, its 21 members extend beyond the Asian-Pacific Rim to include Canada, Chile, Mexico, Peru and the United States, but exclude India (PwC, 2012; APEC PSU, 2013a, 2013b). This is also true of the Trans-Pacific Partnership (TPP) Agreement, which builds on the 2006 Trans-Pacific Strategic Economic Partnership Agreement (P4) between Brunei Darussalam, Chile, New Zealand and Singapore, to include Australia, Canada, Japan, Malaysia, Mexico, Peru, the USA and Viet Nam, but not China, South Korea or India. Because the trans-oceanic scope and composition of APEC and the TPP would detract from comparing the Asian-Pacific Rim with North America and Europe – one of the key tasks of this book – these wider definitions are not pursued here.

A narrower trade bloc, the Association of Southeast Asian Nations (ASEAN) established in 1967, now covers ten states in Southeast Asia (Brunei Darussalam, Cambodia, Indonesia, Laos, Malaysia, Myanmar, the Philippines, Singapore, Thailand and Viet Nam), but excludes China,

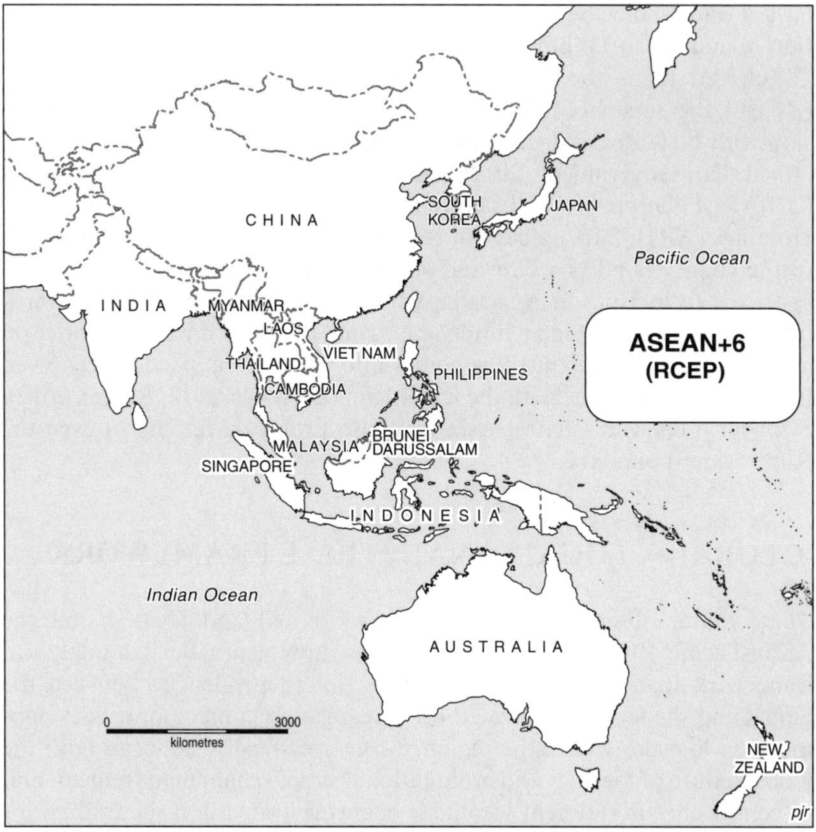

Note: The region encompasses the ten members of the Association of Southeast Asian Nations (ASEAN) – Brunei Darussalam, Cambodia, Indonesia, Laos, Malaysia, Myanmar, the Philippines, Singapore, Thailand and Viet Nam – and the group's six major trading partners comprising Australia, China, India, Japan, South Korea and New Zealand.

Figure 1.9 ASEAN+6 Bloc/Regional Comprehensive Economic Partnership (RCEP)

Japan and South Korea in Northeast Asia (Figure 1.9). Their omission has been remedied to the extent that members of the ASEAN Free Trade Area, established in 1992, have had joint meetings with China, Japan and South Korea (ASEAN+3) since 1997. Also the annual East Asia Summit now includes Australia, New Zealand and India as members (ASEAN+6). Since 2012, moves have been initiated by ASEAN to create a regional free trade area encompassing ASEAN and its six partners into the world's largest trading bloc by 2015 with a GDP of US$19.9 trillion and a population of more than 3.5 billion (Australian Government, 2012a).

Referred to as the Regional Comprehensive Economic Partnership (RCEP), the pursuit of this new trade agreement justifies Australia's inclusion with New Zealand in the wider definition of the Asian-Pacific Rim (Australian Government, 2012b). As the Government of New Zealand's (2010) first National Infrastructure Plan, according to Auckland Regional Holdings (ARH, 2010), does not recognize the many challenges and risks to the country's ports sector and supply chain, attention in this book is restricted to logistics in Australia, where federal, state and local governments are seen as playing a more active role. However a watching brief on logistics developments in India comes into calculation, particularly given the upsurge of its trade with the wider Rim (Brewster, 2012; Regmi, 2012). Stronger links with Central Asia may also prompt a rethink of even the Rim's wider boundary.

'GLOBAL + LOCAL' ANALYTICAL FRAMEWORK

These initial observations on logistics – global and local – and the Asian-Pacific Rim raise a series of issues: how can a flexible analytical framework that accommodates complex interdependencies between the global and the local be provided for investigating contemporary developments in logistics within the region? More specifically, how can both the global nature of logistics and multinational supply chain management, and its significance in different localities, be incorporated into the framework without downplaying or disregarding the importance of the local state?

In addressing these issues the global and local analytical framework developed here allows the incorporation of both international and local networks and linkages (Figure 1.10). Of pivotal importance is the recognition that urban gateway locations situated in complex networks are both global and local (Dick and Rimmer, 2003). These gateways integrate and mediate the two-way global and local flows of goods, people, information and capital. Global flows occur within the 'hinterworld' between gateways (Taylor, 2001; Taylor and Walker, 2004). Each gateway is also linked to local hinterlands by reciprocal flows concentrated along corridors within provinces or nations A and B. Provision is made for global–local interactions and local–global interactions that bypass gateways (for example, resource flows).

Many actors are involved in global and local linkages, and networks ranging from civil society organizations through consumers, labour and states to firms (public enterprises, small and large national firms,

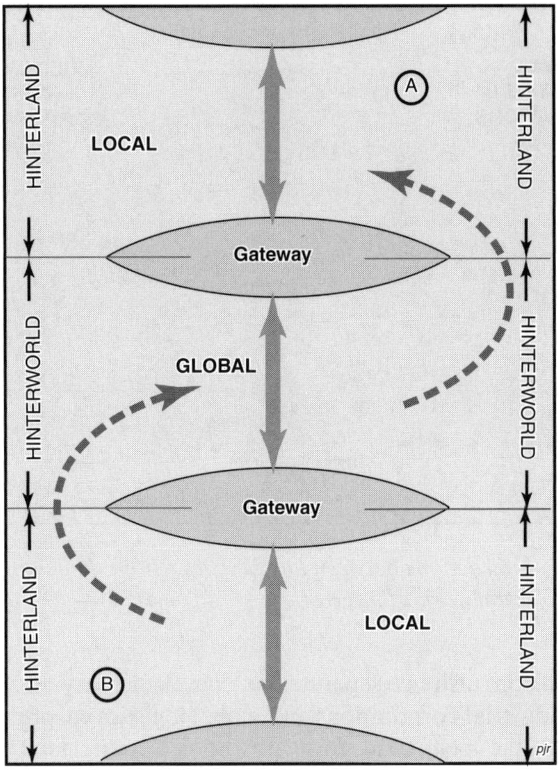

Note: Interactions are shown in the hinterworld between the gateways of regions A and B together with flows within their respective hinterlands, including resource flows (dotted line) that do not pass through the gateways.

Source: Developed from Dick and Rimmer (2003, xvi).

Figure 1.10 Global and local analytical framework

and multinational and global corporations). Ideally, one would like to examine the interrelationships between all actors, but in seeking to unlock global and local perspectives on logistics and supply chain management, the potential cast is narrowed to the leading roles played by states and firms, and the relationships between them: state–firm, firm–firm and state–state (Dicken, 2007).

Within this narrowed compass the emphasis is further tapered to focus on the 'local' state and large corporations, although public enterprises, small and larger national firms will enter and exit depending on the particular scene. Large corporations are pared down, given the focus on

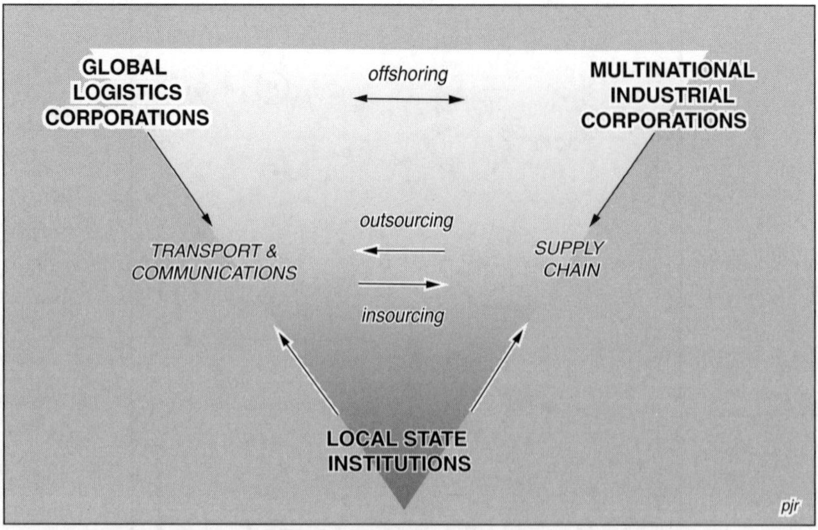

Figure 1.11 Interactions between key players within the triangular framework of interest

logistics, to distinguish two separate, but complementary, networks – multinational industrial corporations and global logistics corporations – that, together with the local state, form this book's triangular framework of interest (Figure 1.11):

- Multinational industrial corporations (MICs) are engaged in the industrial goods transformation network, which extends from natural resources through resource extraction, material processing, parts and components, assembly, wholesale, retail and customers to recycling; the corporations seek to reduce transaction costs in their supply chains that spread across national borders through optimal production, distribution, and location of factories and retail outlets.
- Global logistics corporations (GLCs) operate sea, land and air transport and communications networks that stretch across the globe to provide intermodal freight transport, and just-in-time door-to-door operations for both high-volume and small-lot shipments to meet customer needs and differentiate themselves from rivals.
- Local state institutions (LSIs) make economic planning decisions, involving infrastructure, special economic zones, preferential trade agreements and customs procedures, and market regulation and,

in varying degrees, collaborate with the private sector in ways that affect the architecture of supply chains of both multinational manufacturing and retailing corporations, and the dynamics of global logistics corporations within regional, national, provincial and metropolitan spheres.

Within this interactive framework prime attention is focused on the cross-industry intersection between the coterminous production and logistics networks, where the two actors seek to decrease costs involved in selling in different locations; these costs arise from moving goods, people and information; tariff and non-tariff barriers; and cultural differences (Hamilton, 2005; Rimmer and Hamilton, 2008; Isono, 2011).

At the firm and product level the emphasis within the multinational industrial corporations has been on the supply chain, rather than on the global transport and communications network as such (Figure 1.12). This focus on the supply chain leads to an emphasis on the purchasing systems

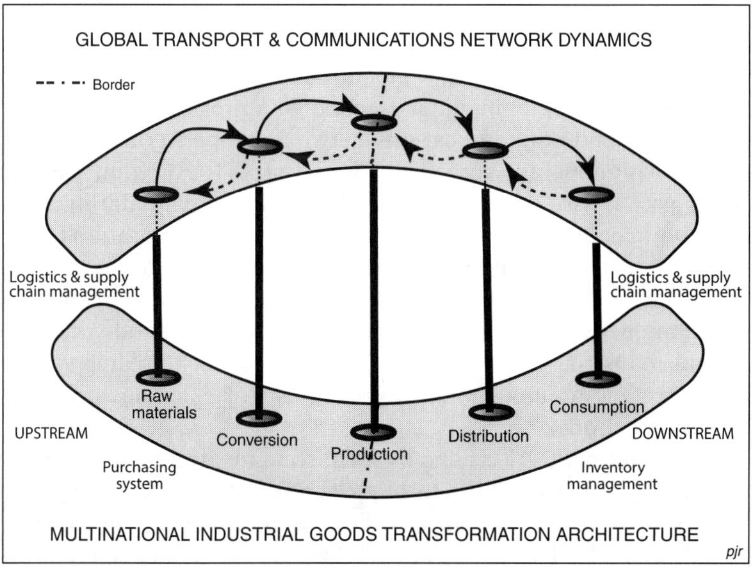

Note: The diagram reflects the relationship between the 'space' of places and the 'space' of flows. Inserting the border leads to the distinction between industrial agglomeration within a country and international fragmentation across countries.

Figure 1.12 Relationship between the multinational industrial goods transformation architecture and the global transport and communications network's dynamics

and inventory management, and inbound and outbound traffic flows. Nevertheless transport and communications network attributes have to be taken into account because, as goods pass through the supply chain, they affect the structure of costs, timing of shipments and conditions of consignments (McMillan, 2009). These attributes underline that global transport and communications infrastructure is of paramount importance to the management of supply chains through its role in connecting fragmented domestic and international production facilities.

Multinational manufacturers and retailers can either provide their own transport and communication needs in-house or, as noted, outsource these services to global logistics corporations. Alternatively, multinational manufacturers and retailers can in-source logistics services by allowing global logistics corporations to act within their organization. This firm focus makes it difficult to integrate the multinational production network based on competition between supply chains with those in the global transport and communications network that favour cooperation between modes.

At a sectoral level it is not possible to have seamless connections between geographically dispersed production networks without looking at the dynamics of the global transport and communications network. Comprising companies (related or unrelated to each other), this transport and communications network propels goods, especially parts and components, across the world; the focal point being on global logistics, with a secondary emphasis on accommodating numerous supply chains across different industries. Corporations within both the production and transport and communications networks create value in the opposite network. The global transport and communications network is essential for the operation of individual multinational industrial corporations. The network itself creates value for transport and communications corporations (for example, airlines and telecommunications).

Planning and policy decisions by local state institutions still influence these world-spanning activities through 'tariffs, tolls, visas, trading quotas and restrictions on border passage', despite international agreements by the International Monetary Fund (IMF), World Trade Organization (WTO) and the World Bank providing the rules and regulations for the capitalist market economy (Walker, 1999, 13). Local institutional control over the gateways governing global and local flows of goods, people, information and money is therefore critical for operators of both global logistics and multinational production networks.

OVERVIEW

The stage is now set for investigating global logistics patterns in Part I of this book, and local logistics processes and policy aspects in the Asian-Pacific Rim within Part II, before widening the region's definition in Part III to accommodate local logistics policies in Australia, and going beyond the Rim's confines to discuss connections with India.

Part I on global logistics examines the Asian-Pacific Rim's position in the world economy by exploring a range of spatial patterns. Chapter 2 analyses the supply chains of multinational manufacturers and retailers, and the extent to which they rely on global logistics corporations, by defining and illustrating the role of third-party logistics providers. Also the global hub-and-spoke system is developed as a yardstick for examining shipping, air transport and telecommunications patterns. Chapter 3 outlines global maritime flows of bulk, liquid and general cargoes before concentrating upon the forces shaping container shipping and port dynamics in the twenty-first century, including the importance of strategic alliances, with particular reference to key shipping companies and terminal operators. Chapter 4 analyses 'global' air cargo and air passenger services, including the significance of strategic alliances and airport infrastructure. Special attention is then paid to the role of airlines as information systems. This leads to a more general discussion of information and telecommunications systems underpinning both air and sea–land transport. Chapter 5 draws upon the data from the preceding chapters on shipping, airline and telecommunications networks to develop the concept of the global 'network of networks'.

Part II explores aspects of local logistics processes in the Asian-Pacific Rim. First, Chapter 6 offers a regional overview by examining the Rim's gateways and corridors. Then Chapter 7 outlines the development of logistics policy within Japan with reference to the activities of key multinational producers and global logistics corporations, and discusses how logistics concepts and technologies are being fashioned and transferred to Southeast Asia to promote greater regional integration. Chapter 8 surveys the spatial structure of the South Korean economy since the Korean War (1950–53) and the emergence of multinational manufacturers, before examining the development of national logistics policies, the appearance of a major South Korean-based global logistics corporation and the importance of logistics in place marketing, with special reference to the gateways of Incheon, Busan, Gwangyang Bay and Gunsan. Chapter 9 demonstrates that any understanding of logistics policy in China requires knowledge of changes in the country's geography and its history over the past 100 years. With this background, the reshaping of China's logistics infrastructure under President Hu Jintao's government during the first decade of the twenty-first century is discussed, before looking ahead to the issues that need to be addressed by his successor, President Xi Jinping's government. Chapter 10 examines the raft of policies designed to bring China, Japan and Korea into an integrated Northeast Asian logistics framework.

In Part III the narrow definition of the Asian-Pacific Rim is widened to encompass Australia's logistics policy, before considering the growing emphasis on interconnecting the Rim with India. Chapter 11 tracks the rise, fall and renaissance of Australia's global logistics corporations, and the way in which newcomers are using connections with the Rim as a springboard to emulate the global reach of the country's earlier logistics leaders. Then in Chapter 12 the proposed linkages between the Rim and India are addressed.

An Epilogue considers how the global hub-and-spoke model can be revamped to incorporate Eurasia, whose economic potential will remain untapped without improvements to, and maintenance of, physical structures, equipment and facilities, and policy, regulatory and institutional frameworks. Extending the Asian-Pacific Rim's logistics networks to meet the rising demand for trading with Central Asia's geographically isolated, inland and remote areas and landlocked countries is seen as a counterweight to the region's reliance on export markets in Europe and North America. Looking ahead to 2050, consideration is given to the likely nature of the revamped hub-and-spoke network by exploring scenarios for both global logistics and local logistics, and the prospects for combining the two. This leads to a reflection on this book's conceptual framework and the need to reformulate the approach for studying multinational industrial corporations engaged in manufacturing and retailing.

PART I

Global context

2. Multinational industrial and global logistics corporations

Multinational industrial corporations (MICs) have arisen since the Second World War (1939–45) from a massive restructuring of individual manufacturing firms and industries accompanying the transformation of both the world and national economies. Until the 1960s and 1970s manufacturing firms and sectors built their entire supply chains to undertake all stages of their productive tasks within a single country. Since the 1980s and 1990s these earlier and shallower factory-centric patterns have been superseded, as retailers have joined manufacturers in unbundling their processes and tasks to stretch their supply chains across national borders to take advantage of the lower costs offshore (Baldwin, 2013). By decentralizing their respective activities on a transnational scale manufacturers and retailers have become multinational corporations geared to marketing products worldwide under common brand names (for example, Dell and Walmart). As their activities have spread across countries, multinationals, including those based in the Asian-Pacific Rim, have been able to take advantage of the reciprocal movements of goods, ideas, technology, capital and technicians between the headquarters economy and factory economies (Athukorala, 2007; Howard, 2010; Kimura, 2013).

As the geographical reach of multinational manufacturers and retailers extended beyond in-house logistics capabilities, their international supply chains, incorporating the Asian-Pacific Rim, have become increasingly complex and prone to greater disruptions (WEF, 2012). To safeguard the reliability of their supply chains, it has become prevalent for these multinational corporations to specialize on their core business competencies, and outsource their logistics activities to professional managers and operators to remain competitive (Figure 2.1). Outsourced logistics activities include distribution and merchandising, storage and management, transport and delivery, information systems, imports and exports, and logistics processing. These transport and logistics functions have become vital for adding value in an array of cross-border manufacturing activities that range from motor vehicles through food and electronics to textiles and apparel (MGI, 2012).

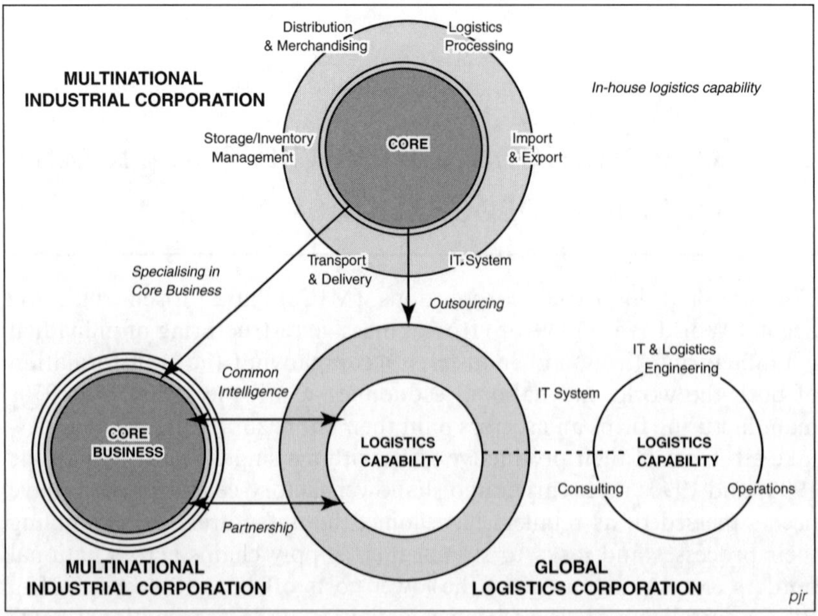

Note: This 'unbundling' of the multinational industrial corporation enables it to concentrate on its core business competencies.

Source: Adapted from Lee (2009).

Figure 2.1 Outsourcing of logistics activities by the multinational industrial corporation to the global logistics corporation

Global logistic corporations (GLCs) have emerged to mobilize transport and communications networks to accommodate the expansion of cross-border trade that is outstripping the growth rate of its domestic counterpart. Their role is to provide the necessary global logistics capability by sharing common intelligence with multinational manufacturers and retailers to provide stable, integrated supply chain solutions. These global logistics providers offer a comprehensive range of services and modes of transport and communications – sea, land and air transport, and telecommunications – to provide value-added services and global logistics capabilities. Services range from domestic and international transport through warehousing and cross-docking to integrated logistics services. The consulting, operational, information technology and logistics engineering services include transport management, value-added warehouse development, dedicated contract management and, above all, vendor-managed inventory (VMI) that can account for 80 per cent of logistics costs. As traditional services are being outpaced by e-commerce, new types of deliveries are being developed by global logistics service providers to meet the needs of online shippers and receivers (that is, consignors and consignees).

A series of issues are raised in this chapter about the interaction between multinational industrial corporations and global logistics corporations. How do the strategies of the two types of corporations differ from each other; how can these differences be reconciled by adopting an integrative approach; and how can a spatial structure be developed to comprehend their activities?

A conceptual framework is provided to address key differences between the multinational industrial corporation and the global logistics corporation. Then each type of corporation is examined separately, before considering how their activities can be integrated and streamlined by examining flows in the global hub-and-spoke network.

CONCEPTUAL FRAMEWORK

The multinational industrial corporation's operational process is designed to add value through manufacturing and retailing. This process is supported by a decision-making system that supplies a marketing strategy in response to demand trends, and an information system that adds further value by facilitating inventory management (Table 2.1). The operational

Table 2.1 Multinational industrial corporations and global logistics corporations and integrative networks and their operational, decision-making and information systems

	Systems		
	Operational	Decision-making	Information
Multinational industrial corporations (MICs)	Products	Marketing strategy	Demand signals (forecasts & inventory)
Global logistics corporation (GLCs)	Carriers	Research institutes	Tracking & tracing shipments
Integrative networks	Sea–land–air freight	Air passenger	Telecommunications

Sources: Rimmer and Hamilton (2005, 2008).

process of the global logistics corporation is also designed to add value, but by transferring freight from one place to another. This process is underpinned by a decision-making system that draws upon the output of research institutes to predict the gap between supply and demand, and an information system that adds further value through tracking and tracing the progress of shipments between shipper and receiver.

The distinction between the two corporate sectors is important because the key to successful supply chain management hinges on integrating the multinational network transforming industrial goods to create 'form value', with the global logistics network generating 'place value' by moving freight from one location to a user at another, and 'time value' by getting it there when needed (Plowman, 1964; Gillen et al., 2008). This operational integration is supported not only by the sea–land–air freight network, but also by an air passenger network allowing corporate personnel to move long distances between dispersed plants for face-to-face interaction and knowledge transfer, and the telecommunications network providing for the transmission of information that adds 'time value' (Figure 2.2). Studying these phenomena has often proved elusive because the two networks have been examined as separate entities with few cross-linkages.

Before discussing the two different types of corporations, their number, nature and location need to be distilled from the 2011 Fortune Global 500 to assess the strength of their footprint within the Asian-Pacific Rim (CNN Money, 2011). This source ranked the world's largest companies according to their gross revenue in 2010. To concentrate on global logistics corporations and multinational manufacturers and retailers, 218 corporations engaged in banking, crude oil production, diversified financials, energy, engineering and construction, health care (insurance, managed care, services), insurance, petroleum refining, temporary help, trading and utilities were removed from consideration. While recognizing that a small number of financial institutions, typified by the United Kingdom's Barclays PLC, control the global economy (Vitali et al., 2011), their omission from this chapter, along with the other nominated categories, follows the practice of AMR Research (now Gartner, Inc.) in identifying the supply chains of multinational manufacturers and retailers (Hofman et al., 2011). The exception in this analysis is that transport and telecommunications corporations are retained and no corporations outside the Fortune Global 500 are added to the mix. This revamping of the data set has a marked impact upon the composition of the top ten corporations among the remaining 282 corporations, by bringing manufacturers, retailers and telecommunications corporations to the fore (Table 2.2).

As the remaining set of 282 firms from the Fortune Global 500 still contained both multinational industrial corporations and global logistics

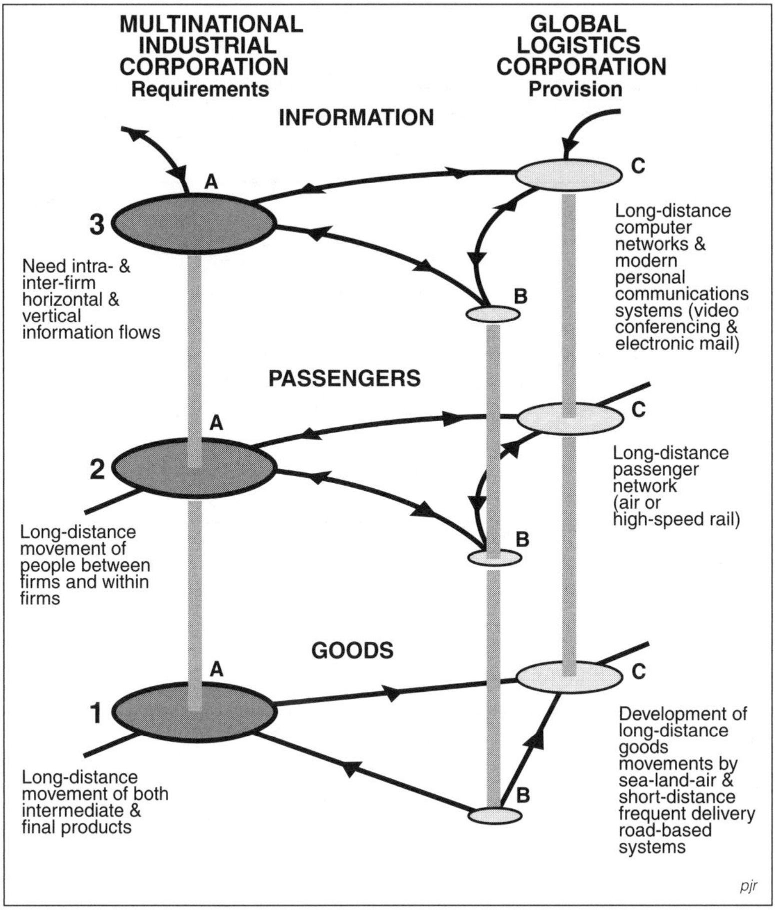

Source: Rimmer (1997a).

Figure 2.2 Transport and communications requirements of multinational industrial corporations and provision by global logistics corporations

corporations, the next step was to separate them. This action involved removing the transport industry group and the entire telecommunications services sector (Table 2.3). Forty-one global logistics corporations were identified; telecommunications services dominated, followed by mail, parcels and freight, and the airlines.

Mapping the headquarters locations of these global logistics corporations suggests that corporate control over logistics is still weighted in

Table 2.2 Effects on the top ten rankings in Fortune Global 500 of removing energy, financials and utilities, 2011

	Original list	Revenue US$ mn	Revised list	Revenue US$ mn
1	Wal-Mart Stores	421 849	Wal-Mart Stores	421 849
2	Royal Dutch Shell	378 152	Toyota Motor	221 760
3	Exxon Mobil	354 674	Volkswagen	168 041
4	BP	308 928	General Motors	135 592
5	Sinopec Group	273 422	Samsung Electronics	133 781
6	China National Petroleum	240 192	Daimler	129 481
7	State Grid	226 294	Ford Motor	128 954
8	Toyota Motor	221 760	Hewlett-Packard	126 033
9	Japan Post Holdings	203 958	AT&T	124 629
10	Chevron	196 337	Nippon Telegraph & Telephone	120 316

Note: Data based on 2010 revenue.

Source: CNN Money (2011).

Table 2.3 Global logistics corporations in Fortune Global 500, 2011

Industry group	Number	Leading firm
Airlines	5	Lufthansa Group
Mail, parcels & freight	8	Deutsche Post
Pipelines	2	Enterprise Products Partners
Railroads	2	Deutsche Bahn
Shipping	3	A.P. Møller-Mærsk Group
Telecommunications services	21	AT & T
Total	41	

Source: CNN Money (2011).

favour of North America and Europe. Both North America and Europe have 15 representatives each, Asia and the Middle East ten, and Oceania one (Figure 2.3). Only the United States among the 12 countries represented reaches double-digit figures, with 15 representatives. As the United States' corporations are dispersed, none of its cities match the concentration of those in Tokyo and Paris, which had five corporations each.

After removing the global logistics corporations, 241 multinational manufacturers and retailers remain. Their supply chain activities range

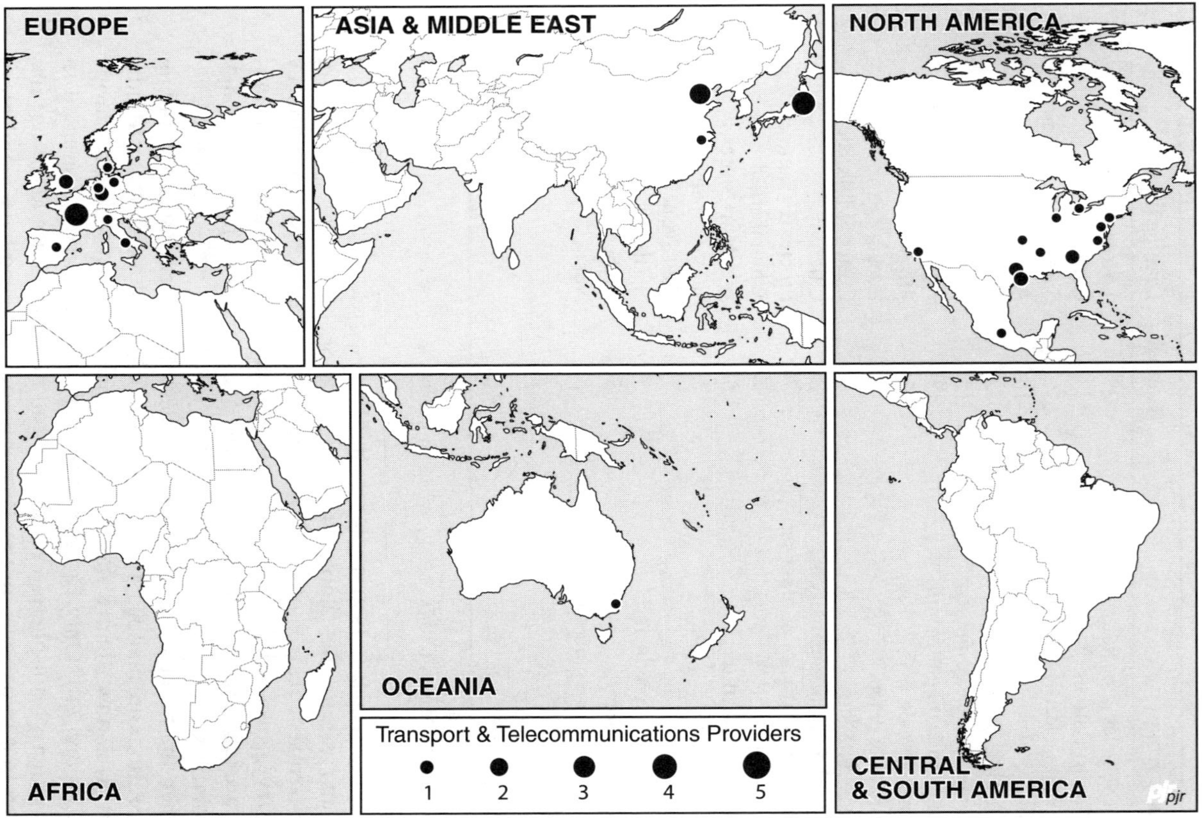

Source: Data from CNN Money (2011).

Figure 2.3 Distribution of the headquarters of global logistics corporations (GLCs), 2010

Table 2.4 Leading groups of multinational industrial corporations in Fortune Global 500, 2011

Industry group	Number	Leading firm
Motor vehicles & parts	29	Toyota Motor
Food & drug stores	23	Carrefour
Electronics, electrical equipment	16	Samsung Electronics
Metals	16	Arcelor/Mittai
Chemicals	15	BASF
Computers, office equipment	15	Hewlett-Packard
Mining, crude oil petroleum	13	Pemex
Pharmaceuticals	13	Pfizer
Aerospace & defence	11	Boeing
Specialty retailers	9	Costco Wholesale
Industrial & farm machinery	8	Caterpillar
Health care: pharmacy & other services	7	Procter & Gamble
Miscellaneous	7	Schlumberger
General merchandise	6	Wal-Mart Stores
Building materials, glass	5	Saint-Gobain
Entertainment	5	Walt Disney
Food consumer products	5	Nestlé
Food production	5	Archer Daniels Midland
Network & other communications equipment	5	Nokia
Other	28	
Total	241	

Source: CNN Money (2011).

across materials, industrials (excluding transportation), consumer discretionary, consumer staples, and information technology sectors and the pharmaceuticals, biotechnology and life sciences industry group. Key industry groups, their number of representatives and leading corporations are identified to illustrate the range of commodities moving through multinational supply chains (Table 2.4).

When the headquarters locations of these manufacturing and retailing corporations are mapped, this shows that a combined Asia and the Middle East (82) is now slightly ahead of both North America (80) and Europe (74) (Figure 2.4). Only five manufacturers and retailers are situated in the southern hemisphere: Oceania (3) and South America (2). None are located in Africa. Seven of the 24 countries represented have ten or more corporations: United States (76), Japan (37), China (23), Germany (18), France (17), the United Kingdom (14) and Switzerland (10). Reflecting

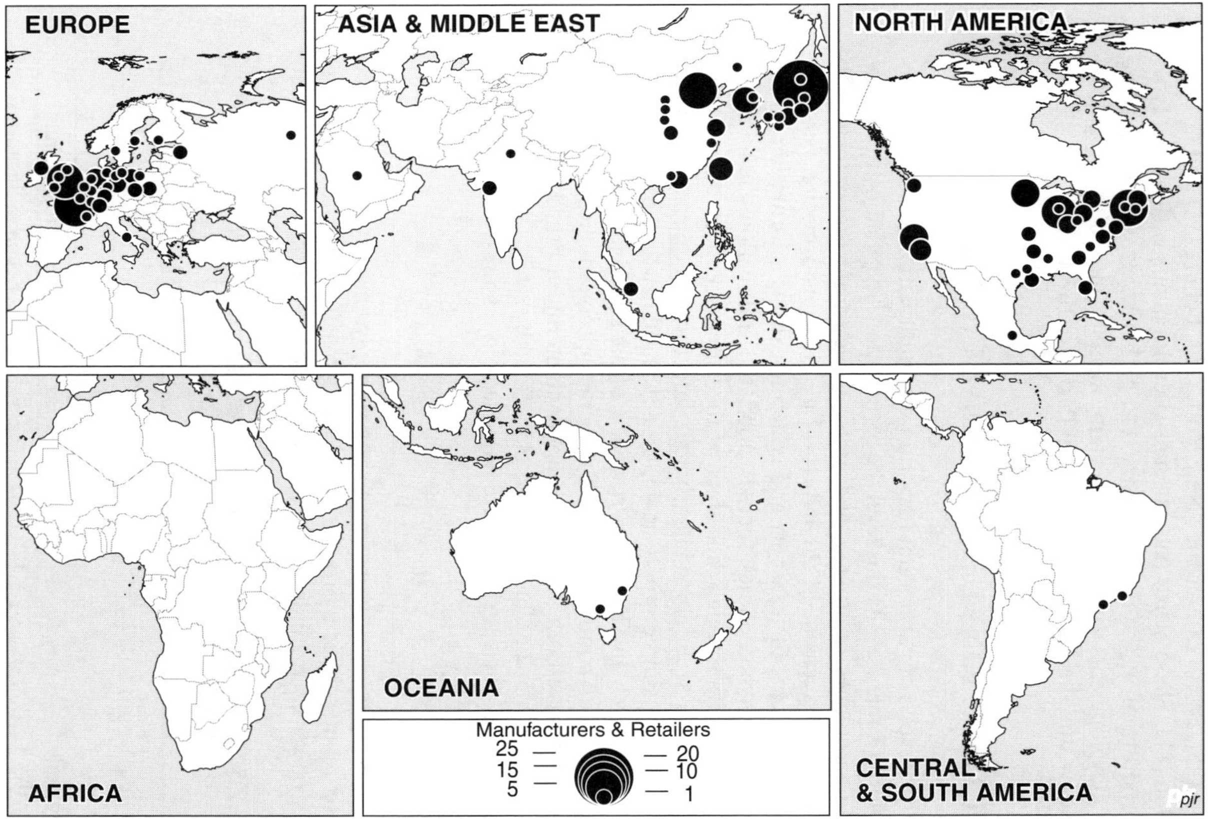

Source: Data from CNN Money (2011).

Figure 2.4 Distribution of the headquarters of multinational industrial corporations (MICs), 2010

different degrees of centralization within individual countries, the leading corporate domiciles among multinational industrial corporations are Tokyo (25), Paris (15), Greater New York (12), Beijing (11) and Greater London (11). These broad patterns mask developments within both types of corporations at the firm, industry and global levels. Comprehending these developments provides important insights into discussing local policies within the Asian-Pacific Rim in Part II of this book.

MULTINATIONAL INDUSTRIAL CORPORATIONS

The firm level is of paramount importance to multinational industrial corporations (Table 2.5). At this level the corporations, typified by those producing aeroplanes, computers and motor vehicles, are preoccupied with inventory management in the industrial goods transformation network; their management of transport and communications information on the movement of commodities focuses upon the traffic flows involved in inbound logistics through each stage of the supply chain. In other words, these capital or technology-intensive manufacturers requiring economies of scale have a simple supply chain, do not readily engage in alliances at an industry level, and have a narrow view of the global logistics network. Their behaviour contrasts sharply with the telecommunications corporations that have both a complex supply chain and a broad view of the logistics network (see Chapter 4). As elaborated by reference to Wal-Mart Stores and Dell Inc., variations are possible between these two extremes.

Wal-Mart Stores

Wal-Mart Stores Inc. maintains a simple supply chain structure but the big-box retailer takes a broader view of the logistics network by exercising its power to regulate traffic flows by 'leaning' on its suppliers such

Table 2.5 Complexity of the multinational industrial supply chain and breadth of logistics network

		Breadth of logistics network	
		Narrow	*Broad*
Supply chain complexity	*Simple*	Manufacturing	Wal-Mart Stores
	Complex	Dell Inc.	Telecommunications

Source: Rimmer and Hamilton (2008).

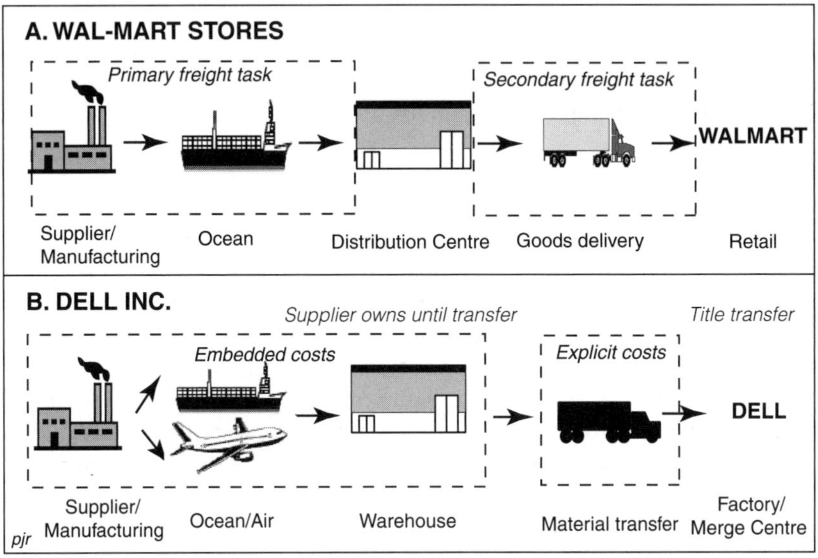

Source: Adapted from Chow (2007).

Figure 2.5 Supply chains: (A) Wal-Mart Stores; and (B) Dell Inc.

as Procter & Gamble (Quelch and Jocz, 2012, 76). Already Wal-Mart controls the secondary freight task involving trucking from warehouse to stores (Figure 2.5A). Wal-Mart has moved to directly control the primary freight task – the supplier-to-warehouse segment of the supply chain – by developing distribution centres to handle different marketing regions. These centres accommodate both offshore shipments through ports or airports that are moved intermodally by container or truck trailer, and direct shipments from larger regional manufacturers. The retailer exerts control either through purchasing produce on an ex-factory gate pricing basis or implementing new service level agreements to control the inbound transport task. Wal-Mart has used its 'whole of chain' solution to drive sustainability initiatives within countries such as carbon reduction targets, zero food waste, water saving and ethical sourcing of products, by requiring all suppliers to subscribe to its 'green' supply chain policy (Walmart, 2011). As a prominent buyer controlling the design and marketing of commodities, notably agricultural products and apparel, Wal-Mart Stores, like other major retailers, is able to set 'pricing points' to determine the location of labour-intensive manufacture of commodities with low barriers of entry. This buyer-driven development has triggered a major sourcing shift to the Asian Pacific Rim, particularly China. This shift has been accompanied by the overseas expansion of Walmart's retailing activities to Africa, Europe and the Rim, notably Japan, China and India, following successful penetration of the adjacent markets of Canada and Mexico (Gereffi and Christian, 2009; Walmart, 2013).

Dell Inc.

Dell has conversely a more complex supply chain or 'value consortium' of international partners and sophisticated distributors but has retained a simple logistics network (Figure 2.5B). The corporation seeks to minimize total costs by combining the location of intensive production, where goods are produced at low cost, with a strategy of postponing the delivery of finished goods to enable them to meet the specific demands of local customers (that is, customization) (Kapuscinski et al., 2004). This 'postponement' strategy hinges on combining flexible production and high-speed transport with information systems, including the use of Twitter to alert customers to new upgrades (Quelch and Jocz, 2012, 115). Dell has revamped elements of its supply chain by switching from airfreight to ocean transport and substituting its 'direct-to-consumer' policy by including retailers in its distribution network, particularly in developing countries where customers do not have credit cards. Now Dell's supply chain more closely resembles that of other manufacturers, which use 'total landed cost analysis' in procuring materials from overseas suppliers and shipping them through ocean (or air) networks into the warehouse. The embedded costs in this primary freight task comprise materials, freight, warehouse and any other charges incurred in not meeting the terms and conditions of sale. Under this vendor-managed inventory the supplier owns the material until the title transfers to the manufacturer once the material is moved in the secondary freight task from the warehouse to the factory or merge centre (that is, explicit costs). While the total landed cost in this regime determines the source of material, the choice of route is decided by total logistics cost.

The selection of Wal-Mart Stores and Dell to illustrate variations from the manufacturing norm of a simple supply chain and narrow view of the logistics network stems from their prominence as supply chain innovators. This status is confirmed in annual surveys undertaken by AMR Research and Gartner, Inc. between 2004 and 2013 that rank corporate supply chains based on the weightings of public financial information (for example, return on assets, inventory turns and revenue growth), in-house and peer opinion, and innovation excellence such as time-to-value (Table 2.6). Wal-Mart Stores, together with P&G, one of its principal suppliers, was ever-present in the top 15 rankings. Apart from being

Table 2.6 Top 15 rankings of the supply chains of multinational industrial corporations, 2004–05 and 2007–13

	2004	2005	2007	2008	2009	2010	2011	2012	2013
Dell	1	1	–	3	2	5	2	4	11
Nokia	2	4	1	2	6	–	–	–	–
P&G	3	2	3	4	3	2	3	5	6
IBM	4	3	4	5	4	8	14	–	–
Wal-Mart Stores	5	8	6	6	7	4	7	9	13
Toyota Motor	6	5	5	7	10	–	–	–	–
Johnson & Johnson	7	6	14	–	12	14	–	–	–
Johnson Controls	8	10	–	–	–	–	–	–	–
Tesco	9	9	8	12	15	–	–	–	–
PepsiCo	10	–	15	11	9	6	9	12	–
Nissan Motor	11	–	–	–	–	–	–	–	–
Woolworths	12	13	–	–	–	–	–	–	–
Hewlett-Packard	13	–	–	–	–	15	–	–	–
3M	14	–	–	–	–	–	–	–	–
GlaxoSmithKline	15	–	–	–	–	–	–	–	–
Samsung Electronics	–	7	10	9	8	7	10	13	8
Intel	–	11	–		–	–	–	7	5
Anheuser-Busch	–	12	7	10	–	–	–	–	–
Home Depot	–	14	–	–	–	–	–	–	–
Motorola	–	15	12	–	–	–	–	–	–
Apple	–	–	2	1	1	1	1	1	1
Best Buy	–	–	9	14	–	–	–	–	–
Cisco Systems	–	–	11	8	5	3	6	8	7
Coca-Cola Company	–	–	13	13	13	13	11	6	9
Nike	–	–	–	15	14	–	–	14	14
Schlumberger	–	–	–	–	11	–	–	–	–
RIM	–	–	–	–	–	9	4	–	–
Amazon.com	–	–	–	–	–	10	5	2	3
McDonald's	–	–	–	–	–	11	8	3	2
Microsoft	–	–	–	–	–	12	12	–	–
Colgate-Palmolive	–	–	–	–	–	–	13	11	10
Unilever	–	–	–	–	–	–	15	10	4
Inditex	–	–	–	–	–	–	–	15	12
Starbucks	–	–	–	–	–	–	–	–	15

Note: Abstracted from the annual top 25 ranking (there was no ranking in 2006).

Sources: Friscia et al. (2004), Friscia et al. (2008, 2010), PR Newswire (2006, 2009), Gartner (2013a) for the years 2011, 2012 and 2013 at http://www.gartner.com/technology/supply-chain/top25.jsp.

excluded in 2007 when a financial restatement was in progress, Dell (2010) did return to a prominent position, despite being superseded as number one first by Nokia and then, following the rise of e-commerce players, by Apple.

Summary

Together the powerhouses Wal-Mart Stores and Dell reflect the shift from the traditional linear push supply chain model that accepts demand, injects product innovation as an externality, and employs deterministic optimization algorithms (for example, linear programming) to a customer-centric pull model that shapes demand, embeds product innovation and incorporates variability by using probabilistic optimization algorithms (Figure 2.6). This demand-driven supply chain network is marked by a circular, self-renewing system covering supply, demand and product management to better gauge, shape and respond to shifts in market

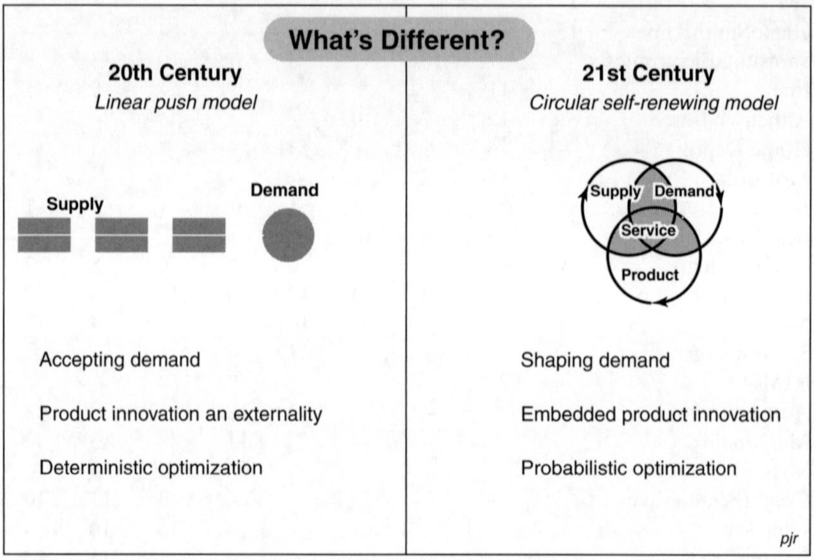

Note: The push factory-based model of the twentieth century is replaced by the demand-driven supply networks (DDSN) of the twenty-first century with a customer-centric pull model.

Source: Friscia et al. (2004, 3).

Figure 2.6 Change in design from (A) linear push model to the (B) circular self-renewing model

Table 2.7 Changes in relative importance of inventory, transport and information in switching from pull to push supply chain systems

Supply chain system	Inventory %	Transport %	Information %
Push	70	20	10
Pull	15	35	50

Source: Estimated from pie charts in Tables 34a and 34b in AASHTO (2002, 49).

demand from a customer, production and fulfilment perspective. The new design model recognizes the superior ability of a corporation to manage proactively rather than to merely respond to shifts in demand; to offer a networked rather than a linear approach to global supply; and to embed product innovations in operations rather than isolate them in a laboratory (Hofman et al., 2011). The outcome from adopting this demand-driven model is a nimbler multinational industrial corporation engaged in a constant process of reinventing itself to adapt its operational strategy so that it can grasp short-lived or unpredicted business opportunities. There is a strong relationship between competency in supply chain management with customer satisfaction and shareholder value (Slone et al., 2010, 4–6; Ellinger et al., 2012).

In switching from a linear 'push' to demand-driven 'pull' supply chain systems, multinational industrial corporations substitute low-cost efficient freight transport services and information for high-cost inventory (Table 2.7). Time spent in the transport network substitutes for time in the warehouse. Nevertheless streamlined warehouses, regional and satellite distribution centres, and local outlets still play key roles in the international supply chain. Any difficulties manufacturers and retailers have in evaluating their international supply chain's performance can be attributed to their management focus being primarily at the firm level, and their analytical framework having a narrow view of global logistics.

GLOBAL LOGISTICS CORPORATIONS

The operational behaviour of global logistics corporations shifts from a competitive stance through to a cooperative position with changes in the level of engagement. At a firm level there are numerous competing transport and logistics companies that can be used to transport goods between supplier and receiver based on a contract or waybill. At an industry level there are strategic alliances among leading international carriers in air, shipping, rail, road and airline operations to optimize the use of transport space; also there is the integration of different modes in multimodal services that allow logistics providers to differentiate services to attract a premium price (that is, a value-adding strategy). At a global level, transport and logistics corporations cooperate to propel the movements of goods around the world and create seamless connections between the geographically dispersed supply chain activities of multinational industrial corporations, and provide the different facilities, services and infrastructure they require.

Multinational industrial corporations that provide their own services in vehicles (owned or rented) as shippers or consignees are referred to as first-party logistics (1PL) providers. This differentiates them from the global logistics providers comprising:

- the actual carriers – airlines, shipping lines, railways and road transport – which are referred to as second-party logistics (2PL) providers; and
- the integrators of supply chain management functions covering transport, warehousing, cross-docking, inventory management, packaging, freight forwarding and customs brokerage that are bundled together to meet a customer's specific needs based on market conditions or delivery requirements for products or materials, which are referred to as third-party logistics (3PL) providers (see RWBL, 2007; Armstrong & Associates, 2009).

Fourth-party logistics (4PL) providers are also identified to cover consultants operating in partnership with multinational logistics corporations to engineer supply chain solutions – the process described as 'insourcing'.

To complicate matters further a shipping company can also act both as an owner of an airline (2PL) and as a freight forwarder (3PL) engaged in arranging storage and transport of merchandise on behalf of shippers. Cargo integrators (3PL) can own airlines or shipping lines (2PL), prompting a distinction between asset and non-asset operators. Given these overlaps, 'pure' third-party logistics providers are difficult to define. Nevertheless it is helpful to restrict discussion here to third-party logistics activities and to give separate consideration to the carriers, and adjacent infrastructure operators and service providers such as port and airport authorities, railway and road transport operators, consultants and software companies, in Chapters 3 and 4. This decision allows an exploration of the way the Internet is changing the way in which both information and goods are exchanged. As electronic communication replaces physical communications, there is a marked decline in the traditional mail business and a boom in online trade (e-commerce), which is boosting parcel businesses.

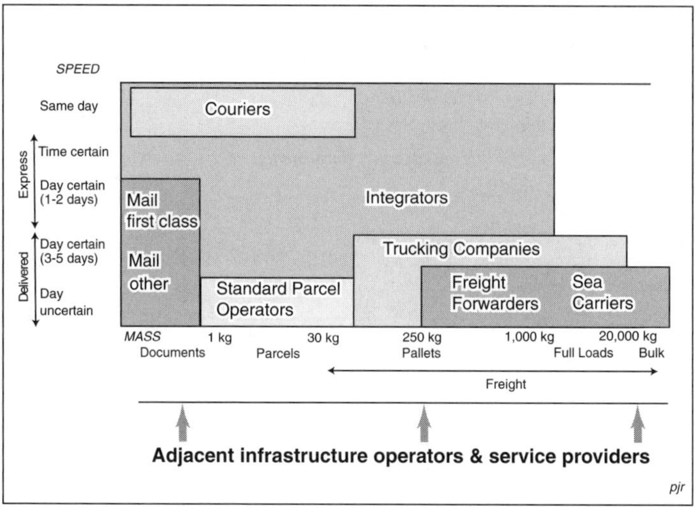

Source: Based on Bakker (2007).

Figure 2.7 Speed and mass characteristics of different types of logistics sectors

Global logistics activities reflect the consignment's mass, and speed of the required delivery. Within this framework a range of activities can be identified: express and delivered mail services for documents under 1 kg; courier services offering time-definite, same-day and day-definite deliveries for documents and parcels under 30 kg; standard parcel services with an uncertain delivery time for parcels under 30 kg; trucking companies able to carry palletized or full-load consignments between 30 kg and 20000 kg; and freight forwarders and sea carriers able to handle consignments from 250 kg to over 20000 kg (Figure 2.7).

This range of activities pursued by third-party logistics providers has been fashioned into three different spheres: post and parcel operators with services for documents and parcels weighing less than 30 kg; express operations offering a range of same-day services for commodities up to 1000 kg; and freight transport for consignments from 250 kg to over 20000 kg (Figure 2.8). As depicted, each sphere of operation is trying to expand its activities into adjacent spheres.

Within this framework third-party logistics corporations are seeking to develop their network strategy by focusing on both strategic and financial activities. They are actively seeking to maintain their mail services because they generate cash. Within their respective continents in which they are

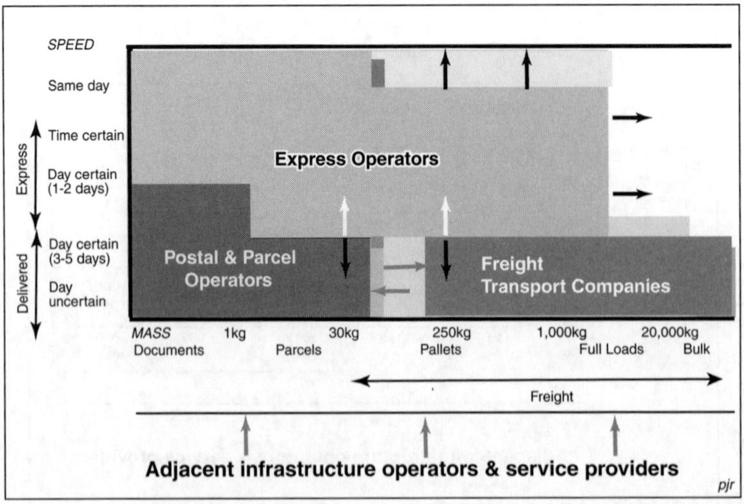

Source: Based on Bakker (2007).

Figure 2.8 Expansion of the domains of postal and parcel operators, express operators and freight transport companies

domiciled, these corporations are seeking to grow their existing business, and accelerate new business to provide cash and create value. Outside their home region they are seeking to explore, build and create value within the Asian-Pacific Rim and other emerging regions by enhancing their intercontinental connectivity, so long as it is above the weighted average cost of capital (WACC).

Armstrong & Associates (2013b) rank third-party logistics service providers annually on their gross revenue (Table 2.8). Since 2006, DHL Supply Chain & Global Forwarding has dominated the top ten rankings following its takeover of the British company Exel, one of many mergers and acquisitions of companies over the decade (Armstrong & Associates, 2013c). DHL has one-third more revenue than the three players jockeying for the second position: Kuehne + Nagel, Nippon Express and DB Schenker Logistics. In turn, the individual revenues of these three corporations are more than double that of most of the remaining companies in the top ten. Narrow margins between these firms account for the volatility in the rankings shown during the first two decades of the twenty-first century.

Not all of the top ten third-party logistics providers are regarded as global players. Nippon Express and CH Robinson are seen as belonging to a group of regional companies. Conversely, Deutsche Post DHL,

Table 2.8 Ranking of top ten third-party logistics providers on gross revenue, 2003–12

Company	HQ	2003	2004	2005	2006	2007	2008	2009	2010	2011	2012
		$ bn	$ bn	$ bn	$ bn	$ bn	$ bn	$ bn	$ bn	$bn	$ bn
DHL	DE	5.7	8.5	9.5	31.0	37.9	37.1	32.5	30.5	32.2	31.6
Kuehne + Nagel	CH	6.9	9.3	10.7	14.9	18.6	20.1	16.0	19.5	22.2	22.1
Nippon Express	JP	4.0	–	–	–	–	–	15.4	18.5	20.3	20.3
DB Schenker	DE	6.4	8.9	10.7	14.0	21.1	21.6	15.7	19.0	20.7	19.8
CH Robinson	US	3.6	4.3	5.7	6.6	7.3	8.6	7.6	9.3	10.3	11.4
Hyundai GLOVIS	KR	–	–	–	–	–	–	–	6.3	8.6	9.8
CEVA Logistics	US	–	–	–	4.6	9.3	9.3	7.6	9.1	9.6	9.3
UPS Supply Chain Solutions	US	4.1	5.3	7.7	8.0	–	9.8	7.5	8.9	8.9	9.1
DSV Solutions	DK	–	–	–	–	7.0	7.2	6.9	7.6	8.2	7.8
Sinotrans	CN	–	–	–	–	–	–	–	–	–	7.5
Panalpina	CH	4.6	5.3	6.3	7.7	8.7	9.9	–	6.9	7.4	–
SDV	FR	–	–	–	–	–	–	5.6	–	–	–
Agility	KW	–	–	–	4.9	–	6.8	5.5	–	–	–
Geodis	FR	–	–	–	–	7.0	8.0	–	–	–	–
Li & Fung	HK	–	–	–	–	11.9	–	–	–	–	–
Toll	AU	–	–	–	–	7.8	–	–	–	–	–
Expeditors	US	–	–	3.9	4.6	–	–	–	–	–	–
NYK Logistics	JP	–	–	–	4.2	–	–	–	–	–	–
Exel	UK	8.3	11.6	13.4	–	–	–	–	–	–	–
TNT	NL	4.7	4.8	4.2	–	–	–	–	–	–	–
Schnieder	US	–	3.4	3.9	–	–	–	–	–	–	–
P&O Nedlloyd	UK	4.8	6.7	–	–	–	–	–	–	–	–

Sources: Foster and Armstrong (2004, 2005, 2006), Armstrong & Associates (2008, 2013d), Popescu et al. (2010, 224), USDOT (2009), Armstrong, Richard (2012), Burnson (2012).

Table 2.9 Ranking of top ten global freight forwarders, 2012

Rank	Provider	Gross revenue	Ocean	Airfreight
		US$ billion	Thousand TEUs[1]	Thousand tonnes
1	DHL Supply Chain & Global Forwarding	31.6	2840	2327
2	Kuehne +Nagel	22.1	3473	1093
3	DB Schenker Logistics	19.8	1905	1095
4	Sinotrans	7.5	8237	417
5	Panalpina	7.1	1388	801
6	Nippon Express	20.3	719	774
7	CEVA Logistics	9.3	783	550
8	Expeditors International of Washington	6.0	868	730
9	UPS Supply Chain Solutions	9.1	500	862
10	SDV (Bolloré Group)	7.0	770	510

Note: Freight forwarders are ranked using a combined overall average based on their individual rankings for gross revenue, ocean twenty-foot equivalent units (TEUs) and airfreight metric tons.[1] TEUs shown are a combination of freight forwarding, non-vessels operating common carrier (NVOCC), booking agent and customer broker activities.

Source: Armstrong & Associates (2013d).

Kuene + Nagel, DB Schenker, UPS Supply Chain Solutions and CEVA Logistics are recognized as global supply chain managers (Armstrong & Associates, 2013d). Even among the latter group there are marked differences between market segments: forwarding (air and ocean freight), mail, and supply chain contract logistics solutions (Table 2.9). DHL Supply Chain & Global Forwarding leads the international forwarding segment which has been more profitable since the 1980s than the ocean carriers and airlines on which the forwarders rely (Damas, 2010). Much of the profitability has stemmed from the international express market offering time-certain, same-day and day-certain international services.

International Express Market

In 2010 only two of the top ten third-party logistics providers – Deutsche Post DHL (DPDHL) and UPS (United Parcel Service) – featured in the international express market with time-definite and day-definite pick-up and delivery door-to-door services for urgent documents and goods. Their global networks are analysed here, together with those of the unranked

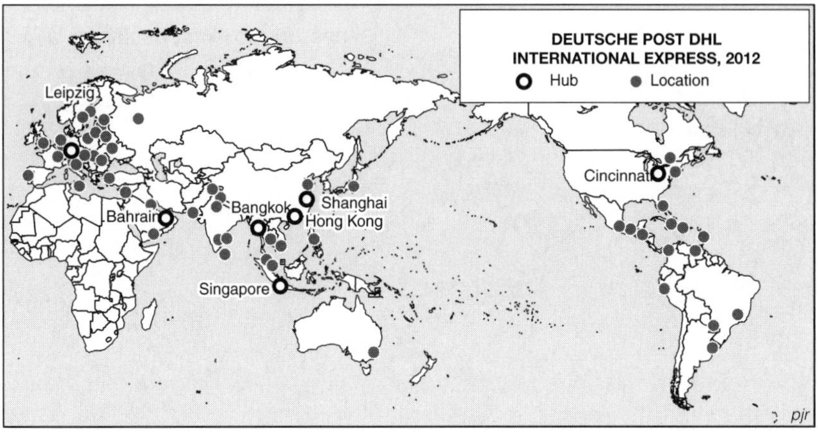

Note: DHL has separate mail and forwarding networks, which have a smaller and larger footprint respectively.

Sources: DPDHL Global (2012), DPDHL (2012b).

Figure 2.9 DPDHL's international express network, 2012

FedEx (Federal Express) and TNT (Thomas Nationwide Transport), before making comparisons between the four companies, which have enjoyed a marked growth in their parcel business stemming from the e-commerce boom.

Deutsche Post DHL's courier and express network originated in the United States as DHL in 1969 and, after DHL had extended its international operations, Deutsche Post acquired a majority ownership in 2001, completed the purchase in 2002 and absorbed DHL into its international express division. In 2004 the company entered the US domestic market with the acquisition of Airborne Express, but the company decided to abandon its efforts to compete with FedEx and UPS and close its facility in Wilmington, Ohio, and subcontract its deliveries. By then the DHL brand had been extended by DPDHL from international express to the global forwarding and supply chain divisions. In 2012 the combined mail and logistics group within headquarters in Bonn had 470000 employees and covered 220 countries and territories. Its international express division with 100000 employees and 2.6 million customers has a global footprint, with Leipzig serving as its European regional hub, Cincinnati for the Americas, Bahrain for the Middle East, and Hong Kong together with Bangkok, Shanghai and Singapore for the Asia Pacific (Figure 2.9).

UPS's network reflects the company's decision to transform a private

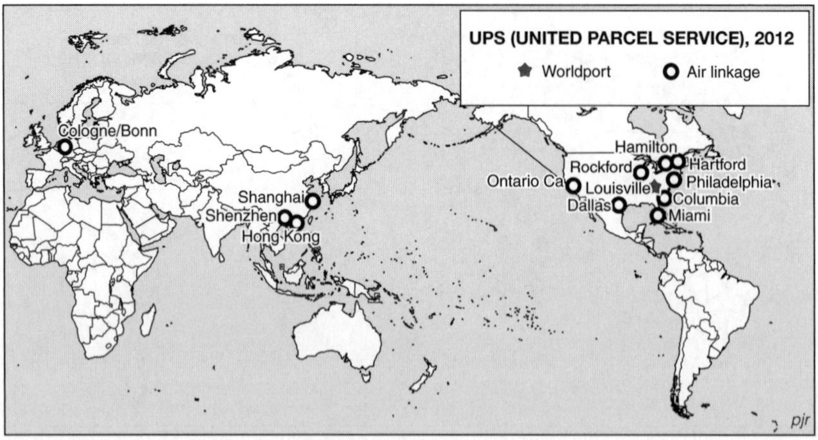

Source: Based on information in UPS (2012).

Figure 2.10 UPS's global network, 2012

messenger and delivery service founded in Seattle in 1907 into the world's largest small-package delivery company, matching DPDHL's coverage of 220 countries and territories, with domestic deliveries in 56 countries (Figure 2.10). The company's international express network is centred on its 'Worldport' hub in Louisville, Kentucky with a capacity to handle 416000 packages per hour. Seven other regional US air hubs and one in Canada supplement this facility. The company's largest international hub in Europe is at Cologne Bonn Airport. Other regional international hubs include Miami for South America, and Hong Kong, Shanghai and Shenzhen on the Asian-Pacific Rim.

FedEx Express's air cargo network provided by 660 dedicated freight aircraft hinges on its global 'superhub' in Memphis, Tennessee, extending to 220 countries and territories (FedEx, 2012). Originally founded in Little Rock, Arkansas in 1971, FedEx moved to Memphis two years later to gain better local government support for the company's global ambitions. Since then the corporation has established a national hub at Indianapolis and five regional hubs within the United States (Anchorage, Fort Worth, Miami, Newark and Oakland) (Figure 2.11). International hubs have been located at Cologne (Central and Eastern Europe), Guangzhou (Asia-Pacific), Miami (doubling for South America), Paris (Europe, the Middle East and Africa) and Toronto (Canada). The Guangzhou hub was opened in 2009 to replace Clark Airport in the Philippines; Figure 2.11 suggests that the transition was still in progress

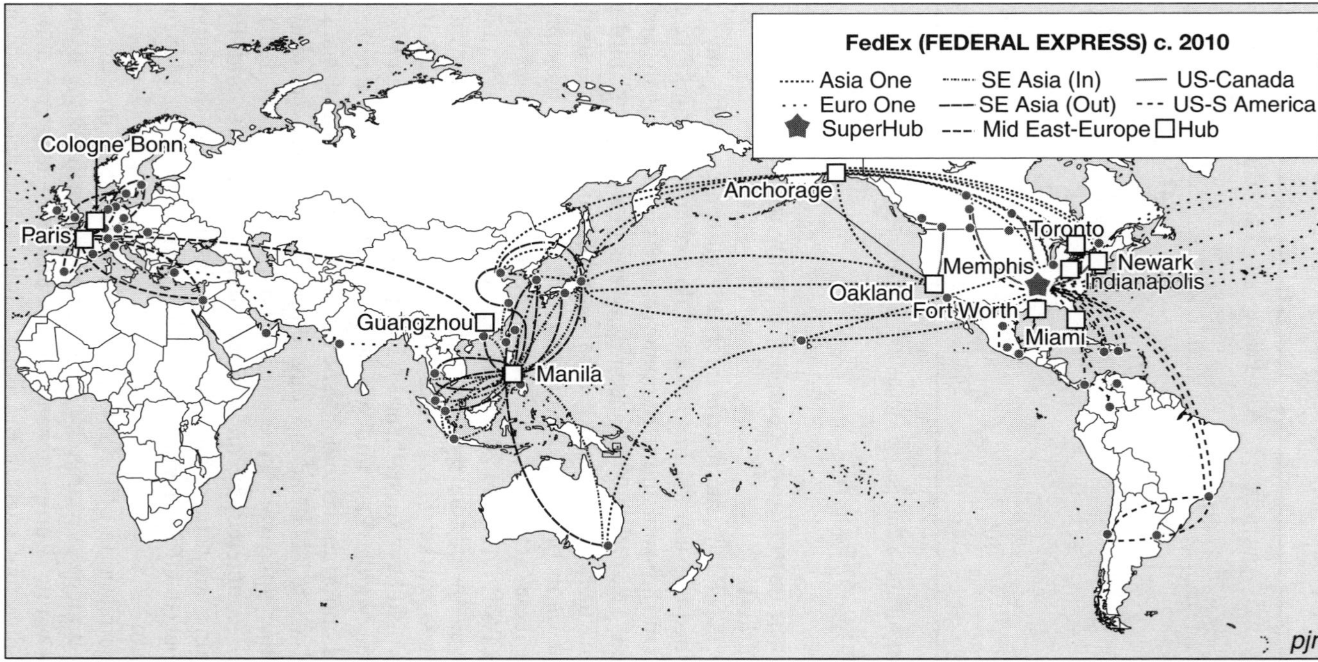

Source: ARM (2012).

Figure 2.11 FedEx route map, ca. 2010

Table 2.10 International express freight market, 2010

	Americas	Asia-Pacific	EEMEA	Europe
	%	%	%	%
DHL	13	36	47	38
FedEx	51	21	6	11
UPS	32	10	12	23
TNT	1	0	17	16
EMS	–	12	–	–
Subtotal	97	79	82	88
Total	100	100	100	100
US$ million	5387	5430	544	5788

Note: EEMEA Eastern Europe, the Middle East and Africa; EMS Express Mail Service.

Source: DPDHL (2012a, 68–9).

in 2010 when this map was compiled to show routes tailored to serve specific markets.

In 2010, TNT was the fourth international express company, originally founded in Australia in 1946 and taken over by Koninklijke KPN N.V., the Dutch postal and telecommunications company, 50 years later (see Chapter 11). Until 2007 the company was in the top ten third-party logistics providers. In 2007 the company sold off its logistics activities to concentrate on its postal and express activities. After 2010 the company demerged these activities and created TNT Express as a separate company (TNT, 2011). In 2012 TNT Express was subject to a takeover by UPS, which would have left only three global players in the international express market (TNT, 2012). As is evident from Table 2.10, the takeover would have strengthened UPS's position in Europe and Eastern Europe, the Middle East and Africa; it would also have increased the company's opportunities in domestic activities within Australasia, China and Brazil where TNT had a strong foothold. This takeover could have led to further upheaval in the international express market had UPS's move been countered by an alliance between DPDHL and FedEx. This remains conjecture, however, as in January 2013 the European Union blocked UPS's merger with TNT Express after a nine-month investigation.

Since the rejection of the takeover, TNT has restructured by adopting a new strategy in March 2013, which involves maintaining its overall leadership within Europe through its extensive regional air and road networks, divesting assets in Brazil and China, and reducing exposure to

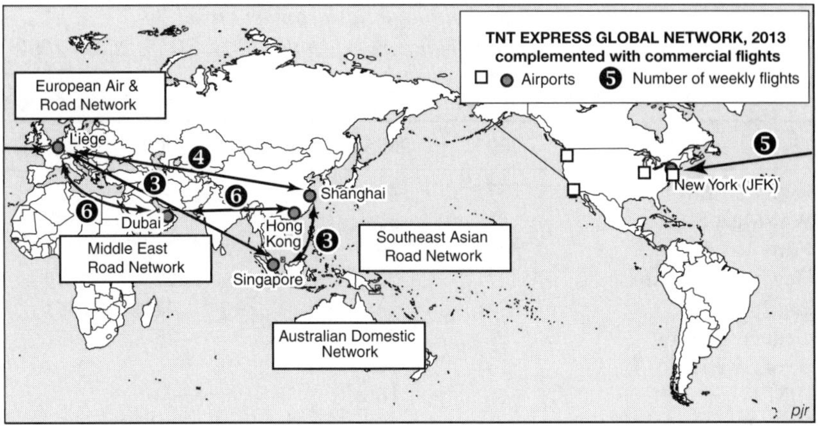

Source: TNT (2013a).

Figure 2.12 TNT Express's global air network complemented with commercial flights, 2013

intercontinental fixed air capacity (TNT, 2013a). TNT's European hub in Liège is connected through its own worldwide air fleet of 51 aircraft to link New York, Dubai, Singapore, Hong Kong and Shanghai with an array of weekly services (Figure 2.12). Complemented by commercial aircraft, these services enable the company's 68 000 employees to serve over 200 countries worldwide, and 61 countries through direct TNT operations. Domestic road networks are also operated in both the Middle East and Southeast Asia, and the company still pursues a broader range of express operations within Australia. TNT claims that its worldwide capabilities in intercontinental coverage and transit time for parcels are still comparable to the three other express companies and offer an edge in 'economy services' (TNT, 2013a).

The four leading companies in the international express market, together with other major third-party logistics providers such as Kuene + Nagel, DB Schenker and CEVA Logistics, manage the supply chain networks of a growing number of multinational industrial corporations listed in the Fortune Global 500. Their number include major motor vehicle manufacturers, notably General Motors, Ford Motor, Daimler, Volkswagen and BMW; technology manufacturers typified by Hewlett-Packard; and retailers such as Wal-Mart Stores and P&G, a major supplier of product ranges, including personal care, household cleaning, laundry detergents, prescription drugs and disposable nappies. The number of third-party logistics

Table 2.11 Number of third-party logistics providers used by multinational industrial corporations, 2003, 2005, 2007, 2009 and 2011

	2003	2005	2007	2009	2011
General Motors	37	43	43	49	51
Wal-Mart Stores	33	30	32	37	49
Ford Motor	27	30	36	31	41
Hewlett-Packard	27	26	27	29	39
P&G	20	22	27	42	53
General Electric	17	21	21	26	–
Georgia-Pacific	16	16	–	–	–
IBM	16	16	–	–	–
DuPont	14	–	–	–	–
Home Depot	14	15	21	–	–
Altria Group	13	–	–	–	–
PepsiCo	13	–	25	30	35
Sears, Roebuck	13	–	21	–	–
Coca-Cola	12	–	–	–	–
Sara Lee	12	15	–	–	–
Target	12	–	–	–	–
Xerox	12	–	–	–	–
General Mills	11	–	–	–	–
Delphi	10	–	–	–	–
Safeway	10	–	–	–	–
Daimler	–	32	31	32	30
Volkswagen	–	28	30	37	42
Unilever	–	24	24	27	36
Siemens	–	19	–	–	30
BMW	–	17	21	–	31
Nestlé	–	16	–	29	42
Royal Philips Electronics	–	16	–	–	32
Toyota	–	16	–	–	–

Note: Variable minimum for inclusion: 2003 – 10 and over; 2005 – 15 and over; 2007 – 20 and over; 2009 – 25 and over; 2011 – 30 and over.

Sources: Armstrong & Associates (2004, 2010, 2013d), Armstrong, Evan (2008) Armstrong, Richard (2005, 2012).

providers employed by multinational corporations in the Armstrong & Associates biennial survey has increased over time (Table 2.11). This raises the issue of how multinational corporations and global logistics corporations are integrated.

Table 2.12 Comparisons of key features of the supply/value chain and the global logistics network

	Supply chain management	Global logistics network
Process	Sequential	Mediating
Value creation	Market needs Firm (Shipper) Firm–Network	Firm (Carrier) Network
Value basis	Distinctive competencies	Network architecture Firm
Analytical level	Firm/group Firms within industry	Country Region
Locational emphasis	Goods transfer – product manufacturing	Logistics network arena

Source: Rimmer and Hamilton (2005, 2008).

INTEGRATION

As is evident from the separate analyses of the transactional activities of industrial corporations and the marshalling operations of logistics corporations, there are marked differences between supply chain management and the global logistics network (Table 2.12). Whereas the latter is a mediating procedure, the former is a sequential process in which value is added cumulatively at every segment of an end-to-end product or service delivery (that is, the value chain). Value in the supply chain derives from market needs, or the firm itself, or interactions between the firm and the global logistics network; while value in the global logistics network originates at the level of the firm, the industry alliance or the network itself. The basis of value in the supply chain arises from the industrial corporation's distinctive competencies, but in the global network it stems from the logistics corporation itself, the alliance's relative strength or network dynamics. Analysis of supply and value chain management occurs either at the firm level or industry level, compared with the focus on either the country or region in investigations of the global logistics network. The locational emphasis in the supply chain is on product manufacturing and the goods transfer process, whereas in the global network it is on the logistics arena.

These itemized differences between the supply and value chain management and the global logistics network explain why it is difficult to integrate them. The dissimilarities stem from a clash in the rules of engagement, involving transactions between the two networks. By its very nature, the

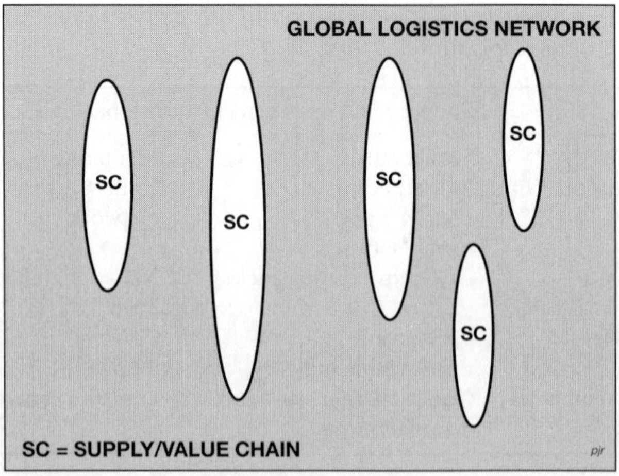

Source: Developed from Rimmer and Hamilton (2008).

Figure 2.13 An array of multinational supply chains within the global transport and communications system

multinational industrial transformation network seeks to be competitive, whereas the global transport network is intrinsically cooperative.

The difficulties in integrating the two networks stem from there being little or no overlapping congruence between the two systems (Sandberg, 2007). In moving beyond the interlinked chains at an industry level to larger and denser patterns at a cross-industry level in supply chain management, the global logistics network assumes paramount importance. As was the case in the traditional formulation of logistics, the industrial transformation network is subsumed within the global logistics network interconnecting the movement of goods and services across the world.

Moving beyond this simple traditional formulation, an array of multinational supply chains – long and short – are seen in Figure 2.13 as being nestled within the broader global logistics network. Reflecting the span of the world's economic system, the global transport and communications network determines the maximum extent of any multinational supply chain. The larger transport and communications network can accommodate innumerable supply chains within this nested model.

This framework suggests that supply chain management still gets priority at a firm level but must take a wider view by incorporating global network attributes that affect the cost structure, timing of shipments and conditions of consignments as goods progress through the system. Conversely, the critical focus in the global logistics network is on accommodating numerous competing supply chains that cross industries. Thus both sides need to look at supply chain management and global logistics.

If you examine supply chain management encompassed within a global logistics network, attention shifts from firm-level attributes to the network's dynamics. As is evident in switching from 'push' supply chain systems followed by traditional manufacturing firms to the 'pull' system pursued by retailers, the industrial corporation's priority changes from inventory management to an emphasis on accessibility and use of logistics services. Interest is centred upon network promotion and contract management, service provisioning and infrastructure operations such as integrated logistics clusters where intermodal terminals are co-located with distribution centres:

> These clusters include firms providing logistics services such as third-party logistics providers (3PLs), transportation carriers, warehousing companies and forwarders; the logistics operations of industrial firms, such as the distribution operations of retailers, manufacturers (for both new products and after-market parts) and distributors; and the operations of companies for whom logistics is a large part of their costs. (Sheffi, 2012, 53–54)

As the objective of these logistics clusters is to minimize the sum of supply chain costs, the stress is on delivering value and driving growth rather than on mass throughput.

CONCLUSION: GLOBAL HUB-AND-SPOKE SYSTEM

The division of corporations into two entities – industrial and logistics – contributes to a conceptual framework for exploring the measures required to reduce the cost of transporting products to markets. As illustrated by the case studies of Dell and Wal-Mart Stores, this conceptual framework is designed primarily to accommodate the increased demand for supply chain and logistics services triggered by a growth in exports and local consumption, particularly in the Asian-Pacific Rim. Arising from this analysis, there is an opportunity to further refine the conceptual framework examining how multinational industrial corporations and global logistics corporations interact, because speed, productivity and reliability hinge on their collaboration.

The interactive approach can be elaborated by paying more attention to global flows of people, information and money to describe the

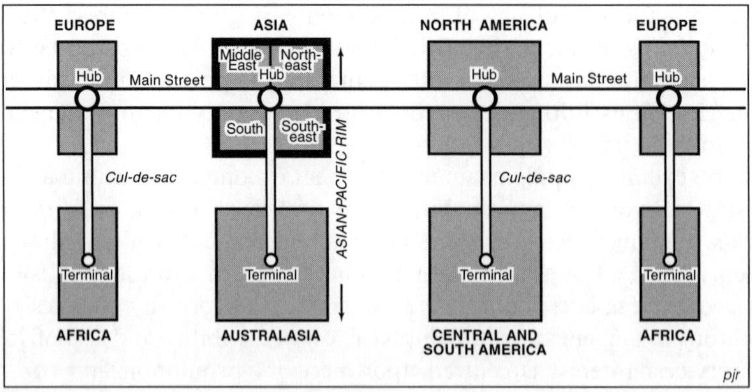

Note: Main Street, hubs and cul-de-sacs are shown together with the wider definition of the Asian-Pacific Rim that includes Australasia.

Source: Rimmer (2001).

Figure 2.14 The global hub-and-spoke network

economic world 'as it really is'. This elaboration focuses on the need to study sea–land, air transport and telecommunications systems, and gateway and corridor structures. These transport and communications patterns are designed to meet the infrastructural needs of multinational industrial corporations for the short- and long-distance movement of intermediate and final products, the long-distance movement of people within and between production and marketing sites, and horizontal and vertical information flows within and between organizations.

The simplest structure that global logistics providers can design to meet the needs of multinational logistics corporations is the global hub-and-spoke network (Figure 2.14). This is constructed by stripping the world to its bare essentials: Africa, Asia and the Middle East, Australasia, Europe, North America, and Central and South America. Then an east–west transcontinental axis is added to link Asia and the Middle East, Europe and North America. This principal axis is conveniently described as 'Main Street'. Three north–south offshoots from hubs on this global-spanning axis link 'cul-de-sacs': Europe to Africa, Asia to Australasia and North America to Central and South America.

Investigation is warranted into the extent to which the global hub-and-spoke system is reflected in container shipping, air transport and telecommunications networks (Chapters 3 and 4). Then considera-tion can be given as to how their key structural elements can be integrated into gateways and corridors to comprise the global 'network of networks' (Chapter 5). Once this task is completed, the way in which the local state has used gateway and corridor strategies in national logistics policy frameworks can be examined, with specific reference to the narrower and wider versions of the Asian-Pacific region (Parts II and III).

3. Maritime networks

Providing a vital link in world trade, global maritime logistics activities allow multinational manufacturers and retailers to sustain their international outsourcing activities. Rather than cover all aspects of the complex system of maritime logistics, attention is focused on containerization and specialized cellular container vessels. Since the 1980s their growth and span, rising productivity and declining freight rates, and continuous improvement in seamless door-to-door services have led to the restructuring of logistics networks, changes in port ranking, repositioning of local distribution centres and intervention of regulatory authorities. A new economic geography has emerged in which manufacturers and retailers, less constrained by the cost of transport, are able to extend their supply chains overseas, especially to take advantage of the growth in Asian-Pacific Rim economies.

A series of issues are raised by the transformation wrought by the globalization of maritime logistics. How have truly global ocean shipping companies evolved to meet the clamour of multinational manufacturers and retailers for a one-stop shipping concept, which incorporates intermodal transport linking railway, road and waterway? How have local port authorities, given the high cost and constraints on constructing port facilities, responded to the technological and organizational changes required to accommodate the introduction of mega-size containerships and increasing competition from rival hub ports? How have terminal operators assumed a global role to overcome the disconnection between the global shipping companies and local port authorities and, in the process, increased their market share and competitive positions, while still collaborating with each other? How have regulators affected the governance and transparency of the administration, economics and operation of container shipping, ports and terminals? Finally, how, and to what extent, has a global hub-and-spoke system materialized in container shipping in response to increasing industrialization, population growth, technological change, trade liberalization and expansion of the world economy?

These issues are addressed in this chapter by focusing upon the role of four key stakeholders – shipping companies, port operators, terminal operators and regulators – in accelerating corporate developments in container shipping as part of changing global trade strategies. Restructuring of ocean shipping to accommodate containers is examined with an emphasis on company consolidation and economies of scale in ship construction. Then the impact of containerization on seaports is analysed by invoking the 'Anyport' and universal port pattern models to discuss how ports across the world have sought to develop their physical infrastructures, especially container terminals and related facilities, to increase their productivity and efficiency. These models accommodate inter-port competition, increases in transhipment cargo, and attempts by ports to expand their hinterlands by introducing inter-modal rail and barge terminals, motivated by the prospect of developing their inland locations into hubs and free trade zones. This analysis leads to a consideration of the increasing role of ports in multinational supply chain management and global logistics network structures. Hybrid global–local concepts are introduced to examine the emergence of terminal operators stemming from the reforms being attempted by many authorities in port governance, deregulation, and private and public partnerships. The degree to which the emerging container system corresponds to the global hub-and-spoke model is assessed in the conclusion.

MARITIME LOGISTICS

Container shipping is put into context by examining the structure and environment of maritime logistics that accounts for 90 per cent of world trade (ICS and ISF, 2012; Valentine et al., 2013). This task involves analysing how different stakeholders interact by identifying the key macroeconomic drivers such as demand and supply, and their political underpinnings (Figure 3.1). Demand for shipping stems from sellers and buyers (that is, shippers and receivers) that, in turn, reflect demographics, notably population growth and degree of urbanization; and economics, including foreign direct investment, capital flows and outsourcing stemming from the fragmentation of geographical production processes. Ocean shipping companies provide an array of 50 000 commercial vessels and incorporate ports into their trade lanes that collectively comprise their overall networks (UNCTAD, 2012). Regulators supply the framework that governs ocean shipping activities and ports, and support both markets and transparency. Key among their global activities, exercised through the United Nations and its London-based International Maritime Organization (IMO), are concerns with the international navigation of the high seas established under the 1982 United Nations Convention on the Law of the Sea (UNCLOS) that defines the rights and responsibilities

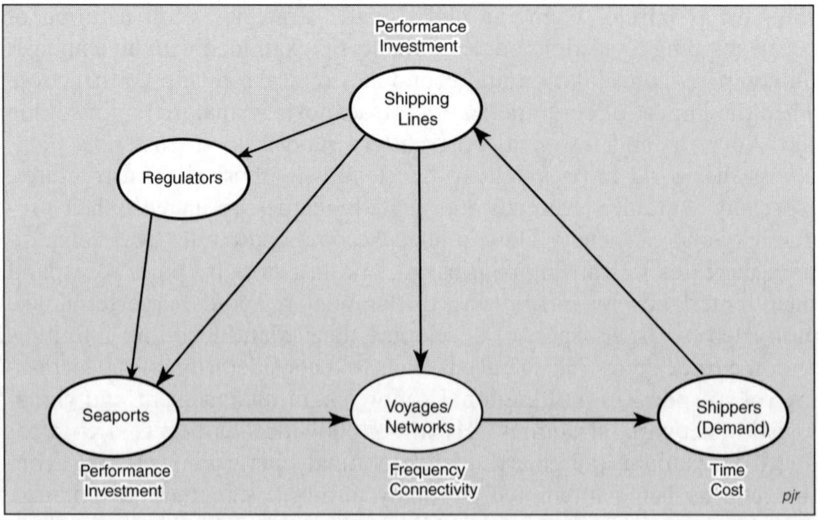

Note: Circular causality leads to evolutionary change in voyage structures/shipping networks. Offering larger and more frequent services attracts shippers and, in turn, an increasing number of shippers attract more shipping lines because demand increases.

Figure 3.1 Key stakeholders in maritime logistics

of nations, and safety of life at sea, including piracy and protection of the maritime environment from pollution. Responsibility for developing labour standards applicable to seafarers rests with the UN's Geneva-based International Labour Organization (ILO). Enforcement of these regulations lies with the flag states where the ships are registered; this enforcement regime is supplemented by Port State Control (PSC), under which national officials have the power to undertake unannounced safety inspections, and detain foreign ships not complying with international manning, equipment, maintenance and operational standards.

Fierce price competition and short-term instability are marked in ocean shipping because it is a service activity at the beginning of the 'roundabout' production process, involving the transfer of capital goods and the application of skilled labour resources between several specialized enterprises (Figure 3.2). Requiring a reliable, safe, prompt and low-cost transport system, multinational manufacturers and retailers draw upon the space offered by ocean shipping companies to meet consumer demand for logistics services (that is, as an external function). In turn, ocean shipping companies draw upon supplies of producer services offered by ports, terminal operators, harbour transport firms, shipbuilders, finance and insurance

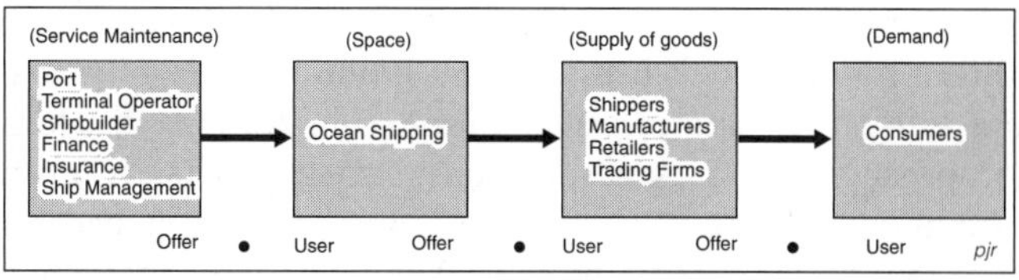

Source: Yamada (1997).

Figure 3.2 The 'roundabout' production process

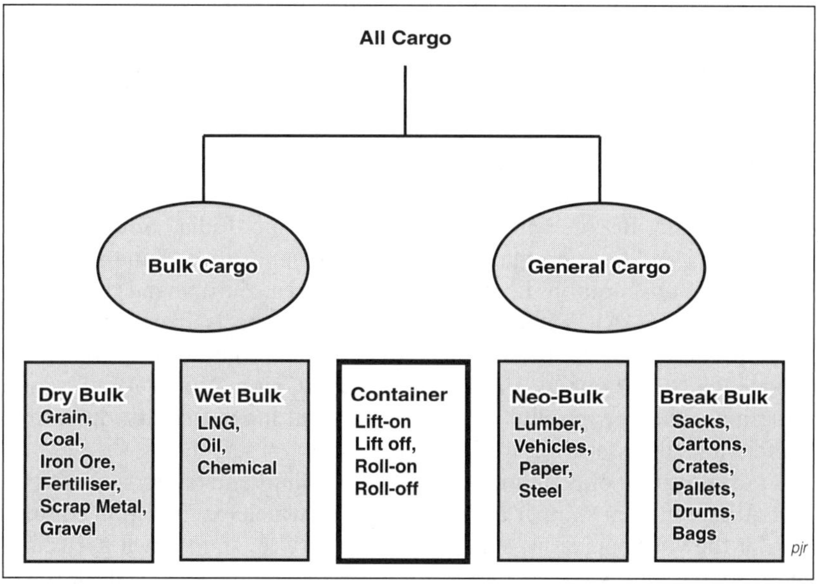

Note: The categorization is fluid because containers are being used for the transport of commodities regarded previously as bulk and dry cargoes.

Source: Based on McMillan (2006: 9).

Figure 3.3 Categorization of maritime cargoes

companies, and ship managers to meet user requirements (that is, as an internal function). Price competition is marked within ocean shipping, because it is at the beginning of this 'roundabout' production process.

Shipping operations within this roundabout production process are categorized into bulk or general cargo sectors based upon the types of commodities carried (Figure 3.3). The bulk sector is divisible into 'wet bulk' such as crude oil, chemicals and petroleum products; and 'dry bulk' commodities, notably coal, iron ore and grain. The general cargo sector (including refrigerated cargo) is separable into three subsectors: 'break bulk', comprising cargo in sacks, cartons, crates, pallets, drums and bags that are manhandled using a ship's slings or shore cranes; 'neo-bulk', covering cargo that makes use of specialized shipping to carry lumber, motor cars, paper and steel; and containerized cargo that has largely superseded break bulk cargo by being packed into standardized boxes (containers) for roll on/roll off (ro-ro) in the short-sea trades or lift on/lift off (lo-lo) in the deep-sea trades. These bulk and general cargo sectors have different import and export patterns, and operational structures.

Bulk Sector

Bulk commodities such as crude oil, iron ore, coal and grain, are dependent upon the location of oilfields or refineries, mines and farmlands. For example, dry bulk ships carry iron ore derived in great quantities from Australia and Brazil, with lesser amounts from India, South Africa, Mauritania and Peru, to meet the massive demand from China and other Asian locations, notably Japan and South Korea, Europe and the Middle East (Figure 3.4A). Tankers move crude oil exports from exploration or processing areas in the Persian Gulf, Africa, South America and the North Sea to markets in Asia, the European Union, North America and Australia. Their propensity for oil spills is resulting in the introduction of double-hulled vessels (Figure 3.4B).

Transportation of commodities in dry bulk ships and tankers relies upon a contract between shipper and cargo owner, which expires upon completion of the voyage (that is, similar to a taxi service, and known as 'tramping'). As the bulk sector is highly competitive, volatile and cyclical, prices (freight rates) vary widely over time, even weekly, according to variations in supply and demand. There is much emphasis by researchers, typified by Clarkson Research Services (Clarkson, 2011a, 2011b) and Drewry Shipping Consultants (DSC, 2011a), on estimating the gap between supply and demand, and forecasting trends in freight rates to manage huge financial risks. Over time the carriers have grown larger, and the minimal infrastructure required for loading and discharge has become more capital-intensive and automated. Ship management options to overcome impediments to fulfilling fixtures, such as a blockage of the Malacca Straits, devolve on either increasing speed, which is heavy on fuel costs, or adding additional ships (Rimmer and Lee, 2007). Thus, in principle, bulk operations have changed little since the mid-nineteenth century: the ship is still the prime asset with a strong resale value and its performance is gauged in tonne-kilometres.

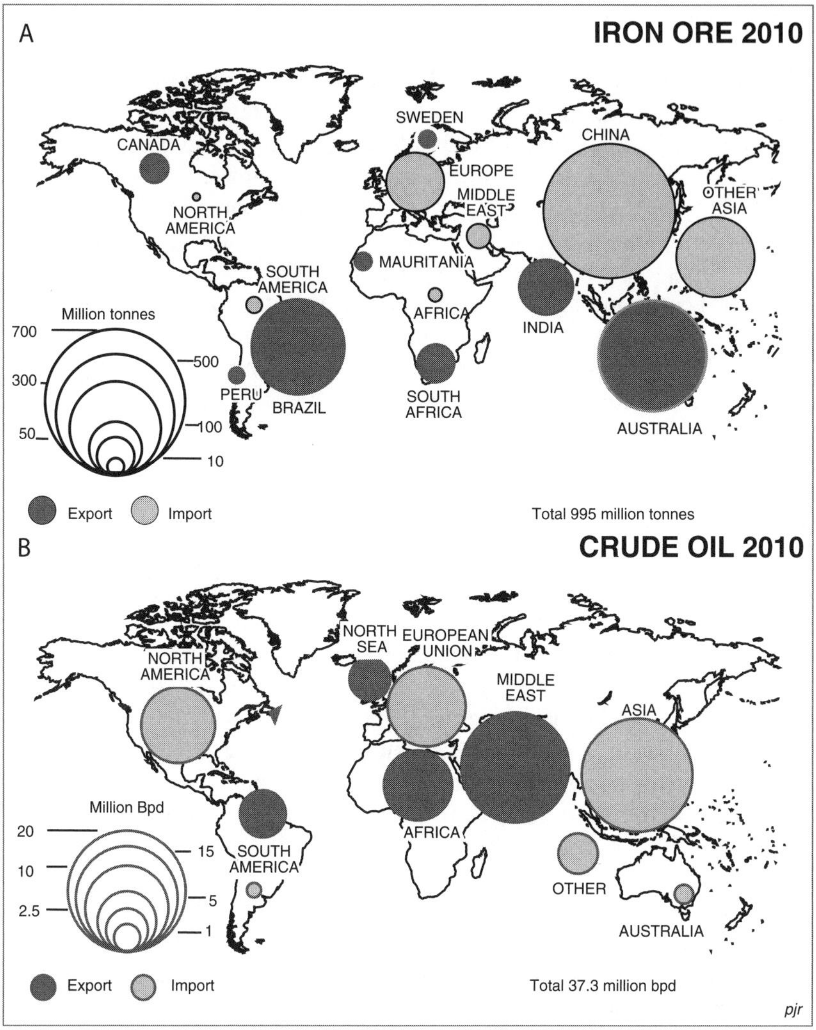

Source: Clarkson (2011a, 2011b).

Figure 3.4 Export and imports of (A) iron ore, 2010; and (B) crude oil, 2010

General Cargo Sector

General cargo is handled by liner shipping, which provides regular services between specified ports, according to advertised schedules and freight rates, and is open to all with items to carry (that is, similar to public transport). Extensive equipment is required to handle general cargo, in terms of ships, equipment and agencies that raise issues of capital concentration and pose barriers to entry. Since the Calcutta Conference of 1875, when a few competing shipowners agreed on a uniform tariff and allotted sailings to each vessel, metropolitan liner shipping companies, based in Europe, Japan and the United States, have cooperated between themselves in cartels (conferences) on specific east–west routes, making it difficult for independents to enter the trade lane and compete.

General cargo in bags, barrels and boxes was carried in the ship's hold and stowed according to destination. The ship's slings or port cranes were used for loading and unloading. As this was a labour-intensive process, ships spent most of their time in port waiting to load or discharge cargo. Port congestion and delays in meeting schedules led to higher inventories, and raised transport and warehousing costs that, in turn, hampered world trade. Demonstration of the feasibility of putting general cargo into steel boxes (containers) by Malcolm McLean and the Matson Line in 1956 revolutionized liner shipping (Levinson, 2006). Pioneered in the domestic trades of the United States and Australia, the concept was extended to the deep-sea trades (Parliament of the Commonwealth of Australia, 1968). Consortia were formed among liner shipping companies to offset the costly adoption of cellular ships, and manage service patterns across the North Atlantic and capacity across key routes such as Australia–UK and Japan–USA. Liner conferences were still used to take care of freight rates through revenue pooling arrangements based on conference tariffs.

Stimulated by the requirements of the US Navy during the Vietnam War (1959–72), containers were standardized into a twenty-foot equivalent unit (TEU) and a forty-foot equivalent unit (FEU) so that investments could occur in cellular ships and cranes. Since then general cargo has been packed into standard containers or high-cube 45-foot variants, transferred to and from the ships using shore cranes, and packed or stuffed and unpacked or stripped away from the waterfront. As this process reduced labour requirements, decreased damage and minimized time in port, both shipping and port efficiency were improved and freight rates lowered. By stimulating the growth of trade flows, containerization became a profitable worldwide system during the 1970s. Independent shipping lines outside the conference sought entry and provided stiff competition to existing carriers.

A 'second container revolution', beginning in the 1980s, involved the introduction of round-the-world services, and the adoption of intermodalism by integrating maritime and inland transport such as barge, rail and truck (Broeze, 2002). Round-the-world services were triggered by the

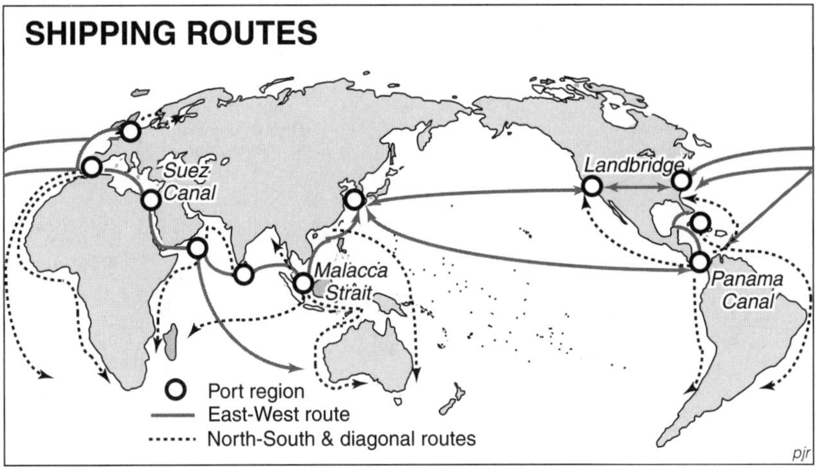

Source: Developed from Notteboom (2011).

Figure 3.5 The trunk, round-the-world route for container services

rapid industrialization of the Asian-Pacific Rim. In response the east–west shipping route was strengthened to connect diverse nodes of production and consumption between Europe and Asia, via the Suez Canal and the Malacca Straits, and Asia and North America across the Pacific, and through the Panama Canal (Figure 3.5). Complementary north–south connections and diagonal feeder links were also developed. After 1984 an alternative route to the Panama Canal was established by a 'landbridge', which used double-stack trains to carry containers between ports on the east and west coasts of North America.

Intermodalism has necessitated the transformation of the ocean carrier's vertical structure by incorporating the appropriate hardware to discharge the additional responsibilities of marine terminal manager, linehaul operator of compatible container trucks and rail wagons, and forwarding agency (Figure 3.6). These added tasks also streamlined the sector's horizontal structure by providing the necessary information software, including bar codes, to enable the container carrier to move from being a point-to-point operator into becoming a fully fledged door-to-door operator. This seamless service meets the demand from shippers for a one-stop logistics supplier offering consolidation and deconsolidation services, and supplying value-added services such as labelling and ordering processes.

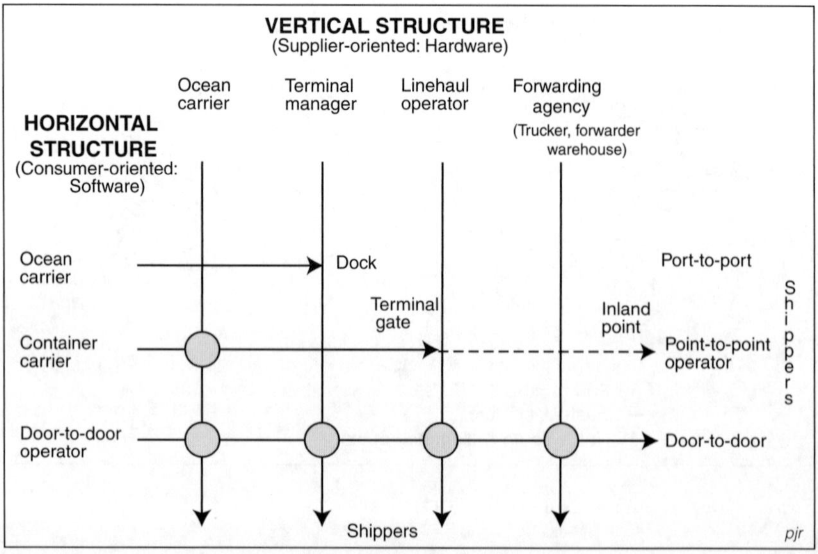

Note: The process through which the shipping company has moved from being solely an ocean carrier into also becoming terminal manager, linehaul operator and forwarding agency by developing subsidiaries to progressively move the focus of its operations from dock-to-dock through terminal-to-terminal and point-to-point to door-to-door operations as an integrated logistics package.

Source: Based on Yamada (1997).

Figure 3.6 Intermodalism

The 'total transport service', catering for the just-in-time management needs of multinational industrial corporations on a single contract, has resulted in containerization being characterized by worldwide seaborne operations and agency network, and a global outlook, vision and employment policies. Not only did the global logistical system lower the cost of transporting goods, but it also boosted international trade and production by enabling producers of final and semi-final manufactured products such as computers and textiles to extend their supply chains overseas. Underpinning these supply chains, the container network, rather than the ship, has become the prime asset. The cost of diverting ships does not cover the economic losses incurred in disrupting the supply chains (Rimmer and Lee, 2007). This development has had a profound impact upon the status of individual container shipping companies, whose performance is measured not only in tonne-kilometres performed but also in meeting just-in-time schedules that favour speed in transit rather than cost per tonne-km.

CONTAINER SHIPPING COMPANIES

Container shipping companies have been outperformed financially by other economic sectors since being transformed into door-to-door operators with the number of bad years outweighing the good ones (Fossey, 2007). This lacklustre economic performance has been attributed to short-term instability arising from the combination of a capital-intensive door-to-door operation and unreliable revenue flows, which stem from variability in owning and leasing assets in the 'roundabout' production process. Nevertheless there have been relatively few bankruptcies, because many companies withstand the financial insecurity by being part of multidivisional firms with interests in either bulk shipping or non-maritime activities such as finance and manufacturing.

Profitability has been sought by shipowners through successive generations of ever-larger container ships to lower the cost per TEU, because owners believe that they can outperform rivals by deploying larger vessels (Figure 3.7). Until the late 1980s container ships were dictated by the length, width and draught of the Panama Canal (Panamax). By1988 the size of the more fuel-efficient vessels carrying 4500–5000 TEUs and then 6000–8000 TEUs exceeded these dimensions (Post-Panamax and

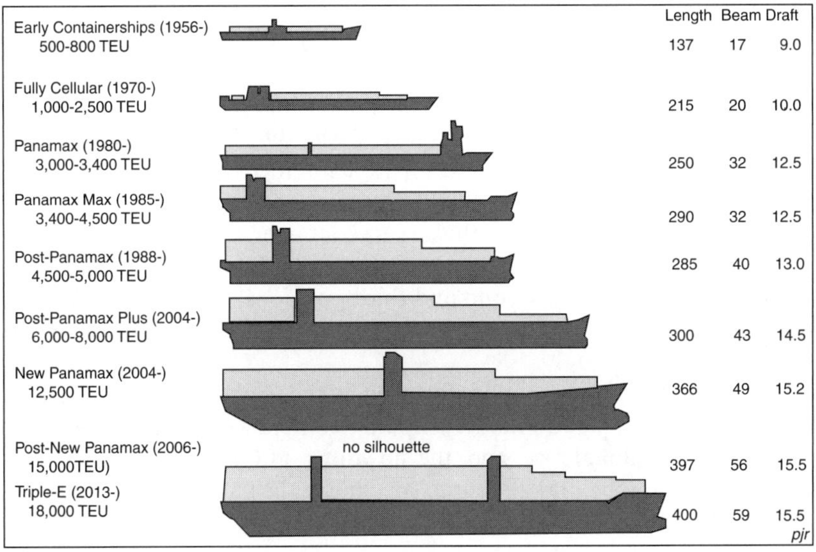

Source: Based on Rodrigue et al. (2013, 19).

Figure 3.7 Evolution of the container ship

Post-Panamax Plus). Plans for a new set of locks created new dimensions for container ships capable of transiting the Panama Canal (New Panamax). By 2006 Post-Panamax ships exceeding these new dimensions were introduced to carry 15000 TEUs to reduce cost per TEU. In 2013 a new ship type, the Triple E, added to length and beam limits to carry 18000 TEUs. These additions have not stabilized the market environment, but triggered fierce price competition, further undermining the sector's profitability and prompting volatility in the rankings of individual container shipping companies.

This volatility is apparent among the top 20 container shipping companies between 1980 and 2010 (Table 3.1). Their share of the world's container shipping slot capacity increased from 26 per cent in 1980 to 73 per cent in 2010 (Notteboom, 2004; CI, 2013). The concentration of power among the top 20, measured by the proportion held by the four largest companies (that is, the C-4 ratio), declined from 1980 to 1990, but rose again in both 2000 and 2010, suggesting a reversal from a looser towards a tighter oligopolistic market (Sys, 2007). This reversal can be interpreted by examining changes in the geographical distribution of the top 20 firms at decadal intervals (Table 3.1). In 1980 North American and European companies dominated the rankings, led by Sea-Land. By 1990 the early pacesetters from the 'developed north' had given way to carriers from the 'undeveloped south', as Asia, particularly the Asian-Pacific Rim, had the largest slot capacity and nine of the top 20 companies, headed by Evergreen Marine Corporation, as they capitalized on their cost advantage, government support, strong maritime infrastructure and aggressive growth strategies (Hawkins and Gray, 2000, 39–47). In 2000 Asia still had the largest slot capacity and greatest number of top 20 companies, despite the adverse effects of the Asian Financial Crisis (1997–98), but Europe's Maersk had become the largest container shipping company. By 2010 Maersk retained the top spot, followed by Switzerland's MSC and France's CMA CGM in second and third positions, and also Europe had the greatest regional slot capacity, while Asia still accounted for 12 of the top 20 companies.

The 2010 rankings were still influenced by the Global Financial Crisis of 2008–09 (Figure 3.8). Container shipping companies had been adversely affected by the global recession, the slowdown in GDP growth, increased bankruptcies among manufacturers, decline in the motor vehicle, retailing and textile sectors, and increased financial instability manifest in exchange and interests rates. Cargo volumes were reduced, freight rates declined, debts were unpaid, and costs and interest rates increased, which led to decreased revenue and profitability. Already troubled by overcapacity, the companies reacted by laying-up vessels in anchorages, developing

Table 3.1 Top 20 container shipping companies, 1980, 1990, 2000 and 2010

Company	HQ	1980		1990		2000		2010	
		TEU mn	#	TEU mn	#	TEU mn	#	TEU mn	#
North America									
Sea-Land	New York	0.07	1	0.12	2	–	–	–	–
US Line	Charlotte	0.02	9	–	–	–	–	–	–
APL	Oakland	0.02	10	0.07	6	–	–	–	–
Farrell	New York	0.02	12	–	–	–	–	–	–
Trans Freight	New York	0.01	14	–	–	–	–	–	–
CP Ships	Calgary	–	–	–	–	0.15	9	–	–
Subtotal		0.14		0.19		0.15		–	
Europe									
Hapag-Lloyd	Hamburg	0.04	2	0.05	10	0.11	17	0.55	5
OCL/P&O	London	0.03	3	0.05	12	0.31	3	–	–
Maersk	Aarhus	0.03	4	0.09	3	0.64	1	1.97	1
CMA CGM	Marseilles	0.01	15	0.03	19	0.12	11	1.21	3
Nedlloyd	Rotterdam	0.01	17	0.04	15	–	–	–	–
Hamburg Sud	Hamburg	0.01	18	–	–	–	–	0.36	13
Ben Line	London	0.01	20	–	–	–	–	–	–
Baltic SC	St Petersburg	–	–	0.04	16	–		–	
Scan Dutch	Copenhagen	–	–	0.03	18	–	–	–	–
Delmas Vieljeux	Le Havre	–	–	0.03	20	–	–	–	–
MSC	Geneva	–	–	–	–	0.24	5	1.64	2
Subtotal		0.14		0.36		1.42		5.73	
Asia-Pacific									
NYK Line	Tokyo	0.02	5	0.08	4	0.17	8	0.36	14
Evergreen	Taipei	0.02	6	0.13	1	0.35	2	0.59	5
OOCL	Hong Kong	0.02	7	0.06	7	0.13	10	0.38	12

Table 3.1 (continued)

Company	HQ	1980		1990		2000		2010	
		TEU mn	#	TEU mn	#	TEU mn	#	TEU mn	#
Asia-Pacific									
Mitsui OSK	Tokyo	0.02	11	0.07	5	0.12	15	0.38	11
NOL/APL	Singapore	0.01	13	0.04	17	0.21	6	0.59	4
Yang Ming	Taipei	0.01	16	0.05	13	0.12	14	0.32	17
COSCO	Beijing	–	–	0.05	9	0.21	7	0.55	7
Hanjin	Seoul	–	–	0.05	11	0.25	4	0.44	10
K-Line	Tokyo	–	–	0.05	12	0.12	13	0.36	15
Hyundai	Seoul	–	–	–	–	0.11	16	0.29	18
China Shipping	Shanghai	–	–	–	–	0.08	19	0.47	8
Pacific Int'l	Singapore	–	–	–	–	–	–	0.25	19
Subtotal		0.10		0.58		1.87		4.98	
Other									
Zim	Tel Aviv	0.02	8	0.04	14	0.13	12	0.32	16
Safmarine	Cape Town	0.01	19	–	–	–	–	–	–
UASC	Kuwait	–	–	–	–	0.07	20	0.19	20
CSAV	Valparaiso	–	–	–	–	0.09	18	0.53	11
Subtotal		0.03		0.04		0.29		1.04	
Top 20 total		0.41		1.17		3.73		11.75	
World total (TEU)		1.58		3.02		6.54		16.09	
Top 20 (%)		26		39		57		73	
C-4 index %		41		36		42		46	
World ships (no.)		–		4969		7093		7947	

Note: Nine of the container shipping companies listed in 1980 have ceased operation. The US Line went bankrupt in 1988 and its ships were taken over by Sea-Land; Ben Line ships were sold in 1991; Trans Freight and Farrell Line became part of the OCL/P&O Group that was taken over by Maersk and led to the creation of Maersk Line.

Source: CI (2001, 2011), Fossey (2007), Notteboom (2004).

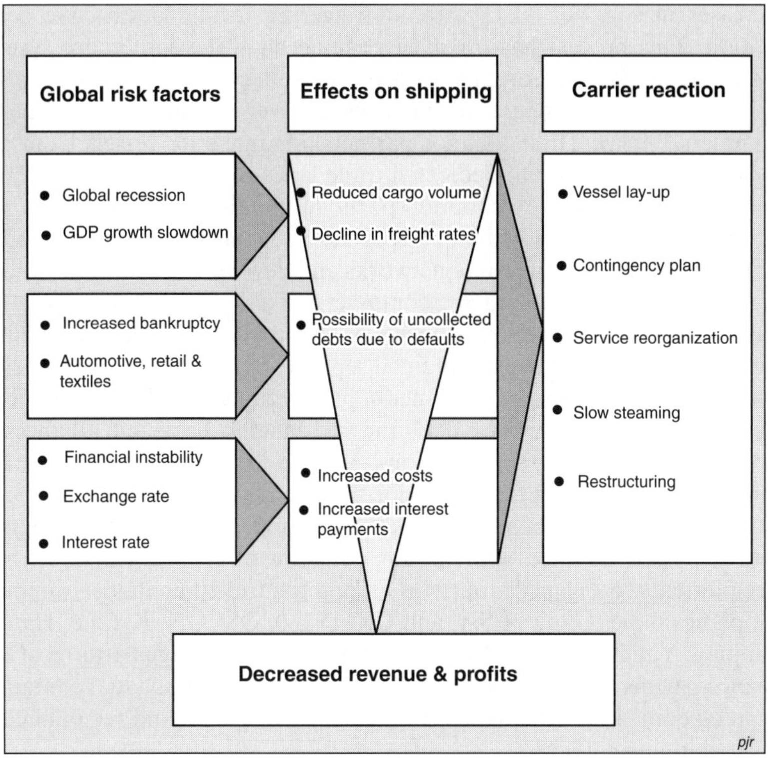

Source: HJS (2009, 9).

Figure 3.8 Recession strategies used during the Global Financial Crisis, 2008–09

contingency plans (for example, postponing or cancelling deliveries of new ships) and reorganizing services. Slow steaming has been adopted by reducing speed from 22 to 16 knots to save 70 per cent in fuel costs, but extra ships were required to fulfil fixtures within the same time scale. Also the companies have restructured in such a way that reliance upon the top 20 rankings can be misleading because they mask the way they have allied with each other across regional borders.

Container shipping companies have collaborated intra- and inter-regionally to lower operational costs, secure economies of scale and reduce the risks associated with capital investment in door-to-door networks. Progressive enlargement in the scale of organization and a further concentration of power have been linked with larger ships to achieve further decreases in cost per TEU without triggering further destructive competition. This process has involved pushing back the conference system and transforming the original consortia's full commercial ventures by developing new-style operating alliances to cover slot-sharing agreements (Rimmer, 1998a). These alliance partnerships integrate vessels from the participating carriers into dedicated trade lanes to provide weekly scheduled services that feature common ports, terminals and transit times. As exemplified by Japan's Mitsui OSK Lines Ltd, these arrangements have enabled carriers to refine route networks and develop telecommunications services for tracking and tracing containers on a door-to-door basis.

However, the alliance structure has not been able to guarantee stability because the partners have maintained separate marketing and sales structures, and their own inland clearance depots, terminals and feeder services. Since the creation of the Global, Grand and Maersk–Sea-Land alliances in the mid-1990s to gain greater economies of scale, market share and market power, there have been further major bouts of restructuring (Figure 3.9). By 2010 this process of merger and acquisition, and further concentration of power, coupled with the introduction of ever-larger ships, had precipitated two distinct groupings among the top 20 container shipping companies – the 'Gang of Six' and CKHYE (COSCON, K-Line, Hanjin Shipping, Yangming Line, Evergreen Line). As the voyage patterns of the alliance partners are complex, attention is focused on individual container shipping companies to illustrate the structure of global and regional container shipping networks.

Global and Regional Shipping Networks

A comparison is made of the global services of the two largest companies, Maersk Line and Mediterranean Shipping Company (MSC), by focusing on their hub ports. MSC is considered first, because greater detail is available on Maersk Line's network that had been bolstered by the takeover of P&O (Peninsular and Oriental Steam Navigation Company) Nedlloyd. Although these networks are comprehensive, the companies still relied upon intra-regional shipping companies such as the Thailand-based Regional Container Lines (RCL), which did not feature among the top 20 container shipping companies but provided important supplementary services for their operations.

In 2010 MSC operated 464 vessels with a capacity of 1.6 million TEU. Eschewing merger and acquisition, the privately owned shipping line, owned by Gianluigi Aponte with headquarters in Geneva, had expanded organically since 1970 from a small conventional shipping operator with a fleet of second-hand ships, a narrow service network and limited services

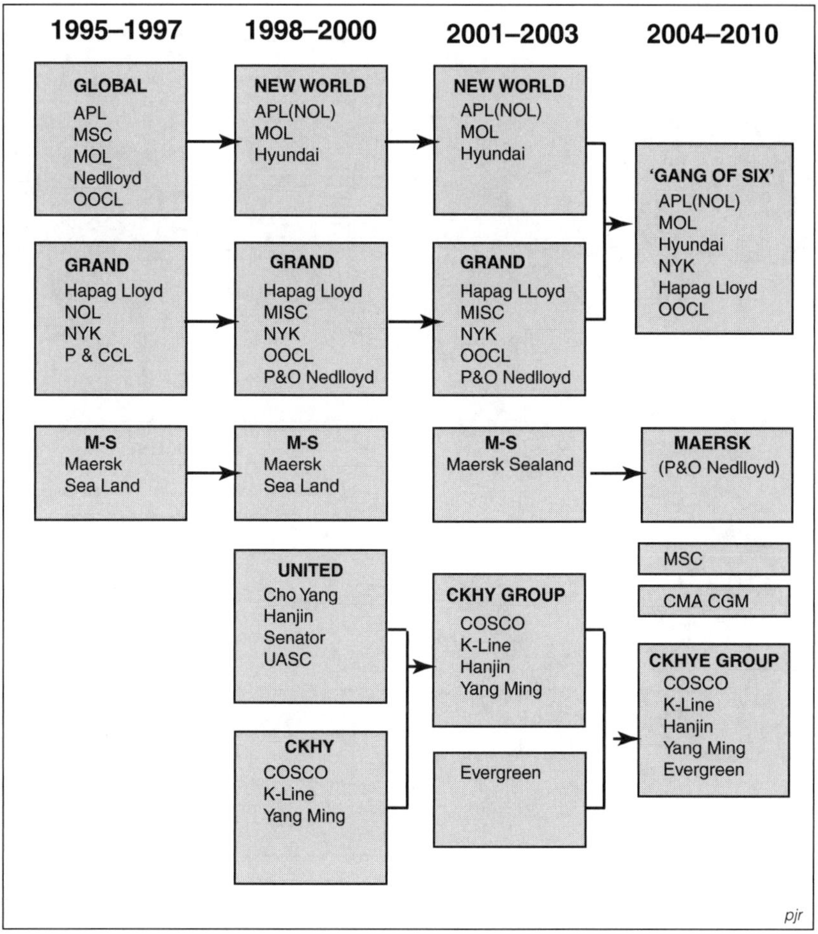

Figure 3.9 Dynamics of strategic alliance formation, merger and acquisition among container shipping companies, 1995–2010

to Africa, into a global carrier serving 340 ports worldwide in six continents, with 421 dedicated local offices in 145 countries employing 30000 people. The company's shipping network, comprising 200 direct and combined weekly services, was orchestrated from 11 hubs: Antwerp, Le Havre, Gioia Tauro, Algeciras, Valencia, Piraeus, Salalah, Jebel Ali, Singapore, Christobal/Balboa and Freeport (Figure 3.10A).

Maersk Line, part of the Danish transport and energy business conglomerate AP Møller-Maersk, had a different set of transhipment hubs:

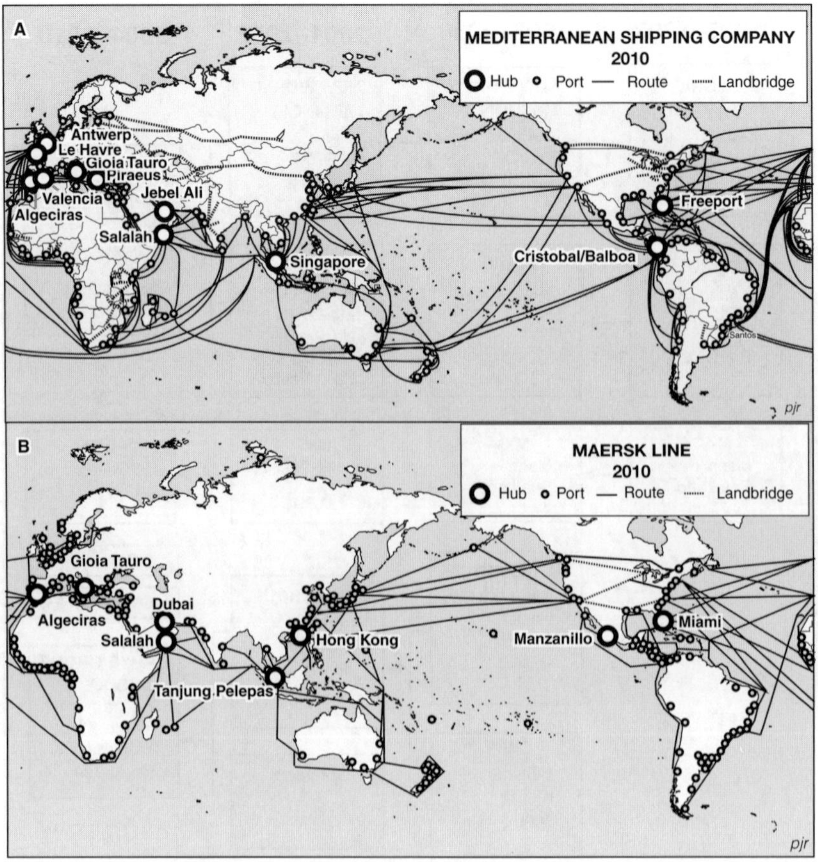

Source: Maersk Line (2011); MSC (2012).

Figure 3.10 (A) Mediterranean Shipping Corporation (MSC) container shipping network, 2010; and (B) Maersk container shipping network, 2010

Algeciras, Gioia Tauro, Salalah, Dubai, Tanjung Pelepas, Hong Kong, Manzanillo and Miami (Figure 3.10B). Their task was to provide a 'balanced' global coverage by integrating the east–west and north–south routes of the complex and diversified container shipping network (Frémont, 2007). With more than 600 vessels and 22 000 employees stationed around the world in 325 offices in 125 countries, the company affected every major port (Maersk Line, 2011).

A more detailed analysis of Maersk Line's network reveals that the

Table 3.2 Distribution of Maersk's trade lanes, 2010

	Mainline	Feeder
East–West Routes		
Asia–Europe	24	–
Atlantic: North America–Europe, Mediterranean, Middle East and Indian Subcontinent	18	–
Trans-Pacific	18	–
Europe–Middle East	10	–
Far East–Middle East	4	–
Subtotal	74	–
Intra-Regional Feeders		
Intra-Asia	–	24
Intra-Europe	–	72
Middle East	–	8
Subtotal	–	104
North–South		
Africa	42	12
Central America & the Caribbean	17	3
Oceania	14	1
South America	34	12
Subtotal	107	28

Source: Maersk Line (2011).

dominant east–west route comprised 74 trade lanes led by Asia-Europe followed by the transatlantic and trans-Pacific routes; these trade lanes were supported by 104 feeders in Asia, Europe and the Middle East (Table 3.2). There were 107 north–south trade lanes dominated by those connecting Africa and South America; 28 feeders in Australia, Africa and South America underpinned them.

Even with the complex network of feeder services operated by their own vessels to provide containers for ever-larger mother ships sailing on mainline east–west routes, the large companies needed to supplement their services by drawing upon specialist, intra-regional feeder shipping companies such as RCL that linked transhipment and feeder ports. In 2010, RCL's feeder fleet with a total capacity of 50 000 TEUs ranged in size from 500 TEUs to 2600 TEUs, covered more than 60 ports within its Asian-Pacific Rim network, and carried containers owned by mainline carriers and independent shippers (Figure 3.11). Although RCL had 34 service patterns, only the 22 incorporating Singapore are shown to highlight the location's pivotal importance as a container port (see Chapter 6).

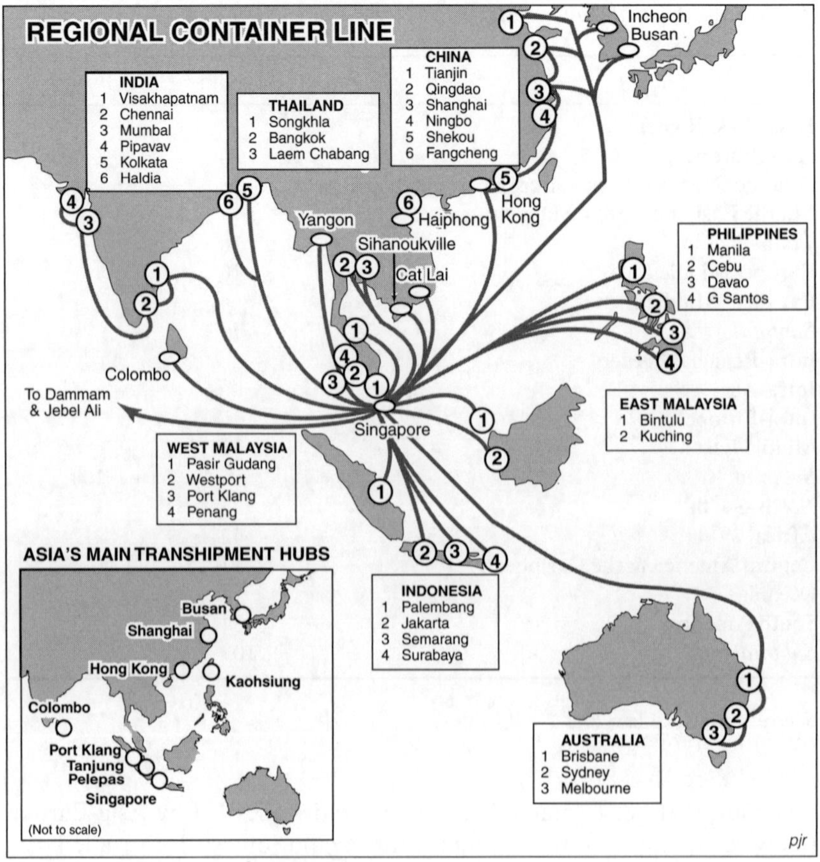

Source: RCL (2013).

Figure 3.11 Regional Container Lines: main ports of call from Singapore, 2010

SEAPORTS

Containerization has prompted changes in both the internal structure of seaports and the evolution of spatial patterns of port locations to handle the more than fifteenfold increase in throughput from 35 million TEUs in 1980 to 545 million TEUs in 2010 (CI, 1970–2013). Changes within ports can be accommodated within the 'Anyport' model, which provides a framework for studying intra-port development and competition

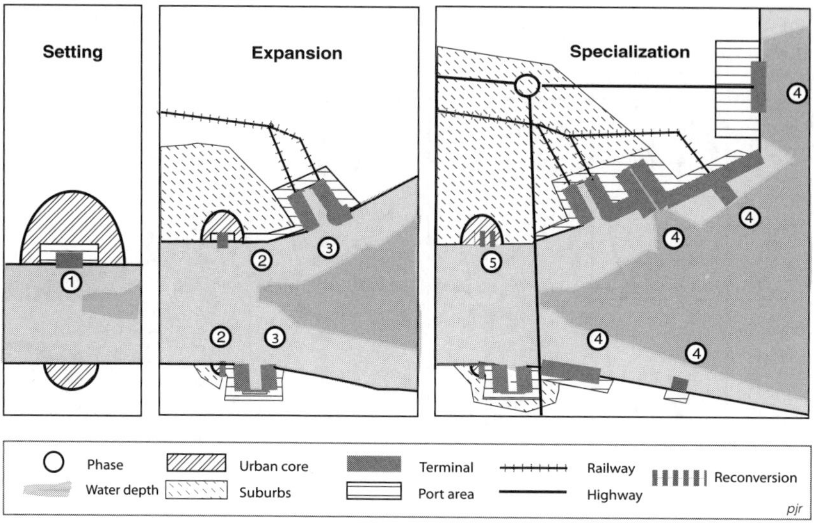

Note: The diagram shows the original setting of the port (phase 1); the expansion of the port beyond the urban area (phases 2 and 3); and specialization with the completion of terminal facilities offering deeper water (phase 4) and the reversion of the original port setting to recreational use (phase 5).

Source: Adapted from Rodrigue et al. (2013).

Figure 3.12 'Anyport'

(Figure 3.12). Over time the port has expanded from the original facility, handicapped by lack of space and opposition from dock labour, and moved progressively towards deeper water, leading to the disconnection between city and port. Specialized terminals have been constructed to meet the needs of particular vessels and cargoes, and the original port facilities have been converted to recreational use. This Anyport model is limited because the dynamics of comparative advantage are not within the port itself, but stem from the universal pattern of a few large and many small ports, which has emerged from the improvement of internal accessibility within countries and the accompanying process of dominance ranking through which a port hierarchy emerges.

In discussing competition, cooperation and a mixture of the two (that is, co-opetition) between seaports, the universal pattern, embodied in the idealized sequence of seaport development from the scattered ports along the coastline, needs to be considered (Figure 3.13). Before the onset of containerization the processes of penetration and port piracy had arisen from expanding transport routes, which facilitated port hinterland

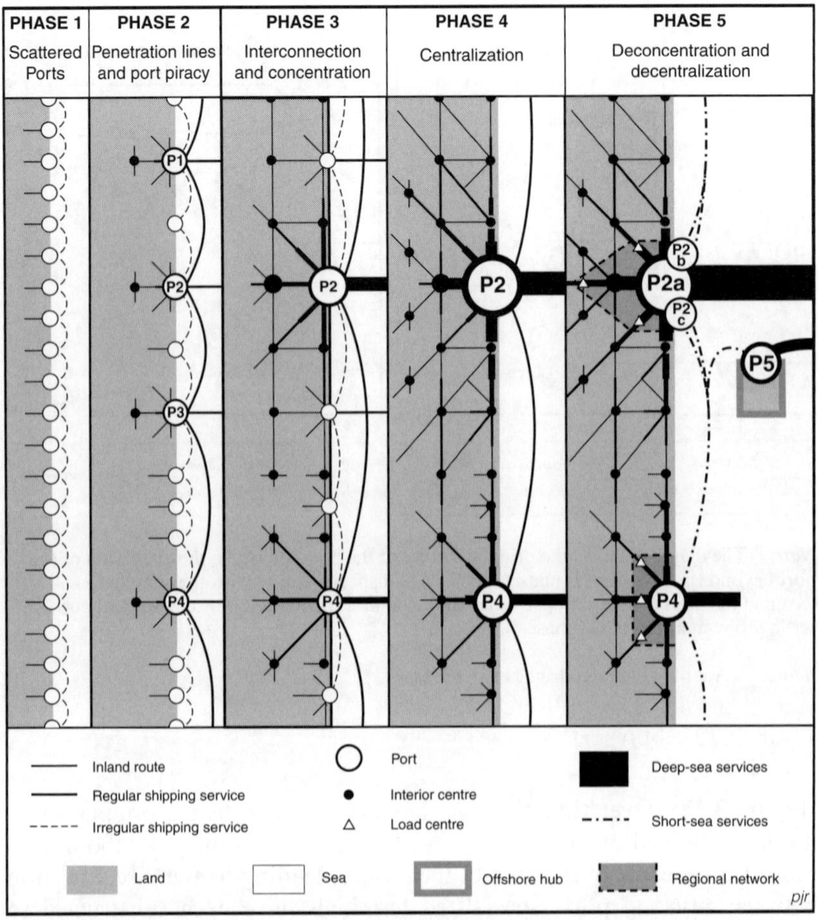

Note: The diagram shows the progression of Ports P2 and P4 from scattered ports through to centralization brought about by improvements to land and sea transport; the deconcentration of Port P2's activities (a, b and c) to accommodate larger ships; the survival of P4 in a decentralized location (often with government support); and the emergence of P5 as an offshore hub to accommodate even larger ships.

Source: Rimmer and Comtois (2009).

Figure 3.13 Universal port patterns

capture. Also interconnection and concentration had occurred, producing centralization (Rimmer and Comtois, 2009). The initial generation of purpose-built container ships, requiring deeper water and dedicated facilities, necessitated the addition of an extra phase to the original model.

This new phase accommodates both the deconcentration of port activities within metropolitan areas, that provide opportunities for collaboration and partnerships between separate authorities, and the decentralization of activities to support regional development in a 'greenfield' site to provide the deeper water required by larger ships (McLaughlin and Fearon, 2013).

The wide-ranging changes in the size of container ships and the complexity of multinational, modular production–distribution chains required little modification to the universal model. Initially, the adoption and spread of container technology reinforced concentration and centralization and then accommodated generations of purpose-built container ships by invoking an offshore hub. Since their introduction in the 1990s, offshore hubs have offered depths of at least 15 metres, room for expansion, lower labour costs and scope for the development of specialized logistics zones.

These alterations in port morphology are reflected in marked changes in the location of the world's top 25 container ports. In 1970, 13 of them were in Europe, eight in North America, two in Japan and two in Australia. Since then an examination of the top 25 container ports at decadal intervals between 1980 and 2000 shows that marked shifts have occurred in regional port numbers and throughput since the beginning of the second container revolution (Table 3.3). The strong position of ports in Europe and North America has been progressively whittled away with the emergence of a rash of ports in Asia and the Middle East, particularly around the Asian-Pacific Rim. These changes are attributed to intense competition between ports in Europe stemming from the overlay and intersection of hinterlands in Northern Europe and the Mediterranean, and in North America from the erosion of captive hinterlands across borders and between port ranges. Within Asia, land-based regionalization has been limited by the heavy reliance on key ports serving mega-urban manufacturing centres on or near the coast, particularly as China lacked the array of corridors and inland terminals characteristic of Europe's inland waterways and North America's railroad system (Rodrigue and Notteboom, 2013). This situation has prompted the Chinese government to undertake heavy investment in both maritime and land-based infrastructure and to seek to make greater use of the Yangtze River (see Chapter 9).

By 2010, 18 of the top 25 container hubs were in Asia and the Middle East (17 in the Asian-Pacific Rim), four in Europe and three in North America; there was no representation in Africa, Oceania, or Central and South America (Figure 3.14). For the first time Shanghai had surpassed Singapore to become the world's leading container port. Shanghai's position stems from China's growth in exports, increasing demand for

Table 3.3 Top 25 world port rankings 1980, 1990, 2000 and 2010

	1980		1990		2000		2010	
	TEU	#	TEU	#	TEU	#	TEU	#
North America								
New York	1.9	1	1.9	9	3.0	13	5.3	20
Oakland	0.8	7	1.1	19	–	–	–	–
Seattle	0.8	8	1.2	18	–	–	–	–
Baltimore	0.7	13	–	–	–	–	–	–
Los Angeles	0.6	16	2.6	6	4.7	7	7.8	16
Long Beach	0.6	19	1.6	12	4.6	8	6.3	18
Honolulu	0.4	23	–	–	–	–	–	–
San Juan	0.4	24	1.4	16	2.4	20	–	–
Tacoma	–	–	0.9	22	–	–	–	–
Subtotal	6.2		10.7		14.7		19.4	
Europe								
Rotterdam	1.9	2	3.7	3	6.3	5	11.1	10
Hamburg	0.8	6	2.0	8	4.2	9	7.9	15
Antwerp	0.7	10	1.5	14	4.1	10	8.5	14
Bremen	0.7	12	1.2	17	2.7	17	4.9	23
Le Havre	0.5	21	0.9	25	–	–	–	–
Bordeaux	0.5	22	–	–	–	–	–	–
Felixstowe	0.4	25	1.4	15	2.8	16	–	–
Gioia Tauro	–	–	–	–	2.7	18	–	–
Subtotal	5.5		10.7		22.8		32.4	
Asia								
Hong Kong	1.5	3	5.1	2	18.1	1	23.5	3
Kaohsiung	1.0	4	3.5	4	7.4	4	8.9	12
Singapore	0.9	5	5.2	1	17.0	2	28.4	2
Kobe	0.7	9	2.6	5	2.3	22	–	–
Yokohama	0.7	11	1.6	11	2.3	21	–	–
Keelung	0.7	14	1.8	10	–	–	–	–
Busan	0.6	15	2.3	7	7.5	3	14.2	5
Tokyo	0.6	17	1.6	13	2.9	15	4.3	25
Manila	–	–	1.0	21	2.9	14	–	–
Bangkok	–	–	1.0	22	2.3	23	5.1	22
Nagoya	–	–	0.9	24	–	–	–	–
Shanghai	–	–	–	–	5.6	6	29.1	1
Port Klang	–	–	–	–	3.2	11	8.9	13
Tg Priok	–	–	–	–	2.5	19	4.7	24
Yantian	–	–	–	–	2.1	24	–	–
Qingdao	–	–	–	–	2.1	25	12.0	8
Shenzhen	–	–	–	–	–	–	22.5	4
Ningbo	–	–	–	–	–	–	13.1	6

Table 3.3 (continued)

	1980		1990		2000		2010	
	TEU	#	TEU	#	TEU	#	TEU	#
Guangzhou	–	–	–	–	–	–	12.6	7
Tianjin	–	–	–	–	–	–	10.1	11
Tg Pelepas	–	–	–	–	–	–	6.5	17
Xiamen	–	–	–	–	–	–	5.8	19
Dalian	–	–	–	–	–	–	5.2	21
Subtotal	6.7		26.6		78.2		214.9	
Other								
Jeddah	0.6	18	–	–	–	–	–	–
Dubai	–	–	0.9	23	3.1	12	11.6	9
Melbourne	0.5	20	–	–	–	–	–	–
Top 25 total	19.5		48.9		118.8		278.3	
Top 25 (%)	53%		58%		53%		55%	
World total (mn TEUs)	36.5		84.2		225.3		503.5	

Source: CI (1970–2013).

'western goods' and its location at the head of the Yangtze River, the main corridor for goods from the interior (see Chapter 6). Singapore is unlikely to regain its position because of competition from both Port Klang and Tanjung Pelepas in Malaysia, and an increasing number of direct calls to Laem Chabang (Bangkok) and Tanjung Priok (Jakarta) that have been boosted by free trade agreements with Europe and North America. Hong Kong remained in third position ahead of neighbouring Shenzhen, but Busan's fifth position was threatened by Ningbo, adjacent to Shanghai. Taiwan's Kaohsiung also faced increased competition from Xiamen and the decision of locally based companies to switch from relaying cargo through the port to direct services to and from ports in Mainland China.

Consolidation of the positions of Asian and Middle Eastern ports in the traffic league stem from their European and North American counterparts bearing the brunt of the Global Financial Crisis (2008–09). Rotterdam and Antwerp were the main European ports ahead of Hamburg and Bremen/Bremerhaven, because they were more competitive than their rivals for transit traffic to and from inland ports in Europe, including those in Germany, and all-water transit traffic from Russia and Scandinavia. In North America, Los Angeles and Long Beach on the west

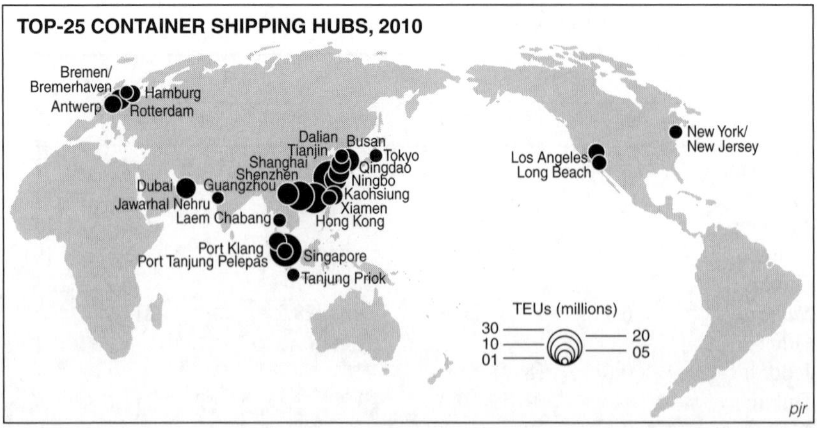

Source: CI (2013).

Figure 3.14 Location of the world's top 25 container hubs, 2010

coast and New York/New Jersey on the east coast of the USA maintained their positions in the top 25, buoyed by the strong growth in imports from the Asian-Pacific Rim.

These container ports are now seen as key elements in the value-added supply chains of multinational manufacturers and retailers (Wang et al., 2007; Hall et al., 2011). As outlined by Ross Robinson (2002), the port: (1) functions as a third-party service provider that intervenes in the supply chains as a market-focused entity; (2) operates as one element, among other logistics entities, in the import–export chain between producer and consumer designed to add and derive value; (3) offers superior value to shippers in a market segmented on the basis of the value propositions of shippers; and (4) competes with other ports as a market-focused firm or entity embedded in the constellation of chains of supply focused on the port. In short, supply chains compete, rather than individual ports. Since ports are but one link in the supply chain, the real beneficiaries of port efficiency are not only multinational manufacturers and retailers, but also consumers at the final destination benefitting from the lower cost of trade. Before these gains can be derived from the containerization of ports, much depends on overcoming the disconnection between the liner shipping corporations operating in the global arena and public sector officials managing ports at the local level.

TERMINAL OPERATORS

The reform of terminal operations has been instituted to overcome this disconnection, which arises from public sector officials not fully comprehending the global ramifications of freight passing through their jurisdictions, and shipping corporations not giving sufficient consideration to the local effects of their world-spanning operations (Maring, 2001). Terminal operations have been either retained under public control and run as commercial businesses, or developed under private management (Notteboom and Rodrigue, 2012). Corporatization has led to local commercial terminal operators expanding their activities to overseas locations (that is, 'lo-globalization'). Privatization has resulted in global business interests moving into local terminal operations (that is, 'glocalization') (Reveley and Tull, 2008). An expanded global–local framework is developed to incorporate these hybrid concepts (Figure 3.15). Reference is made to specific examples to illustrate the differing origins of terminal operators.

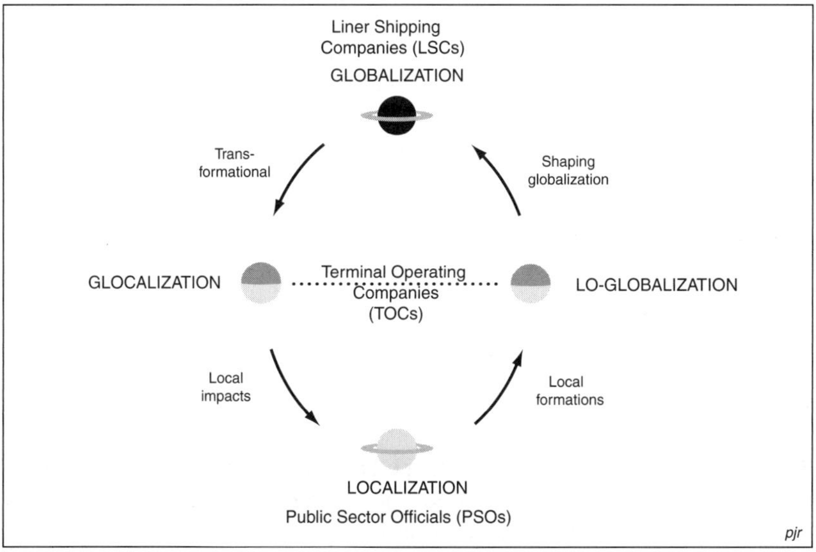

Note: Global logistics corporations create terminal operating companies in local locations and local logistics operations create terminals operations in global locations.

Source: Rimmer (2007).

Figure 3.15 Glocalization and lo-globalization

Lo-globalization

The 'lo-globalization' concept took off from Hong Kong, where there was already a split between the administrative activities of public service officials, and the privately owned stevedoring and operations of the Hong Kong International Terminals (HKIT) established in 1969. HKIT is the flagship of the century-old Hong Kong & Whampoa Dock Company (HKWDC), which is part of the multinational conglomerate operated by Li Ka-Shing's Cheung Kong Holdings Ltd with interests in energy, retailing and telecommunications. In 1994, HKWDC established the subsidiary Hutchison Port Holdings (HPH) to enable the company to prepackage its port operating skills and export them. By 2010 the resultant international network, developed through vertical integration, comprised direct investment in 315 berths within 51 ports, spanning 25 countries across four continents (Figure 3.16A). These activities handled 73 million TEU worldwide and employed 30000 people (DSC, 2011b).

The Port of Singapore followed Hong Kong's lead and offered a variant of the 'lo-globalization' concept. In 1996 the administrative activities conducted by public service officials were hived off to the Maritime and Port Authority (MPA) of Singapore, and the stevedoring activities corporatized during the following year and vested in the PSA Corporation Ltd. Since then PSA International has also become one of the world's leading terminal operators with a portfolio of investments in 29 port projects in 17 countries across Asia, Europe and the America to accommodate the expanding fleet of mega-size container vessels (Figure 3.16B). In 2010 the PSA (Port of Singapore Authority) group of ports handled over 64 million TEUs of which the company's Singapore flagship was responsible for almost 28 million TEU (PSA, 2011). The bulk of PSA's revenue was drawn from Southeast Asia (59 per cent) followed by Europe (28 per cent), Northeast Asia (7 per cent) and others (6 per cent).

Glocalization

The 'glocalization' concept covers the shift of global container shipping companies into the investment and operation of local terminals to offset the diminishing prospects of cutting costs at sea, due to rising inland logistics costs involved in repositioning containers. This move is part of a grander vertical integration plan to move backwards into acquiring shipyards, container production facilities and bunkering, and forwards into storage, freight forwarding, ownership of road and rail facilities and local distribution.

This glocalization process is illustrated by APM Terminals (APMT),

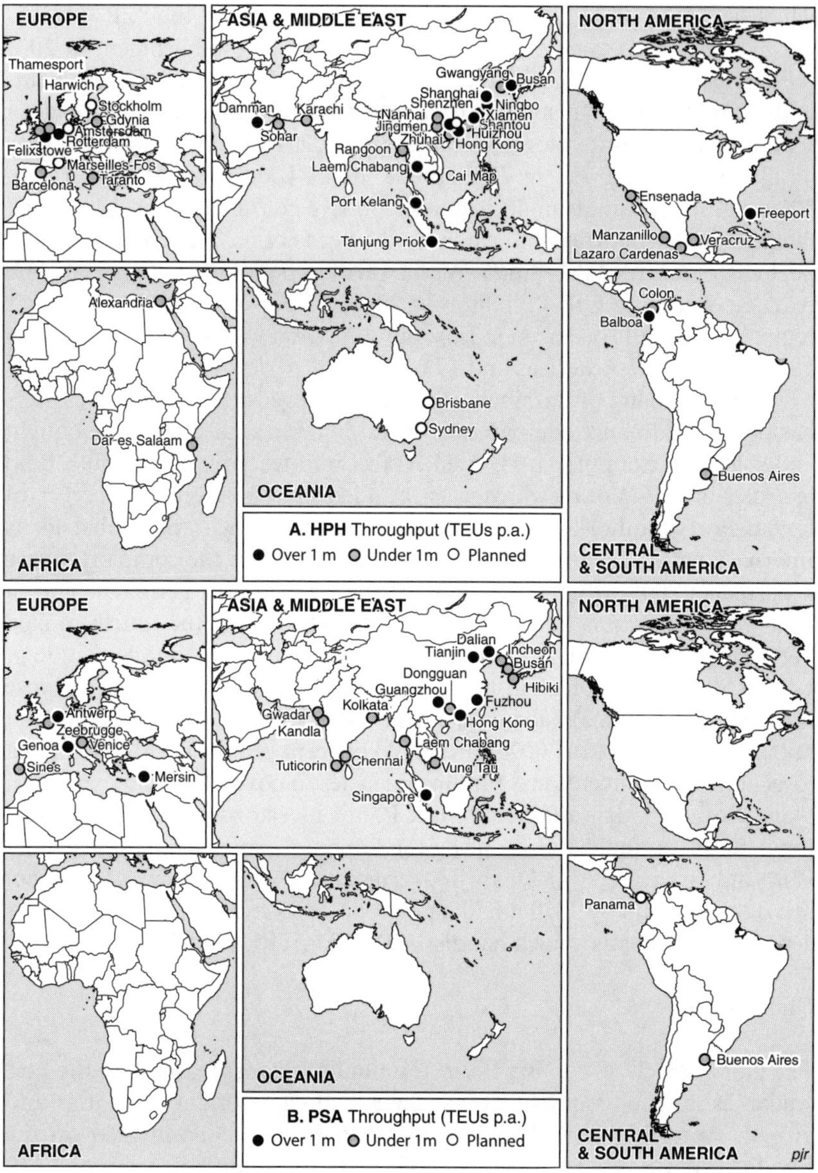

Sources: DSC (2011b), HWL (2011), PSA (2011).

Figure 3.16 Location of owned and managed terminals (A) Hutchison Whampoa, 2010; and (B) PSA, 2010

which is operated as an independent business unit by the A.P. Møller-Maersk (APMM) Group (Figure 3.17A). Since its establishment in 2001 APM Terminals has sought to complement its 'global port' arrangements with terminals and an inland services network to provide door-to-door services and integrated logistics packages. In 2010, APM Terminals, with its global headquarters in The Hague, had 24000 employees operating 50 container terminals in 40 countries on five continents, and 120 inland facilities in 64 countries that cater for the needs of 60 liner companies and port customers (APMT, 2012). With a throughput of 60 million TEU and revenue exceeding US$4.2 billion in 2010, 37 per cent of the company's regional crane lifts occurred in Europe, compared with 27 per cent in Asia, 18 per cent in the Americas and 17 per cent in Africa.

The profitability of terminals operated by stevedores and ocean carriers has prompted finance companies to invest in them as an asset to be bought and sold. For example, the United Arab Emirates' sovereign wealth fund invested in DP World, which was founded in 2005 from the merger of Dubai Ports Authority, originally established in 1995, and Dubai Ports International in 1999 (DPW, 2013). Expansion from the company's base occurred in 2005 with the purchase of the CSX World Terminals and in 2006 with the acquisition of the terminal activities of the fourth-ranked P&O for US$3.9 billion (Figure 3.17B). Controversy over the acquisition of United States assets on security grounds prompted the company to dispose of American terminals acquired in the P&O deal to AIG, a local asset management group. In 2007 shares in 20 per cent of DP World were issued to Islamic and conventional funding agencies to cover debt and expansion plans. Both Moody's and Standard & Poor's investor services downgraded these bonds to 'junk' status during the Global Financial Crisis (2008–09). With aid from the Abu Dhabi Government, DP World recovered from this dilemma, and by 2010 it had a portfolio of 49 terminals in 31 countries across six continents, which handled 49 million TEUs (DSC, 2011b).

Global Reach

The global reach of the 'Big Four' terminal operators featured in the case studies is not uniform. Reflecting their distinctive origins, histories and growth strategies, both Hutchison and PSA have concentrated on the Far East and Southeast Asia; APMT is more evenly balanced; and DP World is strongest in the Middle East but represented in all continents (Table 3.4). As they do not own each terminal in their portfolios, their relative strengths have been blurred by strategic joint ventures between global carriers and local port terminal groups to reduce risk. For example, CMA CGM, Cosco, K-Line, MSC, Nippon Yusen Kabushiki Kaisha

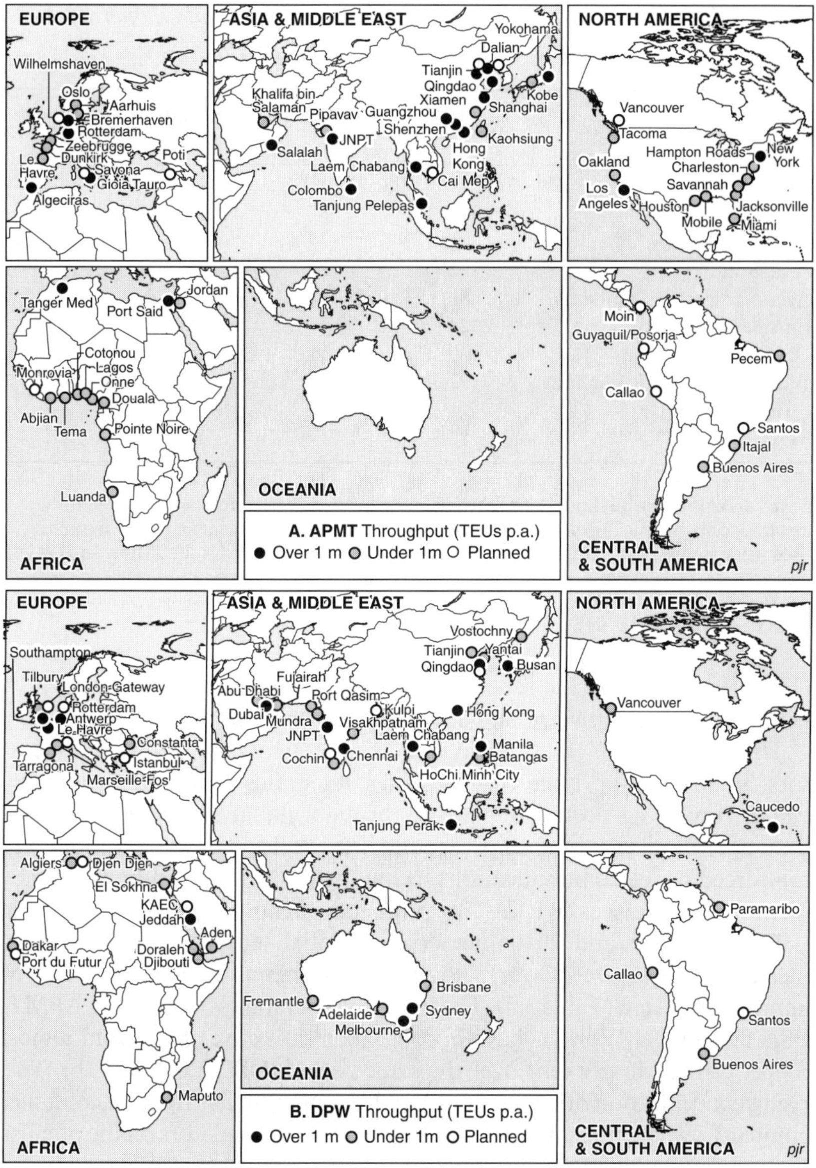

Sources: DSC (2011a), APMT (2012), DPW (2013).

Figure 3.17 Location of owned and managed terminals: (A) APMT, 2010; (B) DP World, 2010

Table 3.4 Regional throughputs of the four leading terminal operators according to their terminal portfolios, 2010

	HPH %	PSA %	APMT %	DPW %
Africa	1	0	13	4
Americas	13	1	19	5
Asia–Middle East	2	0	5	39
Asia–South	2	2	7	13
Asia–Far East & Southeast	58	81	29	20
Europe	24	17	28	10
Oceania	0	0	0	9
World container throughput (mn TEUS)[1]	72.7	64.3	60.2	49.5
Markets share (%)	13.3	11.8	11.0	9.1

Note: [1]As total throughput is a relatively crude measure where an operator may, for instance, only have a 25 per cent share in the ownership of a terminal an equity figure is used when a more sensitive indicator is required. This figure in TEUs for 2010 was: HPH 45 mn; PSA 42.3 mn; APMT 31.6 mn; and DPW 32.6 mn.

Source: DSC (2011b, 21).

(NYK) and PIL (Pacific International Lines) have partnerships with PSA International in Antwerp, Singapore and Zeebrugge.

The outcome of these activities is a network of terminal operators, financed by private equity, which integrates multinational supply chains, involving deep-water ports, through global shipping companies that operate ever-larger ships around the world. These operations are reinforced by telecommunications technologies, including radio frequency identification devices (RFIDs) for precision tracking of cargo movements.

Between 2005 and 2010 the top ten global terminal operators have increased their share of world container throughput from 55 per cent to almost 65 per cent (Table 3.5). The Big Four operators – Hutchison, APMT, PSA and Dubai World – have boosted their collective share from almost 39 per cent to 46 per cent over the same period (DSC, 2006, 2011b). This rising concentration of ownership, coupled with a similar trend in container company ownership, has attracted the attention of regulators on the premise that markets should be contestable and allow the entry of new players.

Postscript

Analyses of container shipping companies, seaports and terminal operators have a short shelf life (see Figure 3.9). Although MSC has eschewed

Table 3.5 Throughput of top ten global terminal operators, 2005 and 2010

		2005			2010	
		TEU	World throughput		TEU	World throughput
		mn	%		mn	%
1	Hutchison	51.8	13.0	Hutchison	72.7	13.3
2	APMT	40.4	10.1	PSA	64.3	11.8
3	PSA	40.3	10.1	APMT	60.2	11.0
4	P&O Ports	23.8	6.0	DPW	49.5	9.1
5	Cosco	14.7	3.7	Cosco	48.3	8.8
6	DP World	12.9	3.2	MSC	19.4	3.6
7	Eurogate	12.1	3.0	Eurogate	12.3	2.2
8	Evergreen	8.7	2.2	SSA Marine	9.1	1.7
9	MSC	7.8	2.0	Evergreen	8.9	1.6
10	SSA Marine	7.3	1.8	Hanjin	8.5	1.6
	Top 10	219.8	55.1	Top 10	353.2	64.7
	Top 24	267.4	67.0	Top 25	409.3	75.0
	Total	399.1	100.0	Total	546.0	100.0

Note: The figures exclude container throughput at terminals where the operator's shareholding is less than 10%. These figures may have been revised in subsequent editions.

Source: DSC (2006, 2011b).

alliances in the past, the introduction of the Daily Maersk Service between key Asian and European ports in 2011 prompted the company to ally with France's CMA CGM controlled by the Saadé family. In 2012 Maersk Line's decision to order ten 18000 TEU Triple E container ships for the pendulum service between Asia and Europe, to maximize economies of scale, realize greater cost efficiency and achieve environmental sustainability, encouraged a deeper alliance between MSC and CMA CGM. By 2013 this development had blossomed into an in-principle operational alliance between Maersk Line, MSC and CMA CGM on the east–west trade routes (DMR, 2013). This 'P3' network, covering 255 ships with a combined capacity of 2.6 million TEUS and 29 loops, has been introduced in 2014. As each of the participating companies has its own preferred seaport hubs and terminal operators, the anticipated consolidation or rationalization of port calls to focus on those with quay facilities and cranes capable of handling the ultra-large container ships operated by this vessel-sharing alliance is expected to have major repercussions on shippers, the two rival alliances, intra-regional feeder services and intermodal connections, seaports and terminal operators. The expected widespread impact has attracted the interest of Beijing, the European Union and United States regulators, whose approval for the new alliance is required (P&H, 2014).

REGULATORS

Regulators of the global container shipping sector comprise individual states, regional organizations such as the European Union and its member states, and international bodies, notably the International Maritime Organization. Over time there has been a shift within this multilevel governance structure from state to private control, accompanied by a rise in the significance of regional and international policies, to regulate the sector.

State control, protecting national container shipping champions by regulation, subsidy and discrimination, has been lessened with increased overseas investment in container shipping and terminals, and the change to 'open registries' distancing the choice of flag from national policymakers. Moves towards liberalizing regulatory controls, and privatizing government-owned container shipping companies and terminals to create a 'level playing field' on the basis of 'fair competition', have been accelerated by the European Union's decision to open up the trading bloc's maritime market to all member states and reduce state interference in container shipping and ports (that is, restricting state intervention to the provision of public goods where the market mechanism fails to provide them). International Maritime Organization regulations governing container shipping safety, environment and security are automatically operationalized by the European Union to encourage shipowners to register their vessels under the EU flag rather than use open registries.

Tensions may arise where the policy jurisdictions of individual states, regional organizations and international authorities differ. One area of contention involves the application of competition (or anti-trust) law to the maritime sector, especially changes to the regulation of liner shipping stemming originally from policy changes in the United States trades to promote a more market-driven, efficient shipping industry. In 1998 the US Ocean Shipping Reform Act (OSRA), amending the US Shipping Act of 1984, continued to transform the country's highly regulated, common carriage system into a more flexible individualized system of one-on-one confidential transport contracts between carriers (shipping lines) and shippers (exporters and importers). In 2008 the European Union went further by removing the block exemption of liner shipping conferences from anti-monopoly practices within two years. But, suggesting that liner shipping may still need special treatment, the European Union reduced the permitted threshold for a consortium or alliance on a particular route from 35 per cent to 30 per cent. Despite this development, Australia, Canada, China, Japan, Singapore, the United States and other jurisdictions have persisted with their more pragmatic national policies towards liner shipping conferences, often in the face of opposition from their local shipper councils. Without the harmonization of maritime shipping rules, the container shipping sector has still not been subjected to 'global' regulation.

THE GLOBAL HUB-AND-SPOKE SYSTEM REVISITED

The global hub-and-spoke system is well entrenched in hierarchical container shipping networks driven by economies of scale, scope and density (Ng and Wilmsmeier, 2012). There have been many changes since the system's inception among shipping companies, port authorities, terminal operators and regulators. By 2010 the Asian-Pacific Rim had become the undisputed main generator of containers. The region's outbound trade lanes linking Europe and North America outstrip those on the return legs, and dwarf those involved in exchanges between Europe and North America (Figure 3.18). Asia–Australasia had the strongest north–south connection, and Asia–South America had the largest diagonal trade between the Northern and Southern Hemispheres. Intra-Asia had the

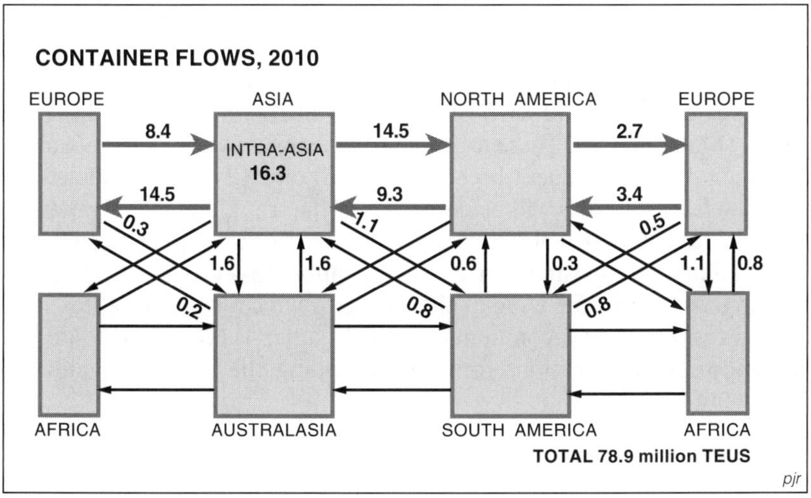

Source: Compiled from CI (2013).

Figure 3.18 Container network, 2010

greatest internal trade, which was almost as extensive as the transatlantic and the trans-Pacific trade combined. There were no marked container flows between Africa, Australasia and South America.

This global pattern hinges on hubs located at strategic locations on 'Main Street' acting as control points to orchestrate major flows between Asia, Europe and North America, and offers a wider geographical coverage. Additionally, the hubs link the 'mainline', multi-port services on the north–south, diagonal and direct routes connected to terminals in the 'cul-de-sacs' of Australasia, Africa, and South and Central America. Also, intra-regional feeder services depend upon the hub configuration for transhipments to and from larger vessels; these are upgradeable from feeder to mainline operations, as occurred with the development of direct services to China. Thus hubs have enabled container shipping companies to deploy vessels of different capacities to match prevailing traffic demand and offer an extensive range of services to multinational manufacturers and retailers across the market spectrum.

Additional flows, anticipated from the potential markets of Brazil, Russia, India, China and South Africa (BRICS), are driving growth in seaborne trade and global value chains. Their emergence is expected to change the competitive hierarchy of container ports and terminals as container shipping companies seek further economies of scale in larger ships and refine their door-to-door networks. Rising long-term gross domestic product (GDP) levels, coupled with the adoption of open markets, are also expected to increase the volume of trade passing through the global hub-and-spoke system. Speculation is also growing about containerships whose dimensions would exceed the Suez Canal (Suezmax) and even a larger vessel carrying 30000 TEU that may be too large for the Malacca Straits (Malaccamax). These technological changes are unlikely to lead to a more stable environment because they will intensify the cascade effect, since the largest vessels will be deployed on the trunk east–west route and the displaced vessels will be relegated to the north–south, diagonal and feeder routes. The existence of this global hub-and-spoke system in maritime logistics raises the issue of the extent to which it is also represented in air transport and telecommunications (Chapter 4) because the outcome has important implications for comprehending the nature of gateways (Chapter 5).

4. Aviation and telecommunications networks

Global air transport and telecommunications services compete with and complement global shipping services. Although air transport and telecommunications networks are distinguished by well-connected hubs their hierarchies differ, resulting in them being considered separately, except for reference to the impact of the Internet on the aviation sector (Tranos, 2011). After discussing the general characteristics of air transport services, given this book's emphasis on logistics, subsequent analysis in this chapter focuses initially on air cargo movements, even though passengers contribute between 70 and 90 per cent of an airline's revenue.

In 2011, air cargo accounted for an estimated 40 per cent of international trade by value, despite carrying only 2 per cent of the total goods by mass (ICAO, 2013). Air cargo has not only outpaced the worldwide growth rate of air passengers and gross domestic product (GDP), but has also expanded at an even greater rate in lesser-developed countries, where road conditions are poor and cargo security is lax. This rapid growth stems from a reduction in the cost of transporting cargo by air from using the belly capacity of wide-bodied passenger aircraft; growth in knowledge-intensive goods such as computers and electronic goods, with higher value to weight ratios, comprising a greater share of international trade; and the adoption of agile supply chain management practices that use the aircraft as a 'virtual warehouse' to meet the premium on speed, flexibility and freight security.

The overriding issue in discussing air cargo, air passenger and telecommunications in this chapter is the degree to which the global hub-and-spoke system, evident in container shipping, has permeated their respective operations. Is there a 'Main Street' in air cargo, air passenger and telecommunications? Are there 'cul-de-sacs' in these different modes? And to what extent are these patterns reflected in the operations of major players?

To address these issues a snapshot is taken of the global air cargo, air passenger and Internet networks in 2010. Paying particular attention to the top 25 hubs in each category, these geographical patterns are interpreted in terms of growth trends, operational characteristics, major players and key developments, including strategic alliances. Differences in the operational needs of air cargo and passenger operations are considered in the context of airline management and operations, with reference to case studies of the Australian airline Qantas Airways and Singapore Airlines, before considering airport cities and airport city-regions or 'aerotropolises'. Then the structure of Internet flows and hubs are examined, and this is followed by a brief assessment of the likely effects of the new generation Internet on manufacturing and retailing, and logistics operations.

AIR TRANSPORT SERVICES

Since the mid-1970s air transport services have been transformed in response to the expansion of international trade and foreign direct investment, greater economic integration, the international fragmentation of production, and airline deregulation and liberalization. Between 1977 and 2011 the number of aeroplanes tripled from nearly 6500 to almost 20000 (Tinseth, 2012). Multiple stops have been replaced by point-to-point services. Air travel has changed from being an expensive luxury item into an affordable proposition at one-third the 1977 price, the number of average weeks' earnings required to fly from London to Sydney declining from 12 weeks to one week (Clark, 2007). Low, stable fuel prices have been superseded by high, volatile fuel prices. Load factors have increased from 61 per cent to 78 per cent. The pre-1980s American and European-centric spatial structure of air traffic with a colonial outlier in Southeast Asia has been transformed into a diverse and globally balanced pattern. Since then a Middle Eastern hub has been inserted and the Southeast Asian hub replaced by a fully fledged Asian hub (Figure 4.1).

Above all, regulated services have yielded to more competitive services, as the broad network airline business model has been swapped for a low-cost carrier or hybrid business model. The traditional broad network airline business model comprised heavily unionized, large carrier groups. These traditional flag carriers have operated international routes governed by bilateral air service agreements negotiated under the 1944 Chicago Convention covering passenger and cargo services, routes, designated airlines and capacity, and fares between nation-states (Table 4.1). This international regulatory regime specified nine freedoms of the air and established the intergovernmental International Civil Aviation Organization (ICAO) to oversee them.

Traditional or 'legacy' carriers have been affected by the liberalization of regulatory policies that provided full market access to start-up carriers.

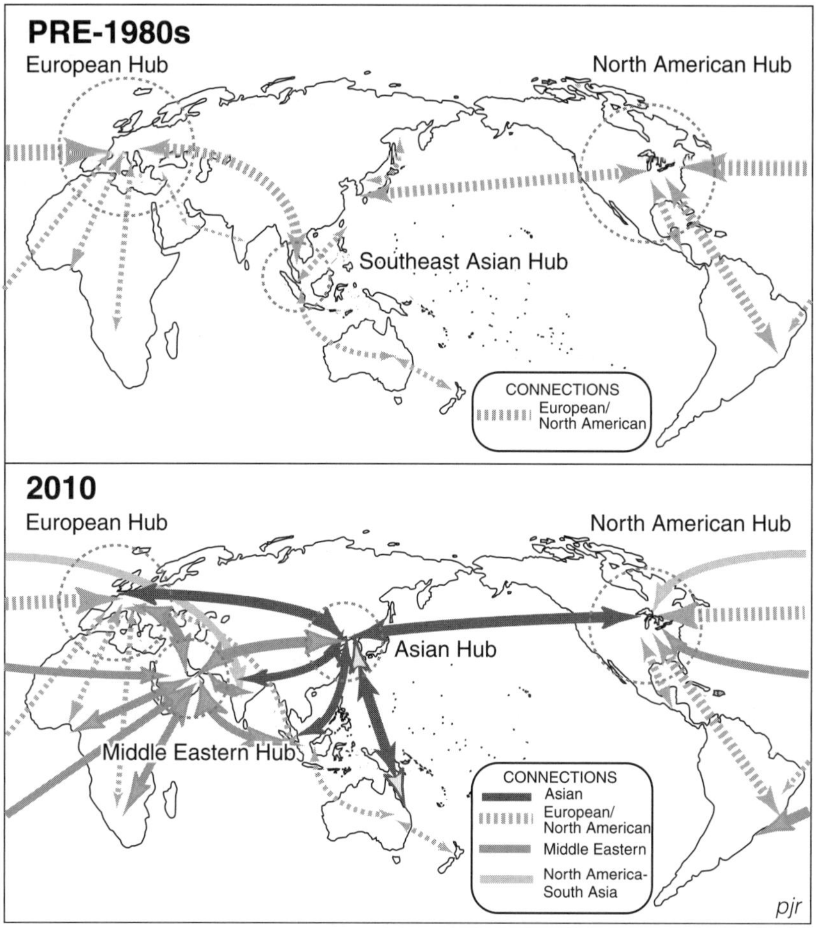

Source: Adapted from Clark (2007, 6, 8).

Figure 4.1 Air transport's spatial structure ca. 2010 compared with pre-1980s

Deregulation and liberalization occurred domestically within the United States (1978) and Canada (1988) before an 'open skies' agreement (1995) was signed between the two countries (Table 4.2). Designed to induce greater competition to satisfy the needs of passengers for better services and lower fares, the 'open skies' single aviation agreements spread to Australia and New Zealand (1996) and then to multilateral agreements within the European Union (1997) and the Association of Southeast Asian

Table 4.1 Air freedom rights and privileges

Freedom	Right or privilege to:	Example
First	Fly over a foreign country, without landing there	Frankfurt–Madrid, as a German company, overflying France
Second	Refuel or carry out maintenance in a foreign country on the way to another country	Frankfurt–Madrid, as a German company, but stopping for fuel in France
Third	Fly from one's own country to another	Frankfurt–Paris, as a German company
Fourth	Fly from another country to one's own	Paris–Frankfurt, as a German company
Fifth	Fly between two foreign countries during flights while the flight originates or ends in one's own country	Madrid–Paris–Frankfurt, as a German company
Sixth	Fly from a foreign country to another one while stopping in one's own country for non-technical reason	Madrid–Frankfurt–Paris as a German company
Seventh	Fly between two foreign countries while not offering flights to one's own country	Madrid–Paris as a German company
Eighth	Fly between two or more airports in a foreign country while continuing service to one's own country	Nice–Paris–Frankfurt as a German company
Nine	Fly between two or more airports in a foreign country without continuing service to one's own country	Nice–Paris as a German company

Note: Most nations exchange first and second freedoms through an International Air Services Transit Agreement. The other freedoms, when available, are usually established between countries in bilateral or multilateral air services agreements. The third and fourth freedoms are always granted together. The eighth and ninth freedoms (cabotage) have been exchanged only in limited instances.

Source: Lufthansa (2012).

Nations (ASEAN). Governments have sought agreements with these regional blocs, as exemplified by the open aviation agreement between the United States and the European Union (2007) that allows airlines to fly between any two cities. As these agreements are still limited in scope, liberalization is still partial at an international level and there is still no

Table 4.2 Bilateral versus open skies agreements

Type of agreement	Service capacity	Service frequency	Fares	Extended traffic rights
Traditional bilateral agreement	Restrictions on which airlines can operate	Restrictions on what markets airlines may serve/number of flights that can be flown	Restrictions on pricing	Restrictions on operations to and from additional countries
Open skies agreement	No restrictions on the number of airlines that may operate, nor restrictions on what markets airlines may serve	No restrictions	No restrictions on pricing	Allowance for open rights to and from additional countries

Source: US GAO (2004a, 11).

'free-for-all', with the European Union imposing an emissions trading system for aviation in 2012.

The legacy carriers have responded to the greater competition unleashed by the unbundling of the traditional air sector by adopting a hub-and-spoke network and shedding jobs (US GAO, 2004b). Although hubbing incurs a 90-minute-plus passenger time penalty, compared with flying non-stop, this strategy has permitted legacy airlines to increase scheduled frequencies. Offering multiple daily flights on competitive routes has allowed the legacy carriers to retain a strong market share of business passengers and customer loyalty through their frequent flyer programmes, airport lounges and higher level of cabin services (for example, meals and in-flight entertainment).

The other effect of deregulation and liberalization has been to allow the entry of new 'low-cost carriers' (LCCs), typified by Southwest Airlines based in the United States, Ryanair in Ireland and Air Asia in Malaysia (CAPA, 2009). The LCCs offer point-to-point services to avoid hubbing, more flights using smaller jets (A-320s and B737-300s) and faster turnarounds (less than 60 minutes) by not using air bridges, avoiding peak hour congestion and using secondary airports. For example, Air Asia uses Senai in Johor Bahru, Malaysia, to connect with Soekarno Hatta in

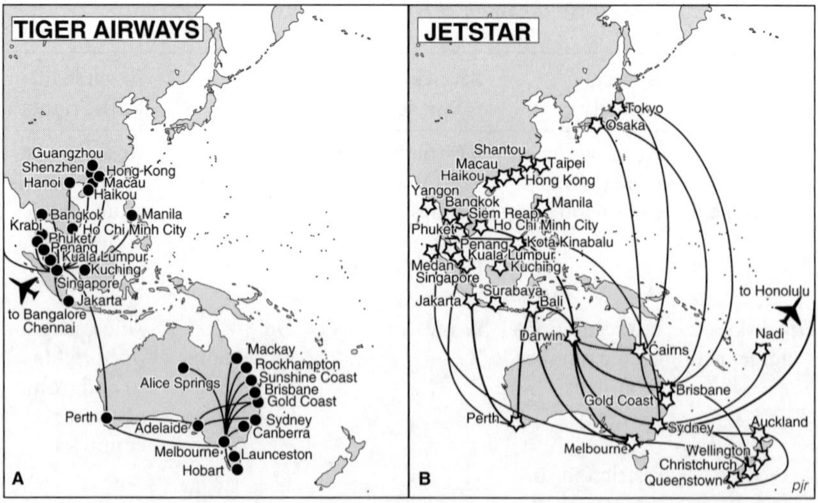

Sources: Data from Tiger Airways (2011), Jetstar (2013).

Figure 4.2 Low-cost carriers: (A) Tiger Airways (Tigerair) operated by Singapore Airlines, 2010, and (B) Jetstar Airways by Qantas Airways, 2010

Jakarta, Indonesia. Also the LCCs use the same aircraft type and concentrate on short-distance routes. Their 'no-frills' services are characterized by a single passenger class, a simple fare scheme that increases prices as the flight fills up, unreserved seating, direct sales over the Internet and optional paid-for food. By 2011 the LCCs had accrued 14 per cent of the world market compared with the 60 per cent held by the legacy carriers (Tinseth, 2012).

Competition from the LCCs has prompted the legacy airlines to develop their own copycat low-cost carriers, sometimes referred to as 'faux' LCCs. For example, Qantas and Singapore Airlines have stakes in the low-fare regional operators the Jetstar Group and Tiger Airways (Tigerair) respectively (Figure 4.2). Since 2004 Jetstar has extended low-fare flights from serving Australia's domestic destinations to short- and long-haul services based in New Zealand, Singapore and Viet Nam, using 100 aircraft carrying 20 million passengers in the financial year (FY) 2011 (Jetstar, 2013). Also established in 2004, Tigerair has extended its pan-Asian services to destinations within a five-hour radius of Singapore using 21 aircraft to carry almost 6 million passengers in FY 2011. Tigerair's domestic services in Australia are now linked with Virgin Australia and the combined operation competes against Qantas/Jetstar.

Besides having the hybrid, two-brand growth strategy to compete for premium, business and leisure markets, the legacy airlines have introduced new-generation aircraft. Higher oil prices since the mid-2000s have prompted the legacy carriers to bring forward fleet renewal and upgrade to more fuel-efficient, very large passenger aircraft (for example, A380-800 and B747-B Intercontinental). Also the mid-sized, wide-bodied Boeing 787 Dreamliner has been introduced to carry 200–350 passengers, which can link China and the United States without hubbing. Other potential 'hub busters' include the Boeing 777-200LR (Long Range) that can offer non-stop service over 17 500 km. While this would allow the carriage of 240 passengers in less than 20 hours between London and Sydney, the restricted payload and relatively small time savings over one-stop flights of less than 24 hours has precluded its introduction by Qantas (Figure 4.3). Still this technical possibility represents a marked improvement on the pre-Second World War thrice-weekly flying boat service that made 32 stops and took nine days between Sydney and London, carrying 15 passengers and five crew members. Clock golf and quoits were offered on the promenade deck to break the tedium of the journey (Rimmer, 2005a).

Even with the introduction of new-generation aircraft, no single airline can create a global network offering a seamless service, because the international regulatory regime restricts access to overseas markets and limits foreign ownership. As the introduction of 'open skies' regimes has heightened competition, legacy airlines have sought, with the approval of domestic authorities, to cooperate with other partners in strategic alliances or quasi-mergers to meet the needs for seamless travel triggered by economic globalization. The three largest alliances – Star, Sky Team and Oneworld – are global networks of carriers that allow members to streamline costs and share revenue (Table 4.3). Although these alliances commenced in the late 1990s as code-sharing arrangements, they are being transformed into closer-knit partnerships to cut costs by co-locating at airports, coordinating frequent-flyer programmes, joint sourcing of fuel, spare parts and inflight service material, sharing information technology (IT) systems and undertaking joint investments in a common IT platform. By 2010 the Star Alliance had a market share measured in revenue passenger-kilometres (RPKs) of 31 per cent, followed by Sky Team with nearly 20 per cent and Oneworld with almost 18 per cent (WATS, 2011). As the alliance networks wield considerable market power, authorities are closely monitoring anti-competitive concerns arising from partnerships and inter-alliance rivalry on specific routes (for example, transatlantic).

LCCs and strategic alliances, coupled with economies of scope from

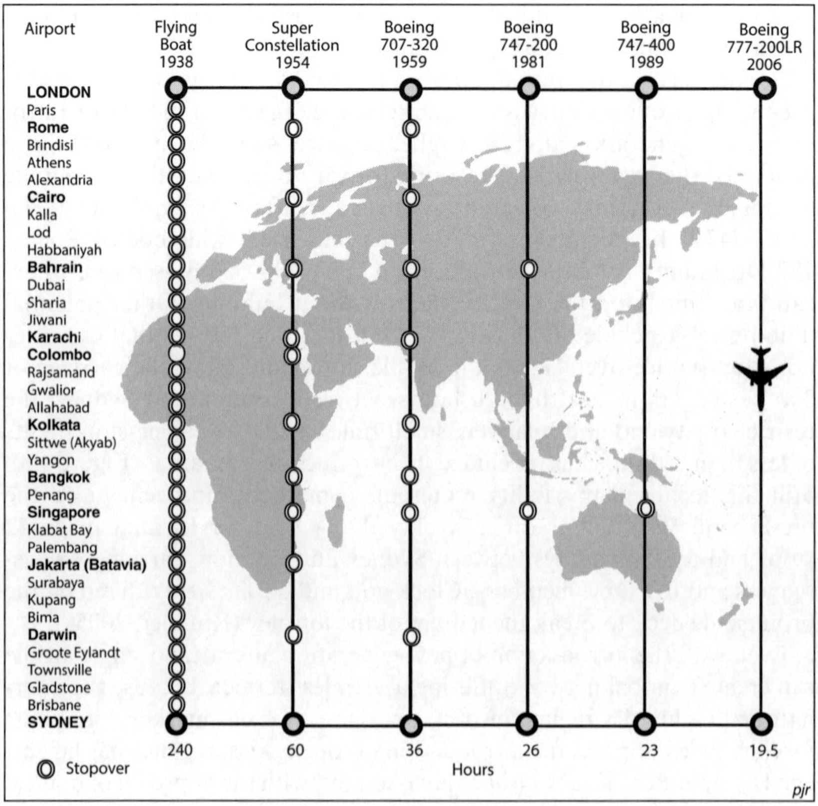

Sources: Data from Rimmer (2005a), Magill (2007).

Figure 4.3 Effects of changes in technology on travel time between London and Sydney

cost saving in producing air passenger and cargo services together, have affected the air transport sector's structure. In 1977 all top ten airlines were large network carriers based in Europe and North America and accounted for one-third of the global fleet (Table 4.4). Since then four of the US-based top ten airlines in 1977 – Eastern, TWA (Trans World Airlines), Northwest and Pan Am – have ceased operation. By 2011 the top ten airlines accounted for one-quarter of the global fleet, when one of them was based in China, two were low-cost carriers, and FedEx (Federal Express) was a cargo carrier.

Having passenger and cargo carriers in the same mix underlines that there are common features between the two operations (Figure 4.4).

Table 4.3 Airline passenger alliances, 2010

	Oneworld	Sky Team	Star Alliance
Members	12	15	28
Founded	1999	2000	1997
Countries	147	173	181
Destinations	766	926	1180
Lounges	550	490	990
Revenue (US$ bn)	92.4	97.9	150.7
Market share (%)	23	25	29
Passenger (RPKs bn)	729	752	1189
Market share (%)	18	20	31
Employees (thousand)	277	399	400
Headquarters	Vancouver (New York 2011)	Amsterdam	Frankfurt

Source: Oneworld (2011), Sky Team (2011), Star Alliance (2011).

Table 4.4 Comparison of the top ten airlines in fleet size in 1977 and 2011

	1977			2011		
	Airline	Country	Type	Airline	Country	Type
1	United	US	NET	Delta	US	NET
2	American	US	NET	United	US	NET
3	Eastern	US	NET	American	US	NET
4	TWA	US	NET	Southwest	US	LCC
5	Delta	US	NET	ExpressJet	US	NET
6	British Airways	UK	NET	FedEx	US	CAO
7	Northwest	US	NET	China Southern	CN	NET
8	Air Canada	CA	NET	US Airways	US	NET
9	Air France	FR	NET	Lufthansa	GE	NET
10	Pan Am	US	NET	Ryanair	IR	LCC

Note: CAO – cargo aircraft only; NET – network carrier; LCC – low-cost carrier.

Source: Tinseth (2012).

These are the airline and the airport, which together comprise the network to meet the demand from both shippers, and business and leisure passengers. The key drivers of air traffic demand are GDP and the value of international trade. Global commercial airline services are judged on

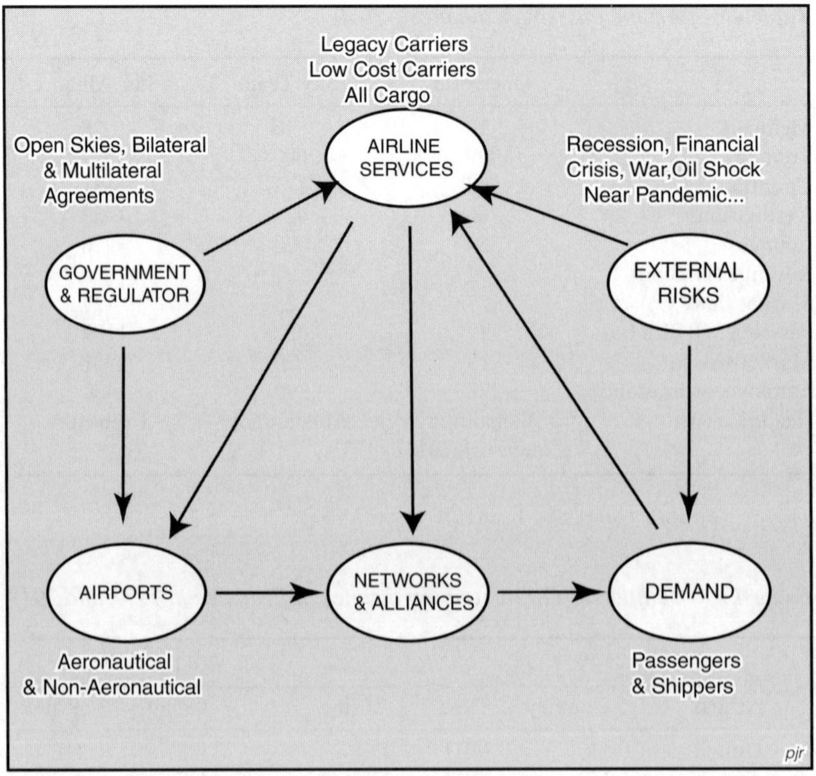

Figure 4.4 Key elements of the business and regulatory policy environment within which air transport operates

their operating profitability, airport infrastructure on performance and investment in aeronautical and non-aeronautical services (for example, duty-free shops), and the network on frequency of service and connectivity. As noted, this system is set within a national and an international regulatory framework involving bilateral and multilateral agreements. Since 1980 this system has been subject to external risks such as recessions, financial crises, wars, oil shocks, a near pandemic, volcanic ash clouds and 9/11. Nevertheless this remarkably resilient system maintained an annual growth rate of 5 per cent between 1980 and 2011 (Tinseth, 2012).

Within this broad aviation structure there are variations stemming from differences in the nature of air cargo and air passenger services. Air cargo differs from air passenger services in its preference for late night and early morning arrivals and departures rather than daytime departures and

Table 4.5 Differences between air cargo and air passengers

Cargo	Passenger
Night/early morning departure/arrival	Daytime departure/arrival
Less sensitive to time, routes & stops	Sensitive to time, routes and stops
One way	Round trip
Limited shippers	Unspecified public travellers
Need ramp services	No further ramp services
Loading/unloading	Self-loading and unloading of able-bodied
No cabin services	Cabin services
Door-to-door and intermodal service	Airport-to-airport service
Annual growth rate (tonnes)	Annual growth rate (passengers)
2010–14 8.1 % (IATA)	2010–14 5.3 % (IATA)
Annual growth rate (FTK)	Annual growth rate (RPK)
2010–30 5.4 % (Boeing)	2010–30 4.9 % (Boeing)

Note: IATA – International Air Transport Association; FTK – freight tonne-kilometres; RPK – revenue passenger-kilometres.

Sources: Petersen (2007), WATS (1995–2010, 2011).

arrivals (Table 4.5). Air cargo is less sensitive to time, routes and stops than passengers, who favour increased frequencies and flying non-stop. Cargo handlers are more responsive to the need to shift loads from one aircraft to another, breaking down and rebuilding pallets, and transhipment costs, while passengers are more concerned that the waiting time for connecting flights should be as short as possible, albeit in an attractive airport environment offering work stations, duty-free shopping and leisure activities.

Cargo flows are generally unidirectional, whereas passenger movements are more balanced, because they involve round trips. Other differences are that air cargo is limited to shippers, rather than unspecified travellers drawn from the public; loading and unloading is obligatory, whereas able passengers can load themselves; door-to-door intermodal cargo services are involved, rather than the airport-to-airport services provided to passengers; and no cabin service is required. Forecasts of annual growth rates suggest that in both the short and long term air cargo will be more robust than passenger traffic. Not only does it reflect the increase in the mass and value of goods being transported, arising from the growth in international just-in-time production and third-party logistics, but also air cargo has a key role to play in the revolutionary way in which products

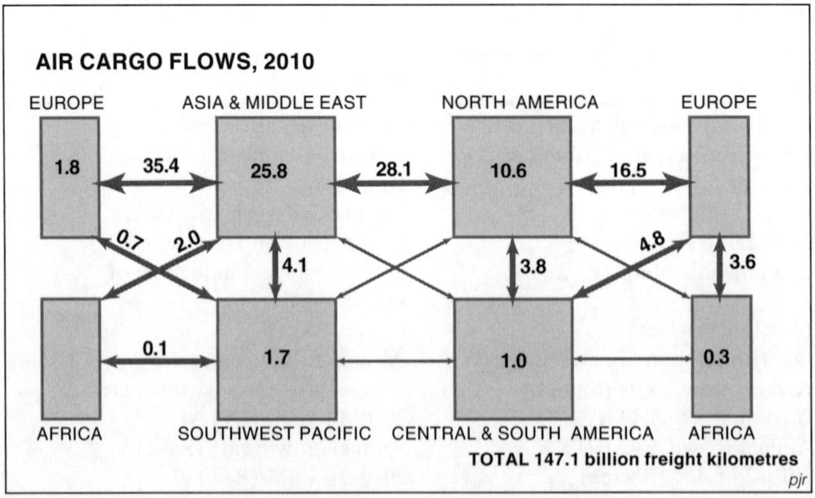

Source: Data from WATS (2011).

Figure 4.5 Air cargo network, 2010

purchased on the Internet using e-commerce can be delivered. This physical Internet relies on 'fast-cycle logistics' to capitalize on 'economies of speed' (Kasarda, 2013a, 2013b).

AIR CARGO

In 2010 the air cargo network mirrored the importance of 'Main Street' in the global hub-and-spoke system, but the relative weightings of the trade lanes differed in importance from container shipping (Figure 4.5). The leading route was between Asia and Europe, followed by the trans-Pacific. This pattern reflected the powerhouse performance of the Asian-Pacific Rim in the spectacular rebound of air cargo demand after the Global Financial Crisis (2008–09), which saw the industry shrink by 20 per cent in freight tonne-kilometres (FTK). 'Main Street's' least patronized link was the transatlantic route that echoed the then stuttering United States recovery and weak economic conditions in Europe. The diagonal link between Europe and South America was stronger than the Asia–South West Pacific link, which was the largest north–south connection linking 'Main Street' to the 'cul-de-sacs'. East–west air cargo movements between Africa, the Southwest Pacific and Central and South

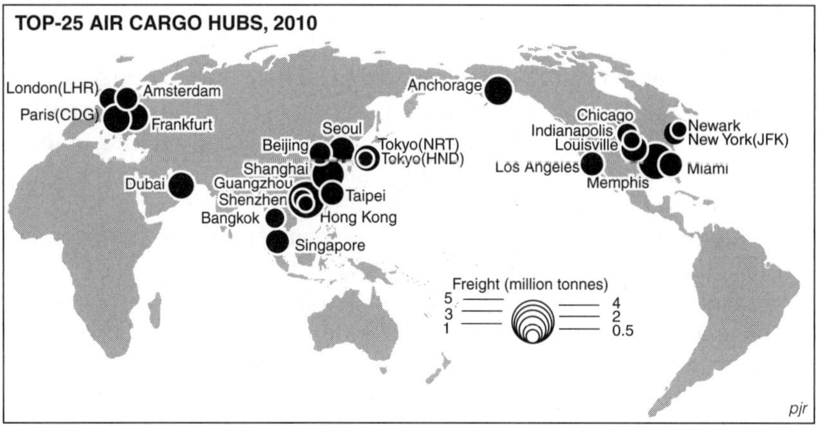

Source: Data from WATS (2011).

Figure 4.6 Top 25 air cargo hubs, 2010

America were negligible. Again, underlining its growing economic importance, the Rim's intra-regional movements were more than double those within North America and dwarfed those in Europe. These differences may reflect the Rim's greater reliance on wide-bodied passenger jets, with large cargo belly holds, operating on dense intra-regional freight routes; North America's dependence on dedicated air express carriers using a mix of wide-bodied and narrow-bodied aircraft to supplement truck and rail; and Europe's greater use of surface transport (Zhang et al., 2011, 813–14).

By 2010, 12 of the top 25 air cargo hubs, based on the tonnage of international and domestic freight, were located in Asia and the Middle East, compared with nine in North America and four in Europe; other regions were unrepresented (Figure 4.6). This distribution reflects both the importance of the Asian-Pacific Rim, especially China, as the world's prime cargo generator. Following the upsurge of transit cargoes from China, stemming from replenishment orders after the Global Financial Crisis (2008–09) and a new wave of high-tech electronic components, Hong Kong became the world's leading cargo hub, followed by Shanghai (Pudong) in third position, ahead of a host of Rim airports meeting a large demand generated by local traffic and transhipments: Seoul, Tokyo (Narita), Singapore, Taipei, Beijing, Bangkok, Guangzhou. Shenzhen and Tokyo (Haneda). Dubai came to prominence as an intermediate hub between the Asian-Pacific Rim and Europe to accommodate dedicated cargo planes that have a shorter range than their passenger counterparts (Chapter 5).

The other feature in the 2010 air cargo pattern was the prominence of hubs in the United States that are closely related to the activities of air express couriers: Memphis, the world's second-ranking hub, is FedEx's 'superhub', and Indianapolis and Newark are the company's regional hubs; Louisville is UPS's (United Parcel Service) world hub; and Anchorage serves as an intermediate transhipment hub for both companies in connecting North America and the Asian-Pacific Rim (see Chapter 1). Without the presence of these hubs to augment Chicago, New York, Miami and Los Angeles, the United States would have experienced a much greater exodus from the top 25 air cargo airports since 1995 because Europe only had a net loss of one over the period, with Paris, Frankfurt, Amsterdam and London maintaining their status as key air cargo centres (Table 4.6).

By 2010 the air cargo sector's operations had been reorganized to accommodate the changes reflected in the global network. An examination of the top 25 airlines in terms of scheduled freight tonne-kilometres (FTK) reflects the dominance of Asia and the Middle East in cargo traffic, with 13 of the airlines domiciled there, compared with five in North America, five in Europe and one each in Australasia and South America (Table 4.7). Another feature was the strength of the couriers or integrators, Federal Express and UPS Airlines, which oversee the entire door-to-door shipment process by acting as forwarder and carrier. These integrators are in the process of extending from express services into general cargo, door-to-door, intermodal delivery services. They outrank not only the heavy lift non-integrator cargo carriers such as the Luxembourg-based Cargolux and the New York-based Polar Air Cargo in freight tonne-kilometres, but also the combination cargo–passenger carriers with dedicated freight aircraft, typified by Korean Air, and passenger operators, reliant upon the services of freight forwarding agents or third-party logistics providers to orchestrate their landside operations with shippers and fill their belly space (Reynolds-Feighan, 2013).

These differences between carriers have resulted in an argument for the negotiation of separate air traffic rights for all-cargo operators, including all-express integrators, because of their differing routing preferences and operational priorities from passenger airlines (Zhang et al., 2011). Although 100 of the over 400 'open skies' agreements granted cargo rights, more remains to be done to overcome constraints and operational restrictions, including night curfews, partial ground-handling entitlements and onerous customs regulations (ICAO, 2013). Progress has been made in relations between China and the United States, the two largest freight-generating countries, towards having unlimited air cargo operations, which has led to the establishment of hubs by FedEx in Guangzhou and UPS Airlines in Shanghai to offset China's shortfall in the availability of all-cargo aircraft (Zhang, 2009). The greater availability of air cargo stemming from China has prompted Hong Kong's Cathay Pacific Airlines, Korean Air and Taiwan's EVA Air and China's 'Big Three' airlines – Air China, China Eastern and China Southern – to follow their United States counterparts in establishing separate cargo and passenger operations to take advantage of any liberalization of air cargo services and advances in regional integration. Cathay Pacific's air cargo subsidiary has entered into an alliance with DHL to provide express services to gateways within the Asian-Pacific Rim (Chapter 6).

Regional differences have also resulted in the creation of two air cargo alliances among combination airlines in 2000 to provide the seamless coordination and delivery of international services to over 500 airports worldwide. The largest group is Sky Team Cargo, comprising Korean Air and China Southern in Asia, Aeroflot, Air France, Alitalia, Czech Airlines and KLM in Europe, and Aeroméxico and Delta Airlines in North America; one drawback is that the American partners do not possess their own cargo fleet. A second group, the WOW Cargo Alliance, comprises Singapore Airlines in Asia and SAS in Europe. Lufthansa, a founding member, and Japan Airlines have left WOW because, without an American partner, the group cannot offer sufficient benefits. As Skyteam and WOW parallel strategic alliances in air passenger transport, they raise similar issues for regulatory bodies on price and consumer welfare.

AIR PASSENGER TRAFFIC

In 2010 the global hub-and-spoke system was also prominent in the world scheduled air passenger traffic. The relative strengths of the lanes in the air passenger network, measured in billion passenger-kilometres derived from 131 airlines participating in *WATS: World Air Transport Statistics*, differed from air cargo, but still highlighted the importance of 'Main Street' (WATS, 2011). The transatlantic route edged the connection between Europe and Asia, with the trans-Pacific being the least patronized link on 'Main Street' (Figure 4.7). The diagonal route between Central and South America and Europe was slightly stronger than the Western Hemisphere's leading north–south route. East–west routes linking Africa, the Southwest Pacific and Central and South America were much weaker. Asia and the Middle East had the strongest intra-continental flows ahead of the

Table 4.6 Top 25 air cargo hubs, 1995, 2000, 2005 and 2010

	1995		2000		2005		2010	
	mn tonnes	#	mn tonnes	#	mn tonnes	#	mn tonnes	#
North America								
Los Angeles	1.60	2	2.04	3	1.94	8	1.75	14
Miami	1.58	3	1.64	10	1.75	12	1.84	12
New York JFK	1.57	4	1.82	6	1.66	14	1.34	19
Chicago	1.24	7	1.47	13	1.55	15	1.38	18
NY Newark	0.91	13	1.08	18	0.95	21	0.86	23
Dallas FW	0.77	14	0.90	20	–	–	–	–
Atlanta	0.77	15	0.89	21	0.77	25	–	–
San Francisco	0.70	16	0.87	22	–	–	–	–
Philadelphia	0.49	19	–	–	–	–	–	–
Honolulu	0.41	21	–	–	–	–	–	–
Seattle/Tacoma	0.40	22	–	–	–	–	–	–
Boston	0.40	23	–	–	–	–	–	–
Denver	0.38	24	–	–	–	–	–	–
Minneapolis	0.36	25	–	–	–	–	–	–
Memphis	–	–	2.49	1	3.60	2	3.92	2
Anchorage	–	–	1.80	7	2.55	3	2.65	5
Louisville	–	–	1.52	12	1.82	11	2.17	10
Indianapolis	–	–	1.17	17	0.99	20	1.01	22
Dayton	–	–	0.83	24	–	–	–	–
	11.58		18.52		17.58		16.92	
Europe								
Frankfurt	1.46	6	1.71	8	1.96	7	2.28	7
London HR	1.13	9	1.40	14	1.39	17	1.55	16
Amsterdam	1.01	11	1.27	15	1.50	16	1.54	17
Paris	0.93	12	1.61	11	2.01	6	2.40	6
Zurich	0.44	20	–	–	–	–	–	–
	4.97		5.99		6.86		7.77	
Asia								
Tokyo NRT	1.66	1	1.93	4	2.29	4	2.17	9
Hong Kong	1.48	5	2.27	2	3.43	1	4.17	1
Seoul	1.22	8	1.87	5	2.15	5	2.68	4
Singapore	1.12	10	1.71	9	1.85	10	1.84	11
Tokyo HND	0.66	17	–	–	0.80	23	0.82	24
Bangkok	0.66	18	0.87	23	1.14	19	1.31	20
Shanghai	–	–	–	–	1.86	9	3.23	3
Taipei	–	–	1.21	16	1.71	13	1.77	13
Osaka	–	–	1.00	19	0.87	22	–	–
Beijing	–	–	0.77	25	0.78	24	1.55	15

Table 4.6 (continued)

	1995		2000		2005		2010	
	mn tonnes	#	mn tonnes	#	mn tonnes	#	mn tonnes	#
Asia								
Guangzhou	–	–	–	–	–	–	1.14	21
Shenzhen	–	–	–	–	–	–	0.81	25
	6.80		11.63		16.88		21.49	
Middle East								
Dubai	–	–	–	–	1.31	18	2.27	8

Sources: ACI (1995–2010, 2011).

Table 4.7 Top 25 airlines by total scheduled freight tonne-kilometres, 2010

	Billion FTK		Billion FTK
Federal Express	15.7	KLM	3.7
UPS Airlines	10.2	**Asiana Airlines**	3.4
Cathay Pacific Airlines	9.6	**China Eastern Airlines**	3.2
Korean Air	9.5	Delta Airlines	3.2
Emirates	7.9	**China Southern Airlines**	3.1
Lufthansa	7.4	**Qatar Airways**	3.0
Singapore Airlines	7.0	LAN Airlines	3.0
China Airlines	6.4	**Thai Airways**	2.9
EVA Air	5.2	**Japan Airlines**	2.9
Cargolux	4.9	Qantas Airways	2.6
Air France	4.7	American Airlines	2.6
British Airways	4.5	United Airlines	2.5
Air China	4.2		

Note: Airlines domiciled within the Asian-Pacific Rim and the Middle East in bold.

Source: WATS (2011, 90).

sluggish economies of North America and Europe; the internal domestic markets within the southern hemisphere were still comparatively small.

In 2010, 11 of the top 25 air passenger 'super' hubs were located in North America compared with nine in Asia and the Middle East, and five in Europe; none were located in Africa, the Southwest Pacific or Central and South America (Figure 4.8). Reflecting the heavy reliance of North

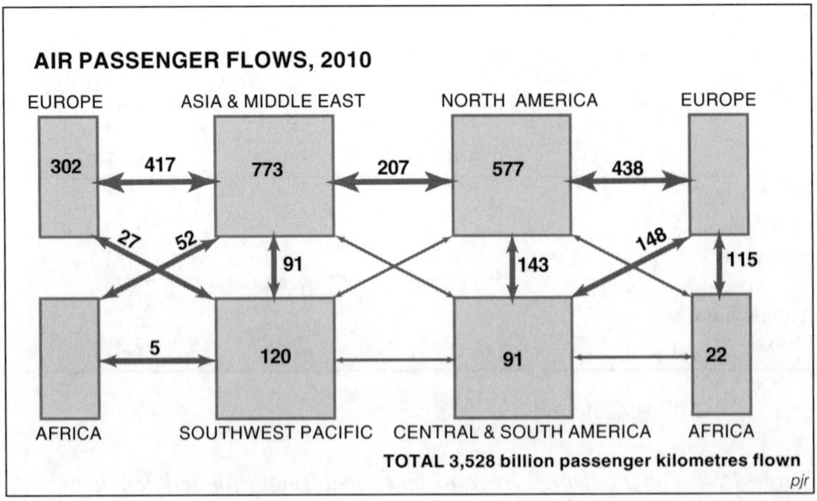

Source: Data from WATS (2011).

Figure 4.7 Scheduled air passenger network, 2010

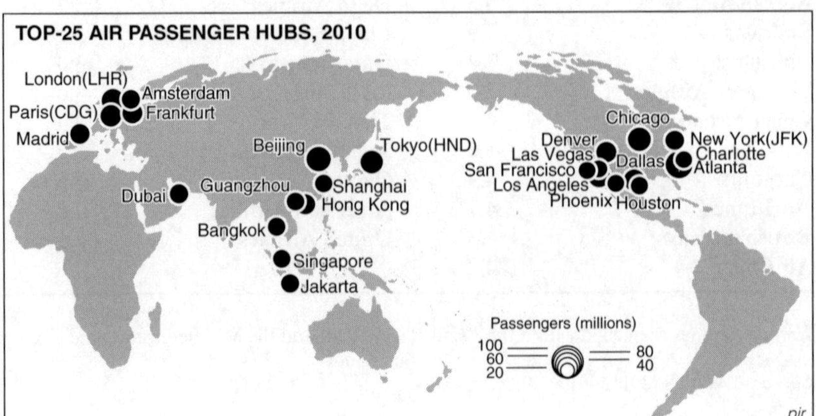

Source: Data from WATS (2011).

Figure 4.8 Top 25 scheduled air passenger hubs, 2010

America on domestic air transport, Atlanta ranked as the world's busiest airport and Chicago (O'Hare) ranked third, based on the Airport Council International's results for 2010 (ACI, 2011). With the rapid growth in China's international and domestic traffic, Beijing became the world's second-busiest airport and Shanghai (Pudong) had risen rapidly in the rankings to twentieth position. London (Heathrow) was the highest-ranking European airport ahead of Paris, Frankfurt, Amsterdam and Madrid, although it still remained the world's busiest airport in international passengers handled.

In 2010 North American airports still outnumbered those in Asia in the top 25, but the mobility gap between the two regions had sharply decreased over the previous 15 years (Table 4.8). Since 1995 the number of top 25 airports in North America had progressively declined at each five-yearly interval from 17 to 11 with the exodus of Boston, Detroit, Miami, Minneapolis, Newark, Seattle and St Louis offsetting the addition of Charlotte. The number of top 25 airports on the Asian-Pacific Rim had almost tripled, with the routinization of air travel, from three to eight with the addition of Beijing, Bangkok, Jakarta, Guangzhou, Shanghai and Singapore augmenting Tokyo and Hong Kong to compensate for the loss of Seoul. Europe had no net loss over the period with the second airport in Paris being replaced by Madrid and London's second airport, Gatwick, flitting in and out of the rankings.

In 2010, 13 of the top 25 passenger airlines were domiciled in North America and Europe, 11 in Asia and the Middle East and one in the Southwest Pacific (Table 4.9). Eight of the top ten airlines were still based in the North Atlantic region, the exceptions being Emirates and China Southern Airlines. Their presence, coupled with nine other Asian and Middle Eastern airlines, presages their rise in the rankings. As illustrated by comparing Singapore Airlines with the Australian-based airline, Qantas Airways, much depends on their headquarters location within the global-hub-and spoke system.

Qantas Airways and Singapore Airlines

Qantas Airways and Singapore Airlines offered a classic comparison, especially when the former was confined to international flights and had no domestic activities (Rimmer, 1996a). Both airlines had similar output characteristics with long stage lengths and large aircraft. In 1992 this situation was changed. While Singapore Airlines remained majority owned by the Singapore Government's investment arm, Temasek Holdings, Qantas was privatized with foreign ownership limited to 49 per cent, foreign airlines to 35 per cent and the largest foreign shareholder to 25 per cent.

Table 4.8 Top 25 air passenger hubs, 1995, 2000, 2005 and 2010

	Passengers handled							
	1995		2000		2005		2010	
	Mn	Rank	Mn	Rank	Mn	Rank	Mn	Rank
North America								
Chicago	67.3	1	72.1	2	76.5	2	66.8	3
Atlanta	57.3	2	80.2	1	85.9	1	88.3	1
Dallas FW	54.3	3	60.7	5	59.2	6	56.9	8
Los Angeles	53.9	5	66.4	3	61.5	5	59.1	6
San Francisco	36.3	8	41.0	9	32.8	23	39.3	23
Miami	33.2	9	33.6	19	–	–	–	–
Denver	31.0	10	38.7	11	43.4	11	52.2	10
New York JFK	30.3	12	32.9	21	41.9	13	46.5	14
Detroit	29.0	13	35.5	16	36.4	20	–	–
Las Vegas	28.0	15	36.9	12	44.0	10	39.8	22
Phoenix	27.8	16	36.0	15	41.2	14	38.6	24
Minneapolis	26.8	18	36.8	13	36.8	19	–	–
Newark	26.6	19	34.2	18	34.0	22	–	–
St Louis	25.7	21	30.6	25	–	–	–	–
Houston	24.7	23	35.3	17	39.7	17	40.5	21
Boston	24.7	24	–	–	–	–	–	–
Seattle	22.8	25	–	–	–	–	–	–
Charlotte	–	–	38.3	11	–	–	38.3	25
Orlando	–	–	30.8	24	34.1	21	–	–
	599.7		740.0		667.4		566.3	
Europe								
London	54.1	4	64.6	4	67.9	3	65.9	4
Frankfurt	37.5	7	49.4	7	52.2	8	53.0	9
Paris	28.0	14	48.2	8	53.8	7	58.2	7
Paris ORY	26.6	20	–	–	–	–	–	–
Amsterdam	24.9	22	39.6	10	44.2	9	45.2	15
Madrid	–	–	32.9	20	41.9	12	49.8	12
London LGW	–	–	32.1	23	32.8	24	–	–
	171.1		266.8		292.8		272.1	
Asia								
Tokyo HND	45.8	6	56.4	6	63.3	4	64.2	5
Seoul	30.7	11	36.7	14	–	–	–	–
Hong Kong	27.4	17	32.8	22	40.3	16	50.3	11
Beijing	–	–	–	–	41.0	15	74.0	2

Table 4.8 (continued)

	Passengers handled							
	1995		2000		2005		2010	
	Mn	Rank	Mn	Rank	Mn	Rank	Mn	Rank
Asia								
Jakarta	–	–	–	–	–	–	44.4	16
Bangkok	–	–	–	–	39.0	18	42.8	17
Singapore	–	–	–	–	32.4	25	42.0	18
Guangzhou	–	–	–	–	–	–	41.0	19
Shanghai	–	–	–	–	–	–	40.6	20
	103.9		125.9		216.0		399.3	
Middle East								
Dubai	–	–	–	–	–	–	47.2	13

Sources: ACI (1995–2010, 2011).

Table 4.9 Top 25 IATA and non-IATA airlines by total scheduled passenger-kilometres, 2010

	Billion		Billion
Delta Airlines	206.9	**Air China**	85.5
American Airlines	201.9	**Singapore Airlines**	84.9
United Airlines	164.7	*Ryanair*	*81.8*
Emirates	**143.9**	Air Canada	77.5
Lufthansa	129.7	KLM	76.1
Continental Airlines	128.1	**China Eastern Airlines**	72.7
Southwest Airlines	*126.6*	**Japan Airlines**	63.2
Air France	125.2	**Korean Air**	59.7
China Southern Airlines	110.5	**All Nippon Airways**	56.1
British Airways	105.5	**Thai Airways**	55.5
Qantas Airways	99.9	**Qatar Airways**	52.7
US Airways	94.7	IBERIA	51.2
Cathay Pacific Airlines	87.3		

Note: Airlines domiciled in the Asian-Pacific Rim and the Middle East are shown in bold; non-IATA members are shown in italics.

Source: WATS (2011, 89).

Following deregulation in Australia Qantas acquired domestic flights and, like Singapore Airlines, developed a low-cost subsidiary. Despite these changes, the comparison between the two airlines is still valid for highlighting the differences between Singapore Airlines based on 'Main Street' and Qantas Airways headquartered in a 'cul-de-sac' location.

Singapore Airlines is a single-fortress-hub airline that seeks to be a 'global' airline by offering the world's longest non-stop daily commercial flights between Singapore and New York with its A340-500 services. Qantas is an end-of-line carrier in a 'cul-de-sac' location that has to use an intermediate hub on 'Main Street' en route to Europe because the maximum limit for current planes on the route is a flight time of 15 hours (Figure 4.9). Having to make a stop put Qantas's role as an independent long-haul airline at a great disadvantage compared with Singapore Airlines. This disadvantage has been compounded by Singapore Airlines (SIA) being able to draw upon 'behind the hub' traffic in Asia, whereas Qantas has been limited to New Zealand and the Pacific Islands. Even if Qantas could overcome this locational disadvantage, its direct European destinations had been reduced to London and Frankfurt with code shares to Helsinki, Paris and Rome. Travel to other European destinations required two stops. SIA's 'starburst', in contrast, offered 12 European locations from Australia's state capitals two or three times daily with a single stop in Singapore.

Qantas has been most vulnerable to competition on the UK/Europe ('Kangaroo') route not only from Singapore Airlines but also from Emirates, which offered six one-stop flights to a variety of European destinations via Dubai. Initially, Qantas responded to this competition on the UK/Europe route by dropping connections via Bangkok and Hong Kong, serviced by older planes, in favour of a partnership with British Airways, and concentrating on its A380 services to Europe through Singapore. On other routes Qantas has been able to rely on protection from the Australian Government that has restricted the number of flights by foreign carriers on bilateral routes. For instance, the Australian Government has precluded Singapore Airlines from flying to the United States via Australian airports, a route Qantas shares with Delta Airlines, United Airlines and Virgin Australia. In response Singapore Airlines has allied with Virgin Australia to offset its disadvantage of being unable to fly via Australia to the United States, and introduced Tiger Airlines (Tigerair) in Australia to provide a domestic feeder for its European services.

As Qantas experienced continued losses on its UK/Europe routes, a more radical strategy was sought to offset the disadvantage of operating from a 'terminal location'. This proposition was to establish Qantas's own locally based hub in Asia with a possible base in either Kuala Lumpur

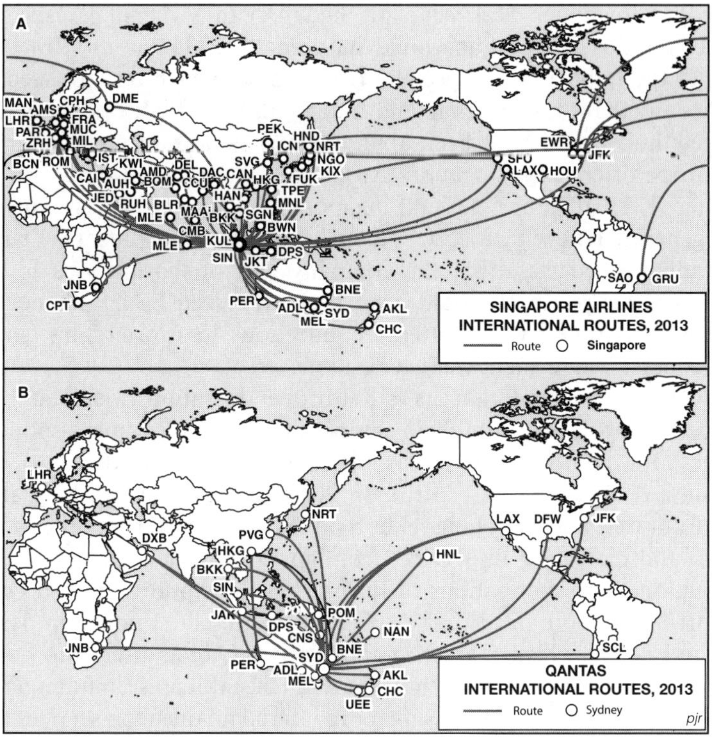

Notes:
Singapore Airlines' Silk Air routes, and Qantas' Jet Star services and connections through Dubai through its partnership with Emirates are omitted.
International Air Transport Association (IATA) codes: AMS Amsterdam; ADL Adelaide; AKL Auckland; AMD Ahmedabad; AUH Abu Dhabi; BCN Barcelona; BKK Bangkok; BLR Bangalore; BNE Brisbane; BOM Mumbai; BWN Brunei; CAI Cairo; CAN Guangdong; CCU Kolkata; CHC Christchurch; CMB Colombo; CNS Cairns; CPH Copenhagen; CPT Cape Town; DAC Dacca; DEL New Delhi; DFW Dallas/Fort Worth; DME Moscow; DPS Bali (Den Pasar); DXB Dubai; EWR Newark, New York; FRA Frankfurt; FUK Fukuoka; GRU Sao Paulo; HAN Hanoi; HKG Hong Kong; HND Tokyo Haneda, Tokyo; HNL Honolulu; HOU Houston; IST Istanbul; JAK Jakarta; JED Jeddah; JFK New York; JNB Johannesburg; KIX Kansai; KUL Kuala Lumpur; KWI Kuwait; LAX Los Angeles; LHR London Heathrow; MAA Chennai; MAN Manchester; MEL Melbourne; MIL Milan; MLE Male; MNL Manila; MUC Munich; NAN Nandi; NGO Nagoya; NRT Tokyo Narita; NKG Nanking; PEK Beijing; PER Perth; POM Port Moresby; PVG Pudong (Shanghai); ROM Rome; RUH Riyadh; SAO Sao Paulo; SCL Santiago; SFO San Francisco; SGN Ho Chi Minh City; SIN Singapore; SYD Sydney; TPE Taipei; UEE Queenstown; ZRH Zurich.

Sources: SIA (2013), Qantas (2013).

Figure 4.9 Passenger networks of: (A) Singapore Airlines, 2013; and (B) Qantas Airways, 2013

or Singapore under Malaysian or Singaporean ownership respectively (Harbison, 2011). The hub would have enabled Qantas to attract both 'behind the hub' traffic, especially from China, which was serviced by a single daily flight to Shanghai, and India with three flights per week. Also the new hub would have been able offer the same 'starburst' of services to Europe offered by Singapore Airlines. This strategy would also have countered the alliance between Singapore Airlines and Virgin Australia, and generated new traffic, to partially offset complaints by Qantas's Australian-based staff that the company was offshoring jobs to Asia. Although this prospect would have been enhanced by an alliance with Malaysian Airlines, which offered connections to Amsterdam, Istanbul and Rome, no agreement was ever established.

As Qantas claimed that its UK/Europe operations were unable to compete or operate profitably in competition with government-sponsored airlines, the company's overseas operations were considered to be in 'terminal decline' (ACCC, 2013). In 2013 Qantas responded by allying with Emirates, and switching its hub on 'Main Street' from Singapore to Dubai and increasing its services from 45 to 100 per week. Rather than the five one-stop destinations to Europe via Singapore – two on Qantas aircraft to London and Frankfurt – Dubai offered 33 non-stop destinations in Europe, which apart from the flight on Qantas aircraft to London (Heathrow), and code shares to Rome and Helsinki, uses Emirates aircraft to and from Dubai. Whereas Singapore offered no one-stop services to the Middle East or North Africa, the partnership with Emirates provides 31 non-stop services. Also the replacement of multiple partners by a single partner offered customers a more integrated proposition.

In March 2013 the Australian Competition and Consumer Commission (ACCC) did not accept that Qantas International was either in 'terminal decline', or that it was adversely affected by having to compete with state-owned airlines in Asia and the Middle East. Nevertheless the Commission approved the company's agreement with Emirates for five years. While the Commission considered the arrangement had material, but not substantial, public benefits – increased frequencies, improved connectivity, reciprocal access to frequent-flyer programmes and increased fleet flexibility – any detriments would be minimal on the UK/Europe route. The Emirates–Qantas alliance will still have to compete with a large number of airlines hubbing on Abu Dhabi, Hong Kong, Seoul, Singapore, Tokyo and several Chinese cities. While Qantas will improve its services to Asia at more convenient times by retaining a minimal UK/Europe connection via Singapore, Singapore Airlines will continue to compete aggressively to maximize passenger traffic on the Australia–Europe route fed by Virgin Australia's domestic services, which had absorbed Tigerair. Singapore

Airlines is also concentrating more on the Asian-Pacific Rim to ensure Singapore's position as a key aviation hub on 'Main Street'. Speculation remains, ignored when Qantas allied with British Airways, that a merger with Singapore Airlines might have provided a better long-term solution for an airline based in a terminal location.

AIRPORTS

Both air cargo and passenger growth surpassed global GDP growth in 2010 and projections by Boeing suggest a positive outlook for air transport demand through to 2031 (Tinseth, 2012). This underlines the need to expand and modernize airport infrastructure to accommodate operational, traffic handling and commercial services, without necessarily having access to public funds, a situation requiring the empowerment of both private and public airports to generate returns on investment. Over time the objectives of running an airport have changed. The original public utility rationale was to stimulate national and regional economic development by generating a self-sustaining airport operation by servicing air cargo and air passengers (that is, the basis for constructing North Texas's Dallas/Fort Worth Airport in 1967). Using public–private partnerships, the new rationale is guided by the profit objective, which is intent on maximizing returns from non-aeronautical business activities. The last objective has been associated with the development of an airport city and its subsequent transformation into an airport-integrated region, or aerotropolis, that generates community benefits from jobs and taxes within a 25 km radius.

Airport City to Aerotropolis

Airport hubs have become the focus of activities aimed at developing the surrounding area within a 5 km radius into a unique business and tourism destination. These 'airport cities' are contrasted with the 'aerotropolis', which is a full-blown regional development model developed by John Kasarda (2000–2001, 2013a). Within this model the airport city morphs into the central business district that is enclosed by a traffic circle with runways, terminal, multimodal transport, office, hotels and cargo, shopping arcades and information infrastructure (Figure 4.10). Radial expressways emanate from this ring road into the wider region that offers locations for time-sensitive manufacturing and commerce (for example, computer repair manufacturers). Recognizing the need for agility and

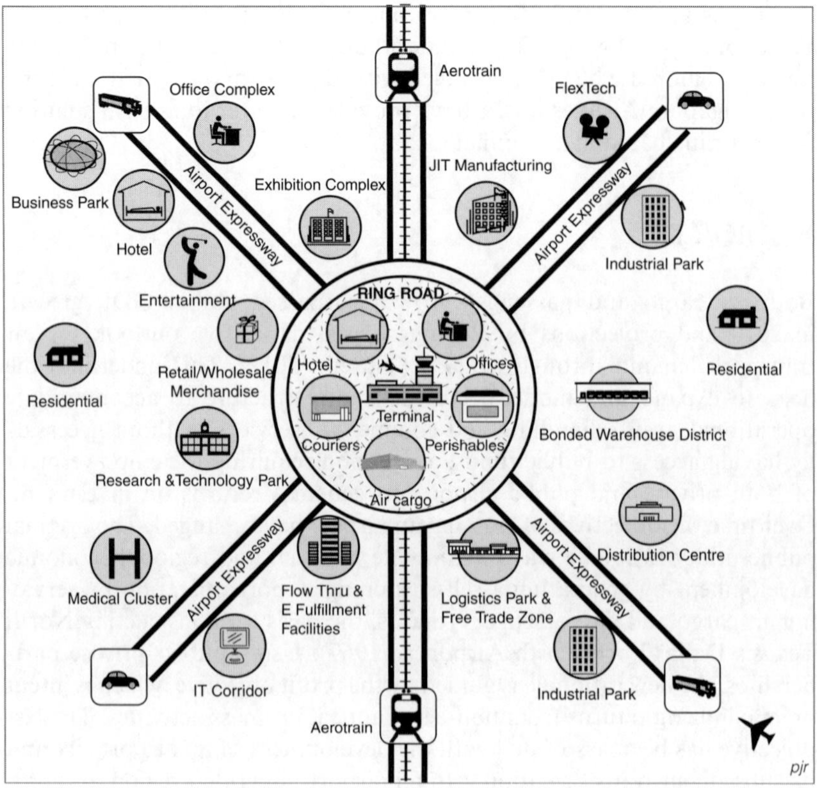

Source: Based on the original aerotropolis schematic in Kasarda (2010, 29).

Figure 4.10 Aerotropolis' structure

accessibility, these activities include industrial parks for processing goods, and logistics and distribution parks.

Attention is focused on the different locational patterns of 'airport cities' and 'aerotropolises'. By 2011 John Kasarda (2011) had designated 16 airport cities: seven in Europe, seven in North America, and one each in Africa and Australia (Figure 4.11). Typified by London Heathrow and Los Angeles, airport cities were conspicuously absent in Asia and the Middle East. This situation will not be altered by the planned development of 16 other airport cities because their locations are still concentrated in Europe and North America.

Airports within the Asian-Pacific Rim have preferred the aerotropolis model. By 2011, 24 aerotropolises had been identified by John Kasarda

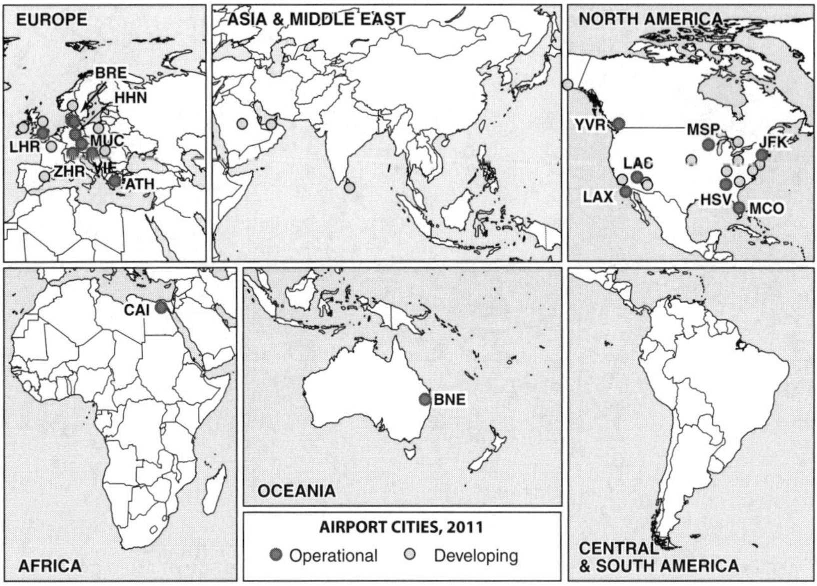

Note: Key for operational airport cities: ATH Athens; BNE Brisbane; CAI Cairo; BRE Bremen; HHN Frankfurt; HSV Huntsville; JFK New York; LHR London Heathrow; LAS Las Vegas; LAX Los Angeles; MSP Minneapolis-St Paul; MUC Munich; MCO Orlando; YVR Vancouver; VIE Vienna; and ZRH Zurich.

Source: Data from Kasarda (2011).

Figure 4.11 Location of airport at the centre of operational and developing airport cities, 2011

(2011): ten in North America, eight in Asia and the Middle East, five in Europe and one in South America (Figure 4.12). Of the 30 being planned, 13 are in North America, 12 in Asia and the Middle East, three in Africa, and one each in Europe and South America.

The prototype for aerotropolis development in Europe has been Amsterdam's Schiphol Airport. The Airport's environs attracted a world trade centre, two five-star hotels and class A office buildings, which not only accommodated financial and consulting firms, but also boasted rentals higher than the traditional central business district. There are also business parks adjacent to expressways with industries making use of logistics and distribution.

Representative of the aerotropolis in North America are the hubs operated by FedEx in Memphis and UPS in Louisville that allow for next-day delivery. Developing aerotropolis locations in North America

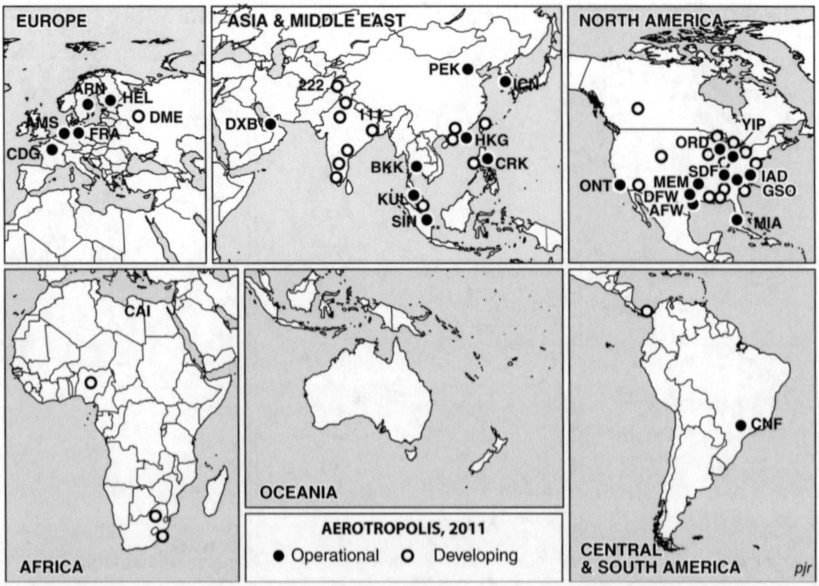

Note: Key for operational aerotropolises: AFW Fort Worth Alliance; AMS Amsterdam; ARN Stockholm; BKK Bangkok; CDG Paris Charles de Gaulle; CNF Tancredo Neves; CRX Clark; DFW Dallas-Fort Worth; DXB Dubai; FRA Frankfurt; GSO Piedmont; HEL Helsinki; HKG Hong Kong; IAD Washington Dulles; ICN Seoul Incheon; KUL Kuala Lumpur; MEM Memphis; MIA Miami; ONT LA-Ontario; ORD Chicago O'Hare; PEK Beijing; SDF Louisville; SIN Singapore; and YIP Detroit Willow Run.

Source: Data from Kasarda (2011).

Figure 4.12 Location of airport at centre of operational and developing aerotropolises

include both greenfield sites, typified by Denver International Airport, and brownfield sites such as the proposed Pinnacle Aerotropolis on the periphery of Detroit, which will offer office space, laboratory and research facilities and high-tech warehouse space complemented by luxury hotels, golf courses, cycling tracks, restaurants and shopping centres. A common complaint by developers in the United States is that environmental rules and regulations often preclude the rapid transformation of developing a site into a fully fledged aerotropolis.

These barriers have been less substantial in the Asian-Pacific Rim, where a rash of aerotropolis locations have been created, and in the development of isolated examples in the Middle East and South America. Perhaps the Rim's classic aerotropolis is Bangkok's Suvarnabhumi Airport, replete with golf courses, shopping malls and cinemas, although rival political factions hindered its realization following two periods of occupation of the facilities by rival protesters. This experience has not deterred the interest of prospective developers in both China and India.

The aerotropolis concept, elaborated by John Kasarda and Greg Lindsay (2011) in *Aerotropolis: The Way We'll Live Next* is not without its critics. Will Self (2011), for instance, has argued that the concept masquerades as a new urban paradigm, when it is essentially the product of boosterism-cum-planning. Also the aerotropolis proposition does not consider the costs involved by authoritarian governments in Asia sweeping away existing settlements to facilitate its rapid implementation. Further speculation is rife upon the likely impact of rising oil prices, carbon emissions and the prospect of the aerotropolises becoming tomorrow's ghost towns.

John Kasarda (2013b) has rebutted this speculation, arguing that there is no evidence that rising fuel prices or greenhouse gases will limit aviation's long-term growth and airport-related developments. Also there are accessible areas of open land for new 'greenfield' airport sites in Asia and the Middle East (for example, Hyderabad and Doha). These sites offer the prospect of not only combatting urban sprawl through the planning of mixed-use residential communities, but also enhancing job creation and income generation.

The remaining contentious issue is John Kasarda's (2013b, 1) premise that 'airports will shape business location and urban development in the 21st century as much as highways did in the 20th century, railroads in the 19th and river, canals and ports in the 18th'. This single-mode proposition overlooks the prospect of a more complex multilayered hub or gateway comprising synergies between all transport modes and the Internet. However, before outlining the gateway concept, there is a need to examine the location, structure and throughput of telecommunications traffic.

TELECOMMUNICATIONS

Considerable care must be taken in assuming that the new electronic spaces are analogous to physical transport spaces, because the routes are invisible. Telecommunications routes comprise a set of interconnected, privately owned superhighways or backbones that jump from major city to major city; there are no on-ramps to the superhighways from either suburban or rural locations (CPrompt, 2010). On this occasion attention is restricted to the flows through the network rather than on corporate control exhibited by the geographical spread of the headquarters of the top-ranking telecommunications companies (Rimmer, 1999).

In 2010 'Main Street' was overshadowed in global Internet geography by movements within Europe (Figure 4.13). This phenomenon stems from a reliance on international bandwidth, measured in gigabits per second (Gbps). The measurement reflects the high level of cross-border movement between Europe's 50 sovereign states, and the relative sparseness of flows within Asia and North America. Nevertheless 'Main Street' is still marked, although the relative importance of its individual components differs from the aviation patterns. The North America–Europe connection is the strongest intercontinental connection, with the Europe–Asian Pacific component conspicuously weaker, suggesting that routinized flows of information are dictated as much by cultural forces as economic factors. This proposition is supported by the strength of the north–south connections between North America and Central and South America, and, to a lesser extent, between Francophone Europe and Africa. Thus, downplaying the international movements within Europe, the dominant feature is the pivotal role played by North America in global Internet geography. Under the Obama administration the United States is trying to perpetuate this position by seeking to obtain longer and stronger intellectual property protection in regional trade agreements such as the Trans-Pacific

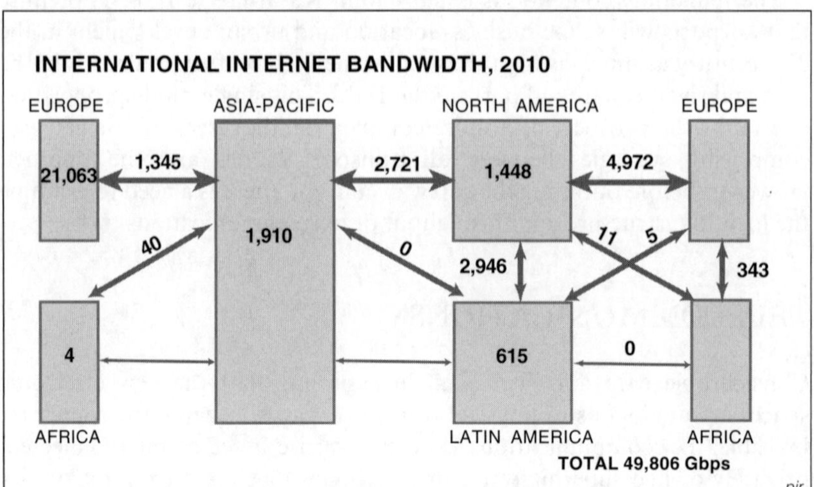

Source: Data from TG (2011).

Figure 4.13 International Internet network, 2010

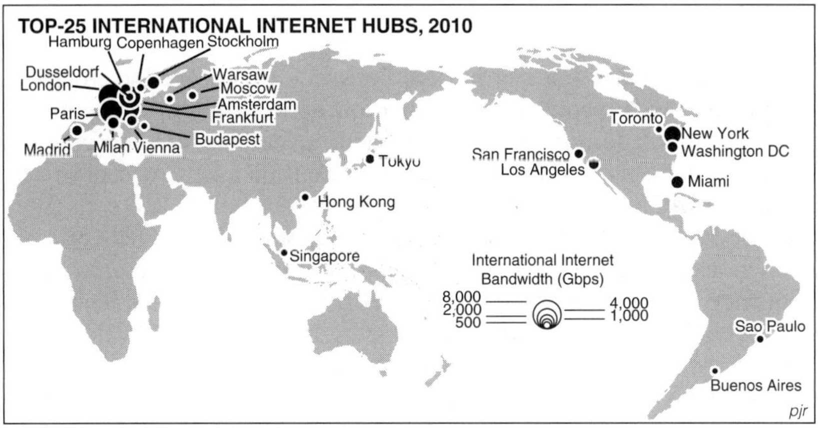

Source: Data from TG (2011).

Figure 4.14 Top 25 international Internet hubs, 2010

Partnership (for example, by pushing for copyright term extensions and digital enforcement provisions for Hollywood and the record industry).

An examination of the top 25 Internet hubs in 2010, gauged in terms of Internet bandwidth connected across international borders to metropolitan areas at mid-year, also exhibits a distribution very different from aviation patterns (Figure 4.14). Again, arising from the nature of the data, 14 of the highest-capacity international Internet hub cities are in Europe, six in North America, three in Asia and two in South America. None are in Africa or Oceania. London, Frankfurt, Paris and Amsterdam comprise the four leading hub cities ahead of New York and Miami, with Tokyo being the highest-ranked Asian-Pacific Rim hub city in fourteenth position (Tranos, 2013). These rankings have been remarkably stable since 2005.

Even extending the analysis to the top 50 Internet hub cities in 2010 does not reduce the preponderance of European cities, as a further 12 would be added. However there were an additional six Asian-Pacific Rim cities, reflecting the region's emerging importance in a shift from the past Eurocentric and United States-centric telecommunications patterns (Malecki and Wei, 2009). This prospect raises the issue as to whether the new-generation Internet, described by the International Telecommunications Union (ITU, 2005) as the 'Internet of Things' (IoT), will have a profound effect upon the structure of global telecommunications geography by enabling communications both between people and 'things', and between 'things'.

Next Generation Internet

The next-generation Internet has the potential to improve the efficiency of moving goods, people and information between multiple regions by reducing costs, and provide new value-adding features by improving the quality of delivered products and services. Sensors and actuators will be embedded within physical objects such as packets, pallets and containers that are linked to the Internet through wired and wireless networks by an identical protocol. By storing information such as routing on radio frequency information identification (RFID) tags and related identification technologies rather than on bar codes, the static objects will become dynamic by allowing them to make intelligent decisions and control the supply chains through which they move, based on information derived from readers or a global positioning system (EC/EPoSS, 2008; Nettsträter et al., 2010; Hribernik et al., 2010). The packets, pallets and containers will be able to sense their physical environment, communicate their location and automatically replenish damaged parts. This rich stream of data flowing to the computer from this activity will be subject to deeper analysis and visualization using software algorithms to assist in better decision-making by logisticians.

These state-of-the art technologies will enhance global logistics processes by: (1) monitoring the quality of shipment conditions such as vibrations, container openings and ensuring refrigeration is maintained in the cold chain for insurance purposes; (2) searching for items in automated warehouses; (3) detecting storage incompatibilities involving flammable goods; and (4) tracking fleets through space and time by controlling the routes for 'delicate goods' such as medical drugs, jewels or dangerous items (Libelium, 2012). Also it will be possible for multinational manufacturers and retailers to address inefficiencies in their supply chains by monitoring storage conditions along the chain, and providing tracking and tracing of commodities (for example, meat and poultry from the farm through the supply chain to the supermarket shelves). Not only will the new technologies enable the global logistics provider to optimize movement between multinational manufacturer and retailer, but also the item itself will be able to check back to decide on whether to continue on its journey, or transfer to another track to satisfy a more pressing demand among an array of receivers.

Thus the new-generation Internet will provide global logistics service providers with the ability to shape and organize the movement of packets, pallets and containers in a decidedly more efficient and target-oriented way. The most likely effect of the new technologies on the spatial structure of telecommunications will be to intensify intra-regional and inter-regional flows through the network.

CONCLUSIONS

The analyses of air cargo, air passenger and telecommunications confirm that the global hub-and-spoke system underpins all three networks designed to accommodate flows of goods, people and information. 'Main Street' and the 'cul-de-sacs' persist in each mode to connect places and people, although the weighting of intra- and inter-regional flows and hubs differs markedly between them.

Having identified individual modal networks and their hubs there is a need to further discuss how they interact with each other in the global 'network of networks' that unites the physical and virtual worlds. Featuring gateways and corridors, this interactive network of networks enables logistics services to be provided, physical goods to be developed, manufactured and retailed, and people to be transported and ideas conveyed. The next generation of the Internet and the introduction of computing power to everyday items will heighten the monitoring of this global 'network of networks' and pinpoint any deficiencies.

5. The network of networks

Container shipping, airfreight, air passenger and telecommunications patterns display marked variations from each other. This is not entirely unexpected because their driving forces differ. Container shipping responds to the scarcity of resources; airfreight activity to the inclusion of speed in servicing dispersed production activities; air passengers to gross domestic product (GDP), income growth and, increasingly, to environmental concerns; and telecommunications to marked cultural differences. Nevertheless all manifestations are underpinned by the global hub-and-spoke system.

As global hub-and-spoke networks allow for economies of scale by consolidating flows from a set of geographically dispersed services onto trunk connections within the hub, the system is the most economically viable arrangement for private interests and preferred to a mesh network topology in which each of the network's nodes is interconnected with every other. Any disruptions in container shipping, air cargo, air passenger or telecommunications services due to a massive node failure have the potential to be economically and socially catastrophic for the supply chains of multinational manufacturers and retailers, and may have a significant spillover effect on second-tier cities (Grubesic and Murray, 2006; Grubesic and Matisziw, 2008). For example, an unexpected three-year shutdown of the ports of Los Angeles and Long Beach in the United States 'would reduce real (inflation-adjusted) GDP by between 0.35 per cent and 0.55 per cent, or $45 billion to $75 billion, per year. That reduction translates into daily costs ranging from $125 million to $250 million' (CBO, 2006, 2).

This latent vulnerability in modal hubs, and their inherent survivability and reliability, is compounded when they are co-located, involving the prospect of multiple node failure in what is becoming the global 'network of networks'. This prospect raises a series of perennial issues: how can multiple nodes and their connections in the global 'network of networks' be conceptualized? And how can these multiple nodes and their connections be identified and ranked?

An initial response is to shift the emphasis from the unidimensional modal networks to develop a three-dimensional multilayered network that accommodates nodes and their multiple modal connections as centres for international trade and communications. A procedure is developed for recognizing the relative size of this set of multilayered nodes to determine the key gateways – the multimodal exit and entry points through which goods, people and information move beyond local markets. The next step is to describe the salient characteristics of gateways with reference to a case study of Dubai Logistics City. Then the nature of the linear trade corridors linking the gateways to major markets through international movements of goods, people and information can be discussed. Finally, gateway and corridor strategies are brought together as interlinked systems of regional significance for connecting global and local commerce. As illustrated by reference to Canada's spatial planning initiative, gateways and corridors can be developed as an integrated package of long-term investment and policy measures to advance economic development.

MULTILAYERED NETWORKS

The shift from the modal networks to the global 'network of networks' has been prompted by the demands of multinational manufacturers and retailers for an array of logistics services. They are concerned with the long-distance movement of intermediate and final products, but also as part of the trade–investment–service nexus with both the long-distance movement of people within and between production facilities, and intra- and inter-firm horizontal and vertical information flows (Baldwin, 2011). In response, global logistics corporations have sought to provide for the long-distance movement of goods and frequent short-distance deliveries, high-speed air transport for business travel, and long-distance computer networks and personal communications systems.

This challenge of dealing with multiple hubs and their connections in sea–land, air and telecommunications networks led to the development of the network of networks that integrates the three different modes: sea–land, air and telecommunications (Figure 5.1). In this representation A, B and C are separate gateways with different platform levels for handling sea–land, air and information flows. The links between them are the corridors accommodating movements of goods and resources, people and information. Goods and resources are analogous to solids, people to liquids, and information to gas.

The figure has 'stocks' for each layer: capital, labour and resources in sea–land transport; complex knowledge involving face-to-face transfer associated with air passenger transport (that is, business travel); and routinized information linked to telecommunications. Of course, telecommunications may also allow the transfer of knowledge products (for example,

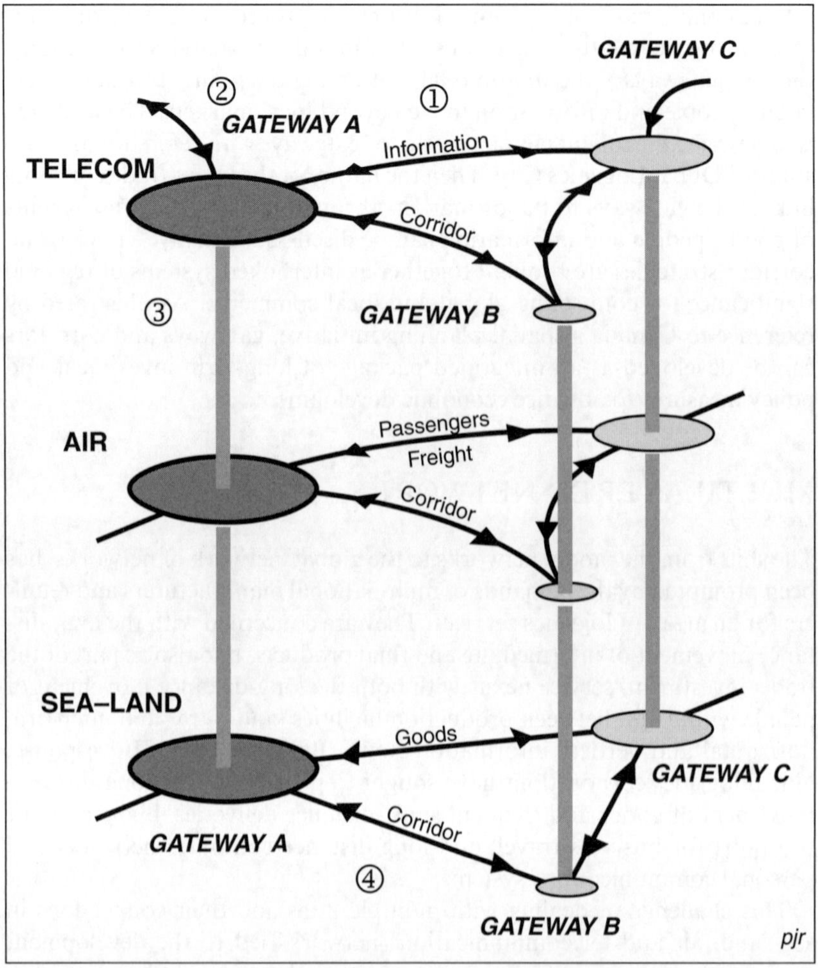

Note: 1. Inter-gateway economic interdependencies are intensifying; 2. Global functions are clustering; 3. Trade flows are dematerializing with informationalization and virtualization; and 4. Physical flow structures (gateways and corridors) are becoming more important.

Source: Adapted from Rimmer (2004a, 2004b).

Figure 5.1 Three-dimensional (3-D) multilayered gateway

downloading software, recorded music, text documents and e-games) and accommodate the tele-transaction of investments and face-to-face contact. The mixed functional role of each layer is a reason why they linked together in this representation encompassing the 'physical gate', the 'knowledge gate' and the 'virtual gate'.

Synergies are possible between sea–land, air and telecommunications levels (that is, physical, knowledge and virtual platforms). While container shipping competes with airfreight, it experiences similar logistical characteristics and dynamic market forces to the aviation industry. In turn, telecommunications are critical for cargo and passenger booking systems, and offer a substitute for some passenger movements. Conversely, telecommunications are also stimulators leading to more travel and a higher level of exchange activities.

These synergies are critical because increasingly profits will not be derived from goods or passengers but from the use of telecommunications (that is, profits are higher up the tree). The new commercial currency is derived not only from the 'traffic rights' but also from access to 'information rights'. Acquisitions of airlines are made not only for the seats they offer but also for the information they hold on passengers in their frequent-flyer schemes. This has prompted the employment of 'data miners' using artificial intelligence to extract meaningful patterns and rules from the large data sets possessed by airlines on the habits of their passengers (for example, car hire and hotel bookings) to inform business decisions.

This transformation of data into information for management decision-making has also resulted in global logistics corporations recognizing the scope for cross-investment in other modal sectors. Container shipping corporations have invested in air cargo and passenger activities; those specializing in air transport have invested in telecommunications.

Having established the multilayered gateway, the framework can be used simultaneously to explore two of Kathy Pain's (2007a) paradoxes:

1. The intensification of economic dependencies between gateways worldwide and the simultaneous concentration of global logistics functions in a single gateway within each region (that is, network extension and concentration).
2. The dematerialization of trade flows through 'informationalization' and 'virtualization', and the increasing importance of physical flow structures (gateways and corridors) and face-to-face contact (that is, network flows and materialities).

Even advanced logistics, which are considered to be the most virtualized of producer services, are 'often "invisible", hidden in retail and distribution networks ... remain located close to gateways and their transportation corridors' (Pain 2007a, 7).

Gateways offer bases for global logistics corporations to manage their operations because they are the 'spaces' through which flow commodities, airfreight, air passengers and information, including capital transactions. The gateways are also the 'places' of capital accumulation on a world scale, their market size, catchment area's growth potential, and geographical location being attractive to multinational manufacturers and retailers for their headquarters and sophisticated control and research functions (Rimmer and Dick, 2013). As commanding components of the global economic system, the gateways reflect the economic power they control.

The multilevel gateways have become the major regional operational bases for global logistics service providers such as DHL, FedEx (Federal Express), TNT (Thomas Nationwide Transport) and UPS (United Parcel Service) that offer integrated transport and telecommunications services for multinational manufacturing and retailing corporations (Chapter 2). Although the operational sites of global logistics service providers are geographically dispersed, they are attracted to gateways because of new agglomeration economies within host countries and opportunities for communicating with other gateways throughout the world (Rodrigue, 2012). 'Intangible' investment networks reinforce this attachment to gateways (Olivier, 2005). Already gateways in the United States and Europe are being seen as the new competitive units in the global economy.

In the United States more than two-thirds of the anticipated population growth between 2010 and 2050 will be in ten emerging gateways supported by eight super-cities (extended metropolitan areas), plus regional nodes and regional networks (Figure 5.2). The gateways are seen as instruments for achieving the country's third millennium goals by boosting global competitiveness through investment in infrastructure and logistics, and enhancing national cohesion by reconnecting declining regions (KCCG et al., 2005). The logistics clusters in these gateways are expected to grow and offer good pay and upward mobility, particularly as the sector is less susceptible to offshoring than manufacturing (Pisano, 2006; Sheffi, 2012, 53–54).

In Europe planners have used gateways to underpin the European Spatial Development Perspectives (European Commission, 1999), supporting a polycentric pattern of balanced development (Figure 5.3). This policy reflects a shift from the earlier definitions of the logistics arenas of the Golden Triangle linking Amsterdam, London and Paris; the Blue Banana stretching from London to Milan that is shifting eastwards and raising logistics issues; and the European 'bunch of grapes' centred on

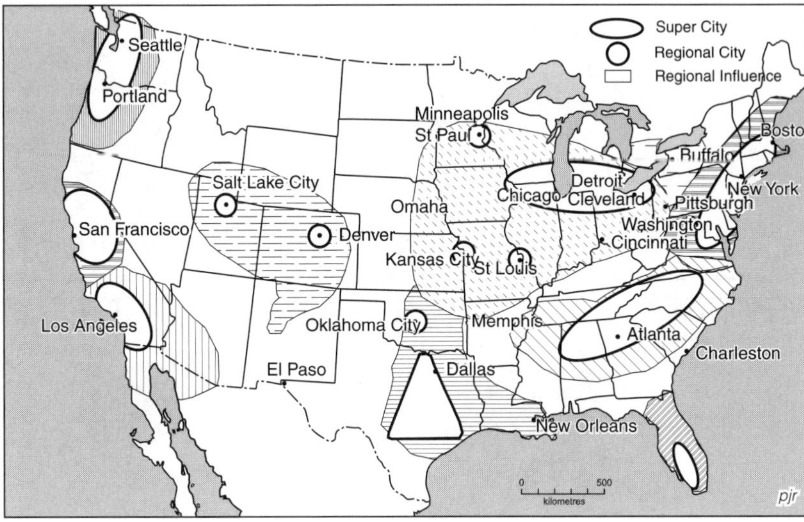

Note: The ten gateway areas are shaded.

Sources: Adapted from KCCG et al. (2005), NCA 2050 (2005).

Figure 5.2 Emerging global gateways in the United States

airports in cities with populations over 2 million (BBSR, 2011). The new focus is explicitly based on gateways. This new spatial policy framework seeks to limit development within the Pentagon area defined by London, Paris, Milan, Munich and Hamburg and to encourage the growth of 'global integration zones' in peripheral areas to address the imbalances. Rather than accept these nominated gateways in Europe and North America as given, the opportunity is taken to rank them against their counterparts in the Asian-Pacific Rim.

GATEWAYS

As the world ranking of container shipping, international air cargo, international air passenger and Internet hubs reflect the premium which global logistics service providers place on nodality, an examination of the world's top 25 representatives in each category in 2010 provides a useful guide to the relative strength of individual gateways (Table 5.1). In distilling this statistical material, multiple hubs in the same location are treated as a single entity. For example, Shanghai's two container

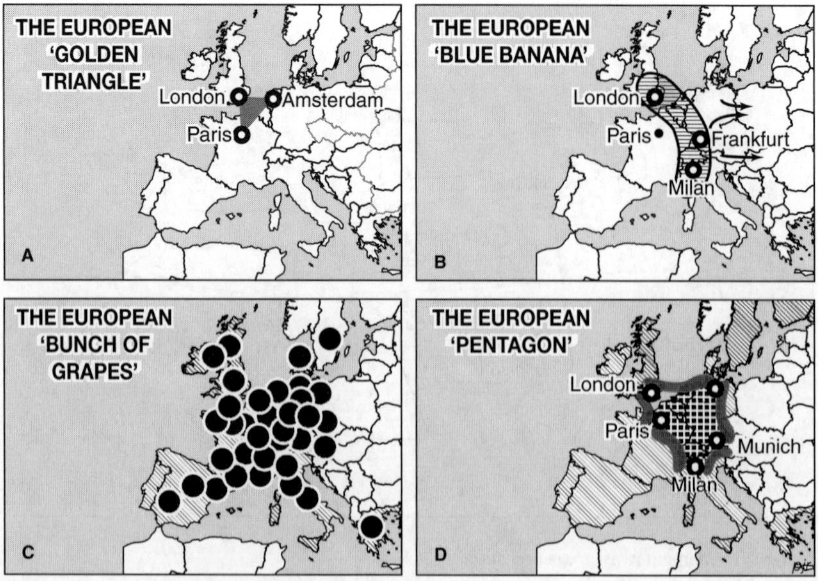

Source: Adapted from BBSR (2011).

Figure 5.3 European spatial frameworks: (A) The European 'Golden Triangle'; (B) The European 'Blue Banana'; (C) The European 'Bunch of Grapes'; and (D) The European 'Pentagon'

shipping hubs – top-ranked Shanghai and sixth-ranked Ningbo – are seen as being part of the same logistics platform. Then in determining multilayered gateways, container ports, air cargo and air passenger hubs within 100 km radius are grouped together (for example, Amsterdam/Rotterdam, Bangkok/Laem Chabang, Beijing/Tianjin, Brussels/Antwerp, Kuala Lumpur/Port Klang and Los Angeles/Long Beach). Also the multiple international container ports within a similar radius are dealt with similarly, even though they included entities outside their administrative boundaries (for example, Hong Kong/Shenzhen/Guangzhou and Singapore/Tanjung Pelepas).

The next step is to remove from the analysis the 36 hubs that appear only once: eight container-shipping hubs (that is, the port cities), six air cargo hubs, seven air passenger hubs, and 12 Internet hubs. In examining this remaining collection of hubs it is recognized that container shipping has lost some of its importance in determining gateways. London, for example, is no longer represented among the top 25 container ports.

Table 5.1 Multilayered gateways, 2010

	Modes							
	Container shipping		Air cargo		Air passenger		Internet	
	Rank	Mill. TEUS	Rank	Mill. kg	Rank	Mill. Pax	Rank	Gbps
FOUR								
Singapore	2	28.4	11	1.8	18	42.0	21	830
Tanjung Pelepas	17	6.5	–	–	–	–	–	–
Hong Kong	3	23.5	1	4.2	11	50.3	20	885
Shenzhen	4	22.5	25	0.8	–	–	–	–
Guangzhou	7	12.6	21	1.1	19	41.0	–	–
Amsterdam	–	–	17	1.5	15	45.2	4	5757
Rotterdam	10	11.1						
Los Angeles	16	7.8	14	1.8	6	59.1	11	1509
Long Beach	18	6.5	–	–	–	–	–	–
New York	20	5.3	19	1.3	14	46.5	5	3850
Newark	–	–	23	0.9	–	–	–	–
Tokyo	25	4.3	9	2.2	–	–	14	1306
Tokyo (HND)	–	–	24	0.8	5	64.2	–	–
THREE								
Shanghai	1	29.1	3	3.2	20	40.6	–	–
Ningbo	6	13.1	–	–	–	–	–	–
Dubai	9	11.6	8	2.3	13	47.2	–	–
Beijing	–	–	15	1.6	2	74.0	–	–
Tianjin	11	10.1	–	–	–	–	–	–
Bangkok	–	–	20	1.3	17	42.8	–	–
Laem Chabang	22	5.1	–	–	–	–	–	–
Paris	–	–	6	2.4	7	58.2	3	6527
Frankfurt	–	–	7	2.3	9	53.0	2	7218
London	–	–	16	1.6	4	65.9	1	7723
TWO								
Hamburg	15	7.9	–	–	–	–	13	1326
Jakarta	24	4.7	–	–	16	44.4		
Miami	–	–	12	1.8	–	–	6	2167
Chicago	–	–	18	1.4	3	66.8	–	–
Madrid	–	–	–	–	12	49.8	10	1511
San Francisco	–	–	–	–	23	39.3	15	1260

Notes:
TEU – twenty-foot equivalent units; Pax – passengers; Gbps – Gigabits per second of internet bandwidth connected across international borders to metropolitan areas.

Table 5.1 (continued)

Omitted container shipping hubs: Busan (5), Qingdao (8), Kaohsiung (12), Port Kelang (13), Antwerp (14), Xiamen (19), Dalian (21), Bremen/Bremerhaven (23); air cargo hubs: Memphis (2), Seoul-Incheon (4), Anchorage (5), Louisville (10), Taipei (13), Indianapolis (22); air passenger: Atlanta (1), Dallas/Fort Worth (8), Denver (10), Houston (21), Las Vegas (22), Phoenix (24), Charlotte (25); Internet hubs: Stockholm (7), Milan (8), Washington (9), Vienna (12), Dusseldorf (16), Moscow (17), Copenhagen (18), Sao Paulo (19), Toronto (22), Budapest (23), Warsaw (24), Buenos Aires (25).

Sources: CI (2013), ACI (2011), TG (2011).

This observation led to the threshold for gateways being set as having a presence in at least two of the four top 25 categories.

On this score 19 multilayered gateways were identified in 2010. Present in all four categories were Singapore, Hong Kong, Tokyo, Los Angeles, New York, and Amsterdam/Rotterdam. Seven gateways were represented in three categories: Shanghai-Ningbo, Dubai, Beijing-Tianjin, Bangkok-Laem Chabang, Paris, Frankfurt and London. The remaining six gateways were present in two categories: Hamburg, Jakarta, Chicago, Miami, Madrid and San Francisco. All multilayered gateways are located in the northern hemisphere (Figure 5.4). This raises the issue of how to promote unimodal hubs and invest them with additional facilities so that they can attain gateway status.

Reservations have been expressed about the use of air and telecommunications traffic for the designation of gateways (Pain, 2007a, 2007b). Nevertheless the results from this exercise mesh closely with the so-called 'world cities' identified on the basis of advanced producer services by the Globalization and World Cities (GaWC) Research Network at Loughborough University (GaWC, 2008). Sixteen of the gateways are ranked as 'alpha cities'; only Dubai, Hamburg and San Francisco have 'beta cities' status. Unlike other categorizations the classification used here does not begin with a pre-set list of centres; there is the prospect of promotion and relegation. Therefore, it is possible to proceed from this analysis to identify the key characteristics of gateways acting as centres for international trade and communications before proceeding to discuss corridors.

Gateway Characteristics

Arising from the preceding analysis, gateways can be cast as extended metropolitan regions, comprising many cities and hubs. Gateways have risen to prominence with the change in focus from local hierarchical relations to the

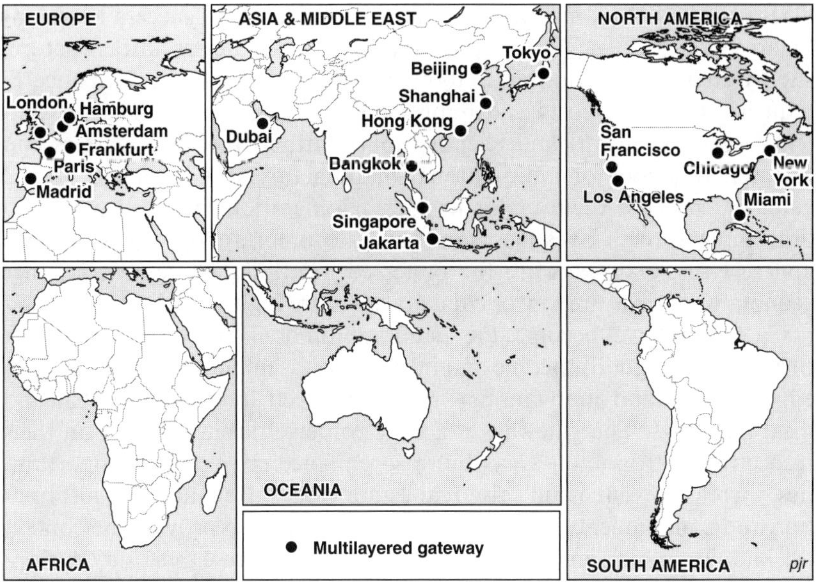

Figure 5.4 Multilayered gateways, 2010

world economy, triggered by a shift from manufacturing to advanced producer services (finance, insurance and real estate) and supported by world-spanning transport and communications networks. By possessing sea, air and telecommunications spoke-like connections to both their hinterlands and the rest of the world (hinterworld), the gateways have captured a substantial share of the local trade mass. Although the spokes of the network permit geographical dispersal, gateways remain the command centres.

By acting as central points for the collection, sorting, transhipment and distribution of goods, gateways provide agglomeration effects; offer platforms for cooperation and competition; and integrate infrastructure services, information and human capital, and strategic alliances, both vertical and horizontal. As such, gateways are key facilitators in multinational supply chains by promoting the continuity of circulation. They increase productivity through providing the opportunity to expand markets by lowering costs, internalizing externalities of upstream and downstream agents, and allocating risk optimally.

Gateways are being driven by the evolution of the supply chain, reflecting displacement of local production by international production, specialization at the production stages, and concentration of mass to realize economies of scale. Incentives to invest in gateways are strongly determined by their market structure. Critical to their success is a combination of strategic location, connectivity, world-class infrastructure, supply-chain orientation and, above all, their efficiency performance in reducing transport costs and improving customer service. The proximity of seaport, airport and teleport nodes attracts the headquarters and research functions of multinational manufacturers and retailers to the gateways because these major urban agglomerations are well placed to draw direct foreign investment, and generate imports and exports of goods and services. Gateways are the preferred locational choice when either economies of scale are low or capacity costs are high.

Gateways have become the main multimodal entry or exit points through which goods, people and information – embodying skills, knowledge transfer and innovations – move between interlinked global and local networks. The gateways not only confer efficient logistics on their respective metropolitan areas but also enhance employment opportunities, increase revenue and raise real estate values. Reliant upon information and communication networks, the gateways also provide the context for knowledge-rich environments and high-quality research and development (R&D) facilities (universities and research centres) for cutting-edge research. Their greater contact opportunities influence accessibility to markets, people and ideas. This privileged status enables the gateways to provide an important impetus to development by promoting the sale of goods, individual accessibility and knowledge transfer.

The gateways, through logistics and information transfer, have therefore become key areas of social functioning and interaction by integrating infrastructure, service information and human capital. All of these activities facilitate flows and, as demonstrated in Figure 5.5, there is a need to concentrate on high-value-added services because physical infrastructure no longer provides a sufficient base. On the lower platforms, provided by roads and highways, ports and airports and railways and inland ports, major players in value-added logistics can be supported: tier 1 covering warehousing and third-party logistics providers, and tier 2 including information technology providers and fourth-party logistics providers. Locating these activities in logistics parks buttresses value-added supporting services supplied by insurance firms, brokers and legal services. On this superstructure major players can locate higher-value-added services, including corporate headquarters and banks, to underline that gateways are the 'places' of capital accumulation on a world scale.

A critical challenge to decision-makers is how to make these gateways – straddling global and local markets, and functioning within a regional framework – more efficient components of the multinational supply chain. If gateways are to maintain and develop their position, attention has to be

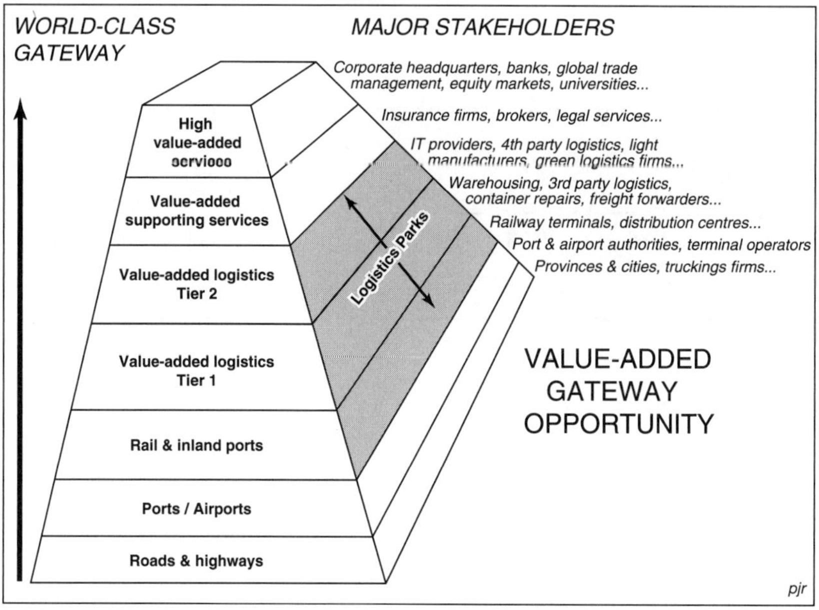

Source: Developed from information in La Fortune (2010).

Figure 5.5 Major players in the multilayered gateway

paid to their governance so as to integrate the physical, knowledge and virtual elements into a 'smart' gateway.

Governance

Consideration has to be given to Kathy Pain's (2007a) third paradox involving the disjunction between gateway hinterworlds and hinterland governance:

3. The space of flows (virtual and material) does not coincide with the territorial space of governance.

As shown in Figure 5.6, the hinterworld's space of flows – virtual and material – exceeds the territorial space of governance and raises issues of cross-border cooperation.

This spatial format also helps in comprehending the importance of coordination among key logistics players to achieve efficiency throughout

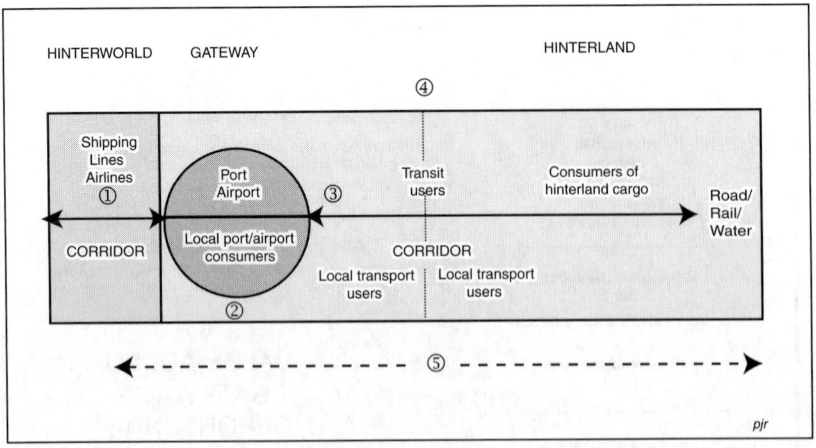

Note: 1. Oligopolistic market structure of shipping lines and airlines. 2. Congestion at ports and airports. 3. Multimodal transportation and congestion (port/road-rail arrangement). 4. Intergovernmental coordination between port and corridor regions (multimodal transport facilities under different jurisdictions). 5. Ownership structure (public/local government, private) – trend to privatization.

Source: Zhang (2007), Rimmer (2011).

Figure 5.6 Gateway–corridor/hinterland–hinterworld network

the supply chain. Both forward and reverse flows of goods can be traced through the gateway and hinterworld–hinterland system. In the former case goods imported from the rest of the world are shipped through the gateway (seaport or airport) and transported along a corridor to the hinterland, either singly or in combination, by road, rail or inland waterway to connect an inland hub (De Langen et al., 2013). The split between modes varies between gateways according to both geographical location and infrastructure.

The framework can be used to explore a range of matters pertinent to transport and logistics including the oligopolistic structure of shipping lines and airlines (Zhang, 2007). Attention can also be centred upon the effects of congestion pricing at gateways on the hinterland's road pricing, the impacts of highway pricing on the gateway with particular reference to capacity investment, and road congestion and social welfare (Yuen et al., 2008). These congestion delays at gateways require shippers and receivers to increase inventories and constrain the growth of hinterlands.

Multimodal transport and congestion involving the integration of port and road–rail arrangements can be explored. Studies can be made of different jurisdictions controlling separate components of the multimodal transport chain – national, provincial and metropolitan – and seeking to maximize their own interest. There is also an opportunity to examine the ownership structure of transport and logistics facilities and track the trend towards privatization.

All members of the logistics chain engaged in this multi-stage process, including the gateway, contribute to the overall cost of shipments that includes both transit time and reliability. After controlling for distance, David Hummels (2001) finds that every additional day in transit reduces the possibility of the United States sourcing cargo from that location by 1–1.5 per cent, and time lost in travel is equivalent to an *ad valorem* tariff of 16 per cent. These issues are pertinent to Dubai Logistics City, which has been artificially induced as a multilevel gateway to fill a missing gap between Asia and Europe.

Dubai Logistics City

Dubai World Central is developing Dubai Logistics City as a multilevel gateway to the 'wider Middle East', which encompasses Southern Europe, the Commonwealth of Independent States (CIS), India and Africa (Figure 5.7). This region has a potential market of 2 billion customers within a 3–4-hour flight range. The gateway itself has been developed as a Free Zone incorporating Al Maktoum International Airport and Aviation City, which are adjacent to Jebel Ali Port. Already Dubai is a regional centre for re-export, retailing, leisure and banking, and is seeking to enhance its standing in information technology.

The Logistics City is being developed as a multilevel gateway, covering 21.5 sq km, with all transport modes, logistics and value-added services being located in a single customs bonded and free zone environment that includes light manufacturing and assembly (for example, high-tech electronics, spare parts, health care, consumer goods, relief aid and a range of value-added goods). This facility offers: multimodal transport; management by logistics professionals; flexible supply chain solutions; an understanding of customer needs; freedom to choose logistics service providers; upgradeable infrastructure to accommodate value-added services; and 'room-to-grow' through its land reservation policy. The City's added attractions are that it offers a secure investment with no taxes and liberal visa regulations for foreign personnel.

Logistics City's management seeks to be the 'best-of-the-breed' integrated logistics provider, serving a world-class supply chain and logistics community, while positioning Dubai as the region's logistics gateway of choice. This goal allows multinational industrial corporations to optimize their supply chains in three different ways:

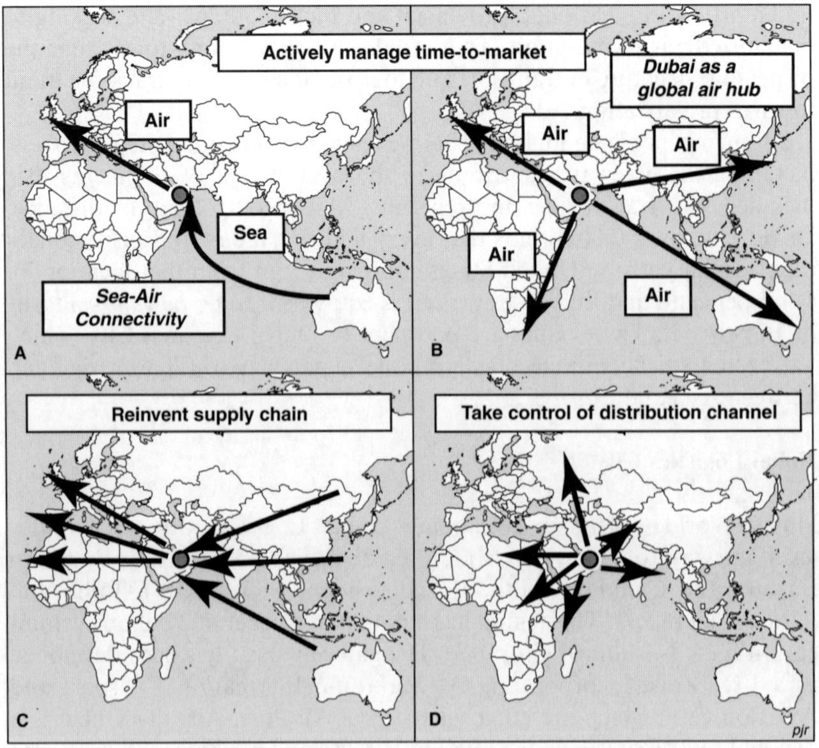

Note: This situation offers the opportunity for actively controlling the time to market by using: (A) sea-air connectivity; and (B) the global air hub. The location also provides manufacturers and retailers the opportunity for: (C) reinventing the supply chain; and (D) controlling the distribution channel.

Source: Adapted from Proffitt (2006, 3–6).

Figure 5.7 The positioning of Dubai Logistics City

1. To actively manage time-to-market by using: (a) sea–air connectivity to reduce transport costs, reroute shipments after dispatch, speed up orders and pack and label in transit; and (b) Dubai as a global air hub to merge shipments from different continents and daily connect remote markets with Europe and Asia.
2. To reinvent the supply chain by merging products and components from Asian sources, localizing products to individual European, African and Middle Eastern markets by postponing assembly, increasing flexibility, lowering the risk of inventory and using competitive labour costs.

3. To take (or regain) control of the distribution channel by establishing a base for supplying goods into the wider region, centralizing control and inventory, and controlling the distribution channel by getting closer to customers, decreasing stock levels and stock-outs, increasing customer service, and better controlling pricing and promotions.

Thus the Logistics City's management is seeking to attract logistics service providers and forwarders engaged in airfreight shipments; third-party and contract logistics service providers offering value-added services; and trading companies and producers which need light manufacturing as part of the order fulfilment process. All three sets of participants will offer or make use of warehousing and distribution services and multimodal transport requirements.

CORRIDORS

Land-based corridors that are centred on inland transport routes between gateways provided by trunk railways, highways and waterways have attracted considerable attention in outlining the emerging global spatial economy. Ruth Banomyong (2007a, 4) recognizes four different types of corridors traversing national borders that offer a less political approach to regional economic development:

1. The transport corridor that physically links an area or region.
2. The multimodal corridor that has more than one mode of transport that can physically link the corridor (for example, road and rail).
3. The logistics corridor that not only physically links an area or region but also harmonizes the corridor's institutional framework to facilitate efficient flow and storage of freight, and movement of people and related information (for example, by removing bottlenecks at border crossings).
4. The economic corridor that is able to attract investment and generate economic activity along the less-developed areas in the corridor, provided that physical linkages and logistics facilitation are already in place.

International funding agencies focus most attention on the economic corridor (Kunaka, 2010).

The economic or development corridor represents the final stage to be attained in promoting regional economic cooperation, because it requires physical linkages and logistics facilities to be in place so that they can attract investment and generate vibrant economic activities in lagging

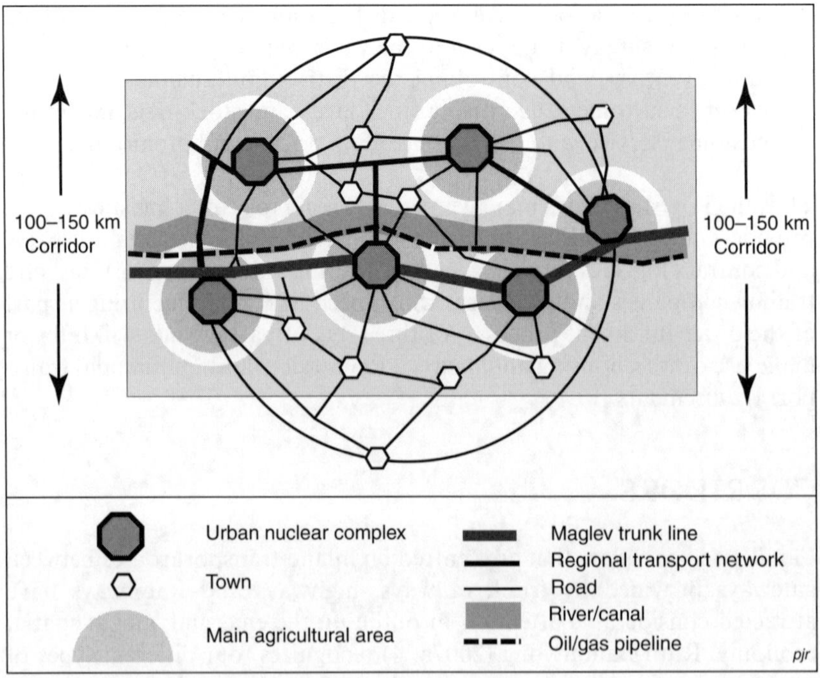

Source: Adapted from Schiller Institute (2012).

Figure 5.8 Development corridor concept

areas by lowering distribution costs and improving land supply for economic activities. As highlighted by the Schiller Institute (2012), these trunkline routes are perceived not only as a continuous strip of land for moving goods, people and information but also a potential 100–150 km wide zone for urban activities and high-density agriculture, mining and manufacturing production along their length (Figure 5.8). A magnetic levitated train route, paralleled by electrical transmission lines, fuel pipelines, optical cables and water supply conduits, is seen as the highest expression of the 'development corridor' concept.

Mapping these development corridors provides an opportunity to outline a global land transport system, which complements shipping routes and links six continents (Figure 5.9). A world 'landbridge' is envisaged that connects five continents, with the exception of Australasia. An intercontinental link for freight shipments, involving a tunnel underneath the Bering Strait between Siberia and Alaska, would not only shorten the

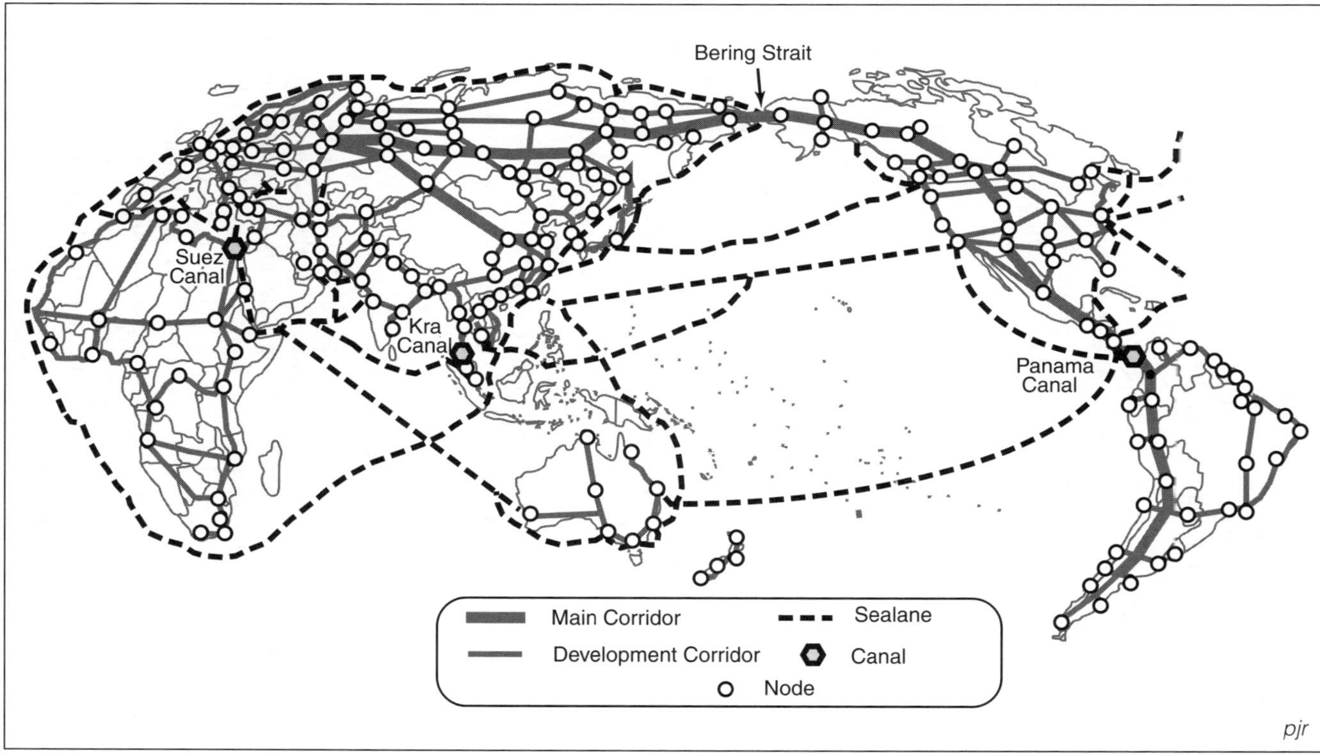

Sources: Adapted from Emerson and Vinokurov (2009), Schiller Institute (2012).

Figure 5.9 Inter-continental land transport corridors

trip between Eurasia and America but also accelerate economic integration and development, particularly in the northern regions of Canada, the Russian Federation and the United States. Meanwhile much reliance is placed on the core Paris–Berlin–Vienna Triangle; optimization of Central Asian and Eurasian land transport corridors; the north–south trade corridors linking the Western Hemisphere; a raft of railway projects for Africa and the Middle East; and a ring-rail plan for Australia.

Already, elements of this grand vision are occurring in North America and Europe, and are being planned in the Asian-Pacific region. Following the North American Free Trade Agreement between Canada, Mexico and the United States, north–south trade corridors are supplementing traditional east–west routes (Figure 5.10).

The development of the Trans-European Networks (TENs) is providing for the interconnection and inter-operability of national networks (Figure 5.11). Plans are afoot for the Asian Highway (AH) and the Trans-Asian Railway (TAR) to integrate Asia (Chapter 12). There are also plans for complementing the Asian initiatives by linking TENs with six new logistics corridors under the Central Asia Regional Economic Coöperation (CAREC) programme to bring about the economic integration of Eurasia by linking them to maritime networks (see the Epilogue).

What is often missing from this big picture is the failure to link logistics corridors to their gateways. Too much emphasis is focused on national borders that are associated with barriers to the flow of goods. Even if we dispensed with these national borders a distinct core-and-periphery structure would still evolve of its own accord together with regions of industrial specialization. This pattern of agglomeration may persist over time, even when trade costs fall due to complex interdependencies between the locational decisions of firms.

GATEWAYS AND CORRIDORS

Gateways and corridors must be considered together with hinterland and hinterworld relations as the basic ingredients of spatial planning (Figure 5.12). Otherwise the preoccupation with land-based networks will lead to the failure to recognize that airports and seaports are also at the border (Rimmer and Dick, 2012). These 'at-border' issues that occur at airports, seaports and land borders involving cross-border movement of business migrants, labour and tourists can be resolved through international organizations. The primary obstacles are the 'behind-the-border' issues that occur in the main gateways. As noted, these involve oligarchic structures, congestion, multimodal transport, intergovernmental

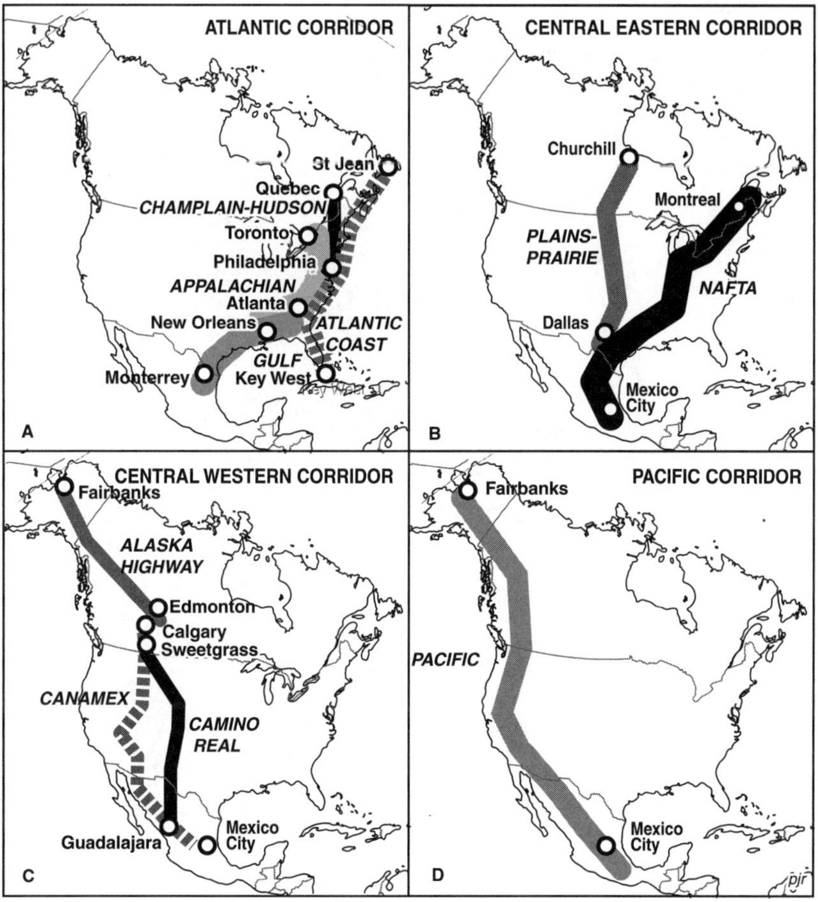

Note: (A) Atlantic Corridor; (B) Central Eastern Corridor; (C) Central Western Corridor; and (D) Pacific Corridor.

Source: Adapted from NAFI (2008).

Figure 5.10 North American trade corridors

coordination and ownership structures. Their resolution should deliver higher returns to business than those likely to be derived from the further liberalization of border barriers to trade and investment. The concepts of gateways and corridors are used as spatial tools to formulate logistics policies in Europe and North America, but to date have been less instrumental in the Asian-Pacific Rim.

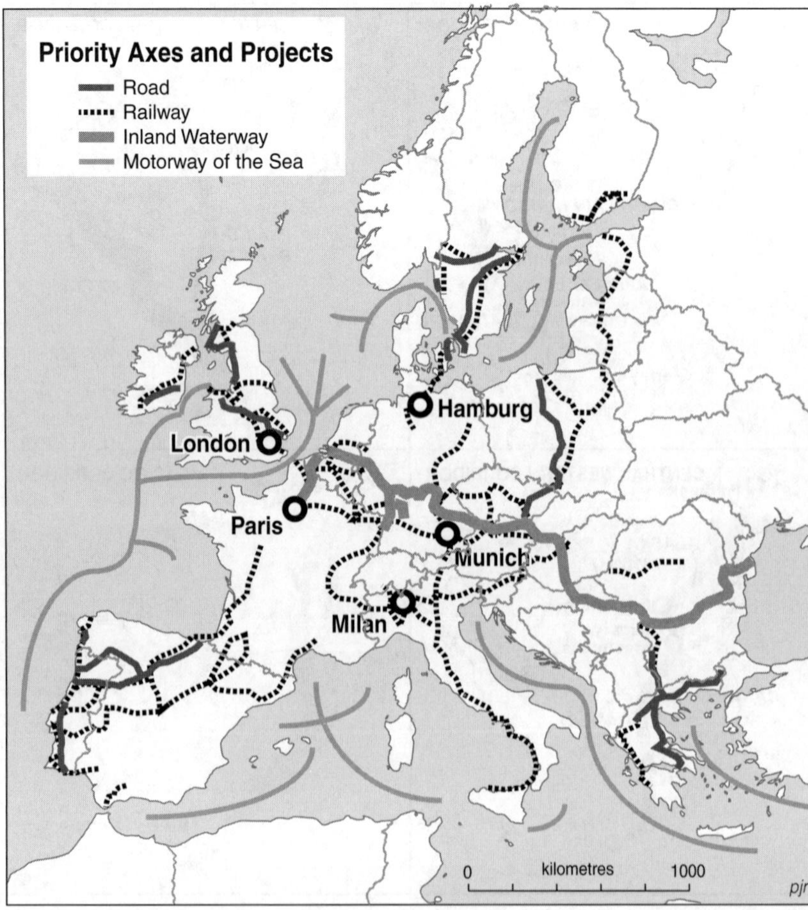

Source: Adapted from EI Euroinfrastructure.eu (2010).

Figure 5.11 Thirty priority axes and projects under the Trans-European Transport Network (TEN-T)

In Europe the North West Metropolitan Area 'Spatial Vision' Group combines the pivots of the Pentagon areas – London, Paris, Frankfurt, Amsterdam and Brussels – as gateways and relevant segments of the TENs network as logistics corridors (NWMA Spatial Vision Group, 2000). The policy strategy is to extend these corridors to stimulate peripheral growth outside the Pentagon. A drawback to this cocooned approach is that it excludes both external material and virtual flows, which are part of the

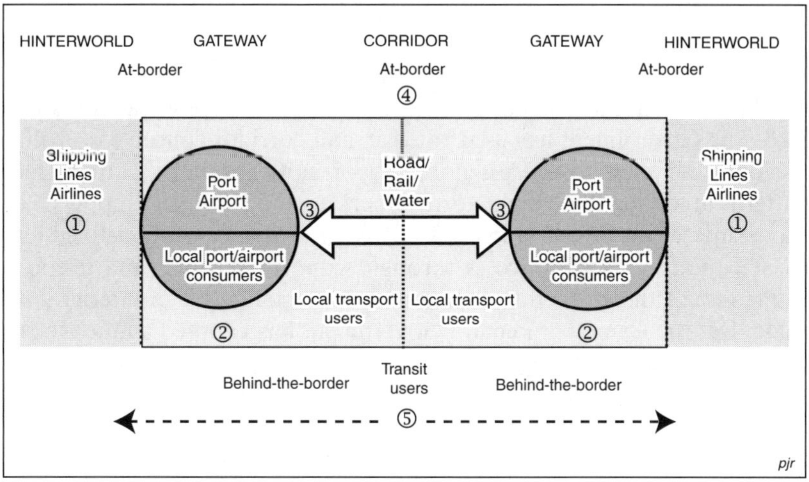

Note: 1. Oligopoly market structure involving shipping lines and airlines. 2. Congestion at ports and airports. 3. Multimodal transportation and congestion (port/road-rail arrangement). 4. Intergovernmental coordination between port and corridor regions (multimodal transport facilities under different jurisdictions). 5. Ownership structure (public/local government, private) – trend to privatization.

Sources: Zhang (2007), Rimmer (2011).

Figure 5.12 Inter-gateway corridor network

global network organization underpinning the knowledge economy (Pain, 2007a).

The Coalition for America's Gateways and Trade Corridors (CAGTC, 2012) is an interest group that lobbies for increased investment in infrastructure (including intermodal connectors). Freight gateways and trade corridors have often been devolved to regional and local jurisdictions in the United States, but nevertheless the Maritime Administration (2008) has detailed a National Port Gateway and Freight Corridor Strategy and significant freight provisions have been made by the Government of the United States in *Moving Ahead for Progress in the 21st Century* (USDOT, 2012). These actions may have been prompted by the Canadian Federal Government's initiative to reappraise the role of logistics in regional development and national transport policies. Canada's initiative has led to gateway and corridor plans being developed as integrated packages of long-term investment and policy measures that provide national benefits.

The Canadian Asian-Pacific Gateway and Corridors Initiative

Since the mid-2000s the Canadian Federal Government has sought to develop an integrated spatial approach in its policy on physical infrastructure. The Government has used gateway and corridor concepts to realign the logistics system to address global opportunities and likely future trade patterns involving the Asian, North American and European supply chain traversing 'Main Street' (Figure 5.13). A gateway is usually defined as a coastal metropolis with access through seaports, airports and teleports to the rest of the globe that captures a substantial share of international trade. But the Canadian Federal Government has adopted a much looser definition covering a range of centres over a wide geographical area.

In 2006 the Government's initial policy thrust was to leverage the country's advantages in connecting North America to the Asian-Pacific Rim by developing the Asia Pacific Gateway Initiative to meet the increased demand for supply chain and logistics services arising from Asian exports and to benefit from satisfying China's demand for services

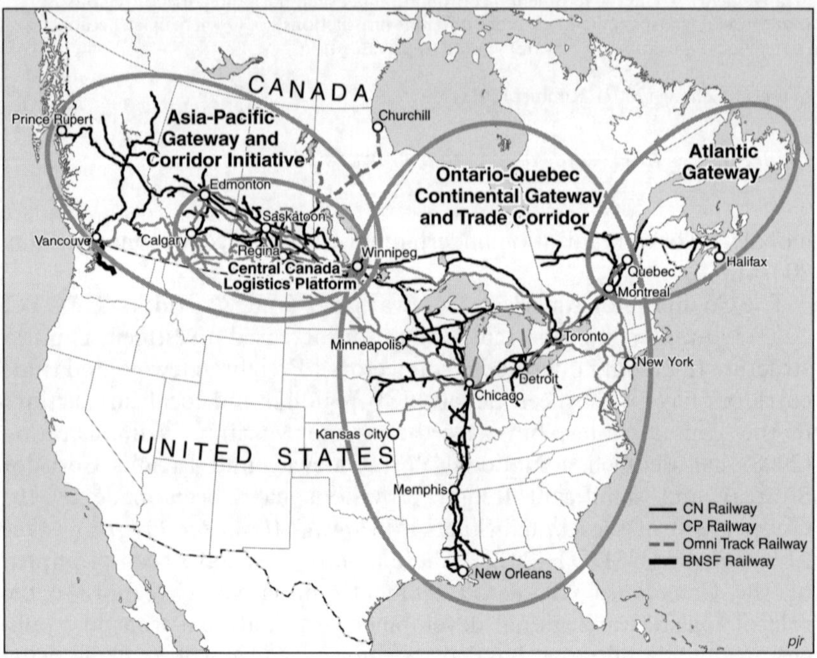

Source: Transformed from La Fortune (2010).

Figure 5.13 Canada's gateways and corridors

and resources stemming from that country's rising domestic consumption (Government of Canada, 2007). In response to these trading opportunities the Asia-Pacific gateway and corridor comprises the logistics infrastructure network that encompasses ports in the Lower Mainland of British Columbia (notably the Port of Vancouver) and Prince Rupert, principal road and rail connections that extend across western Canada and south to the United States, land border crossings, and major Canadian airports.

Also in 2006 the Atlantic Gateway was conceived as an east coast counterpoint to the Pacific Gateway to capitalize on the shortest all-weather route to Europe, and Central and South America, and Asia via the Suez Canal. This initiative incorporates the ice-free deepwater port of Halifax, and intermodal connections crossing Canada's east coast provinces not only link to the rest of Canada but also to extend deep into the United States consumer markets. Under very favourable conditions Chicago can be reached from Halifax in 2 hours 30 minutes by non-stop direct flight, 36 hours transit time by non-stop truck and 74 hours by double-stack container train (Halifax Gateway, 2012).

In 2007 the Ontario–Quebec Continental Gateway Initiative was promulgated to provide the lynchpin between the Pacific and Atlantic gateways. The twin provinces produce almost 60 per cent of Canada's gross domestic product and comprise an identical share of the country's population, including the two largest cities of Toronto and Montreal. The region's multimodal transport connections are fully integrated with their United States counterparts to warrant the extension of the gateway's footprint across the border to New Orleans. Within a 1000 km radius, 135 million consumers can be reached within 24 hours.

These separate initiatives were incorporated into the Canadian Federal Government's National Policy Framework for Strategic Gateways and Trade Corridors (Government of Canada, 2010). The framework is designed to provide a perspective on the national logistics system, an institutional framework for future governance and a system-wide approach. Investments in Canada's gateway–corridor network are designed to develop innovative ways of increasing the competitiveness of the country's multinational manufacturers and retailers by facilitating intermodal traffic flows on a North American scale and capturing value-adding opportunities from improved reliability, speed and productivity (Stalk and McMillan, 2013).

An Arctic Gateway has also been mooted to accommodate the prospects of resource development and viable international shipping avenues brought about by climate change, but this is not yet part of the National Policy Framework. Another possible spin-off is the prospect of collaboration with, and between, the Western Provinces of British Columbia, Alberta, Saskatchewan and Manitoba through the proposed development of a Central Canada Logistics Platform in which Calgary, Edmonton, Regina, Saskatoon and Winnipeg feature as key hubs.

Thus the Government of Canada's National Policy Framework provides an opportunity for exploring the economic foundations of the gateway and corridor concepts. The policy is underpinned by literature covering relevant theories, opportunities and issues, academic research, national and international experiences, and implications for logistics and infrastructure policies to realize associated development prospects. Deriving a series of key precepts from the Canadian experience provides an important springboard for exploring local logistics policies within the Asian-Pacific Rim (Table 5.2). Lessons can be drawn on the importance of research and development, analysis and long-term planning, legislative frameworks, public investment in infrastructure and public–private partnerships. There is also practical advice on border congestion, increased

Table 5.2 Key precepts derived from Canada's gateway and corridor strategy

- Designed to strengthen a region's competitive position in global commerce by creating reliable, efficient and secure connections between gateways, permitting seamless and fast movement
- Regional policy framework for strategic gateways and trade corridors that will guide future actions
- Strategically located gateways and border crossings to play a vital role in fostering competitiveness
- Support for limited number of gateway strategies and for intermodal corridors to enhance trade competitiveness and regional transport network
- System based approach that tackles infrastructure, policy, governance and operational issues in an integrated public and private sector strategy
- Vision of a spatial economy in which competitiveness is advanced by efficient, safe and secure transport systems that support the region's success in the rapidly changing world of international commerce
- A regional policy framework that will provide focus and direction for strategies that foster the development and optimize the use of the transport and energy systems of regional significance for international trade
- A regional economic policy that is tailored to the geography and regional realities
- Provision of transport infrastructure – building blocks, gateways and corridors
- Systems approach that places emphasis on integration of a range of planning skills and labour markets

Source: Government of Canada (2007).

aviation capacity, and issues involving gateways, hinterlands and corridors. Guidance is also provided on planning future corridors, systematic intermodal solutions and public–private partnerships.

CONCLUSION

Recognition of multilayered gateways and their associated corridors has provided a framework within which the supply chains of multinational manufacturers and retailers and global logistics corporations interact within hinterlands and the hinterworld. While corporations seek the legal security of gateways, especially for intellectual property, they simultaneously pursue weakly governed jurisdictions to minimize scrutiny and tax liability over their less-value-creating activities such as fabrication (Rimmer and Dick, 2013; Baldwin, 2013). These local state jurisdictions have only been given passing reference in this global overview that spans interactions between multinational manufacturers and retailers, and global third-party logistics providers, shipping lines and seaports, airlines and airports, and telecommunications.

Moving from the global to an Asian-Pacific Rim perspective brings these 'local' state institutions into greater prominence and raises issues of governance and regulation, land use and urban planning, environmental footprints, and security, risk and information management. There is an opportunity for examining 'local' logistics policy-making at regional and national levels. According to Ruth Banomyong (2007a, 3), this focus involves 'the process of planning, facilitating, implementing, integrating, and controlling the efficient and effective flow and storage of freight, and movement of people and information within and between logistics systems for the purpose of enhancing traders' competitiveness in order to increase national and/or regional competitive advantage'. Much of this policy-making at national, provincial and metropolitan levels is focused on developing both gateway and corridor infrastructure to streamline interactions with global logistics players so that the 'local' focus meshes with the wider global structure.

These strategies reflect that a global revolution is under way within the movements of goods and services, which not only offers new development opportunities but also, at times, creates infrastructure capacity constraints in both gateways and corridors, suggesting that some transport and telecommunications systems are inadequate for future needs. By integrating technology and intelligence into the physical transport infrastructure, there is an opportunity to reduce environmental impact, improve capacity, and make transport systems more efficient, safe and secure.

PART II

Local policies: Asian-Pacific Rim

The Asian-Pacific Rim is now central to any discussion of the role of logistics within the global economy: it is the world's premier manufacturing centre, particularly for motor vehicles and electronics, and an emerging giant in outsourced logistics services (Armstrong & Associates, 2013e). As there are no exact bounds to the Rim, this study of 'local logistics' shifts between stricter and looser definitions of the region depending on their appropriateness to the particular matter in hand. The stricter definition covers the 'Main Street' arc stretching from the Russian Far East to the Indonesian archipelago, which is also referred to as East Asia and subdivided for convenience into Northeast Asia and Southeast Asia (Figure II.1).

This Asian-Pacific Rim is not only separated from other regions by oceans and difficult terrain, but also split by cultural and linguistic groups, and divided by national boundaries where data on logistics are collected. These boundaries are intersection points for the Rim's 17 political jurisdictions that involve economies within both Northeast Asia and Southeast Asia. Taiwan is considered as part of China in the statistics provided by the World Bank, and the Russian Far East is excluded from consideration (Table II.1). The jurisdictions differ widely in surface area, population, and in total and per capita gross national income (GNI) and in terms of purchasing power parity (PPP). Their boundaries are also associated with barriers to the flow of goods, not only stemming explicitly from import tariffs and quotas, but also arising implicitly from inconsistent regulatory and legal standards, and other irritating delays linked with border crossings. The boundaries pose obstacles to logistics development, even where no formal barriers exist, as restrictions on movements of people persist well after formal barriers to trade in goods have been lowered.

Even if we dispensed with national borders and considered trade flows across unbounded economic space, discrete areas of industrial specialization and urbanization would still evolve of their own accord, and exhibit distinct core-and-periphery patterns. These urban-industrial agglomerations in the Asian-Pacific Rim are becoming increasingly important within the world economy. Many of the region's leading multinational manufacturers, especially those engaged in the production of motor vehicles and electronics, and foremost retailers have their headquarters within these agglomerations. Among the top ten Asian-Pacific supply chains, Flextronics with headquarters in Singapore, Acer in Taipei and Seven & I Holdings (Seven-Eleven) in Tokyo are discussed in Chapter 6; Toyota in Toyota City/Nagoya and Sony in Tokyo in Chapter 7; Samsung, LG and

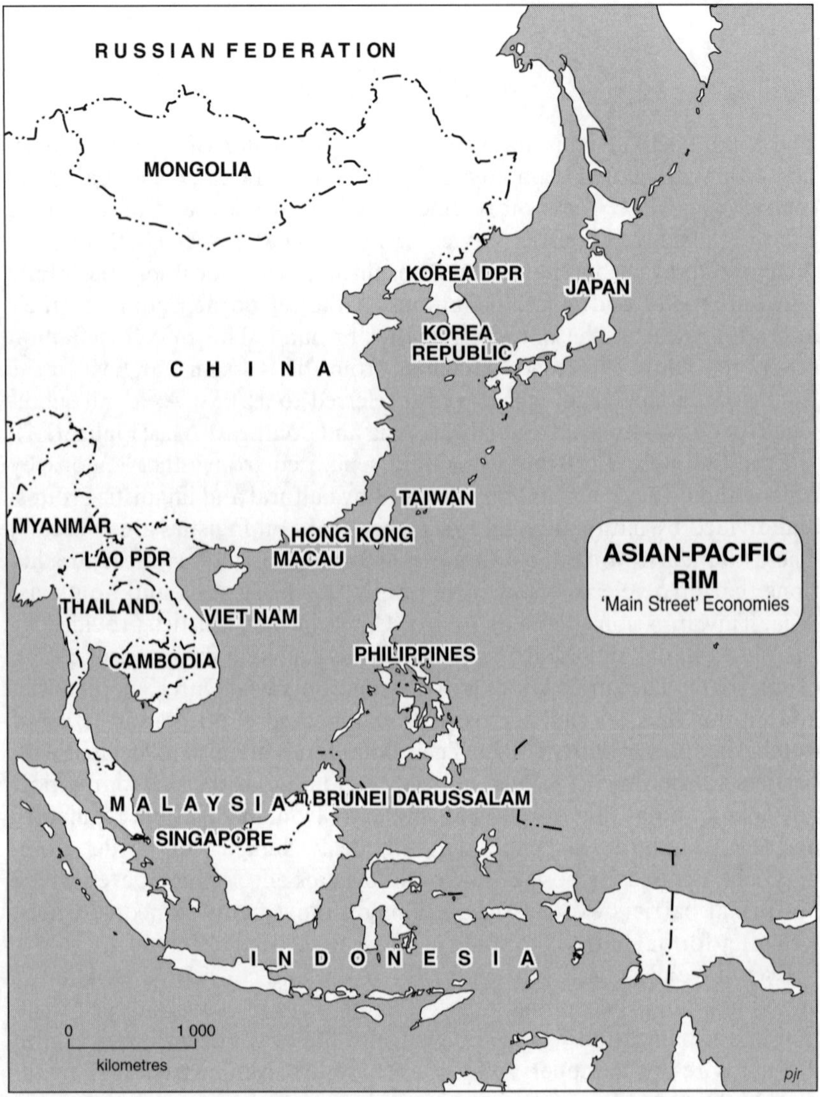

Figure II.1 The Asian-Pacific Rim's 'Main Street' economies

Table II.1 Surface area, population and gross national income of Asian-Pacific Rim economies, 2010

Country	Surface area	Population	Gross national income purchasing power parity (PPP)	
	sq. km	number	total	per capita
	thous.	million	US$ billion	US$
Northeast Asia				
China	9600	1344	11361	8450
– Hong Kong SAR	1	7	364	51490
– Macao SAR[1]	0	1	31	57060
Japan	378	128	4541	35530
Korea DPR	121	24	n.a.	n.a.
Korea Republic	100	50	1510	30340
Mongolia	1564	3	12	4360
Subtotal	11764	1557	–	–
Southeast Asia				
Brunei Darussalam[2]	6	0.4	20	49790
Cambodia	181	14	32	2260
Indonesia	1905	242	1099	4530
Lao PDR	237	6	16	2600
Malaysia	331	29	438	15190
Myanmar	677	48	n.a.	n.a.
Philippines	300	95	395	4160
Singapore	1	5	310	59790
Thailand	513	70	583	8390
Viet Nam	331	88	287	3260
Subtotal	4482	597.4	–	–
Total	16246	2154.4		

Notes:

1 2010 data.
2 2009 data.

Source: World Bank (2012a).

Hyundai in Seoul in Chapter 8; and Lenovo in Beijing in Chapter 9 (Table II.2). Given their domiciles, these brand-name manufacturers and retailers are reliant upon diverse local logistics services.

In a bid to capture the diversity of local logistics within the Asian-Pacific Rim, albeit within the context of an emerging global system, interest is centred upon changes occurring at both regional and national levels. At the regional level various loose arrangements have been developed to give the Asian-Pacific Rim some political substance such as the wide-ranging

Table II.2 Top ten Asian-Pacific supply chains, 2010

Rank	Company	HQ	Return on assets[1] %	Inventory turns[2] no.	Revenue growth[3] %	Composite score[4]	World ranking
1	Samsung	Seoul	9.8	16.9	22.5	3.98	10
2	Hyundai	Seoul	9.8	17.1	8.4	1.86	28
3	Lenovo	Beijing	1.0	20.9	6.5	1.63	35
4	Honda	Tokyo	2.5	6.7	–10.5	1.32	53
5	LG	Seoul	0.7	22.3	4.6	1.30	55
6	Acer	Taipei	4.8	10.7	10.0	1.26	59
7	Toyota	Toyota City	1.0	11.5	–8.5	1.21	65
8	Seven & I Holdings	Tokyo	2.4	20.7	–3.1	0.90	69
9	Flextronics	Singapore	–16.9	8.3	1.9	0.85	94
10	Sony	Tokyo	0.2	6.6	–5.8	0.59	105

Notes: Companies with headquarters in Australia and India are excluded from the list and Honda, the motor vehicle manufacturer, is not used as a case study.

1. Return on assets (ROA): [(2010 net income / 2010 total assets) * 50%] + [(2009 net income / 2009 total assets) * 30%] + [(2008 net income / 2008 total assets) * 20%]
2. Inventory turns: 2010 cost of goods sold / 2010 quarterly average inventory
3. Revenue growth: [(change in revenue 2010–2009 * 50%] + [(change in revenue 2009–2008) * 30%] + [(change in revenue 2008–2007) * 20%]
4. Composite score: (peer opinion * 25%) + (Gartner opinion*25%) + (ROA*25%) + (inventory turns * 15%) + (revenue growth * 10%)

2010 data was used where available. Where 2010 data was unavailable, latest available full-year data was used. All raw data was normalized to a ten-point scale prior to composite calculation.

Source: Bloch and Hofman (2011).

Asia-Pacific Economic Cooperation (APEC) forum and the ten members of the Association of Southeast Asian Nations (ASEAN) together with its combinations ASEAN+3 (China, Japan and South Korea) and ASEAN+6 (adding Australia, India and New Zealand). Some of the narrower representations have been used to suggest that the Rim is a unified and cohesive subsystem of the world economy. Representing the Rim in this way overlooks marked variations in logistics performance between the 15 regional economies surveyed by the World Bank in terms of the Logistics Performance Index (LPI) in 2007, 2010 and 2012 (Arvis et al., 2007; Arvis et al., 2010, 2012). In 2012 performances ranged from first-ranked Singapore to 140th-ranked Mongolia with 40 per cent of the leader's score (Table II.3).

Table II.3 Ranking of Asian-Pacific Rim economies on the World Bank's Logistics Performance Index and indicators, 2012

Country	Rank	Score[1]	%[2]	Country	Rank	Score	%
Singapore	1	4.13	100	Philippines	52	3.02	64.8
Hong Kong SAR, China	2	4.12	99.9	Viet Nam	53	3.00	64.1
Japan	8	3.93	93.8	Indonesia	59	2.94	62.2
Taiwan, China	19	3.71	86.6	Cambodia	101	2.56	50.0
Korea Rep	21	3.70	86.2	Lao PDR	109	2.50	48.0
China	26	3.52	80.5	Myanmar	129	2.37	43.8
Malaysia	29	3.49	79.8	Mongolia	140	2.25	40.0
Thailand	38	3.18	69.6	Korea Dem. Rep.	n.a.	n.a.	n.a.

Notes:
1. Based on the Logistics Performance Index (LPI), which is a multidimensional assessment of logistics performance rated on a scale of 1 (worst) to five (best).
2. Percentage of the highest performer (i.e. Singapore).

Source: Arvis et al. (2012).

At best, national economies are crude units for comprehending shifts in logistics. Nations are political or military entities and it does not necessarily follow that they are also the salient entities for assessing logistics performance. Viewing the Asian-Pacific Rim as an aggregation of countries also draws attention away from the significance of 'gateways' within the Rim, such as Singapore and Hong Kong ranked in first and second position in the World Bank's Logistics Performance Index for 2012. At the very least the transformation of the logistics arena within the Asian-Pacific Rim should be conceived in terms of gateways and corridors (Chapter 6).

But to examine logistics within the Asian-Pacific Rim as an entity with its own gateway and corridor structure and dynamics is to diminish the regulatory role of the nation-state, which still retains considerable power over the structures of production, distribution and consumption (Figure II.2). The actions open to the nation-state reflect that its objectives are concerned with social responsibility, adding value and efficiency; its decision types cover governance, hardware and software and logistics functions; and its policy targets cover both global and local logistics corporations, and multinational manufacturers and retailers. Rethinking the changing function of the nation-state within the integration and globalization of the Rim has also led to attention being focused on local logistics.

As it is not possible to cover all 15 'local' economies identified in the

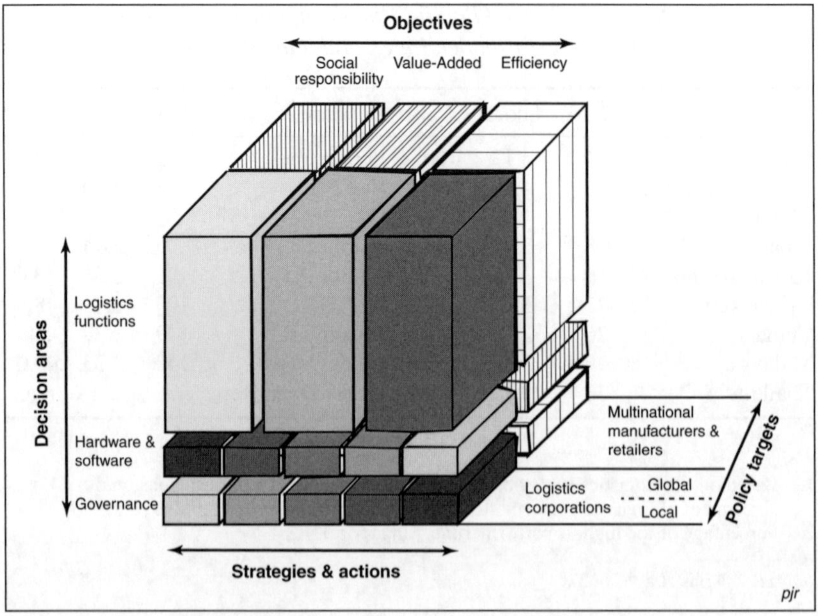

Source: Based on Seo (2011, 20).

Figure II.2 Three directions for the nation-state to develop strategies and actions: objectives, decision areas and policy targets

World Bank's survey, attention is focused primarily on logistics policies within three economies: Japan (Chapter 7), South Korea (Chapter 8) and China (Chapter 9). Striking differences in policy-making between the three economies stem from Japan's short-lived governments, South Korea's five-year rotation of presidents, and China's five-year plans and ten-year presidential eras (premiers and presidents are referred to by their family name followed by their given name). Nevertheless, narrowing the focus to three countries does provide an opportunity to examine the World Bank's logistics performance indices for 2007, 2010 and 2012 in greater depth (Table II.4). In all three years Japan ranked ahead of South Korea and China on all six key pointers that contribute to the indices: customs, infrastructure, international shipments, logistics quality and competence, tracking and tracing, and timeliness. Nevertheless the gap between Japan and South Korea and China on these counts narrowed between 2007 and 2012. During this period Japan experienced a progressive decline in its overall score and status, especially pronounced in logistics quality and competence, whereas South Korea and China narrowed the gap on most counts.

Table II.4 Ranking of Japan, South Korea and China on the World Bank's Logistics Performance Index and indicators, 2005, 2010 and 2012

	Japan			Korea			China		
	2007	2010	2012	2007	2010	2012	2007	2010	2012
Customs									
Rank	11	10	11	25	26	23	35	32	30
Score	3.79	3.79	3.72	3.52	3.33	3.42	2.99	3.16	3.25
Infrastructure									
Rank	6	5	9	28	23	22	30	27	26
Score	4.11	4.19	4.11	3.22	3.62	3.74	3.20	3.54	3.61
International shipments									
Rank	9	12	14	25	15	12	28	27	23
Score	3.77	3.55	3.61	3.44	3.47	3.67	3.31	3.31	3.46
Logistics quality & competence									
Rank	5	7	9	24	23	22	27	29	28
Score	4.12	4.00	3.97	3.44	3.64	3.65	3.40	3.49	3.47
Tracking & tracing									
Rank	5	8	9	22	23	22	31	30	31
Score	4.12	4.13	4.03	3.63	3.83	3.68	3.37	3.55	3.52
Timeliness									
Rank	7	13	6	19	28	21	36	36	30
Score	4.08	4.26	4.21	4.11	3.97	4.02	3.68	3.91	3.80
Logistics Performance Index									
Rank	6	7	8	25	23	21	30	27	26
Score	4.02	3.97	3.93	3.52	3.64	3.70	3.32	3.49	3.52

Sources: Arvis et al. (2007), Arvis et al. (2010), Arvis et al. (2012).

As the country-specific performance data for each year are not strictly comparable, attention is concentrated on 2012. An examination of domestic time and cost data for Japan, South Korea and China for 2012 reveals that Japan has the shortest lead time but the highest costs for imports and exports in both the port and airport and the land supply chains (Table II.5). South Korea and China have comparable lead times but China is cheaper on all counts.

Table II.5 Time and cost data for Japan, South Korea and China, 2012

Item	Unit	Japan	South Korea	China
Export time & cost				
Port or airport supply chain				
Distance	Km	392	300	162
Lead time	Days	1	3	3
Cost	US$	931	572	454
Land supply chain				
Distance	Km	75	300	215
Lead time	Days	1	3	3
Cost	US$	707	500	645
Import time & cost				
Port or airport supply chain				
Distance	Km	171	300	133
Lead time	Days	1	3	4
Cost	US$	935	707	453
Land supply chain				
Distance	Km	75	300	171
Lead time	Days	1	3	3
Cost	US$	866	500	637

Source: Arvis et al. (2012)

Other data on the quality of the logistics experience suggest that South Korea has moved ahead of Japan (Table II.6). China lags behind both economies on most counts, notably the low number of shipments meeting quality criteria, the number of forms required and the rate of physical inspection.

A key focal point in government circles within China, Japan and South Korea is how to build an efficient logistics system to make the best use of trade-related infrastructure (that is, the well-managed distribution of goods, services and related information passing through the supply chains of manufacturing and retailing firms). Without rail and road connections between the three countries, goods are transported mainly by sea, but the shift from bulky items towards lighter and higher-value products has seen them being sent increasingly by air. There is a strong reliance upon road transport within all three countries, but in China products are also being manufactured and consumed increasingly within inland areas. Given the greater efficiency of rail transport over 500 km compared with trucks, multimodal arrangements are becoming crucial to building a countrywide distribution system that reduces trade costs to inland areas. Benefits from

Table II.6 Quality of logistics experience in Japan, South Korea and China, 2012

Item	Unit	Japan	South Korea	China
Shipments meeting quality criteria	%	93	97	69
Number of agencies: imports	No.	3	1	3
Number of agencies: exports	No.	3	1	3
Number of forms: imports	No.	4	2	6
Number of forms: exports	No.	4	1	5
Clearance without physical inspection[1]	Days	0	1	2
Clearance with physical inspection	Days	1	1	4
Rate of physical inspection	%	3	3	17
Multiple inspection	%	2	1	5

Note:
1. Time taken between the submission of an accepted customs declaration and customs clearance.

Source: Arvis et al. (2012, 47–50).

lower costs of traded goods and reduced road accidents stemming from the improved distribution system will have to offset the negative impacts of any displacement of people and environmental damage.

After exploring national logistics systems in China, Japan and Korea, all three economies are considered together to address how investments in the region's physical infrastructure should be located to increase their efficiency and effectiveness in enhancing cooperation and integration (Chapter 10). This issue allows gauging the extent to which a logistics strategy can be outlined for the Asian-Pacific Rim in a fashion similar to policies developed for the European Union and the North American Free Trade Area. More specifically, the focus is on Northeast Asia to see if the subregion comprising China, Japan and South Korea can reach the levels of integration attained in Southeast Asia.

6. Gateways and corridors

The Asian-Pacific Rim's gateways and corridors provide building blocks for comprehending local logistics. Key elements are the scale and efficiency of the gateway's port and airport infrastructure, and corridor capacity from gateway to market and within the urban area. Along with combined gateway–corridor reliability and information systems linking operators, these elements are integral components in any system designed for reducing life-cycle costs by eliminating steps in the handling of goods through the logistics network.

Gateways and corridors within the Asian-Pacific Rim, like their counterparts in Europe and North America, have been given new institutional roles and functions to provide policy tools for national governments and regional bodies to reshape the logistics arena and redistribute economic activities (World Bank, 2005; Kunaka, 2010; Kunaka et al., 2012; Mustafa and Kunaka, 2012). This redistribution process is so designed that manufacturing and retailing are not concentrated in gateways, but spread along the corridor to encompass smaller cities and lagging rural areas.

Before discussing this recasting of gateways and corridors in the Asian-Pacific Rim, a series of issues has to be addressed. How has the Rim's logistics arena changed over time? How can regional gateways and aspiring gateways (proto-gateways) be identified and ranked? And how will these gateways and proto-gateways be interlinked by a series of corridors?

Outlining the Asian-Pacific Rim's distinctive commercial history sets the scene for discussing the logistics arena's development. The relative merits of individual gateways and proto-gateways within the Rim have already been explored to determine where manufacturers and retailers should locate (e.g. Kotler et al., 2002; Oum and Park, 2004). A series of case studies of gateways and their subregional economies and leading corporations are therefore undertaken to illustrate pertinent logistics features, which have been underplayed in comparative surveys. Attention is focused upon Singapore/Sijori (Singapore–Johor–Riau), Hong Kong/Pearl River Delta, Taipei/Taiwan, Shanghai/Yangtze River Delta and Tokyo/Kanto. Then the essential characteristics of the corridors linking the gateways are explored before examining the nature of economic space aided by invoking comparisons with spatial planning in Europe.

THE LOGISTICS ARENA

The Asian-Pacific Rim's logistics arena is essentially a product of the globalization process. This process is largely associated with changes in the modes of production and consumption, and successive revolutions in transport and communications since the mid-nineteenth century (Chapter 1). These changes have helped to develop new markets and accelerated the turnover of capital. Since 1850 each set of innovations has changed the way in which space is organized, and has opened up radically different opportunities for economic development.

In 1850 what is now the Asian-Pacific Rim comprised a closed logistics system centred upon Japan, and an open logistics system in which major nodes were 'port cities' such as Jakarta (Batavia) and Singapore (Figure 6.1). By 1930, improvements in transport and communications had transformed this simple logistics structure. External links with Japan were superimposed upon bilateral colonial networks serving subregional economies with extensive agricultural hinterlands: British Burma pivoted on Rangoon, British Malaya on Singapore, the Dutch East Indies on Jakarta, French Indochina on Saigon, and the American Philippines on Manila. By 1980 the area had become known as the 'Western Pacific'. With the globalization of economic activity expanding markets and deepening economic interdependency beyond state borders, the role of port cities within the Western Pacific had intensified. Within this economy Tokyo – reflecting Japan's ascendancy – had become the dominant regional hub with Bangkok, Hong Kong, Seoul, Singapore and Taipei playing major subregional roles.

During the 1990s the term 'Asian-Pacific Rim' came into vogue to describe the countries stretching from the Russian Far East to the Indonesian archipelago. Following the end of the Cold War in the early 1990s there was enthusiasm for creating a new logistics arena within the Rim based on identifying key economic subregions (Figure 6.2). Tokyo was still the dominant hub. Japanese commercial interests saw the national capital as the pivot of an East Asian corridor stretching from Sapporo via Seoul to Hong Kong and, hypothetically, connecting with an emerging Southeast Asia corridor from Bangkok to Singapore. More realistically, with the appearance of China's 'market socialism', was the emergence of the New Golden Triangle pivoted on Hong Kong, Shanghai and Taipei. At the time there was conjecture as to which of the three would become the dominant hub. Meanwhile, several broad economic zones were identified: the North Asia Economic Zone with its Tumen River project straddling the borders of China, Russia and North Korea; and the Indochina project encompassing Cambodia, Laos, Thailand and Viet Nam. This zonal focus

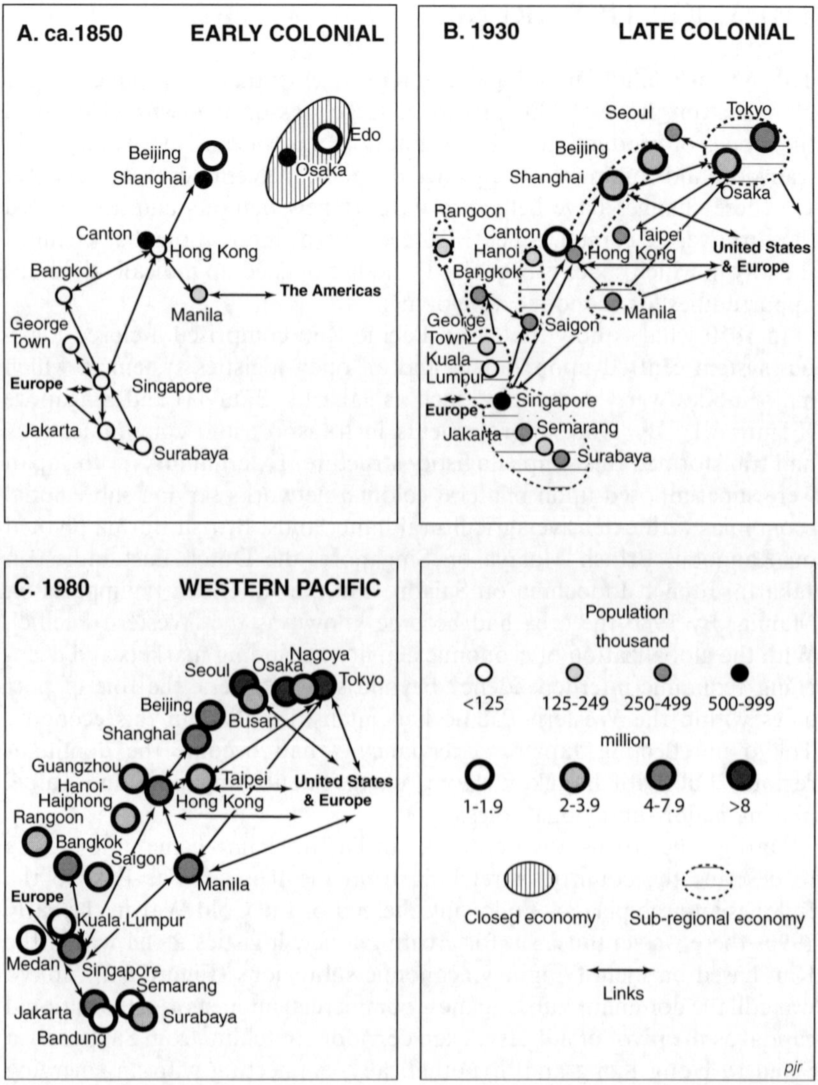

Sources: 1850 figures are from various sources; 1930 from Mitchell (2007); 1980 figures from UN (2010), Dick and Rimmer (2013).

Figure 6.1 Predating the Asian-Pacific Rim: (A) Colonial Era, ca.1850; (B) Late Colonial Era, 1930; and (C) Western Pacific Rim, 1980

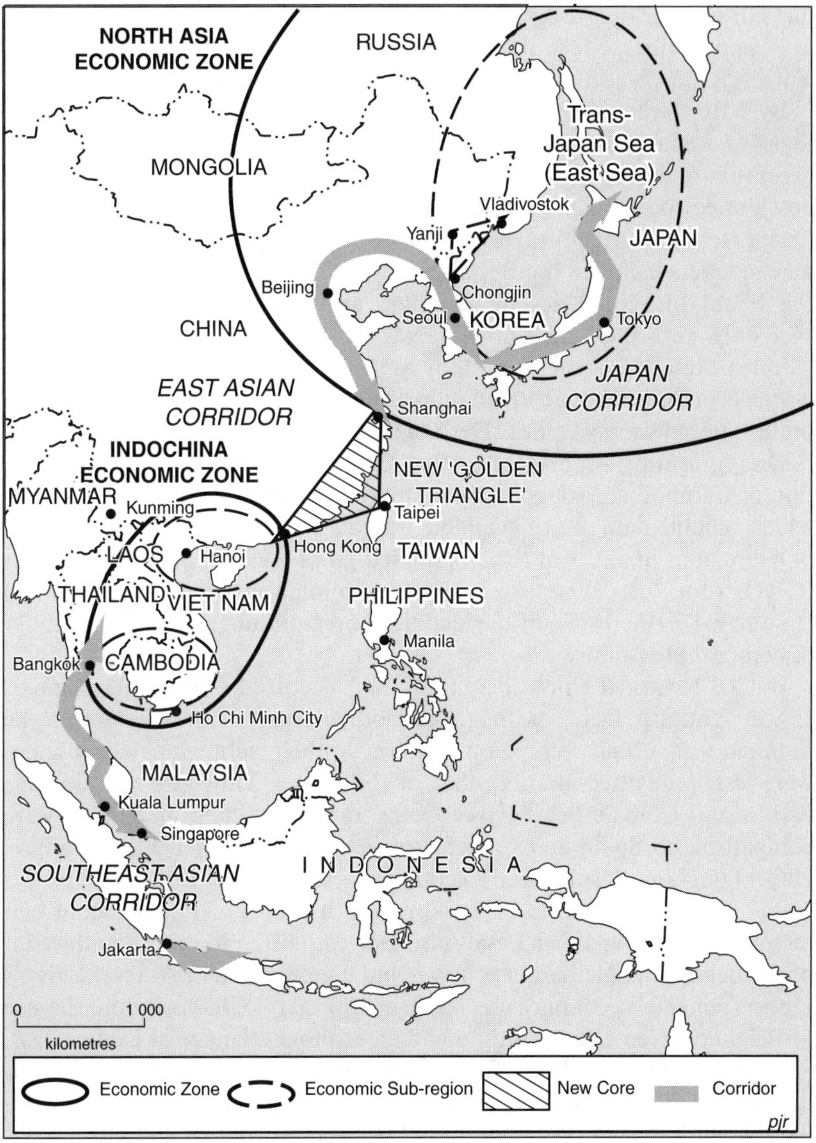

Source: Rimmer (1994).

Figure 6.2 The Asian-Pacific Rim, 1990

has shifted over time as both state and non-state actors have seized emerging opportunities. Most attention was centred on the development of the Tumen River project and the Sino-Russian border area.

By 2010 the focus on the Tumen River project and a host of regional logistics arenas identified in Southeast Asia had lost momentum, with the exception of Singapore–Johor–Riau (Sijori) (Figure 6.3). Two decades of accelerated industrialization have shifted the economic centre of gravity from extensive agricultural areas to coastal subregional economies. These new magnets included the Bohai-Yellow Sea Rim, the Pearl River Delta, the Seoul–Incheon–Kaesong Triangle and the Yangtze River Delta. Not only were these coastal subregions less dependent upon their agricultural hinterlands, but also they are once again closely linked to the world economy through their industrial activities being integrated into multinational supply chains (Derudder et al., 2013; Kimura, 2013).

Disaggregating economies in the Asian-Pacific Rim, with the exception of Cambodia, Mongolia, Myanmar, North Korea and Viet Nam for which reliable data are unavailable, reveals the relative economic weight of subregions in terms of their estimated gross regional domestic product (GRDP) for 2010 expressed in terms of purchasing power parity (PPP) (Figure 6.4). The results of the leading subregions are matched with those of comparable countries.

By 2010 marked shifts in ranking had occurred (Table 6.1). China's Lower Yangtze Delta, with an economy larger than Italy's, was the dominant economic subregion. Although their subregional economies were less than three-quarters that of the Lower Yangtze's size, Japan's Kanto and China's Pearl River Delta, ranking second and third, were comparable to Spain and Canada respectively. China's Beijing–Tianjin–Hebei (*Jing-Jin-Ji*) subregion's economy, was only half that of the Lower Yangtze and comparable to Turkey. South Korea's Greater Seoul had moved ahead of Japan's Kansai subregion into fifth place, with both economies behind the Netherlands in size but ahead of Saudi Arabia. China's Upper Yangtze's economy was larger than Japan's Chubu region, the size of Belgium. Even Greater Busan had an economy the size of Denmark's.

Within Southeast Asia, Greater Singapore has an economy that is larger than that of Greece. Greater Bangkok's economy is almost comparable with that of the Czech Republic, and Greater Manila is on a par with Ireland. Greater Jakarta's economy is slightly less than Morocco's whereas Greater Kuala Lumpur's economy is larger than New Zealand's.

These comparisons highlight that the preoccupation with nation-states masks the importance of key economic subregions. The size of these subregional economies offers a surer guide to the relative strength of individual gateways rather than the figures for the principal cities alone.

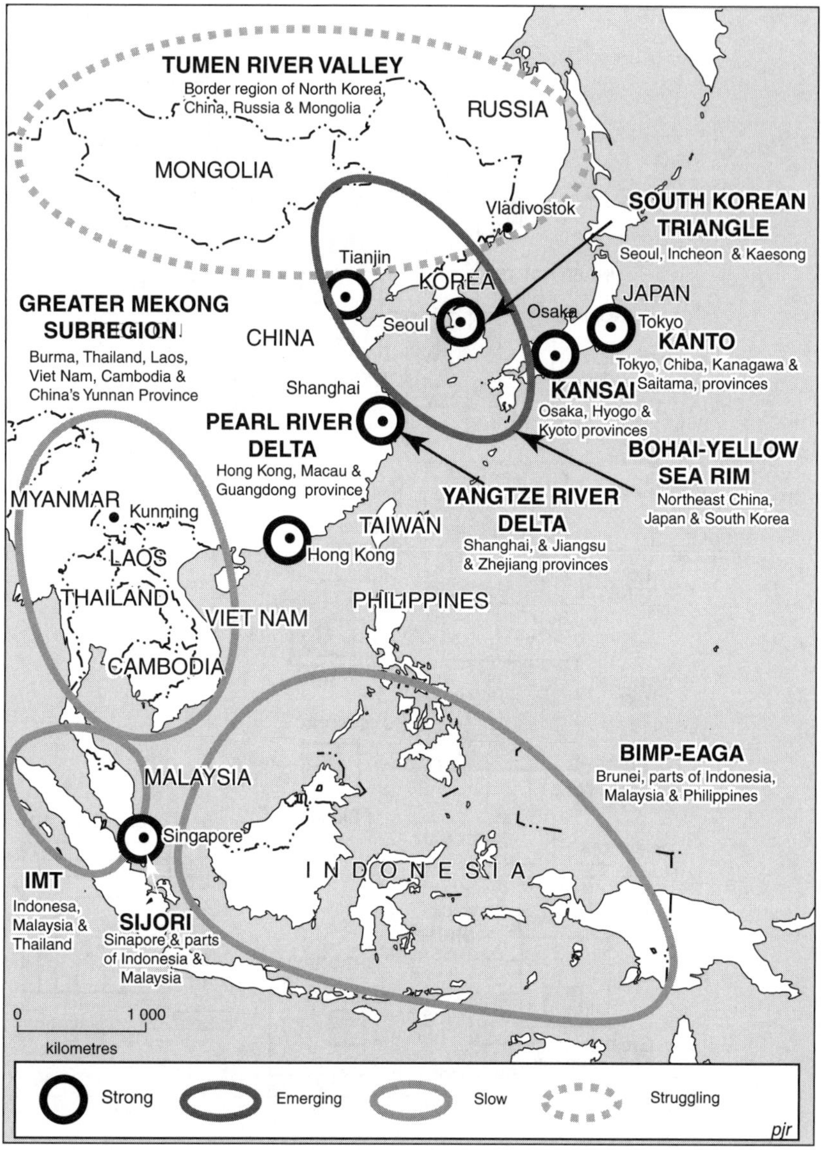

Source: Updated from Rimmer (2004a).

Figure 6.3 The Asian-Pacific Rim, 2010

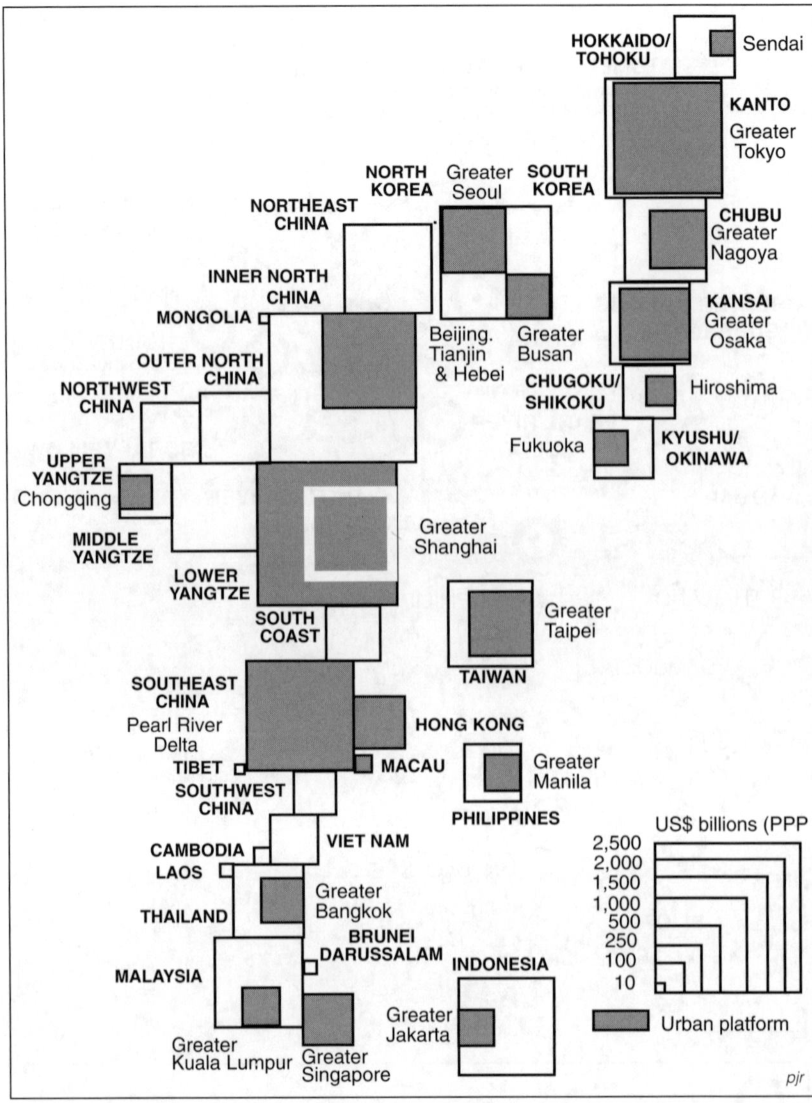

Sources: Calculated from Alpha (2011), BPS (2009), DOSM (2011), NBSC (2010, 2011), NSCB (2011), SB (2010), and World Bank (2011a, 2011b).

Figure 6.4 Estimated gross regional domestic product (GRDP), adjusted for purchasing power parity (PPP), for sub-regions and urban platforms in the Asian-Pacific Rim, 2010

Table 6.1 Leading Asian-Pacific Rim sub-regions and comparable national economies in gross regional domestic product, 2010

Sub-region	GRDP US$ bn	Major city	GCDP US$ bn	Equivalent	GDP US$ bn
Northeast Asia					
Lower Yangtze, China	2001	Shanghai	415	Italy	1908
Kanto, Japan	1434	Tokyo	787	Spain	1478
Southeast China, China	1416	Hong Kong	336	Canada	1327
Beijing, Tianjin & Hebei (*Jing-Jin-Ji*), China	1020	Beijing	336	Turkey	1116
Greater Seoul, South Korea	689	Seoul	340	Netherlands	706
Kansai, Japan	680	Osaka	324	Saudi Arabia	593
Upper Yangtze, China	571	Chongqing	181	Argentina	642
Chubu, Japan	377	Nagoya	308	Belgium	407
Greater Busan, South Korea	241	Busan	74	Denmark	219
Southeast Asia					
Greater Singapore (including Johor & Riau)	331	Singapore	292	Greece	317
Greater Bangkok, Thailand	242	Bangkok	148	Czech Rep	266
Greater Manila, Philippines	176	Manila	136	Ireland	178
Greater Jakarta, Indonesia	168	Jakarta	167	Morocco	178
Greater Kuala Lumpur, Malaysia	150	Kuala Lumpur	58	New Zealand	130

Note: GRDP – gross regional domestic product; GCDP – gross city domestic product; GDP – gross domestic product.

Sources: Calculated from Alpha (2011), BPS (2009), DOSM (2011), NSCB (2010, 2011), NCSB (2011), SK (2011), World Bank (2011a, 2011b).

GATEWAYS

Gateways in the Asian-Pacific Rim are coastal metropolitan areas that have outgrown their earlier roles as ports servicing extensive primary producing hinterlands, to become the focal points of national economies. The transition to an industrial mode of export production, and advances in transport and telecommunications technology, have resulted in the gateways becoming both the main production, wholesaling, insurance and financial centres, and multimodal entry or exit points and distribution centres (that is, a collection of hubs) through which goods, people and information move beyond local and regional markets. The articulation and regulation of these flows is the prime function performed by the gateways (Rodrigue, 1996).

A recurrent dilemma for multinational manufacturing and retailing corporations is to determine which gateways to incorporate into their supply chains. Within the Asian-Pacific Rim, Singapore, Hong Kong, Shanghai and Tokyo are already numbered among the world's leading gateways together with Bangkok, Beijing and Jakarta (Chapter 5). Their elevated status has prompted governments to engage in 'place marketing' to promote the claims of other gateway locations (Kotler et al., 2002). While recognizing China's lower labour and production costs, Japan, for example, seeks to advance the claims of Kansai economic subregion based on the quality of Osaka-Kobe-Kyoto's transport and logistics infrastructure that is deemed superior to that of Hong Kong, Singapore and South Korea (Takeda, 2008; Ernst & Young and JETRO, 2009). As these claims on the relative merits of gateways are couched in the most general terms, a more rigorous approach is required.

Examining centres in terms of the importance of their container shipping, air cargo, air passenger and Internet connections reveals the relative importance of gateways in the Asian-Pacific Rim (Ohashi et al., 2005). Representation in the top 50 world rankings of these four modes (Table 6.2) is used as the basis for determining 'regional gateways' (that is, compared with the top 25 employed in the analysis of 'world gateways' in Chapter 5).

As they are represented across all four modes, this analysis identifies Shanghai, Singapore, Hong Kong, Beijing, Tokyo and Kuala Lumpur as the prime regional gateways (Figure 6.5). Centres with only two or three modes – Bangkok, Manila, Seoul, Jakarta, Taipei and Osaka – are considered to be regional proto-gateways. Those centres with only a single mode are regarded as hubs: the port cities of Busan, Qingdao, Kaohsiung, Xiamen, Dalian, Ho Chi Minh City, Lianyungang, Yingkou, Surabaya and Nagoya; and the sole airport city representative of Chengdu, an inland centre intent on becoming an aerotropolis (see Chapter 4).

Table 6.2 *Asian-Pacific Rim gateways, proto-gateways, port and air hubs, 2010*

	Modes							
	Container shipping		Air cargo		Air passenger		Internet	
	Rank	Mill. TEUS	Rank	Mill. kg	Rank	Mill. Pax	Rank	Gbps
GATEWAYS								
Shanghai	1	29.1	3	3.2	20	40.6	49	288
Ningbo	6	13.1	–	–	–	–	–	–
Shanghai (SHA)	–	–	39	0.5	41	31.3	–	–
Subtotal		*42.2*		*3.7*		*71.9*		*288*
Singapore	2	28.4	11	1.8	18	42.0	21	830
Tanjung Pelepas	17	6.5	–	–	–	–	–	–
Subtotal		*34.9*		*1.8*		*42.0*		*830*
Hong Kong	3	23.5	1	4.2	11	50.3	20	885
Shenzhen	4	22.5	25	0.8	50	26.7	–	–
Guangzhou	7	12.6	21	1.1	19	41.0	–	–
Subtotal		*58.2*		*6.1*		*118.0*		*885*
Beijing	–	–	15	1.6	2	74.0	38	475
Tianjin	11	10.1	–	–	–	–	–	–
Subtotal		*10.1*		1.6		*74.0*		*475*
Kuala Lumpur	–	–	28	0.7	31	34.1	46	308
Port Kelang	13	8.9	–	–	–	–	–	–
Subtotal		*8.9*		*0.7*		*34.1*		*308*
Tokyo	25	4.3	9	2.2	32	33.8	14	1306
Yokohama	36	3.3	–	–	–	–	–	–
Tokyo (HND)	–	–	24	0.8	5	64.2	–	–
Subtotal		*7.6*		*3.0*		*98.0*		*1306*
PROTO-GATEWAYS								
Bangkok	–	–	20	1.3	17	42.8	–	–
Laem Chabang	22	5.2	–	–	–	–	–	–
Subtotal		*5.2*		*1.3*		*42.8*		
Manila	37	3.3	49	0.4	49	27.1	–	–
Seoul	–	–	4	2.7	33	33.6	41	394
Jakarta	25	4.7	38	0.5	16	44.4	–	
Taipei	–	–	13	1.8	–	–	36	510
Osaka			26	0.7	–	–	–	–
Kobe	47	2.6	–	–	–	–	–	–
Subtotal		*2.6*		*0.7*		–		–

Table 6.2 (continued)

	Modes							
	Container shipping		Air cargo		Air passenger		Internet	
	Rank	Mill. TEUS	Rank	Mill kg	Rank	Mill. Pax	Rank	Gbps
HUBS								
Busan	5	14.2	–	–	–	–	–	–
Qingdao	8	12.0	–	–	–	–	–	–
Kaohsiung	12	8.6	–	–	–	–	–	–
Xiamen	19	5.8	–	–	–	–	–	–
Dalian	21	5.2	–	–	–	–	–	–
Ho Chi Minh City	38	4.4	–	–	–	–	–	–
Lianyungang	29	3.9	–	–	–	–	–	–
Yingkou	35	3.3	–	–	–	–	–	–
Surabaya	38	3.0	–	–	–	–	–	–
Nagoya	45	2.5	–	–	–	–	–	–
Chengdu	–	–	46	0.4	–	–	–	–

Note: TEU – twenty-foot equivalent units; Pax – passengers; Gbps – Gigabits per second of internet bandwidth connected across international borders to metropolitan areas.

Sources: CI (2013), ACI (2011), IATA (2011), TG (2011).

Results from this survey mesh closely with other rankings (Table 6.3). All gateways and proto-gateways, except for Osaka, are among 47 cities accorded 'alpha' status in the survey of 'The world according to GaWC' (the Globalization and World Cities Research Network), based on their advanced producer services (GaWC, 2011). Also, all appear among 65 cities in the Global Cities 2010 rankings based on 25 unspecified metrics by A.T. Kearney (ATK, 2011). Apart from Jakarta and Manila, that are excluded from the survey, together with Guangzhou and Shenzhen, all gateways and proto-gateways are ranked in the accessibility component of the Global Power City Index produced by the Mori Memorial Foundation (MMF, 2010) using data on 53 cities. These comparisons suggest that the method used for identifying logistics gateways has some validity, especially as it does not involve a predetermined number of cities, but permits promotion and relegation to and from the list. The most contentious issues derived from this comparison involve the world gateways of Bangkok and Jakarta being regarded as regional proto-gateways; the rise of Kuala Lumpur to

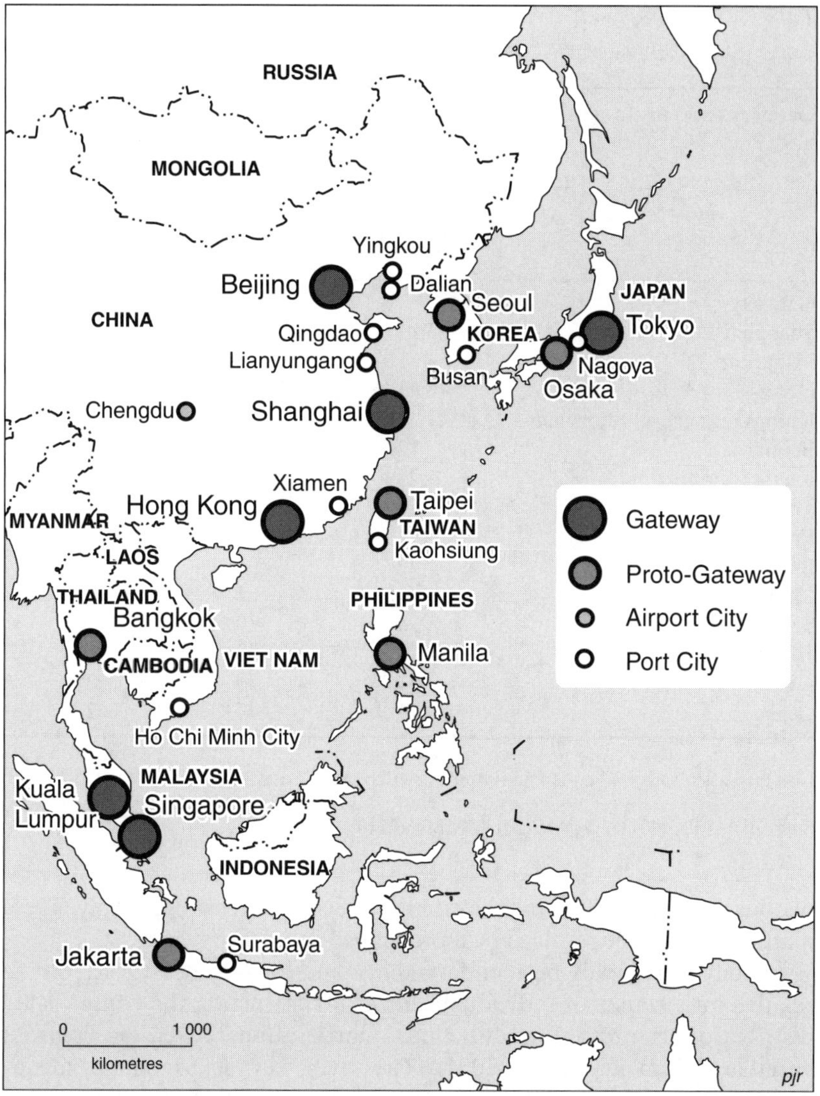

Source: Data from Table 6.2.

Figure 6.5 Gateways, proto-gateways, airport city and port cities in the Asian-Pacific Rim, 2010

Table 6.3 Comparative rankings of major Asian-Pacific Rim gateways and proto-gateways, 2010

Gateways and proto-gateways	Globalization and World Cities (GaWC)	Global Cities Index (GCI)	Global Power City Index (GPCI)
			Accessibility
	Rank	Rank	Rank
Gateway			
Shanghai	7	20	16
Singapore	5	8	4
Hong Kong-Guangzhou-Shenzhen	3/67/106	5/57/62	8/NS/NS
Beijing	12	15	18
Kuala Lumpur	23	48	21
Tokyo	6	3	6
Proto-Gateway			
Bangkok	42	36	27
Manila	54	51	NS
Seoul	24	10	10
Jakarta	26	53	NS
Taipei	43	39	29
Osaka	111	47	22

Note: GaWC also ranked Ho Chi Minh City (70); NS – not selected.

Sources: ATK (2011), GaWC (2011), MMF (2010).

regional gateway status; and the ranking of Seoul as a proto-gateway. These matters can only be resolved by more refined comparative analyses.

A study has already been undertaken, albeit for Northeast Asia, on the relative importance of individual centres for attracting the consolidated distribution centres of multinational corporations based on logistics variables (Oum and Park, 2004). The seven key determinants, identified by questioning the chief executive officers (CEOs) of multinational manufacturing and retailing corporations, were, in order of importance, market size, geo-location, transport facilities, political stability, skilled labour, logistics providers and flexible government. On six of the seven determinants, Japan and Korea ranked ahead of China; market size was the only attribute favouring China. Nevertheless the strength of this single determinant was sufficient for Shanghai to be ranked well ahead of Seoul–Incheon and Tokyo–Yokohama, followed by Osaka–Kobe,

Beijing–Tianjin, Taipei and Busan–Gwangyang Bay; Hong Kong was not included in this particular study.

Rather than repeat this exercise cataloguing the advantages and disadvantages of individual centres for multinational manufacturers and retailers based on logistics variables, in this chapter attention is focused on a series of case studies of gateways and their subregional economies and leading corporations. First, there is an examination of Singapore, Hong Kong, Taipei and Shanghai to explore the nature of inter-gateway competition in logistics. Secondly, there is a study of Tokyo to examine the neglected topic of intra-gateway logistics. Once these tasks are completed, the corridors designed to integrate the gateways into a seamless Asian-Pacific Rim logistics network can be examined.

INTER-GATEWAY COMPETITION

As discussion of inter-gateway competition involving Hong Kong, Taipei and Shanghai invariably draws upon a comparison with Singapore's logistics policies and institutions, there is a need to examine all gateways. Initially, each of the four gateways are considered in turn: Singapore to illustrate the strengths, weaknesses, opportunities and threats to its gateway status; Hong Kong to demonstrate the transformation of a port city into a regional gateway functioning as an intermediary for China; Taipei to exemplify the loss of regional gateway status; and Shanghai to represent the rise of a new gateway to regional prominence. Then an assessment is made of the impact of inter-gateway competition on the four centres and their subregional economies.

Singapore/Sijori

Singapore and its wider footprint cover Johor in Malaysia and the Riau Islands in Indonesia, and are collectively referred to as 'Sijori' (Figure 6.6). The Republic's Government has been seeking to consolidate Singapore's position as an integrated logistics gateway by subjecting its organizational and development capabilities to a rigorous assessment by the Working Group on Logistics (WGL, 2002). This review was undertaken by analysing strengths, weaknesses, opportunities and threats (SWOT). In this SWOT analysis strengths and weaknesses involve internal organizational issues, and opportunities and threats relate to changes in Singapore's environment.

Strengths stem from Singapore's world-class physical infrastructure embodied in Pasir Panjang seaport operated by PSA International Pte

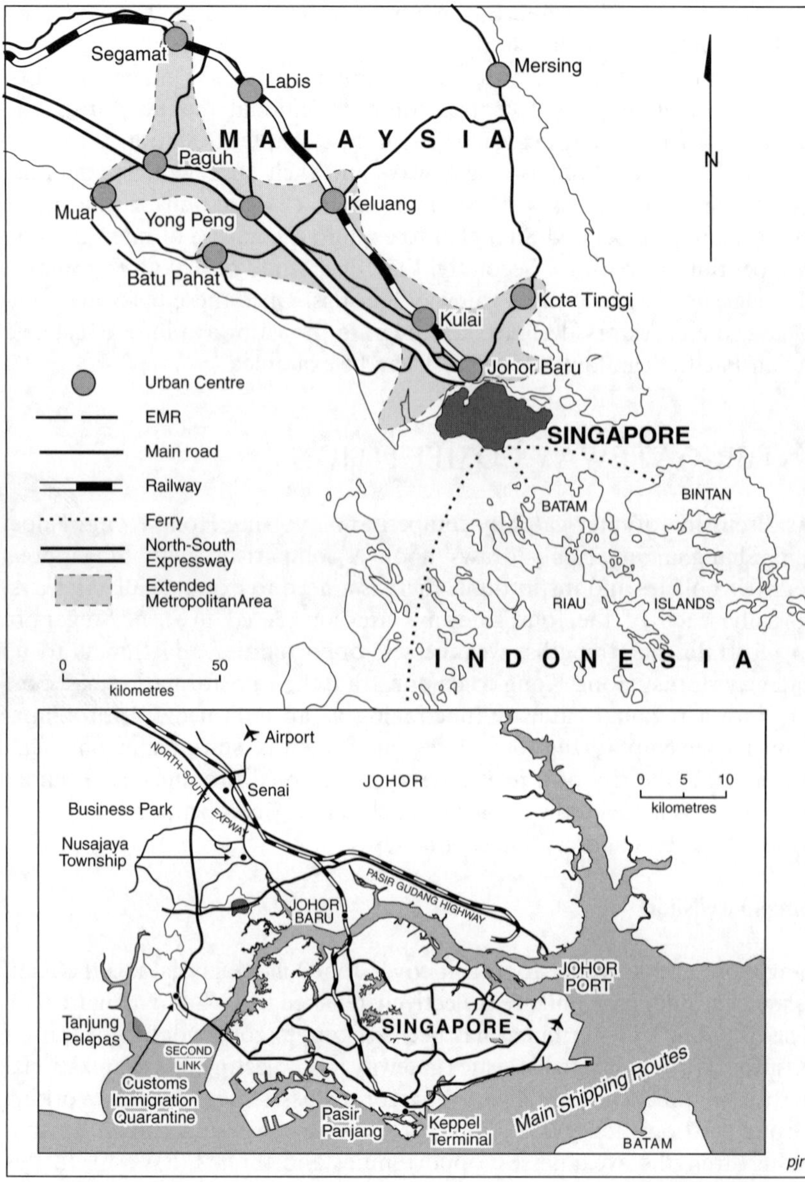

Source: Based on Rimmer and Dick (2009, 66).

Figure 6.6 Singapore, 2010

Ltd, and Changi International Airport and its associated Air Logistics Park; good connectivity to trading hubs and manufacturing bases (by air and sea) enabling it to be a pivotal transhipment centre; the location of major shippers and logistics service providers with regional headquarters and offices; stable political, economic and social conditions; an educated workforce; a strong legal system and business-friendly taxation structure; and a proactive government engaged in opening doors for businesses through bilateral and multilateral initiatives (for example, free trade agreements).

Weaknesses arise from relatively higher operational costs (especially land rental and wages) compared with neighbouring areas; a small geographic space and domestic market; a fragmented industrial base that lacks scale, and few local logistics players possessing global aspirations; some missing elements necessary to form a logistics cluster; lack of responsiveness to customers' needs; a shortage of skilled, experienced and entrepreneurial logistics professionals; and inadequate technological capabilities to carry out a wide range of supply chain management activities.

Opportunities result from the strong growth potential for logistics outsourcing in Asia (estimated by the Working Group on Logistics at US$80 billion in 2012); specialized logistics capabilities dovetailing with other sector expansion plans (for example biomedicals and chemicals); the ability to leverage on Singapore's good connectivity within the Asian-Pacific Rim to provide high value-added supply chain management services, to tap offshore trade conducted by Singapore-based trading companies (estimated at US$120 billion in 2012), and to establish a reputation as a secure logistics hub.

Threats are posed by the relocation of manufacturing and distribution bases to China; and increasing regional competition as other governments such as Malaysia and Thailand seek to transform their hubs into gateways. There are also advances in technology, notably the increase in size of ocean liners and jetliners, which may result in vessel and aircraft operators bypassing Singapore should a trade route become too thin.

With the rise of competition, particularly from Malaysia's Port of Tanjung Pelepas and Senai International Airport, the review suggests that the Singapore Government responds to the SWOT analysis by reinforcing its position as a global integrated hub (Figure 6.7). The three key enablers of this vision are: political, economic and regulatory stability; excellent physical, information and financial infrastructure; and a critical mass of logistics professionals to underpin the maritime, land transport and aviation pillars, plus integrators and supply chain management capabilities and technologies over which a global integrated hub can be built.

Before this vision can be realized, impediments to business have to

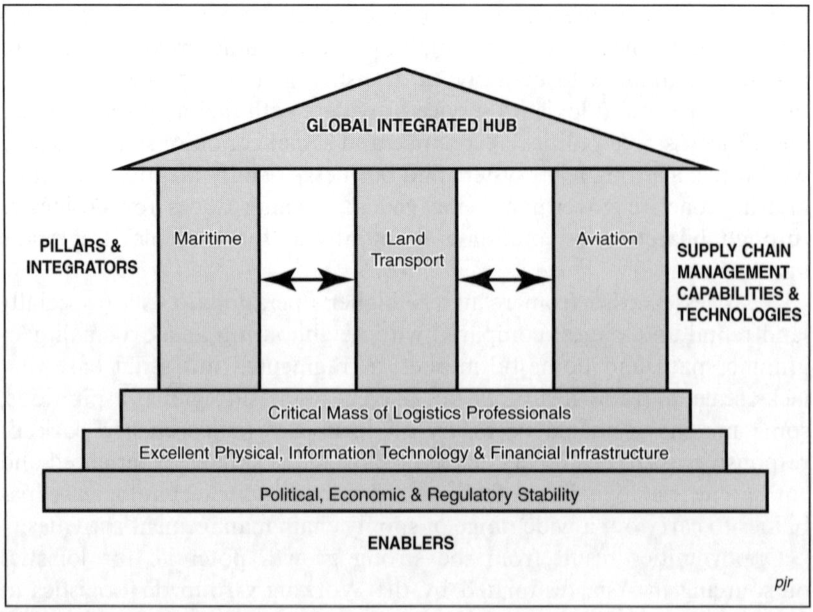

Source: WGL (2002, 5).

Figure 6.7 Singapore's vision of a global integrated hub

be removed. There is an urgent need to manage costs when they are not matched by productivity increases. Propositions designed to bring about these increases include the removal of trade declaration charges; the extension of concessions on seaport dues to all vessels; and a reduction in land premiums and tenure for logistics operations. Extending the free trade zone within company premises and offering greater flexibility to employ foreign workers are suggested measures that could abate policy hindrances.

As, in time, all rivals can match the excellence of its physical infrastructure, Singapore needs additional sources of growth. Thus a major focus is on sourcing knowledge-intensive supply chain management and supporting value-added services for Singapore's broader hinterland in Johor and Riau. The rapid evolution of transport and logistics is such that the highest value is attained not only from moving cargo but also from controlling and optimizing flow of the cargo through information management.

Within a seven-hour flight radius of Singapore, transport and logistics companies can tap 2.8 billion people. This area covers China, India, Viet Nam, Thailand, Australia and Japan, and each market requires a different strategy. Within this hinterland Singapore can function as a virtual logistics hub with knowledge and skills to control information processing, and payments from flows of supply chains that cut across region.

The Working Group's prime recommendation is that the gateway should be recast as the 'brain centre' controlling logistics limbs – the control and planning functions – beyond Singapore. Recommended developments include: (1) a London-Plus (Maritime) Development Framework; (2) information technology to underpin a Logistics Service Centre to attract and root the headquarters of multinational industrial corporations, particularly those engaged in information technology; (3) a supply chain management Nerve Centre for Innovation in sourcing and procurement, supply chain optimization, data hosting and reverse logistics; (4) a secured gateway; and (5) multimodal connectivity by integrating physical and information technology infrastructure (for example Port-Net and Spectrum).

A champion agency is also recommended so that a competitive tax regime can be introduced and the capability to compete in multinational supply chains upgraded. No less than nine government departments have been involved in logistics. This overlapping structure can be replaced by a single agency with the mandate, clout, resources and deliverables to make and coordinate difficult decisions. Such an agency would have strategic and tactical, marketing and promotional, developmental and operational roles.

In 2003 the Maritime and Port Authority was appointed as the champion agency to establish Singapore's international maritime centre to attract the regional bases of international shipping companies and logistics enterprises and boost professional business education in the Republic through its Maritime Cluster fund. By 2013 Singapore had plans for an expanded airport to strengthen its hub position and a consolidated container port capable of handling 65 million twenty-foot equivalent units (TEUs) (Yew, 2013). Also Infocomm Development Authority Singapore and the Civil Aviation Authority of Singapore were nominated as champion agencies for e-freight and tasked with generating paperless air cargo and logistics solutions that boost productivity across the supply chain. These decisions are part of Singapore's Economic Development Board's broader programme of providing incentives to attract major original equipment manufacturers (OEMs) to the Republic as a regional base for overseeing their supply chain operations.

Flextronics International Ltd's Singapore headquarters, for instance, commands an extensive multinational design, manufacturing and logistics network spread across the world's major electronics markets to service OEMs (for example Alcatel-Lucent, Apple, Cisco, Huawei Technologies and Lenovo). Engaged in the provision of electronics manufacturing services, Flextronics, with net sales of US$23.6 billion in 2013, has strengthened its regional and local sourcing base by having 200 000 professionals located in 30 countries in the Americas, Asia and Europe (Flextronics, 2013). The company has used this massive physical infrastructure as the base of a 'platform' on which it has: (1) imposed its logistics services to build a suite of end-to-end supply chain solutions to create new value for customers; and (2) superimposed a real-time information layer to provide improved visibility, risk management and execution to keep pace with shortening production cycle from one week to less than one day (for example to build Microsoft's Xbox videos).

Offering scale, scope and speed, this platform mirrors Singapore's ambition to become a control tower for virtual supply chains. Marked by the absence of factories and advanced cloud tools and apps, Singapore seeks to mimic the Flextronics control tower, which is designed to reduce cost, increase velocity and lower risk, so that the Republic can become the preferred logistics and supply chain management gateway for leading multinational manufacturers across the electronics, chemical and biomedical sectors. As highlighted by Rodney King (2008), this strategy means that Singapore has to lure foreign talent, and retain and, if possible, increase the number of multinationals, against competition not only from Kuala Lumpur but also Hong Kong, Taipei and Shanghai.

Hong Kong/Pearl River Delta

Hong Kong's position as a key international logistics and supply chain base within the Asian-Pacific Rim arose, like Singapore, from its strategic location. This geographical advantage was capitalized upon during the British colonial regime through its free port status, open and transparent regulatory regime, low and simple tax system, free flow of capital and information, efficient customs and world-class infrastructure. Once Hong Kong became an integral part of China's Pearl River Delta, the Special Administrative Region's (SAR) position as a major port city for Mainland China was confirmed with improved access being provided by road, high-speed rail, air and water to major cities in the world's most populous consumer market and largest manufacturing centre. Mainland China was also Hong Kong's largest trading partner and flows of capital and trade had developed local skills and experience in handling projects within Greater China (including Macau and Taiwan). Being the world's top-ranked international air cargo handling centre, third-busiest container port, and a leading cyber-port, coupled with its status as a premier regional financial centre, enhanced Hong Kong's trading efficiency.

The Colonial Government afforded only limited resources to the logistics industry during the 1990s and Hong Kong was in danger of being marooned as a 'port city'. This situation was aggravated when the handover of Hong Kong to China in 1997 coincided with the Asian Financial Crisis (1997–98) and the outbreak of SARS (Severe Acute Respiratory Syndrome). Also the business community anticipated a negative fallout from China's admission to the World Trade Organization in 2001, which was expected to lead to intensified competition for producer services from Guangzhou in the Pearl River Delta. In response the Hong Kong Government identified logistics as one of the main pillars of its revamped economy. This led to the establishment of the Hong Kong Logistics Council as part of a concerted effort to transform Hong Kong from a port city into a multilayered gateway. The Council collaborated with the logistics sector to facilitate this transformation by complementing Hong Kong's port activities with airfreight operations as the Special Administrative Region was within five hours flying time of half the world's population.

Since 1995 Hong Kong International Airport (HKIA) has been the world's top-ranked international air cargo hub with Hong Kong Air Cargo Terminal Limited (HACTL) handling the largest share of its freight. Rather than seek to compete on cost, HACTL has sought to boost efficiency and time reduction throughout the Asian-Pacific Rim. In pursuing this goal much emphasis has been placed on practising 'quality betterment', by establishing benchmarks for land-side services, import cargo breakdown, mishandling rates, and availability rates for the information technology (IT) and industrial automation systems. Quality betterment has been pursued through innovations, including height-checking sensors, the provision of weighing scales at the forwarders' warehouse, and canopies. These initiatives have enabled HACTL to offer a total logistics solution with four interconnected features: better cost control, operational efficiency, seamless connectivity and customized services. Although air cargo accounted for only 1.3 per cent of Hong Kong's total cargo tonnage in 2011, it was an indispensible component of the local economy because it accounted for almost 36 per cent of the total value of Hong Kong's external trade (HKIA, 2012). On an average day 10 800 tonnes of cargo move through HKIA, together with 148 000 passengers and 1000 flights by over 100 airlines to and from 170 cities, including 49 within Mainland China.

Hong Kong's instant appeal in moving from port city to a multilayered gateway lies in its superior transport and communications connectivity with China (Figure 6.8). Goods flow efficiently to and from southern China through Hong Kong to the rest of the world. Services accounted for almost 90 per cent of Hong Kong's gross domestic product (GDP), with trading and logistics being responsible for 26 per cent in 2007, compared

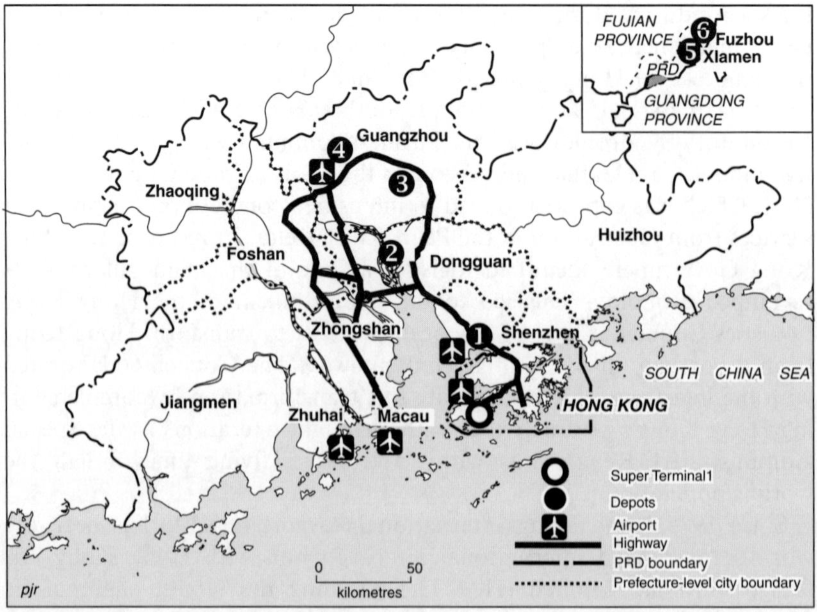

Note: Hong Kong Air Cargo Terminal Ltd (HACTL) operates the super-terminal with a handling capacity of 2.6 million tonnes per year. A wholly owned subsidiary, Hong Kong Air Cargo Industry Services Ltd (HACIS), operates SuperLink China Direct Services, which connects: 1. Shenzhen Airport (SZX); 2. Humen Airport, Dongguan (DGM); 3.Guangzhou Free Trade Zone (ZMY); 4. Guangzhou Airport (CAN); 5. Xiamen Airport (XMN); and 6 Fuzhou Airport (FOC).

Source: Data from HACIS (2012).

Figure 6.8 Super-terminal and inland cargo depots in Southern China, 2010

with 20 per cent for financial services, 11 per cent for professional and other producer services, and 3 per cent for tourism (Wang and Cheng, 2010).

Enhancing Hong Kong's appeal has been its proximity to the Pearl River Delta, which has been a main driver of Mainland China's economic and modernization programme since 1978. Hong Kong's role as a financial and business services provider for the Pearl River's mega-metropolitan region has benefitted from the Delta becoming a dynamic production centre, accounting for two-fifths of China's exports and over one-tenth of its GDP in 2010 (LFRC, 2011a). Besides being a base for the production of electronics and electrical appliances, the Pearl River Delta Region, including Hong Kong and Macau, has a market of 50 million consumers.

Of particular benefit to Hong Kong's logistics services has been the Closer Economic Partnership Agreement (CEPA), a free-trade pact with Mainland China signed in 2003. Apart from a specific reference to liberalizing logistics services, the pact has led to a zero tariff on imported goods from Hong Kong, including food and beverages, textiles and clothing, plastics and plastic articles, pharmaceuticals and chemicals. In 2004 there was a new initiative with the potential to create a larger regional economy in South China – the Pan-Pearl River Delta (or '9+2' cooperation), which comprised nine southern provinces of Mainland China and Special Administrative Regions of Hong Kong and Macau. New highways and railways were built to break down barriers and develop an integrated regional economy of 450 million people. This project had the capacity to expand Hong Kong's catchment area into the Middle and Upper Yangtze. In 2005 the Digital Trade and Transportation Network System complemented this policy, promoting e-logistics and providing a unified electronic platform for seamless and efficient information exchange. Then in May 2009 the CEPA Supplement VI was signed, which further opened up Mainland China to Hong Kong providers of freight forwarding, storage, distribution and rail transport services to counteract the impact of the Global Financial Crisis (2008–09).

Since then Hong Kong's infrastructure has been enhanced by Lantau Logistics Park, which was located strategically between Hong Kong International Airport and the container terminals. A fifth border crossing was added to expand Hong Kong's catchment area and collaboration with the adjacent city of Shenzhen. In 2010 an agreement with Guangdong Province envisaged the further expansion of this catchment area with a Hong Kong link to the Shenzhen–Guangzhou high-speed railway in 2014 and the completion of the 50 km Hong Kong–Zhuhai–Macau Bridge by 2016 (Hou and Li, 2011; Cheung, 2013). Designed to confirm Hong Kong's role as the Delta's leading gateway, these infrastructural investments, coupled with further airport expansion, need to be complemented by the development of warehousing activities and third-party logistics providers offering door-to-door and desk-to-desk higher-value services.

Li and Fung Ltd is one of Hong Kong's largest third-party logistics providers with both a local presence and a global reach. Originally founded in 1906 by To-ming Li and Pak-liu Fung as a trading company in Canton (Guangzhou), the company moved its headquarters to Hong Kong during the 1930s. In 1949 it became an exporter. Since 1979 the company has diversified its activities not only into retailing and marketing but also into third-party logistics. Li & Fung Ltd has become heavily involved in the supply chain management of high-volume, time-sensitive consumer goods such as high-fashion apparel, footwear and home textiles. These value-added logistics activities, involving 12000 partners in the supply chain, extended outwards from Hong Kong to multinational retailers in North America, Europe and Oceania and backwards to sourcing markets in the Asian-Pacific Rim, especially Mainland China. The company's core competency involves: sourcing raw material and components; finding the right locations for the labour intensive assembly; developing practical solutions for quick-response manufacturing; and making private label and branded products shop-ready at the factory level (Feng, 2007; Fung et al., 2008). The company's location in Hong Kong underlines that the Special Administrative Region possesses an advantage in the provision of logistics services over rival sites in the Asian-Pacific Rim. Yet, unlike Li & Fung, most value-added logistics companies in Hong Kong remain small and reminiscent of those serving the local logistics market in Taipei.

Taipei/Taiwan

Since the mid-1990s Taipei's position as a major global gateway has been incorporated in the Republic of China (ROC) government's strategy to develop the island of Taiwan as an Asia-Pacific Regional Operations Centre (APROC) to capitalize on its location between Northeast and Southeast Asia (Figure 6.9). The Centre's policy objectives have been to: liberalize the island's economy and promote internationalization; strengthen the flow of goods; and attract investment by multinational and domestic enterprises (Desevedavy and Thien-Ah-Koon, 2003). This strategy hinged on developing six operational centres for manufacturing, sea transport, air transport, finance, telecommunications and the media (Ho, 2003). Much effort has been focused on seaport and airport developments aimed at upgrading logistics capability. Special emphasis was placed on Taiwan's lower average sailing and flying times to Asian-Pacific locations compared with Hong Kong and Shanghai.

As the 1990s passed without direct shipping and aviation routes to Mainland China, there was much scepticism among multinational industrial corporations that wanted the liberalization of cross-strait trade to process unfinished goods. This lack of direct links resulted in the migration of many of these corporations to Mainland China, particularly those reliant on container shipping rather than those dependent on express air cargo services.

In 1997 offshore shipping centres were established, which allowed five Chinese and five Taiwanese companies to participate legally in cross-strait trade. By 2001 sea and air transhipments of goods were permitted from the offshore centres, but the full implementation of these free port initiatives at the Kaohsiung and Keelung seaports and Taipei's Chiang

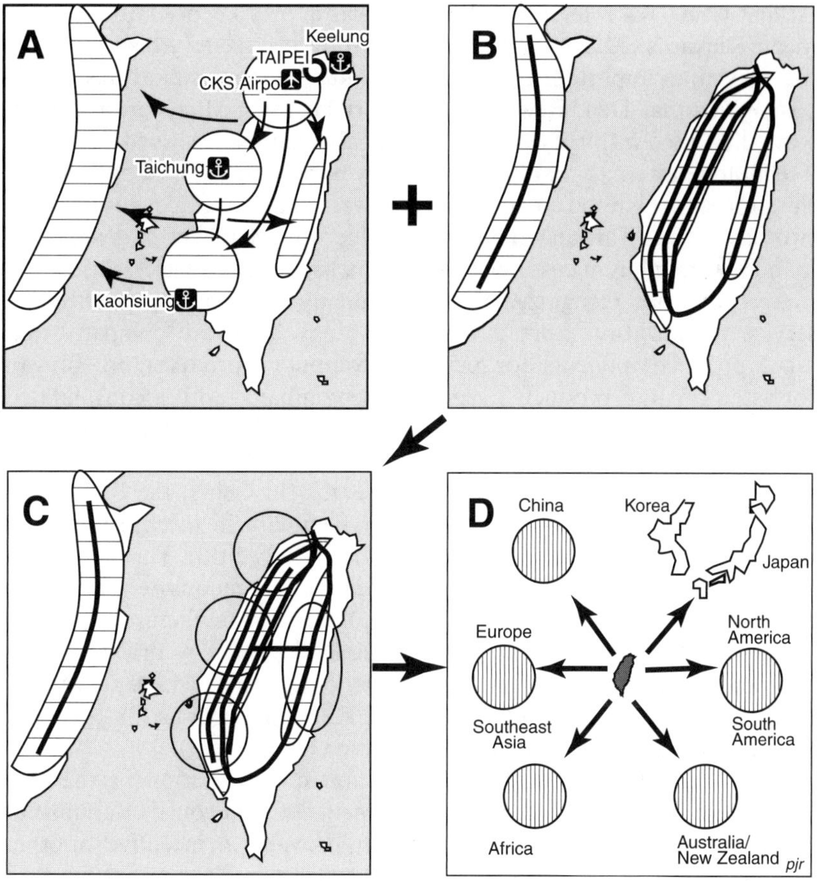

Source: Rimmer (1996b).

Figure 6.9 Plans for revitalizing Taiwan's spatial structure: (A) regions; (B) transport axes; (C) five regions and five transport axes; and (D) regional operating centre

Kai Shek (CKS) International Airport were delayed. By the time the port of Kaohsiung was semi-privatized in 2006 to offer cheaper port facilities than Hong Kong, much of the transhipment trade had already migrated to ports in Mainland China (Rickards, 2012a). Therefore Kaohsiung's revival hinged on foreign carriers being allowed to enter the cross-strait routes, but China has regarded this trade as being domestic.

In 2008 direct flights were permitted between Taiwan and the Mainland.

At that time CKS International Airport was in pressing need of refurbishment (Rickards, 2012b). With additional runways, the refurbished airport has played an important role as a high-value international express cargo base, given that Dell, Hewlett-Packard, IBM, Intel, Microsoft and Sony were all located within its vicinity. Orders, for example, received by Synnex Technology International Corporation by noon were fulfilled by 6.30 pm; this process drew upon components that were in the inventory for less than two days. Thus Taiwan's competitive edge was no longer in generalized manufacturing but in customized software, hardware and accessories.

Acer Inc. has recognized this situation by switching to a consumer service organization from a high-technology hardware company that air-shipped components for personal computers produced in Taiwan for assembly into products overseas. The company, with a consolidated revenue of US$14.8 billion, has disintegrated its vertical supply chain by shifting into branding and marketing and outsourcing final products to multiple contract manufacturers for assembly in China, the Philippines and the Netherlands to provide greater flexibility in inventory control than is possible under a single vendor policy (Acer, 2013). This horizontal supply chain model has enabled the company's headquarters in Taipei to direct goods flow from its original equipment manufacturers (OEMs) based largely in Chongqing within Mainland China by drawing upon information from its subsidiaries in its major markets of Europe, Middle East and Africa (38 per cent revenue in 2012), Pan America (28 per cent), Asia-Pacific (18 per cent) and Greater China (16 per cent).

In June 2010 the signing of the Economic Cooperation Framework Agreement (ECFA) between the governments of the People's Republic of China and the Republic of China (Taiwan) provided an incentive for other multinationals to follow Acer's lead and invest in Taipei as a gateway for Mainland China (LFRC, 2010a). By offering reciprocal tax concessions and open access to service sectors such as logistics, the Agreement promised to further boost two-way trade and investment (Brown et al., 2010). Provided Taiwan's acknowledged shortfall of high-level logistics professionals is resolved, it is possible that the original Asia-Pacific Regional Centre concept could be revitalized. Multinationals would be able to establish their innovation centres and multipurpose operational hubs in Taiwan's relatively high income per capita and trade-driven economy. Under this regime high-value-added research and development, involving design and branding, would be undertaken in Greater Taipei and low-value-added fabrication transferred to Mainland China before the Taiwan-based company reasserts control over the high-value-added area marketing of products, including distribution and sales and after-sales service, in other gateway centres (Figure 6.10). This tacit free trade

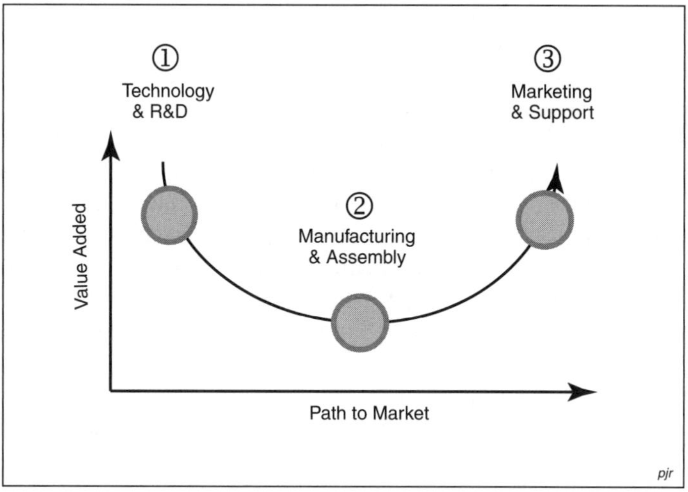

Note: Enunciated by Stan Shih, the founder of Acer Inc., for Taiwan, the curve demonstrates the opportunities to produce higher value added activities upstream (1) and downstream (3) of manufacturing and assembly (2). These higher value activities are attracted to gateway locations.

Sources: Weinberg (2010), Baldwin (2013).

Figure 6.10 The 'smile curve' showing progressive stages in evolution of the value chain

arrangement between Taiwan and China may weaken Hong Kong's re-export business with the Mainland, where Shanghai has been strengthening its overall position as an Asian-Pacific Rim gateway in its own right.

Shanghai/Yangtze River Delta

Shanghai and the Yangtze River Delta's return to prominence as an Asian-Pacific Rim gateway with the greatest gross regional domestic product stems from the Shanghai Municipality imbuing its logistics sector with sufficient competitive edge to challenge the status of Hong Kong, Taipei and Singapore. This has been made possible by the degree of autonomy afforded the Shanghai Municipality (equivalent to a province in status) by China's Central Government. During the 1990s the Municipality was protected from too much political interference in its expansion into the Pudong New Area on the east side of the Huangpu River by the rise of the former Shanghai Mayors Jiang Zemin and Zhu Rongji to power in the Central Government (Lam, 1999).

Since then the Municipal Government has used a combination of preferential policies, and coordinated planning and investment strategies to foster Shanghai's development as a gateway. Logistics companies have been given taxation concessions and priority in the use of land within industrial zones, while less advanced manufacturing industries and property developers have been encouraged to spread into the adjacent provinces of Jiangsu and Zhejiang. By 2005 added value from Shanghai's logistics sector was an estimated US$32 billion, representing 13 per cent of the Municipality's GDP and one-quarter of its service industry that complemented its six key industries: electronics, motor vehicles, petrochemicals, high-grade steel, machinery and biomedicine (Chin et al., 2007, 4; Liu et al., 2011). At the time Shanghai was already the world's number three container port and an air transport and digital hub, but most of its logistics companies were still small-scale operators.

Since the mid-2000s the Municipal Government has sought to develop an integrated logistics network linking inland waterway, rail and sea transport within the country's leading transhipment hub (CDC, 2006, 2007). Becoming the world's number one container port and an efficient international air cargo base, which interconnected the old and new airports, has attracted large state-owned and international logistics enterprises to Shanghai and strengthened the Municipality's standing. By 2009 its status led the Central Government to proclaim Shanghai as an international shipping and financial centre. In 2013 this ranking was reinforced by supplementing the logistics facilities at Pudong Airport Comprehensive Free Trade Zone, Waigaoqiao Free Trade Zone and Waigaoqiao Free Trade Logistics Park by the opening of the Yangshan Free Trade Port Area as the fourth component of Shanghai's Free Trade Zone (Figure 6.11). Although 18 service sectors are listed, foreign-owned transportation, warehousing and postal services are on the 'negative list' of activities precluded from the Zone (China Briefing, 2013).

Fast trains and motorways are being constructed to connect the components of the Shanghai Free Trade Zone to a productive hinterland with an urban population of over 80 million (NBSC, 2011). By 2020 planned motorway developments are expected to reduce travel time between Shanghai's logistics facilities and the inner Yangtze River Delta Region covering the Municipality and the entire provinces of Jiangsu and Zhejiang (Figure 6.12). The high-tech production centres of Wuxi, Suzhou and Jiaxing will be accessible from Shanghai's seaport and airport facilities in less than three hours; the outer region, encompassing the independent metropolitan regions of Nanjing and Hangzhou, in less than five hours; and the Delta's fringe areas in less than 12 hours. These

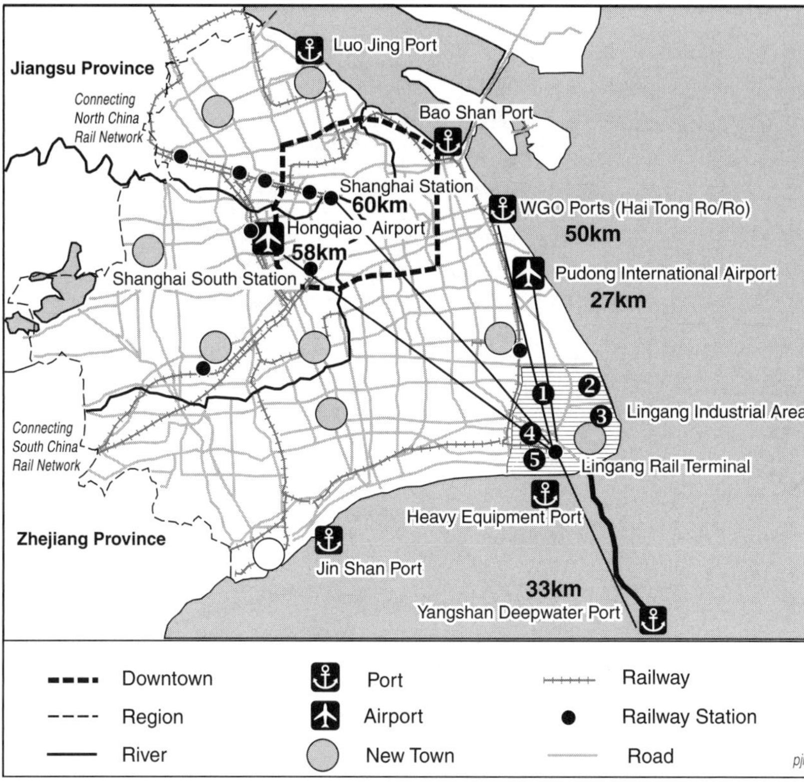

Note: Lingang Industrial Zone: (1) Central Logistics Zone; (2) Hi-Tech Park; Hi-Tech Industries and Training; (3) Harbor New City; (4) Logistics Park; and (5) Heavy Equipment Zone.

Source: Derived from maps in CIMEC (2006), Frost & Sullivan (2007).

Figure 6.11 Shanghai, 2010

infrastructure projects are designed to coordinate development within the mega-metropolitan area and underpin Shanghai's emergence as the Asian-Pacific Rim's premier logistics centre.

Summary

Considerable attention has been given to competition involving Singapore, Hong Kong and Taiwan fuelled by, and in response to, the rise of Shanghai and the Yangtze River Delta as a logistics centre. In this regard

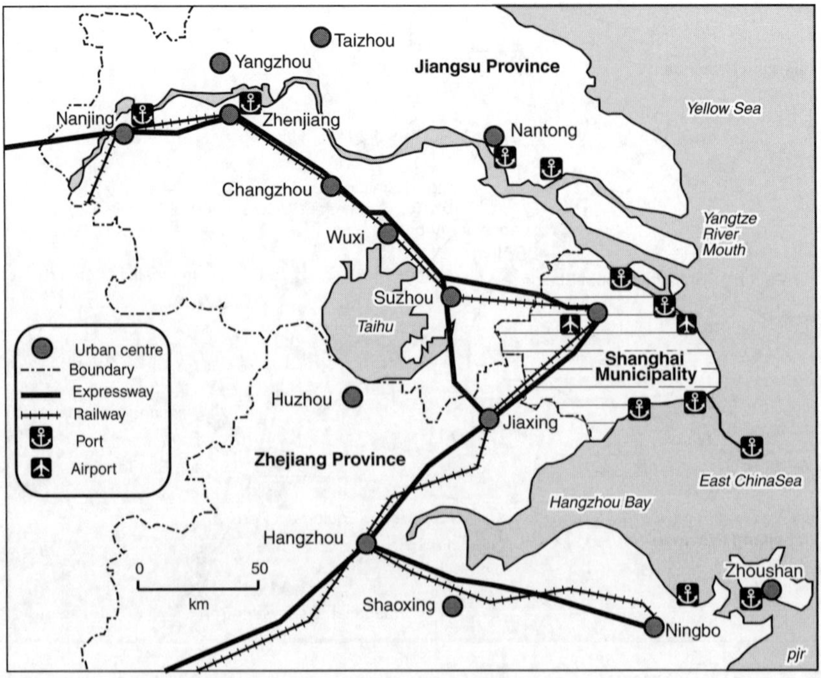

Sources: Compiled from various sources, including CDC (2006, 2007).

Figure 6.12 Shanghai's environs, 2010

Singapore's logistics policies and institutions, and effective ways of combining them to bring about more competitive outcomes, have been designed to counter global logistics corporations and multinational industrial corporations relocating their regional offices to Hong Kong or Shanghai to take advantage of the China market. In head-to-head competition Hong Kong's evolution from port city to multilayered gateway for the Asian-Pacific Rim, coupled with hosting a key third-party logistics provider, has enabled the Special Administrative Region to maintain an edge over Shanghai in logistics and supply chain management. Taiwan is seeking to resurrect its gateway position by promoting the new Taoyuan International Airport as an air cargo and passenger hub, and centre of an aerotropolis due for completion by 2030 (Yeh, 2013). Nevertheless Shanghai has significant advantages over its rivals such as lower operating costs in serving China's domestic market, which will be compounded by the establishment of its new free trade zone. Rather than accelerating the shift from volume-based transport services to higher-valued logistics services, the Hong Kong SAR Government and business community have sought to become more regionally focused in China to offset the threat of being marginalized by Shanghai. There is now an overlap between Hong Kong's logistics hinterland in southern China with Shanghai's hinterland in central China, raising the possibility of the ultimate stand-off between market-dominated and state-driven economies. Meanwhile Shanghai's rise to prominence in central China may end in revitalizing Taiwan's gateway status, because the distance from there to eastern China is shorter than that from Hong Kong. What is missing from these comparisons – other than a deeper consideration of Shanghai's transport connections within the Yangtze River Delta – is any discussion of the importance of intra-gateway logistics.

INTRA-GATEWAY LOGISTICS

Logistic activities within gateways are arguably one of the most critical challenges in the Asia-Pacific Rim due to public underinvestment in mega-metropolitan regions. This task of mobilizing resources from a broader local tax base derived from metropolitan wealth and incomes, coupled with selective borrowing for investment in large-scale infrastructure projects, to overcome the inefficiencies and bottlenecks hindering intra-gateway logistics, has been addressed in Japan, particularly in Tokyo.

Tokyo/Kanto

Tokyo and the wider Kanto subregion, with a population of over 40 million and one-fifth of Fortune Global 500 corporations, is Japan's principal logistics platform (Figure 6.13). Rather than rate Tokyo against other Asian-Pacific gateways, attention is focused on the platform's intra-gateway logistics. This task involves totally optimizing the logistics activities of private companies within the metropolitan area while also considering the traffic environment, traffic congestion and energy consumption.

Intra-gateway logistics in Kanto are heavily dependent upon truck transport that is concentrated within the Tokyo Metropolitan Government (TMG) area. About one-third of the area's daily truck traffic is accommodated on the 300 km expressway system. Nevertheless average rush hour speed is 21 km per hour and on-road parking occasions high congestion levels (TURBLOG, 2011a, 2011b). Other issues include air pollution from

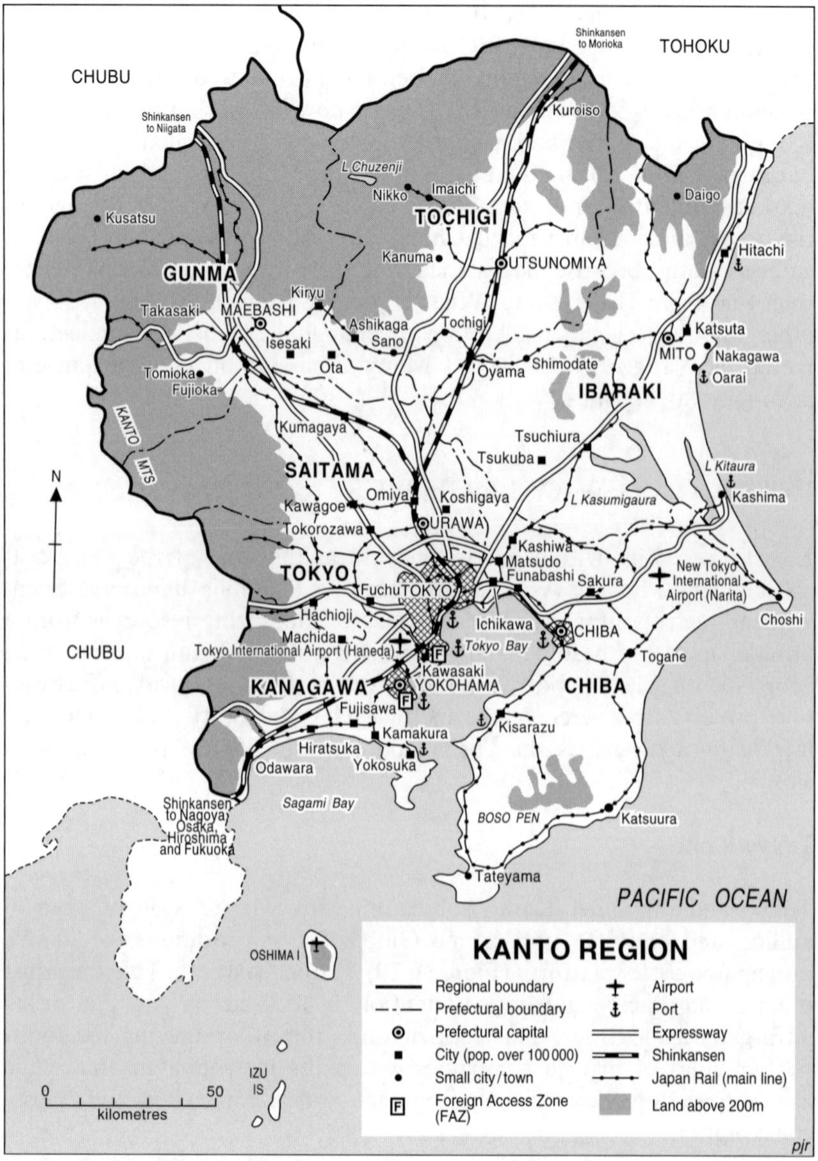

Figure 6.13 Greater Tokyo (Kanto), 2010

Table 6.4 Tokyo's comprehensive logistics vision, 2006

Initiative 1 Establishing Efficient Logistics Network

a. Eliminating bottlenecks in the network
b. Promoting road network development to support logistics
c. Use of cutting-edge technology to create new logistics infrastructure

Initiative 2 Reinforcing Logistics Functions for International Trade

a. Building up the capacity of the Tokyo port as an international trade base
b. Streamlining port operation
c. Dealing with increasing air cargo

Initiative 3 Promoting Development of Logistic Bases for the Tokyo Metropolitan Area

a. Updating functions of distribution estates
b. Creating high-performance logistics bases in the port area
c. Enhancing logistics function in the Tama area

Initiative 4 Promoting Logistics Projects for Local Revitalization

a. Increasing loading /unloading space
b. Supporting local projects toward efficient logistics, including joint delivery
c. Supporting small and medium business that contribute to efficient logistics

Initiative 5 Improving the Environment and Quality of Life in Urban Areas through Better Logistics

a. Reduce adverse effects on the environment through efficient use of networks and bases
b. Enhancing the appeal of Tokyo through smoother flow of large freight vehicles
c. Improving logistics for a safer and secure life

Source: TURBLOG (2011b, 24–7).

greenhouse gas and particle matter emissions, and lack of parking and loading and unloading places.

These issues prompted the Tokyo Urban Development Bureau (TUDB, 2006) to issue its Vision of Comprehensive Logistics (Table 6.4). This framework is designed to provide an efficient logistics network, reinforce logistics functions for international trade, develop logistics bases, promote logistics projects to revitalize local areas, and improve environmental quality. Since then progress has been made in streamlining local logistics plans, the mandatory inclusion of parking lots in buildings, joint delivery projects and environmental improvement measures. All diesel vehicles must comply with emission standards within Metropolitan Tokyo and cannot be over seven years in age. Reflecting Japan's pioneering role in intelligent transport system (ITS) innovations, most trucks use the electronic toll collect (ETC) system and draw upon the Vehicle Information and Communications System (VICS) that offers an advanced incident alert system. Besides providing a more conducive urban environment, other structural conditions include more stable and better skilled truck operators that stem from a regulated trucking industry in which all firms are required to have a minimum of five vehicles; and flexible land use and building standards enabling logistics terminals to be built within six months.

A high level of efficiency in the use of urban space is seen as a prerequisite in intra-gateway logistics. A number of indicators point to this standard being achieved in Greater Tokyo: 'side streets are calm and smooth; delivery trucks are clean and well ordered (multiple compartments, multiple temperatures)'; most office buildings incorporate loading bays; and multistorey logistics terminals are located close to commercial and residential areas (INRETS, 2009, 6). As exemplified by the downtown Parc Tokyo II warehouse of Prologis, a US firm, this multistorey facility, located close to the airport and seaports, is capable of accommodating 40 ft container trucks. Also the premises accommodate third-party logistics providers such as FedEx and DHL and provide a distribution centre for Estée Lauder's cosmetics. Thus Greater Tokyo's integrated metropolitan fabric may help explain why an urban economy, characterized by a unique service of home deliveries, provided by Yamato, Sagawa and Nippon Express and 24/7 convenience stores (*kombinis*) such as Seven-Eleven Japan Co. Ltd and its competitors Lawson Japan and Family Mart, has been sustainable, while they have been too costly elsewhere.

Seven-Eleven Japan Co. Ltd, a subsidiary of Seven & I Holdings Ltd, has 5100 convenience stores in Greater Tokyo, which act as outlets for 3000 processed food, liquor and magazine items, serve as local business-to-consumer (B2C) points and host automatic teller machines (SEJ, 2013). Averaging sales of US$8000 per day, these stores are replenished by distribution centres covering 50–60 stores within a defined area, which are responsible for inventory management in line with demand communicated through point-of-sales data that are analysed overnight. Fresh goods and cooked rice products are delivered up to four times daily in specially designed crates, and frozen products between three and seven times per week in insulated boxes. Over 3800 purpose-built vehicles are used within Tokyo to link distribution centres and stores. Their operation has been outsourced to a trucking company in a bid to reduce variable costs arising not only from fluctuations in fuel price, fleet maintenance and staff, but also from delays in making deliveries, as dedicated parking sites are rare.

Most pilot programmes sponsored by the national government for

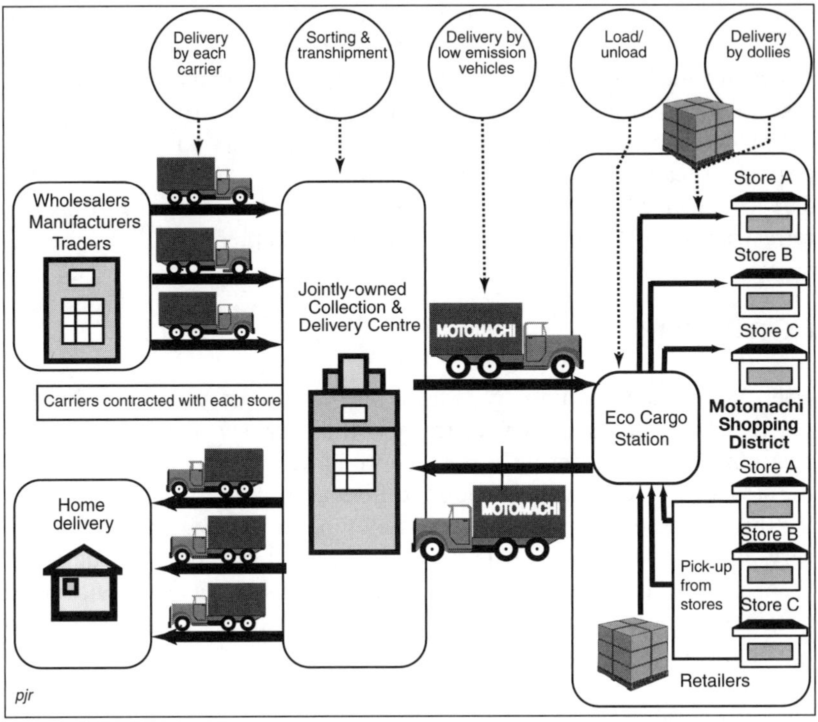

Source: INRETS (2009: 18).

Figure 6.14 Motomachi Shopping Street, Yokohama

enhancing mobility within Tokyo have focused upon these truck parking spaces, and on-street and off-street delivery areas. There has also been some experimentation with using public–private partnership to consolidate goods in Greater Tokyo. Yokohama's Motomachi District is among the nine pilot programmes (Figure 6.14). Goods from many logistics companies destined for the district are received at the logistics centre from which consolidated deliveries are made. It took seven years for this co-operative system to become operational and financially viable (INRETS, 2009; Dablanc, 2013). The system's sustainability hinges on attracting a requisite number of carriers; inexpensive delivery charges; the demand and profitability of the area's customers; and the excellence of the delivery staff and drivers.

The Japanese Government's logistics policy envisions Tokyo as an exemplar for improving the logistics environment in other Asian-Pacific Rim gateways, which have lagged behind best practice in Europe (BESTUFS, 2007). Any improvements in urban productivity from adopting Tokyo's policy would benefit the overseas operations of Japanese manufacturing and retailing corporations located in these gateways. This explains the prominence given in Japan's national planning to Tokyo's ports and airports, because the Global Power City Index 2010 (MMF, 2010) listed Tokyo's inner-city infrastructure as a strength, and international transport infrastructure as a pronounced weakness (see Chapter 7).

CORRIDORS

The Asian-Pacific Rim's gateways and proto-gateways are knitted together by a bundle of surface transport, air transport and telecommunications corridors offering access to both hinterland and hinterworld. As the structure of economic corridors differs according to what is moving, the three types of corridors are discussed separately, because they present very different spatial constructs for institutional collaboration designed to improve their performance and quality of logistics services. Once these differences are examined, the separate analyses can be drawn together to discuss the nature of economic space.

Surface Corridors

Maritime corridors link major channels to Europe, North America and Australasia and connect all gateways, proto-gateways and port cities within the archipelagic Asian-Pacific Rim from the Sea of Okhotsk to the Malacca Straits (Figure 6.15). Within the regional maritime transactional network, heavily reliant on short-distance container shipping and car ferry services, these centres have been developing industrial production complexes within their hinterlands. Fluvial corridors, provided naturally by the Mekong River, Pearl River and the Yangtze River, extend the reach of the region's maritime corridors (Rimmer and Comtois, 2009).

Asian-Pacific Rim economies have been dependent upon expanding their land transport corridors that straddle central transport arteries such as highways or railways between gateways, proto-gateways and port cities. Large areas have been scanned to identify corridors that offer the most direct connections between areas of high existing and projected demand.

A major issue concerning national governments has been that all modes – rail, road and water – have been developed in isolation from each other. There is often no common multimodal transport system that integrates at least two different modes into a door-to-door transport chain. As

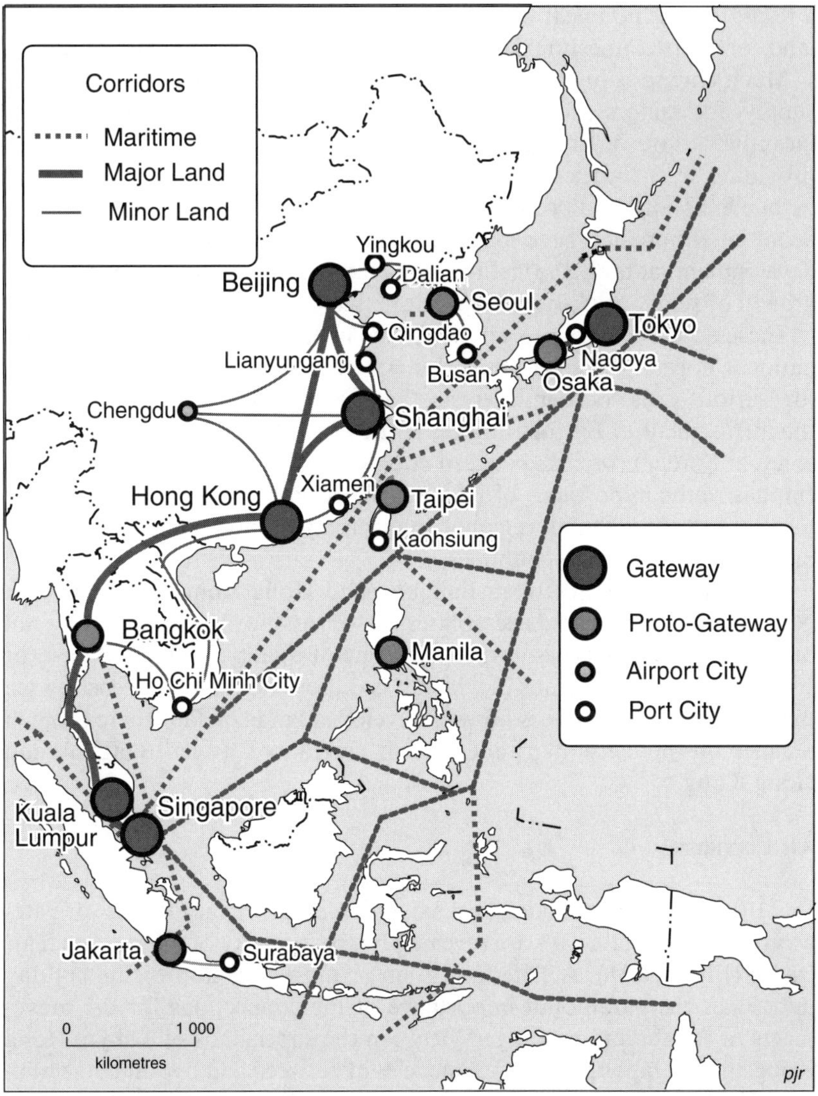

Figure 6.15 Asian-Pacific maritime corridors, and major and minor land corridors, connecting gateways, proto-gateways, air city and port cities, 2010

a result there is no linear orientation of freight and passenger flows along land corridors connecting gateways and proto-gateways to major markets.

Much emphasis in China, for example, has been directed at enhancing supply-side factors such as improving intermodal connections, offering incentives to move from road transport to higher-capacity railways and providing a well-articulated multimodal interchange system to lower carbon emissions and promote 'green logistics' (Kam and Rimmer, 2011). Scant attention has been paid to demand imperatives of multimodal development, notably the institutional factors that continue to nurture the growth of single-truck-owner operators (see Chapter 9).

These domestic concerns are heightened where corridors traverse international borders. Then the corridor becomes a binational trade channel for various cross-border interests that seek to develop or consolidate the infrastructure. By focusing on strategic nodes and special economic zones at border crossings between countries, these cross-border corridors emphasize the importance of bilateral plans, rather than multilateral initiatives, in strengthening regional connectivity and broadening economic opportunities between economies.

The land corridor between Bangkok and Hong Kong traversing Viet Nam, Laos and Thailand exemplifies these cross-border issues. Either rail or road does not exist; is suspect in terms of quality, speed and cost; or stretches across subregions in which it is difficult to match the cost by sea (see Chapter 7). As there is no well-developed land corridor there is much reliance on the dense maritime and air corridors between Bangkok and Hong Kong.

Air Corridors

In 2010 air corridors linking the Asian-Pacific's 'premier league' of gateways and proto-gateways are revealed by the intensity of international air traffic (Figure 6.16). A criterion of ten or more non-stop flights per day underlines the paramount importance of the connections for the movements of freight and passengers between the super-hubs of Tokyo, Hong Kong and Singapore. Lower frequencies of between and five and nine non-stop flights per day integrate the remaining gateways and proto-gateways into the regional air network.

Comparisons of the air network's structure are often made with various manifestations of regional development in Europe. On closer inspection there is no 'blue banana' stretching from Tokyo to Singapore. There is no 'bunch of grapes'. Also there is no 'pentagon' model. Instead, if a line was drawn around the perimeter of the network enclosing key gateways and proto-gateways the structure of a mango can be envisaged.

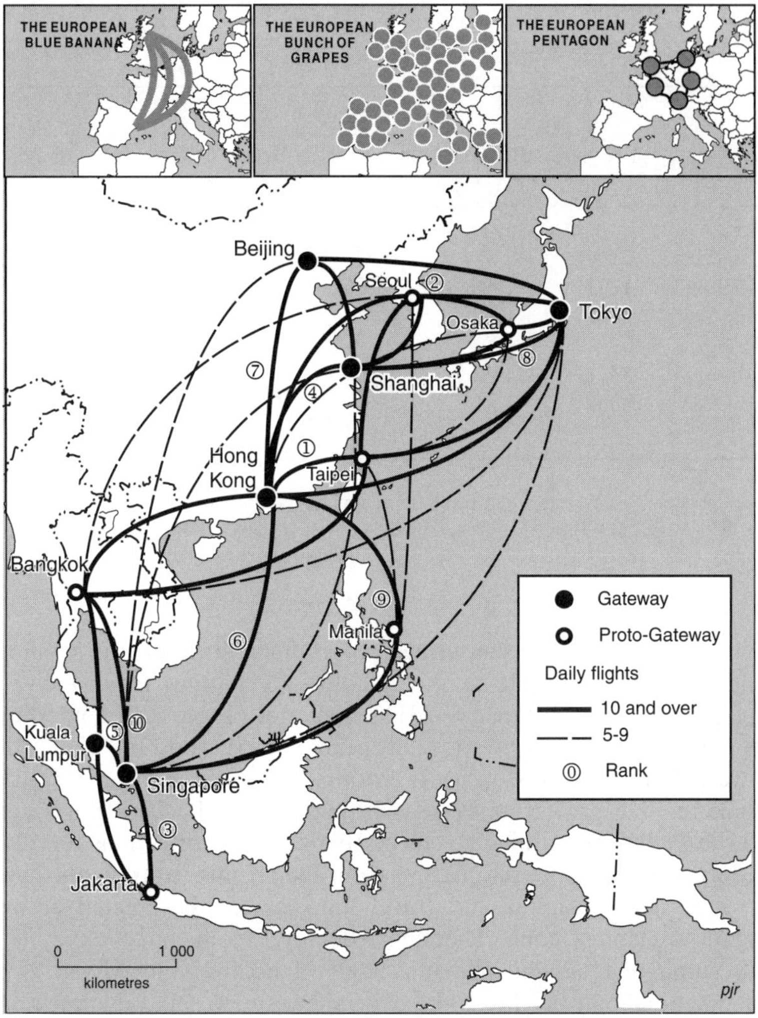

Note: The top ten connections are ranked in terms of the number of daily flights. The five-flights per day threshold excludes corridors linking the capitals of Hanoi (Viet Nam), Naypyidaw (Myanmar), Phnom Penh (Cambodia), Vientiane (Laos), Ulaan Bataar (Mongolia) and the second cities of Cebu (Philippines), Chiang Mai (Thailand), Penang (Malaysia) and Surabaya (Indonesia).

Source: Data from OAG (2010).

Figure 6.16 Asian-Pacific air corridors between gateways and proto-gateways, February 2010 with inset showing European spatial structures

Table 6.5 Distances and flight times between Asian-Pacific Rim gateway airports, 2010

	Time (minutes)					
	Tokyo	Beijing	Shanghai	Hong Kong	Singapore	Bangkok
Tokyo	–	157	133	216	396	344
Beijing	2104	–	81	147	332	245
Shanghai	1781	1089	–	90	281	214
Hong Kong	2891	1971	1208	–	192	128
Singapore	5311	4457	3769	2569	–	106
Bangkok	4608	3290	2867	1723	1416	–
			Distance (kms)			

Note: Assumes an average flight speed for commercial airliner of 500 mph, which is equivalent to 805 km/hr or 343 knots. Exact time may vary depending on wind speeds.

Source: Travelmath (2010).

Within this narrowly circumscribed geographical structure the maximum flight time between gateways is 6 hours 36 minutes from Tokyo to Singapore, a flight distance of 5311 kilometres (Table 6.5). Underlining the inappropriateness of the European comparison, the flight time between London and Moscow is 3 hours 7 minutes, a distance of 2508 kilometres. The greater time lapse within the Asian-Pacific Rim, coupled with limited bilateral air agreements between countries plus an allowance for time spent getting to and from the airport, restricts the extent to which daily business and travel linkages can be created between Singapore, Hong Kong, Shanghai, Beijing, Seoul and Tokyo (Oum and Yamaguchi, 2006; Williams, 2006; Ichikawa and Miwa, 2011). This phenomenon heightens the dependence upon telecommunications connections.

Telecommunications Corridors

In 2010 the telecommunications corridors between the Asian-Pacific Rim's gateways and proto-gateways are revealed by Internet bandwidth connected across international borders to metropolitan areas (TG, 2011). The highest-capacity regional corridor was between Tokyo and Hong Kong, which was followed by Singapore–Hong Kong and Singapore–Tokyo (Figure 6.17). Lower-level corridors outside this triangular structure

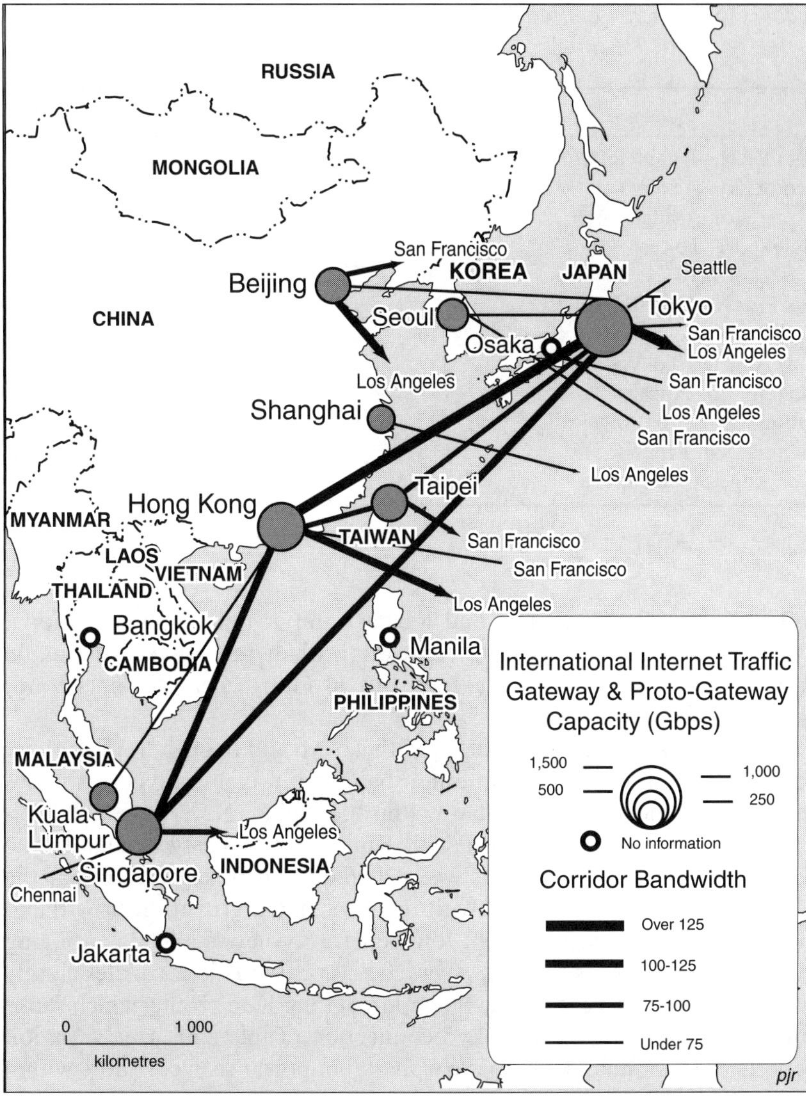

Source: Data from TG (2011).

Figure 6.17 Asian-Pacific international Internet traffic and corridor bandwidth between gateways and proto-gateways, 2010

Table 6.6 Asian-Pacific Rim telecommunications traffic by corridor, mid-2010 (Gbps)

	Bandwidth	Average traffic	Peak traffic
INTERNAL CORRIDOR			
Hong Kong–Tokyo	163	73	95
Hong Kong–Singapore	133	54	76
Singapore–Tokyo	125	60	82
Taipei–Tokyo	101	48	62
EXTERNAL CORRIDOR			
San Francisco–Tokyo	316	144	196
Los Angeles–Tokyo	259	125	166
Beijing–Los Angeles	141	64	93
Hong Kong–Los Angeles	125	53	74
Beijing–San Francisco	115	52	77
Los Angeles–Singapore	108	53	80

Source: TG (2011).

linked Taipei, Seoul, Beijing and Kuala Lumpur hubs into the regional system. No regional corridors connecting Shanghai, Osaka, Bangkok, Manila and Jakarta hubs exceeded the 50 Gbps (gigabits per second) threshold for inclusion.

Both Shanghai and Osaka, along with Tokyo and Beijing, have stronger trans-Pacific international Internet bandwidth connections with Los Angeles and San Francisco than within the region. Nevertheless the collective bandwidth of the Asian-Pacific Rim's corridors grew at a faster rate than trans-Pacific corridors between 2006 and 2010, suggesting that the regional network will expand with the anticipated growth in broadband subscription rates from current low penetration levels and a continuing fall in the Rim's transit prices. Average and peak traffic correlates closely with bandwidth, except for the Singapore–Hong Kong route, which ranks lower than the Singapore–Tokyo connection (Table 6.6). This variation reflects the continuance of Tokyo's pivotal importance in corridors within and outside the Rim.

Summary

As corridors bring different modes – surface transport, air transport and telecommunications – into play, these backbones of regional connectivity within the Asian-Pacific Rim are considered to be multimodal. Most land movements are concentrated within 100 km radius of gateways, and air transport and telecommunications are used primarily to expand operating space not to hinterlands but to other gateways.

This analysis suggests that economic space involving the physical movement of people and goods is more continuous than movements of information. Nevertheless there are marked divergences and convergences between modes. A different time lapse is involved in travelling by sea and air, but both modes have a common start and end point.

Less widely acknowledged is that economic space is also discontinuous. Telecommunications not only transcend economic space but also bring the business cores of gateways into instantaneous contact. The spatial outcome is that these essentially similar city-cores are stacked pancake-like on top of each other (Dick and Rimmer, 2003, 343). In some respects, the cores of the six gateways – Shanghai, Singapore, Hong Kong, Tokyo, Bangkok and Beijing – and the proto-gateways are more adjacent economic spaces than their physical hinterlands.

CONCLUSIONS

This chapter has sought to build up a spatial picture of the Asian-Pacific Rim through an analysis of gateways and corridors. An accurate view of the Rim's emerging spatial economy is elusive because, as in Europe, the roles of gateways and corridors are contested (Pain, 2007a). Some decision-makers see gateways and external (international) corridors as positive because they attract flows into the knowledge economy; others see gateways and internal corridors as negative because they strengthen unequal spatial relationships between places.

The perpetuation of this debate has masked recognition of the new economy in the Asian-Pacific Rim in which gateways and corridors have become important components of an integrated logistics system. This system is aimed at creating the highest level of customer satisfaction by managing value-added activities arising from the spread of markets and the emergence of complex production networks and multistep supply chains. Both gateway congestion and border crossings are impediments to the system's efficient operation. Corresponding institutional frameworks, supported by global logistics service providers, are seeking to overcome these impediments to the door-to-door movement of goods by optimizing the efficient flow and storage of freight, and facilitating both people and related information movements within this system. Rather than elaborate the institutional framework that underpins regional planning designed to facilitate competitiveness in international trade, attention has been centred upon the availability of the physical infrastructures of transport and telecommunications provided by the gateways and corridors to explore the nature of economic space (that is, the 'space' of places).

This chapter highlights that economic space in the Asian-Pacific Rim is not only multidimensional – surface transport, air transport and telecommunications – but also uneven. This unevenness is reflected in the disposition of contours on economic potential maps that give rise to corridors where transactions converge. Thus the search for 'optimal' economic space in the conditions of rapid growth and structural change that pertain in the dynamic Asian-Pacific region is a fruitless exercise (Rimmer and Dick, 2012). Having outlined the nature of the Asian-Pacific's logistics arena and its technological underpinnings, the task ahead is to turn attention to matters of governance by examining logistics policies in Japan, South Korea and China before discussing the prospects for closer integration between them within Northeast Asia.

7. Japan and Southeast Asia

Japanese multinational industrial corporations have exercised a strong influence on international developments in logistics. Toyota Corporation's management philosophy aimed at eliminating manufacturing waste by producing only the right amount and combination of parts at the right place at the right time has had a marked impact upon logistics practice (SFE, 2003–04). Since the 1980s this 'lean thinking' has been embodied in Toyota's production system and linked to 'systems thinking' which led to the 'just-in-time' (JIT) principle and automation being incorporated into common practice around the world. It was not until the promotion of a broader version of supply chain management in the United States and Europe featuring agile and flexible supply chain configurations that Japanese practices lost some of their international appeal. However this loss of influence did not extend to Southeast Asia. After Japanese companies had ingested the broader concepts of supply chain management and developed third-party logistics (3PL) companies, the pitch for influence over economic development in Southeast Asia and the wider Asian-Pacific Rim was reinvigorated. The Japanese International Freight Forwarders Association (JIFFA), founded in 1979, and the Japan Institute of Logistics Systems (JILS), established by the Government of Japan in 1992, have both supported this pitch.

Expertise in supply chain management, albeit with Japanese characteristics, has become a major instrument behind the Japanese push for greater Asian regionalism as a counter to Western, especially 'Anglo-Saxon', ideas and influences. To some extent this is an emotional issue, as 'regionalism' to the Japanese is what 'democracy' is to the United States. There is also a feeling within government circles that, for all sorts of reasons, the Asian-Pacific Rim needs to strengthen its regional ties because these represent both Japan's and the Rim's future. Thus there are strong non-economic political goals behind this emphasis on regionalism and promotion of domestic growth within Asia. Some people argue that it is almost a matter of survival, because the Asian-Pacific Rim cannot compete with major power blocs such as Europe and North America unless a regional competency in logistics is established.

Before discussing Japan's interest in logistics within Southeast Asia, it is important to address developments within the country's domestic scene, particularly with reference to the estimated damage of between US$122 billion and US$235 billion caused by the Great East Japan Earthquake, tsunami and nuclear meltdown of 3 March 2011 (World Bank, 2011c). Even before this most expensive disaster in world history, logistics in Japan was already in a state of transition with three key issues being debated. How can the Japanese logistics sector combat intensifying international competition? How can Japanese-style third-party logistics corporations be developed? And how can the friction among logistics service providers be avoided following the privatization of postal services?

After a broad overview of Japan's rolling logistics policy since its inception in 1997 these issues of international competition, third-party logistics and privatization are discussed in this chapter by examining the geographical spread and activities of Toyota Motor Corporation and Sony Corporation, and four third-party logistics providers: Nippon Express Co. Ltd, Yamato Logistics Co. Ltd, the NYK Group and Nissin Corporation. As the four third-party logistics corporations were the subject of a late 1980s study of freight forwarding in Japan (Rimmer, 1991), attention here is focused on how their logistics strategies have changed since that date in response to global and local developments by examining past, present and likely near-future transitions. Then Japan's interest in the economic development of Southeast Asia is examined by focusing on the Greater Mekong Subregion (GMS), before considering how this emphasis may be widened to encompass other countries within the Asian-Pacific Rim and even beyond to include India (see Chapter 12). Finally, differences between logistics in Japan and Europe are explored to gauge whether there is an emerging universal framework capable of managing multinational manufacturing and retail supply chains.

LOGISTICS POLICIES

Before discussing the evolution of logistics policies in Japan it is important to provide context by outlining the market size and key sectoral trends. Statistical sources in Japan do not define a 'logistics sector' as such, but this is generally taken to encompass companies engaged in truck transport, coastal and ocean-going (international) vessels, air transport, railway, ocean freight and airfreight forwarding and warehousing. These companies are categorized in the standard industrial classification code (SICC) as land transport (5050), marine transport (5100), air transport (5150) and warehousing and harbour transport (5200) (ISNMS, 2007).

Table 7.1 Transport modal split in Japan, 1950–2012

	Tonnes					Tonne-kilometres				
	Road	Rail	Shipping	Air	Total	Road	Rail	Shipping	Air	Total
	%	%	%	%	mn	%	%	%	%	(bn)
1950	63.1	26.9	10.0	0.0	490	8.1	50.0	41.9	0.0	62
1955	69.1	22.5	8.4	0.0	824	11.7	52.6	35.7	0.0	81
1960	75.8	15.1	9.1	0.0	1525	15.0	39.0	46.0	0.0	138
1965	83.8	9.3	6.9	0.0	2616	26.1	30.5	43.4	0.0	186
1970	88.1	4.7	7.2	0.0	5253	38.8	18.0	43.2	0.0	350
1975	87.4	3.6	9.0	0.0	5026	36.0	13.1	50.9	0.0	361
1980	88.9	2.7	8.4	0.0	5981	40.8	8.5	50.6	0.1	439
1985	90.2	1.7	8.1	0.0	5597	47.5	4.9	47.5	0.0	434
1990	90.2	1.3	8.5	0.0	6776	50.2	5.0	44.7	0.1	547
1995	90.5	1.2	8.3	0.0	6643	52.7	4.5	42.6	0.2	559
2000	90.6	0.9	8.5	0.0	6371	54.2	3.8	41.8	0.2	578
2005	91.0	1.0	8.0	0.0	5322	58.6	4.0	37.2	0.2	569
2006	91.3	1.0	7.7	0.0	5431	59.9	4.0	35.9	0.2	579
2007	91.2	1.0	7.8	0.0	5274	60.8	4.0	35.0	0.2	581
2008	91.5	0.9	7.5	0.0	5027	62.0	4.0	33.8	0.2	556
2009	92.0	0.9	7.1	0.0	4716	63.8	4.0	32.0	0.2	522
2010	91.6	0.9	7.5	0.0	4892	54.7	4.5	40.6	0.2	444
2011	91.8	0.8	7.4	0.0	4899	54.1	4.7	41.0	0.2	427
2012	n.a.	n.a.	n.a.	n.a.	4843	n.a.	n.a.	n.a.	n.a.	n.a.

Note: n.a. – not available.

Sources: SB (2013, 390); NS (2013) for 2012.

Market Size and Trends

Most information on Japan's logistics sector is focused on transport measured in tonnes carried or tonne-kilometres travelled (Table 7.1). These data enable us to track three phases in the development of Japan's post-war economy prior to the bursting of the 'bubble economy' (Rimmer, 1998b; Flath 2001; NE, 2006). First, there was the remarkable growth in transport demand during the period of high growth (1945–72) that reflected the development of the heavy and chemical industries in the coastal belt underpinned by the opening of the national highway system in 1963. Second was the period of diminishing growth rate (1973–85) following the first oil shock in the early 1970s. Third, there was a shift into the 'bubble economy' (1985–92) based on high-value-added processing and assembly industries, including electronics and software, which led to the renewed upsurge in transport growth. In 1991 this growth was boosted by changes to the regulation of trucking, which permitted the legal development of a nationwide parcel delivery service and led to a sharp increase in the number of operators to over 60000 and a downward trend in unit costs.

Since the bursting of the 'bubble economy' in the early 1990s the volume of domestic tonnage carried by all transport modes has declined. Transport in tonne-kilometres has also fallen, despite the increased distances involved in integrating and consolidating plants and logistics centres. In the process road transport has risen to almost 64 per cent of the total domestic freight task while coastal shipping has declined to less than 32 per cent and rail has dwindled to around 4 per cent. Road transport accounted for almost all freight traffic within 100 km radius of Tokyo, half of all movements over 500 km and one-fifth over 1000 km (JRF-RC, 2009, 8). This pattern prompted the Government of Japan to adopt a series of environmental and safety measures, including speed limitations on heavy trucks and increased penalties for vehicle overloading, in a bid to trigger greater use of coastal shipping and rail; the tonne kilometres figures for 2010 and 2011 suggest that this modal shift may be occurring.

The policy shift towards coastal shipping and rail reflects the Government's response to a rise in logistics costs as a proportion of gross domestic product after reaching a low point of 8.2 per cent in 2003 (Table 7.2). Since then logistics costs have increased to almost 9 per cent due to higher warehouse costs. These costs are likely to rise given a growing demand for courier services to carry smaller lots and make more frequent deliveries at times specified by the customer, particularly with the growth in home delivery and e-commerce. The efficiency of truck loading has declined and, despite the expansion of the high-standard expressway network, its use by commercial vehicles is still low. Bottlenecks hinder the movement of larger vehicles, especially trucks carrying the increasingly popular 40ft international containers. Access is limited from expressway interchanges to ports and airports and there are missing links in metropolitan expressway ring road systems. When coupled with transport's contribution to global warming, air pollution and growing waste disposal, there is a strong case to support the Government's initiative for seeking to control and reduce logistics costs, especially by promoting advanced information technology within the sector and improving supply chain practices to enhance efficiency.

In 2010 Data Monitor (2011) estimated the size of Japan's logistics market at US$248 billion, a figure that would be greater if the in-house operations of manufacturers and retailers were included. According to

Table 7.2 Composition of Japan's logistics costs as a percentage of gross domestic product, 1991–2007

Year	Transport	Warehousing	Management & administration	Total
	%	%	%	%
1991	6.5	3.5	0.5	10.5
1995	6.3	2.7	0.4	9.5
2000	5.8	2.5	0.4	8.6
2001	5.6	2.5	0.4	8.4
2002	5.6	2.4	0.4	8.3
2003	5.6	2.3	0.3	8.2
2004	5.8	2.3	0.4	8.5
2005	5.3	2.7	0.4	8.4
2006	5.5	2.8	0.4	8.7
2007	5.5	3.0	0.4	8.9

Source: JILS (2010).

this source, truck transport accounted for over 43 per cent and warehousing 35 per cent per cent of the market with sea, rail and air transport (including express services) providing the balance. Comprising over 2.7 million employees, the logistics sector's structure is characterized by a large number of small and medium-sized companies, particularly in road freight transport, water transport and warehousing (Table 7.3). This pattern is attributable to governmental control over supply and demand that has insulated enterprises from true competition manifest in a perfectly competitive market; the relatively small start-up investments required to enter certain transport businesses; and the role afforded them in the logistics sector's multilayered structure as first-tier or second-tier subcontractors. In particular, the shift from licensing to prior approval by government for changes in freight rates has promoted greater integration across the sector. Before examining the logistics sector's structure in more detail through a series of case studies, it is apposite to trace changes in government policy since the late 1990s because they have been designed to promote logistics in a comprehensive and integrated manner. These changes shed light on the nature of internationalization, the emergence of third-party logistics providers, and the impact of information and communications technology.

Table 7.3 Proportions of small and medium-sized enterprises in Japan's logistics sector, 2009

Division	Enterprises		Employees	
	Total	SMEs	Total	SMEs
	(number)	(%)	(thousand)	(%)
Railway transport	5005	97.6	258	69.4
Road freight transport	77237	99.7	1793	92.4
Water transport	3849	99.8	54	92.0
Air transport	813	95.9	53	30.2
Warehousing	11005	99.7	200	89.5
Services incidental to transport	16001	99.9	345	85.5
Total	113910		2703	

Note: Small and medium-sized enterprises (SMEs) are defined as having less than 300 employees; road passenger transport is excluded from the list.

Source: SB (2013, 190–91).

Government Policy

The prime objectives of Japan's initial Comprehensive Logistics Policy Outline (1997–2001) were to supply convenient and attractive logistics services within the Asian-Pacific Rim; promote the low-cost supply of domestic logistics services; and develop suitable corrective measures for resolving energy, environmental and transport problems (Table 7.4). These objectives were supported by key policy measures designed to promote the construction of logistics infrastructure, encourage deregulation and establish an advanced logistics system. Although the international arena received some attention, the major policy focus was primarily on 'local logistics'. Traditionally, Japanese companies had their own logistics departments. After the collapse of the 'bubble economy' in the early 1990s, Japanese multinational manufacturing and retailing corporations began to concentrate on their core businesses, sell their warehouses, and outsource logistics to domestic or foreign providers in return for pledges to keep the jobs of former employees of their abandoned in-house subsidiaries. Although third-party logistics providers had emerged in the United States during the early 1990s, there was no mention of them in government circles within Japan until the late 1990s. Even when these providers are highlighted in developing Japan's rolling logistics policy, there is a desire for providers

Table 7.4 Japan's programme of comprehensive logistics policies 1997–2009

Context	Pillars	Examples
***Comprehensive Logistics Policy Outline*, 1997–2001**		
1. To provide convenient and attractive logistical services in the Asian-Pacific Rim	1. Deregulation and simplification of government procedures (abolition of demand–supply rules)	– International logistics (improving container terminals)
2. To reduce transport costs so as not to diminish competitiveness of Japanese industries	2. Realization of sophisticated logistical systems (including EDI, standardization through unit load and pallet pool and technological innovation in logistics field)	– Intermodal freight transport (improving roads, airports, bridges, tunnels and railways)
3. To cope with negative externalities	Improvement of infrastructure	– Intra-city logistics (improving truck terminals and avoiding traffic accidents)
***New Comprehensive Logistics Policy Outline*, 2001–2005**		
1. Development of globalization	1. Functional reinforcement of distribution hubs	– Maintain international marine container terminals – Promoting 24 hr operating ports – Change to electronic processing and one-stop services for customs procedures
2. Rapid development of information transmission technology	2. Construction of advanced distribution systems	– Computerization of logistics (e.g. EDI and ITS) – Improvements to inter-regional logistics – Comprehensive plan for urban logistics – Modal shift from truck to rail and shipping – Development of reverse logistics

Table 7.4 (continued)

Context	Pillars	Examples
***Comprehensive Logistics Policy Outline*, 2005–2009**		
1. Sub-domestication of freight transport within East Asia to make it a compatible environment for Japanese enterprises	1. International-domestic combined freight transport offering high-speed, seamless and low-cost transport	– Improvement of performance of major international ports and airports – Building up logistics networks in/out country
2. Environmental policy due to Kyoto Protocol coming into effect	2. Efficient and environmentally friendly freight transport	– Promotion of Green Freight Transport – Freight transport management
3. Security policy as part of anti-terrorism measures	3. Freight transport to sustain lifestyle of citizens	– Assurance of safety and stability of logistics system – Prompt response to disasters

Sources: Government of Japan (1997, 2001, 2005, 2007a, 2007b, 2009a, 2009b).

with 'Japanese characteristics' focused on just-in-time systems that, unlike global logistics corporations based in the United States, make use of pallets rather than international containers.

In 2001 the New Comprehensive Logistics Policy Outline (2001–2005) heralded a switch in Japan's policy to global logistics to meet: increased international competition, notably from DHL, FedEx and DB Schenker; the pressing need to reduce environmental problems; and the requirement to contribute to a sustainable society. Establishment of a high-tech and efficient logistics system driven by electronic data interchange (EDI), intelligent transport systems (ITS) and geographical information systems (GIS) were seen as the best means of supporting a globally competitive society. Developing logistics systems to address global warming, air pollution, waste disposal, and safety and security were proposed to combat the range of emerging social issues. Specific encouragement was given in the 2001 Policy Outline to the development of third-party logistics providers by reducing entry requirements and the decision of Nissan Motor

Co. Ltd to sell its logistics subsidiary. The TDK Corporation, Fujitsu Ltd and Snow Brand Milk Products Co followed Nissan's lead. By 2003 third-party logistics business exceeded ¥1 trillion, which prompted the Ministry of Land, Infrastructure and Transport (MLIT) to institute a training programme for small and medium-sized logistics enterprises. As the third-party logistics business was forecast to experience an annual growth rate of over 10 per cent and exceed ¥13 trillion by 2013, this programme not only triggered the growth of local enterprises but also attracted more foreign logistics corporations. Their number included the British company Exel, which purchased Fujitsu's logistics business in 2004, and Prologis, a real-estate company from the United States, which moved into the warehousing market following the easing of regulations on the securitization of assets (that is, the process of converting a pool of illiquid assets such as warehouses into tradable securities).

In 2005 the revised Comprehensive Logistics Policy Outline (2005–2009) was launched to develop a more efficient domestic logistics system by introducing electronic application systems to streamline administrative procedures for import and export processes at ports and introducing international standards for electronic data interchange (EDI); and improving inter-regional logistics by increasing the capacities of freight railways and developing ports, railway freight terminals and other distribution nodes and encouraging professional trucking companies at the expense of private in-house vehicles. There were also recommendations for formulating the Total Plan for Urban Area Logistics that connected airports and ports to highways by access roads, offered support for the improvement of logistics bases along highways, and encouraged the establishment of city and district logistics committees; and supported the training of the human resources needed to promote the further development of third-party logistics providers. Apart from the promotion of environmental policy through the adoption of a 'green logistics' partnership within the logistics sector, strategies were also developed for revitalizing multimodal activities by supporting the JR Freight Corporation, strengthening privatization, developing a tariff system for the trucking industry to cope with price hikes, subsidizing low-emission vehicles, encouraging coastal shipping and offering incentives for grouping companies together, enhancing competition in aviation, deregulating freight forwarding and easing restraints to encourage new entrants into warehousing.

The Comprehensive Logistics Policy Outline (2005–2009) sought to strengthen Japan's international logistics function by establishing super-hubs in Tokyo Bay, Ise Bay and the Port of Kobe to produce higher levels of service at lower cost than South Korea's Busan and Taiwan's Kaohsiung, by 30 per cent (Figure 7.1). Measures to develop the

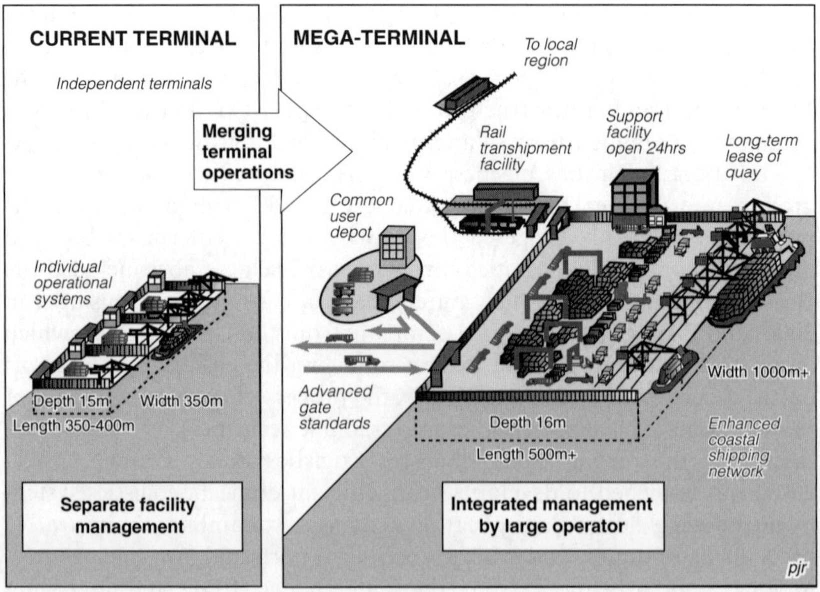

Note: No change has been made to the perspective of the original diagram.

Source: Based on MLIT (2006).

Figure 7.1 Programme to support the development of the next-generation high-standard mega-container terminals, 2006

super-hub ports centred upon the need to: establish terminal operators; promote logistics industry consolidation; reduce costs by enlarging the size of terminals and permitting both public and private participation in terminal development; integrate and computerize terminal management systems; and support increases in vessel size.

Other measures sought to upgrade airfreight services through the expansion of metropolitan area airports in the Chubu, Kansai and Kanto regions. There were also initiatives for promoting international multimodal transport, including the development of a port logistics information system platform, improved operating rates, enhanced port security measures, round-the-clock operations and a one-stop service for import, export and other port procedures (Figure 7.2). These strategies were designed to underpin the Government's vision of the country as an open economic society with a distinct competitive edge.

The development of logistics policies in Japan has provided an important counter to the past preoccupation with passenger movements (that

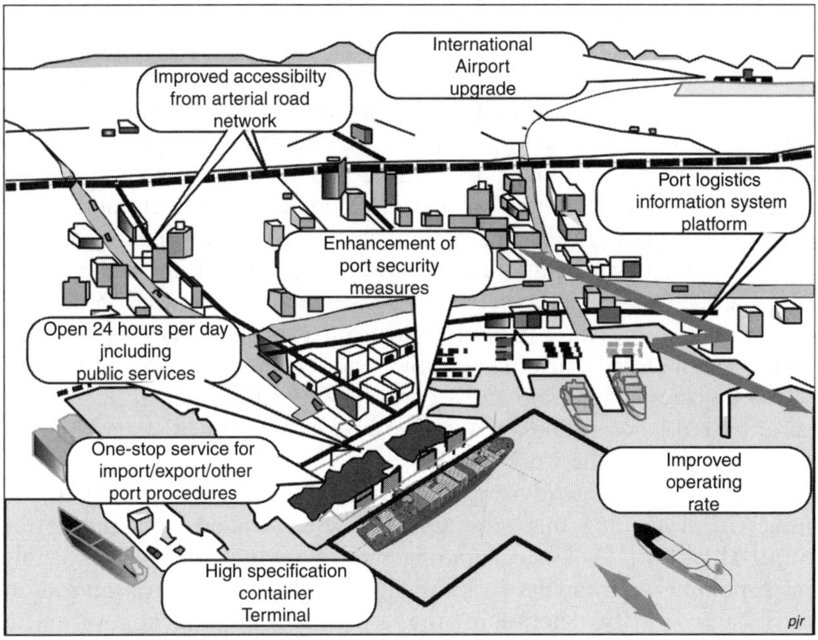

Source: Based on MLIT (2006).

Figure 7.2 Functional reinforcement of international airports and seaports, 2006

is, person trips) and inattention to integration between freight transport modes. Much effort was expended on methods for estimating and evaluating the freight flow on the road network around Tokyo Bay and in other major ports as the basis for establishing an arterial network for international freight (Kono and Okutani, 2006). Nevertheless shortcomings remained, including the need to widen the definition of logistics facilities to encompass stores and offices in addition to warehouses and factories; to include stakeholders in the public sector in addition to business companies; to mitigate the negative effects of the stricter parking laws on trucks introduced in 2006; and to address the labour shortfall of some 400 000 workers, especially in truck transport. In updating policy there has been a recognition that planners should not be preoccupied with vertical linkages but should also consider the horizontal linkages embodied in multinational supply chains, particularly as major manufacturers and retailers have been demanding that global logistics companies use advanced information technology.

In 2009 the Japanese Cabinet endorsed the new Comprehensive Logistics Policy Outline (2009–2013), which heeded the call from multinational manufacturing and retailing corporations with headquarters in Japan to put a premium on further reducing supply chain costs, while maintaining high security levels and responding to the demand for increased logistics efficiency (Government of Japan, 2009a, 2009b). Echoing the 2005 plan, the programme was designed to respond to three sets of changes surrounding logistics: the internationalization of supply chains, that has increased transport requirements following the acceleration in the spread of Japanese-owned factories to other parts of Asia; the need to develop environmental measures in light of the post-Kyoto protocol framework's emphasis on global warming; and the requirement to implement ways in which logistics can be safe and secure by preventing truck accidents and securing sea-lanes, while simultaneously developing a disaster-resistant and resilient traffic network (Table 7.5).

The Government's Advisory Committee covered a range of pertinent topics in developing this programme. These included streamlining the Super-Hub Port Project, upgrading metropolitan airports, completing metropolitan ring-road networks, revitalizing the railways, roll-on/roll-off ferries and security, determining the respective roles of local government and companies, enhancing safety and efficiency in trucks and encouraging the development of an advanced service network (Government of Japan, 2009b). The Committee's deliberations on these topics were distilled into three supporting pillars: the realization of an efficient global logistics system supporting multinational supply chains; an awareness of 'green logistics'; and logistics safety and security.

In July 2009 the Japanese Government adopted the Comprehensive Logistics Policy (2009–13). Two months later, after almost 40 years in office, the Liberal Democratic Party (LDP) lost government to the Democratic Party of Japan (DPJ). Although the Policy remained valid, the new government planned to abolish road tolls, except in Tokyo and Osaka, and delay the construction of roads. Before these proposed changes could be fully implemented, the Government had to grapple with the impacts on Japan's manufacturing and retailing supply chains arising from the earthquake, tsunami and nuclear meltdown of 3 March 2011 (3/11) and disruptive floods in Thailand in July 2011 (METI, 2011, 2012; BMI, 2012). The Government's response to 3/11 was a Strategy for the Rebirth of Japan, which stressed the importance of creating new frontiers based on enhancing the country's high world ranking in logistics, and building flexibility and quicker reaction speeds into disaster-resistant supply chains (NPU, 2011, 2012). In December 2012 the Government reverted from the Democratic Party of Japan to the Liberal Democratic

Table 7.5 Japan's comprehensive logistics policy (2009–13)

Changes Surrounding Logistics

1. *Globalization of Supply Chains*
   - Increasing transport requirements between factories following their spread within Asia, putting a premium on lowering costs
   - High security levels should be maintained together with an increase in logistics efficiency
2. *Need for Environmental Measures in Light of Commencement of the First Commitment Period and Post-Kyoto Protocol Framework*
   - More attention to global warming measures
3. *Requirements to Make Logistics Safe and Secure*
   - Key tasks are prevention of serious truck accidents and the safeguarding of sea-lanes
   - Development of a secure, disaster-resistant traffic network that is capable of a quick recovery when failure occurs

Integrated Logistics Measures (2009–2013)
Three Pillars

1. *Realization of Efficient Logistics Supporting Global Supply Chains*
   - Improvement of regional logistics settings through inter-governmental talks in Asia
   - Establishment of efficient and seamless logistics network
   - Introduction of IT to customs procedures and logistics management as well as establishment of international sharing of information
   - Satisfaction of both security and efficiency enhancement
2. *Realization of Green Logistics*
   - Integrated measures by mode and increased efficiency of transport, including modal shift
   - Ring road development and ITS promotion for smoother traffic
   - Cooperative efforts by local municipalities, cargo owners & carriers
   - Establishment of efficient reverse logistics
3. *Safe and Secure Logistics*
   - Enhanced cooperation between forwarders and carriers
   - Introduction of measures for the safety of heavy trucks and implementation of fleet control
   - Intensive development of traffic safety facilities
   - Promotion of navigation, safety and countermeasures against piracy
   - Disaster penetration/mitigation and securing/cultivating labour force

Note: This is an unofficial translation.

Sources: Government of Japan (2009a, 2009b).

Party under former Prime Minister Abe Shinzō before much progress was made on implementing this Strategy. As logistics is still likely to be central in any response to the continuing post-earthquake recovery process – irrespective of the party in power – it is pertinent to address corporate measures taken to promote an improved distribution system for international trade, third-party logistics and the privatization of postal services before considering the new logistics policy planned for the period between 2013 and 2017.

INTERNATIONALIZATION

Japan's motor vehicle and electronics industries have been the key logistics drivers among domestic players in expanding the country's economic activities overseas. This process of internationalization can be traced by tracking changes in the manufacturing patterns of the Toyota Motor Corporation and Sony Corporation since the 1950s.

Toyota Motor Corporation

Toyota Motor Co. Ltd was originally established as an offshoot of a textile machinery business in 1937, but it did not begin exporting motor vehicles until the late 1950s. By 2010 it was the world's largest motor vehicle manufacturer with 48 overseas manufacturing companies in 26 countries, and sales of over 7 million vehicles in more than 160 countries generating net revenue of US$240 billion (Toyota, 2005–11, 2012a, 2012b). What were the phases in this internationalization process?

During the 1960s and 1970s Toyota's emphasis was on manufacturing in Japan and exporting to the United States and Asia (Figure 7.3). When Toyota achieved an output of 3 million vehicles in 1980 only 200000 vehicles were manufactured overseas in Australia, Brazil and South Africa. From the mid-1980s Toyota's focus shifted to producing overseas where demand for and barriers to imports existed, notably the United States and Western Europe. By 2000 Toyota's strategy had moved towards the establishment of an efficient worldwide production and supply system. This stress has also boosted production in emerging regions, notably Brazil, Russia, China and India, with increasing attention being paid to Africa, Eastern Europe and other parts of Asia.

As part of the creation of Toyota's worldwide production system, the corporation has developed the Innovative International Multipurpose Vehicle (IIMV) Project (Figure 7.4). Since its inception in 2004, the Project has sought to take advantage of the collapse of the currencies in Southeast

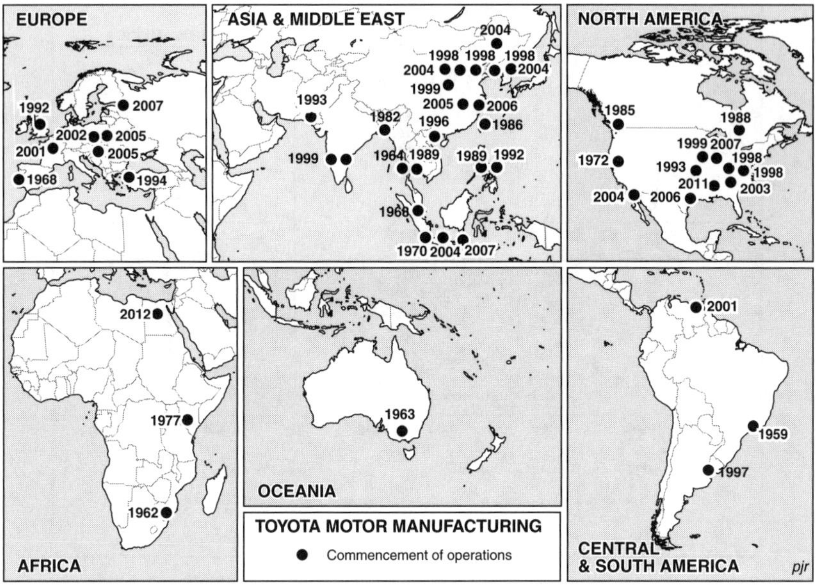

Note: Dates refer to when production commenced at that location.

Source: Based on data from Toyota (2012b).

Figure 7.3 Toyota Motors' production network, 2012

Asia during the Asian Financial Crisis (1997–98) to increase the local procurement of vehicle parts and establish an export structure. As a prime source of car parts, Thailand is the pivot of the system with Indonesia also being afforded an important role in regional complementation in what has become Toyota's second 'mother base' in Asia. The project has grown from its Asian-Pacific Rim supply bases to include Argentina and South Africa in producing pick-up trucks, minivans and sports utility vehicles (SUVs) for sale in 140 countries within Oceania, Europe, Africa, the Middle East, and Central and South America. By 2010, 810 000 IIMV series vehicles were produced, about one-tenth of Toyota's total vehicle sales.

An examination of vehicle production and sales by region between 2005 and 2010 reflects the shift of production and sales away from Japan, North America and Europe towards Asia, particularly the Asian-Pacific Rim, and Africa, the Middle East and Central and South America (Table 7.6). The movement in revenue has not matched the shift in sales towards emerging countries because of the greater proportion of higher-value

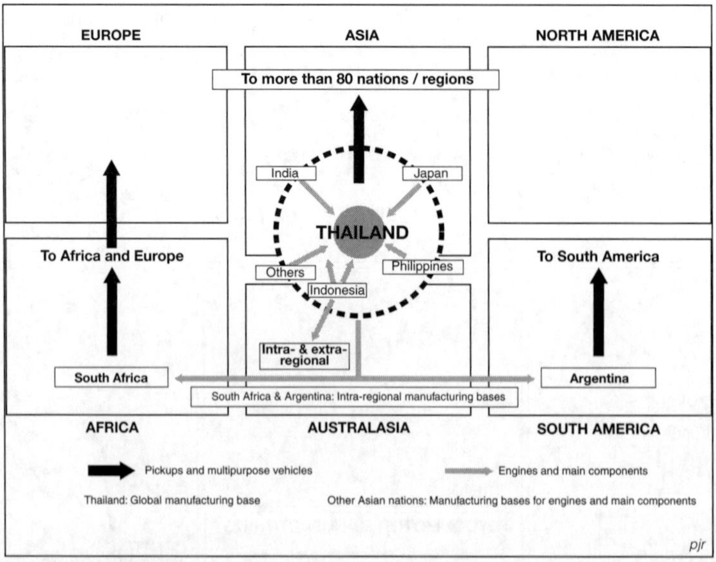

Source: Rimmer (2004a).

Figure 7.4 Toyota Motor's innovative international multipurpose vehicle (IIMV) project

hybrid cars sold in Japan, North America and Europe. Quality issues necessitating the recall of vehicles across the world beset Toyota's sales in 2010; the multinational corporation's response was barely under way when it was then overtaken by a series of calamitous events in 2011 that affected sales, production and revenue.

In 2011 Toyota's supply chain was thrown into disarray by the 3/11 earthquake, ensuing tsunami and nuclear meltdown, which resulted in a temporary halt in production at its domestic factories and delayed worldwide output in June 2011 by 760000 vehicles (Toyota, 2012a, 2012b). Floods in Thailand in July 2011 compounded this issue by reducing output worldwide by a further 240000 vehicles. By March 2012 Toyota's output had recovered due to the corporation's resilient response to these disasters; their net effect on production was reduced from 1 million vehicles to 390000 vehicles. Nevertheless General Motors (GM) surpassed Toyota in 2011 as the world's leading motorcar manufacturer. Also there was a precipitous decline in the corporation's supply chain ranking from its top ten position between 2005 and 2011 to sixty-fifth position in 2012 (Chapter 2). Toyota's response to these disruptions has been to restructure its supply chain by diversifying risk through the decentralization of third- and

Table 7.6 Toyota's vehicle production, sales and revenue by region, 2005 and 2010–12

	Production (Million vehicles)				Sales (Million vehicles)				Revenue by market (US$ bn)			
	2005	2010	2011	2012	2005	2010	2011	2012	2005	2010	2011	2012
	%	%	%	%	%	%	%	%	%	%	%	%
Japan	63	58	52	53	32	30	26	28	40	39	37	39
North America	16	15	19	17	31	29	28	26	33	29	28	25
Europe	8	6	5	5	13	12	11	11	13	11	10	10
Subtotal	87	79	76	75	76	71	65	65	86	79	75	74
Asia	n.a.	15	19	20	n.a.	14	17	18	n.a.	13	16	17
Other	n.a.	6	5	5	n.a.	15	18	17	n.a.	8	9	9
Subtotal	13	21	24	25	24	29	35	35	14	21	25	26
Total	100	100	100	100	100	100	100	100	100	100	100	100
	7.2	6.8	7.2	7.4	7.4	7.2	7.3	7.4	173	204	228	226
	(Million vehicles)				(Million vehicles)				(US$ bn)			

Note: n.a. not available; rounding errors.

Sources: Toyota (2005–11, 2012a).

fourth-tier parts suppliers, and seeking to improve international competitiveness by adhering to its lean thinking practices. Although Toyota recovered quickly from the disruptions to regain its position as the world's largest motor vehicle manufacturer, the recuperation of the country's electronics industry, typified by the Sony Corporation, has taken longer.

Sony Corporation

Sony Corporation recorded its first annual loss since 1985 after the Global Financial Crisis (2008–09). Before then the Corporation, founded in Tokyo in 1946, had blossomed from supplying technologically innovative products, including the transistor radio (1955), the first colour video-cassette recorder (1971), the Walkman personal stereo (1979), the first 8 mm camcorder, (1985), the Playstation (1994) and the first liquid-crystal display (LCD) television (2007) (Sony Corporation, 2008–12). The first annual loss was attributable not only to the Global Financial Crisis but also to Sony's slow reaction to Apple's popular musical entries and the flexibility of its rival's virtual supply chain, the market leadership of

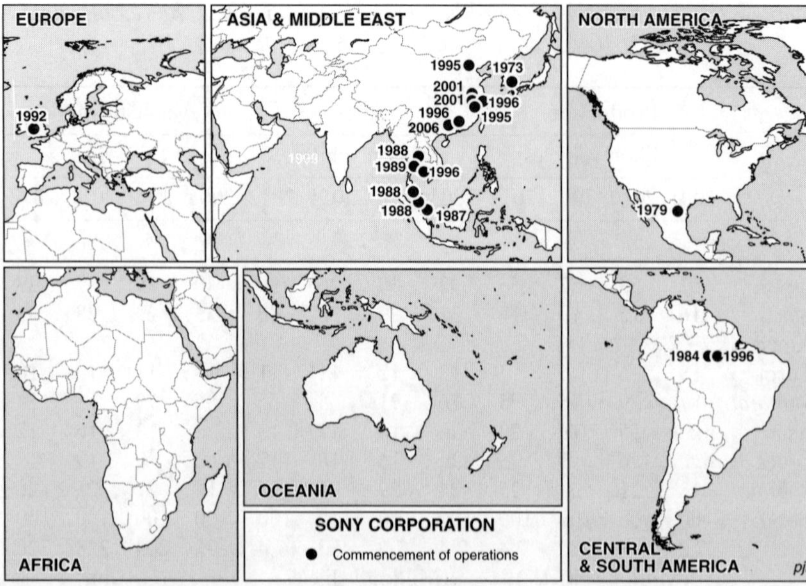

Note: Dates refer to when production commenced at that location.

Source: Data from Sony Global (2012).

Figure 7.5 Sony Corporation's manufacturing operations, August 2012

Samsung in television production, and Nintendo's and Microsoft's devices outselling the Playstation 3 (Ferrari, 2009, 2011).

The loss prompted Sony to restructure its worldwide supply chain that complemented its high-cost operations in Japan with low-cost specialist plants built in Korea in the 1970s, Southeast Asia, Mexico and South America in the 1980s, the United Kingdom in the 1990s and China in the late 1990s and 2000s. Products were also outsourced to contract manufacturers and distributed to 200 countries by sales subsidiaries, unaffiliated distributors and direct sales by the Internet (Figure 7.5). The restructuring of this network was accelerated by the 3/11 earthquake and recurrent annual losses. Since then the number of manufacturing sites in Japan and overseas has been reduced from 57 in 2008 to 38 in 2012, employees by 20000 to 162000 and suppliers from 2500 to 1200. Reallocating the workforce, increasing redundancies and reducing excessive inventories have enabled Sony to reach the target of cutting supply chain costs by 20 per cent. As cost-cutting alone cannot ensure Sony's supply chain capability to sustain efficiency and adaptability for the changed business conditions in consumer electronics and games, much will hinge upon progress towards streamlining the company's sales and operations planning.

Unlike Japan's motor vehicle and electronics manufacturers, the retail sector, which had avoided damage to stores, took time to restart operations after the 3/11 earthquake, because products could not be procured. Its response has been increasingly reliant on third-party logistics providers, which have been afforded a key role in the Government's Strategy for the Rebirth of Japan.

THIRD-PARTY LOGISTICS COMPANIES

Before analysing the corporate networks of specific third-party logistics service providers, it is pertinent to gauge the number of Japanese logistics companies with overseas interests and their patterns of penetration into foreign markets. A guide to the number of logistics companies in Japan is provided by the Japan International Freight Forwarders Association (JIFFA, 2012a). Between 1962 and 2012 the number of locations operated by Japanese overseas affiliated firms and representative offices increased from nine to 1167 locations (Table 7.7). Over this period activities located in North America progressively declined from more than half to less than

Table 7.7 Number of overseas subsidiaries of members of the Japan International Freight Forwarders Association, 1962–2012

	1962–70	1970–79	1980–89	1990–99	2000–09	2010–12
	no	no	no	no	no	no
North America	5	16	49	69	89	96
Asia	4	22	118	378	802	890
Europe	0	5	36	77	120	126
Central & South America	0	2	3	11	19	23
Oceania	0	0	5	8	10	11
Middle East	0	0	0	3	9	11
Africa	0	0	0	2	3	7
CIS	0	0	0	1	2	3
Total	9	45	211	549	1054	1167

Note: CIS Commonwealth of Independent States.

Source: JIFFA (2012a, 6).

one-tenth of the total; those located in Asia increased from two-fifths to three-quarters; and those in Europe declined to one-tenth after enjoying an upsurge in the 1980s. The best showing of 'all other regions' was between 2010 and 2012 when they accounted for one-twentieth of all activities, suggesting a slight dispersion for activities from the Asian–European–North American Triad.

In 2012, members of the Japan International Freight Forwarders Association had 187 overseas affiliated firms and representative offices, and 2110 overseas bases in 1167 locations that were operated by 119000 local employees and 5850 Japanese employees. When mapped by country, it is evident that the Asia-Pacific Rim's strength is derived from China (40 per cent) with Thailand, Singapore, Indonesia, Malaysia, Viet Nam and the Philippines featuring prominently, followed by South Korea, India and Taiwan (Figure 7.6). The United States remained the third-strongest market, accounting for 7 per cent of locations, with the Netherlands, Germany, the United Kingdom and Russia prominent in Europe. As national figures can be misleading, these are augmented by a list of the most-favoured locations for Japanese freight forwarders. In 2012 Shanghai (191 locations) was the clear leader, followed by Hong Kong (83), Bangkok (79), Singapore (53), Jakarta (39), Ho Chi Minh City (37) and Los Angeles (32). If mega-metropolitan regions were taken into account the Lower Yangtze (196 locations) would rank ahead of the Pearl River Delta (134) (see Chapter 6).

With this background on the penetration of Japanese logistics companies overseas, the development of specific company networks over time are examined, based on information provided by JIFFA (2012a) on the date individual companies established their overseas affiliated firms and representative offices. Four logistics service providers – Nippon Express Co. Ltd, Yamato Holdings Co. Ltd, NYK Logistics/Yusen Sea & Air and Nissin Corporation – are chosen from 26 'key' firms to trace the dynamic realignment of Japan's logistics sector in response to the changing needs of shippers, markets and consumers (Figure 7.7). Nippon Express and Yamato are drawn from the land transport sector and NYK Logistics/Yusen Sea & Air from the marine and air transport sectors, which have played pivotal roles in the creation of a post-war integrated logistics market, whereas Nissin from the port and harbour sector has remained aloof from these moves, preferring to develop as an independent company. The differing experiences of these firms demonstrate the degree to which merger and acquisition, and alliances, have been fostered by the Government to create integrated third-party logistics service providers capable of performing in both domestic and international markets.

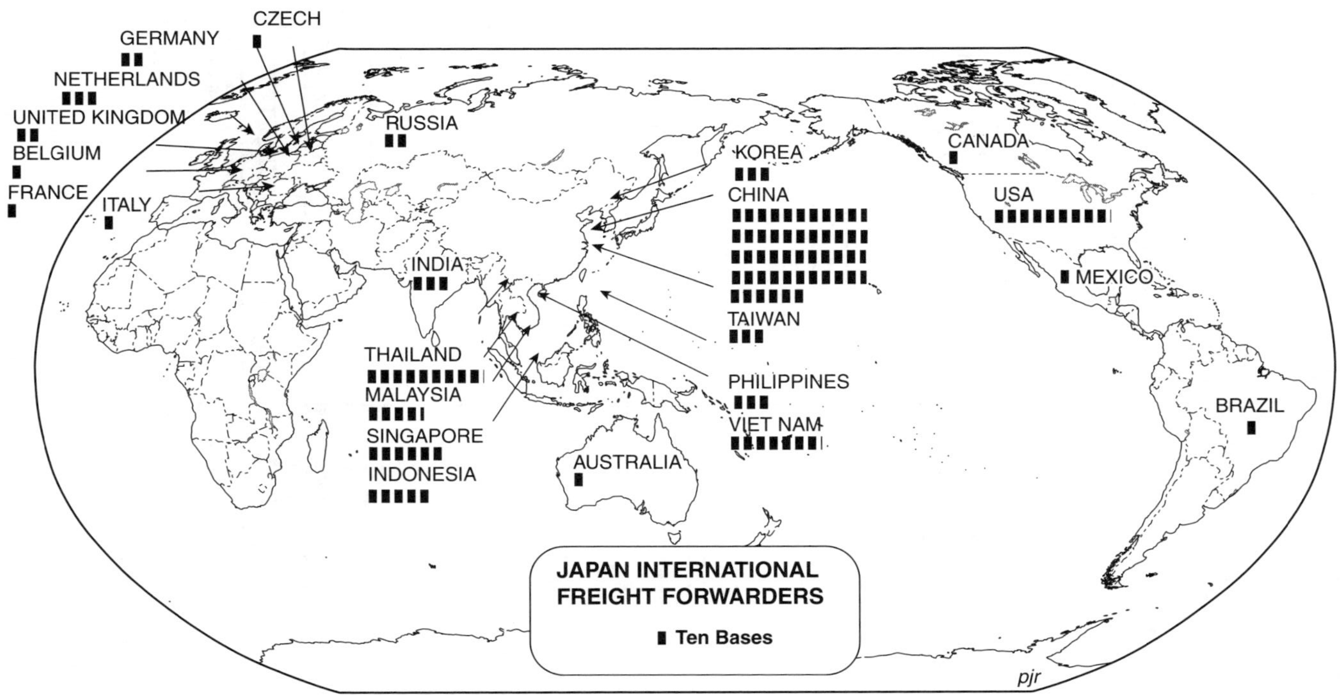

Source: Data from JIFFA (2012a).

Figure 7.6 Location of member companies of the Japan International Freight Forwarders Association, 2012

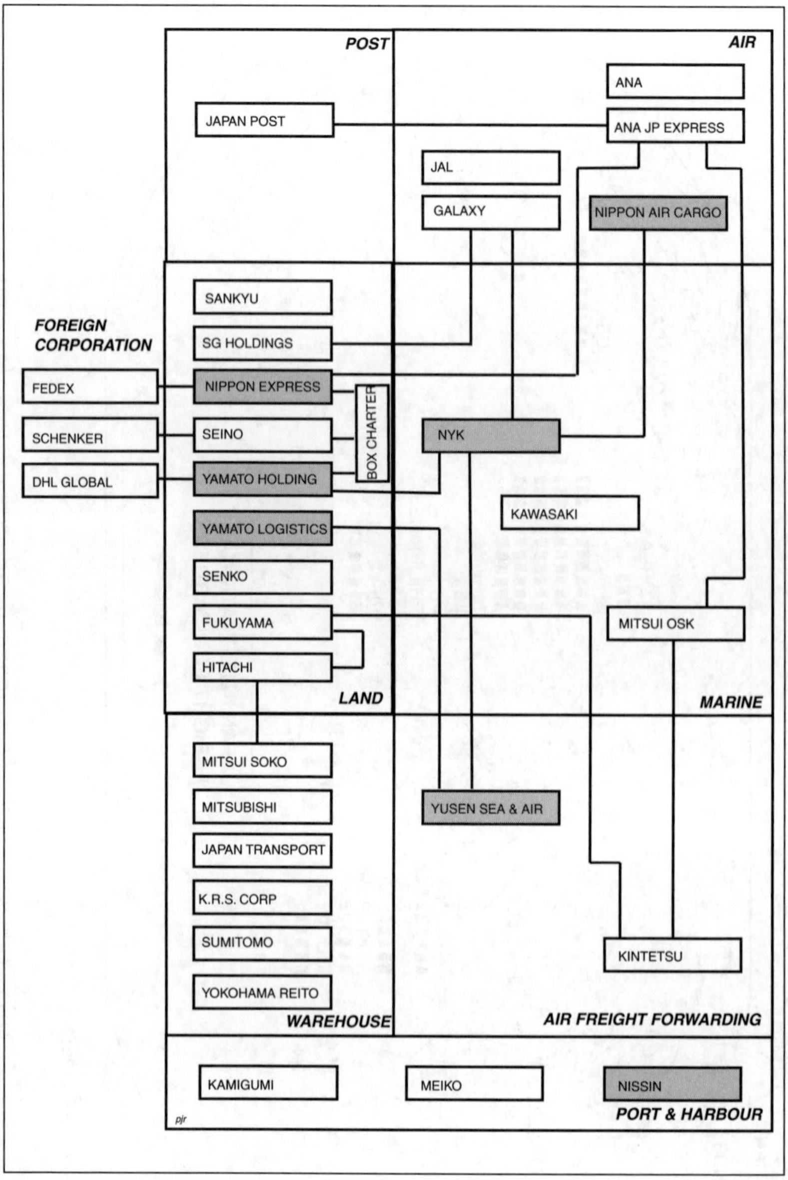

Note: Case studies are shaded.

Source: Adapted from ISNMS (2007).

Figure 7.7 Alignments of logistics companies in Japan, 2012

Table 7.8 Transition of Nippon Express's business scope, services and investment

	Business scope	Services		Investment
		Domestic freight	International freight	
Past	Domestic and international freight to/from Japan	Individual modes of transport	International transport to/from Japan	Strengthening of the capital base and nurturing of group companies
Present	International transport between Japan and three key world markets	Development of third-party logistics	International transport between Japan and America, Asia and Europe	Reinvestment by group companies
Near Future	Business expansion based on each local area around the world	Integrated services, incorporating global financial services		Various means of expansion (e.g. alliances and merger & acquisition)

Source: NE (2007).

Despite differences between companies in their degree of integration, the business histories of all four companies have followed a similar trajectory. As illustrated for Nippon Express, all companies have in the past added an international arm to their domestic business activities; have been transformed in varying degrees into global logistics corporations; and are seeking to restructure their value-added activities to address the lingering fallout from the Global Financial Crisis (2008–09), which sprung from the subprime mortgage problem in the United States, and the Great East Japan Earthquake of 2011 (Table 7.8).

Nippon Express Co. Ltd

As Japan's top-ranking global logistics service provider, Nippon Express (NE, 2012) reflects the company's long involvement in the transport and distribution sector. The company, usually referred to as 'Nittsu', can trace its antecedents to the Land Transportation Company (later the National Transport Company), which delivered freight between railway terminals and customer premises in 1872. In 1928 this company became the International Transport Company specializing in rail freight pick-up and delivery. By 1937 the company adopted its modern guise when it was established as the Nippon Express Co. Ltd, a semi-governmental company. In 1942 Nippon Express was involved in the government merger of transport companies during the Pacific War. After the war Nippon Express was listed as a private company on the Tokyo Stock Exchange under the Express Business Act, 1950. Since then the company's prime focus has been on domestic and international transport to and from Japan. At home Nippon Express has offered rail, road, sea and air services, and developed international transport services by establishing beachheads in New York (1962), Singapore (1973) and the Netherlands (1977) (Figure 7.8). As overseas subsidiaries offered higher margins than those in Japan, this international network has expanded within North America, Asia and Europe.

As Nippon Express had a broad customer base in Japan and was capable of providing a full range of logistics services, the company had shunned inter-company alliances until 2006 when fierce domestic

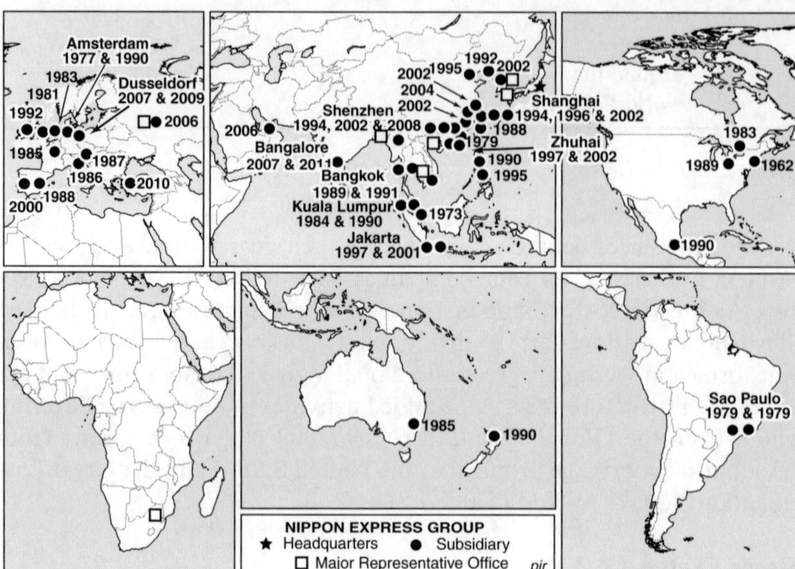

Note: Only places with two subsidiaries are named. Note that the first representative office was established in New York in 1958.

Sources: Data from NE (2005–12) and JIFFA (2012a).

Figure 7.8 Nippon Express' network, 2012

competition prompted it to invest in Box Charter, a joint trucking company established by 14 other companies, including Seino and Yamato, to offer business-to-business (B2B) services. In 2008 Nippon Express went a step further by merging Pelican, its small package delivery service, with Japan Post in a new company, JR Express Co., which brought it into competition with Seino and Yamato (NE, 2008). Before the company changed its reporting structure in 2010, it ranked first within Japan in rail freight (43 per cent market share), warehousing (39 per cent), domestic airfreight (24 per cent) and international airfreight (21 per cent) (NE, 2009). Thus, Nippon Express has moved from its position as a freight forwarder within Japan to become a third-party logistics provider by capitalizing on the group's companies in rail, road, marine and international air transport. By 2011 the company had 388 business bases in 210 cities across 36 countries worldwide.

China has become a prime focus of Nippon Express's international activities since it teamed up with Mitsubishi Corporation in 2007 to develop a countrywide delivery network from the company's Shanghai Delivery Centre to 32 cities. In 2010 this network handled annual imports of 10 000 tonnes of Japanese-made consumer products – office appliances, household goods, TVs and cameras – and provided inter-plant transport for Japanese manufacturers. These efforts have led to the development of the company's overland 'SS7000' route traversing the 7000 km between Shanghai and Singapore (Figure 7.9). This integrated service incorporates

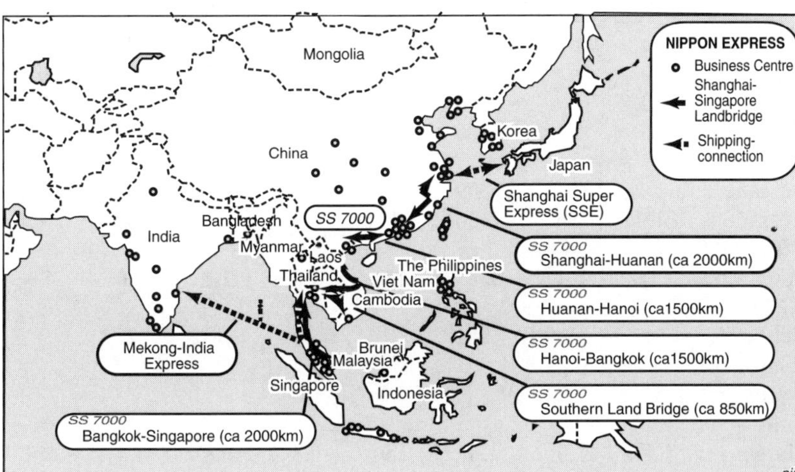

Source: NE (2012, 14).

Figure 7.9 Extending Nippon Express' Asian network to India

roll on/roll off shipping services between Hakata and Shanghai, makes use of high-speed rail within China, and a shipping service between Southeast Asia and India. Fast freight is accommodated by air services connecting Tokyo Haneda, Shanghai and Hong Kong. A link has also been established with China Shipping in CNJ World Logistics Ltd to ship car components from Japan to Europe via China and export cars from the Yangtze River Basin to the rest of the world. Bases have been added in Russia and the Middle East to enhance the company's global network and strengthen the corporation's capital base.

Lower operating margins and rates of returns on assets in a highly competitive and shrinking domestic market have prompted Nippon Express to adopt a lower cost structure, strengthen sales capabilities and optimize its parcel delivery business (Table 7.9). Stagnant conditions in transport and distribution within Japan have resulted in the corporation seeking to leverage its global network and grow its logistics operation into one that can meet the diversifying supply chains of Japanese-based multinational manufacturers and retailers. By 2010 the activities of the Nippon Express Group had crystallized into supplying international logistics services between Japan

Table 7.9 Nippon Express revenue, operating income and net income, FY 2005–12 (US$ million)

	2005	2006	2007	2008	2009	2010	2011	2012
Japan	n.a.	n.a.	14117	16795	16441	15183	15244	15511
Americas	n.a.	n.a.	379	479	465	320	984	1005
Europe	n.a.	n.a.	506	690	652	429	863	908
Asia & Oceania	n.a.	n.a.	806	1013	1061	937	2358	2385
Revenue	16237	15271	15809	18978	18619	16870	19449	19808
Operating income	401	367	426	484	341	403	380	456
Margin (%)	2.5	2.4	2.7	2.6	1.8	2.4	2.0	2.3
Net income after tax	242	159	281	363	154	135	277	327
Margin (%)	1.5	1.0	1.8	1.9	0.8	0.8	1.4	1.7

Note: n.a. not available; rounding errors.

Source: NE (2005–12).

and three world regions: Asia/Oceania (accounting for almost 6 per cent of the company's revenue of US$16.9 billion), Europe (less than 3 per cent) and the Americas (less than 2 per cent) (NE, 2010). In 2010 the burgeoning Asia/Oceania market was split into East Asia with regional headquarters in Hong Kong and South Asia/Oceania organized from Singapore.

The company's strategy in moving to a 'five-polar' focus – Japan, the Americas, East Asia, Europe and South Asia/Oceania – was to expand local operations within each of the markets in a bid to become the world's premier third-party logistics provider. This proposition was based on being a dominant air and maritime freight forwarder without owning either aircraft or ships. While maintaining its focus on transport and distribution, the three-year business plan in 2010 involved raising revenue from overseas local subsidiaries by taking further advantage of the shift of Japanese manufacturers and retailers to overseas locations. Also Nippon Express has introduced its own warehousing, and pick-up and delivery system in overseas markets, and is offering supply chain management services to local clients in such diverse locations as Chicago, Los Angeles, Pilsen (Czech Republic), Torun (Poland), Moscow, Singapore, Guangzhou and Hanoi. In the process the distinctions between domestic and overseas bases, sales systems and products have been eliminated. This strategy of engaging in seamless global logistics requires investment in a variety of non-group activities, including overseas warehousing and safe storage facilities, and intra-regional logistics services. Spurred by the 3/11 earthquake in Japan, the focus is leading Nippon Express to explore overseas partnerships, and mergers and acquisitions with major companies, especially with the likely continuing slump in domestic business and increased local competition, particularly from Yamato which has a markedly different business and profit structure.

Yamato Logistics Co. Ltd

Yamato is Japan's largest provider of express home delivery services with a revenue of US$15.3 billion in a market involving the carriage of almost 3.5 billion individual parcels weighing less than 30 kg (YHCL, 2012). Founded as a trucking company in 1919, Yamato provides an insight into local logistics within Japan, particularly by highlighting the emergence of Japan Post Service Co. as a competitor. Since 1923 Yamato has prospered through a delivery agreement with the major retailer Mitsukoshi. The company did not come into prominence until 1976 when it pioneered private parcel deliveries (*takkyubin* / *ta-q-bin*) as a profitable consumer-to-consumer (C2C) service in Japan, specializing in the safe carriage of skis, golf bags, art and archaeological objects.

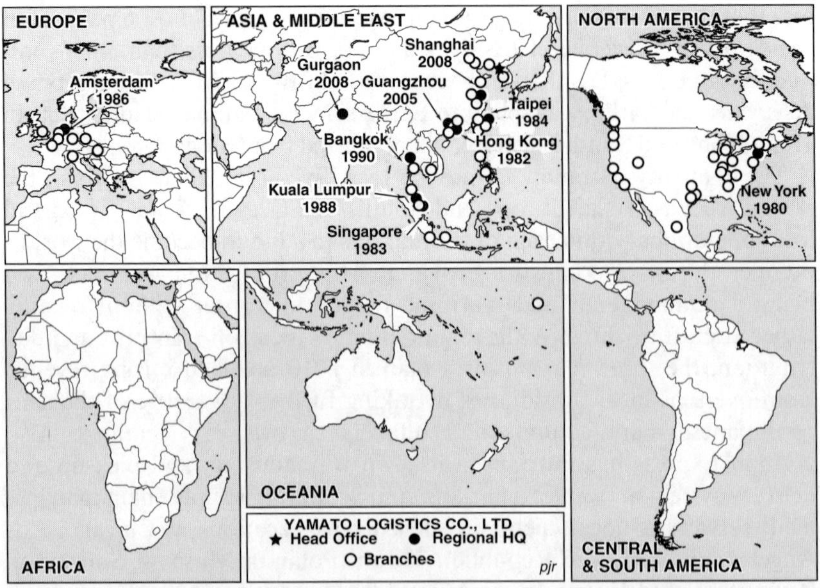

Note: Only regional headquarters are named.

Sources: Data from YHCL (2005–10, 2011, 2012) and JIFFA (2012a).

Figure 7.10 Yamato Logistics Co. Ltd's network, 2012

As regulations confining trucking companies to specific areas precluded the company's nationwide expansion throughout Japan, its focus has been on developing international operations (Figure 7.10). In 1986 Yamato entered into an agreement with United Parcel Service (UPS), which extended its coverage to 39 countries so that it could meet needs of increasing numbers of Japanese people living abroad. Following changes in the regulation of the trucking industry in 1991, Yamato extended its network nationwide, which has provided over 90 per cent of its revenue. While it commenced operations in China during 1993, Yamato's attention was concentrated on expanding domestic delivery services and in 1997 the company initiated its 'Black Cat' (*kuroneko*) mail services. By 2000 the company had expanded into logistics by establishing the Yamato Logistics Produce Co. Ltd to offer manufacturers and retailers a range of business-to-consumer (B2C), business-to-business (B2B) and consumer-to-business (C2B) services. These procurement, delivery and repair services employ information technology (IT), logistics technology (LT) and financial technology (FT), cultivated in the *ta-q-bin* (lit. 'quick home pick-up or delivery') operation, which have enabled Yamato to use a proposal-type marketing approach to differentiate its services from competitors. This approach has included the '*ta-q-bin* collect' and 'cool *ta-q-bin* strategies' and enhanced services such as 'time-period delivery' and 'driver direct'.

Yamato's logistics activities have been affected by the 2003 decision of Japan Post to enter the private sector and compete with express delivery companies through its lower-priced delivery service, Yu-pack. In 2005 Yamato responded to this competition by becoming a holding company, enabling it to develop a range of 'non-delivery' items: Biz-Logistics (inter-company logistics), Home Convenience, E-Business (tracking, security and packing), financial services and truck maintenance. Yamato Holdings Co. Ltd was also concerned that after Japan Post was fully privatized in 2007 the new entity would have an unfair competitive advantage, and approached Japan's Fair Trade Commission, albeit unsuccessfully, to be given equal access to the postal network (JFTC, 2006). Meanwhile Yamoto experienced competition from Sagawa Express in the home delivery market and the company sought to strengthen its position by contributing capital, together with Seino Transportation Co. Ltd, Nippon Express and 12 other companies, to consolidate Japan's domestic trucking business. Also the company entered into an alliance with the Nippon Yusen Kabushiki Kaisha (NYK)'s Yusen Air & Sea Service and expanded its share of the international distribution of small parcels and a direct mail partnership with DHL Global.

By 2010 Yamato's logistics activities had recovered from the Global Financial Crisis (2008–09), which had produced the first annual decline in the number of parcels handled in Japan since the company's inception. In 2011 Yamato (at 42 per cent) maintained its lead in Japan's express delivery market over Sagawa Express (39 per cent) and the combined Nippon Express and Japan Post entity (11 per cent) (YHCL, 2011). Although Yamato's 'non-delivery' activities had grown to almost 20 per cent of the company's income by 2012, it was still heavily reliant upon the express home delivery business (Table 7.10). This door-to-door business was affected not only by domestic economic trends such as a declining birth rate, ageing population, regional depopulation and widespread Internet use, but also fiercer price competition with its rivals following the passing of the Revised Postal Privatization Reform Law in 2012. The new law sought to revitalize Japan Post, as its share of the home delivery service covering magazines, catalogues and form letters to household boxes had dwindled to slightly more than half, with Yamato handling two-fifths of the market (UNI-LC Japan, 2012).

Looking ahead, Yamato has allied with NYK to serve Japanese car, electronics and appliance manufacturers, especially in China, as a step towards integrating domestic collection in Japan with its global transport

Table 7.10 Yamato Group's revenue, operating income and net income, FY 2005–12 (US$ million)

	2005	2006	2007	2008	2009	2010	2011	2012
Delivery	–	–	–	9793	10159	10387	11974	12344
Non-delivery[1]	–	–	–	2444	2586	2519	2897	2996
Revenue	9981	9746	9839	12237	12745	12906	14871	15340
Operating income	575	66	569	681	567	660	773	811
Margin (%)	5.8	0.7	5.8	5.6	4.5	5.1	5.2	5.3
Net income after tax (loss)	315	(204)	286	353	260	347	399	241
Margin (%)	3.2	(2.1)	2.9	2.9	2.0	2.7	2.7	1.6

Note: 1 In 2012 non-delivery revenue from customers covered BIZ Logistics (7%), Home Convenience (4%), E-Business (3%), Financial (4%), Truck Maintenance (2%). Japan accounted for 98 % of operating revenue, USA, 1 % and other regions 1 %.

Sources: YHCL (2005–10, 2011, 2012).

operations. This focus on becoming a global logistics provider centred on the Asian-Pacific Rim was prompted by Japan Post strengthening its international connections, particularly in China, by forging air cargo links with Nippon Express, All Nippon Airlines (ANA) and Mitsui OSK Lines to link Narita, Kansai and Chubu airports with Beijing, Shanghai and Dalian. Yamato has countered by launching *ta-q-bin* parcel services from its Haneda Airport base to Shanghai and Singapore in 2010, and Hong Kong and Malaysia in 2011. Given this competition, Yamato's future growth will hinge on the success of further differentiating itself as a fourth-party logistics (4PL)-style provider by proposing supply-chain solutions to clients and furthering its expansion in the Rim to secure new growth capabilities through its alliance with NYK Logistics Co. Ltd.

NYK Line (Nippon Yusen Kabushiki Kaisha) / Yusen Logistics

The NYK Line, Japan's largest shipping company, originated from a merger of Mitsubishi Mail Steamship Co. and Kyodo Transport Co. in 1885. By 1900 the Mitsubishi core company had expanded its liner services

Table 7.11 NYK Group's revenue, operating income and net income, FY 2005–12 (US$ million)

	2005	2006	2007	2008	2009	2010	2011	2012
Global logistics								
Liner	4231	4590	4815	6590	6003	4000	5517	5046
Logistics	3307	3630	4071	5233	4462	3658	4686	4400
Terminal	1015	948	800	1150	1025	916	1114	1361
Air cargo	0	0	0	920	718	596	935	892
Subtotal	8553	9168	9686	13893	12208	9170	12252	11699
Other								
Bulk	5310	5769	6580	10304	11008	7821	9520	8851
Other	1093	1487	2068	1600	1522	1252	1429	1446
Subtotal	6403	7256	8648	11904	12530	9073	10949	10297
Total	14956	16424	18334	25797	24738	18243	23201	21996
Operating income	1503	1196	889	2016	1475	(194)	1471	(293)
%	10.0	7.3	4.8	7.8	6.0	–1.1	6.3	–1.3
Net income	664	784	551	1139	572	(187)	945	(886)
%	4.4	4.8	3.0	4.4	2.3	–1.0	4.1	(–4.0)

Note: 'Bulk' includes Car Carrier Division, Dry Bulk Carrier Division (Iron ore, coal, grains, etc.) and Tanker Division (Crude oil, petroleum products, LPG, LNG, etc.). 'Other' includes cruise, real estate and other services.

Source: NYK (2005–12).

first into the ports of the Far East and then worldwide. During the interwar period its merchant ships, tankers and liners plied ocean and local sea routes and the company resurfaced after the Pacific War to operate tankers (from 1959), ore carriers (1960) and container shipping (1968) before branching into air cargo services (1978) (NYK, 2007). It is now one of the world's most comprehensive global logistics enterprises with a revenue of almost US$ 22 billion in 2012 (Table 7.11). Over 50 per cent of the revenue is derived from global logistics activities that combine vessels, warehouses, trucks and aircraft to provide services and solutions tailored to the needs of multinational manufacturers and retailers; the balance of its revenue is provided largely by bulk shipping.

NYK's strategy within its global logistics division has been to establish itself as a logistics integrator to offset the volatility of freight rates in container liner shipping (Chapter 3). The company's logistics segment comprised two separate subsidiaries – Yusen Air and Sea Services Co. Ltd

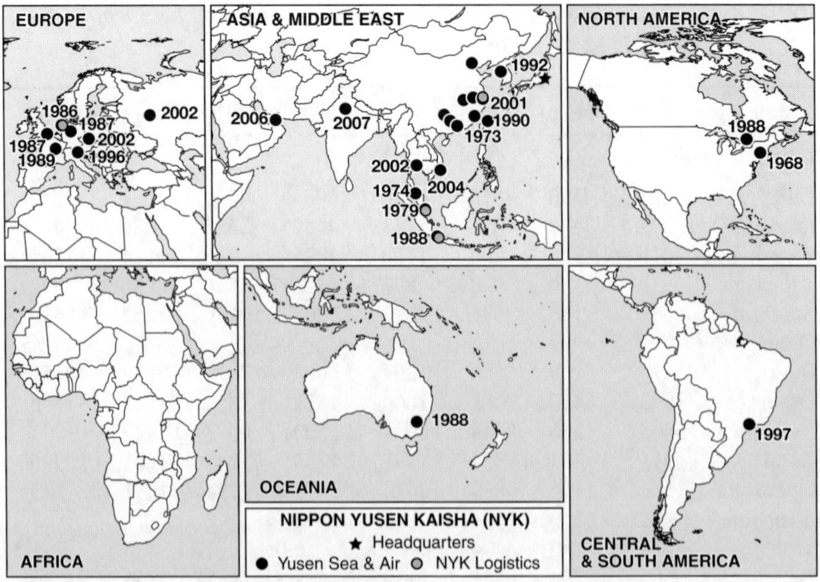

Note: The dates of establishing Yusen Sea & Air and NYK Logistics are shown. The two subsidiaries have since been folded into the Yusen Co Ltd's network.

Source: Data from JIFFA (2012a).

Figure 7.11 Yusen Co. Ltd's network, 2012

and NYK Logistics – which developed separate footprints (Figure 7.11). Yusen was established as an air transport agent in 1955, acquired by NYK in 1959, changed its English name in 1961 and commenced its international airfreight forwarding business in the 1980s. During the same decade NYK set up its own logistics department, Japan Intermodal Transport Co. Ltd, to handle ocean freight forwarding in the Asian-Pacific Rim before expanding into Europe and the Americas during the 1990s, and into Eastern Europe and the BRICS after 2000. In 2001 the NYK Group sought to reposition itself as a 'global logistics megacarrier' and launched the brand name 'NYK Logistics' in 2004, before merging it with Japan Intermodal Transport Co Ltd as an independent subsidiary to meet the difficult task of 'synchronizing' every supply chain with the customer's final demands. Thus, NYK Logistics provided overland transport, warehousing, delivery and ocean freight forwarding and Yusen Air & Sea Services handled air freight forwarding as part of the corporation's focus on order fulfilment and demand satisfaction.

Table 7.12 Yusen Logistics Co. Ltd's logistics centres, pre- and post-amalgamation, 2010 and 2012

Pre-amalgamation (2010)			Post-amalgamation (2012)		
Region	NYK Logistics	Yusen Sea & Air	Region	Yusen Logistics Co. Ltd	
	Locations	Locations		Locations	Warehouses
	no.	no.		no.	Thousand m^2
Japan	23	18	Japan	73	67
Asia/China	78	44	East Asia	76	249
Oceania	7	3	South Asia/ Oceania	115	656
Americas	30	24	Americas	65	424
Europe	59	22	Europe	98	831
	197	111		427	2227

Source: NYK (2012, 43).

This strategy has had mixed results. After the Global Financial Crisis (2008–09) there was a significant drop in overland transport activities and a sharp downturn in air cargo business, prompting NYK to make drastic cost-cutting measures (NYK, 2009a, 2009b, 2009c, 2009d). In 2010 this led to the two subsidiary companies, NYK Logistics and Yusen Sea & Air Services, being integrated into Yusen Logistics Co. Ltd with a workforce of 15000 to provide comprehensive value-added logistics services across 37 countries. No geographical segmentation is given of the new company's activities but it can be inferred from the regional distribution of their logistics centres and the size of their warehouses designed to accommodate food products, apparel, electronic appliances and consumer goods (Table 7.12).

This restructuring of the logistics segment was part of the NYK Group's wider management plan to provide value-added solutions that go beyond traditional shipping by strengthening freight forwarding to offset volatile freight rate fluctuations. As part of this plan NYK is seeking to adopt a light asset business model by reducing its own containership fleet and increasing short-term charters, while expanding the bulk shipping business through long-to-medium-term contracts for car carrying, natural resources and energy transport to generate stable earnings. Looking ahead, the NYK Group is seeking to deepen and redefine the scope of its global contract logistics services to take advantage of the transformation of China and the fresh opportunities offered by Eastern Europe and Russia. This strategy of growing within the Asian-Pacific Rim and then

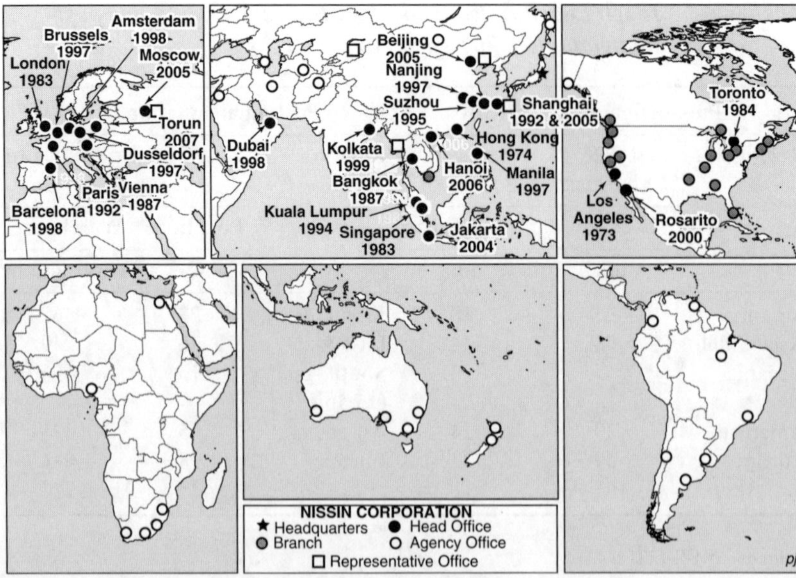

Note: Only 'head offices' are named.

Sources: Data from NC (2005–12), JIFFA (2012a).

Figure 7.12 Nissin Corporation's network, 2012

expanding across the globe has also been echoed among port and harbour companies such as Nissin Corporation.

Nissin Corporation

Nissin Corporation, like other port and harbour service providers, has been able to monopolize local terminal operations and create a highly profitable business as a comprehensive logistics operator without the need for merger and acquisition or alliances. In 1938 the company was established in Yokohama as Nissin Transport Co. Ltd, then became Nissin Trading Co. Ltd in 1946 before becoming Nissin Transportation & Warehousing Co. Ltd in 1950. By 1968 the company had already moved from its port and harbour transport origins by extending into an array of domestic activities, including freight forwarding, customs brokerage, freight transport, airfreight, warehousing, packing and crating, and household removals, before entering into door-to-door operations within Asia, Europe and North America (Figure 7.12). Between 1973 and 1985 regional head offices were established

Table 7.13 Distribution of Nissin Corporation's sales, 2006–12 (US$ million)

	2006	2007	2008	2009	2010	2011	2012
International freight	1048	1100	1387	1148	1007		
Domestic freight	325	317	386	384	371	1668	1569
Other	434	448	500	483	389	649	610
Total	1807	1865	2273	2015	1767	2317	2179
Operating income	36	51	52	36	9	50	46
%	2.0	2.7	2.3	1.8	0.5	2.2	2.1
Net income	16	33	23	15	7	24	23
%	0.9	1.8	1.0	0.7	0.4	1.0	1.1

Note: No geographical segment information is given.

Source: NC (2005–12).

in Los Angeles, Hong Kong and London. When its name was changed to Nissin Corporation in 1985, the company had additional subsidiaries in Asia, Europe and North America. By 2000 there were five subsidiaries in Europe and nine in Asia. Key features have been the development of the corporation's branch network in the United States, to provide the motor vehicle industry with parts, and its deepening strength in China. Not only has the corporation become a third-party logistics (3PL) provider but it is also seeking to become a 4PL provider by offering clients step-by-step assistance in supply chain management, especially in consumer electronics.

The Global Financial Crisis (2008–09) saw Nissin experience a decline in international freight, which had provided three-fifths of its income (Table 7.13). Domestic freight also declined, but not to the same extent. Although there was shift from air to marine freight in international transport, this was unable to compensate for the downturn in exports of motor vehicles prompted by the 3/11 earthquake and the floods in Thailand. Since 2011 these changes have been masked by the integration of international and domestic freight into a single logistics segment. Without any marked recovery in this segment, the corporation has become more reliant on travel services and other non-logistics business.

Nissin's immediate strategy has been to use the corporation's global network, comprising 28 regional head offices, 72 branches and five representative offices in Europe, the Middle East, China and North America, to further develop air cargo and freight forwarding services. Particular attention is being paid to cross-border land transport in Southeast Asia between Thailand, Laos and Viet Nam, and between Mexico and the

United States. Also the corporation will seek to deepen its logistics activities in Central and Eastern Europe, India and Russia. Expansion will also be sought through strategic alliances in China, typified by the corporation's long-standing arrangement with Sinotrans, and its plan to develop further as a 4PL provider.

Summary

These four case studies illustrate how Japan's global logistics corporations have been transformed through alliances, mergers and acquisitions, and cataclysmic events to enable local manufacturers and retailers develop multinational supply chain arrangements. In 2013 their efforts to respond to the post-3/11 earthquake situation were bolstered by the Government of Japan's (2013a, 2013b) fifth Comprehensive Logistics Policy (2013–2017) which seeks to establish an integrated logistics system to support the revitalization and growth of a strong Japanese economy. Reflecting past policies, the future directions target lowering environmental impacts and improving resilience to disasters induced by climate change. Besides affording logistics a pivotal role in improving people's lives, there is an accompanying emphasis on deepening the supply chains of Japanese enterprises in the Asian-Pacific Rim to improve their competitiveness through improvements in trade, customs and quarantine operations (Table 7.14). The government's continuing priority on building a speedy, seamless, cost-effective intermodal distribution system across national borders, especially in Southeast Asia, is to enable the Asian-Pacific Rim to compete on an equal footing with the European Union and members of the North American Free Trade Agreement.

JAPANESE LOGISTICS ACTIVITIES IN SOUTHEAST ASIA

An abiding concern of Japan's comprehensive rolling programme of logistics policies has been a focus on building a seamless distribution system across national borders within the Asian-Pacific Rim. This initiative has been prompted by the shift of production bases from Japan to the Association of Southeast Asian Nations (ASEAN), and the opportunities offered by the growth of the middle class, particularly in Indonesia, Malaysia and Singapore. By 2012 there were 4682 Japanese affiliated companies operating in Southeast Asia, three-fifths of those in the Asia and Oceania region (JETRO, 2013). Most of them were large companies because a major drawback to the business opportunities for Japanese

Table 7.14 Japan's Comprehensive Logistics Policy (2013–2017)

On 25 June 2013, the Cabinet approved the Fundamental Principles of Comprehensive Logistics Policy (2013–2017) in order to present to the public the Government of Japan's guiding principles on logistics and their administration through the collaboration of related ministries and agencies.

Key Points

1. *Logistics that support enterprises' global supply chain*
2. *Logistics with lower environmental burdens*
3. *Logistics with disaster resilience*

Components

Basic directions

The Government of Japan should set the goal of establishing a logistics system that supports the revitalization and growth of a strong Japanese economy (i.e. the realization of optimal logistics operations inside and outside Japan that are devoid of irrationality, waste and inconsistencies).

Future efforts

1. *Realizing streamlined logistics that support industrial activities and people's daily lives*
    - Expanding Japan's logistics systems to logistics clusters in other parts of Asia
    - Improving and effectively utilizing logistics infrastructure to enhance Japan's competitiveness by acquiring locations for establishing new businesses
    - Securing and fostering human resources to support the logistics business
    - Streamlining logistics and improving business structure through collaboration between shippers and logistics providers
    - Logistics that support maintaining and developing people's lives
2. *Efforts toward further reduction of environmental impacts*
3. *Efforts toward ensuring safety and security*
    - Measures against disasters in the logistics field
    - Proper maintenance, management and utilization of infrastructure
    - Achieving a balance between ensuring security and streamlining logistics
    - Ensuring the safety and security of transportation

Future framework to promote logistics policies

The Government of Japan will list specific logistics measures to be advanced into a programme, set a goal with a mid-to-long-term perspective, and prepare a progress schedule to achieve the goal. Based on these efforts, the government will assess the current situations through public-private cooperation, and properly manage the progress using a PDCA (plan-do-check-act) management method.

Note: This is an unofficial translation.

Sources: Government of Japan (2013a, 2013b), METI (2013).

small and medium-sized enterprises in Southeast Asia has been that the region's logistics costs have been double those of Europe (Suenaga, 2004).

The Government of Japan has sought to facilitate the establishment of an ASEAN-wide multimodal transport and logistics network in a bid to reduce logistics costs for the country's manufacturing and retailing enterprises. The Japan External Trade Organization (JETRO, 2008) has identified a network of seven priority cross-border corridors: (1) Bangkok–Kuala Lumpur–Singapore; (2) Bangkok–Vientiane–Hanoi; (3) Hanoi–Guangzhou; (4) Bangkok–Yangon; (5) Bangkok–Phnom Penh–Ho Chi Minh City; (6) Singapore–Jakarta; and (7) Bangkok–Manila (Figure 7.13). Investigations of these corridors by Japanese consultants have been designed to pinpoint bottlenecks, provide policy recommendations to ASEAN countries and facilitate the logistics needs of Japanese companies (e.g. JIFFA, 2012b). The overall aim has been to strengthen 'the competitiveness of the ASEAN region and Japanese companies' (Yoshida, 2006, 3).

JETRO (2008) has also provided basic information on door-to-door costs and transit times for the seven priority routes and illustrated them with reference to specific case studies (JETORO, 2009a). An examination of the cost of moving car parts between Manila and Bangkok, for example, shows that the largest cost is incurred in the Philippines' domestic transport system. Since this survey JETRO has sought to go beyond time and cost considerations by including quality measurements such as the propensity for damage.

These issues have resonated with the Asian Development Bank, of which the Government of Japan is the largest contributor, as both have a shared vision of a prosperous, integrated and harmonious Southeast Asia based primarily on the development of cross-border transport corridors (Faure, 2010). The Bank added four further corridors to JETRO's original seven corridors to complete the network linking key hubs: (8) Bangkok–Kunming–Hanoi; (9) Singapore–Manila; (10) Singapore–Hong Kong; and (11) Hong Kong–Manila (ADB and ADBI, 2009, 90). The 11 corridors have been incorporated in the Bank's subregional framework designed to promote regional economic integration, poverty alleviation and private sector participation in infrastructure projects. The framework comprises: (1) the Greater Mekong Subregion (GMS); (2) the Indonesia–Malaysia–Thailand Growth Triangle (IMT-GT) (Irawady, 2010; Kareem, 2010); and (3) the Brunei Darussalam–Indonesia–Malaysia–Philippines East ASEAN Growth Area (BIMP-EAGA) (see inset, Figure 7.13). Although the Japanese Government's technical cooperation in logistics has spread across all three of the Bank's subregions, its prime target has been the poor quality of the Greater Mekong Subregion's infrastructure. With a land area of 2.6 million sq km and a population of 326 million,

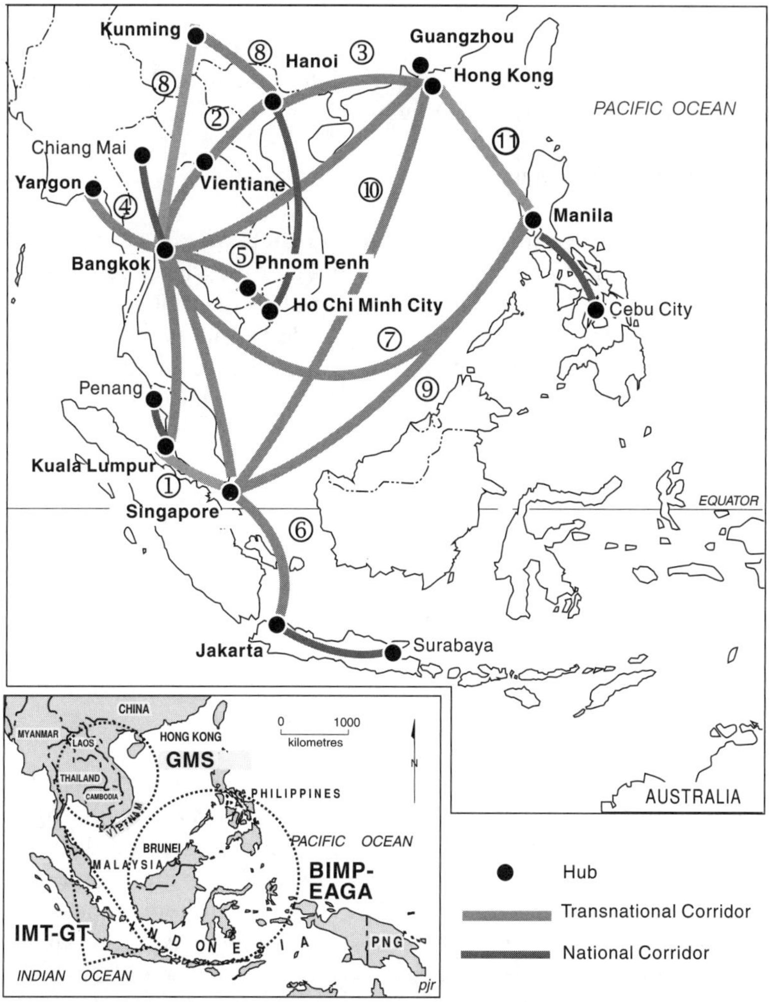

Note: Corridors: (1) Bangkok–Kuala Lumpur–Singapore; (2) Bangkok–Vientiane–Hanoi; (3) Hanoi–Guangzhou; (4) Bangkok–Yangon; (5) Bangkok–Phnom Penh; (6) Singapore–Jakarta; and (7) Bangkok–Manila. Added corridors: (8) Bangkok–Kunming–Hanoi; (9) Singapore–Manila; (10) Singapore–Hong Kong; and (11) Hong Kong–Manila. Subregions: BIMP-EAGA Brunei, Indonesia, Malaysia and the Philippines East Asian Growth Area; GMS Greater Mekong Subregion; and IMT-GT Indonesia–Malaysia–Thailand Growth Triangle.

Sources: Based on ADB (2005), Rimmer and Dick (2012).

Figure 7.13 Southeast Asia's economic corridors with inset showing major subregions, 2012

the subregion covers Cambodia, the Lao People's Democratic Republic (PDR), Myanmar, Thailand and Viet Nam in Mainland Southeast Asia, together with the People's Republic of China's Yunnan Province and the Guangxi Zhuang Autonomous Region.

Greater Mekong Subregion

The Japanese Government's bilateral and multilateral technical cooperation within the Greater Mekong Subregion has been concentrated, in varying degrees, on three economic corridors identified by the Asian Development Bank in 1998 to integrate trade and investment and facilitate the process of shifting from a relative dependence on agriculture into areas of higher-valued production, notably motor vehicle production and electronics:

1. The East–West Economic Corridor running between Da Nang in central Viet Nam and Mawlamyine (Moulmein) in Myanmar to link the South China Sea and the Andaman Sea.
2. The Southern Economic Corridor linking Ho Chi Minh City in southern Viet Nam, Phnom Penh in Cambodia and Bangkok.
3. The North–South Economic Corridor connecting Bangkok and Kunming in southern China (with possible extensions from Kunming to Hanoi and from Hanoi to Guangzhou).

The Japanese Government, together with the Asian Development Bank and its consultants, has devoted much effort to benchmarking the logistics systems capability of the three economic corridors based on their infrastructure, institutional framework, service providers, and shippers and receivers (Banomyong, 2007b, 2008, 2013). Also their door-to-door travel time and logistics costs by land and sea transport have been analysed between the terminal cities in each economic corridor before gauging the potential of improving road transport to reduce them (Table 7.15).

The East–West Economic Corridor was the first to attract the interest of the Japanese Government because it would not only expand 'the manufacturing and sales activities of the locally established Japanese businesses' and logistics companies but also contribute to the investment environments of Thailand and Viet Nam and the economic growth of Laos (Suenaga, 2004, 12). As ocean transport was taking 10–15 days between Bangkok in Thailand and Hanoi in Viet Nam, a land transport (truck) corridor route across Laos to link the two capitals would, provided bottlenecks at border crossings were overcome, shorten transit time for the 1555 km journey to three days. In 2004 the need to traverse

Table 7.15 Door-to-door inter-city transport costs in Southeast Asia's major corridors, 2006

Corridors	Land transport			Sea transport		Remarks
	km	days	cost US$	days	cost US$	
1. North–South						
Bangkok–Hanoi (via Mekong & Kunming)	2719	6	n.a.	10–15	2000	
Hanoi–Guangzhou	1190	2	3000	4–6	560	40ft container including customs
2. East–West						
Bangkok–Hanoi (via Savannakhet & Dongha)	1555	3–4	4200	10–15	2000	40ft container including customs
Bangkok–Yangon	945	3	730	30	1130	10t truck & 20ft container, excluding customs
3. Southern						
Bangkok–HCMC–Vung Tau	913	2	1390	2–3	560	10t truck & 20ft container, excluding customs
4. Malay Peninsula						
Singapore/Kuala Lumpur–Bangkok	1550	3	1673	6	1360	10t truck & 20ft container, excluding customs

Note: In 2006 the cost per ton from Hanoi to Kunming was US$270; the cost per TEU from Haiphong to Kunming was US$1579 (Banomyong, 2007a).

Sources: Banomyong (2007a), JETRO (2008), JICA (2007).

Laos led to adoption of a model Cross Border Transport Agreement (CBTA) (Takeuchi, 2007). Once the feasibility of the East–West Corridor between Bangkok and Hanoi was established by a pilot demonstration project undertaken by the Sumitomo Corporation (METI, 2005), attention turned to linking Bangkok to Yangon (945 km) in Myanmar because the sea route between the two is circuitous. Further, by extending the route beyond Yangon to Mawlamyine it is possible to link the South China Sea and the Andaman Sea.

The Southern Economic Corridor linking the vibrant economic hub of Ho Chi Minh City and Bangkok also attracted strong technical cooperation from the Japanese Government. The benefits of improved land transport are less obvious because 2–3 days door-to-door transport by sea compares with two days by road, although Phnom Penh may develop as an economic outpost due to the attractive backhaul rates on offer (Rimmer and Dick, 2012).

The North–South Economic Corridor, connecting Bangkok and Hanoi via Kunming, attracted less direct technical support from the Japanese Government because the route suggested by the Asian Development Bank strengthened 'vertical' linkages between China and Thailand via Laos (Shiraishi, 2010; Taillard, 2010). Although the route was more roundabout than the direct 'horizontal' East–West route, its potential was deemed greater because of its bigger population, population density and gross regional domestic product (Ishida, 2010; Montague, 2007; ADB, 2008a, 2009). The corridor was expected to attract larger private sector investment to border economic zones and generate greater economic activity among smaller cities and rural areas than the East–West route. The corridor offered the prospect of not only connecting Hanoi to Guangzhou but also linking Shanghai.

The growing presence of China prompted the Japanese Government to strengthen its commitment to the East–West and Southern Economic corridors as the infrastructure development and trade facilitation have had positive impacts on incomes and poverty levels within 20 km of these arteries (Fujimura, 2006; Edmonds and Fujimura, 2006, 2008; Stone et al., 2012). This success prompted the Asian Development Bank (ADB) to redefine and update the GMS corridors. The three original corridors, East–West, Southern and North–South, were expanded to nine by adding the Eastern (Kunming–Ca Mau), Southern Coastal (Vung Tau–Dawei), Central (Kunming-Sihanoukville with branch to Sattahip), Northern (Tamu–Fangcheng), Western (Tamu–Mawlamyine) and Northeastern (Thanh Hoa–Bangkok–Laem Chabang) corridors (Figure 7.14). While the ADB's additional corridors provided the Japanese Government with a greater array of opportunities to invest in multimodal transport corridor projects that created connectivity, its policy shifted towards the adoption of a broader logistics policy framework that identifies the need to invest in gateways.

Japan's Asian Gateway Initiative

Japan's technical cooperation has sought to complement ASEAN's (2007) Roadmap for the Integration of Logistics Services across its ten member

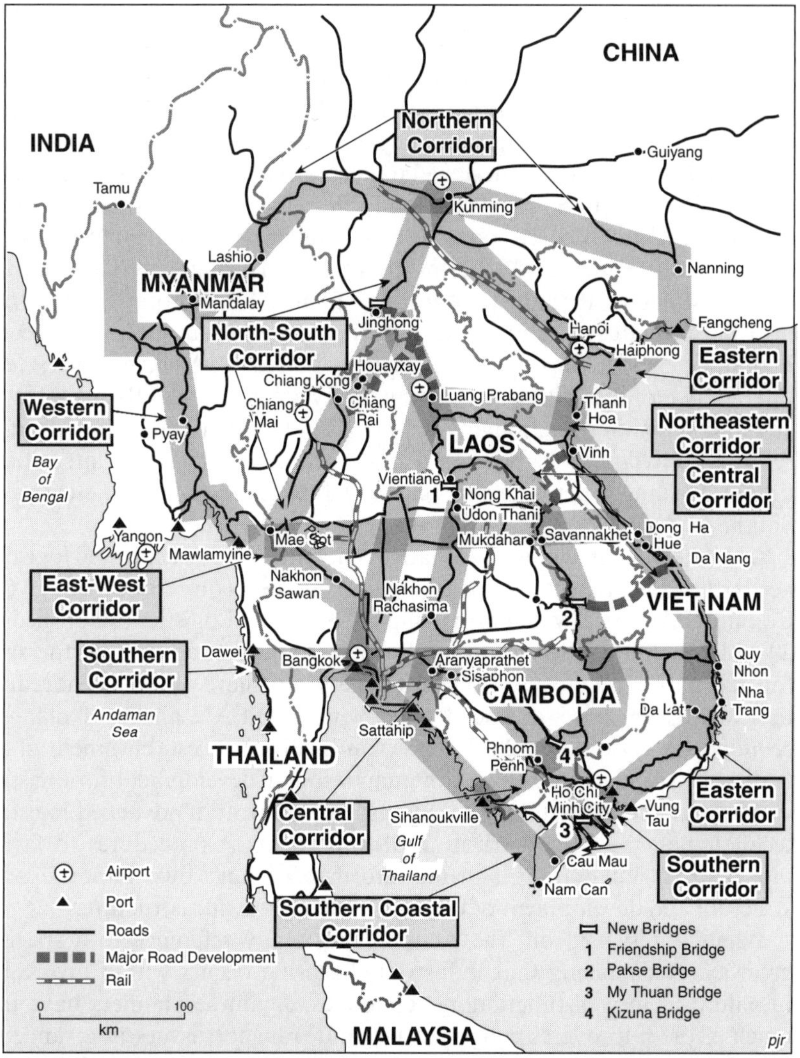

Note: 1. North–South Corridor (NSC): Bangkok to Kunming; 2. Eastern Corridor (EC): Kunming to Ca Mau; 3. East–West Corridor (EWC): Mawlamyine to Da Nang; 4. Southern Corridor (SC): Dawei to Quy Nhon/Vung Tau; 5. Southern Coastal Corridor (SCC): Bangkok to Nam Can; 6. Central Corridor (CC): Kunming to Sihanoukville/ Sattahip; 7. Northern Corridor (NC): Fangcheng to Tamu; 8. Western Corridor (WC): Tamu to Mawlamyine; and 9. Northeastern Corridor (NEC): Thanh Hoa to Bangkok/Laem Chabang.

Sources: Information from ADB (2012a, 2012b).

Figure 7.14 Redefined economic corridors in Greater Mekong Subregion

states and the Master Plan for ASEAN Connectivity, designed to expand the capability and competitiveness of the region's third-party logistics service providers and develop human resources (ASEAN, 2010). These logistics objectives reflect Prime Minister Abe's earlier Council for Asian Gateway Initiative (CAGI, 2007) – a package of ten major policy priorities and seven priority areas – designed to keep Japan at the forefront of logistics development in Southeast Asia (Table 7.16). Three of the Initiative's ten projects are focused on logistics: streamlining trade measures to achieve both security and efficient logistics; transforming agriculture into a successful growth industry through enhanced collaboration with the distribution industry; and creating the prototype Asian Gateway Special Economic Zone to improve the efficiency of logistics. Also, logistics is featured in two of the Initiative's seven priority areas: the 'Big Bang' in travel and transportation embodying a long list of user-friendly, but drastic, reforms to aviation, seaports and trade procedures; and the intensification of exchanges between subregions in Japan and industrial clusters in Southeast Asia.

As Japan's Asian Gateway Initiative echoed ASEAN's expressed logistics needs, the Government of Japan sought to pursue its objectives through the Committee on Asia-wide Partnership for Seamless Logistics established in 2006 (IIST, 2007). The Committee formulated the Action Plan Partnership for International Logistics Competitiveness to achieve a 50 per cent reduction in logistics costs and lead times within ASEAN ahead of planned economic integration by 2015. This plan involves the establishment of an ASEAN-wide logistics network; human resource development for logistics and import/export customs procedures; employment of advanced logistics technologies; the computerization of import/export procedures to facilitate ASEAN integration; and the reform of Japan's own import/export structure and development of customs systems and infrastructure.

What is missing from the Action Plan is any reference to a specific gateway. Recognizing that industrial clustering occurs within proximity of gateways in well-functioning economies, Japanese planners have put much effort into overcoming land use and transport issues in a range of ASEAN's mega-urban regions such as Bangkok, Jakarta and Manila, to streamline the supply and distribution of goods to benefit the offshore activities of Japanese manufacturers and retailers (Rimmer, 1986). Particular attention has been centred on the legendary traffic problems of Greater Bangkok, which is regarded as the pivot of the Greater Mekong Subregion (Supatn, 2011). Japanese motor vehicle and electronics companies, notably Honda, Toyota and Sony, and their component manufacturers, together with Japanese logistics providers such as Sagawa Express, have been attracted to Thailand's 45 industrial estates, particularly those

Table 7.16 Japan's Asian Gateway initiative, 2007: sections related to the logistics sector

Major Policy Priorities

1. Change in aviation policy to achieve 'Asian Open Skies'
   - Form a strategic international aviation network through aviation liberalization with other Asian countries to invigorate regional economies and improve consumer convenience
   - Make Haneda Airport more international; facilitate 24-hour operation of major international airports by promoting the use of late-night and early-morning slots whose usage is currently low
2. Implement a programme for streamlining trade measures

Reforms in customs clearance and other relevant procedures so as to enhance logistic capacity for international trade

   - A major challenge is establishing programmes and systems aimed at achieving both security and efficient logistics
   - Revision of the Program for Streamlining based on the framework of the Partnership for International Logistics Competitiveness Programme
3. Transform agriculture into a successful growth industry during the globalization era
   - Foster collaboration with other industries, such as distribution, logistics, food and financial industries, to enhance managerial capacity concerning sales, finance, etc.
4. Create an 'Asian Gateway Special Zone'
   - Enhancing exchange with Asia by encouraging such initiatives to improve the efficiency of logistics and simplify trade procedures in a way that increases the nighttime use of facilities

Priority Areas

1. 'Big Bang' in travel and transportation – user-friendly but drastic reforms to aviation, seaports and trade procedures
   - Construct additional logistics facilities, in competition with other Asian airports
   - Provide fast and convenient international logistics in Kansai & Central Japan
   - Step up efforts to build a seamless network of land, sea and air transport by accelerating the construction of roads that give access to key airports and seaports
   - Construct a trunk network for international logistics (approx. 34 000 km) by expediting efforts to turn the 47 areas currently not navigable by container trucks of international standard size into navigable ones (within the next ten years)
   - To allow the Super Core Ports to offer world-class seaport logistics services
   - Achieve more efficient and seamless logistics in coastal areas

Table 7.16 (continued)

Priority Areas

- Create large-scale sophisticated logistics centres that work in harmony with container terminals and other facilities
- Promote the development of aids (e.g. nighttime quarantine support facilities, common depots) that contribute to advances in seaport logistics

2. Promote every region of Japan, incorporating the vitality of Asia by providing a way for Japanese regions to dramatically enhance their exchanges with Asian regions
   - Improve road infrastructure in a way that provides better access to tourist attractions and logistics centres
   - Create wide-area logistics networks and enable electronic procedures in order to establish a seamless logistics network

Note: Only major policies and priority areas involving logistics are listed.

Source: CAGI (2007).

concentrated within a 100 km radius of Suvarnabhumi International Airport (Figure 7.15). Not only do the industrial estates offer some 1500 Japanese companies access to the airport and seaports, but the urban agglomeration also provides them with important scale economies and low transport costs (Fujita, 2012).

The quality of economic space in Thailand decays rapidly as one moves beyond the Greater Bangkok gateway. Some non-gateway locations are likely to impose higher overall unit costs for non-agricultural and non-resource developments, place some firms at a competitive disadvantage, and provide serious obstacles to the Thai Government's dreams of efficient decentralized locations. Considerable care needs to taken that the new enthusiasm for land-based infrastructure in cross-border special economic zones is not at the expense of high-yielding investments in vital gateway infrastructure. The apparent need for cross-border infrastructure catered for by the GMS Cross Border Transport Agreement (CBTA) may in large part be a product of the artificial 'distortions' created by national policy regimes (Rimmer and Dick, 2012). For example, the likely outcomes of the cross-border economic zone on the Myanmar–Thailand border are that refugee Burmese labour ends up on the Thai side and firms on the Myanmar side engage in a range of 'smuggling' activities that are illegal in Thailand. If the aim of cross-border special economic zones is to by-pass irksome regulations, this is a good way of undermining national policy. Over time, liberalization and harmonization of

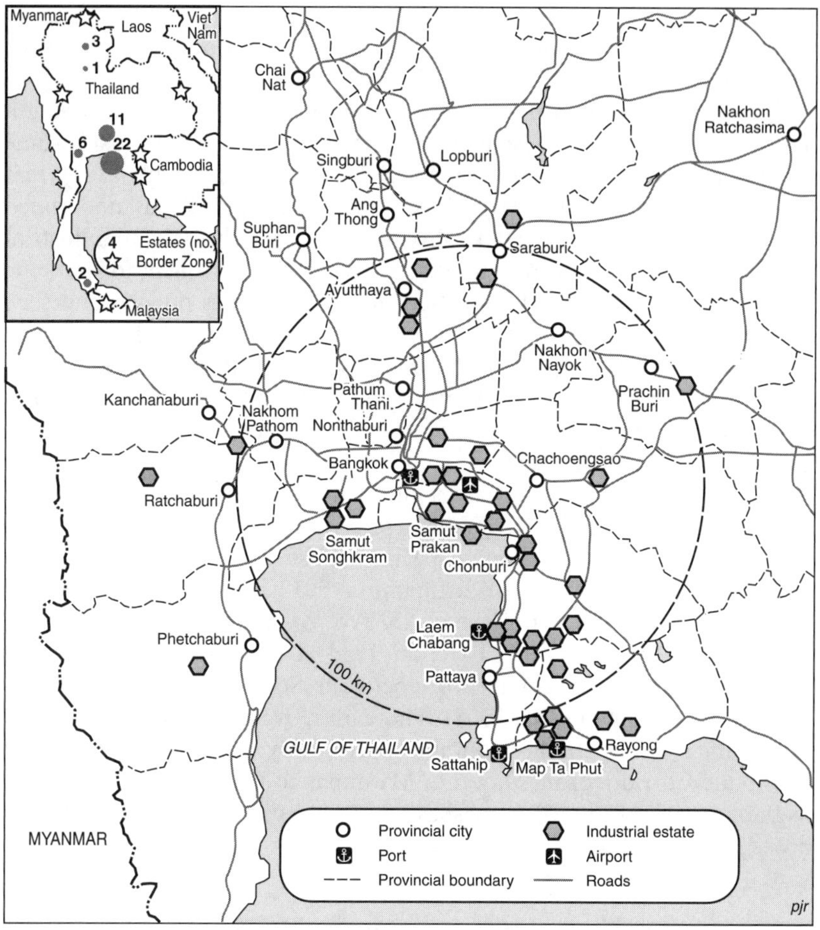

Note: The circle defines the area within100 km radius of the Suvarnabhumi International Airport.

Source: IEAT (2014).

Figure 7.15 (A) Location of industrial estates within Greater Bangkok; and (B) Inset showing the number of industrial estates and cross-border economic zones in Thailand, 2014

ASEAN policy regimes should gradually whittle away these distortions. Meanwhile the best returns are to be derived from large infrastructure projects in the Greater Bangkok gateway, particularly those that combat flooding. Between September and December 2011 Thailand's Great

Flood inundated several industrial estates and disrupted the supply chain of motor vehicle components and computer parts produced by and for Japanese companies.

The short-lived disruptions, reflected in sharp downturns in production and export performance, have exposed the downside risks of just-in-time procurement and production (Chongvilaivan, 2012). Thailand's Great Flood, coupled with the Great East Japan Earthquake, has underlined the importance of dynamic flexibility to Japanese multinational industrial corporations. They have prompted the Japanese Government to stress the importance of disaster risk management in its logistics policies and seek to encourage the development of more resilient supply chains by using a greater range of production bases. Besides targeting less flood-prone regions of Thailand, where the Industrial Estate Authority of Thailand (IEAT) is offering new sites, locations in Cambodia, Laos, Myanmar and Viet Nam are also being canvassed by Japanese Government agencies (Ono, 2009). These searches are spurred not only by recurrent political unrest in Bangkok, but also by Japanese-owned factories located in China being affected by rising wages, especially those engaged in labour-intensive production (Hoshino, 2012; Imamura, 2012; Abe, 2013). As Chinese interests seek to 'structure' these ASEAN economies, consideration is also being given by Japan's External Trade Organization to enhancing multimodal transport connections between Southeast Asia and India (Matsushima, 2008; Fujita, 2008). These initiatives have led to the definition of the Mekong–India Economic Corridor by extending the Southern Economic Corridor from Dawei in Myanmar to Chennai and Bangalore in India, a proposition that meshes with the Asian Development Bank's broader strategy for a seamless Asia (see Chapter 12).

CONCLUSION: DIFFERENCES BETWEEN JAPAN AND EUROPE

Having discussed Japan's rolling logistics policy, the production networks of Toyota and Sony, four case studies of key Japanese logistics providers, and the country's activities in Southeast Asia, this section discusses how Japan's experience in logistics and supply chain management differs from other major players. Why does the application of the key characteristics of global logistics services and multinational supply chain management designed to improve efficiency and profitability – lean logistics, the development of information and communications technology, value-adding, outsourcing, and integrated control – differ when they are applied in Japan?

This issue prompted Masato Shinohara (2006) to undertake a

comparative study of Japanese and European logistics management – represented by the Netherlands – to find out what causes differences between the two, and whether a universal logistics framework can emerge to better manage logistics and expanding multinational supply chains. Explanations for the variations between Japanese and European logistics were sought in the embeddedness of value systems and cultures, and the institutional environment (covering policy, the judiciary and the bureaucracy) and governance, involving both contracts and management policies. Based on the perceptions of logisticians in Japan and the Netherlands, differences were detected in both business practices, exemplified by variations in resource allocation and allotment, and in governance, typified by variations in contracts and management policies.

The key findings of Shinohara's study are that logistics in Japan is dictated by customer satisfaction and long-standing collaboration, whereas logistics in Europe is mainly regulated by logicality and fairness. European perceptions of Japanese practice are that it leads to excessive service and accountability. Conversely, Japanese perceptions of European practice are that it produces less customer service and is overly rigid in its adherence to the terms of the contract. Both areas have sought to adopt the strengths of the alternative conceptual framework. This has led to the Japanization of logistics management in Europe and the Europeanization of logistics management in Japan. As no universal logistics management framework has yet emerged, it is important to continue to distinguish between the global and the local.

8. South Korea

Logistics in South Korea is very much a post-Korean War (1950–53) phenomenon. Times were so parlous after the end of the war that company workers used their own vehicles to make deliveries. Between 1960 and 1990 there was a shift in the balance from the local to the global arena stemming from the rapid transformation of an abject economy, which led to the greater use of road transport at the expense of rail and the emergence of logistics as a key issue. Over this period there was a progressive shift in the economy from having an agricultural base to becoming an industrial powerhouse featuring large national manufacturing corporations engaged in iron and steel production and shipbuilding, and exports of textiles, shoes, cars and nascent consumer electronics, notably household appliances and televisions. As a last resort for attaining market competitiveness, the emerging multinational industrial corporations sought cost reductions from efficient logistics and customer service improvements.

During the 1990s the South Korean Government responded to the logistics needs of an increasing number of multinational manufacturing and retailing companies by seeking to provide the necessary infrastructure through investments in ports and freight terminals, as a means of expanding social overhead capital and encouraging a reverse shift from road to rail-based multimodal transport (Rimmer, 1995; KOTI-KSP, 2012). In 1992 the issue of the Seoul Metropolitan Region being 350 km from the country's major deep-sea port of Busan was addressed. Logistics centres were built, near both the capital and Busan, to relieve growing congestion at the port prior to berths becoming operational at the new port of Gwangyang Bay in 1998, and an array of inland logistics centres being completed to support export-oriented growth (Figure 8.1).

Since the Asian Financial Crisis (1997–98) the industrial era has progressively given way to a post-industrial epoch featuring knowledge-based industries, underpinned by information technology (IT), biotechnology (BT), nanotechnology (NT) and the fusion of all three, to capitalize on South Korea's strengths in technology and design. Although elements of the earlier agricultural and industrial phases persist, particularly shipbuilding, information and communications technology (ICT) has become the main driver of South Korea's sustained economic growth and the

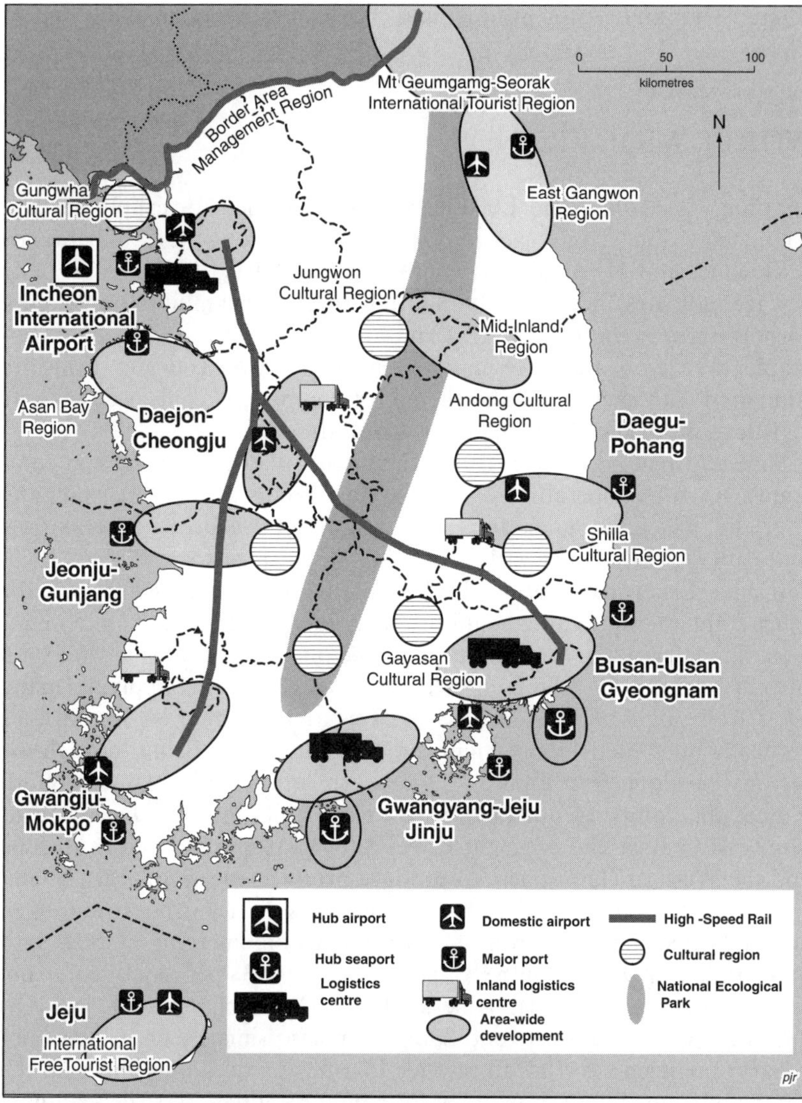

Source: Information from ROK (2001, 121).

Figure 8.1 Location map showing major development regions and projects of the Fourth Comprehensive National Territorial Plan, 2000–2020

country's reputation for product and process excellence rivalling that of Japan.

WORLDWIDE BRANDS

Samsung Electronics and LG Electronics, renowned for cellphones and digital television technologies respectively, rank among the leading brands worldwide, and Hyundai Motor has been revitalized by an infusion of new technologies and design. As South Korean-based multinational retail corporations, exemplified by E-Land, do not have the comparable geographical reach of the three manufacturers, the two electronics firms are compared with each other and the motor company is contrasted with its logistics subsidiary, Hyundai Glovis Co. Ltd.

Samsung Electronics Co. Ltd is the largest of the Samsung conglomerate's 83 firms operating under the Lee family's umbrella company Everland, which accounted for 13 per cent of South Korea's gross exports in 2010 (*The Economist*, 2011). Starting with transistor radios in 1969, Samsung Electronics has evolved from manufacturing televisions for other companies into a high-end producer of consumer electronics items, including televisions, smartphones, mobile phones and tablets, with sales surpassing US$135 billion in 2010 (Samsung, 2011). Supplying many parts from its own divisions, the market-driven, digital e-corporation's vertically integrated supply chain is orchestrated from Seoul through ten regional headquarters (Figure 8.2A). Apart from the nine plants in South Korea, the company operated 31 overseas units in 2010, heavily concentrated in Asia and augmented by scattered plants situated in Europe and the Western Hemisphere to produce products meeting local demand specifications. The corporation's 58 sales subsidiaries in 51 countries in 2010 reflected the move from its earlier focus on emerging markets into industrialized regions: South Korea accounted for 38 per cent of company revenue, Europe and North America 18 per cent each, China 17 per cent and the rest of Asia 9 per cent. Samsung relies primarily on its own subsidiary, Logitech Co. Ltd, to provide logistics services that underpin the company's capacity to draw upon its capital resources, to scale manufacture up very quickly and to supply components to other corporations such as Apple Inc.

LG Electronics Co. Ltd, formerly Lucky Goldstar Co. Ltd, commenced operations in 1958 to manufacture South Korea's first domestic radio (LG, 2009). Since then LG Electronics, supported by overseas research and development facilities in China, Germany, Japan and the United States, has grown into a manufacturer of home entertainment, mobile

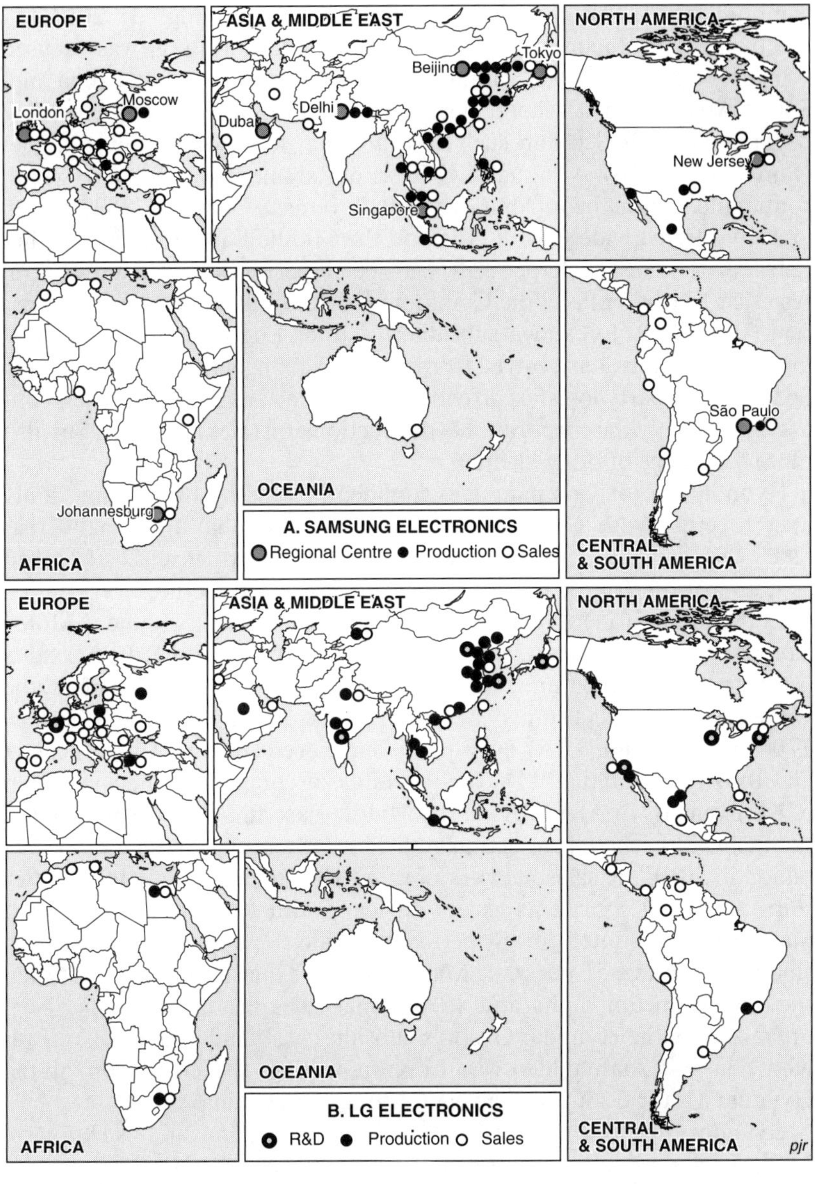

Sources: Data from Samsung (2011), LG (2011).

Figure 8.2 Corporate production networks of South Korean multinationals: (A) Samsung Electronics Co. Ltd, 2010; and (B) LG Electronics Co. Ltd, 2010

communications, home appliances and air conditioning. By 2010 LG Electronics' production network, in contrast to Samsung, was focused primarily on the BRICS countries (Brazil, Russia, India, China and South Africa) and a second tier of middle-income countries emerging beyond the BRICS group such as Indonesia, Mexico, Poland and Viet Nam (Figure 8.2B). Although LG Electronics' sales network traversed all continents, regional contributions to its revenue of almost US$90 billion in 2010 differed widely, with Asia and the Middle East generating 37 per cent, North America 26 per cent, Europe 18 per cent, South and Central America 12 per cent and the Commonwealth of Independent States 5 per cent (LG, 2011). LG's own subsidiary, Pantos Logistics, Korea's largest logistics company, has evolved from an airfreight agent in 1977 into a fully fledged third-party logistics provider with operations in 37 countries, connecting not only the corporation's production and sales networks, but also those of a range of other clients.

Hyundai Motor Company was founded in 1967 by the Chung family and, together with Kia, acquired during the Global Financial Crisis (2008–09), comprises the Hyundai Motor Group, which in 2010 ranked as the world's fourth-largest motor vehicle manufacturer on annual sales (Schmitt, 2011). Excluding Kia's contribution, the Hyundai Motor Company produced over 3.6 million units in 2010: South Korean plants generated 1.74 million units; China 705 000 units, India 600 000 units, the United States 500 000 units, Czech Republic 200 000 units and Turkey 77 000 units (Figure 8.3A). New plants have been added in China, Russia and Brazil (Hyundai, 2011). The assembly of completely knocked down (CKD) vehicles in Africa, Asia, the Middle East and South America was not included in these production statistics. Generating revenue of US$98 billion in 2010, the sales network covered 180 countries and 6000 dealerships across all continents except Africa: South Korea and the United States each accounted for 18 per cent of sales, Europe 13 per cent and emerging markets 51 per cent. Management of the supply chain between the ten production units and 15 national sales headquarters has been organized by the Hyundai Group's subsidiary, Hyundai Glovis Co. Ltd, whose largest shareholder was Eui-Son Chung, the eldest son of the Hyundai Motor Group's Chairman, Mong-Koo Chung.

Hyundai Glovis Co. Ltd was founded in Seoul during 2001 as Hankook Co. Ltd, changed its name to Glovis in 2003, and assumed its current name in 2011 (Hyundai Glovis, 2012). The subsidiary has established its reputation as an integrated global second-party logistics (2PL) provider engaged in the shipment and distribution of Hyundai and Kia motor vehicles on behalf of the Hyundai Motor Group by supplying ocean, air and inland transport, storage, packaging and recycling services. This worldwide

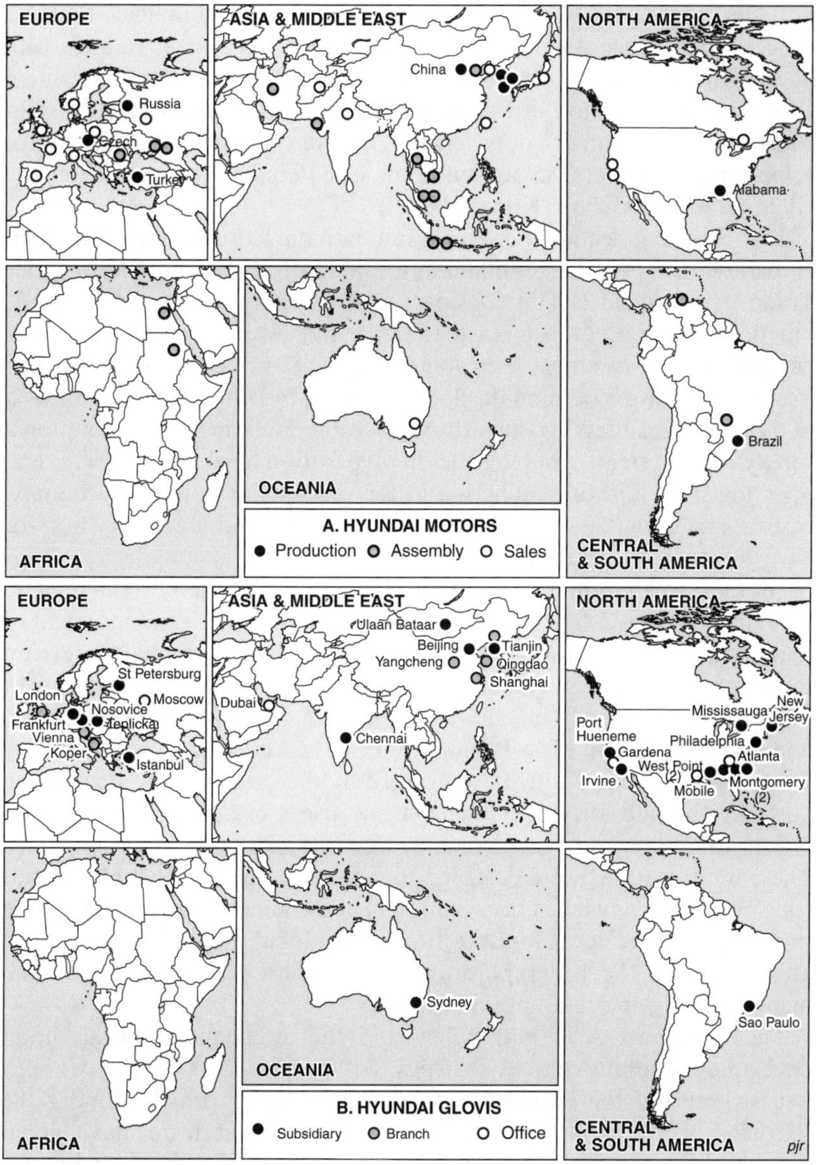

Sources: Data from Hyundai (2011), Hyundai Glovis (2012).

Figure 8.3 Corporate networks of South Korean multinationals and global logistics corporations: (A) Hyundai Motor Corporation, 2010; and (B) Hyundai Glovis Co. Ltd, 2010

provider has 20 subsidiaries, four offices and seven branches that are concentrated in the Asian Pacific Rim, Europe and North America with outliers in Oceania and South America (Figure 8.3B). Although Hyundai Glovis has moved into third-party logistics activities, involving chemicals, construction, consumer goods, energy, machinery, steel and other motor vehicle manufacturers, 85 per cent of its US$16 billion income is from the Hyundai Motor Group (Kim, 2012).

The close connection between multinational corporations and their global logistics providers is contentious in South Korea, because the Fair Trade Commission (FTC) considers that this may lead to unfair trade practices. This situation has led to successive South Korean Presidents being pressured to adjust their logistics policies not only to address this issue but also to accommodate global logistics, by offering links to the rest of the world; seamless logistics, through accommodating the multinational supply chain system; cyber logistics in preparation for the e-commerce era; open logistics, faithfully adhering to the precepts of a market economy; custom-made logistics, to satisfy client demands; and green logistics, for environmental friendliness and safety.

South Korea's initial policy response occurred under President Kim Dae Jung's (1998–2003) 'People's Government' with the announcement of the economy's first National Logistics Plan (2001–20) designed to develop Incheon as a logistics hub for Northeast Asia (Table 8.1). Subsequent modifications and refinements were made to the logistics hub strategy under President Roh Moo-Hyun's (2003–08) decentralized 'Participatory Government', which sought to transform the economy by developing not only the hub airport at Incheon but also mega-ports in Busan and Gwangyang Bay, and Free Economic Zones (FEZs) at all three locations. These modifications were designed to capitalize upon the country's strategic position sandwiched between Japan and China, and to encourage the transformation of local logistics firms into global network corporations able to extend the geographical reach of South Korean multinational manufacturing and retailing enterprises.

The Northeast Asia hub policy and the attendant emphasis upon developing budding global logistics service providers raises two key issues: how did the Northeast Asian hub strategy progress under the Participatory Government? And how far and to what degree have global network corporations emerged in South Korea to exploit the Participatory Government's strategy?

These issues are addressed initially by outlining South Korea's first National Logistics Plan (2001–20) and tracking subsequent modifications. The development of Incheon as an international airport for the National Capital Region, centred on Seoul, is traced and contrasted

Table 8.1 Major logistics policies in Korea, 2001–20

Title	Date	Ministry
Government of the People (1998–2003)		
National Logistics Basic Plan, 2001–2020	*2001*	*Ministry of Construction & Transportation*
Industrial Logistics Innovation Plan	2002	Ministry of Industry & Resources
Participatory Government (2003–2008)		
Northeast Asia Logistics Road Map	2003	Joint Government Ministries
National Logistics System Improvement Measure	2004	Ministry of Finance & Economy
Specialized Logistics Company Promotion Plan	2004	Presidential Committee on Northeast Asian Cooperation Initiative
National Logistics Basic Plan Modification Plan (2006–2020)	*2006*	*Ministry of Construction & Transportation*
Promulgation of Logistics Policy Basic Law and Logistics Facility Law	2007	Ministry of Construction & Transportation
Pragmatic Government (2008–2013)		
Service Industry Advancement Plan	2009	Ministry of Planning & Finance & six other ministries
National Logistics Master Plan, 2011–2020[1]	*2011*	*Ministry of Land, Transport & Maritime Affairs*

Note: [1]This is related to the Metropolitan Logistics Master Plan (2011–2020) and the Provincial Master Plan (2011–2020).

with the mega-ports of Busan and Gwangyang Bay, to elaborate and evaluate aspects of this modified Plan with reference to their attached Free Economic Zones (FEZs) as hosts of multinational industrial corporations. As global logistics corporations play a pivotal role in South Korea's major gateways, special consideration is given to them by focusing upon the rise of Korea's Hanjin Group to assess the degree to which the family conglomerate (*chaebol*) has attained global player status. Then this chapter considers changes to South Korea's logistics policy under President Lee Myun-Bak's (2008–2013) 'Pragmatic Government' and considers the likely trajectory of the new National Logistics Basic Plan (2011–2020) under the Park Geun-hye Government that began its five-year term in 2013.

THE NATIONAL LOGISTICS BASIC PLAN (2001–20)

A key policy goal of Kim Dae Jung's 'People's Government' (1998–2003), following the Asian Financial Crisis (1997–98), was to improve national competitiveness through a core competency in logistics. This emphasis on logistics was an integral part of the Government's plan to move from the then 30-year-old developmental state model, which involved close and opaque business–government relations, to a market-oriented approach to economic growth based upon foreign direct investment and market-friendly, transparent corporate governance (Lee and Hobday, 2003). Apart from easing freight regulations and strengthening customer protection, the strategy underpinning the rolling National Logistics Basic Plan (2001–20), developed by the then Ministry of Construction and Transportation (MOCT), concentrated upon infrastructure development including the opening of Incheon International Airport in 2001. Implementation of this Plan favoured road transport at the expense of other modes; this shift is understated, because annual figures have been restricted to tonnage, as information on tonne-kilometres has not been published in the country's statistical yearbook since 1999 (Table 8.2). In addition, the Government's

Table 8.2 Annual freight traffic by mode, 1998–2011

Year	Rail		Road		Shipping		Aviation		Total
	mn tonnes	%	mn tonnes	%	mn tonnes	%	mn tonnes	%	mn tonnes
1998	53.8	7.7	499.1	71.3	147.0	21.0	0.4	0.0	700.3
1999	43.3	7.6	408.1	71.9	115.2	20.3	0.4	0.1	567.0
2000	45.2	6.7	496.1	73.4	134.5	19.9	0.4	0.1	676.3
2001	45.1	6.3	535.7	74.2	140.5	19.5	0.4	0.1	721.8
2002	45.7	5.9	584.6	75.7	141.7	18.3	0.4	0.1	772.4
2003	47.1	6.2	565.5	74.6	145.3	19.2	0.4	0.1	758.3
2004	44.5	6.6	518.9	76.4	115.6	17.0	0.4	0.1	679.4
2005	41.7	6.1	526.0	76.5	119.4	17.4	0.4	0.1	687.4
2006	43.3	6.3	529.5	76.6	117.8	17.1	0.4	0.1	690.8
2007	44.6	6.2	550.3	76.9	120.1	16.8	0.3	0.1	715.2
2008	46.8	6.4	555.8	76.2	127.0	17.4	0.3	0.0	729.6
2009	38.8	5.1	607.5	79.2	120.0	15.7	0.3	0.0	766.7
2010	39.2	5.0	619.5	79.6	119.0	15.3	0.3	0.0	778.0
2011	40.0	5.1	633.9	80.8	110.1	14.0	0.3	0.0	784.3

Note: No figures have been given for tonne-kilometres since 1999.

Sources: MLTM (2009), SK (2013).

Plan sought to control the location of freight terminals, create logistics information networks, rationalize warehousing and storage systems, and standardize pallets and packing to improve loading productivity. Little attention was paid in the Plan to creating an integrated multimodal transport system, establishing further inland container depots, developing specialized logistics personnel, or fostering global network corporations, despite additional support through the Logistics Innovation Plan augmented by the Ministry of Industry and Resources in 2002.

Roh Moo-Hyun's 'Participatory Government' (2003–08) sought to address the initial National Logistics Plan's shortcomings (Jung, 2008). This action was spurred by both: (1) external threats stemming from the 'nutcracker crisis' of being sandwiched between China and Japan, and the prospect of intensifying competition from emerging logistics hubs in the Asian-Pacific Rim; and (2) persistent internal weaknesses arising from the economy's declining growth potential due to deindustrialization and low productivity in the services sector, other than air transport, construction and engineering, and an unsatisfactory business environment (regulations, labour disputes, high land prices and poor living conditions for foreigners). The Government responded by making a series of modifications to its overall economic strategy by making logistics a core concern of the country's economy in a bid to take advantage of new investment opportunities in China and diminish the continuing technology gap with Japan.

In August 2003 the Joint Government Ministries put forward the National Logistics Road Map (2003), which, together with the Ministry of Finance and Economy's National Logistics System Improvement Measure, sought to promote South Korea as Northeast Asia's logistics business centre. The centre's rationale was that it would supply business, logistics and information services to neighbouring China and Japan, and would connect with other regional economic zones in the Asian-Pacific Rim. Opportunities would also be provided to attract the headquarters of global logistics corporations to the hub and offer a regional gateway for multinational industrial corporations to establish bases near seaports and airports. Companies would have the prospect of supplying value-added services, notably manufacturing, assembly, processing, and packing and labelling that use raw materials, components and goods accumulated throughout Northeast Asia. Although the region's economic zone includes both China and Japan, has a population of 1.5 billion within a four-hour flight distance of Seoul, and its share of world production is expected to increase to 30 per cent in 2020, compared with less than 21 per cent at the beginning of the millennium, there has been no distinctive logistics hub serving Northeast Asia's diverse subregions because it is neither a single market nor a unified one.

The Participatory Government sought to plug this gap in Northeast Asia's logistics arena by making South Korea as a whole one of the required business hubs, and seeking to derive value from the transhipment of goods, people and information passing to, from and through the country's airports, ports and teleports, and free economic zones (PCNABH, 2003; PCNACI, 2004). Four main tasks were identified:

1. The expansion of logistics infrastructure to develop strategic hubs by executing the second stage of Incheon International Airport and providing a second connecting bridge and airport railway; building 29 new berths at Busan New Port (opened in 2006) and 21 new berths at Gwangyang Port that sit astride the world's main container shipping trunk route; and strengthening the international rail network to connect with Trans-China Railway (TCR), Trans-Manchurian Railway (TMR) and Trans-Siberian Railway (TSR) via North Korea.
2. The establishment of an efficient logistics network by improving freight transport systems with increased investments in railways to move away from road-based infrastructure; increasing railway efficiency through upgrading (for example, electrification and multi-tracking); and developing multimodal transport.
3. An improvement in logistics productivity by standardizing equipment (for example, pallets), automating warehousing and stevedoring, and 'informationalizing' logistics by integrating advanced technologies into the sector; expanding the network to interconnect with related local trade, clearance, financial and overseas systems; and developing human resources through the sponsorship of academic programmes and boosting the capabilities of professionals.
4. The enhancement of the logistics industry's competitiveness by minimizing economic restrictions and maximizing consumer protection, adopting an integrated logistics company certification system, diversifying the functions of warehousing and storage units, and providing strong government support to promote third-party logistics (3PL).

A key feature of the Participatory Government strategy was to establish and plan an array of logistics nodes beyond the inland container depots (ICDs) and integrated freight terminals (IFTs) built under previous regimes (Table 8.3).

Activities at the port were to be replicated inland, as rail transport from the pier to the customs house was designed to offer simplified bonded transport at the new Honam, Chungbu and Youngnam inland logistics

Table 8.3 Logistics facilities in South Korea, 1993–2014

Region	Location	Type	Opened	Distance from Seoul km	Size thous. sq. metres	Funding model
Seoul	Uiwang	ICD	1993	30	750	BOT
Seoul	Gunpo I	IFT	1997	23	380	BOT
Busan	Yangsan	IFT	1999	400	320	BOT
Busan	Yangsan	ICD	2000	400	950	BOT
Honam	Jangseong	ILB	2005	270	520	BOO
Chungbu	Cheongwon/ Yeonji	ILB	2010	121	480	BOO
Youngnam	Chilgok	ILB	2010	248	450	BOO
Seoul	Gunpo II	IFT	2012	23	350	BOO
Seoul	Paju	ILB	2013	54	390	BOO
Seoul	Pyeongtaek[1]	IFT	2014	67	420	BOO

Note:

1. Under construction. ICDs (inland container depots) are logistics strongholds built in strategic transport locations for roads and railways in order to reduce traffic problems between off-dock container yards and ports. IFTs (integrated freight terminals) handle loading, unloading, classification, information processing and the packing of freight using more than two transport modes (i.e. freight trucks and railroads). ILBs (inland logistics bases) incorporate both an ICD and an IFT. Funding models: BOT – build, operate, transfer; BOO – build, own, operate.

Sources: ESCAP and KMI (2007, 80), MLTM et al. (2009, 35–6); Seo (2011), KOTI-KSP (2012).

bases to be constructed under the build, own, operate (BOO) arrangements rather than the previous build, own, transfer (BOT) arrangements (Figure 8.4A). These inland logistics bases, offering one-stop logistics services, were to be afforded regional roles in handling containers when they were opened. A major task for the Participatory Government was to plan the integration of these inland logistics bases into an efficient hub-and-spoke system.

The major network developed by the Participatory Government in South Korea has been underpinned by an array of planned secondary distribution centres (Figure 8.4B). When these centres, combining freight terminals with wholesale premises, retail shops, and information and financial facilities are completed, they will total 12 million sq m.

In 2006 the Participatory Government incorporated these comprehensive infrastructure developments, underpinning the Northeast Asia logistics business centre concept, into the National Logistics Basic Plan

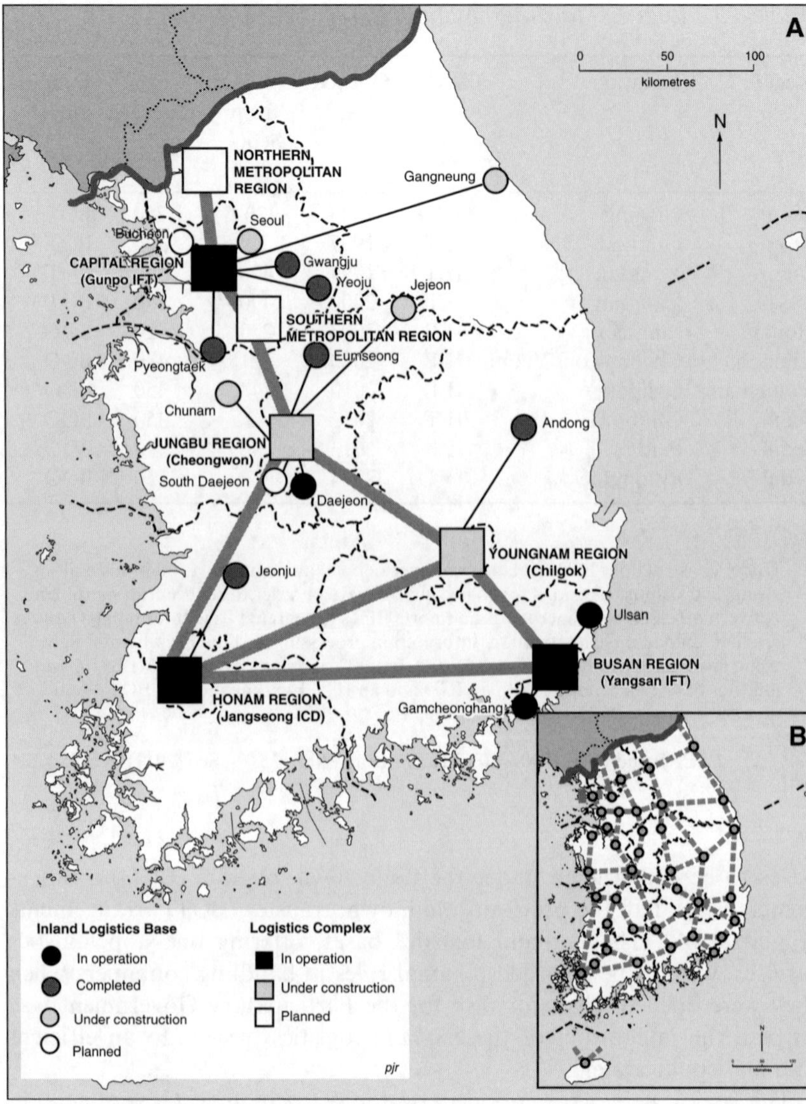

Source: Information from MLTM et al. (2009, 67).

Figure 8.4 South Korea's hub-and-spoke logistics system: (A) inland container depots (ICDs), integrated freight terminals (IFT) and inland logistics bases (ILB); (B) secondary distribution centres

Modification Plan (2006–11) to underline the strategic necessity of having a core national competency in logistics (Jung, 2008). Under this new Plan airport and seaport facilities were to be upgraded to world-class levels and their hinterlands developed; advanced information systems were to be established to enhance the competitiveness of airport and seaports through dramatic improvements to customs and simplification of tran-shipment procedures; the domestic transport system was to be revitalized through increased allocation of government investment in the mass transit system; future action plans were to be targeted at expanding logistics hardware; and logistics companies were to be promoted.

Before examining the strategies for promoting logistics companies, attention is focused on reviewing the Northeast Asia hub project under the Participatory Government that was designed to attract multinational manufacturing and retailing corporations into the Free Economic Zones. Here normal trade barriers have been eliminated to facilitate overseas trade and commerce through tax reduction, deregulation, labour flexibility, financial support, international schools and international hospitals (Figure 8.5). Surrounding the international airport at Incheon and the mega-ports at Busan and Gwangyang Bay, these zones were designed to provide a new growth engine to upgrade the South Korean economy and capitalize on the country's advanced IT infrastructure, sophisticated industries, educated workforce, domestic market and pivotal position in Northeast Asia.

CLUSTERS

A common element in the Participatory Government's Northeast Asia hub strategy has been heavy investment in value-added logistics services, together with manufacturing, distribution and trade, designed to develop 'clusters' of economic activities. Rather than pursuing a policy of balanced regional development, a selective and concentrated programme of 'place marketing' was adopted focused on three Free Economic Zones, nominated in 2003 and 2004 as the leading areas for 'globalization' (Table 8.4):

1. Incheon is a metropolitan city with a population of 2.6 million, which is part of the National Capital Region that has 46 per cent of the country's population, almost 48 per cent of gross domestic product (GDP), almost 50 per cent of the workforce and more than 50 per cent of manufacturing firms.
2. Busan-Jinhae (Bujin), second only as an economic centre to the National Capital region, is a typical post-industrial city with a population of 3.6 million, that has lost its past strengths in footwear

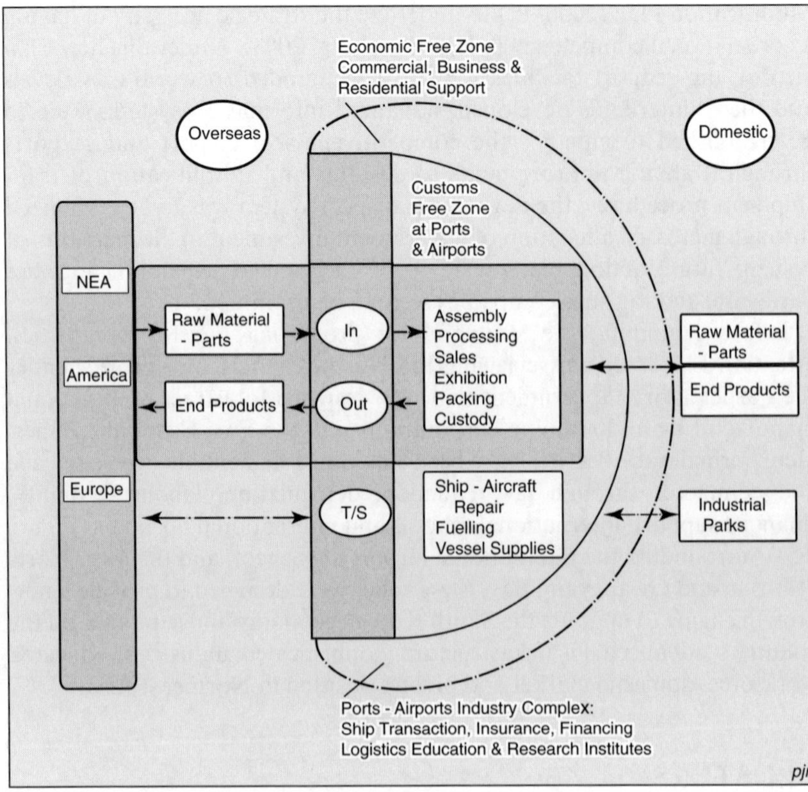

Note: NEA Northeast Asia; T/S transshipment.

Source: Based on MLTM et al. (2009, 17).

Figure 8.5 Logistics hub concept

and textiles, lacks high-value-added industries and headquarters functions, and is reliant on port logistics for its growth strategy.

3. Gwangyang Bay Area is a raw greenfield site, which is designated as a mega-hub port and logistics centre with a current population of 289 000.

Before evaluating the performance of the Northeast Asia hub project as a whole, it is pertinent to detail the selection and concentration of activities on the three zones with their very different socio-economic environments and challenges.

Table 8.4 The original free economic zones established in South Korea, 2003–04

	Incheon	Busan-Jinhae (Bujin)	Gwangyang Bay Area
Area (km^2)	209	105	89
Airports/ Ports	Incheon Int'l Airport Incheon Port	Busan Port/ Busan New Port	Gwangyang Port
Development period	2003–20	2004–20	2004–20
Designated industries	• Airport logistics • Land development • Int'l business • Tourism, leisure • Cutting-edge industries • Manufacturing	• Maritime logistics • Cutting edge parts & materials • Manufacturing (motor cars, shipbuilding) • Tourism, leisure	• Maritime logistics • Fine chemicals • New materials • Tourism, leisure
Website	www.ifez.go.kr	www.bjfez.go.kr	www.gfez.go.kr

Source: MLTM et al. (2009).

Incheon

Incheon, through its proximity to eastern China, is being marketed as an 'outpost of globalization'. The metropolitan city is being redesigned and rebuilt to house logistics activities on reclaimed land 50 km from downtown Seoul at a cost of US$5 billion (Figure 8.6). The strategy of combining both a 'competitive city' and a 'knowledge-based city' into a single urban development is being pursued through the five 'port' components that comprise the Pentaport project (Rimmer, 2004b):

1. The Incheon International Airport, particularly as a node for air freight in Northeast Asia.
2. The revitalization of the Port of Incheon, which, though experiencing a great tidal range, is being developed by the Port of Singapore Authority (PSA) as part of a 'gateway cluster' (together with the airport) to offer access to northern China.
3. A business port to attract the Asian-Pacific Rim headquarters of multinational manufacturing and retailing corporations.

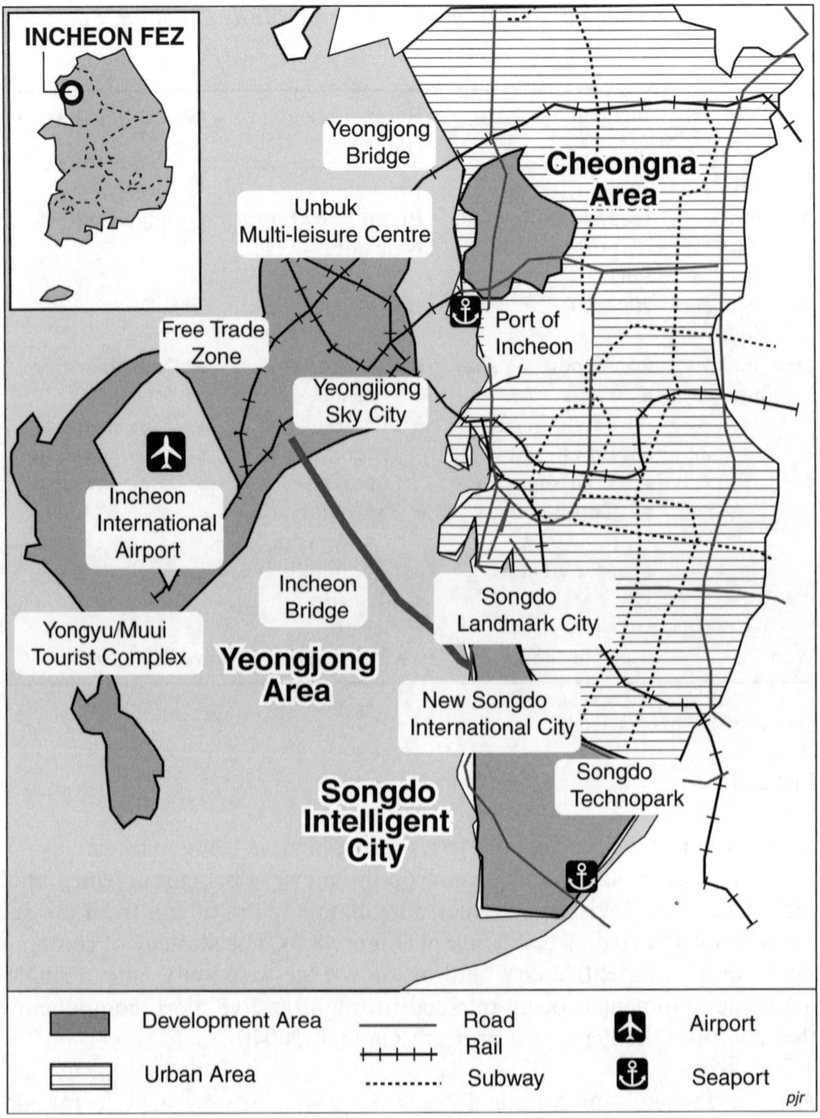

Source: Information from KFEZ (2012).

Figure 8.6 Incheon Free Economic Zone (FEZ)

4. A financial port for multinational banking corporations.
5. A leisure port as a magnet for tourists from China.

These activities are focused on three separate, but interlinked, growth poles within the metropolitan city that are earmarked for major projects to be completed by 2020: Yeongjong surrounding Incheon International Airport as an Airport City base for logistics, tourism and leisure; Songdo Intelligent City for knowledge-based industry, including a techno park based on advanced IT infrastructure, a bio-tech complex and an international business district; and the Cheongna reclaimed area for an international financial centre, tourism and leisure complex, floral distribution centre and entertainment venue.

Busan

Busan-Jinhae (Bujin) economic zone, given its proximity to Japan, is being marketed on two counts: maritime logistics based on the function of Busan Port and Busan New Port as a gateway for maritime cargo in Northeast Asia, a regional headquarters for global shipping corporations, and the establishment of an international logistics cluster; and cutting-edge parts and research and development (R&D) with various material clusters supporting the shipping, machinery and motor vehicle industry, notably Renault-Samsung, and the development of knowledge-based machinery (mechatronics). These activities are split between six districts: upgraded logistics, distribution and international business functions in Busan New Port; logistics and leisure in Ungdong; mechatronics and public service, educational and R&D facilities in Dudong; cutting-edge industry and R&D enhancements in Jisa; logistics in West Busan; and aviation logistics and parts and material industry improvements in Myeongji (Figure 8.7A). Their economic prospects hinge on Busan New Port becoming a maritime logistics centre for Northeast Asia serving both China and Japan (OECD, 2004).

Gwangyang Bay

Gwangyang Bay is being marketed as an international maritime logistics centre involving both cargo destined for northern China and the National Capital Region and the value-added activities of global network corporations such as Hutchison Port Holdings; as a materials handling cluster to strengthen the competitiveness of POSCO steelworks, oil and petrochemical industries at Yeosu Industrial Complex and serve as an advanced base for shipping on the 'golden' route linking both the Chinese and Japanese

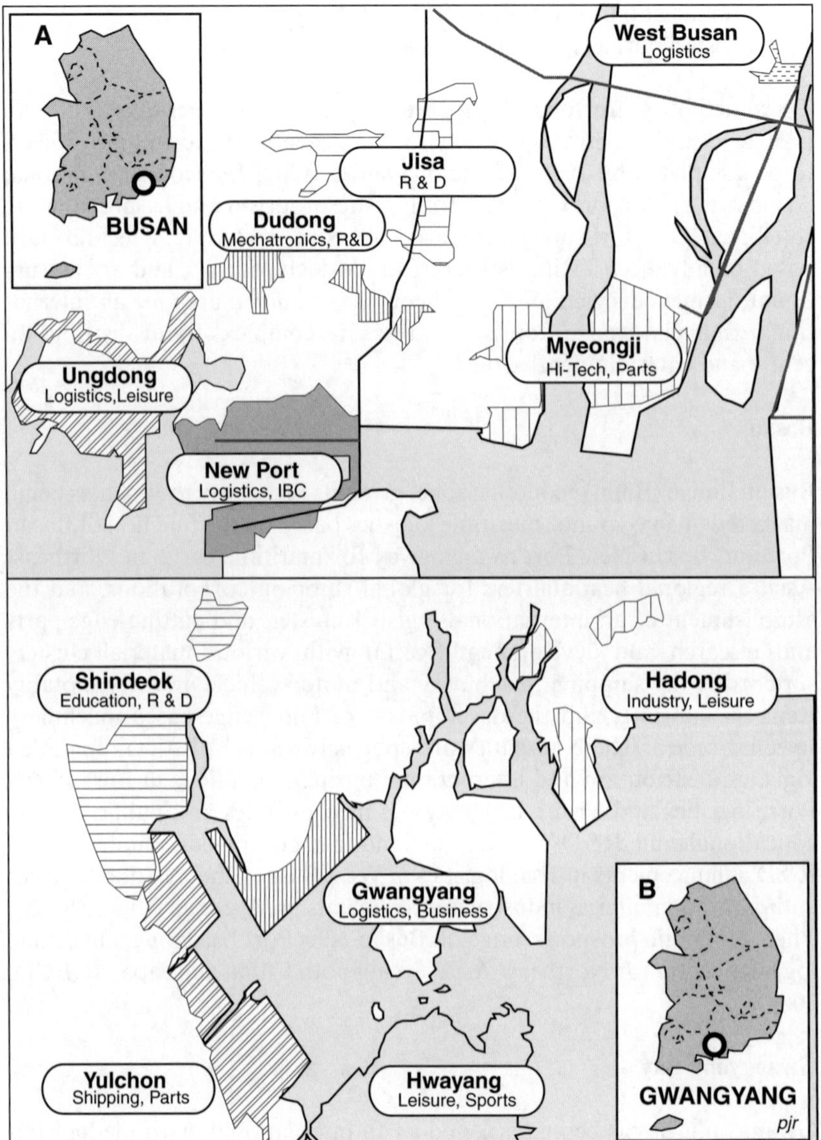

Source: Information from KFEZ (2012).

Figure 8.7 (A) Busan-Jinhae Free Economic Zone (FEZ); and (B) Gwangyang Bay Area Free Economic Zone (FEZ)

markets; and through tourism and leisure tied to the development of the southern coastal belt and the construction of an international resort (Figure 8.7B). These activities are spread over five separate districts: Gwangyang is at the heart of the zone, not only because of its central geographical location but also because of the location of the container port; Yulchon is designated for shipbuilding, manufacturing, petrochemical, and steel-related industries, Hwayang is to serve as a focal point for tourism; and Shindeok and Hadong function as residential complexes for foreign investors and employees of multinational firms.

Summary

It is probably too early to evaluate the overall performance of the three Free Economic Zones initiated during the Participatory Government's regime and their contribution to the Northeast Asia hub concept. Nevertheless these zones have been subject to a series of ongoing criticisms within South Korea, particularly by those resistant to change and deregulation (Jung, 2008). These criticisms have targeted the overpreoccupation with hard infrastructure provision in airports, seaports and freight terminals. The critics have highlighted the failure to develop an extended tax base to finance these long-term action programmes from increased economic activities, thereby reducing the heavy reliance on central government support. There is also an alleged lack of distinctiveness in the individual strategies for Incheon, Busan and Gwangyang Bay. Apart from logistics, all three have relied on similar businesses, R&D, and tourism and leisure activities. Above all, they have failed to develop their own 'brand value', which is crucial when competing against special economic zones in neighbouring countries.

When planning these zones perhaps there was too little recognition by the Participatory Government of Richard Florida's (2002) observation that professionals take their identities from where they live (location) rather than from where they work (corporation). Candidates for jobs check out surrounding streets, the parks and the nightspots, and look for outdoor recreation, the music scene and high-energy activities. There has been a pressing need for the inclusion of unique and aesthetically pleasing 'motivation-attractions' to be included in the FEZs (Sorensen, 2003). Without them it has been difficult to convince international symbolic analysts engaged in 'problem solving, problem identifying and strategic brokering activities' that Incheon, Busan and Gwangyang Bay are 'cool' places to live and work (Reich, 1991, p. 483).

Incheon has been afforded a financial role by the Participatory Government and has been actively seeking to improve the environment for international business, education and medical services, but there has been little difference in the composition of activities in Busan and Gwangyang Bay. This lack of variation may explain why they have been less successful than Incheon in attracting foreign investment and tenants. Even in Incheon foreign investment has been primarily in land and port development projects rather than in global logistics activities. This situation has been attributed to the lack of attention to the nature of each area's distinctive socio-economic environment when outlining the 2006 National Logistics Basic Plan. Also there has been a failure to streamline the governance of the FEZs, remove legal and institutional obstacles, and appreciate that firms or, better still, their supply chains, not cities, compete (Christopher, 2005, 122). While the Participatory Government sought to address these criticisms, particularly in light of the aggressive expansion of airports, seaports and special economic zones in China, it also pursued a parallel policy of seeking to transform local logistics companies into global corporations.

SEARCHING FOR GLOBAL LOGISTICS PLAYERS

The impetus to develop global logistics players based in South Korea came from the Presidential Committee on the Northeast Asian Cooperation Initiative (PCNACI, 2004). The Committee recognized the shortcomings of local logistics firms in comparison with their global counterparts. South Korea's logistics sector was fragmented, with local firms offering transport-oriented services rather than comprehensive logistics services catering for the whole supply chain. As noted, the leading Korean firms such as Samsung Electronics' Logitec, Pan Korea Express (LG Electronics) and Hyundai Glovis were closely linked to major multinational manufacturers and did not offer services for a range of industries or regions.

South Korean logistics was also distinguished by the small scale of business, with average sales of the top seven firms being less than 11 per cent of those of the top seven global logistics corporations in 2003 (Table 8.5). The logistics sector was characterized by low-value-added services stemming from a preoccupation with delivery, and neglect of assembly and processing; this shortcoming was compounded by South Korean firms offering about 20 types of services compared with over 40 services supplied by global logistics corporations. The small third-party logistics market, reflecting low levels of outsourcing and a high degree of unreliability, together with the absence of government support for comprehensive logistics services to respond to global trends, led the Committee to promote strategies for developing global logistics corporations.

Table 8.5 Comparison of turnover of global logistics corporations and South Korean logistics firms, 2003

Global			Korean		
#	Company	Sales (2003)	#	Company	Sales (2002)
		100 mn KRW			100 mn KRW
1	EXEL	108 996	1	Korea Express	11 000
2	Ryder System	52 740	2	Hanjin	6154
3	Geodis	39 848	3	Pan Korea Express	4000
4	C.H. Robinson	38 676	4	Hyundai Logistics	3876
5	Schneider	30 472	5	K.P.D.	3455
6	Expeditors	26 956	6	CJ GLS	3400
7	USFreightways	26 956	7	Hansol CSN	2925
	Total	324 644		Total	34 810
	Average	46 378		Average	4973

Source: PCNACI (2004).

The Presidential Committee's aim in promoting global logistics corporations offering a high-volume logistics service with professional know-how was envisaged as an incremental three-stage process. Stage 1 (2005–09) was focused on expanding the third-party logistics market and attaining economies of scale, so that market restructuring could concentrate on developing comprehensive logistics companies. Stage 2 (2010–14) was centred on the growth of comprehensive Asian-Pacific Rim logistics companies. Stage 3 (after 2014) would be reached when South Korean-based logistics corporations competed with their global counterparts.

In response to the manifest shortcomings of local logistics companies, the Presidential Committee promoted a globalization strategy and a certification system through the 2004 Specialized Logistics Company Plan to nurture competitive, integrated logistics companies. This Plan also recognized the need to have representative foreign enterprises based in South Korea such as DHL and FedEx, because they generated added value in the global market. Under the Plan, integrated global logistics corporations, provided certain requirements were met, were offered generous support, including tax incentives, so that they could serve as models for aspiring local companies.

The prime incentive for global logistics corporations is the offer of 100 per cent exemption from corporate tax for the first three years until 2014, with a 50 per cent reduction for the following two years (that is, similar to the tax incentives provided to foreign companies in the Free Economic Zone). To qualify for these incentives an integrated global logistics

Table 8.6 Comparison of turnover between global logistics corporations and South Korean logistics firms, 2005

Global			Korean		
#	Company	Turnover US$ million	#	Company	Turnover US$ million
1	USPS (United States Postal Service)	122122	1	Hanjin Shipping	8600
2	DPWN (Germany)	76411	2	Hyundai Shipping	7169
3	UPS (US)	48876	3	STX Pan Ocean	4016
4	FedEx (US)	43736	4	SK Shipping	2277
5	Maersk (Denmark)	39368	5	Yuko Car Carriers	2238
	Total	330513		Total	24300
	Average	66102		Average	4860

Source: Lee and Mun (2008, 2).

corporation has to have sales exceeding 3 trillion won (US$270 million); an established information system, inventory management and tracking system with more than 10 per cent of sales invested in the information system over a three-year period; overseas logistics centres and an established domestic presence, by being represented in five cities and provinces within South Korea with a storage area exceeding 10000 m^2 and in more than seven foreign countries together with affiliations to local logistics companies; and more than 100 workers.

In 2005 the argument in favour of transforming Korean national network companies into global logistics corporations was reinforced by an updated comparison with United States Postal Service (USPS), Deutsche Post, United Parcel Service (UPS), FedEx and Maersk (Table 8.6). This comparison showed that the average turnover of Korea's five leading firms had declined to less than 8 per cent of their global counterparts compared with almost 11 per cent in 2002. The Ministry of Construction and Transportation responded to this situation with the 2007 Promulgation of Logistics Policy Basic Law and Logistics Facility Law.

By 2007 South Korea's logistics sector comprised two distinct components: shipping companies and the in-house subsidiaries of manufacturing corporations (Table 8.7). The distinction between the two components is blurred because Hanjin Shipping occurs in one sector and the Hanjin Business Group in the other. Also Korean Airlines are part of the Hanjin Group, suggesting the 'true' size of the country's logistics companies may be larger than suggested. There is therefore a need to delve into the nature

Table 8.7 Top 20 logistics companies in South Korea, 2007

Shipping	100 million Korean won	Manufacturing and retailing corporations		100 million Korean won
		Parent	Subsidiary	
Hanjin Shipping	69 360	Hyundai Motor Co.	Glovis	25 102
STX Pan Ocean	48 734	Geumho Asiana Group	Korea Express	12 669
Hyundai Merchant Marine	48 456	Samsung Electronics	Samsung Electronics Logitech	11 399
Korean Line Corporation	19 713	LG Electronics	Pantos Logistics	10 203
SK Shipping	18 712	Hanjin Business Group	Hanjin	7598
EUKOR Car Carriers Inc.	15 823	Hyundai Business Group	Hyundai Logistics	5640
Samaun Logix	10 907	CJ Group	CJ-GLS	5194
Daeyang Shipping	7244	–	Sebang	4612
Heunga-A Shipping	4833	LG Group	Hi Logistics	2705
KMTC	4519	*Subtotal*		85 122
Sinokor Merchant Marine	4172	Total		337 595
Subtotal	252 473			

Source: MLTM et al. (2009).

of business organizations in Korea to ascertain the degree of synergies between subsidiaries.

Family governance is the prime characteristic of the Korean business group or *chaebol* (Figure 8.8). Also the family dominates the structure of the *chaebol* set within the context afforded by reciprocal links with government and banks; conglomerate ownership of banks has been forbidden since 1982 (Lim, 2003; Kim, 2005). A holding company comprises the subsidiaries which, despite cross-holdings, operate formally as independent entities. Within the group there is extensive diversification as a wide range of discrete products and services are produced, as the family conglomerate seeks to further diversify its activities. These features are explored with reference to the Hanjin Group, South Korea's largest logistics company, ranked twelfth among conglomerates by the Fair Trade Commission in 2012 (KKW, 2012).

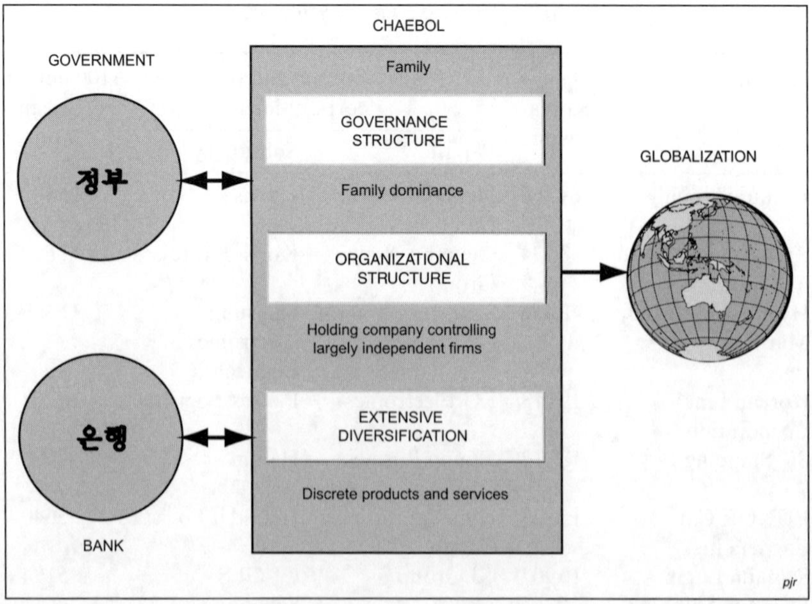

Figure 8.8 Key elements of the structure of the South Korean family conglomerate or chaebol

The Hanjin Group

The late Chung-hoon Cho founded the Hanjin Transportation Co. Ltd on 1 November 1945 in the aftermath of the Second World War (Figure 8.9). Beginning with a single truck in Incheon, the company prospered from a transport contract set in 1956 with the US Army during the Korean War and another a decade later with the US Forces in the Vietnam War (1962–75) that was organized by his younger brother Chung-kun Cho (also known as Charley Cho). These contracts provided the foundation for key business acquisitions that led to the coalescence of the Hanjin Group, comprising Hanjin Shipping, Korean Air, Hanjin Heavy Industry and Construction (HHIC), and Hanjin Freight Express. With the diversification of interests covering air, land and marine logistics, shipbuilding and finance and insurance, Chung-hoon Cho progressively brought his four sons into the business: Yang-ho Cho replacing the founder's younger brother at Korean Air, Nam-ho Cho at Hanjin Heavy Industries and Construction, the late Soo-ho Cho at Hanjin Shipping and Jung-ho Cho at Meritz Securities.

A poor safety record at Korean Air, coupled with concern over the company's finances during the Asian Financial Crisis (1997–98), led

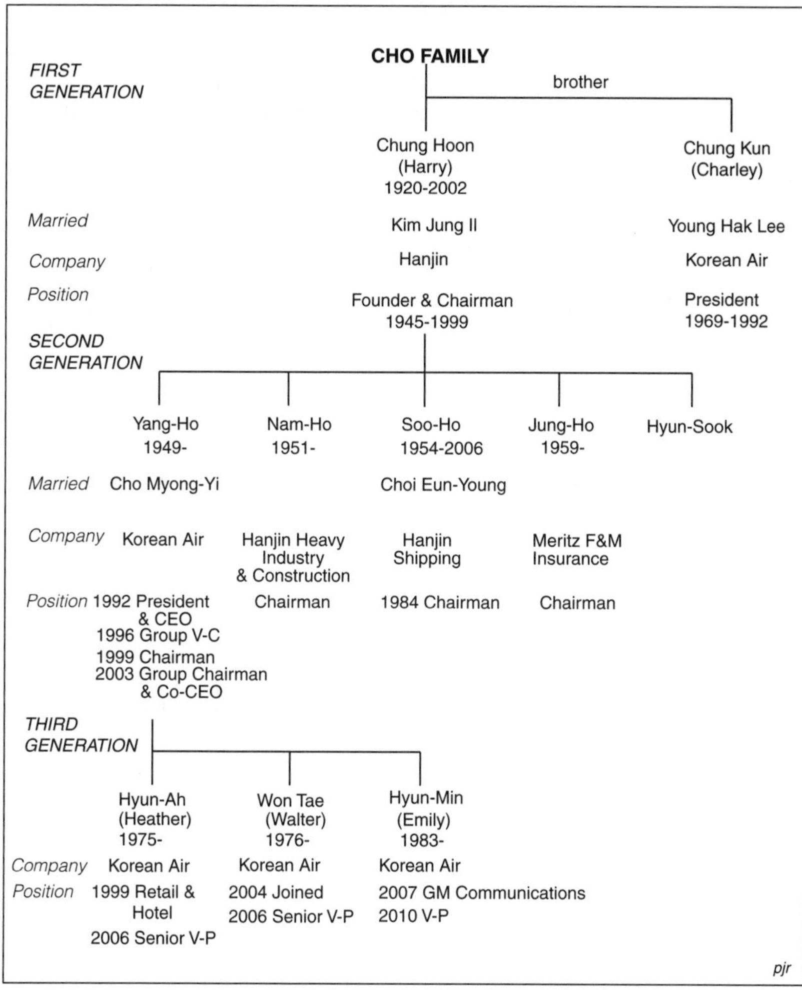

Figure 8.9 The Cho Family

to government intervention under President Kim Dae Jung's People's Government that prompted the founder to take responsibility for the company's shortcomings and to concentrate on chairing the Group until his death in 2002. His eldest son, Yang-ho Cho, became chair of the Group which survived intact until 2005. Then Nam-ho Cho removed Hanjin Heavy Industries and Construction and Jung-ho Cho separated Meritz from the Group. Interest centres on the degree to which the Hanjin Group has since globalized its activities by studying how the international

Table 8.8 The composition of the Hanjin Group, 2005

Land	*Hanjin Transportation Co. Ltd	Information & Communication	Hanjin Information & Telecommunications Co. Ltd
Air	*Korean Air Lines Co. Ltd		Total Passenger Service System Co. Ltd
	*Korea Airport Service Co. Ltd		Cyber Logitec Co. Ltd
Marine	*Hanjin Shipping Co. Ltd		Cyber Sky Co. Ltd
	Keoyang Shipping Co. Ltd (merged 2008)		Global Logistics System Korea Co. Ltd
Tourism, Hotel, Real Estate	Hanjin Travel Service Co. Ltd	Social Welfare (Health)	Inha University Hospital
	KAL Hotel Network	(Education)	Jungseok Education Foundation
	Air Total Service		Hangkuk Aviation University
	Jungseok Enterprise Co. Ltd		Inha University Foundation
			Korea Research for the 21st Century

Note: *Companies listed on the stock exchange.

Source: Hanjin Group (2005).

networks of Hanjin Shipping and Korean Airlines have changed over time, before assessing the extent of synergies between them and their subsidiaries (Table 8.8).

Hanjin Shipping (HJS)

Snapshots of the route networks of Hanjin Shipping in 1995 and 2010 are used to gauge the degree to which its container operations have stretched across the globe to facilitate South Korea's participation in the expansion and integration of the world economy (HJS, 2010). By 1995 HJS had developed a skeletal round-the-world network that stemmed from the

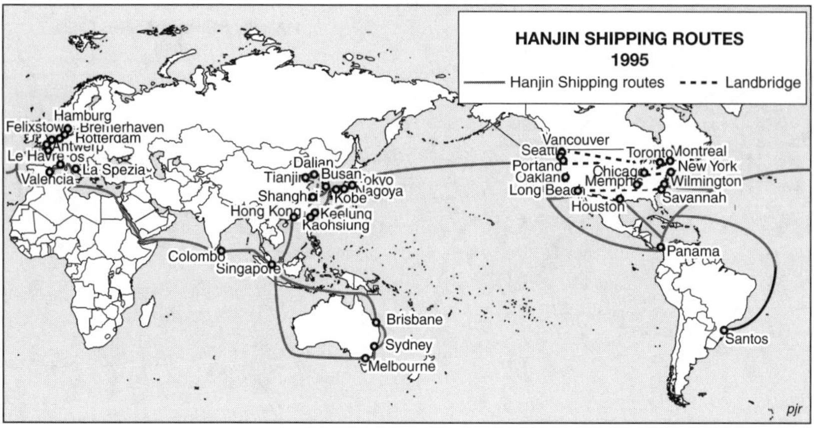

Source: Information from HJS (1995).

Figure 8.10 Hanjin Shipping Co. Ltd's container service routes, 1995

merging of routes started by Hanjin Container Lines Ltd (1975) in the Middle East (1977), trans-Pacific (1979), East Coast North America (1986) and Japan (1986) with those resulting from a merger with Korea Shipping Corporation (1988) such as the Europe–USA via Asia pendulum (1991), transatlantic (1991), China–Europe Express and the Mediterranean (1995) (Figure 8.10). Network intensification was restricted to the United States where HJS connected West Coast ports of Seattle and Long Beach to inland areas by a double-stack train and serviced the East Coast ports through a series of all-water routes. As there were only single route connections to Australia and South America and none to Africa, Hanjin Shipping fell short of offering a global service.

By 2010 HJS had broadened its coverage with 57 liner services covering six continents (Figure 8.11). This extension follows the introduction of direct calls to China (1996); the acquisition of a majority interest in DSR-Senator Line (1997); creation of an around-the-world service – the United Alliance – with DSR-Senator, Cho Yang Shipping Co. and United Arab Shipping Co.; and, after surviving tax evasion charges (1999), the establishment of Hanjin Logistics (2000) to offer door-to-door services. Much of this extended coverage stemmed from Hanjin's CKHY alliance established in 2001 with COSCO Container Lines of China, K-Line of Japan and Yangming Line of Taiwan, which collectively offered express container services and shared space to provide lower operating costs. While the extent of Hanjin's business network stemming from membership of the

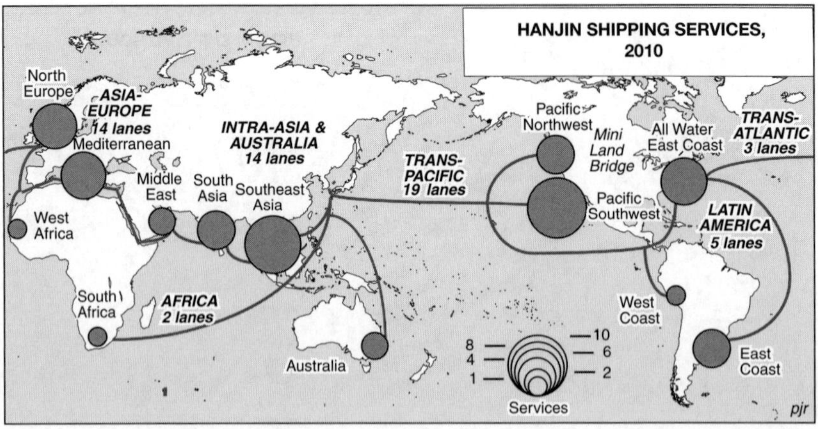

Source: Information from HJS (2011).

Figure 8.11 Hanjin Shipping Co. Ltd's container network, 2010

world's largest strategic alliance does not match that of Maersk (AP Møller Group), the company has become a global carrier covering 80 ports in 35 countries with regional headquarters in New York, Hamburg, Shanghai and Singapore. Also there are 200 overseas offices in 53 countries on six continents that produce 90 per cent of its revenue. These shipping services are supported by Hanjin's third-party logistics activities focused on a special business unit in Seoul opened in 2008 and 12 dedicated terminals worldwide. Although the corporation has plans to increase the number of these logistics hubs, the slowing down of the container industry and rapid decrease in consumer consumption following the Global Financial Crisis (2008–09) has led to greater reliance on sharing liner services and terminals with its CKHY partners. Meanwhile consideration is being given to the development of joint logistics services with Korean Air.

Korean Air

To assess the extent to which operations of Korean Air have been globalized, an additional snapshot of the network in 1982 (when it was known as Korea Air Lines, KAL) is added to those for 1995 and 2010. In 1982 the sparse network reflected the company's extension from the original Asian beachheads established after its acquisition by Hanjin from the South Korean Government in 1969 – Bangkok, Hong Kong, Saigon, Tokyo and Taipei – across the Pacific using Boeing 747s in the 1970s to the inclusion of Europe and the Middle East with Boeing 707s in the early 1980s (Figure 8.12A). As travelling abroad from Korea was then restricted, the founder, Chung-hoon Cho, and his brother concentrated on carrying air cargo and developing Seoul as a transit hub for Japan, but were unable to capitalize on South Korea's Great Circle position offering the shortest distance between two places because the airline was prevented from flying over the then Soviet Union.

By 1995 the network mirrored the intensification of services to Asia, North America and across Russia to Europe together with the addition of routes to Australia and South America (Figure 8.12B). This intensification

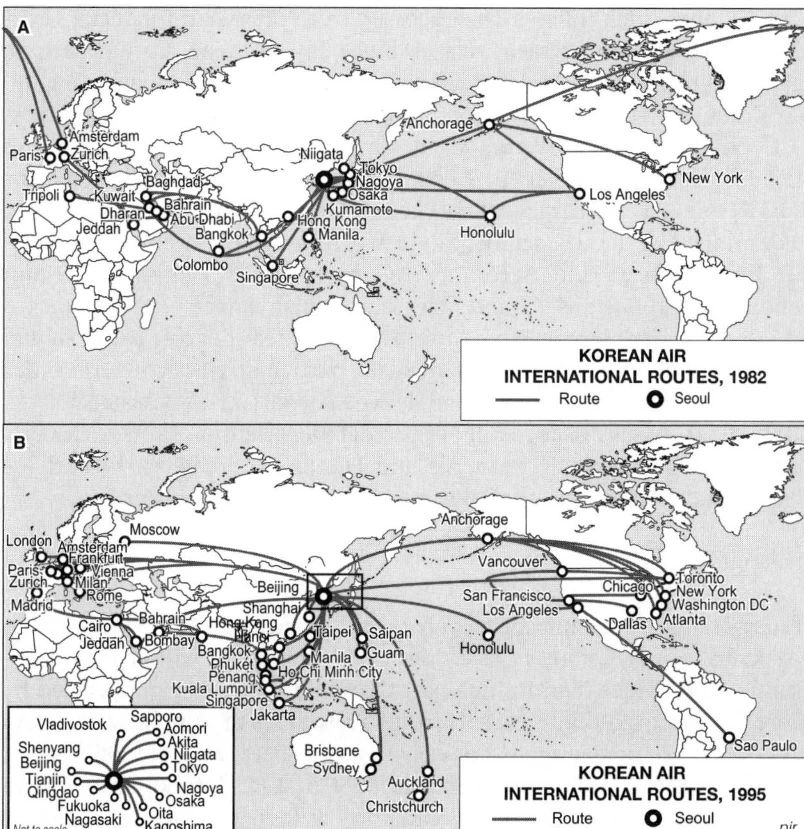

Sources: Information from Davies (1997), KAL (1994).

Figure 8.12 *(A) Korea Air Lines (KAL) network, 1982; (B) Korea Air Lines (KAL) network,1995*

reflected the easing of travel restrictions by the South Korean Government and a bid to offset the entry of a second Korean carrier, Asiana Airlines. Despite this competition, Korean Air still persisted with its surging freight operations centred on Los Angeles, New York and Tokyo and hubbing on Seoul. Consequently Korean Air failed to meet the strict definition of a global carrier as one that 'operates hubs in several countries' (Tretheway, 1991, 49).

In 2010 Korean Air's network would still fall short of this definition as a global carrier, despite serving 120 cities in over 39 countries across six continents with a fleet of 120 airplanes, because it is still focused on its Incheon hub (Figure 8.13). Yet this definition underplays Korean Air's actual global reach following its recovery from the Asian Financial Crisis (1997–98) and poor accident record. Since 2000 Korean Air has been an inaugural member of the 11-member Sky Team strategic alliance, including Delta, Air France and China Southern, which gave customers access to 13133 daily flights covering 856 destinations in 169 countries, and over 20 hub airports (Chapter 4). Furthermore Korean Air has become the world's biggest air cargo carrier in international airfreight-kilometres, underpinned by the six-member Skyteam Cargo Alliance, including Delta, Air France Cargo and Aeroméxico Cargo, and its Tianjin-based joint venture with Sinotrans, Grand Cargostar. This reliance on airfreight for one-third of company revenue raises the issue as to the role cargo should play in determining global carrier status, particularly as Korean Air has developed a Central Asian hub at Navoi Airport in Uzbekistan (KAL, 2011, 2012). As this issue is still open to debate, attention shifts to discussing synergies between Korean Air and Hanjin Shipping, particularly as they provide the basis for defining a truly global logistics company.

Synergies

If the possible interconnections were taken into account the Hanjin Group would have had few peers as a logistics corporation within the Asian-Pacific Rim. Other than to highlight the Sky-Bridge System operated by Korean Air Cargo that uses the Group's resources in shipping and trucking, the degree of synergy is not easy to assess between Hanjin Shipping, Korean Air and Hanjin Transportation Co. Ltd. Providing an ocean service that interconnects the Korean ports of Incheon and Busan and the Chinese ports of Dalian, Shanghai, Tianjin, Qingdao, Weihai and Yantai with air services to Europe and North America, the Sky-Bridge System suggests the potential for a Korean-based global logistics corporation.

These physical services are underpinned by the development of Hanjin Group's information and communications services. In particular, the

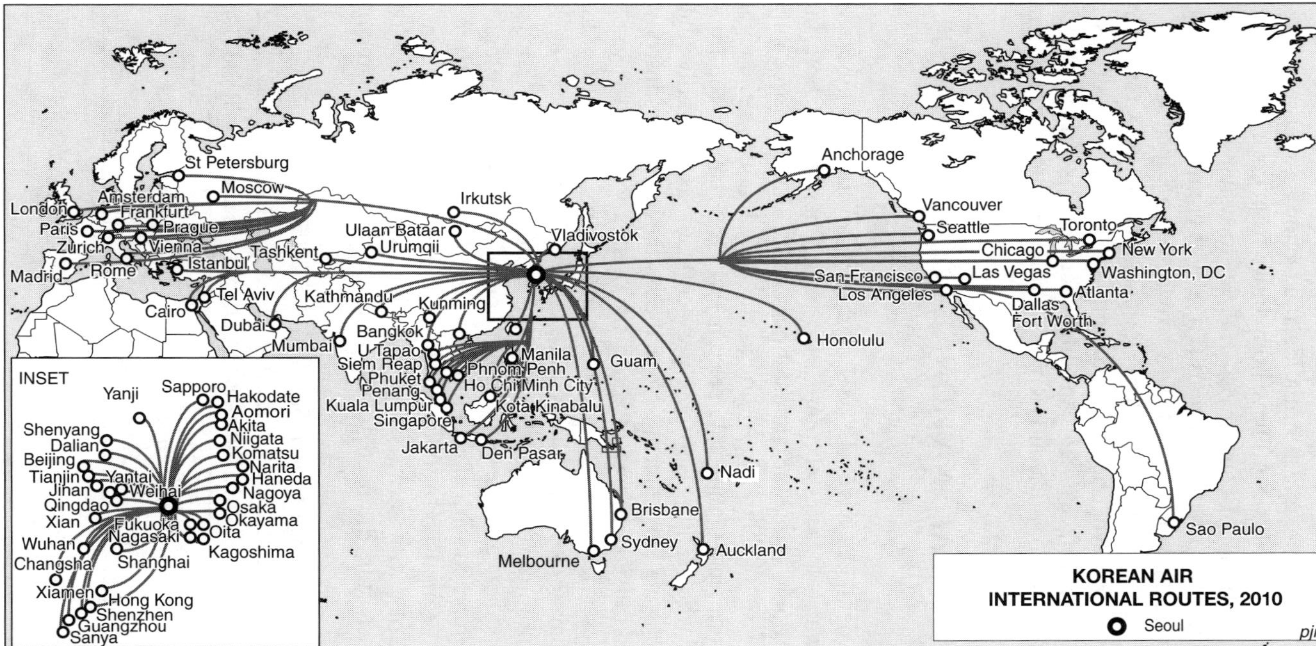

Source: Information from KAL (2010).

Figure 8.13 Korean Air Lines (KAL) network, 2010

Hanjin Information Systems and Telecommunications Co. Ltd (HIST, 2012) has sought to integrate information and technology between subsidiaries and their customers. Staff have been drawn from Group subsidiaries to create a professional IT company specializing in system integration (SI) and geographical information systems (GIS). The company is seeking to become a world leader in IT logistics to provide value-added services.

Any assessment of the size of logistics corporations in South Korea needs to take these synergies into account. As family connections are always close to the surface in Korean conglomerates, it is difficult to determine the likely trajectory of South Korea's global logistics corporations.

LOOKING AHEAD: NATIONAL LOGISTICS MASTER PLAN (2011–20)

In 2008 President Lee Myun-Bak's Pragmatic Government inherited a situation in which logistics accounted for over 4 per cent of both businesses and national sales, and almost 4 per cent of the workforce during the previous year (Table 8.9). Although the added value of the eighth-ranking logistics sector (almost 36 per cent) was less than the top-ranked retailing and wholesaling sector (38 per cent), it was markedly higher than manufacturing (23 per cent). Nevertheless the logistics industry was still beset by a range of persistent issues: the orientation towards second-party logistics services that reflected the major shippers' mistrust of local third-party logistics services; the inability of small companies to engage in cross-border trade; the limited home market dominated by a few large logistics companies; and the poor reputation of South Korean logistics companies compared with their global counterparts in competitiveness, value-added creation and service levels. Also the logistics hub concept still lacked clarity, with several issues involving the Free Economic Zones unresolved including the need to relate targeted industries to regional

Table 8.9 The logistics sector in South Korea, 2007

Classification		All industries (A)	Logistics sector (B)	Ratio (B/A)
Companies	no.	3 189 181	171 587	4.5
Employees	no.	15 728 028	566 835	3.6
Sales revenue	bn KRW	1 864 067	82 342	4.4

Note: KRW – Korean won.

Source: MLTM et al. (2009).

logistics patterns; overcome the preoccupation with hardware (memory sets and handsets) and neglect of software aspects, including legal barriers; and heed the call to streamline administration responsibilities between the central government and the Free Economic Zones. Above all, the prime shortcoming of the preceding Roh Moo-Hyun administration was the absence of a principal agency to drive the logistics policy (Jung, 2008).

Responsibility for addressing these logistics issues under the Pragmatic Government became the task of a new super ministry – the Ministry of Land, Transport and Maritime Affairs (MLTM) – created by amalgamating existing ministries to enhance the competitiveness of the logistics sector through the efficient working of the air, land and sea transport systems. The MLTM, aided by the Korea Transport Institute (KOTI), has sought to establish new directions for promoting logistics by outlining three policy goals: (1) to secure added value from global logistics; (2) to establish an integrated logistics system; and (3) to strengthen the competitiveness of domestic logistics companies (Seo, 2009). These goals are pursued though five strategies designed to: (1) attract the Northeast Asian headquarters of global network corporations; (2) develop a new business model within an integrated Northeast Asian economic zone; (3) improve and establish new hardware and software for strengthening service capability; (4) encourage domestic logistics companies to cross borders; and (5) expand the domestic logistics market.

These goals and strategies were incorporated in the National Logistics Basic Plan Modification (2011–20) that seeks to address changes in South Korea's internal and external environments by going beyond the sole emphasis on efficiency in adding the values of 'eco-friendliness' and safety to guide structural reorganization (Jeong and Roh, 2010; KOTI-KSP, 2012). Domestically, the Ministry has already modified policies to address the growth of 'green logistics' and the integration of land, sea and air transport to create an intermodal transport system. Further policy modifications have been made to respond to changes that have emerged in the logistics arena since the announcement of the 2004 Specialized Logistics Company Promotion Plan, notably shifts in the global logistics market stemming from mergers and acquisitions, a greater emphasis on security, variations in oil prices, and any lingering impact of the Global Financial Crisis (2008–09). Further structural adjustments are also necessary to address the shortcomings arising from the preoccupation of the Northeast Asia hub strategy with cargo volumes per se, rather than addressing the challenges and potential benefits from South Korea's geographical position squeezed between China and Japan.

Reflecting the Pragmatic Government's preoccupation with construction, an early decision was made during the Global Financial Crisis (2008–09) to

Table 8.10 Characteristics of the three new free economic zones in South Korea, 2008

	Yellow Sea	Saemangeum Gunsan	Daegu-Gyungbuk-do
Area (km^2)	55	67	40
Airports/ports	Pyeongtaek Port Dangin Port	Gunsan Port Gunzang New Port	Daegu International Airport
Development period	2008–25	2008–30	2008–30
Designated industries	• Logistics • Cutting edge manufacturing (motor cars, IT & bio-technology) • Electronics Information • Biotechnology	• Manufacturing (motor cars, shipbuilding & machinery) • New & renewable energy • Tourism & leisure (catering to Chinese clients)	• International education • Medical complex • Textiles, Fashion • Games, Software • Manufacturing (parts & materials, IT)
Website	www.yesfez.go.kr	www.sgfez.go.kr	www.dgfez.go.kr

Source: MLTM et al. (2009).

accelerate regional infrastructure spending. The three existing Free Economic Zones – Busan, Incheon and Gwangyang Bay – were augmented by adding three new ones: Yellow Sea (Pyeongtaek-Dangjin), Saemangeum–Gunsan and Daegu-Gyungbuk-do (North Gyeongsang Province). All three new regional clusters are being developed as 'test-beds' for experimenting with corporate deregulation to revive the sluggish domestic economy and stimulate renewed foreign company interest in South Korea (Table 8.10). The Presidential Commission on Regional Development (PCRD) suggested that Saemangeum-Gunsan should be developed into the Koreanized 'Dubai of Northeast Asia' with a specific focus on logistics.

Saemangeum-Gunsan Free Economic Zone

Saemangeum–Gunsan Free Economic Zone is located on the west coast 270 km from Seoul in the North Jeolla Province (Figure 8.14). Since its initiation both central and provincial governments have sought to reinvigorate the flagging local provincial economy by reclaiming the Saemangeum

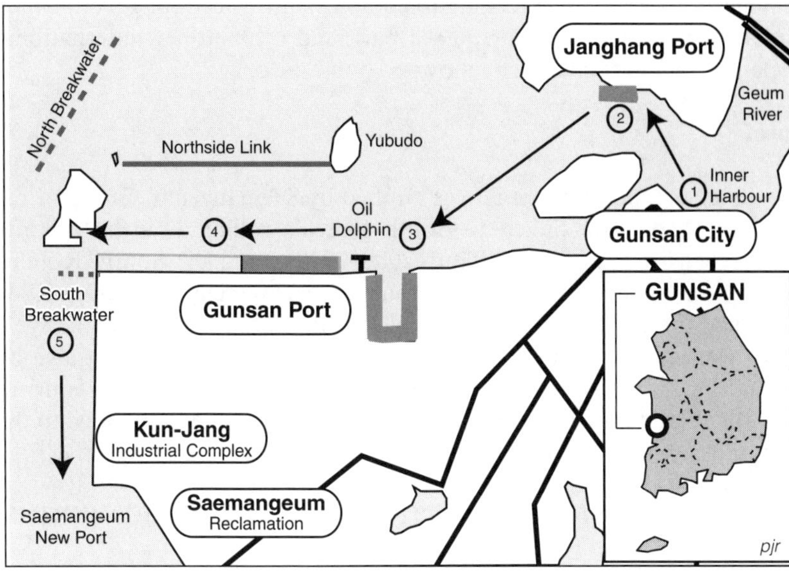

Sources: Information from Rimmer (2008), KFEZ (2012).

Figure 8.14 Saemangeum Gunsan Free Economic Zone (FEZ)

wetlands for agricultural use (Rimmer, 2008). Despite opposition from conservationists, a 34 kilometre seawall had by 2010 transformed the 400 sq km wetlands habitat of migratory birds into 28 300 ha of farmland and a 11 800 ha freshwater reservoir at cost of 2.4 trillion won (US$2.6 billion). The Pragmatic Government has bundled the Saemangeum project together with the pre-existing city of Gunsan, a river port whose wharves have migrated in classic 'Anyport' fashion from its original location in search of greater depths towards the mouth of the Geum River (Chapter 3). The 'rebadged' Saemangeum–Gunsan Free Economic Zone is in now in the process of being developed as a centre for logistics, future-oriented new industries, and leisure-recreational purposes that are linked to further specialized port activities planned outside the Geum River as part of the Saemangeum land reclamation and development project. Sanmangeum New Port will offer 20 m depths and be capable of handling 330 000 dwt ships and, together with the new state-run Kun-Jang industrial complex covering 2010 ha, will cater for exports, processing, and the distribution of transhipped cargoes. On completion, the complex is designed to take advantage of China's growing economy, which currently suffers from inadequate logistics facilities. The provincial government is seeking to complement the central government's initiatives with new harbours, a sea park and a brand new international airport or, at the very least, a renovated domestic one.

Envoi

The construction-based initiatives typified by Saemangeum–Gunsan Free Economic Zone are linked to South Korea's rolling Fourth National Comprehensive Territorial Plan, 2000–2020. In 2009 South Korea's Presidential Committee on Regional Development (PCRD, 2011) prompted the embellishment of this plan, not only by identifying the West Coast Belt and the Kunjang–Saemangeum reclamation area but also by promoting the South Coast Sun Belt, the East Coast Energy–Tourism Belt, the Inland Belt and the North–South Border Peace Belt linked to the Kaesong Industrial Zone (Figure 8.15). In 2012 five more prospective Free Economic Zones were identified and incorporated in the Second Revised Fourth National Comprehensive Territorial Plan, 2011–2020 (KRIHS, 2013).

These initiatives raise issues about the construction agenda's environmental footprint and the need to address 'green logistics', which as yet is not well established in South Korea (Roh, 2012). Parallels can be drawn between South Korea's mega-infrastructure agenda, and the regional initiatives of the Japanese 'construction state', which over six decades since the end of the Pacific War has switched emphasis from Tennessee Valley-style river-basin schemes, through industrial complexes and technopolises to leisure resorts (McCormack, 2001). Pursuing this comparison should spark a debate on how South Korea's 'new digital economy', marked by high-speed information transfer and an emphasis on conservation and sustainability, intermeshes with developmentalist policies focused on mega-infrastructure port and harbour projects for boosting logistics and provincial economic growth.

Various efforts were made by Lee's Pragmatic Government in the aftermath of the Global Financial Crisis (2008–09) to promote logistics as one of the new economy's growth engines so that South Korea excelled in the provision of higher-valued-added services. As outlined in the 2009 Service Industry Advancement Plan, developed by the Ministry of Finance and Planning and six other ministries, logistics and ten other services were seen as the key to South Korea's future growth, employment and well-being. Designed to create jobs, to offset the progressive switch from heavy manufacturing to labour-saving technology-intensive industries, this emphasis on increasing employment and productivity in the lagging service sector has been reflected in the new National Logistics Basic Plan (2011–20).

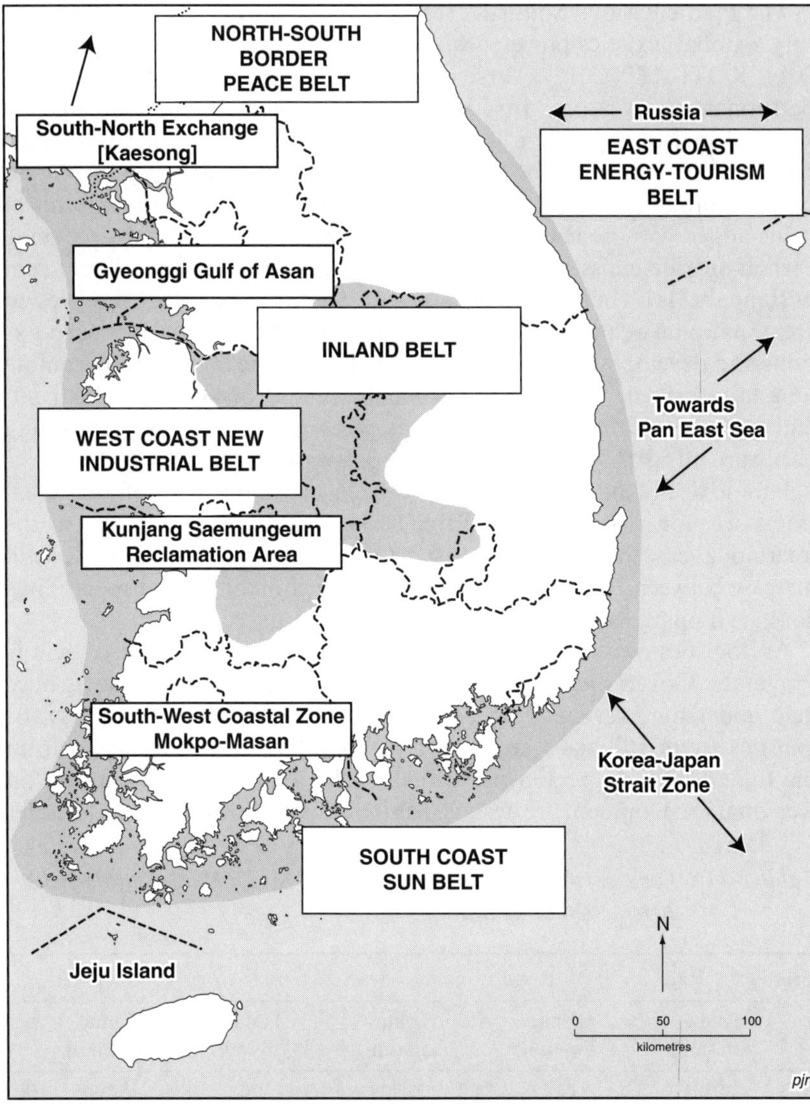

Sources: Information from PCRD (2011), KRIHS (2013).

Figure 8.15 South Korea's supra-economic regions identified by the Presidential Committee on Regional Development

The Plan envisions South Korea as being one of the twenty-first century's global logistics powers leading to low-carbon 'green growth' (Seo, 2011; KOTI-KSP, 2012). Three objectives, together with their associated performance indicators, are identified in this quest for a Korean-style national logistics system: a logistics hub that leads the Northeast Asian economy by improving the domestic sector's cost competency by 3.6 per cent per annum; a logistics sector that will attain fifth position in terms of value-added within the domestic economy; and sustainability by reducing carbon dioxide emissions in the national logistics sector by 16.7 per cent of standard BaU (business as usual) rates. These objectives are designed to create national wealth by nurturing Korean-based global logistics corporations and developing a core competency in domestic logistics; to promote long-term growth by ensuring sustainability and boosting employment; and to improve the national logistics sector's efficiency by developing hardware infrastructure and improving software infrastructure.

Paradoxically, no marked shift in the relative importance of individual transport modes is envisaged (Table 8.11). Despite being heralded as the intermodal era, the domestic transport task undertaken by all modes will increase between 2011 and 2021, with the exception of sea transport. Thus coastal shipping will remain an underutilized resource.

As logistics was but one of a range of services promoted by the Pragmatic Government, the sector lost the pivotal position that it once held under the previous Roh Moo-hyun Government. Nevertheless the logistics sector still has a key role to play in Northeast Asia. Apart from the Inland Belt, the regions identified by the Presidential Committee on Regional Development are designed as logistics platforms for cross-border

Table 8.11 Forecast freight volume by mode in South Korea, 2011, 2012, 2016, 2020 and 2021

Year	Rail		Road		Sea		Air		Total	
	Tonne-km (mil)	%	Tonne-km (mil)	%	Tonne-km (mil)	%	Tonne-km (mil)	%	Tonne-km (mil)	%
2011	11391	7.4	114458	74.3	27998	18.3	157	0.10	154005	100
2012	11693	7.5	116864	74.6	27998	17.9	163	0.10	156719	100
2016	12903	7.7	126486	75.5	27998	16.7	188	0.11	167575	100
2020	14305	8.0	137054	76.3	27998	15.6	219	0.12	179577	100
2021	14656	8.0	139696	76.5	27998	15.3	227	0.12	182577	100

Note: Rounding errors

Source: Seo (2011, 13).

cooperation. The Committee recognizes the pressing need to interconnect North and South Korea, and benefit from economic opportunities in the People's Republic of China through its emphasis on the West Coast New Industrial Belt.

This task is left to the Park Geun-hye Government, which came to power in 2013 with the declared policy of connecting to the transcontinental logistics network that links Northeast Asia and Europe. As South Korea's successful export-oriented growth model may be running out of steam as an employment generator, the new administration is likely to target the underdeveloped logistics sector as a source of higher-paying jobs to overcome the financial crunch being experienced by the country's debt-laden, middle-income families (Choi et al., 2013). A survey of corporate opinion by the Korea Chamber of Commerce & Industry (KCCI, 2013) on the Park Government's likely policy directions has identified distribution and logistics as one of the key service areas warranting attention in a labour market challenged by single-income family structures and a low fertility rate. Many of these opportunities in the logistics sector will attract the *chaebol* rather than independent small and medium-sized third-party enterprises. Progress on this matter will be closely monitored by the Government of the People's Republic of China, because the country is expected to experience similar problems to South Korea, when its own export-oriented growth model leads to hiring fewer workers and it seeks to expand and strengthen its logistics sector to generate employment.

9. China

The People's Republic of China's logistics sector has been given unprecedented attention since the announcement of the country's 10th Five-Year Plan (2001–05). The Plan sought to 'develop the producer service industries by introducing new forms of enterprises and advanced technology; developing [supply] chain operations, logistics and distribution, agency system, multi-modal transportation; and upgrading the traditional transport circulation industry, transportation industry and postal industry' (LFRC, 2004, 1). Any understanding of the priority given to the logistics sector requires an appreciation of the country's geography, and at least 100 years of history. Charting a path through China's modern history from the founding of the Republic of China in 1911 is not an easy task until the establishment of the People's Republic of China in 1949 when it becomes possible to discuss logistics during the successive eras of Mao Zedong, Deng Xiaoping and Jiang Zemin before concentrating on Hu Jintao and looking ahead under Xi Jinping. Initially, however, it is important to examine the pivotal role played by Dr Sun Yat-sen, the founding father of modern China.

In 1922 Sun Yat-sen, a former Minister of Railways, provided a vision of an integrated transport system to underpin China's international development (Sun, 1928 [1922]). The scenario was based upon establishing the great northern, central and southern ports focused on the Bohai Rim, the Yangtze River Delta and the Pearl River Delta respectively, with a progressive dispersion of the railways away from these maritime hubs to inland settlements (Figure 9.1). This vision persisted, but the blueprint was largely unfulfilled for 50 years under 'warlordism', the Nationalist Government, and the People's Republic of China under Chairman Mao Zedong.

Mao Zedong's era (1949–76) was marked a faithful adherence of Sun Yat-sen's railway plan to underpin the planned economy but there was a relentless pursuit of self-sufficiency and relocation of economic activities away from the three designated coastal clusters, arising from fear of attacks by either the United States or the then Soviet Union. Military logistics became prominent. The People's Liberation Army under General Hong Xueshi had established a logistics unit during the Korean War (1950–53),

Note: The plan shows the location of the Great Northern Port, Great Eastern Port and Great Southern Port.

Sources: Sun (1928 [1922]), Rimmer (1997b).

Figure 9.1 Dr Sun Yat-sen's railway plan, 1921

which was credited with fighting the United States army to a standstill. Although the China National Foreign Transportation Corporation, better known as Sinotrans, had been established in Beijing–Tianjin, Guangzhou and Shanghai as early as 1950, the modern notion of business logistics remained virtually non-existent until the last quarter of the twentieth century (Wang, 2005). After the 1978 market reform and the opening up of China's economy under Deng Xiaoping and, following the deterioration of his health in 1995, by his successor Jiang Zemin, business logistics took root (Lam, 1999; Wang, 2007).

The Deng Xiaoping era (1978–93) was marked by a sense of direction, missing from Sun Yat-sen's earlier vision. Economic development was refocused upon the three metropolitan clusters, particularly the Pearl River Delta (Lam, 1995). Transport and warehousing were still dominated by state-owned organizations, notably Sinotrans and the China Postal Administration, which introduced the Express Mail Service (EMS) in

1980 for international deliveries. As China's domestic logistics sector was so underdeveloped, Tsingtao Beer was forced to concentrate on overseas markets for expansion. With heightened awareness of barriers to logistics and their adverse impact on industrial modernization, there was a marked change under Deng Xiaoping from a totalitarian state to one in which Central Government directives remained but market influences surfaced. Under this new regime the Central Government coordinated all three levels of government – national, provincial and local – and allowed both state-owned and private transport enterprises to tender for, and carry out, projects to meet the increased demand, stemming from rising manufacturing exports and primary imports generated by the string of newly created special economic zones (SEZs) along the coast.

Global logistics corporations, notably DHL in 1981, FedEx (Federal Express) in 1984, and UPS (United Parcel Service) and TNT (Thomas Nationwide Transport) in 1988, were permitted to enter China to capitalize on their affiliation with multinational manufacturers (for example, UPS and Motorola). The newcomers were not allowed to engage in road transport pick-up and deliveries that had become the preserve of local private enterprises. In a bid to acquire technical know-how from these global logistics corporations, Sinotrans established joint ventures with DHL and FedEx in 1986, and TNT in 1988. Only a minority foreign shareholding was permitted in these joint ventures and the Chairman or General Manager had necessarily to be a citizen of the People's Republic of China (Cen, 2005). After the late 1980s China allowed foreign shipping companies to enter its seaports to accommodate the expansion of international trade based upon the import of raw materials such as coal and iron ore, and the export of textiles and apparel, household appliances and electronics. From 1990 container ships were permitted to enter China's ports to handle the increasing trade (Wang, Charles, 2006).

The Jiang Zemin era (1993–2003) was distinguished by accelerated export-led economic growth and attention being lavished on China's east coast ports (Lam, 1999; Kuhn, 2004). Reflecting Jiang's leadership of the Shanghai Faction, the Shanghai metropolitan area was allowed to reassume its leading role in China's economy. Meanwhile Premier Zhu Rongji sought to reform state enterprises beset by outmoded infrastructure, overstaffing, lack of customer orientation, and poor service levels. Although the state-owned EMS of China Post was still dominant, further changes were permitted to allow greater foreign participation in logistics, particularly as more multinationals had established production bases in China (Niehues et al., 2007). In 1995 China's first true third-party logistics provider was established when Procter & Gamble outsourced its supply chain management to PG Logistics. As multinationals sought to penetrate China's huge consumer market with their brands, a foreign majority-based joint venture between Shenzhen ST-Anda Logistics and Singapore's Semb-Corp Logistics was permitted to operate a nationwide distribution service with 30 regional distribution centres (STAL, 2009). In 1996, after the establishment of Sinotrans's joint venture with UPS, FedEx was allowed to move into an arrangement with a private company, EAS International Co Ltd. Following the return of Hong Kong to China in 1997, Kerry Logistics was permitted to enter the mainland market and introduced clients to just-in-time and supply chain management practices; its entry ended the claims of logistics service providers based in the former colony to be recognized as a separate category (Nor, 2011). In 1998 DHL was the first foreign company to be granted a 'Class A' licence to supply international freight forwarding; this arrangement was later extended to other foreign freight forwarders and shipping companies as there was a rapid growth in demand for logistics services spurred by rising exports of industrial manufactured goods.

Changes to the international express market during the Jiang Zemin Era did not fully satisfy export-oriented multinational industrial corporations. While the multinationals could outsource their logistics requirements in dealing with foreign trade, they found China's highly fragmented and underdeveloped domestic logistics sector substandard. Not only were there countless drivers of overloaded and poorly maintained trucks, but also more than an estimated 500 000 road transport and warehousing operators, 7000 barge companies and 3000 licensed freight forwarders (foreign and domestic), and over 600 licensed shipping agencies (LCG, 2005). The Chinese Government still subdivided the logistics sector into a number of subsectors such as low-value-added transportation and warehousing, within which activities were strictly controlled. Further air, waterway and road capacities were restricted, railway freight services unreliable, information technology (IT) support services absent, logistics facilities and equipment poor, and the resultant high freight rates being compounded by local protectionism, corruption, and unpredictable roadblocks. The journey time between Chongqing to Shanghai (about 1450 km) – ten days by rail – equalled the length of time it took these goods to travel the 11 910 km from Shanghai to Los Angeles by sea, three-fifths of the costs being incurred before the goods reached the port of export (Carruthers et al., 2003; Kledal, 2005).

In 2001 the State Council's response to the critical domestic situation was to give unprecedented attention to logistics in the 10th Five-Year Plan (2001–05) in a bid to overcome the regional disparity between the coastal east and the interior in a truly national logistics network. The Plan sought to liberalize the logistics sector and encourage more foreign investment in the establishment of local logistics enterprises; promote the development of third-party logistics providers and consolidation of domestic operators; improve the business environment (for example, customs); develop logistics infrastructure (air, sea and road); and facilitate the establishment of common standards and IT applications. Although larger trucks were permitted, stricter licensing of drivers, tighter weight restrictions and increased tolls were imposed.

Also in 2001 China's Government committed to entering the World Trade Organization (WTO) within four years and promised to fight corruption, eliminate red tape and progressively remove restrictions on wholly owned foreign logistics enterprises as part of its policy of diversifying the sector. According to this schedule, only air, water and commercial rail operations would be beyond the reach of foreign logistics operators by the end of its implementation period (Figure 9.2).

By 2002 the task of overseeing the prioritization of logistics and China's entry into the WTO for the next decade was bequeathed to Jiang's

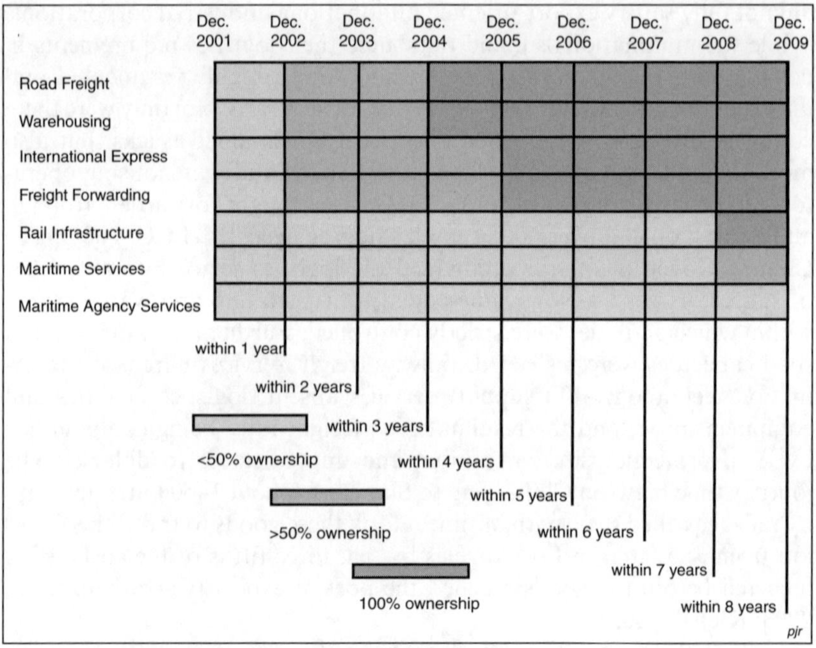

Sources: Updated from USDA (2003), Pang (2005), So (2005), Hejazi (2006).

Figure 9.2 Progressive changes in regulations after China's accession to the World Trade Organization, 2001

successor, President Hu Jintao, and the Premier, Wen Jiabao (Lam, 2006). This transfer of power raises several issues. How successful have new public policies been in changing the structure of the logistics sector during the Hu Jintao era (2003–13)? More specifically, how far has the logistics sector shifted its prime focus from rudimentary transport and warehousing activities to become more broadly based providers of supply chain solutions? And how far has the provision of third-party logistics services been expanded to focus on customer needs and technological capabilities? In turn, how have the shifts in structure influenced market conduct? How has the sector's overall performance been affected by changes in the interactions between structure and market conduct? Finally, after this decadal analysis of the logistics sector's structure, conduct and performance, what unresolved logistics issues remain for Hu's successor, President Xi Jinping?

These issues are addressed by analysing the structure, market conduct and performance of China's logistics sector during the Hu Jintao era (Figure 9.3). After briefly discussing supply and demand and public policies, China's fragmented logistics structure is analysed by focusing upon case studies of key providers drawn from in-house operators, state-owned

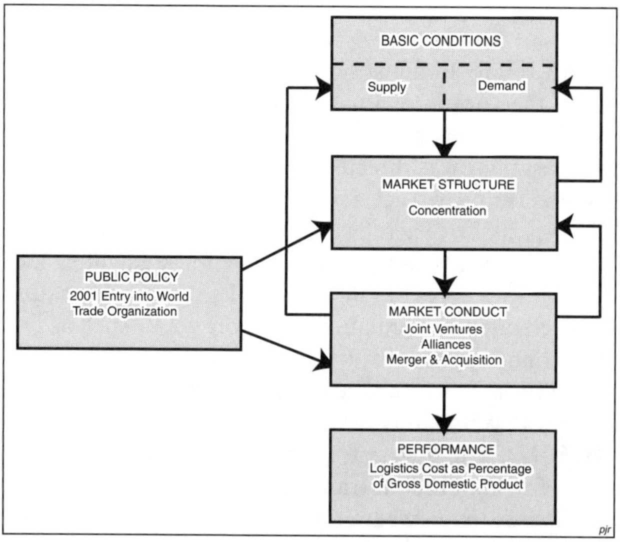

Note: The diagram is an elaboration of Joe Bain's (1959) industrial organization approach.

Source: Based on Scherer and Ross (1990 [1970], 5).

Figure 9.3 The structure–conduct–performance approach

logistics enterprises, privately owned logistics enterprises and global logistics corporations. Discussions of market conduct centre upon joint ventures, strategic alliances, franchising, and merger and acquisition (M&A) strategies used primarily by global logistics corporations. Domestic providers are also progressively employing these M&A strategies. In assessing whether the changes in structure and market conduct have improved the logistics sector's performance, reliance is placed upon a series of aggregate measures provided by the China Federation of Logistics and Purchasing (CFLP, 2004–2013a, 2004–2013b, 2005–13c); these measures are also summarized in reports by the Li and Fung Research Centre (LFRC), now renamed the Fung Business Intelligence Centre (FBIC), which has been given the responsibility of publishing the CFLP's monthly China Logistics Prosperity Index that commenced in May 2013 (FBIC, 2013a). Finally, unresolved issues affecting China's logistics sector under Xi Jinping are discussed.

THE HU JINTAO ERA (2003–13)

Supply and Demand

In 2003 the Hu Jintao administration inherited an ambitious programme for expanding the supply of logistics services and improving their efficiency, including a greater role for the private sector (Wang, 2003). Significant investment was directed at transport infrastructure to remove bottlenecks and improve accessibility (Wang, Qingyun, 2006; ADB, 2008b; FHWA, 2008). There was much reliance on traditional road depots, railway marshalling yards and warehouse facilities located adjacent to the downtown cores of inner cities (JLL, 2008). Specialized logistics facilities to accelerate the circulation of export goods such as double-stack trains, inland container depots (dry ports), integrated logistics centres and cold chain facilities, characteristic of Germany, Japan, South Korea and the United States, were barely developed (Nogales, 2004; Beresford et al., 2012; TPRI, 2012). There were few dedicated logistics centres for trucks, logistics parks for multimodal transport, or automated, standard or specialized warehouses. Even where logistics parks had been built there were criticisms that provincial and local governments were using them as 'cash cows' because they profited from the sale of land on which they were built (LFRC, 2006a). Also there was a shortage of third-party logistics providers that led many manufacturers and retailers to distribute their own products. Freight forwarders, offering combined transport on single freight documents for a through transport fee, had to register with the local transport administrative department, while the logistics company providing agency services for a fee had to file with the Ministry of Commerce (Liu, Bing-lian et al., 2013).

This lack of specialized facilities, the lagging development of third-party logistics enterprises and cumbersome regulations were exposed by the rapid growth of economic output, and expansion in the scale of industrialization and foreign trade that increased the demand for logistics services. China became number one in the world for 100 products drawn from ten industries, including coal, steel, cement, chemicals, building materials, textiles, home appliances and electronics (Liu, Bing-lian et al., 2011, 2013). Many industrial clusters were also established, including those specializing in high-value apparel (LFRC, 2006b, 2010b). Some products, notably electronic products and motor vehicles, required specialized logistics services and drove the number of multimodal logistics parks from 205 in 2005 to 475 in 2008 to accommodate their needs (LFRC, 2006a; NDRC and CFLP, 2009).

The downturn in foreign trade during the Global Financial Crisis (2008–09) affected China's logistics market, especially throughput at the leading container ports of Shanghai and Shenzhen. In response the Government stimulated domestic consumption, which had a beneficial effect upon the sales of cars, home appliances, building materials and retail chains (LFRC, 2012a, 2012b). These rising sales induced logistics demand for additional transport and specialized warehousing facilities, bonded logistics centres and public information platforms. Foreign real-estate investors such as the Goodman Group and Prologis were attracted to build distribution centres. Investments varied according to commodity, as instanced by Quanzhou Medicine and Food Logistics Co in Hunan Province expending more on automated storage for pharmaceuticals and tobacco than an apparel producer (TPRI, 2012, 208). Most consumption was still concentrated in the highly developed coastal eastern region, but demand was shifting as retail chains – supermarkets and specialty stores for cars, pharmaceuticals and real estate – established branches and distribution centres in the fast-growing central region and the less economically developed western region. As the patterns of demand changed, particularly with the accompanying transfer of factories, including those operated by Flextronics and Dell, to take advantage of cheaper land and labour inland, growing freight traffic put heavy pressure on the existing logistics infrastructure.

In assessing how the Hu Jintao administration coped with the supply–demand equation, initial attention is given here to tracking key changes in government policy related to the logistics sector before assessing their impact on the sector's structure, conduct and performance. An examination is made of the Opinions of the State Council – synonymous with the Central People's Government – chaired by Premier Wen Jiabao and comprising all heads of government departments and agencies. There is not scope for discussing the separate Opinions of the Ministries of Commerce, Railways and Transport; plans for the national layout of individual transport modes (air, rail, road, inland waterways, coastal shipping and pipelines); 11 national-level plans featuring the development of logistics in specific regions (for example, the Central Region, Pearl River Delta and Yellow River Delta); agreements for incorporating Hong Kong, Macau and Taiwan into Greater China's logistics system (see Chapter 6); schemes for progressing logistics 'informatization', and the standardization of logistics terms and calculation of logistics costs; strategies for improving logistics education to overcome the sector's chronic shortage of professionals; the logistics of emergencies such as the 2008 Wenchuan earthquake in Sichuan and the 2010 Yishu earthquake in Qinghai Province; or the logistics of special events, notably the 2008 Beijing Olympics and Expo 2010 Shanghai (Liu, Bing-lian et al., 2011, 2013; TPRI, 2012). Even the Opinions of the State Council, given their extensive and detailed nature, have necessarily to be truncated in outlining public policy.

Public Policy

During the Hu Jintao Era the State Council, together with its macroeconomic planning agency, the National Development and Reform Commission (NDRC), devoted much effort to streamlining China's logistics management system to improve national competitiveness and narrow regional disparities (Table 9.1). The logistics sector was spread across many government departments. These included air transport, communications (road and water), post and rail, that cast their individual national plans within the targets set by the country's five-year planning framework. Related departments such as commerce, finance, information, taxation and trade also expressed opinions on the logistics sector. In 2005 an attempt was made to coordinate the activities of nine ministries and two commissions following the 'Notice of the National Reform Commission of the PRC on the Establishment of a Joint Conference System for National Modern Logistics'. A set of national assessment rules were established for classifying individual logistics service enterprises (PRC, 2005).

Since 2005 a series of policies have been proclaimed to guide the development of China's logistics sector following the Opinions of the State Council on Promoting the Modern Logistics Sector. A new feature, added to the string of 13 free trade zones, was the creation of bonded

Table 9.1 State Council Opinions on the logistics sector during the Hu Jintao era (2003–13)

Year/month	Legislation
2001	**10th Five-Year Plan (2001–05)**
2004/08	Opinions of the State Council on Promoting the Modern Logistics Sector
2006	**11th Five Year Program for National Economic and Social Development (2006–10)**
2007/03	Opinions of the State Council on Expediting the Development of the Service Sector
2007/11	Opinions of the State Council on Promoting a Sound and Rapid Development of Modern Transportation
2007/12	Opinions on the State Council Concerning Accelerating the Development of Modern Transportation
2008/03	Opinions of the State Council on Implementation of Policies & Measures to Expedite Development of Service Industry
2009/02	Opinions of the State Council of the Releasing of Plans for Adjusting and Revitalizing the Logistics Industry (2009–11)
2011/03	**12th Five-Year Plan (2011–15)**
2011/06	Opinions of the State Council on the Releasing of Plans for Adjusting and Accelerating the Logistics Industry
2011/08	Opinions of the General Office of the State Council on the Policy of Accelerating the Healthy Development of the Logistics Industry
2012/07	Opinions on Strengthening Road Transport Safety
2012/07	Opinions on Promoting the Development of Civil Aviation
2012/08	Opinions of the State Council on Further Reformation of the Distribution Sector and Acceleration of the Development of the Distribution Sector

Sources: LFRC (2003, 2004, 2006a, 2007, 2008, 2009, 2011b, 2012a, 2012b).

logistics centres in coastal and inland locations to attract or generate international goods flows. The strategic status of the logistics sector was raised further in the State Council's Outline of the 11th Five-Year Plan for National Economic and Social Development (2006–11). Logistics was given national planning status in investments for transport infrastructure designed both to revitalize the Northeast region's old industrial base and to underpin the westward movement of manufacturing away from the coast. Great importance was also attached to the development of rural markets and an improved circulation system for agricultural products through the establishment of logistics distribution centres.

In 2007 further enhancement of the logistics sector was embodied in the Opinions of the State Council on Implementation of Policies and Measures to Expedite Development of Service Industry, which sought not only to reform both the railways and civil aviation, but also to encourage the further development of third-party logistics (3PL) providers. The streamlining of China's logistics management system was taken a stage further during the following year when the Ministry of Transport was established as part of a programme of super-ministry reform. The new super-ministry integrated departments concerned with civil aviation, communications (road and water), post and urban public transport. Although this amalgamation was designed as a step towards replacing the focus on unimodal transport with a multimodal approach, the Ministry of Railways maintained its independence. Its exclusion limited the new super-ministry in its task of 'drawing out strategies and plans of logistics development as well as related policies and standards and supervising the implementation' (Ma, 2010,10). Also the Ministry of Commerce was still free to offer separate advice on expediting the development of modern logistics in the 'circulation' sector, including wholesaling and retailing. Nevertheless the Transport super-ministry made plans to increase modern technology use, balance regional development, improve multimodal transport and promote 'green logistics' to respond to the requirements of sustainable development. The Global Financial Crisis (2008–09) overtook China before this agenda could be advanced.

In response to the Crisis that depressed consumption in China's key overseas export markets, the Opinions of the State Council of the Releasing of Plans for Adjusting and Revitalizing the Logistics Industry were issued to elevate the logistics sector to a national strategic level, increase logistics efficiency and reduce logistics costs (LFRC, 2009). The programme initiated by the NDRC covered five development goals, ten major missions, nine key initiatives – including coal, cold chain for agricultural products, commercial logistics, emergency logistics, logistics standards, multimodal transport, logistics parks and urban distribution – and nine supportive measures. Given its complexity, attention is concentrated here upon the key proposal for the well-planned layout of the logistics sector, which identified nine major logistics clusters (Figure 9.4). Regulations were formulated for the development of modern logistics in the Southern Region and development plans were issued for express logistics services in the Northern Region, the Pearl River Delta and the Yangtze River Delta.

This regional framework was to be knitted together by ten major logistics corridors: five running in a north–south direction and five tracking in an east–west direction. Grafted on to this network were 38 logistics hubs. They were divided into 21 'national hubs', which formed the backbone of

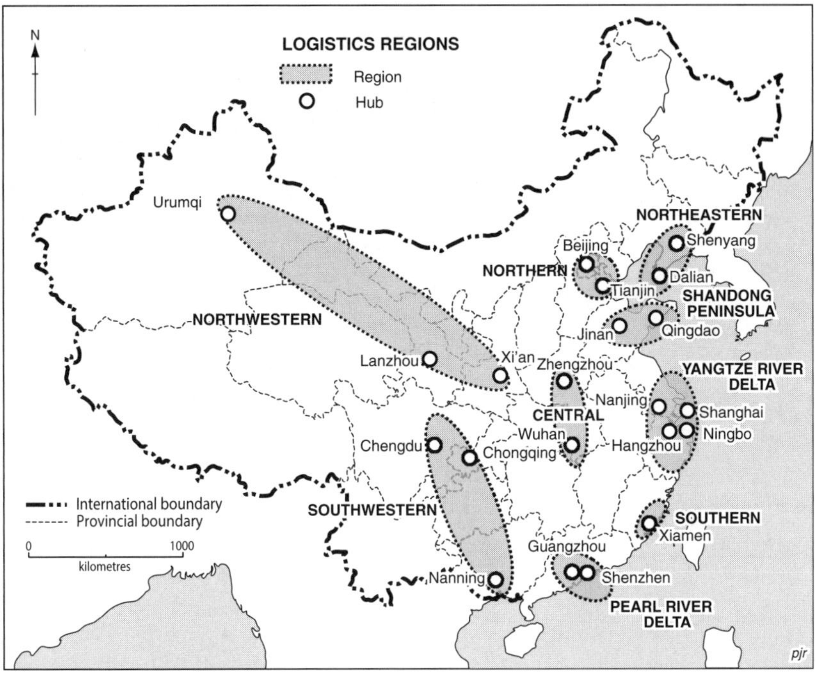

Source: Data from LFRC (2009, 21).

Figure 9.4 China's logistics regions, 2009

the logistics regions, and 17 'regional hubs' (Figure 9.5). The distinction between national and regional hubs was dropped and their total number increased to 42 with the addition of Qinhuangdao, Tatung, Xuzhou and Zhanjiang (LFRC, 2012b). Some of the inland hubs such as Kunming, Shijiazhuang, Xi'an and Chengdu were to be developed as 'dry ports' (Beresford et al., 2012).

As illustrated by Chengdu's 'four parks' and 'four centres' plan, the Central Government relied on both city and provincial governments to implement its guidelines for modernizing logistics facilities (JLL, 2008; Guo, 2012). In Chengdu these facilities are to be moved progressively from the inner-city area to four logistics parks linked to the airport and railway marshalling yards and four logistics centres adjacent to major highways to accommodate all aspects of the trucking industry (Figure 9.6).

These upgraded hubs, together with the designated corridors, provided the framework for the further development of inter-regional networks in the 12th Five-Year Development Plan (2011–15). The Plan's nine directives

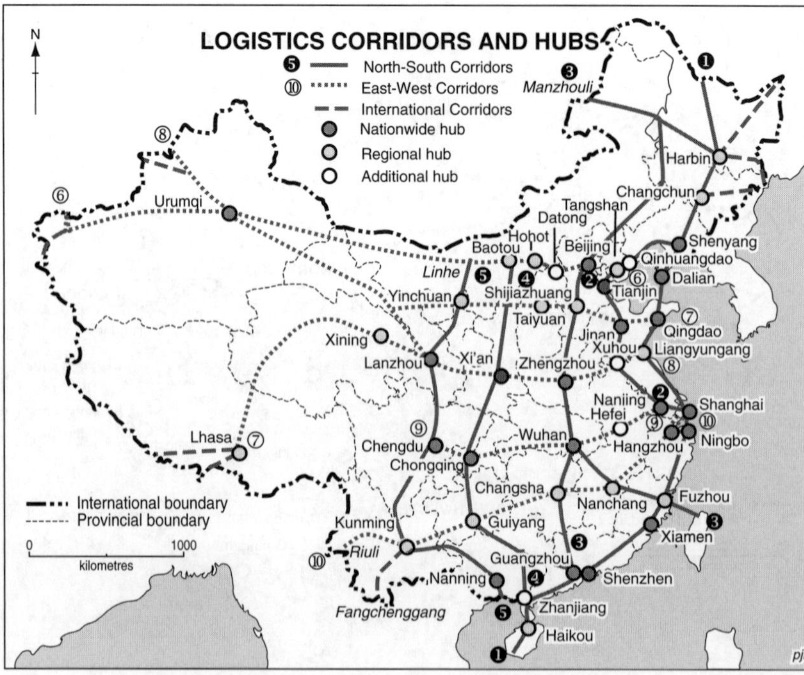

Source: Data from LFRC (2009, 21–3).

Figure 9.5 China's logistics hubs and corridors, 2010

included: developing third-party logistics; facilitating the seamless transition to multimodal transport; constructing public logistics information platforms for sharing information between different cities; and enhancing the competitiveness of logistics enterprises as global service providers by supporting radio frequency identification (RFID) technologies (LFRC, 2011b, 60).

By 2011 the original set of Opinions that established the logistics network – corridors and hubs – in response to the Global Financial Crisis had expired. A fresh set of Opinions of the State Council on the Releasing of Plan for Accelerating the Logistics Industry offered eight new measures for the sector's healthy development; a ninth measure was added later (LFRC, 2012a). These measures sought to promote an integrated multimodal transport system to reduce energy consumption and emissions, while providing a better operational environment, especially for long-distance trucking services, which were the acknowledged backbone of China's economy. Drawing upon the Ministry of Finance and State

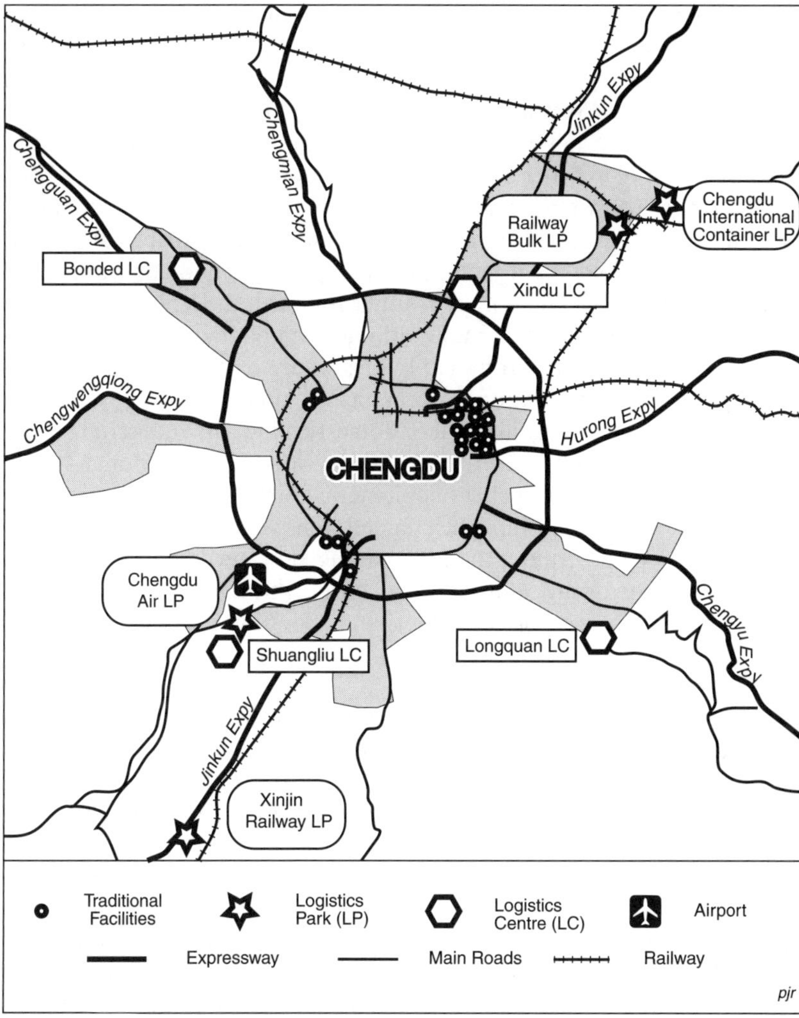

Sources: Data from JLL (2008), TPRI (2012).

Figure 9.6 Chengdu's four logistics parks and four logistics centres, 2010

Administration of Taxation's experience from a Shanghai pilot project, a reduction of the tax burden on logistics corporations was given together with preferential treatment for their activities in land use allocation. In 2012 major policies from the State Council related to the logistics sector were the Opinions on Strengthening Road Transport Safety and Opinions on Promoting the Development of the Civil Aviation Industry; there was also an emphasis on encouraging private investment in the logistics sector.

The era's final Opinions of the State Council on Further Reformation of the Distribution Sector and Acceleration of the Development of the Distribution Sector sought to modernize China's supply chain network to reduce the ratio of logistics costs to gross domestic product (GDP) (LFRC, 2012b). Apart from strengthening of urban–rural connections and city deliveries, improving logistics facilities by adding large distribution centres and agricultural cold chain facilities, and injecting cloud computing and bar codes to push the technology frontier forward, the key emphasis was on optimizing the design of multinational supply chain networks. This final policy mandate was prompted by the failure of Chinese manufacturers to spread their production geographically, preferring to stay close to their supplier base. Only a handful of domestic blue chip industrial corporations had moved out from China and developed multinational supply chains (Pan, 2008). Besides Haier appliances, Huawei telecommunications and Tsingtao Beer, their number included Lenovo computers, which had some issues in transforming the loss-making state-owned business into a profitable, fast-growing multinational corporation producing personal computers (PCs), smartphones, tablets and televisions.

Lenovo Group Ltd

In 2005 Lenovo acquired IBM Personal Computers to provide the electronics company instant access to many foreign companies and institutions and number three ranking after Dell and Hewlett-Packard in the global PC market. Apart from adopting English as the common corporate language, the Chinese chairman relocated to IBM's operational base in Morrisville, North Carolina, USA, and the American Chief Executive Officer (CEO) moved to Singapore. Research and development (R&D) was divided between company headquarters in Beijing and Morrisville and marketing was located in Bangalore. Orchestrating the multinational company proved difficult as executives in the less profitable US market received greater remuneration than those in the fast-growing domestic market (Quelch and Jocz, 2012, 207–8). Results were initially disappointing as Taiwan's Acer surpassed the company in third position in the worldwide global personal computers market (Gartner, 2013b). Since then the US$30 billion technology company employing 27000 people with customers in over 160 countries has responded by consolidating its position in the Asian-Pacific Rim through its joint ventures with NEC in Yonezawa, Japan, from 2011 and Compal in Hefei from 2012. A hybrid supply chain model has been developed with an advanced analytical capability to orchestrate the mix of 11 in-house plants and 24 outsourced

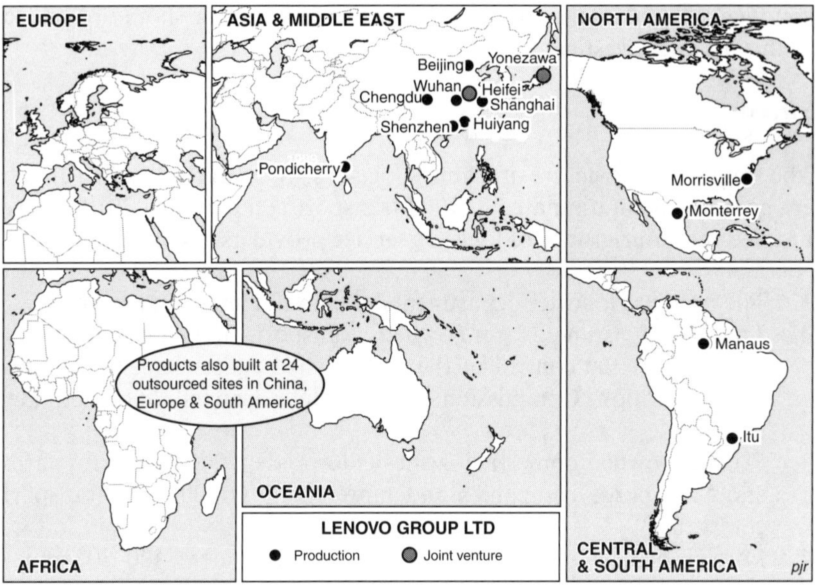

Sources: Data from Zapko (2009, 2012).

Figure 9.7 Lenovo's hybrid production network, 2010

manufacturing plants (Figure 9.7). The wider deployment and investment in in-house production has enabled Lenovo to strengthen control, and deliver greater agility in the end-to-end supply chain compared with conventional companies totally reliant on outsourcing (Zapko, 2009, 2012). By 2012 Lenovo had leapfrogged Dell and Acer and moved into second position to challenge Hewlett-Packard in the depressed worldwide personal computer market by establishing a growing presence in emerging markets in the Asian-Pacific Rim and South America, especially Brazil. Accounting for over 40 per cent of its shipments, China has remained Lenovo's most profitable market (Lenovo, 2012). Nevertheless the company has experienced adverse cost issues in China stemming from the country's fragmented and inefficient logistics sector, which has made it difficult to serve third- and fourth-tier cities.

The failure of domestic companies to follow Lenovo's lead in establishing multinational supply chains has been variously attributed to the dearth of managerial resources, inability to escape national culture, lack of business plans and strategies, difficulty in adapting to overseas environments, absence of due diligence and reciprocity problems (Shambaugh, 2012). Given Lenovo's difficulties in serving the domestic market, the structure, conduct and performance of the China's logistics sector should be added to this list and investigated.

Structure

The fragmented structure of China's logistics sector during the Hu Jintao era comprising an estimated 750 000 transport companies in 2010 can be distilled into four groups of logistics service providers (Table 9.2):

1. The in-house logistics departments of manufacturers and retailers.
2. Traditional Chinese state-owned transport and logistics enterprises under the control of the state-owned Assets Supervision and Administration Commission of the State Council (circa 50 key players).
3. Privately owned domestic logistics enterprises (2000 freight forwarders, 5000 barge companies and more than 700 000 road transport companies).
4. Foreign-owned global logistics service providers (20–30 major international companies).

As the relative advantages and disadvantages of the four segments have been well established, sample firms are used here to draw out differences in scale and service scope in terms of their logistics capabilities, to gauge the effect on performance of the public policy changes during the Hu Jintao era.

The selection of sample firms was designed to focus on their geographical coverage within China. This priority stemmed from extended supply chains into and out of China overstretching local logistics capabilities. Structural weaknesses were even exposed in distributing simple consumer products such as beer within China's multi-tiered urban system; only Tsingtao Beer and China Merchants Logistics, for example, employed sophisticated management techniques within the country's 'cottage' logistics system (Dai and Zhou, 2008).

In-house operations

During the Hu Jintao era manufacturers in China continued to operate their own logistics arms because of concerns about the service quality and services charges of third-party logistics providers and loss of control over logistics management (FBIC, 2013b). Their number included: Huizou TCL, a consumer electronics manufacturer headquartered in Guangdong Province; Shanghai Bright Dairy & Food Co. Ltd, a distributor of dairy and food products; the Taiwan-based RT-Mart, a leading hypermarket

Table 9.2 Types of logistics enterprises in China

Type	Case studies	Pros	Cons	Developments
Logistics subsidiary of large enterprise	Haier Logistics	Specialist know-how Good network coverage	Difficult to develop external client base Future strategic plan & positioning affected by mother company	Operate independently from mother company
State-owned	COSCO Logistics	Large-scale Pan-China network Good relationship with government	Overstaffing Low operational efficiency Not consumer-oriented	Improve efficiency by merger & acquisition
Privately-owned	Kerry EAS Yuan Cheng Datian W. (DTW) Group S.F. Express Anji Automotive Logistics Corporation	Clear market segmentation in terms of location, services and targeted customers Relatively efficient Rapid growth	Limited fixed assets Lack of funding for market expansion Constrained by internal management & company structure	Form strategic partnership with other competitive counterparts or investors
Foreign players	DHL Express UPS Global- TNT Express FedEx Corp	Strong overseas network Good logistics operational know-how Widespread adoption of IT	Relatively weak domestic network in China Limited scope of business in China High operating costs in China	Expand their Mainland market by merging or forming partnerships with local players

Note: Columns pros, cons and developments may not apply specifically to individual case studies, which have been added to the Table, because they are referred to in the text.

Sources: LFRC (2012a, 12), Huang and Kadar (2002–03).

chain in China; and Wuhu Annto Logistics Co. Ltd in Anhui Province, founded in 2000 as a subsidiary of the Midea Group Co. Ltd, a manufacturer and marketer of home appliances. As annual reports on these companies provided scant information on the geographical coverage of their logistics activities, Haier Logistics was chosen to exemplify in-house operations because an array of secondary sources were available to fill out its profile (Chen et al., 2004; Haier, 2011; Khanna and Palepu, 2010; McIntire and Lim, 2010).

Haier Co. Ltd, a state enterprise, established Haier Logistics as a subsidiary in 1999 to overcome the underdevelopment of third-party logistics enterprises and limited retail infrastructure that hindered the distribution of its products. The parent company had been founded 15 years earlier as the Qingdao Refrigerator Factory, a single-model refrigerator producer. During the 2000s the building of a global brand and diversification into the research, development and sale of washing machines, water heaters, computers and televisions transformed the loss-making state corporation. The corporation invested in factories in less-developed countries to escape pressures from rising material and manufacturing costs on China's eastern seaboard and to maintain profit margins. By 2010 the company had a worldwide supply chain network with 61 trading companies, eight design centres, 29 manufacturing plants, 16 industrial parks, over 800 suppliers and 24000 employees; its products were sold in over 178 countries through 58800 sales and support partners (Figure 9.8). In 2011 Haier was the world's leading major appliance brand with a turnover of US$23.2 billion, 90 per cent of which was drawn from Mainland China, the interior of which was still likened by Haier (2011) to one of the company's markets in a developing country and requiring attention to local logistics.

Haier Logistics Co. pioneered a separate logistics business in China to distribute small home appliances such as refrigerators and televisions (TVs) to the country's third- and fourth-tier markets. During the 2000s the subsidiary's task was to streamline the supply chain to achieve higher factory throughput at minimal cost and provide better customer service. Re-engineering the company's business by centralizing the handling of customer orders, previously dispersed across different divisions and profit centres, Haier Logistics switched from made-to-stock to made-to-order, implemented just-in-time management and shortened cycle times. Much effort was expended on supply chain visibility by extracting data and using it to improve volume growth, delivery predictability and delivery turnaround time. By minimizing inventories to six days for raw materials and less than ten days for finished goods, the parent company became the epitome of 'lean' manufacturing in China. Trucking goods to 42 distribution centres nationwide has enhanced responsiveness to customer demand

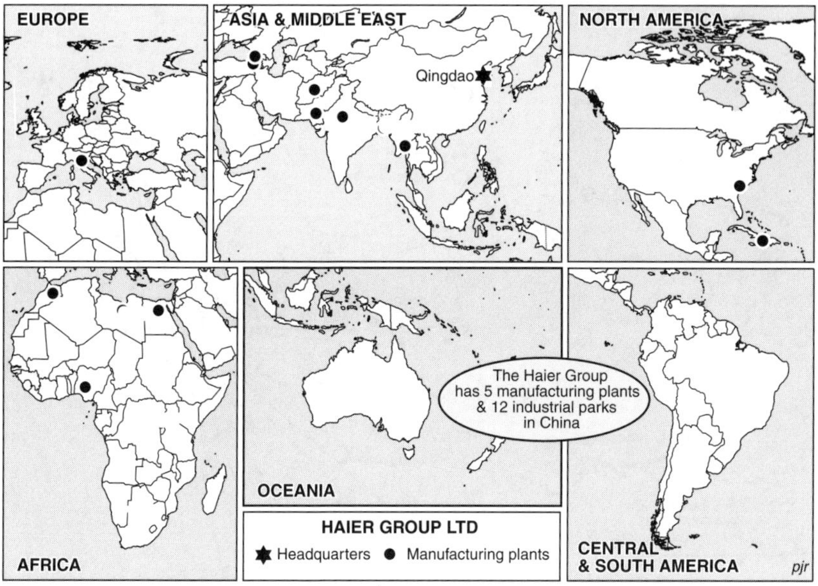

Source: Data from McIntire and Lim (2010).

Figure 9.8 Haier's international network, 2010

and enabled cash-on-delivery payments (Figure 9.9). This strengthening of Haier's logistics network has also allowed the company to take advantage of the administration's Grand Development Strategy of the Western Region, which has attracted multinationals to Xi'an and the Chengdu–Chongqing economic zone. In 2011 Haier Logistics was reabsorbed into the parent company. Two-thirds of the parent company's revenue came from its logistics business in China and one-third from sales of washing machines and water heaters.

Largely supplying services to internal customers, in-house logistics enterprises, including Walmart China, possessed the advantages of in-depth knowledge and enjoyed the support and network coverage of parent companies. Nevertheless in-house companies often lacked economies of scale and, unlike Haier Logistics and Walmart China, found it difficult to attract external clients, particularly when the non-market-driven strategies pursued by their parent companies affected their future positioning. Some companies spun-off or sold their logistics divisions but, as noted, Haier reabsorbed its subsidiary because of the edge it gave the company over its competitors, notably Midia and TCL Corporation. Other companies had already moved from in-house logistics into modern integrated third-party

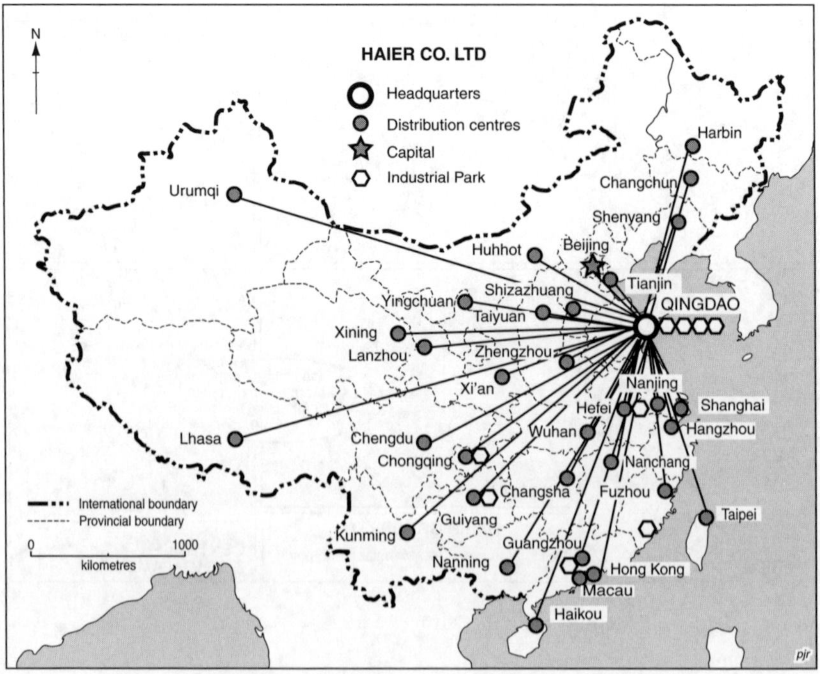

Note: Some locations on the original schematic map used for this figure are either obscured by overprinting or not identified precisely.

Source: Updated from Liang (2004).

Figure 9.9 Haier's domestic network, ca. 2008

logistics management such as Wuhu Annto Logistics, which has contracts with large domestic electronics manufacturers and more than 200 receiving/delivery points concentrated in the Yangtze and Pearl River Deltas. The most common service outsourced was transport and distribution, encompassing four-fifths of all firms surveyed (CL and GSCC, 2012; LFRC, 2012b; FBIC, 2013b). Outsourcing transport services arose from specialization within the motor vehicle, electronics, fast-moving consumer goods (FMCG) and pharmaceutical sectors. This trend to outsourcing also prompted the traditional state-owned transport enterprises to add third-party logistics to their business profiles.

State-owned logistics enterprises

Traditional state-owned logistics enterprises, engaged in both transport and warehousing, reacted to the changes in public policy during the Hu

Jintao era by restructuring and modernizing their business models to improve cost-efficiency and maintain their dominant position within the logistics sector. The three major players were:

1. China Ocean Shipping (Group) Company (COSCO), engaged in international shipping and freight forwarding.
2. Sinotrans, the largest freight forwarder in China, with a significant share of sea, air freight and inland waterway markets following the acquisition of Changjiang Shipping Corporation which operated services on the Yangtze River.
3. China Shipping Container Line (CSCL), also prominent in international shipping and freight forwarding.

All three companies possessed an extensive domestic network, with operations distinguished by competitive pricing, strong connections with provincial and local governments, and immunity from local protectionism imposed by provincial governments and disputes over regulations.

The 'Big Three' maintained their dominant position, despite their overall share of the sales revenue of China's top 20 logistics companies declining from 80 per cent in 2005 (including the Changjiang Shipping Corporation) to less than 60 per cent in 2010 (Table 9.3). Reflecting the volatility in China's logistics industry, 12 of the top 20 enterprises in 2010 were not ranked in 2005. Nevertheless the grip of state-owned enterprises on the top 20 ranks was intensified because most new entrants were owned by either central or provincial government instrumentalities. As highlighted by the establishment of COSCO's logistics arm, state-owned enterprises extended into other activities.

COSCO Logistics was founded in 2002 to complement the parent company's investments in marine terminals, container depots and information and communication technology to offset the intensification of competition from foreign operators following China's entry into the WTO (Rimmer and Comtois, 2002, 2005; COSCO, 2013a). The new subsidiary offered third-party logistics services in China to 400 business outlets across 29 provinces, municipalities and autonomous regions. Headquartered in Beijing, the subsidiary comprised companies located in Beijing, Dalian, Guangzhou, Ningbo, Qingdao, Shanghai, Wuhan and Xiamen that serviced other state-owned industrial corporations such as Guangdong Changchong Electronics Co. Ltd. These regional operations used a diverse array of road vehicles, barges and railways to move white goods, motorcars, power plants and chemicals within their respective hinterlands (Figure 9.10). In 2007, contrary to argument that the size of China's

Table 9.3 Sales revenue of China's top logistics enterprises, 2005 and 2010

	Enterprise	2005 RMB billion	Enterprise	2010 RMB billion
1	China Ocean Shipping (Group) Co.	119.5	China Ocean Shipping (Group) Co.	143.6
2	China Shipping (Group) Co.	81.0	SINOTRANS & CSC Holdings Co. Ltd	91.6
3	Sinotrans	45.2	China Shipping (Group) Co.	64.2
4	China Changjiang Shipping Corporation (CSC)	18.0	Xiamen Xiangyu Group Co. Ltd	25.7
5	China National Materials Storage and Transportation Corp. (CMST)	12.8	China Railway Material Co.	22.7
6	International Cargo Transport of China Ltd	5.7	China National Materials Storage and Transportation Corp. (CMST)	22.0
7	China Railway Express Co. Ltd	5.4	Hebei Logistics Industry Group Ltd	18.4
8	Shandong International Transportation Corp. Maritime (Group) Co. Ltd	5.1	Henan Coal & Chemical Industry Co.	16.2
9	China Merchants Logistics Group Co. Ltd	3.9	China Petroleum Transportation Corp.	14.6
10	Kerry EAS Logistics Ltd	3.7	The S.F. Express Company	11.4
11	Yuan Cheng Group Co. Ltd	3.9	China Railway Container Transport Co. Ltd	10.6
12	Shanghai Pan Asia Shipping Co. Ltd	3.2	Anji Automotive Logistics Company	10.0
13	Guangdong Nan Yue Logistics Co. Ltd	3.1	Shuohuang Railway Development Co. Ltd	9.6
14	SINOPEC Pipelines Transport & Storage Co.	3.0	International Cargo Transport Limited of China	8.6
15	Tianjin Datian W Group Company Ltd	3.0	China Minmetals Logistics Corp.	8.0
16	Qingdao Haier Logistics Co. Ltd	3.0	China Railway Express Co. Ltd	7.7
17	Zhenhua Logistics Group Co. Ltd	2.8	Yunnan Logistics Industry Group	7.5
18	China Petroleum Transportation Corporation	2.4	Beijing Huayou Natural Gas Co. Ltd	7.1
19	China Post Logistics Co. Ltd	2.0	SITC International Holdings Co. Ltd	6.0
20	Suzhou Longxing Logistics Co. Ltd	1.8	SINOPEC Pipelines Transport & Storage Co.	6.0
		328.5		511.5

Sources: LFRC (2007, 12–13; 2012a, 11).

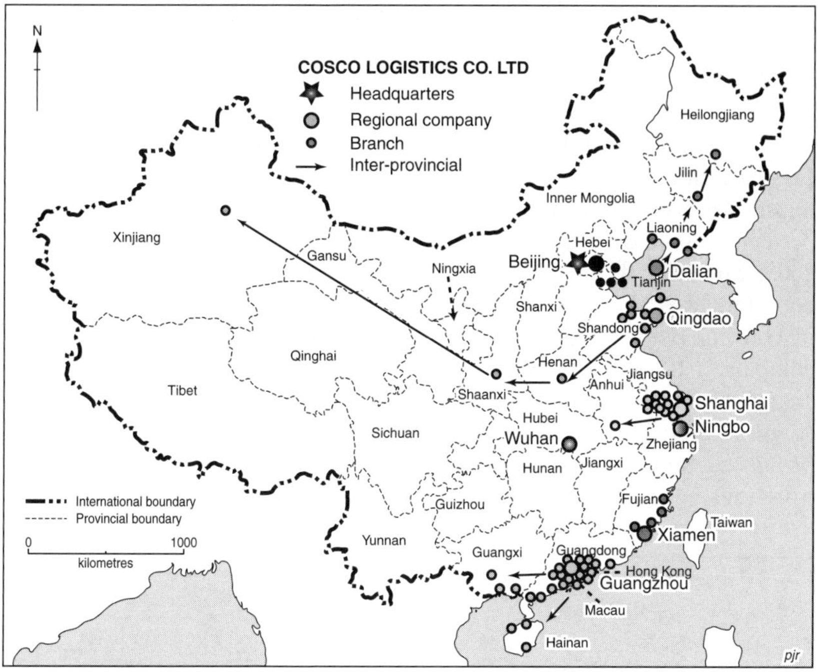

Note: COSCO's network encompasses all provinces; only regional companies and their branch offices are shown here.

Sources: COSCO (2013a, 2013b).

Figure 9.10 COSCO Logistics Co. Ltd's domestic network, 2012

market was a disincentive to create global logistics champions, COSCO Logistics used its domestic expertise and home-country advantage as a springboard to set up logistics operations in Hong Kong, Western Asia and North America; the company also operated a double-stack train in North America (Rimmer and Comtois, 2009; Zhang et al., 2010). Prospects for COSCO and the other members of the Big Three state-owned corporations have remained brighter than for their smaller counterparts with a provincial or local focus, and privately owned domestic logistics enterprises.

Privately owned domestic logistics service providers

The other response to changes in public policy has led to an increase in the number and size of privately owned third-party logistics providers seeking to capitalize on the accelerated growth of China's logistics market. Several examples are drawn here from the top 20 logistics service providers in 2005 and 2010 to illustrate the diversity and changing nature of the issues facing the non-state group.

In 2005 the top 20 logistics service providers included Kerry EAS Logistics Ltd, an offshoot of Kerry Logistics, the Hong Kong third-party logistics service provider owned by the Kuok Group, which took a 70 per cent stake in China's EAS International Transportation Ltd (BTM, 2005; So, 2005; KL, 2013). The new subsidiary was able to develop a comprehensive Pan-China logistics platform with distribution centres in Harbin, Beijing, Tianjin, Shanghai and two in Shenzen. By 2010 the company's trucking network had nodes in Harbin, Shenyang, Beijing, Jinan, Xi'an, Shanghai, Wuhan, Chengdu, Guangzhou and Shenzhen (Figure 9.11). This network linked branches and offices in all of China's provinces, supported by 4000 staff, 2000 vehicles and 386000 sq m of warehousing. In turn, the company's China focus was incorporated into

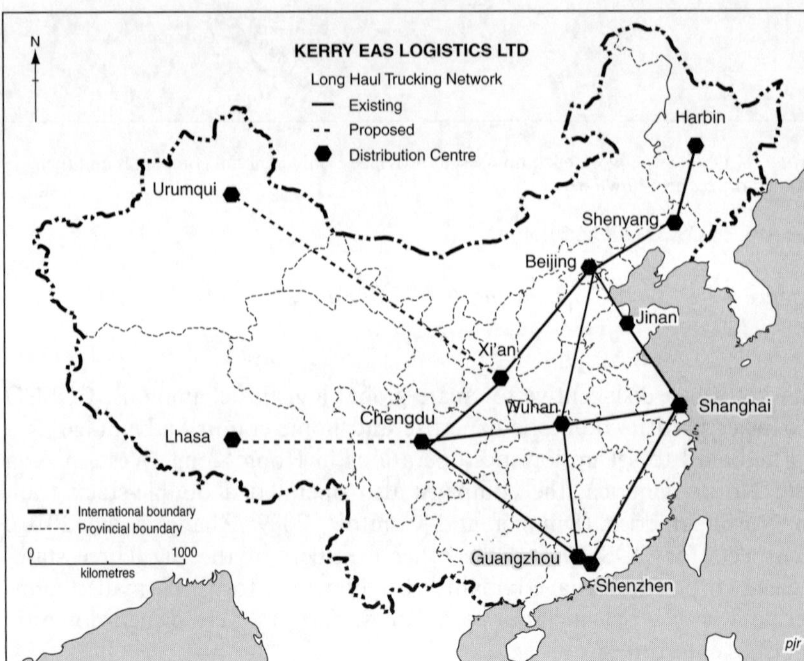

Source: So (2005), CSCI (2012), KL (2013).

Figure 9.11 Kerry EAS Logistics Ltd's network, 2010

its Asian-Pacific network, still orchestrated from its Hong Kong base, which has representation in Indonesia, Malaysia, Thailand and Viet Nam.

Companies like Kerry EAS Logistics Ltd, according to the CFLP survey, Development of Non-State Owned Local Logistics Enterprises, had forged alliances with local manufacturing enterprises; established integrated logistics services; engaged in franchised operations to meet the higher demand for logistics services and greater differentiation among them; taken advantage of the opportunities afforded by the entry of multinational corporations into different business sectors and industries; developed a capital base and a network covering at least 30 cities in China; boosted the government's tax revenue and created jobs; and acquired IT capability to improve their supply chains (LFRC, 2007,11). These developments were also borne out by an examination of the geographical coverage of the Shanghai Yuan Cheng Group that, like Kerry EAS, was also ranked among the country's top 20 logistics companies in 2005 with revenues in excess of 2 billion RMB (Table 9.3).

Shanghai Yuan Cheng Group Company (SYCG, 2013), founded in 1988, offered integrated domestic logistics services across all modes. By 2005 the company had expanded into international logistics operations by air and sea. In 2009 the company received financial support from China Guangda Investment Management Co. Ltd to fund expansion (Liu, Bing-lian et al., 2011, 33). By 2010 the company had almost 600 outlets in China, controlled more than 4000 vehicles, employed 10000 people and possessed 40 million sq m of warehouse space. Also the company operated six express trains for high-value freight and express post, six airlines for parcels, five scheduled trains for regular services and 12 container trains. Employing advanced logistics and supply chain management systems, the company's reach covered all provinces and most prefectural level cities. Very detailed descriptions of both branches and delivery and non-delivery areas were provided online to clients (Figure 9.12).

The growth of privately owned firms such as Shanghai Yuan Cheng Logistics has been variously attributed to their focus on one or two key industries, light-asset nature and higher level of efficiency than state-owned enterprises (LCG, 2005). Sustaining their growth and profitability hinged on being price–service competitive, acquiring sufficient financial support, attracting managerial talent and devising an appropriate organizational structure. Like Tianjin Datian W. Group Ltd, they were also key targets of foreign companies wanting to expand into the China market.

Tianjin Datian W. (DTW) Group Ltd ranked fifteenth among the top 20 providers in 2005. In 1992 it was established as Tianjin Hua Tian Air Freight Forwarding Company, a state-supported logistics operation. By 1999 the venture's express service network was transformed into a joint

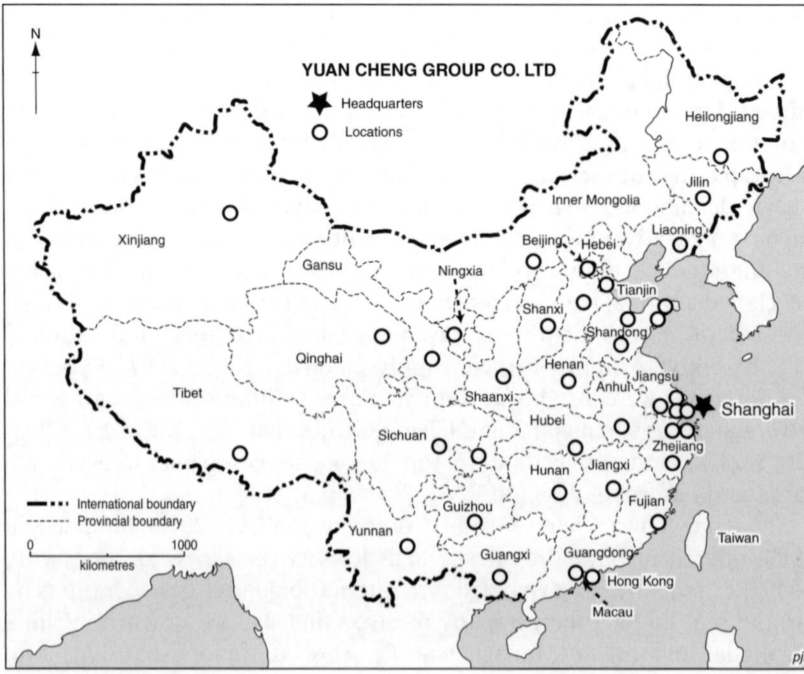

Source: SYCG (2013).

Figure 9.12 Yuan Cheng Co. Ltd's 'molecular' logistics network, 2012

venture with FedEx. Then in 2007 the foreign collaborator bought out the comprehensive domestic courier logistics network serving 76 locations (Figure 9.13). Since then the DTW Group has moved its headquarters to Beijing and developed as an integrated logistics operator using its own fleet of trucks to provide intercity express services between 26 cities and less-than-truckload (LTL) intercity services between 80 cities (TDTW, 2013).

By 2010 Tianjin DTW had disappeared from the top 20 ranking, together with Kerry EAS and Yuan Cheng, which had not kept pace with the growth of their state-owned rivals. Moreover, these road-based companies had been outpaced by the rapid growth in revenue, deliveries and employment in the country's express parcel delivery market during the late 2000s (Table 9.4). Driven by 193 million online shoppers, particularly those living in lower-tier cities, the leading of 'e-tailing' sites such as the Alibaba Group's Taobao.com and Tmall.com, and JD.com have sought, with varying success, to create a nationwide logistics network

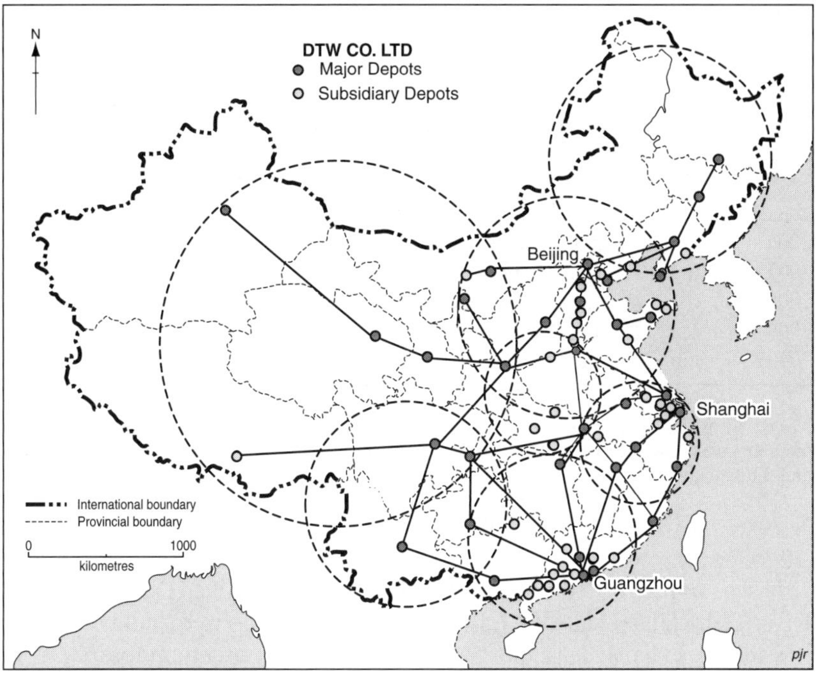

Note: The figure shows major and subsidiary depots and regional spheres of influence prior to the takeover of the company's domestic air service.

Sources: TDTW (2007, 2013).

Figure 9.13 Tianjin Datian Wu Liu's logistics network, 2007

(KW, 2012; FBIC, 2013b). By 2010 these trends had led to Shenzhen Shun Feng Express Group Co. Ltd (SF Express) becoming the leading privately owned company in the top 20 rankings.

SF Express had expanded its pick-up and delivery network since its establishment in 1993 to span Greater China by incorporating Hong Kong (1993) and Taiwan (2007) into its domestic network, and advancing into Singapore (2010), Korea, Japan and Malaysia (2011), and the United States (2012) (SF Express, 2013). By 2012 the company operated 5000 service branches and its geographical reach extended to 31 provinces, municipalities and autonomous regions and nearly 300 large and medium-sized cities (Figure 9.14). Most branches were in the eastern and central provinces with the company's warehouses being located largely in coastal areas, as two-thirds of demand for express delivery services in

Table 9.4 China's parcel delivery market, 2006–09

Year	Companies		Revenue		Deliveries		Employment	
	Number	Annual growth	RMB	Annual growth	Number	Annual growth	Number	Annual growth
		%	billion	%	billion	%	thousand	%
2006	2422	20.0	30.0	25.0	1.1	22.4	22.7	36.3
2007	n.a.	n.a.	34.3	14.3	1.2	9.1	23.4	3.1
2008	n.a.	n.a.	40.8	18.9	1.5	25.0	24.0	2.6
2009	n.a.	n.a.	47.9	17.4	1.9	26.6	n.a.	n.a.
2010	n.a.	n.a.	57.5	20.0	2.3	21.1	n.a.	n.a.

Note: Statistics refer to express operators with annual revenues over RMB 200 million, including state-owned, private and foreign companies, compiled by the State Post Bureau and the National Bureau of Statistics.

Sources: Liu (2009), Jiao et al. (2013, 138).

2011 was concentrated in the Bohai Rim, Yangtze River Delta and Pearl River Delta (Jiao et al., 2013, 141). Although these services had been made possible by extensive use of franchisees that paid a premium to operate in the company's livery, SF Express was in the process of buying back these franchises to exert greater direct control over the quality of services. This enabled the company to position itself nearer the top end of the express market to meet the growing demand for high-end food products and door-to-door cold chain delivery. These activities attracted higher fees and escaped the price wars that afflicted its rivals. In 2014 the company proposes to operate domestic and international airmail express services from Hangzhou Xiaoshan Airport to consolidate its position.

By 2011 SF Express, together with the state-owned China Post's EMS (Express Mail Service) and the franchisors Shanghai Shentong Express Ltd and Shanghai Yuantong Express Co. Ltd, accounted for two-thirds of the fast-growing, but fragmented, domestic express delivery market worth an estimated 84 billion RMB (US$13.4 billion) (KW, 2012). All three privately owned franchisors had failed to establish their own online retail operations due to low orders and uncompetitive products. Their importance among 6800 licensed operators suggested that they were increasingly able to expand their geographical reach. Despite competition from distribution companies such as Rugenda established by the clothing company Vancl, and Ozzo by the computer parts company Newegg, the three franchisors were well positioned for a second attempt at entering the online retail market (SE, 2012; FBIC, 2013b). By developing better technological

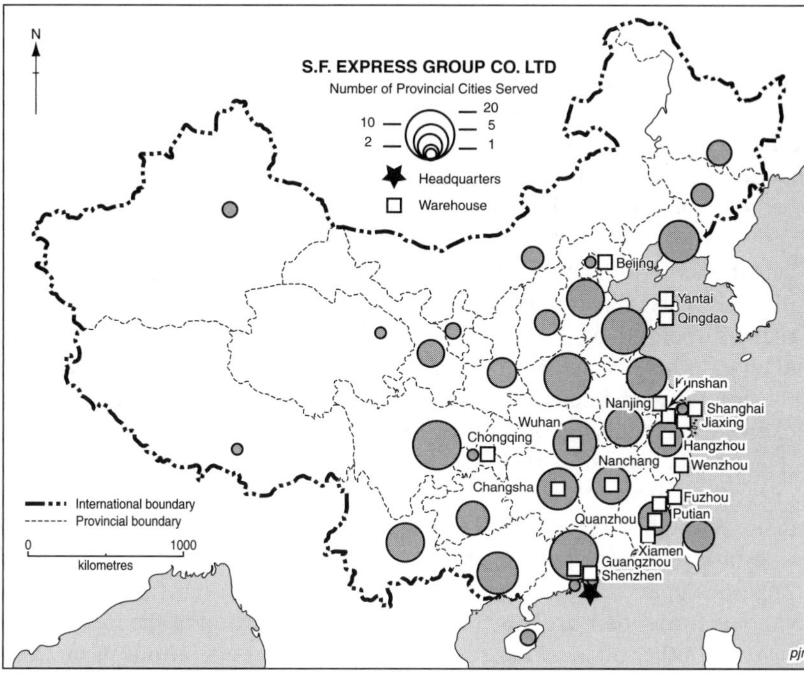

Note: The 1500 county-level cities or districts serviced are not mapped.

Source: SF Express (2013).

Figure 9.14 Shanghai S.F. Express Co. Ltd's logistics network, 2012

platforms, they could offer complex supply chain solutions comparable to those of global logistics corporations, a phenomenon attributed to their connections (*guanxi*) with both the commercial sector and public officials at all levels of government.

Many other smaller scale, privately-owned delivery enterprises, often unlicensed and without a national network, capital and connections, survived the lack of economies of scale, value-added functions and information management by filling a particular niche. The smaller enterprises sought to avoid competition with state-owned enterprises such as EMS and larger non state-owned enterprises, particularly SF Express, by focusing upon both labour-intensive activities and local markets within the same city or province. They were reluctant to adopt modern vehicles and global positioning systems (GPS), which would have improved inventory and customer tracking controls to help reduce the costs incurred in supply chains. The need for heavier investment in plant and equipment and higher taxes and increased fuel prices saw some of these point-to-point route carriers, operating on paper-thin margins, exit the sector.

Beyond these smaller private enterprises were the independent long-distance owner-operators that were deeply embedded within China's socio-economic fabric. Although profit margins were meagre, owning a truck, often purchased with help from family and friends, offered economic opportunities for rural–urban migrants to enter the formal economy. Their trucks were heavily used, with co-drivers being employed, together with a sleeper cab, to maximize road time (Barboza, 2011; Katz, 2011). Truckers operated between their home bases and depots located in provincial cities, where cargo was manhandled and trip turnaround was invariably slow. On-time delivery times were affected by the failure to speedily clear road accidents and severe traffic jams.

New loads were sought by truckers from brokers whose function was to negotiate deals at the lowest possible price on behalf of their clients, usually manufacturers or third-party logistics providers, with whom they had established personal connections by paying a deposit to insure these companies against loss. Once a broker had secured the freight against rival bids from other brokers, the origin and destination of the freight was advertised either on blackboards outside shop-front operations or on electronic screens within spacious freight transaction halls such as Changsha Zhongnan Freight Transport Market, which housed scores of separate booths, replete with computers and fax machines (TPRI, 2012, 208). Drivers tendered for the loads displayed on the screens or negotiated with the broker and, if successful, paid a fee for the service.

The driver–broker relationship did not extend beyond the single-trip transaction. Although the unregulated truck operators were agile as to the shape and size of cargo, flexible on route, responsive to last-minute demands and, above all, price-competitive, they had no beneficial connections with public officials, which was why some preferred to pay a 'licence fee' to operate for a larger private company (Kam and Rimmer, 2011). Overloading was commonplace. The truck's cargo bed, with or without sides, was lengthened or widened to carry additional goods on top of the freight, secured by ropes and tarpaulins. As alternatives to paying tolls and bribes, some truckers, assisted by a paid local guide, used back roads or travelled by night to circumvent traffic police and truck inspectors. Their resultant low-cost structures enabled individual truck operators to compete favourably with the less nimble railway and waterway operations (McArthur and Rao, 2009). This advantage applied even over the 2000 km distance between Mianyang in Sichuan Province and Hefei in Anhui Province, where the all-road option was

Table 9.5 Cost and journey times for carrying household appliances by different transport modes between Mianyang and Hefei, 2009

Item	Unit	Road		Road-Rail		Road-Water	
		40-foot	200 cubic metres	40-foot	200 cubic metres	40-foot	200 cubic metres
Cost	RMB	6000	20000	7700	26000	9000	30000
Cost per cubic metre	RMB	100		130		130	
Total time	Days	4		5		7	

Source: TPRI (2012, 246–7).

cheaper than the road–rail and road–water combinations (Table 9.5). While global logistics corporations did not normally use the services provided by independent truck operators, they too benefitted indirectly from their presence by being able to charge higher fees for their more 'reliable' and 'higher-quality' services.

Global logistics corporations

China's accession into the WTO during the Hu Jintao Era improved the environment for global logistics corporations (GLCs) offering third-party logistics services. The GLCs possessed extensive international networks, offered IT integration, supplied quality services and management, and had conspicuous brand names. Nevertheless their operations were still handicapped, in varying degrees, by high cost structures, regulatory restrictions, infrastructural bottlenecks at key hubs, limited network coverage and a lack of local knowledge, experience and connections (that is, social capital or *guanxi*). Usually their customers were multinational manufacturers and retailers with headquarters located outside China, including Carrefour SA and Wal-Mart Stores Inc.

The GLCs dominated three major logistics segments in China:

1. International express services, illustrated by those provided by DHL, FedEx, TNT and UPS (Chapter 2).
2. International shipping and freight forwarding services, typified by those supplied by APL Logistics, Maersk Logistics and OOCL (Oriental Overseas Container Line), which had strong operational expertise, advanced IT capabilities and one-stop global logistics services (Chapter 3).

Table 9.6 Characteristics of the 'big four' global network corporations in China, 2012

	DHL-Sinotrans	FedEx	TNT	UPS
Entry (Agency)	1981	1984	n.a.	1988
JV Sinotrans	1986	1986	1988	1996
JV Terminated	–	1995	2003	2004
JV Partner	–	EAS (1995–99) TDTW (1999–2005)	Machplus World wide Express (2004)	Yangtze River Express
Wholly-owned	–	2006	2003	2005
Regional HQ	Beijing	Guangzhou	Shanghai	Shanghai
Staff (est.)	9200	9000	3500	6000
Branch Offices (+additions)	50 (+20)	89 (+32)	25	45
Network (Cities)	401 (international) 128 (domestic)	300	200	200
Target (Cities)	n.a.	n.a	1100	n.a.
Market Share (estimated)	33 %	20 %	Less than 10 %	20 %
Notes	Offers 500 000 sq.m. for supply chain customers	23 flights per week between China & USA	TNT-Hoau extensive road service in China (sold in 2013)	192 flights per week between China & USA

Sources: Cen (2005, 19), LFRC (2007, 8), Niehues et al. (2007, 5), DHL (2012), FedEx (2013), UPS (2013), TNT (2013b).

3. Specialized logistic services for particular commodities such as motor vehicles.

The dominance exerted by GLCs over particular segments is illustrated by their strong presence in international express delivery services where the 'Big Four' global integrators – DHL, FedEx, TNT and UPS – accounted for 80 per cent of China's international market, leaving China Post and privately owned enterprises with the balance (Table 9.6). The GLCs were strongly represented in the Bohai Rim, Yangtze River Delta and Pearl

River Delta, reflecting that these clusters had 30 per cent of the country's population, almost half the national GDP, 75 per cent of foreign direct investment (FDI) and 84 per cent of international trade (TPRI, 2012). Some specialization occurred within the express delivery services group, with DHL focusing on transporting medical products, FedEx on high-value spare parts and UPS on high-value technology items. The GLCs were not well represented in either the highly regulated rail cargo sector or the emerging e-commerce market (FBIC, 2013b).

This domination by the GLCs limited the opportunities for both state-owned and non-state-owned enterprises, not only in express delivery but also in shipping and freight forwarding where foreign enterprises, typified by Maersk Logistics, had been adept at facilitating physical door-to-door transport, adding value, managing the supply chain and logistics, and optimizing the supply chain. These outcomes contradicted the Central Government's 2004 initiative to promote the logistics sector's development by encouraging large state-owned enterprises in China to become market leaders and non-state enterprises to participate in third-party logistics activities.

In 2006 the National Development and Reform Commission (NDRC), Ministry of Commerce (MOC) and CFLP undertook a Joint Study on 'The Impact of the Entry of Foreign Enterprises on China's Logistics Industry and Some Policy Recommendations'. This study advised the government to restrict GLC entry into the logistics sector because their global reach and financial power would inevitably prevail over local enterprises (LFRC, 2007). In 2009 a new Postal Law of the People's Republic of China covered packages below 50 kg within cities and packages less than 150 grams between cities. This law prevented wholly owned foreign enterprises such as UPS Co. Ltd from engaging in handling letters, and having 'free passage' of express vehicles and 'parking rights' in urban areas; these activities were reserved for China Postal Service and Logistics (Liu, 2009; KPMG, 2011; Jiao et al., 2013, 142).

UPS Inc.'s headquarters were based at Shanghai Pudong International Airport. Since 2004 these headquarters had supported not only the corporation's international transport and warehousing activities, but also its supply chain solutions services located in 23 business centres purchased from Sinotrans for US$100 million (UPS, 2006, 2013). In 2010 UPS moved its Asian-Pacific Rim operations from Clark Base in the Philippines to Shenzhen Bao'an Airport at a cost of US$180 million. Only after regulators had approved a US$1.6 billion loan to China Postal Service and Logistics in 2012 was UPS licensed to operate delivery services in five hubs or gateways: Shanghai, Guangzhou, Shenzhen, Tianjin and Xi'an (Figure 9.15). Except for Xi'an, this was not an exclusive right because

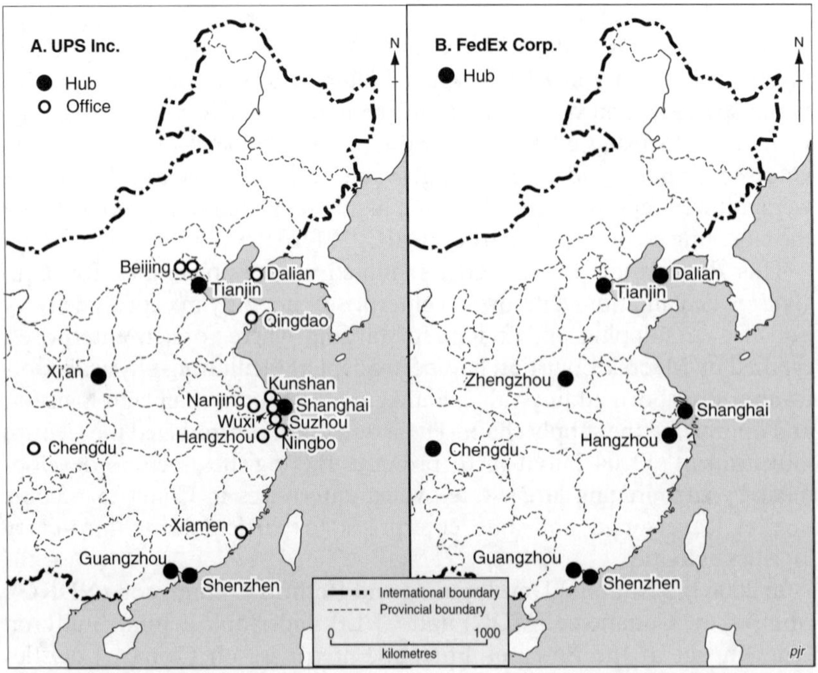

Note: UPS offices shown are either under the name of UPS Supply Chain Solutions or Fritz Logistics (Tianjin) Ltd

Sources: UPS (2013), FedEx (2013).

Figure 9.15 Logistics networks of: (A) UPS Inc.; and (B) FedEx Corporation in China, 2012

FedEx had also been given access to these gateways and additional rights to key logistics clusters of Chengdu, Dalian, Hangzhou and Zhengzhou. Outside these nominated gateways, freight had to be handed to domestic operators to reach the final destination.

Summary

As China's four logistics subsectors differed in service scope from single functions to complex multi-functions, they were not able to provide the full range of logistics capabilities. This led to changes in market conduct, which were designed to compensate for shortcomings in agility, supply chain integration, domestic coverage, industry-specific knowledge, international logistics and domestic transactional logistics, by forging linkages between the four subsectors.

Market Conduct

An examination of market conduct during the Hu Jintao era is here focused primarily upon the strategies used by global logistics corporations in the express delivery, shipping and freight forwarding, and specialist logistics sections. The prime strategies used by GLCs were joint ventures, strategic alliances, franchising, and merger and acquisition; these strategies were also used by other segments of China's logistics sector to overcome the rigidities of its fragmented and inefficient structure.

Joint ventures between GLCs and their Chinese counterparts offered quicker market entry in a logistics market purportedly worth US$120 billion (DHL, 2012). The classic case was DHL China, which has pursued its growth in China within a joint venture with Sinotrans to marry modern management practices, aggressive promotion strategies, advanced technical support and high-quality service with local knowledge and talent. Giving access to China's domestic express, forwarding and supply chain market from airport hubs in Beijing Capital and Shanghai Pudong International Airports, the joint venture with Sinotrans has been renewed until 2052. In 2010 DHL entered the domestic express delivery market with a 50 per cent a stake in the air carrier Sinotrans A-Plus Express (APEX); a year later the joint venture was sold to Shenzhen Unitop Logistics Co. Ltd, a domestic freight forwarder (Appel, 2012).

Joint ventures in shipping and freight forwarding are illustrated by US-based YRC Worldwide Inc. (formerly known as Yellow Roadway Corporation). In 2005 YRC Worldwide and JHJ International Transportation Co. Ltd, a Shanghai freight forwarder with 1700 employees in 64 locations, had entered into an equal partnership for US$46 million (YRCW, 2008). Then in 2008 YRC Logistics Asia Ltd purchased a 65 per cent equity interest for US$48 million in Jiayu Logistics Co. Ltd's less-than-truckload (LTL) business with over 30000 customers, 1400 employees and in 170 locations (YRCW, 2009). As the minority party held the position of General Manager, decisions on developing the truckload and LTL business were often vetoed. Although the veto power was removed from the minority shareholder, YCR Worldwide subsequently sold the business to its joint venture partner but still retained its partnership with JHJ International Transport (YRCW, 2010, 2011).

Partnerships in specialized logistics were exemplified by the 2002 joint venture between TNT Logistics and Anji Automotive Logistics Co. Ltd, a subsidiary of the state-owned Shanghai Automotive Industry Corporation (SAIC). The joint venture was formed to provide third-party logistics services for Shanghai Volkswagen which used China as both a source and destination market (Bliss and Haddock, 2008). In 2006 TNT Logistics was sold to Apollo Management L.P. and Anji-TNT Logistics was rebranded as Anji-CEVA Logistics (Anji, 2013; CL, 2013). The new company became the largest motor vehicle logistics company in China with over 5 million vehicles being handled in 2010 (Jiang, 2013). By 2012 China's Anji-CEVA integrated network for car sales, services and imports served 204 cities and over 3000 destinations using road, rail and water transport options (Figure 9.16).

As direct investment in China through joint ventures was a time-consuming process, it became the preferred option only for those with little experience in the logistics market. GLCs sought to establish wholly owned operations to boost the range of logistics services on offer by using three different routes to achieve greater independence: strategic alliances such as that between FedEx and Tianjin DPW to offer airfreight operations within China; franchising as pursued by TNT, which provided a

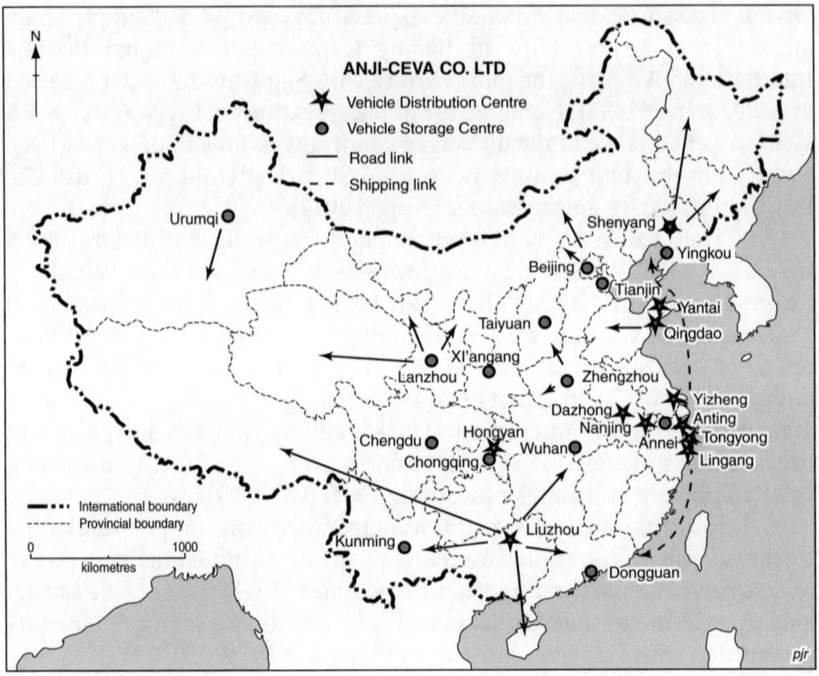

Note: The company makes use of 3000 trucks, 348 box cars, three river steamers on the Yangtze, five ships and two roll-on/roll-off facilities at Shanghai's Waigaoqiao port.

Sources: Anji (2013), Anji-CEVA (2013).

Figure 9.16 Anji-CEVA Automotive Logistics Co. Ltd's network, 2012

special training programme to boost the skills of franchisees; and merger and acquisition, which offered GLCs the quickest route to achieve independence and an extension to their networks.

Merger and acquisition was fraught with obstacles ranging from political interference, the protection of state-owned companies, intellectual property matters, limited understanding of local needs, lack of information for due diligence and China's fragmented market (Niehues et al., 2007, 11). Nevertheless the GLCs had accumulated considerable experience in taking over express delivery companies that had a strong presence in China. For example, Deutsche Post World Net (DPWN) acquired DANZAS in 1999, DHL Express in 2002, Airborne in 2004, and Exel in 2005, and TNT acquired Wilson in 2003 (Cen, 2005: 53; HC, 2007). As illustrated by TNT, this merger and acquisition experience led to the restructuring of its logistics networks in China.

TNT has an investment holding company based in Shanghai (Pang, 2005; Lombard, 2006). In 2007 the company proceeded with the 100 per cent takeover of the Hoau Logistics Group, which was China's largest enterprise engaged in LTL express services after China Post (Figure 9.17). This merger and acquisition provided TNT-Hoau with a large land-based transport network within China with 1260 depots and 56 domestic hubs covering more than 500 cities (EFT, 2009). Hoau provided TNT with the necessary experience in overcoming local protectionism following the company's decision to divest itself of its logistics business and concentrate upon its mail delivery network business. As TNT was prevented from merging its operations with UPS by the European Union regulators, the company decided to maintain its presence in Beijing, Shanghai, Wuhan and Zhongshan, but disposed of Hoau domestic road operations in China to the Hong Kong-based Citic Group in 2013.

FedEx, like UPS, has invested heavily in China. In January 2006 FedEx purchased a 50 per cent stake in FedEx–DTW International Priority Express and DTW's domestic express network for US$400 million to create a wholly owned foreign enterprise, albeit with strong local management. Since 2009 FedEx has established an Asia-Pacific Rim hub at Guangzhou Baiyun International airport, a domestic hub at Hangzhou Xiaoshan Airport serving 400 domestic cities via Okay Cargo Airlines, and a main international gateway at Shanghai Pudong Airport with other international gateways in Beijing and Shenzhen. Also the company has folded its domestic express division into its international operations. Although FedEx offered both a combined air–ground time-definite service and a ground-only service to more than 100 cities within China, its share of the price-sensitive market did not exceed 1 per cent, a figure that still disturbed some of its Chinese competitors (KW, 2012).

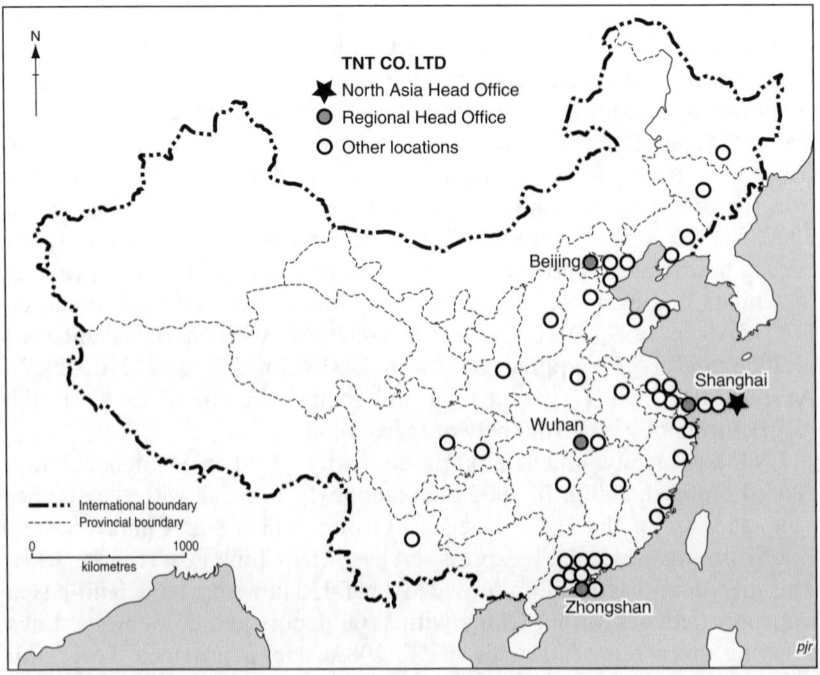

Sources: TNT (2013b), cf. Pang (2005), Lombard (2006).

Figure 9.17 TNT Express locations in China, 2013

Outside the 'Big Four', the German-based DB Logistics, owner of Schenker AG, acquired Bax Global in 2006 to augment 14 offices and seven logistics centres in China (Millar, 2007). Then in 2007 a string of United States logistics firms made acquisitions: Tianjin Baoyan Logistics was purchased by Schneider Logistics (Tianjin) Ltd; and the third-party logistics provider Shanghai Chic Logistics was bought for US$60 million by Menlo Worldwide, a subsidiary of United States-based Con-way Inc., which had a third-party logistics network covering almost 80 cities (KPMG, 2011). In 2012 CEVA Ground, a joint venture between CEVA Logistics and the Shanghai J.Y. Group Company, became a wholly owned subsidiary by buying out the latter's 30 per cent share (CL, 2013).

GLCs did not monopolize the merger and acquisition strategy, as it also extended to state-owned enterprises. In 2005 China Post Logistics Co. Ltd merged with China Courier Service Corporation operating Express Mail Services (EMS) to boost the overall performance in the hotly contested domestic market. Then in 2006 China Railway Express Co. Ltd merged with China Railway Parcel Express Co to consolidate their activities in China's highly fragmented domestic market that had low entry barriers. In 2009 Sinotrans merged with the Changjiang National Shipping (Group) Co. Ltd; and China Post Group's China Express Delivery Service Company and China Post Logistics Co. Ltd were merged into China Post Express Delivery Co. Ltd. By 2010 the State Council was actively encouraging further merger and acquisition to extend the scale of operation and development of specialized logistics services (Wang, 2013, 13–14).

After 2005 there were also instances of merger and acquisition among non-state and in-house enterprises following the opening-up of the express delivery sector (Table 9.7). In 2005 the Hong Kong-based Kerry Logistics Network (KLN) took a 70 per cent stake for US$47 million in EAS International Transportation Co. Ltd. Then in 2006 the Singapore-based 3PL Keppel Transport & Telecommunications acquired a 35 per cent stake in Wuhu Annto Logistics, attracted by the company's network of 90 transportation, warehousing and distribution facilities; this stake was resold to the majority shareholder in 2013 as Keppel sought to move into port and third-party logistics. In 2009 the international freight forwarder NTS Logistics Management Co. Ltd acquired the domestic LTL carrier Tong Cheng Logistics to become reportedly the country's largest integrated non-state logistics enterprise with a network of 60 cities. In 2012 NTS Logistics merged with Damco China Ltd, part of the AP Møller Maersk Group (NTS, 2013). This vigorous merger and acquisition activity and the formation of strategic alliances were not the preferred options among family-run logistics service providers, however, which sought to grow organically.

Performance

Gauging the effects of changes in structure and market conduct on the performance of China's logistics sector during the Hu Jintao era (2003–13) is dependent upon annual statistics provided by the China Federation of Logistics and Purchasing (CFLP, 2004–13a; CCTA, 1986–2012; CIFA, 2013). As past performance details are restricted to the annual sales of the largest providers, the analysis is limited to distilling the Federation's aggregate measures into time series to detect trends in market size and efficiency.

Market size

China's logistics sector's market size and the demand for its services were reflected in the rise of total logistics value, derived from goods produced in or entering the country (Table 9.8). Between 2001 and 2012 the total value of final products to end-users increased more than ninefold from 19450 million RMB to 177300 million RMB, with year-on-year rate of

Table 9.7 Selected merger and acquisition activity in China, 2006–11

Year/ month	Buyer	Seller	Activity	Share (%)	RMB Million
2012/08	Shentong Express	Haihong (Hainan Airlines)	Acquisition	60	200 (US$25 mn)
2011/07	Singapore Post Ltd	Shenzhen 4PX Express Pte Ltd	Shareholding	20	60
2011/06	Shenzhen Uni-top Industry Co.	Sinotrans-Apex (50-50 JV)	Acquisition	100	n.a.
2010/07	Hangzhou Baishi Network Ltd [BES Huizhou]	Shanghai Huitong Express	Shareholding	70	n.a.
2010/06	DHL	Sinotrans A Plus Express (Apex)	Acquisition	100	300
2010/06	Haihong (Hainan Airlines)	Shaoxing Zhejiang Yuanzhi Logistics Co., Ltd	Joint venture	51	n.a.
2010/05	Haihong (Hainan Airlines)	TTK Express	Shareholding	60	120
2010/03	Alibaba[1] (owner Jack Ma)	Stars Express (owner Chen Peng)	Shareholding	30	50
2007/03	TNT Hoau Logistics Group Co. Ltd	Hoau Logistics Group Co. Ltd	Acquisition	100	878
2006/01	FedEx	Tianjin Datian W. DTW Domestic Express Network	Shareholding Acquisition	50 100	3200 (US$400 mn)

Note:
1. Alibaba/Stars Express joint venture went bankrupt in 2012.

Sources: Brekelmans and Sunderland (2012a, 2012b).

growth rates consistently being above those for GDP. Slackening only during the Global Financial Crisis (2008–09), this growth stemmed largely from the acceleration of China's manufacturing activities, with industrial products rising to over 90 per cent of logistics value from 2009. Despite

Table 9.8 Composition and growth of logistics value in China, 1991–2012

Year	Industrial products	Imported Goods	Other[1]	Total	Growth
	%	%	%	RMB billion	%
1991–1995	79.5	n.a.	n.a.	n.a.	n.a.
1996–2000	82.9	n.a.	n.a.	n.a.	n.a.
2001	n.a.	n.a.	n.a.	19451	–
2002	n.a.	n.a.	n.a.	23259	19.6
2003	n.a.	n.a.	n.a.	29549	27.0
2004	84.6	n.a.	n.a.	38383	29.9
2005	86.0	11.3	2.7	48058	25.2
2006	86.7	10.6	2.7	59598	24.0
2007	87.8	9.7	2.5	75228	26.2
2008	88.8	8.7	2.5	89991	19.6
2009	90.4	6.9	2.7	96650	7.4
2010	90.2	7.5	2.3	125413	29.7
2011	90.2	7.5	2.4	158354	26.3
2012	91.4	6.5	2.1	177316	11.9

Note:
1. Comprises agricultural products, recycled materials and consumer products; n.a. not available.

Sources: CFLP (2004–13a, 2004–13b), LFRC (2004, 2006a, 2007, 2008, 2009, 2011b, 2012a, 2012b), FBIC (2013b).

the country's emergence as a consumer market for overseas producers, imported goods did not keep pace with industrial products; also the combined total of agricultural products, recycled materials and consumer products never exceeded 3 per cent.

The double-digit growth of China's economy generated additional demand for logistics services. This was reflected in the coefficient of logistics demand, derived from dividing the total logistics value by the country's GDP (Table 9.9). Calculation of this coefficient showed that the logistics service requirement in producing one unit of national GDP increased from 2.0 units in 2001 to 3.4 units in 2012. Although there were temporary reversals in the trends during the Global Financial Crisis (2008–09), the subsequent recovery to higher levels shows that market demand has been resilient.

A measure of the logistics sector's market between 2003 and 2012 was reflected in the rapid growth of total value-added by the logistics sector from 911 billion RMB to 3600 billion RMB (Table 9.10). The sector's

Table 9.9 Coefficient of logistics demand in China, 2001–12

Year	Coefficient	Year	Coefficient
1991–1995	1.6	2006	2.8
1996–2000	1.7	2007	3.0
2001	2.0	2008	2.9
2002	2.3	2009	2.8
2003	2.5	2010	3.2
2004	2.8	2006–10	2.9
2005	2.6	2011	3.4
2001–2005	2.4	2012	3.4

Note: The coefficient of logistics demand is the total logistics value as a proportion of gross domestic product.

Sources: CFLP (2004–13a, 2004–13b), LFRC (2004, 2006a, 2007, 2008, 2009, 2011b, 2012a, 2012b), FBIC (2013b).

Table 9.10 Total value-added of China's logistics sector, year-on-year growth and contribution to tertiary sector, 2003–12[1]

Year	Total value added	Year-on-year growth	Contribution to tertiary sector	Share in GDP
	RMB billion	%	%	%
2003	911	–	16.2	6.7
2004	1078	18.3	16.6	6.7
2005	1227	13.8	16.8	6.7
2006	1412	15.1	16.7	6.7
2007	1793	27.0	16.6	6.7
2008	2153	20.1	16.4	6.8
2009	2310	7.3	16.1	6.9
2010	2700	16.9	16.0	6.9
2011	3200	18.5	15.7	6.8
2012	3548	10.9	15.3	6.8

Note:
1. Total logistics value is defined as products being produced in or entering China during the recorded period.

Sources: CFLP (2004–13a), LFRC (2004, 2006a, 2007, 2008, 2009, 2011b, 2012a, 2012b), FBIC (2013b).

significance was also underlined by its relatively stable contribution to the tertiary sector and share of GDP.

Efficiency

A measure of changing efficiency in the logistics sector during the Hu Jintao era has been provided by total logistics cost as a proportion of GDP (Table 9.11). As the percentage had dropped from 24 per cent in 1991 to less than 20 per cent in 2001, there were expectations that during the Hu Jintao era it would fall to less than 17 per cent by 2010 (LFRC, 2006a). This did not materialize because the figure has remained stubbornly around 18 per cent; a trend suggesting China would take over 30 years to reach the comparable level of the United States and Japan at between 8 and 10 per cent. This situation is attributed, at least in part, to the tertiary sector only accounting for two-fifths of the economy, compared with two-thirds in advanced capitalist countries (LFRC, 2007, 6). High tolls on the highways, accounting for 20–30 per cent of trip cost, and poor railway freight services have also contributed to the situation; drivers' logs on the

Table 9.11 Total logistics cost as a percentage of China's gross domestic product, 2000–12

Year	Total logistics costs/ GDP	Year-to-year reduction	Total logistics cost savings
	%	%	RMB billion
1991–95	22.8	–	–
1996–2000	21.7	–	–
2001	18.8	0.6	63.4
2002	18.9	–0.1	–11.5
2003	18.9	0.0	–2.7
2004	18.1	0.8	24.4
2005	18.6	–0.5	35.5
2006	18.3	0.3	n.a.
2007	18.4	–0.1	n.a.
2008	18.2	0.2	n.a.
2009	18.1	0.1	n.a.
2010	17.8	0.3	n.a.
2011	17.8	0.0	n.a.
2012	18.0	–0.2	n.a.

Note: n.a. not available.

Sources: CFLP (2004–13a), LFRC (2004, 2006a, 2007, 2008, 2009, 2011b, 2012a, 2012b), FBIC (2013b).

route to Mongolia reported official and unofficial tolls costing 16 RMB (US$2.60) per kilometre (Batson, 2008; TPRI, 2012).

The total logistics costs in this analysis were derived from an amalgam of transport, inventory and management. Between 2001 and 2012 the total cost increased more than fourfold from 2028 billion RMB to 9400 billion RMB, with double-digit year-on-year growth (Table 9.12). The composition of total costs underlines that transport is still the dominant contributor but inventory costs have increased. Although management costs had been expected to rise with outsourcing and the increased deployment of the services of 3PL operators, this had not materialized, suggesting improvements in the efficiency of supply chain operations had occurred.

This rising importance of inventory costs led to the annual National Survey on Logistics Market being undertaken by the NDRC and Nankai University between 2006 and 2011 (Table 9.13). While the survey found increasing receptivity to outsourcing over this period, no consistent signs of improvement were detected in the circulation efficiency of the industrial and commercial enterprises due to the Global Financial Crisis (2008–09) disrupting the average inventory period (LFRC, 2012b; FBIC, 2013b). More than half of the industrial and commercial enterprises surveyed held their inventories for more than 30 days, which is attributed to

Table 9.12 Components of total logistics cost in China, 2001–12

	Components			Total	Growth
	Management	Inventory	Transport		
	%	%	%	RMB billion	%
2001	n.a.	n.a.	n.a.	2028	n.a.
2002	n.a.	n.a.	n.a.	2199	8
2003	14	30	56	2498	14
2004	14	29	57	2911	17
2005	14	31	55	3386	16
2006	13	32	55	3841	14
2007	13	33	54	4541	18
2008	13	35	53	5454	16
2009	12	33	55	6080	12
2010	12	34	54	7098	17
2011	12	35	53	8410	19
2012	12	35	53	9370	11

Note: n.a. – not available; rounding errors.

Sources: CFLP (2004–13a), LFRC (2004, 2006a, 2007, 2008, 2009, 2011b, 2012a, 2012b), FBIC (2013b).

Table 9.13 Average inventory period for industrial and commercial enterprises, 2006–11

Enterprise	Days						Average
	>10	1–20	21–30	31–60	61–90	<90	
	%	%	%	%	%	%	Days
Industrial							
2006	10.6	17.7	18.8	25.3	16.5	11.1	46.6
2007	10.2	18.5	19.2	26.6	15.4	10.1	45.2
2008	9.8	9.9	21.7	27.6	16.1	14.9	52.0
2009	9.5	10.6	23.4	28.9	15.4	12.2	48.9
2010	9.5	11.2	23.7	32.4	13.5	9.7	45.9
2011	9.0	9.5	23.0	32.5	26.0		48.1
Commercial							
2006	14.5	19.1	19.7	22.1	14.3	10.3	41.6
2007	16.1	20.2	20.8	23.3	10.4	9.2	39.7
2008	11.1	19.8	20.1	28.8	10.7	9.5	42.3
2009	11.4	21.3	20.1	29.8	9.3	8.1	40.1
2010	14.8	23.9	18.6	25.7	9.1	7.9	38.0
2011	15.0	19.0	17.0	29.0	20.0		41.6

Note: In 2011 no breakdown is given for inventories over 60 days into 61–90 days and over 90 days.

Sources: LFRC (2004, 2006a, 2007, 2008, 2009, 2011b, 2012a, 2012b), FBIC (2013b).

poor warehousing and inventory management. Nevertheless an overall improvement in logistics efficiency was supported by China's rising ranking in the World Bank's logistics performance index from 30th in 2007 to 26th in 2012. The ranking suggested that there was still scope for improved inventory and customer tracking controls to reduce costs incurred in supply chains, the need for more emphasis on environmentally sustainable transport systems to reduce dependence on imported oil, and greater stress on the integration of individual modes of transport.

Summary

The performance measures underline the growth in market size and improvements in efficiency in China's logistics sector during the Hu Jintao era. They were underpinned by increasing investments in the logistics sector's total fixed assets from 728 billion RMB in 2004 to 3232 billion RMB in 2011, a figure boosted in 2008 as part of a stimulus package to offset the impact of the Global Financial Crisis (Table 9.14). Between 2004 and 2011 the

Table 9.14 Composition of fixed asset investments in China's logistics sector, 2004–11

	Transport	Warehouse & storage & postal services	Wholesale	Total	Growth
	%	%	%	RMB billion	%
2004	82	6	12	728	–
2005	83	4	13	929	28
2006	80	4	16	1217	23
2007	77	5	18	1428	17
2008	75	6	19	1751	23
2009	76	7	17	2569	47
2010	76	7	17	3068	19
2011	68	9	23	3232	5
2012	65	10	25	4011	24

Sources: CFLP (2005–13c), LFRC (2005, 2006a, 2007a, 2008, 2012c).

composition of the fixed assets changed, with wholesaling and distribution and, to a lesser extent, warehousing, storage and postal services, accounting for an increasing share at the expense of transport. Nevertheless, transport still accounted for over three-fifths of the total, reflecting continued investment by the Chinese Government in civil aviation, highways, inland waterways, railways and seaport infrastructure, the bulk of the outlay being related to logistics (Chen and Lee, 2013; FBIC, 2013c).

Between 2000 and 2010 the length of highways tripled and that of expressways more than quadrupled (Table 9.15). The railway network – ranking second in the world after the United States – increased by one-third and the percentages of both electrified track and double-track lines rose. Since 2008 there has been greater capacity for rail freight operations as high-speed passenger trains commenced running on 10000 km of dedicated track by 2012. Also the quality of 'high-standard' inland waterways increased, the pipeline network tripled, and specialized systems for moving coal, containers, grain, oil and ore were established. Over the decade the integrated network (excluding air routes) expanded, but seamless movement between modes was still not well developed, resulting in supply chains still being assembled in an inefficient and piecemeal fashion. Only 1 per cent of China's massive port throughput of containers was combined with rail for transport inland; a reflection of the segmented management of logistics facilities, bottlenecks in rail infrastructural capacity and the low credit levels of operators (Liu, Wei-lin et al., 2013).

Table 9.15 Length of different transport modes in China, 2000, 2005, 2010 and 2015

Mode	Unit	Actual			Planned
		10th Plan		11th Plan	12th Plan
		2000	2005	2010	2015
Integrated network[1]	thous km	n.a.	3688	4320	4900
Highway	thous km	1680	3345	4008	4500
– expressway	thous km	16	41	74	106
Railway	thous km	69	75	91	120
– double track[2]	%	37	39	45	50
– electrified[2]	%	25	31	45	60
Inland Waterways (higher grade)	thous km	n.a.	82	102	130
Pipeline	thous km	25	44	79	150
Coastal berths (deep water)	no.	n.a.	1113	1774	2214
Civilian airports	no.	135	142	175	230

Notes:

1. Excludes civil aviation routes and international shipping routes;
2. Information on double tracking and electrification for 2000, 2005 and 2010 from NBSC (2013).

Sources: NDRC (2012), NBSC (2013).

The massive investment in logistics infrastructure was designed to accommodate the upsurge in domestic freight traffic (Table 9.16). Although the tonnage doubled between 2000 and 2010, there was no marked modal shift; road transport maintained over three-quarters of the total, inland waterways increased and rail declined. Nevertheless there was greater volatility between modes in the distance travelled in freight tonne-kilometres, which tripled between 2000 and 2010, the increase being particularly marked after 2005. Road transport boosted its share of freight movements from almost 14 per cent to over 30 per cent largely at the expense of rail and, to a lesser extent, coastal shipping, which was engaged in transporting coal, metal ores and building materials.

The 12th Five-Year Development Plan for an Integrated Transportation System (2011–15) provided no overall fixed investment target for logistics, but forecast an extension of the integrated transport network to increase by 14 per cent from 4.3 million to 4.9 million km (NDRC, 2012; FBIC, 2013c). Other than a slight rise in pipeline movements at the expense of

Table 9.16 Freight traffic in China, 2000, 2005 and 2010

Mode	Freight tonnage (million tonnes)			Freight task (billion tonne-km)		
	2000	2005	2010	2000	2005	2010
Road	10388	13418	24481	613	869	4339
Rail	1786	2693	3643	1377	2073	2764
Inland Waterway	946	1712	3208	666	1112	2243
Coastal shipping	276	485	581	1707	3855	4600
Air	2	3	6	5	8	18
Pipeline	187	310	499	64	109	220
	13585	18621	32418	4432	8026	14184

Sources: NDRC (2012), NBSC (2013).

road transport, no marked modal shifts are anticipated. Nevertheless the transport task is expected to increase by 41 per cent from 32000 million tonnes in 2010 to 46000 million tonnes in 2015; freight tonne-kilometres are expected to grow at an identical rate from 14200 to 20100 billion tonne-kilometres. Although there is no breakdown by region, these figures underline that pressure will increase on the domestic logistics sector's performance during the Xi Jinping administration.

THE XI JINPING ERA (SINCE 2013)

Unresolved Issues

This chapter has used the structure, conduct and performance framework to examine China's logistics sector during the Hu Jintao era (2003–13) that began soon after China's entry into the WTO and ended with the country being the world's largest producer of motor vehicles. The framework's application is justified by the lack of financial information on the performance of individual logistics service providers during this period in which the scale of the sector's infrastructure was expanded and the quality of facilities improved to accommodate the huge increase in trade and investment. Even the use of this time-honoured framework has been constrained by limited data on vertical integration and diversification, level of concentration, economies of scale and entry barriers, sources of absolute cost advantage, and pricing behaviour. Having illustrated the changing geographical spread of logistics activities in China, product diversification and company restructuring by using a range of sample firms, the unresolved issues that remain to be addressed by the Xi Jinping administration need to be identified.

The new administration will be able to draw upon the Report from China's Transport Planning Research Institute (TPRI, 2012), *Transport Efficiency through Logistics Development*, which was sponsored by the Asian Development Bank. The report examined the structure, market conduct and performance of China's logistics sector based on case studies of selected commodities, including parcels and packages, and survey reports on four provinces along the Yangtze: Zhejiang, Anhui, Hunan and Sichuan. 'Even after infrastructure investments on a scale and at a pace greater than anywhere else in the world', the report found China's logistics sector still suffered from over-regulation, a fragmented service market and inefficient use of existing facilities, which have been responsible for 'low efficiency and reliability, poor safety, and lack of sustainability' (TPRI, 2012, 2–3). This report's recommendations for overcoming these dilemmas by improving the productivity of the logistics section has been distilled into a second document by the Asian Development Bank (ADB, 2012c), entitled *Transport Efficiency through Logistics Development: Policy Study*, which offers a set of guidelines to address policy, regulatory, operational and infrastructural issues (Table 9.17).

In March 2013 the 18th National People's Congress (NPC) of the Communist Party of China addressed the main policy question arising from the continued presence of multiple jurisdictions, other than the Ministry of Transport, monitoring logistics developments. Putting the Ministry of Railways operations under the control of the Ministry of Transport and creating the China Railway Corporation to manage commercial activities has removed a barrier to the creation of a truly multimodal system (FBIC, 2013c). Already the corporation has plans to streamline the railway's cargo handling practices, introduce rail courier services to expand the scope of business and launch door-to-door services. However the Ministry of Commerce is still free to promote the application of modern logistics technology to boost domestic consumption, including distribution networks with logistics parks, public distribution centres and terminal nodes. Nevertheless this step towards overcoming multiple jurisdictions, which complicate coordination, hinder standardization and impede communications along the supply chain, will allow the new administration to establish a logistics section within the Ministry of Transport to concentrate upon short-term regulatory matters, medium-term operational problems and long-term infrastructural challenges.

Regulatory matters stem from China's licensing system, which requires

Table 9.17 Asian Development Bank's policy proposals for transport efficiency through logistics development in China, 2012

1. Improve the Policy Framework (S)
- Improve the policy direction for logistics development
- Improve the regulatory framework
- Promote unified technical standards
- Strengthen the government's strategic role in transport and logistics investment

2. Market Regulation (S)
- Improve the output of domestic freight forwarders and truck brokers
- Introduce mechanisms to enhance honesty and trust in freight markets
- Create a sound logistics and insurance regime
- Improve the system of import/export control
- Adjust the supervision regime for logistics operators
- Improve urban distribution regulation

3. Effective Transport and Logistics Practices (M)
- Promote drop-and-pull transport operations
- Promote multimodal transport development
  - — Reduce control over rail container transport
  - — Accelerate the development of inland waterway container transport
  - — Create the right environment for multimodal transport to succeed

4. Infrastructure (L)
- Accelerate the development of inland waterway transport
- Emphasize comprehensive planning in logistics park construction
- Accelerate the development of a national container network
- Establish mechanisms to coordinate infrastructure development

Note: S = Short-term; M = Medium-term; and L = Long-term.

Source: ADB (2012c, 32–40).

logistics service providers to apply for multiple licences, often from different central government departments, and pay numerous taxes prior to operation. Affecting market conduct, these requirements are compounded by the need to purchase licences from each local government or hire appropriately licensed trucks for delivery within urban centres that, in turn, are limited by curfews on times of operation and growing congestion that precludes on-time deliveries. Policies governing truck size and bridge limits vary widely, and official tolls imposed by local governments to pay for road and bridge building, and unofficial taxes by traffic police, erode profits and result in circuitous routing patterns to avoid these imposts.

Operational problems arise from the market dynamics of China's logistics services sector. While the Government and its advisors favour the implementation of multimodal transport, the domination of China's logistics service structure by small truck owner-operators militates against its realization (Kam and Rimmer, 2011). The local know-how and services at affordable prices provided by small trucking firms enable them to compete favourably against cheaper rail and water transport. So long as the small trucking firms are commercially sanctioned, institutionally encouraged and fortified by the sector's higher echelons, and bolstered by the westward movement of manufacturing and retailing, their influence upon China's logistics service sector is likely to persist and pose a direct threat to the implementation of multimodal transport. Any attempt to change the structure to create an integrated national logistics sector poses a dilemma for a government that prioritizes social harmony, because the truck owners are so deeply embedded within China's social fabric.

Infrastructural challenges stem from the continuing concentration of logistics infrastructure in coastal areas and the anticipated faster growth in regional GDP by 2020 within central and western China (Figure 9.18). As manufacturers and retailers move westwards to the growth areas of Hefei, Wuhan, Chongqing, Chengdu and Xi'an, a widening imbalance in movements between inbound raw materials and outbound finished goods flows from China's 'rebalancing' agenda is expected to result in further empty truck movements. Some local warehousing will have to be upgraded in the expanding logistics regions, cold chain facilities provided, loading docks supplied, express delivery streamlined and the over-reliance on manual operations overcome. Planning guidelines will be required, especially as some landlords seek to maximize rents by allocating only part of a site to warehousing, thereby precluding the most appropriate design of logistics facilities. As part of an emphasis on environmentally sustainable transport systems, there will be a need to make greater use of inland waterways and the national container network, combining rail haul and road pick-up and drop, to reduce China's dependence on imported oil. The Asian Development Bank's recommendations on the need for massive injections of capital into the logistics sector to deepen domestic integration and raise efficiency through the adoption of the best operational practices and consolidation of its structure echo those of the *China 2030* report, co-authored by the World Bank and the Development Research Center of the State Council (World Bank and DRCSC, 2012, 148, 176).

As these regulatory, operational and infrastructural issues will affect the logistics sector's performance, a new set of directives and action programmes, albeit following Marxist-Leninist traditions, will be required

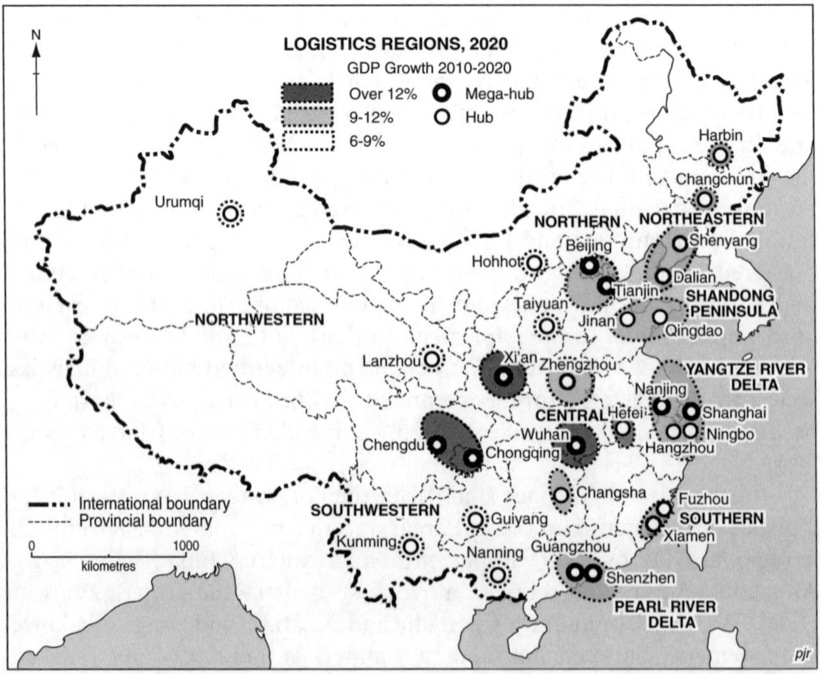

Note: Based on a concentrated urbanization scenario, this refined set of logistics regions pinpoints the accelerated development of the Yangtze River Valley and the area around Xi'an. A clutch of gateways or logistics mega-hubs, expected to handle one billion tonnes per annum, are distinguished from ordinary cluster hubs.

Sources: Information from MGI (2009), EIU (2012), MQ (2013).

Figure 9.18 Logistics regions and gateways in China, 2020

from Xi Jinping's leadership to create fresh visions and directions and set future economic targets. Opinions on the logistics sector from the State Council, led by Premier Li Keqiang, should provide another round of public policy responses to address the issues identified. Their overarching goal should be to create a consistent set of regulations to overcome conflicting standards, a competitive multimodal environment employing pricing, taxation and fiscal incentives, and optimization of the existing infrastructure for managing supply and demand based upon the coordination of physical planning developments. Then the logistics sector, comprising larger, more efficient and innovative companies or collectives, will be able to support enterprises moving up the value chain and competing in the digital economy; underpin the westward migration of manufacturing; meet growing domestic demand from a new middle class by moving away from export-led capital investment toward household consumption, productivity and efficiency; and assist the creation of a low carbon economy (Huang, 2013; Pettis, 2013). Also attention will need to be given to China's cross-border connections, particularly with Japan and South Korea, because they offer opportunities for expanding the geographical reach of the country's logistics service providers and enabling the country to become more competitive internationally (Chapter 10).

10. Northeast Asia: regional logistics policy

No attempt is made here to outline a logistics policy for the entire Asian-Pacific Rim. Rather, attention is focused on Northeast Asia, which has lagged behind Europe, North America, South America and Southeast Asia in establishing an integrated regional logistics market. In the new millennium interest has been revived in developing a joint logistics policy between China, Japan and South Korea because progress has been so tardy on the more difficult task of establishing a trilateral free trade agreement, customs union or common market. Since November 2012 the three countries have been negotiating a China–Japan–South Korea Free Trade Agreement (CJK FTA) to be implemented within two or three years. While talks continue at regular meetings on this formal mechanism covering tariffs, investments and services, attention is meanwhile being focused on strengthening economic interdependence and intensifying social exchanges within Northeast Asia through informal mechanisms that involve developing an efficient logistics network. Offering a less political approach to regional development, these mechanisms include the identification of transnational economic corridors and the development of special economic zones straddling border areas, offering a fall-back position should unresolved territorial issues derail completion of a trilateral Free Trade Agreement.

Before examining this new interest in developing a regional logistics policy, a series of issues have to be addressed. Why has so little been achieved in developing an integrated logistics market in Northeast Asia that accounts for one-fifth of the world's gross domestic product (GDP)? What lessons can be derived from considering other regional associations in designing an integrated logistics market in Northeast Asia? How has an integrated logistics arena in Northeast Asia been designed by regional scientists? And how can institutional and financial mechanisms be advanced for Northeast Asia to support this emerging integrated logistics arena?

In addressing these issues attention is focused initially on Northeast Asia's policy context to account for the paradox between the lack of progress, and the irrepressible urge among political leaders, intellectuals, manufacturers and retailers in China, Japan and South Korea from the late 2000s to develop a new, cooperative Northeast Asian logistics market. Then lessons can be drawn from the experiences of other regional associations: the North American Free Trade Agreement (NAFTA), the European Union (EU), the Union of South American Nations (UNASUR) and the Association of Southeast Asian Nations (ASEAN) where marked progress has been made in designing institutional arrangements to support logistics development. Steps recommended by regional scientists towards reshaping the logistics arena in Northeast Asia to overcome the physical and institutional gaps are considered before concluding with a discussion of regional governance and financing infrastructure.

POLICY CONTEXT

The desire for an integrated logistics market in Northeast Asia is deep-rooted. Pan-Asian sentiment was evident before the Sino-Japan War (1894–95) and Russo-Japan War (1904–05) and propelled Japan into a colonial role in Formosa (Taiwan) and Korea. In 1913 a plan was mooted for a Japan–Korea Tunnel under the Tsushima Strait to link the respective railway systems, but little progress was reported until Japan's invasion of China in 1937 (Rimmer, 2006b). In 1938 the tunnel plan resurfaced under the Japanese colonial regime to replace the ferry between Shiminoseki and Busan that enabled travellers to connect with the railway running through Seoul and Pyongyang to Mukden (Shenyang) in Manchuria. A map produced by the Construction Bureau of Japan's Ministry of Railways, which was published in the *Fukuoka Shimbun* in 1938, demonstrated that the Japan-to-Korea connection had the potential of joining Tokyo to Singapore – provided the missing rail links were completed – a vision that still permeates thinking among Japanese scholars about the long-term spatial structure of the Asian-Pacific Rim's logistics arena (Figure 10.1).

In 1940 Japan's Railway Construction Bureau undertook initial drilling activities for the Tsushima Tunnel. By then Imperial Japan had focused on developing an orbital railway network linking Korea, Manchuria and the Russian Far East (Figure 10.2). With the defeat of Japan in the Pacific War this proposition, underpinning the country's Greater East Asian Co-prosperity Sphere, not only evaporated but also triggered a backlash in China, and in 1948 split Korea into the socialist north and the capitalist south at latitude 38 degrees north. Since then the dream of a regional integrated logistics market lay dormant until the end of the Cold War in the late 1980s because each country pursued its own national strategies and economic policies with little regard to the wider regional structure.

The attraction of a more integrated and liberalized logistics market in

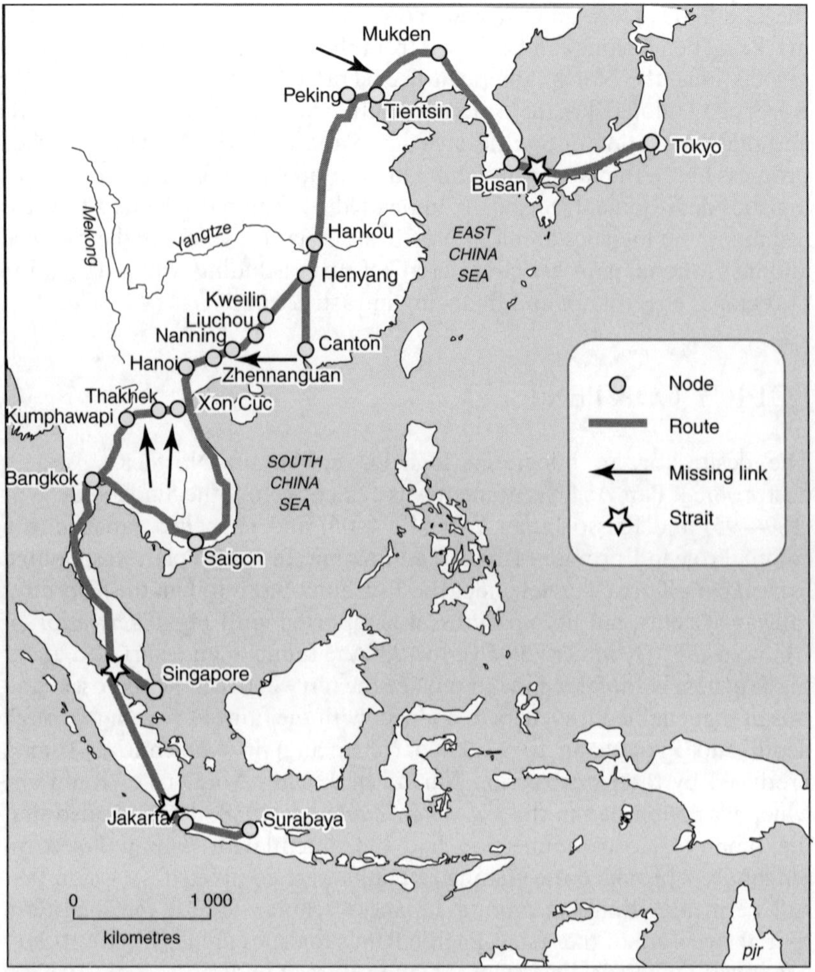

Source: Fujihashi (2010).

Figure 10.1 Japanese Imperial Government's vision of a railway linking Asia's Pacific Rim prior to the Asia-Pacific War (1941–45)

Northeast Asia is that it will end long-standing contradictions between China, Japan and South Korea that have hindered the development of a more embracive economic community. Although building 'a common house' for Northeast Asia, modelled on the North American Free Trade Agreement and the European Union, remains a desirable outcome as a

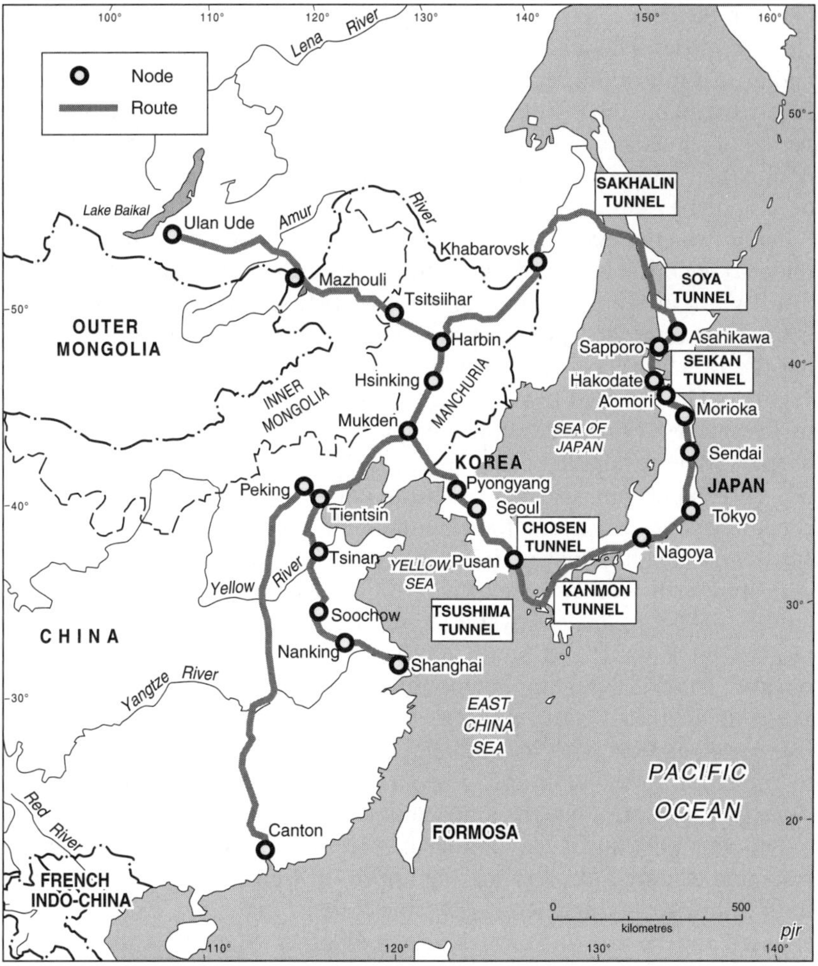

Source: Henshu (1986).

Figure 10.2 Japanese Imperial Government's orbital railway route, ca. 1940

means of overcoming the past history of war and confrontation spread over hundreds of years, little advancement has been made towards an integrated logistics policy. Progress has been stunted by distrust between China, Japan and South Korea and the attitude of the United States that, until its newfound interest in the Asian-Pacific Rim, has vacillated between benign neglect and negativity. Nevertheless each of the four principal countries – China, Japan, South Korea and the United States – has had a turn in leading regional logistics policy development in Northeast Asia (Rozman, 2004; Rimmer, 2005b; Calder and Min, 2010). Once their period of leadership passed, the individual countries refocused on consolidating their national strategies rather than on enhancing Northeast Asian development.

Japan was the initial helmsman. During the early 1990s the country's regional scientists were enthused with creating an arena around the 'Japan Sea Rim' to increase regional cohesiveness (Mitsuhashi, 2000; Nakagawa, 2005). The approach offended South Korea, which countered by defining the Bohai–Yellow Sea economic area. This resistance prompted the Japanese Government to switch its policy to employ local forces designed to foster cross-border development by sidestepping entrenched political barriers. The resultant border fever was contagious because it infected not only Japan but also neighbouring countries. China pursued special economic zones straddling the country's northeast, the Russian Far East, Japan and North Korea; and South Korea opted for a 'northern strategy' with its North Korean counterpart. Japan's initiative foundered on the naivety of its provincial governments; China's expansionary tactics were resisted by Russia; and South Korea's conciliatory approach came to naught. These failures were compounded by disinterest from the United States in Northeast Asian activities. Nevertheless Japanese regional scientists have persisted with streamlining their strategies for a 'seamless' Asia to capitalize on the country's deepening economic ties within Northeast Asia; their blueprint has remained an influential guide (Figure 10.3).

Between 1994 and 1998 China came to the fore as the new leader by resuming trading links and seeking improved transport connections with both South Korea and Russia. As the Asian Financial Crisis (1997–98) exposed the failure of South Korea and other economies to maintain global banking standards, China was able to demonstrate its emerging role as a responsible economic partner at this critical juncture. Nevertheless the advent of a common front was undermined by the persistence of mutually accusative Sino-Japanese relations and the antipathetic attitude of the United States and the International Monetary Fund towards an Asian Monetary Fund to underpin regional approaches by Japan and South Korea. This setback did not hinder China from developing its own regional logistics strategies. Major economic zones were designated 'red areas' and other significant economic zones 'yellow areas' and the primary (red) and secondary (yellow) routes linking them were identified; purple routes were added to complete the wider network (Figure 10.4). Within this framework the country's logistics priorities had already shifted from

Note: Routes 5 and 6 are the main corridors for connections with Japan. The Japanese Government's policy advisers would like to develop Route 3, particularly the section intersecting with Route 5 at Harbin, to develop the inland area of Northeast Asia.

Sources: Kayahara (2004), Rimmer (2005b), KOTI (2009), Arai (2013), ERINA (2013).

Figure 10.3 Japan's vision for transport corridors in Northeast Asia, 2002

the Pearl River Delta to the Yangtze River Delta to bolster China's global position. It was but a short step from this framework to demonstrate how China's spatial planning principles could be extended to Japan and Korea to establish the Northeast Asian logistics arena (Rimmer, 2003).

Then between 1999 and 2002 South Korea took the lead by joining Japan and China in ASEAN+3 in the hope that its mediating role would translate into joint logistics activities in Northeast Asia. Rapprochement was sought with North Korea through the then South Korean President's 'Sunshine Policy'. Kim Dae Jung's initiative was aimed at knitting together the severed Korean railway network and casting a united Korea as the logistics hub for Northeast Asia and the beginning of an 'Iron Silk Road'. Spatial planning steps towards realizing these goals led to the

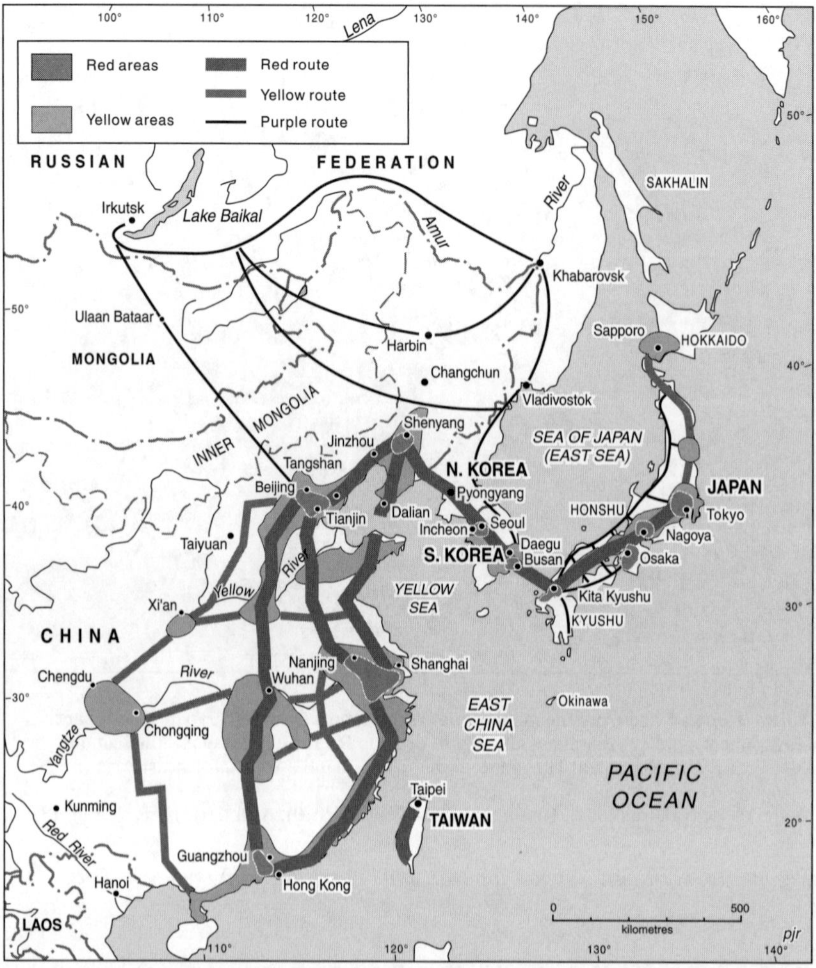

Note: 'Purple routes' were added to show how corridors in Northeast Asia could be integrated into the framework.

Source: Rimmer (2003).

Figure 10.4 Extrapolating China's spatial strategies, comprising red and yellow areas and corridors, to Japan and Korea, 2000

definition of transnational development axes affording links to China, Japan and the Russian Far East (Figure 10.5). These connections were part of a wider vision espoused by Kim's East Asian Vision Group, the East Asian Study Group and the Network of Northeast Asian Think

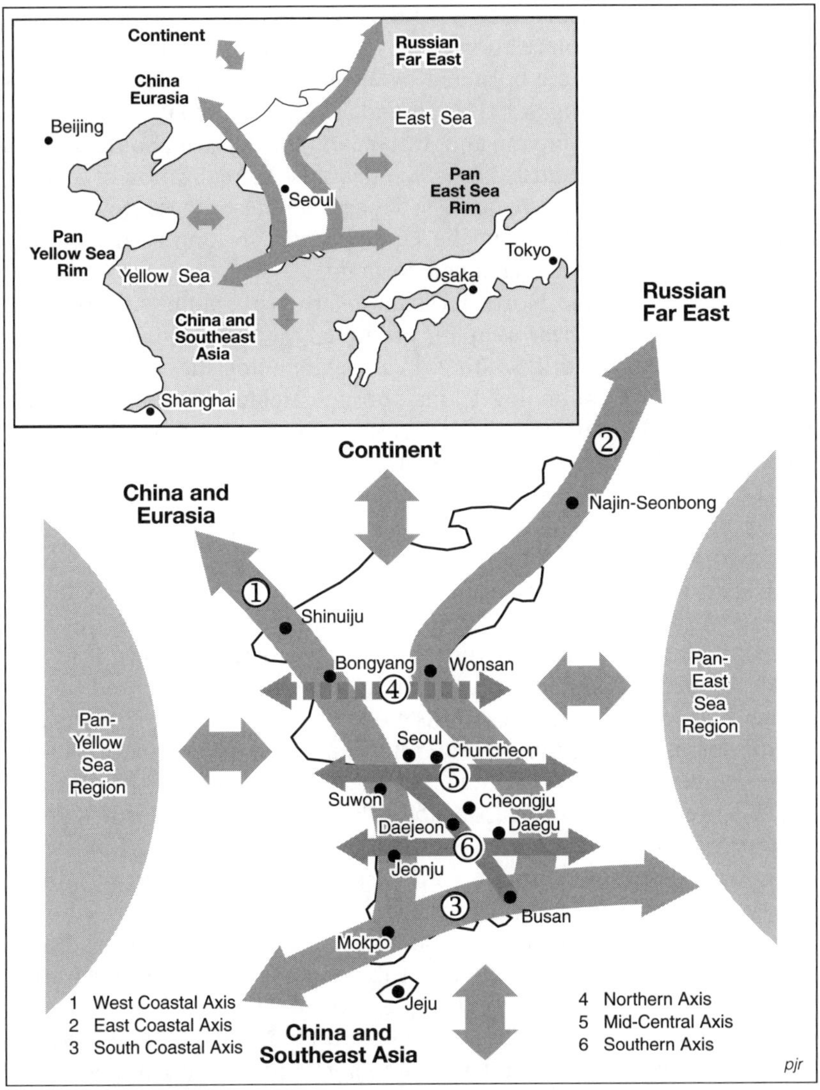

Note: The Plan identifies four points of international contact.

Source: ROK (2002).

Figure 10.5 Corridors linking Northeast Asia stemming from South Korea's Revised Fourth National Comprehensive Plan (2006–30)

Tanks (NEAT). As Kim hailed from Korea's west coast region, particular emphasis was placed on relations with China by declaring it an 'open territory'. These plans were bolstered by a flurry of intercity arrangements hosted by Dalian, Qingdao, Tianjin and Yantai in China; Kita Kyushu and Shimonoseki in Japan; and Busan and Incheon in South Korea. Although they were regarded as a step towards the realization of a wider Mediterranean-style East Asian logistics arena, none of these cross-border activities stirred interest from the United States so long as the nuclear threat from North Korea remained dormant.

In October 2002 the North Korean government's admission that the country possessed nuclear weapons prompted the Bush administration in the United States to stifle South Korea's regional logistics initiatives and shift attention to containing China through tighter collaboration with Japan. By raising barriers to regionalism in Northeast Asia, the United States exposed the unpreparedness of China, Japan and South Korea to integrate their logistics activities. China had not endorsed a Northeast Asia policy, and Japan was anxious about North Korea's intentions and tried to counter China's influence by wresting the initiative from the Network of Northeast Asian Think Tanks by establishing a Council on East Asian Community (CEAC). Meanwhile the United States used its geographical detachment from the region to defend its own role as a broker in logistics matters between China, Japan and Korea, and to seek greater business opportunities for its global logistics service providers and multinational manufacturers and retailers. Nevertheless the Six-Party Talks established in 2003 between China, the United States, North and South Korea, Japan and Russia not only sought to end North Korea's nuclear programme through negotiation, but also promised a framework for enhancing a joint logistics policy. Before discussing this proposition it is pertinent to discuss what institutional mechanisms can be derived from the experiences of regional associations in North America, Europe, South America and Southeast Asia to assist the ongoing process of integration in Northeast Asia that has eventually to extend beyond the 'Big Three' – China, Japan and South Korea – to incorporate Mongolia, North Korea and the Russian Far East, and accommodate United States interests.

LESSONS FROM OTHER REGIONAL ASSOCIATIONS

Most logistics activity occurs within states but there is an increasing amount occurring in the spaces between countries in Northeast Asia opened up by globalization. As this increasing activity cannot easily be dealt with by the respective national governments, regional logistics issues require collective decision-making and cooperative resolutions. Comparative studies of regional organizations, therefore, can assist decision-makers in Northeast Asia in developing policy-relevant knowledge about new forms of regional governance and cooperation.

The 1994 North America Free Trade Agreement led to the progressive removal of tariffs on goods shipped between the US and Canada in 1998, and between the US and Mexico in 2008, to harmonize their land-based logistics systems and make them interoperable. This Agreement's immediate impact on removing artificial barriers to trade resulted in a sharp increase in goods movement by land transport, creating delays and congestion at both the US–Canadian and US–Mexican borders (see Figure 5.10 in Chapter 5). A review of differing technical standards between the three countries highlighted that they acted as non-tariff barriers and increased costs. Much effort has been focused on these inconsistencies because their removal permitted the use of intelligent transport systems to speed up inspections at border crossings (Higginson, 2013). The resultant increased trade has led to the north–south transport corridors matching the importance of the traditional east–west trade routes, and has created an integrated commercial economy in North America. A 15-year controversy over allowing trucks from Mexico and the United States to travel on each other's highways was not resolved until 2011. As the driving force behind North America's experience has been primarily economic, rather than institutional, the lessons to be drawn in Northeast Asia stress the need to integrate trade and economic responsibilities with policies for security and investment in logistics infrastructure.

The European Union's experiences with transnational projects stem from developing the Trans European Transport Network (TEN-T) projects that cover road, rail and inland waterway networks, ports and airports (see Figure 5.11 in Chapter 5). This top-down activity demonstrates that creating a framework for regional infrastructure cooperation across borders requires an honest broker to forge a coalition of interests and high-profile coordinators to monitor implementation. Although transport has been a key area of the Union's agenda since the Treaty of Rome (1958), no common logistics market was stipulated in the original legislation aimed at creating a 'combined' transport network by 2020. The Directorate-General of Transport's task was focused initially on removing institutional and technological barriers to cross-border movements to allow people and goods to move easily and cheaply throughout the European Community. As exemplified by air traffic management, progress was slow and complicated in the 1980s because individual countries had not transferred authority to the regional body. During the 1990s greater integration was spurred in Europe by the intervention of strong regional organizations, notably the European Commission and the European Court of Justice, which increased competition and allowed a shift to a more appropriate policy network. The European Commission was instrumental in replacing 20 different safety and control systems by mandating a standard European Rail Transport Management System (ERTMS).

The Union of South America's bottom-up experience in developing logistics policy demonstrates the benefits of regional integration and infrastructure that can stem from creating a forum for dialogue and cooperation. In 2000 the Initiative for the Integration of the Regional South American Infrastructure (IIRSA) was conceived at a meeting of the heads of 12 countries in Brasilia. The objective was not only to physically integrate South America but also to coordinate and harmonize economic regulations and policy frameworks to facilitate the movement of goods and increase inter-regional trade. A key element in achieving the aim of reducing high logistics and transport costs was to conceive projects as part of ten development axes or regional development plans that transcend national borders and promote the integration of economic sectors across neighbouring countries. These projects include the Interoceanic Highway linking the Pacific Coast countries, notably Chile and Peru, with Argentina and Brazil, facilitating better connections to ports from isolated interior areas and Bolivia (Figure 10.6). As IIRSA does not finance projects, the Inter-American Development Bank (IDB) plays an important role in filtering out unproductive projects, coordinating national and subnational agencies, increasing stakeholder participation and minimizing the impact on people displaced by large infrastructure projects.

The Association of Southeast Asian Nations (ASEAN), comprising ten member countries, has experience in formulating and adopting a regional logistics policy with a methodology that could be replicated in Northeast Asia (Banomyong et al., 2008). Since ASEAN's inception in 1967, transport and communication have been afforded a key role in promoting regional trade and investment as the basis of generating a thriving economy. Given the nature of the terrain and economic disparities, the funding of regional infrastructure has been difficult. As individual members are responsible for funding their own infrastructural projects, ASEAN's task has been to seek greater coordination among them through a series of five-year transport action plans. Within this planning framework the Greater Mekong Subregion (GMS) has been created as an informal institution among Cambodia, Laos, Myanmar, Thailand, Viet Nam and China's Yunnan Province and Guangxi Zhuang Autonomous Region to facilitate cross-border transport (see Chapter 7). This emphasis on subregional transport has led to an appreciation of the need to support a regional logistics system. The key features of the ASEAN Strategic

Note: These transnational territories are deemed to be in need of infrastructure investment to create new development opportunities for their respective populations, a prospect that has led to opposition about their likely environmental consequences.

Sources: IIRSA (2012), Action 2030 Institute (2009).

Figure 10.6 Development axes in the Union of South America

Transport Plan (2011–16) are the Asian Highway and the Singapore–Kunming Railway, together with the further implementation of the roadmap for the integration of logistics services (Figure 10.7). Overall responsibility for the supervision, coordination and implementation of these plans to ensure an efficient and integrated regional transport system rests with the ASEAN Senior Transport Officials Meeting (STOM).

Lessons for Northeast Asia from the experience of other regional associations are instructive on the functions of strong regional administrative

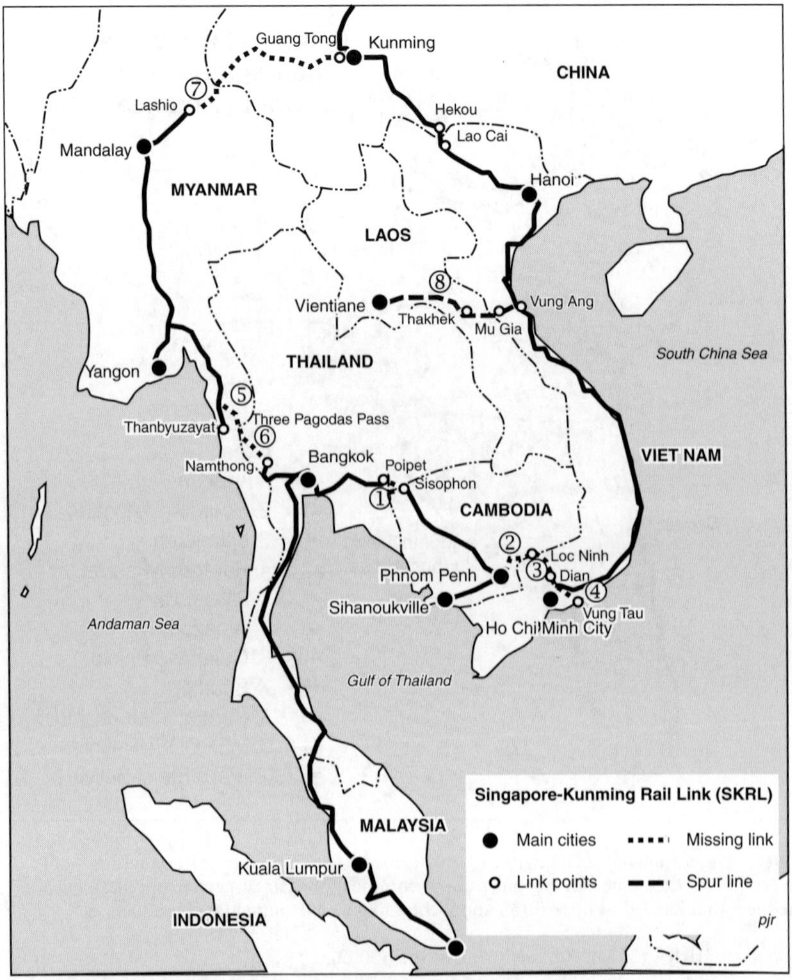

Note: As part of a plan to mobilize resources that improve physical, institutional and people-to-people connectivity within ASEAN, this flagship project is designed to complete 4067 km of missing links and a spur line to Vientiane in Laos. Numbers refer to: (1) Poipet–Sisophon (48 km) by 2013; (2) Phnom Penh–Loc Ninh (254 km) by 2015; (3) Loc Ninh–Ho Chi Minh (129 km) by 2020; (4) Mu Gia–Vung Ang (119 km) by 2020; (5) Thanbyuzayat–Three Pagoda Pass (110 km) by 2020; (6) Three Pagoda Pass–Nam Tok (153 km) by 2020; (7) Lashio–GuangTong (858 km) no date given; and (8) Vientiane–Thakek–Mu Gia (466 km) by 2020. Not shown is the Aranyaprathet–Klongluk (6 km) section due for completion in 2014.

Source: ASEAN (2010, 14).

Figure 10.7 The proposed Singapore–Kunming Rail Link (SKRL) route network

organizations, the roles of financial organizations, and the variety of methodologies for implementing regional logistics policies. Nevertheless these models do not provide an institutional blueprint for a region such as Northeast Asia that does not possess either cross-border or intergovernmental structures. Northeast Asia must develop a many-sided process of 'hard' and 'soft' regulation based upon laws, principles and norms, institutions, policies, and voluntary codes of conduct that are apposite for the spatial economy's own geography and realities. Although South Korea is fulfilling the classic small-country mediating role in logistics matters by promoting maritime, airline and telecommunications agreements, much remains to be done. China's stance is focused on the narrower view of the Asian-Pacific Rim (ASEAN+3), whereas Japan prefers to encompass the wider Rim and maintain its strategic links with the United States, which at the beginning of President Barack Obama's second administration in 2012 announced a 'pivot' or 'rebalancing' towards Asia (Agnew, 2012).

TOWARDS GREATER LOGISTICS COOPERATION IN NORTHEAST ASIA

Since the mid-2000s there have been signs of increased intergovernmental collaboration in logistics within Northeast Asia. Although political relations between China, Japan and South Korea are still punctuated by rival claims over disputed islands, there are deepening trade connections and intensifying cross-border networks and supply chains between the three to complement the strength of their involvement in the global trading system. Large Japanese manufacturing and retailing corporations, for instance, have established offshore bases in Dalian, Shanghai and Zhenjiang, and source materials in both Busan and Seoul. These integrated industrial clusters highlight the contrast between globalizing business service networks and Northeast Asia's fractured political-territorial space, exemplified by North Korea's open defiance, an ongoing territorial dispute between Japan and Russia, and Japan's suspicion of China's growing assertiveness.

Within this fractured political-territorial space, Japanese and South Korean economic ties have, at best, improved slowly and incrementally, and China–Taiwan relations have been more relaxed since 2008. These developments have been accompanied by the further growth of local, informal cross-border intercity linkages. The Global Financial Crisis (2008–09) spurred these deepening connections because it gave birth to a series of summit conferences on logistical matters. The failure to denuclearize North Korea and stifle missile tests following the breakdown of the Six-Party Talks in 2009, confrontations between North and South Korea, and recurrent border disputes have not derailed progress towards a more integrated regional logistics network to underpin a Northeast Asian economic community and facilitate growing trade interdependence.

These developments presage a spell of joint leadership between China, Japan and South Korea in regional logistics matters. Efforts in Northeast Asia to establish a regional committee or institutional mechanism to set priorities and agendas for an integrated logistics market have borne fruit (Rimmer, 2011). The Chinese, Japanese and South Korean governments are now participating in a trilateral annual Ministerial Conference on Transport and Logistics. The declared intention of these gatherings is to provide a seamless logistics system, establish environmentally friendly logistics, and achieve a balance between secure and efficient logistics (MOT et al., 2008). In 2011 the collaboration of China, Japan and South Korea led to the Northeast Asia Logistics Information Service Network (NEAL-NET) that will enable key players in the supply chain to trace the movements of containers and vessels (NEAL-NET, 2012). This arrangement is seen as the prelude to the realization of sea–land intermodal transport movements among the three countries using an operational system based on transferring towed trailers to and from ferries (Lee, 2013).

These Conference deliberations have been assisted by the work of regional scientists in mapping out how Northeast Asia's logistics pattern could develop. Japan's National Institute for Research Advancement (NIRA, 2006) launched a Grand Design for Northeast Asia (Figure 10.8). As it featured a Big Loop Railway, it was reminiscent of the 1938 orbital railway and built on earlier initiatives. On this occasion, however, the Grand Design was developed in league with China's Institute for Spatial Planning and Regional Economy (ISPRE), and the Korea Research Institute for Human Settlements (KRIHS).

This transnational collaboration has continued with joint recognition of the Beijing–Seoul–Tokyo (BESOTO) Corridor Vision, which highlights Seoul's pivotal position (Figure 10.9). Regional scientists conceive the mega-region as a potential international urban business, financial and consumption arena (NIRA, 2007; Ichikawa and Miwa, 2011). Their concept is concerned with creating a 'one-day' business travel zone, based on knitting together the existing air shuttle with high-speed rail transport networks and short-sea ferries to reduce travel times and widen access within the Corridor. Both Kansai (Osaka–Kyoto–Kobe) and Shanghai should be added to the list of pivotal centres, so that parallels can be drawn with the European Pentagon, and access between the Corridor and the rest of the world improved.

Further collaboration between the maritime think tanks in China, Japan

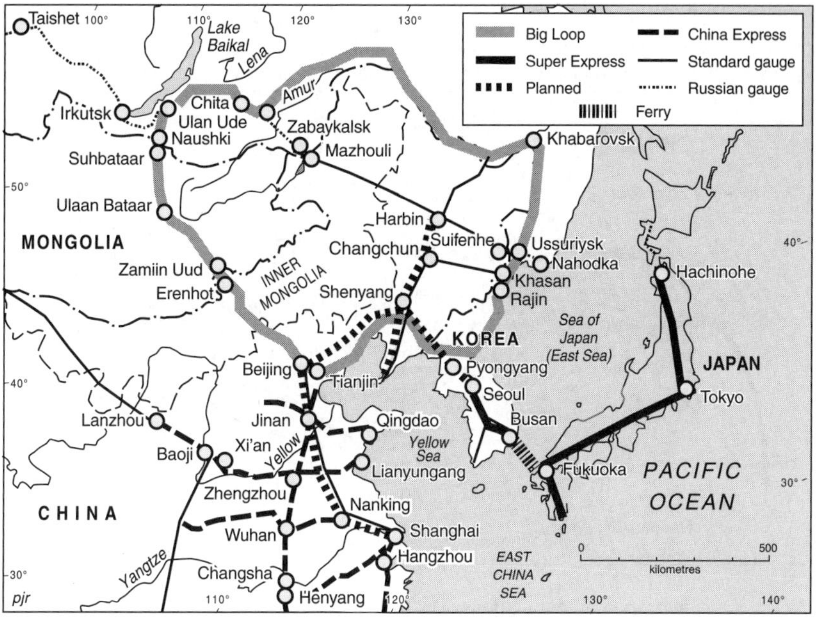

Source: Adapted from Sawai (2004, 6).

Figure 10.8 The 'Grand Design' for logistics cooperation in Northeast Asia, 2005

and Korea has produced a logistics variant of the Beijing–Seoul–Tokyo–Shanghai–Osaka (BESOTOSHAOS) Business Circuit based on resurrecting the 'techno-superliner' with a speed of up to 50 knots and basing it in Kyushu, Japan, to create a 'one-day' cargo delivery zone (Kim, 2009). Both the ports of Qingdao and Shanghai could be reached in less than 28 hours (Figure 10.10). Such a service would reduce both the real response time to satisfy shipper demand and lead times within a just-in-time system. Nevertheless high energy consumption, low cargo capacity and a high level of charges are likely to militate against the techno-liner's implementation.

A distillation of the work of spatial planners shows how Northeast Asia's logistics pattern may develop by 2020 (Figure 10.11). This pattern has a strong emphasis on major international axes connecting China, Japan, Mongolia, North Korea and the Russian Far East. Cross-border linkages are focused on four subregions: (1) the Northern Inland; (2) the Pan-Japan (East) Sea; (3) the Pan-Yellow Sea; and (4) Japan–Korea Straits. The third and fourth arenas have the strongest cross-border

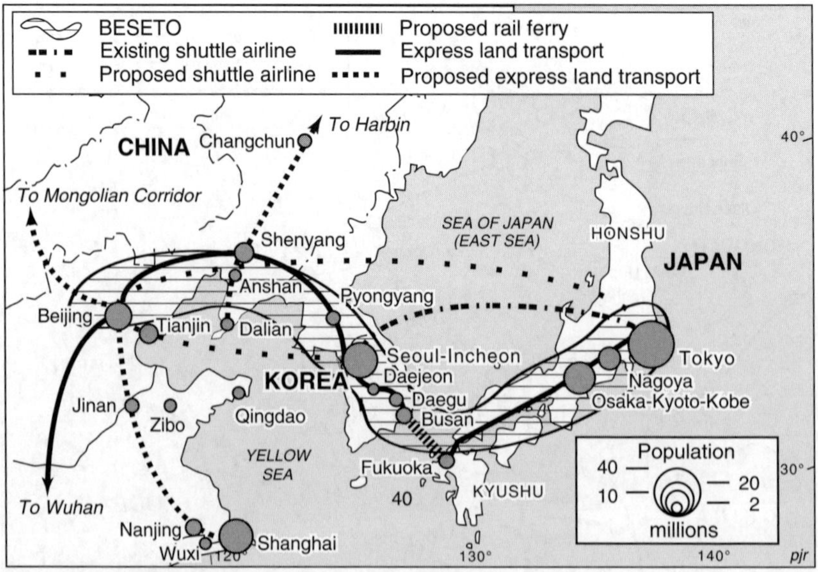

Note: Only metropolitan populations over 2 million are shown.

Sources: Updated from Kim et al. (2003), WG (2012).

Figure 10.9 The BESOTO Corridor concept and high-speed transport, 2010

exchanges and linkages. An emphasis on corridors within these arenas suggests that the spatial planners have taken their cues from the networks developed in North America, Europe, South America and Southeast Asia.

Within this broad framework some Japanese interests are still seeking an undersea tunnel between Kyushu and the Korean Peninsula as part of Japan's push towards a 'Seamless Asia'; South Korea is prioritizing connections between Busan and Fukuoka as an exemplar of intercity logistics cooperation involving the private sector; and Russia is seeking to augment its gas network with oil pipelines and investments in upgrading transport linkages within eastern Siberia and Sakhalin. Meanwhile China has reinforced Tianjin's status as the focus of the country's third growth engine, after Shenzhen in the Pearl River Delta and Pudong in the Lower Yangtze, by designating the Tianjin Binhai New Area as a national economic zone to enhance its global standing; this may have the unintended spin-off of boosting trade and cross-border production with Japan and Korea within the Pan Yellow Sea arena.

The Chinese Government is also casting Tianjin as the logistics gateway

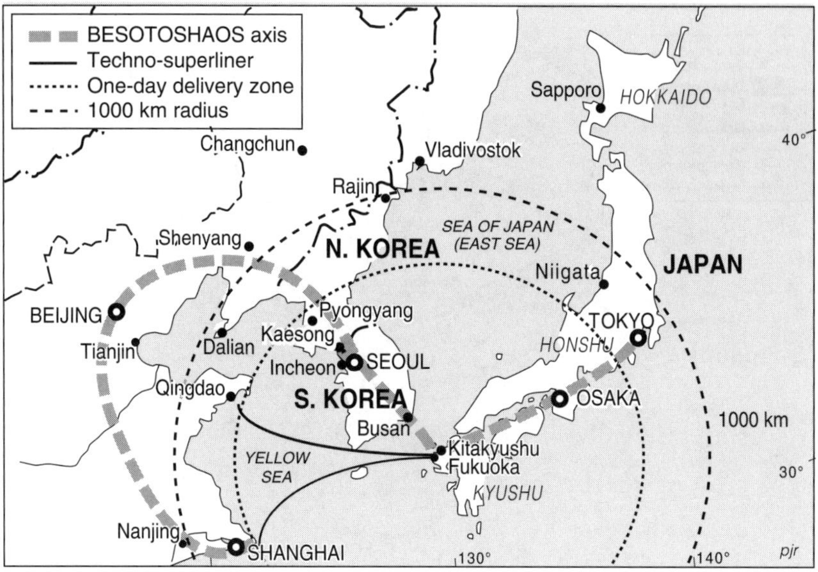

Source: Adapted from Kim (2009).

Figure 10.10 High-speed international logistics network using ferries and roll-on/roll-off shipping

to the country's lagging northeast region. Improved transport connections are planned to revitalize the area through the construction of an eastern border railway between Dalian and Suifenhe, the Changchun–Hunchun Expressway, and a road link from Hunchun to the North Korean port of Rason (Raijin–Sonbong). Also China is linked through the border city of Dandong to North Korea's Shinuiju Special Administrative Zone. The only connection between North Korea and South Korea is in the Kaesong Industrial Park. Located in the southern part of North Korea within 70 km of Seoul, the 15 enterprises employ 40 000 local workers augmented by 500 engineers from South Korea.

Once these physical linkages and logistics facilities are in place and operational, the persuasive argument is that the cross-border corridors in remote and inland areas will attract investment and generate vibrant economic activities in less-developed areas by lowering distribution costs and improving land supply for economic activities. For example, the corridor from Tianjin to Ulan Ude is of critical importance to landlocked Mongolia because it links the country with both China and Russia (Figure 10.12). An examination of the transport costs and transit time between Tianjin

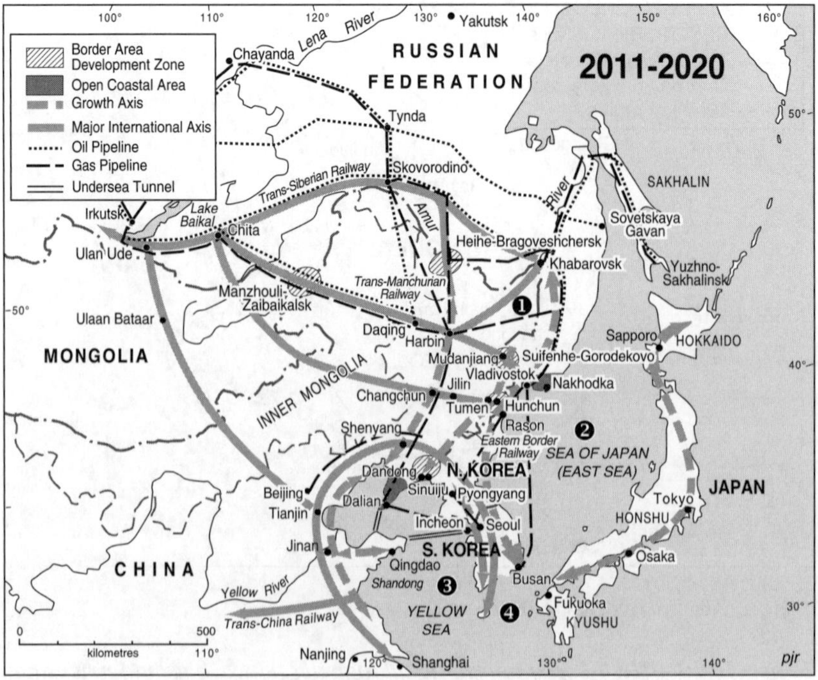

Source: Updated from Rimmer and Jun (2000, 407).

Figure 10.11 Development axes in Northeast Asia, 2011–20. Sub-regions: 1 Northern Inland; 2. Pan Japan (East) Sea; 3. Pan Yellow Sea; 4. Japan-Korea Straits

and Ulan Ude highlights that road is the most expensive mode, but rail costs could be undercut by a rail–road combination. The key features of the cost–distance graph are the high charges incurred in negotiating the China–Mongolia and the Mongolia–Russia borders.

The Mongolian case focuses attention on cross-border transport and logistics infrastructure, but this preoccupation with corridors traversing international borders in Northeast Asia is not without its problems. These issues stem from too narrow a focus on land border infrastructures, which risks a double misallocation of resources stemming from a neglect of both vital urban infrastructure and more modest, but no less essential, infrastructure in rural areas.

What is missing from the analysis is any recognition that for most international sea and air movements, the gateway is also the border (Rimmer and Dick, 2012). The functional efficiency of gateway ports, airports and

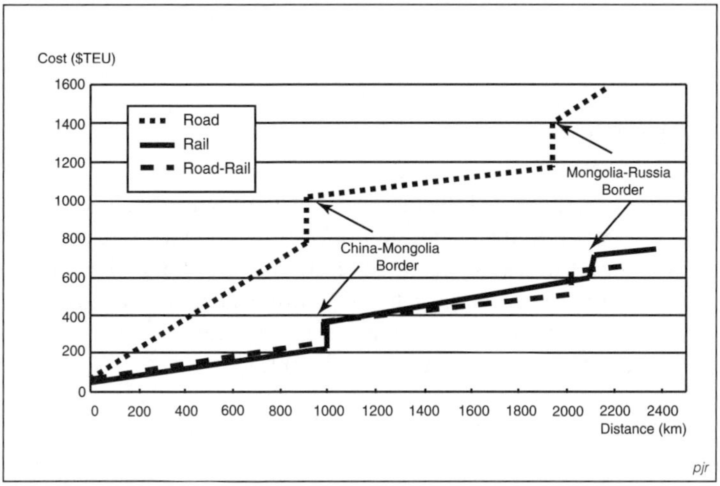

Source: Adapted from KOTI (2009, 55).

Figure 10.12 Estimated cost per twenty-foot equivalent container unit and transit time from Tianjin to Mongolia, 2010

teleports (or lack thereof) has a great impact on logistics costs, particularly as there are no land connections between China, Japan and South Korea. Arguably the fixation with land-based cross-border infrastructure has attracted attention away from the inefficiencies of coastal gateways, which are inextricably linked as part of integrated supply chains. The most critical challenge in Northeast Asia is how to make the gateways more efficient.

Addressing the inefficiencies of gateways and identifying bottlenecks hindering door-to-door logistics are of paramount importance to Northeast Asia's regional development. It should be possible to produce a gateway and corridor initiative not dissimilar to the Government of Canada's (2010) National Policy Framework for Strategic Gateways and Trade Corridors that reflects the geography and regional realities of Northeast Asia (see Chapter 5). This initiative would comprise integrated packages of long-term investment and policy measures to guide future actions. These packages would advance the development of a limited number of strategically located gateways and cross-border trade corridors to overcome obstacles in the regional logistics network and strengthen Northeast Asia's competitive position in global commerce. In logistics it does not matter where the obstacle is – gateway, corridor or at the border – the question is to try and locate it, estimate the cost of its impact and determine the cost of removing it to permit seamless and fast movement.

CONCLUSION

This chapter has addressed the historical reasons why a logistics policy has not been developed in the fractured political-territorial space of Northeast Asia. As the trust necessary for a coherent logistics policy has not always been forthcoming, lessons on institutional mechanisms have been drawn from the experiences of a range of existing regional associations in North America, Europe, South America and Southeast Asia. Then the trend towards greater logistics cooperation since the mid-2000s was discussed with a critical examination of bundles of transport and logistics activities in Northeast Asia at national and provincial levels. Following leadership transitions in China, Japan, South Korea and the United States since 2012, there is renewed hope that further progress will be made towards a logistics policy for Northeast Asia based upon adopting a gateway and corridor initiative (Tanner et al., 2013). However, before the new leaders can realize regional policy objectives, there is a need to provide a broader institutional framework in which all players at national and provincial levels participate, and to overcome the lack of funding for facilitating infrastructure investment.

Regional Governance

Governance issues are likely to emerge in logistics that can support or challenge the sovereignty upon which national governments customarily base their authority. The scope of these issues extends beyond the actions of their financial, planning and transport agencies to include a broad range of stakeholders. Besides local governments and their complementary agencies, the stakeholders could extend to civil society, cross-border interest groups, non-governmental organizations and private businesses (Lee et al., 2013).

Short of a China–Japan–South Korea Free Trade Agreement coming up with a robust logistics policy, an intergovernmental council for cross-border cooperation in Northeast Asia would offer the best prospect of pursuing joint logistics projects to facilitate freight flows, promote trade and enhance the capacity of gateways. Already progress has been made in developing bilateral maritime agreements between China and South Korea, and Japan and South Korea (Rosenberg, 2005). South Korea also has narrow bilateral air agreements with China and Japan, which its government hopes to transform into cross-border 'open-skies' agreements (Oum, 2008).

Developing more formal institutional arrangements governing cross-border activities involving different permutations of China, Japan, the Koreas, Mongolia, the Russian Far East and the United States is a more difficult task. This challenge may require a body similar to the European Union or the Inter-American Development Bank in South America to play a brokering role in building consensus between countries. The World Bank, the Asian Development Bank, the oft-mooted Northeast Asian Bank for Development and Cooperation, or China's proposed Asian Infrastructure Investment Bank (AIIB) announced by Xi Jinping in October 2013 could develop the necessary knowledge of geographical conditions and economic realities required to identify, prioritize and prepare viable logistics projects in Northeast Asia. This systems approach would place an emphasis on a range of policy and regulatory issues, land use planning, labour markets, research and development, analysis and long-term planning, the climate for private sector investment and public investment in infrastructure.

Financing Investment

Bearing in mind that infrastructural investment cannot solve all issues, the task of an integrated regional logistics policy framework in Northeast Asia is to develop the most rigorous financial plan to attract the world's private savings into productive economic infrastructure. Projects need to be related to each other and double-checked to determine whether calculations under- or overestimate the cost of obstacles or their removal in mobilizing resources for infrastructure networks (Rimmer and Dick, 2012). Of particular importance is the need to improve the local government tax base within gateway regions.

Regional logistics projects in Northeast Asia are unlikely to satisfy conventional cost–benefit standards. They require political objectives and political support. This will only occur if China, Japan and South Korea encourage and welcome a process of closer relations among themselves and Mongolia, North Korea and the Russian Far East. As cross-border projects are expensive, national budgets will have to carry the financial burden. Efforts will be made to involve the private sector by creating a business-friendly environment for investment.

Much technical work is required to develop a more rigorous cost–benefit analysis to overcome the obvious limitations of both the 'national' calculus for setting infrastructure priorities and the 'transnational' calculus, which can skew investment to cross-border projects at the expense of domestic needs (Rimmer and Dick, 2012). A regional institution in Northeast Asia must be prepared to undertake this task. Although the budgetary costs of projects are an important barrier to implementation, political or software obstacles can be equally significant. Overcoming information asymmetry among shareholders deserves serious attention.

Coordination problems are likely to arise in Northeast Asia because the costs of and benefits from transnational projects and socio-economic impacts are rarely symmetrical across countries. Harmonizing regulations, national laws, administrative procedures and international conventions on rail and road modes are a prerequisite. Early in the process coordination must extend to subnational governments and groups affected by the project.

Having discussed the cross-border and interorganizational structures to manage Northeast Asia's gateways and corridors, and the financing of material and virtual infrastructures, there is a need to return to the Asian-Pacific Rim. This involves going beyond the narrow definition of China, Japan and South Korea in ASEAN+3 to the broader concept of the Rim that encompasses Australia and New Zealand and emphasizes the wider region's connections with India.

PART III

Local policies: the wider Rim and beyond

A looser definition of the Asian-Pacific Rim accommodates the 'cul-de-sac' featuring Australia and New Zealand and allows consideration of the extension of 'Main Street' through improved connectivity with India. By adding India to ASEAN+3 (China, Japan and South Korea), their combined forecast contribution to world income in 2017 would increase from US$214 billion to US$251 billion (Francois and Wignaraja, 2008). Also by making brief reference to New Zealand in discussing Australia, this looser definition accommodates ASEAN+6 (Table III.1).

Only four of the top 25 Asian-Pacific supply chains in 2010 were located in this wider area: three in Australia and one in India. Their composition is different from the top ten supply chains in the narrower definition of the Asian-Pacific Rim (Table III.2).

In Australia, BHP Billiton and the Rio Tinto Group are major resource companies with dual headquarters in the United Kingdom. Their activities are focused primarily on exporting bulk shipments of bauxite, coal and iron ore through dedicated ports (Figure III.1). In contrast, Woolworths Ltd, the country's largest supermarket and grocery store, is not only involved in imports through the major container ports of Melbourne, Sydney, Brisbane, Fremantle and Adelaide but is also engaged in inter-state movements between these centres. Given the specialized nature of

Table III.1 Key indicators of economies within the wider Asian-Pacific Rim, 2011

Country	Surface area	Population	Gross national income purchasing power parity (PPP)	Gross domestic product	
	sq. km		per capita	total	Annual
	Thous.	million	US$	US$ trillion	%
Australia	7741	22.6	46 200[1]	1372	1.8
New Zealand	268	4.4	29 935[1]	143[1]	1.9[1]
India	3287	1241	1410	1848	6.9

Note: [1]2010

Source: World Bank (2012b).

Table III.2 Top-25 supply chains: Australia and India, 2011

Rank	Company	HQ	Return on assets[1]	Inventory turns[2]	Revenue growth[3]	Composite score[4]	World ranking
			%	no.	%		
1	Rio Tinto	London/ Melbourne	9.4	2.5	27.3	1.69	33
2	BHP Billiton	Melbourne/ London	13.9	2.0	3.0	1.58	37
3	Woolworths	Sydney	10.9	11.1	5.9	1.58	38
4	Tata Motors	Mumbai	0.7	5.6	47.3	1.17	69

Notes: 2010 data was used where available. Where 2010 data was unavailable, latest available full-year data was used. All raw data was normalized to a ten-point scale prior to composite calculation.

1. Return on assets (ROA): (2010 net income / 2010 total assets) *50%) + ((2009 net income / 2009 total assets) * 30%) + ((2008 net income / 2008 total assets) * 20%)
2. Inventory turns: 2010 cost of goods sold / 2010 quarterly average inventory
3. Revenue growth: ((change in revenue 2010–2009) * 50%) + ((change in revenue 2009–2008) * 30%) + ((change in revenue 2008–2007) * 20%)
4. Composite score: (peer opinion * 25%) + (Gartner opinion*25%) + (ROA*25%) + (inventory turns * 15%) + (revenue growth * 10%)

Source: Bloch and Hofman (2011).

both BHP Billiton and Rio Tinto, Woolworths is used to discuss supply chain issues in Australia.

India's sole top 25 representative is Tata Motors, the country's largest motor vehicle manufacturer with headquarters in Mumbai and revenue of US$20 billion in 2010 (Tata, 2012). The world's largest bus and fourth-largest truck manufacturer has six domestic plants producing an array of passenger cars, a presence in South Korea from having taken over Daewoo Motors (2004), and in the United Kingdom from its buyout of Jaguar Land Rover from Ford (2008), together with assembly lines in Morocco, South Africa, Spain and Thailand (Figure III.2). Within India the company has its own logistics arm to meet the well-documented challenges posed by rising rural sales, poor infrastructure and inadequate multimodal transport that have prompted recommendations for a switch from road to rail, a greater use of inland waterways and construction of logistics parks (Gupta et al., 2009; Gupta et al., 2010; AL, 2013). Unlike motor vehicles, there is no major electronics firm in India comparable to Sony in Japan, Samsung and LG in South Korea, and Lenovo in China. This absence of a major electronics firm highlights the need to focus on the country's external connections, particularly the quality of its air links, to account for this situation.

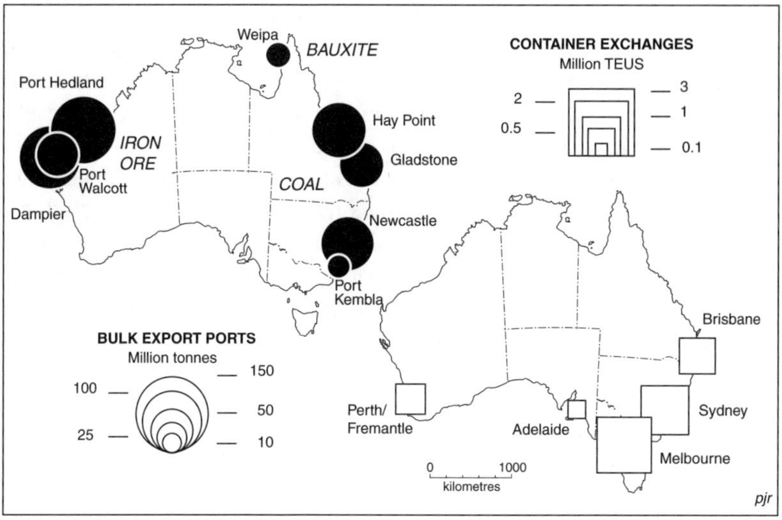

Source: Data from BITRE (2009a).

Figure III.1 Bulk exports and container exchanges within Australia's port-oriented system, 2006–07

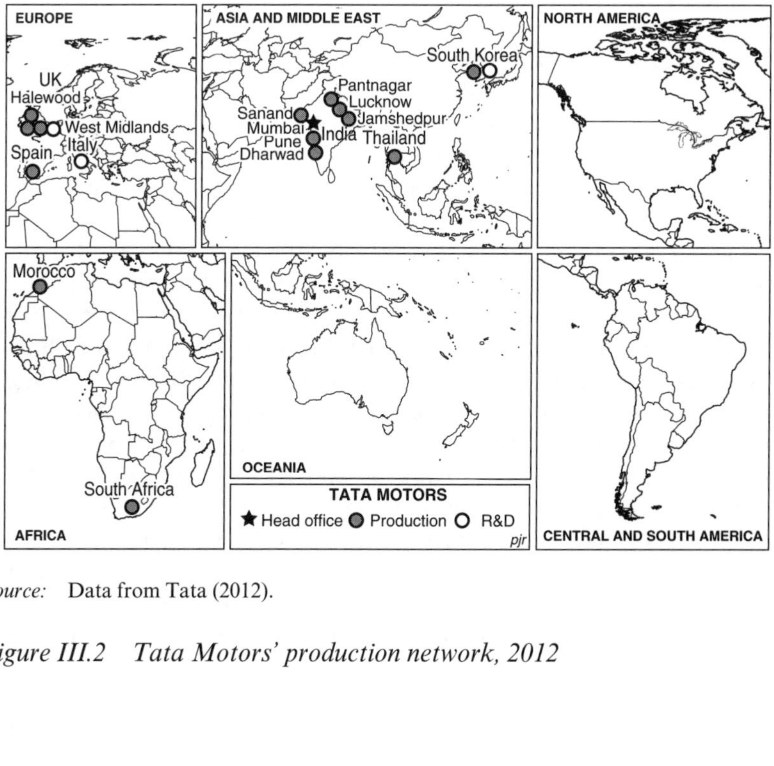

Source: Data from Tata (2012).

Figure III.2 Tata Motors' production network, 2012

Loosening the definition of the Asian-Pacific Rim to incorporate Australia and the Rim's connections with India has the additional benefit of being able to examine logistics policy under federal governments. Unlike China, Japan and Korea where the central government is at the level of the state, there are two or more levels in federal governments. Australia's federal government, comprising six states and two territories, was originally established in 1901, whereas India's federal government, covering 28 states and seven territories, was established in 1947 and re-established in 1950. Within Australia the states exercise considerable political power and are active in pursuing their own logistics policies, but in India the central government exerts greater power in relation to the states. As the trade-off between the political power of the states and the federal government's control over finance is critical to any understanding of logistics policy in Australia, this situation is elaborated further. But federal–state relations are not pursued in India where the focus is concentrated upon the issue of improving its connections with the Asian-Pacific Rim.

AUSTRALIA

An examination of Australia's logistics landscape discusses how further economic development of the Asian-Pacific Rim has affected the country's position in the global logistics arena (see Chapter 11). Huge distances from international markets continue to have a profound effect upon the economic development of a country with a population of almost 24 million in a land area of 7.7 million km^2 (Figure III.3). In 1955 less than 22 per cent of the world's gross domestic product was within 10000 km of Australia's capital of Canberra, compared with 98 per cent within the same radius from London (Ewing and Batterby, 2003). By 1998 Australia's figure had increased to 34 per cent but the country was still ranked thirty-ninth in trade intensity out of 40 countries, with only New Zealand placed below it. As the country's geographical isolation accounted for two-fifths of the 20 per cent gap in labour productivity between Australia and the United States, arguments for the 'death of distance' appear premature (Batterby, 2006).

Great distances between mainland state capital cities and their associated regional centres, strung out over 30000 km in coastal conurbations, compound the country's relative geographical isolation. As outlined in the Australian Government's White Paper *Australia in the Asian Century*, the country's position has improved during the new millennium with the further development of the Asian-Pacific Rim's economy (Australian Government, 2012b). Nevertheless the reorientation of the country's transport and logistics system to accommodate the Rim's greater importance

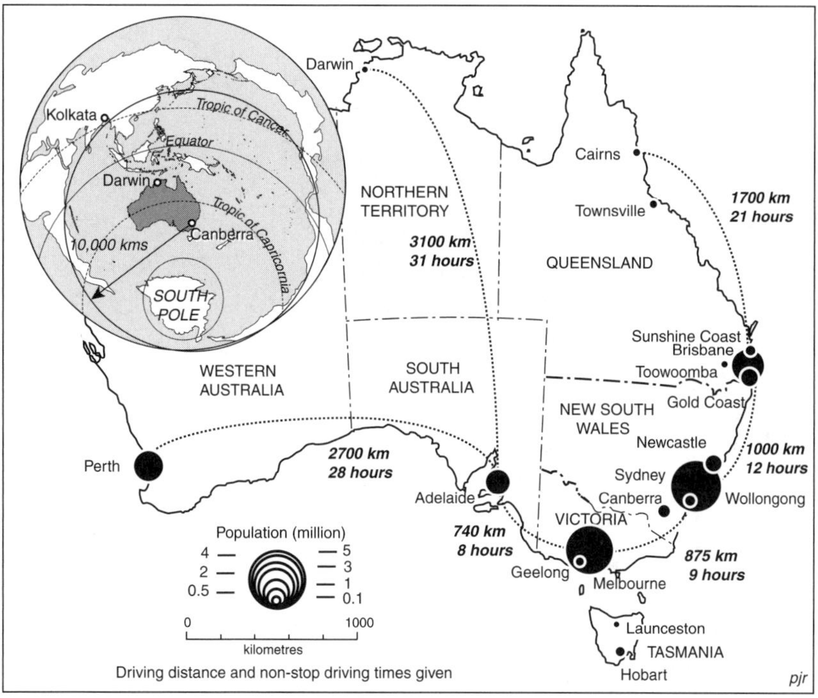

Note: Road distances and time differences between Australian cities and associated regional centres in kilometres and hours. Populations are shown for cities over 100 000. Inset shows area of the Asian-Pacific region within 10 000 km distance of Australia.

Figure III.3 Australia and the Asian-Pacific Rim, 2012

has been slow. Despite being the only continent under the control of a single country, the movement, storage and handling of goods and materials across the entire logistics chain, from producer to consumer, and from point of origin to final disposal, is still not well integrated nationally to deal with the high urban density, and remoteness and rural issues that characterize Australia (ATC, 2009; ISC, 2002, ix; NTC, 2009a).

These observations have not stopped Asian-Pacific Rim visionaries extending their development corridors to encompass Australia and New Zealand (Figure III.4). An economic corridor extending from Cairns to Adelaide is envisaged to complement those identified in the narrower definition of the Rim. Much of the enthusiasm for incorporating Australia into the Rim came from Japanese business interests at the height of the late 1980s boom. They sought unsuccessfully to provide the corridor with a fast rail backbone and a rash of intelligent cities or ‘technopolises’. Since

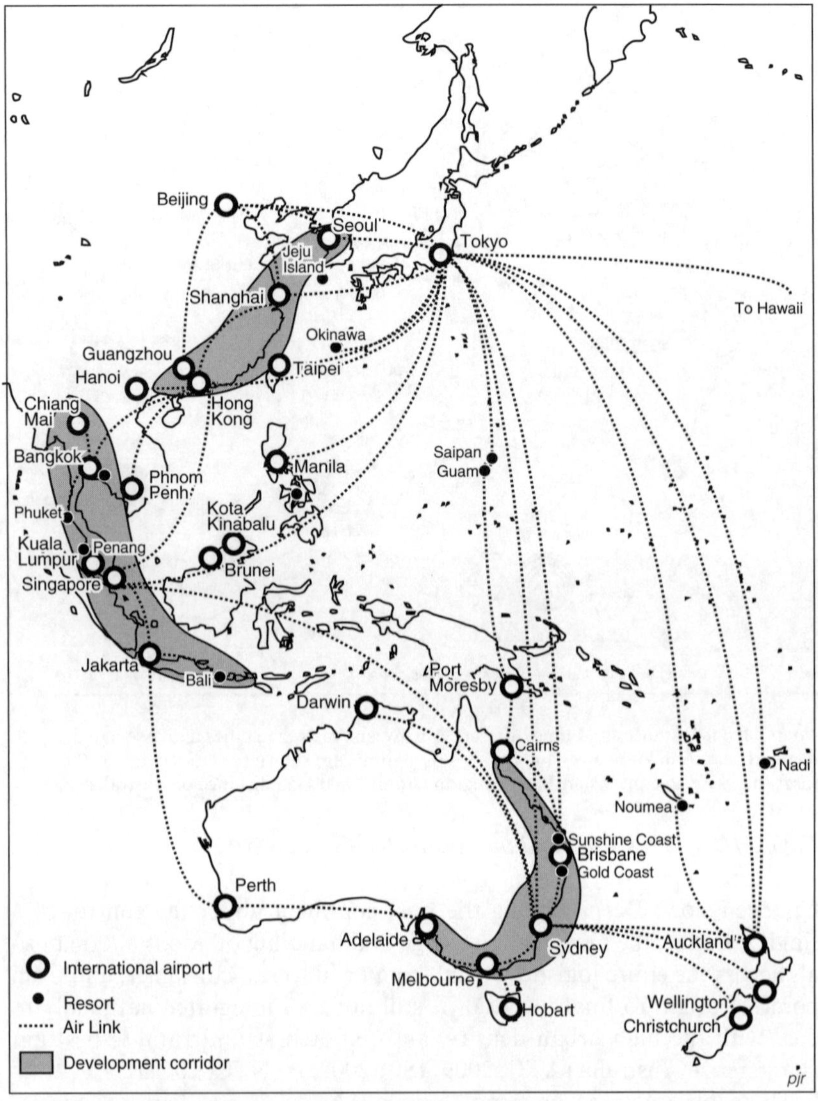

Figure III.4 *Development corridors in the wider definition of the Asian-Pacific Rim*

then Japanese multinational corporations have turned more towards India as an essential link in the world's value chain, particularly in the vehicle market where their car companies accounted for almost half of India's passenger vehicle market in 2013 (Fujita, 2008; LM and WSJ, 2013).

INDIA

An examination of India's logistics landscape in Chapter 12 discusses steps being taken to capitalize on the Government's 1991 'Look East' policy. This policy switch was prompted by the Government's abandonment of its import-substitution strategy to offset the lack of progress on cross-border multimodal transport among members of the South Asian Association for Regional Cooperation (SAARC), comprising Afghanistan, Bhutan,

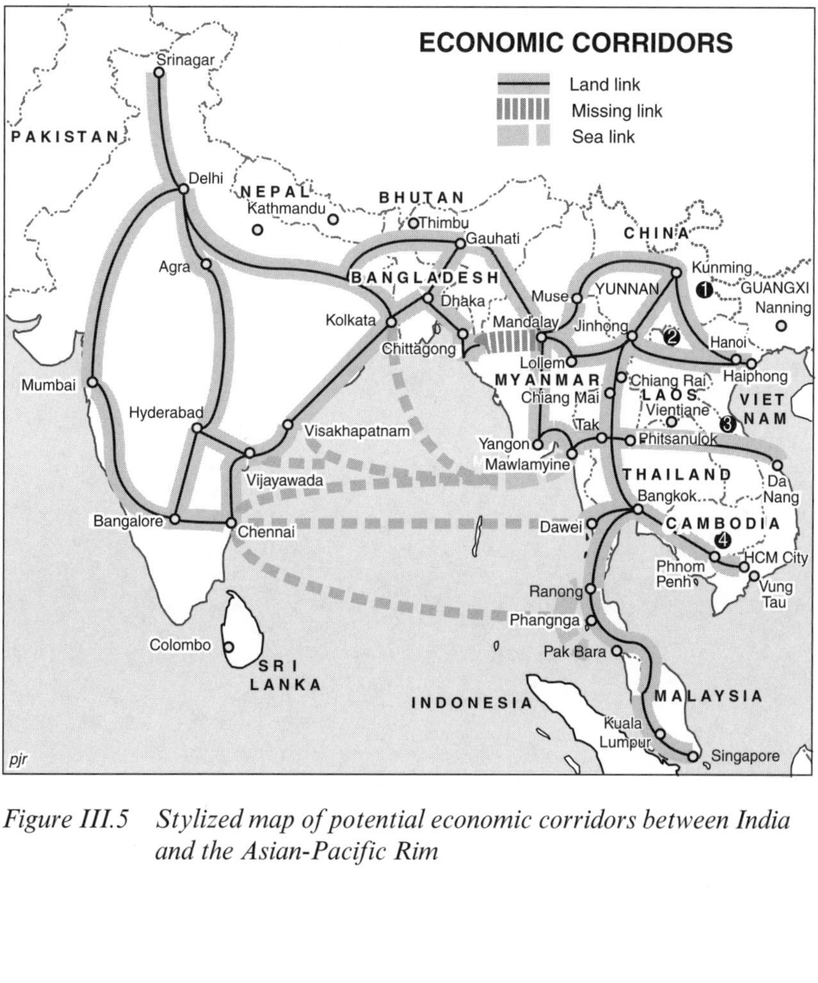

Figure III.5 Stylized map of potential economic corridors between India and the Asian-Pacific Rim

India, Nepal, Pakistan and Sri Lanka (De, 2008; Bhattacharyay and De, 2009; Rahmatullah, 2010; Dayal, 2013). Assisted by Japanese expertise, this policy seeks to overcome the cross-border infrastructural bottlenecks and complicated customs procedures between India and the Asian-Pacific Rim in order to accommodate increasing trade, derive synergies from the fragmentation of production networks and offer greater access to international markets (ADB and ADBI, 2013).

A spatial design for infrastructure and industrial placement to deepen economic integration and narrow development gaps between India and the Asian-Pacific Rim would have to consider four possible economic corridors that cut across the north–south corridor between Kunming and Singapore: (1) Hanoi–Kunming–Mandalay and then by land routes through India; (2) Hanoi–Jinhong–Mandalay and then by land routes through India; (3) Da Nang–Phitsanulok–Tak–Mawlamyaing port and then by sea to ports in India; and (4) Ho Chi Minh City–Phnom Penh–Bangkok and Dawei port and then by sea to Chennai, with the Thai ports of Ranong, Phangnga and Pak Bara offering alternatives should connections through Myanmar prove unfeasible (Figure III.5).

These corridors are regarded as key components of a larger Eurasian logistics system. Also they are seen as major elements in the revamped global hub-and-spoke system in 2050 (see Epilogue).

11. Australia

Since 2000, attempts have been made by the Commonwealth (Australian or Federal) Government to overcome the past uncoordinated and mode-centric approach to key logistics issues. A policy framework more conducive to the logistics sector is being developed, covering issues of inventory management, supply chains, outsourcing strategies and market drivers. Under this evolving national policy, the Commonwealth Government, in concert with state and local governments, has sought to influence the efficiency of logistics services through critical investments in transport and communications infrastructure, including further progress on the national divided highway system and rolling out a national broadband network. Supported by pilot studies into intermodal transport, meat and livestock, grain and coal supply chains, this policy is designed to: (1) develop world-class logistics services; (2) influence the efficiency of supply chains; and (3) alter the balance of market power exerted and accumulated by individual suppliers, logistics service providers and retailers by securing scarce market assets in infrastructure, information and property (FLCWA, 2009; NTC, 2008a, 2008b, 2008c, 2009a, 2009b, 2009c, 2009d; GTA, 2013).

A series of issues are raised by these investments that impinge on the competitive dynamics of the Australian logistics sector. How has power shifted in the supply of logistics services in Australia? How have major retailers in Australia taken control of the demand for logistics services between supplier and the customer's warehouse, and affected the distribution of market power within supply chains between suppliers of retail products and logistics service providers? And how have governments reacted to the effects of these changes in the market for logistics services on the performance of the national economy?

A conceptual framework is developed to trace the trajectories of major logistics services providers to offer a historical perspective on the present Australian logistics sector by drawing upon a series of past studies. Then shifts in market power brought about by changes in demand are addressed by examining the strategies of two major retailers seeking to wrest control of the primary freight task from goods suppliers. Consideration is then given to significant challenges posed by the absence of a national logistics policy providing consistent regulation and coordinated infrastructure investment, and implementation, across all jurisdictions and all modes.

SUPPLY

Any understanding of the Australian logistics sector devolves on comprehending the organizational sequence that has produced three of the world's earliest global logistics corporations: Brambles, Mayne Nickless and Thomas Nationwide Transport (TNT) (Figure 11.1). After the Second World War Mayne Nickless (founded in 1886) together with single truck companies, notably TNT (established in 1946) and Brambles (established in 1956) sought venture capital to escape their provincial status by

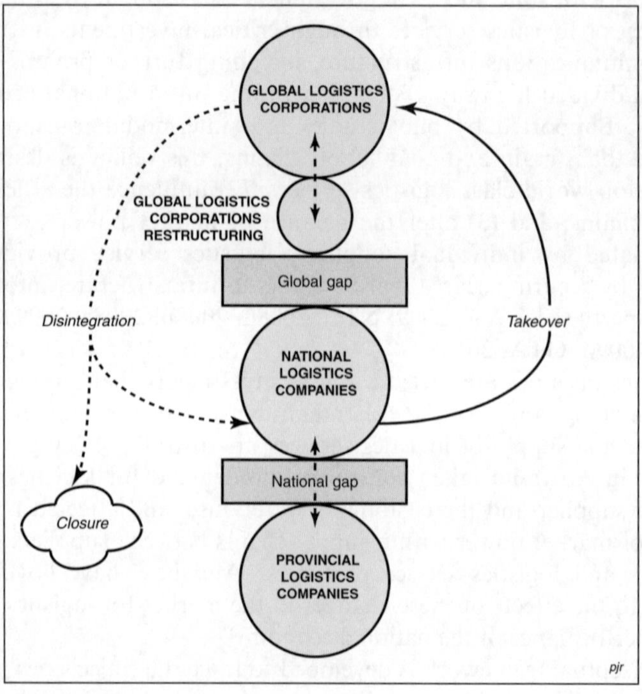

Note: This process is generalized from the Australian experience of transforming national logistics champions into global logistics corporations.

Source: Adapted from Clarke (1985, 89).

Figure 11.1 Organizational segmentation, restructuring and corporate interaction

crossing the 'national gap' through merger and acquisition to dominate non-bulk transport across all states, modes and services, and extend their interests to New Zealand. Other privately operated road transport companies were small, except for Finemores, Linfox and Scott that provided specialist services such as handling outsize containers (Rimmer, 1970). As Australia provided a 'cash cow' for the 'Big Three' companies, they were able to use their dominant domestic market positions and accumulated know-how to obtain international capital to bridge the 'global gap' and expand into Europe, North and South America, and Asia and skip steps in the restructuring process through merger and acquisition (Rimmer, 1977; Rimmer and Taylor, 1987; Wynne, 2001). These pioneering global logistics corporations possessed worldwide investments across all modes (air, rail, road and sea) in break-bulk, bulk and express freight, and a wide range of activities, including customs clearance, warehousing and materials handling. As experienced by the Australian-headquartered global logistics corporations, a reversal of this process is also possible, involving a return to the status of national logistics company or undergoing total disintegration.

In 1992 the dominant position of the Big Three in Australia was undermined. Mayne Nickless and TNT, controlling 85 per cent of non-bulk freight transport and 90 per cent of air express services, were convicted of colluding and running a price-fixing cartel in contradiction of the Trade Practices Act 1974 (Sd+D, 2004, 21; Rimmer, 1996c; Wynne, 2001; Dick, 2007). Since losing their 'cash cow', the Big Three did not have the capital to take advantage of rail reforms within Australia that permitted greater private participation. Nor were they in a position to diversify their operations or create integrated logistics solutions to capitalize on Australia's growing outsourced logistics market, valued at A$41 billion in 2002–03, that had attracted overseas express transport operators such as Exel (Sd+D, 2004, 1). Their fortunes differed: Mayne Nickless abandoned freight transport altogether, and moved first into health care and then into communications, before disintegrating; TNT was sold to the Dutch Post Office (Koninklikje PTT Nederland, KPN) in 1996 and only its express freight services were retained in Australia; and Brambles, not involved in the court case, merged with the industrial services arm of GKN plc (formerly Guest Keen & Nettlefolds) in 2001 and became a dual-listed company in Australia and the United Kingdom, and survived as a corporate entity by specializing in supplying pallets.

The Big Three's discarded assets allowed second-tier companies in Australia such as Linfox and Toll to grow rapidly and compete for domestic market leadership (Table 11.1). Between 1989 and 2005 Toll, which had become a public company in 1991, acquired no less than 45 companies,

Table 11.1 Revenue generated by selected Australian logistics service providers, 1999–2000 and 2002–03

Company	1999–2000	2002–03
	$A million	$A million
Toll Holdings	1360	2603
Queensland Rail	1035	2227
P & O Transport	n.a.	1495
Linfox Transport	618	1065
Pacific National	n.a.	1000
TNT Australia	814	742
Mayne Nickless	943	–[1]
Brambles	931	n.a.

Note: n.a. not available; [1] Abandoned freight transport.

Sources: BTE (2001, 26–7), Sd+D (2004, 22–3).

largely within Australia and New Zealand (Toll, 2011). Along with the stevedoring company Patrick Corporation, Toll took the opportunity to move into privatized rail transport. As the new market leaders, Toll and Patrick differed from the 'Big Three' in that the individuals running them had significant personal investment in the companies, and from the family companies such as Linfox in that the value of their personal wealth was related to the company's share prices. The prime focus of both Toll and Patrick was on merger and acquisition, including the takeover of smaller firms unable to meet the rigours of providing daily round-the-clock services. Although the prime focus of their operations differed, both Toll and Patrick engaged in joint ventures in rail and air transport as part of their strategy to provide integrated logistics services covering all modes, warehousing and distribution, stevedoring, project management and fleet management. Their national offerings stand in sharp contrast to the vast number of road-specific transport services.

In 2006 Toll Holdings acquired Patrick Corporation Stevedores, which prompted the Australian Competition and Consumer Commission (ACCC) to intervene because the single company would have controlled large parts of Australia's transport system. The outcome was that Toll was required to devolve its port, stevedoring and rail assets to a new and separate company, Asciano Ltd, and the 'new' Toll Holdings company was to concentrate upon freight forwarding so that it could coordinate services along the multimodal supply chain. This new focus enabled Toll Holdings to continue to build upon its domestic logistics activities before following in the footsteps of the 'Big Three' and attracting international capital to cross the 'global gap'. In 2006 Toll acquired the Singapore third-party logistics (3PL) SembLog that had assets in China, India, South Korea and Thailand. This acquisition enabled the company to follow Linfox's 20-year foray into the Asian-Pacific Rim's market and be among the second generation of Australian-based global logistics corporations.

Linfox Logistics and Toll Holdings

Both Linfox Logistics and Toll Holdings are based in Melbourne. The former is a privately owned company started by a single truck operator, Lindsay Fox, after the Second World War and had an annual turnover in excess of US$3 billion in 2011 (Linfox, 2011). The latter is a publicly listed company with a revenue of US$8.5 billion that can trace its roots to a local transport company founded in Newcastle in 1886, but has largely been built through merger and acquisition by its then Chief Executive Officer, Paul Little, between 1986 and 2011 (Toll, 2012). Having established their activities in Australia and New Zealand, both of these companies are now seeking to export their expertise to compensate for the decline in the growth of domestic freight volume.

Half of Linfox's 14000 staff are now located in the Asian-Pacific region as the company operates logistics services in China, Hong Kong, India, Indonesia, Malaysia, Singapore, the Philippines, Thailand and Viet Nam, and seeks to develop stronger connections with international brands, notably the British supermarket operator Tesco and US companies such as Campbell, Kellogg, Kraft, Mars and Procter & Gamble that are expanding in the region (Figure 11.2). As is evident in the opportunities to carry iron pellets from China's largest mine in Xinjiang Province for local processing, serving Tata and Bluescope Steel in India, and undertaking Unilever's distribution in six Asian countries, Linfox considers that the Asian-Pacific region's market of 2 billion people has sufficient growth potential and has declared it has no interest in expanding into Europe and the United States (Linfox, 2011).

Toll Holdings with 35000 employees has gone global in scope. The company prioritizes not only the Asian-Pacific Rim, particularly through its supply chain capability in Greater China, but also Europe and the Middle East, to rank twenty-third among global freight forwarders in 2010 (Armstrong & Associates, 2012). The corporation justifies this move by stressing the increased demand stemming from globalization, the need to satisfy customers looking for transnational solutions, and that merger and acquisition has become more difficult after acquiring an additional 42 companies between 2006 and 2010 (Toll, 2011). The strategy's rationale is

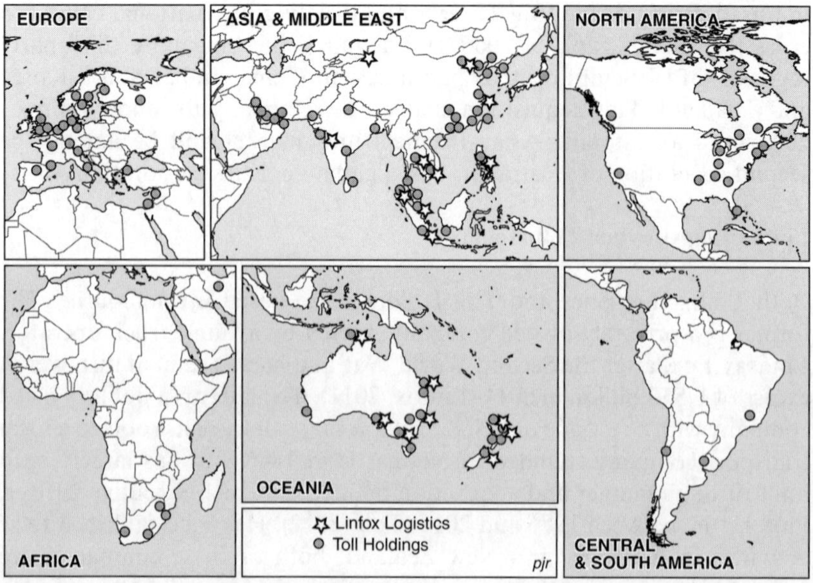

Sources: Linfox (2011) and Toll (2011).

Figure 11.2 Office distribution of Linfox Logistics and Toll Holdings

dictated by the need to accelerate the company's critical scale of operations to satisfy customers located outside the Asian-Pacific Rim buying from the region, and to acquire companies in consignee markets. In response, Toll has adopted a light-asset mode in seeking to shift from value-added services as a third-party logistics provider, by becoming a lead logistics provider, and moving into offering advanced services as a fourth-party logistics provider. In the process Toll has reshaped its organizational structure into four divisions: global resources, global express and domestic freight, global contract logistics and global forwarding. These divisions are managed by personnel recruited from leading logistics service providers such as Kuehne + Nagel, DHL, Panalpina and UPS (United Parcel Service) in Toll's bid to become a global niche forwarder centred in the Asian-Pacific Rim.

DEMAND

In Australia manufacturers have historically managed the movement and inventory of products from factory or warehouse directly to the retailer's stores. An extremely competitive road transport and warehousing industry, comprising almost 45 000 enterprises, offers both small and large businesses the opportunity to outsource these activities to reduce costs and improve consumer responsiveness (IBISWorld, 2010). Nevertheless about three-quarters of Australian businesses in the mining, agricultural, manufacturing and service sectors, typified by the supply chains of BHP Billiton, the Australian Wheat Board (AWB), the carmaker GM Holden Ltd, and the retailer David Jones, still conduct their logistics activities in-house to maintain control of the business task. This situation, coupled with expected growth in the freight task, offers third-party and fourth-party logistics service providers an opportunity to extend beyond air, sea and rail transport and courier services into non-transport activities such as managing the customer's supply chain in such a way as to push any inefficiencies and costs back to the suppliers (Alpha, 2004).

The outsourcing of logistics activities in Australia is dependent upon the extent to which the big manufacturers and retailers exert their buying power, and take greater control over the logistics chain to reduce internal inventory, coordinate input delivery, and increase demand visibility to improve consumer responsiveness. The top 20 manufacturers, accounting for over 50 per cent of grocery products, are in a position to operate vendor-managed inventories in supplying large volumes to retailers (Sd+D, 2004, 39). Where manufacturers have been lagging in optimizing transport and introducing efficient load systems, major Australian retailers, in contrast, have sought supply chain reforms to offset cost pressures by rationalizing their distribution systems, by using more direct sourcing from overseas to exert greater control over suppliers and cut costs across stores, distribution centres and transport divisions by eliminating wholesalers wherever possible. Major retailers have developed their own distribution centres and are in a position to directly control the primary freight task: the supplier-to-retailer's warehouse segment of the supply chain (Figure 11.3). This control is exerted through either purchasing produce on an ex-factory gate pricing basis or implementing new service-level agreements to influence the inbound transport task (Huntley, 2006; PwC, 2006). The major retailers already controlled the secondary freight task from retailer's warehouse to the stores.

Coles and Woolworths

Coles and Woolworths, the two vertically integrated major supermarket chains in Australia, exemplify these developments to reduce costs. Coles (a division of Wesfarmers) and Woolworths are Australia's largest retailers stretching across food and grocery, liquor, petrol, general merchandise

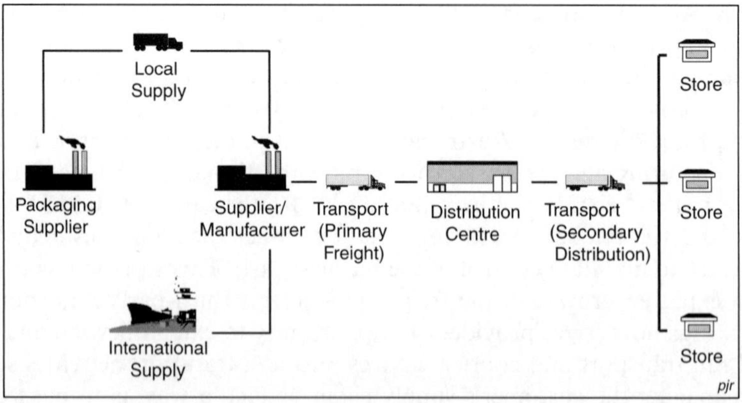

Source: Based on information from Huntley (2006).

Figure 11.3 Primary and secondary freight tasks

and consumer electronics. They have followed trends in the European Union and the United States designed to take greater control of the logistics chain to facilitate the increased use of outsourcing and prescriptive agreements with national logistics service providers, notably Linfox and Toll. As they account for over 70 per cent of packaged goods sales and 50 per cent of fresh produce sales such as meat, fruit and vegetables, the two companies claim to have used their 'whole of chain' solution to drive sustainability initiatives within Australia such as carbon reduction targets, zero food waste, water saving and ethical sourcing of products (ACCC, 2008, xv). Both companies are in a position to export their wholesaling and management expertise to the Asian-Pacific Rim; Woolworths already has a network of consumer electronic stores in partnership with the Tata Group, India's largest conglomerate.

Both Coles and Woolworths are in the process of streamlining their distribution and warehousing practices to further reduce costs and lower prices by taking advantage of improvements in information and communications technologies, and a reduction in transport costs along Australia's main intercity corridors. Within Australia the respective logistics divisions of the two companies operate a primary freight transport management system, and meet packaging and barcode requirements using radio frequency scanning, automated storage and retrieval systems, and high-speed sorting technology across a national network of distribution centres.

To offset the costs of warehousing and storage in every state capital city, the two companies are shifting from state-based platforms to a national

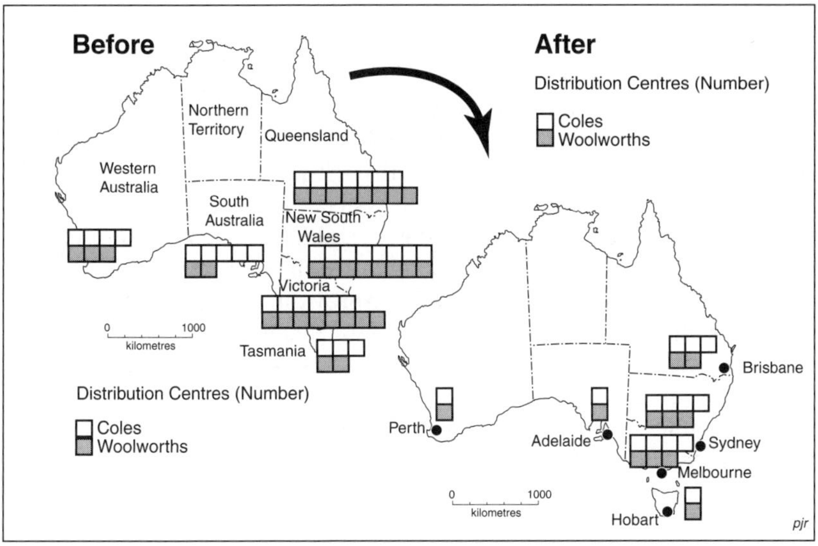

Sources: Based on information from Huntley (2006), WOW (2010a, 2010b, 2011).

Figure 11.4 Changeover of Coles and Woolworths from a state platform to a national distribution system, 2005–2010

Australian distribution network, which involves serving customers across a land mass the size of Europe with catchment areas more diverse than the United Kingdom. Within Australia, Woolworths has reduced its number of distribution centres from 31 to 11 since 2006, and Coles from 33 to 14 since 2007, to handle food and fast-moving consumer goods (Figure 11.4). Coles and Woolworths have established national distribution centres in both New South Wales and Victoria to obtain competitive leverage and strategic advantage from serving the entire country. This shift is leading to larger, centralized warehouses and greater use of cross-dock facilities for their logistics needs. With the anticipated increase in freight flows this concentration of activity, without local planning, will affect both congestion and the community amenity network. The rationalization of logistics systems to reduce costs may also affect the development of a national freight strategy by altering the spatial demand for transport and storage infrastructure. Concerns have been raised about the future resilience of food supply chains in response to natural disasters or other major disruptive events, given the major influence on the supply chain exerted by the reduced number of distribution centres operated by integrated supermarkets (DAFF, 2012).

POLICY

Australia has had no national transport and logistics policy comparable to Japan, South Korea or China (Chapters 7, 8 and 9). Under Australia's federal system, transport and logistics policy and regulatory responsibilities span across Commonwealth, state and territory, and local governments. Differences between these regulatory systems mean that national logistics corporations can face inconsistent regulations, creating unnecessary inefficiency and cost. With the Commonwealth Government limiting its attention to its constitutional domain of providing cross-border transport between states, much effort is based on influencing the unguided planning and policy developments by state and territorial, and local governments.

A flurry of activity in the early 1990s to develop intergovernmental cooperation in transport occurred through the National Road Transport Commission (NRTC), the Council of Australian Governments (COAG) and the Australian Transport Council (ATC), which in 1997 led to the creation of a Designated Interstate Railway Network and the Australian Rail Track Corporation (ARTC) to improve connectivity (Table 11.2). Otherwise state and territory-based Freight Councils, also established in 1997, have been relied on to bring together all players in the export chain, from shipping lines and airlines to producers and manufacturers, to improve the efficiency and quality of transport and logistics.

In 2000 a national solution was sought by the then Commonwealth (Liberal–National) Government by instituting the Freight Transport Logistics Industry Action Agenda 'to identify and address impediments to growth and the opportunity to create a sustainable internationally competitive freight transport logistic industry' (DOTARS, 2002, 1). Comprising a core group of participants from the freight logistics industry and its stakeholders, the Industry Steering Committee was appointed by the then Commonwealth Minister for Transport and Regional Services in 2001 to prepare an Action Agenda for Australia's freight transport logistics industry, following a preliminary analysis of its structure, conduct and performance (BTE, 2001). In 2002 this led to the launching of the Australian Logistics Industry Strategy, which comprised two documents, the final report of the Steering Committee (the Action Agenda) and the Government Response from the then Minister for Transport and Regional Services (ISC, 2002).

As the National Transport Commission had superseded the National Road Transport Commission in 2003 to develop nationally consistent regulatory and operational reforms relating to road, rail and intermodal transport, the Action Agenda addressed five priority areas: leadership, infrastructure, people, innovation and sustainability, all critical to

Table 11.2 Key government bodies engaged in transport and logistics in Australia

Body	Date	Members	Function
National Road Transport Commission (NRTC)	1991	Five non-Executive Commissioners and one Executive Commissioner (CEO), who collectively report to the Australian Transport Commission (ATC)	To develop monitor and maintain uniform or nationally consistent regulatory and operational reforms relating to road, rail and intermodal transport (e.g. regulators in heavy vehicle and road safety areas and pricing reform).
Council of Australian Governments (COAG)	1992	The Prime Minister, State Premiers, Territory Chief Ministers & the President of the Australian Local Government Association (ALGA)	COAG's Reform Council is pursuing a microeconomic reform agenda to deliver a seamless national economy through plans for deregulation priorities, regulatory reform and competition reforms (including infrastructure, transport policy and road reform plan).
Australian Transport Council (ATC)	1993	Commonwealth, State, Territory and New Zealand Ministers	Consult and provide advice to governments on the coordination and integration of all surface transport and road policy issues at a national level.
Standing Committee on Transport (SCOT)	1993	Chief Executives of Commonwealth and State road and transport agencies	Provide advice on a range of policy and technical matters, with assistance from a number of subcommittees.
Australian Freight Councils Network (AFCN)	1997	Operate within each state jointly funded by Commonwealth and State Governments with support from the Australian Logistics Industry	Industry driven forum bringing together all players within Australia's freight logistics chain.

Sources: ATC (2009), COAG (2007), DITRDLG (2008).

Australian companies being sought as participants in multinational supply chains. Leadership was designed to boost Australia's economic performance by coordinating supply chain resources to share the value generated by the chain based on investment and risk. In 2004 infrastructure was to be revitalized through the *AusLink White Paper* (DOTARS, 2004) to provide a long-term strategic approach to intergovernmental planning and accelerated development of a seamless land transport infrastructure focused on freight corridors and intermodal terminals (Figure 11.5). Recruitment, and education and training, were sought through the establishment of a not-for-profit Transport and Logistics Centre (TALC) in Sydney to act as 'think tank' for new ideas in capability building by providing advice on workplace planning and skills development. Innovation was to be pursued through technology and knowledge by using e-logistics

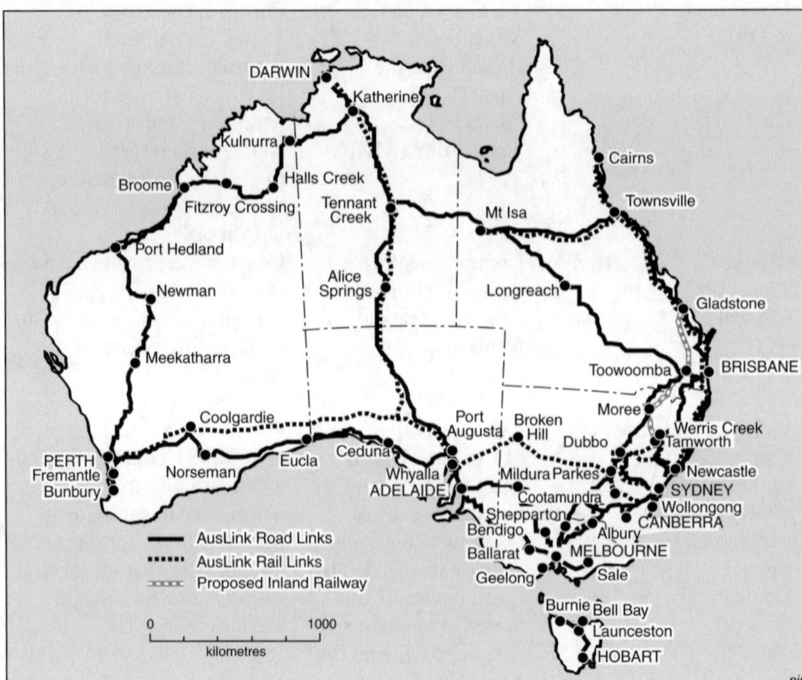

Note: The program sought to transcend the focus of transport planning in Australia on a single mode with integrated planning across all modes.

Source: DOTARS (2004, 17).

Figure 11.5 The AusLink program, June 2004

to address interconnectivity between systems and enhancing the quality of data and analysis. Sustainability was looked for in the promotion of environmental accreditation among manufacturers and retailers, and logistics service providers. Security was added later as a sixth priority area.

Continuing reliance on the Australian Freight Councils Network (AFCN) to drive the Action Program, and identify and address constraints, was not a feasible proposition since Australia's freight task, accounting for 9 per cent of gross domestic product (GDP), was projected to double over the period between 2000 and 2020 (BTE, 2001). This led to the National Transport Commission's (NTC, 2006) report '*Twice the Task*' that recommended a more integrated approach to transport planning, investment, regulation and pricing across national supply chains and for all modes over a 20-year period. In particular the proposition was designed to address the greater impacts of road transport's growth on congestion in urban areas, in, near or between ports, intermodal terminals, and outer industrial suburbs.

In response, the Australian Logistics Council (ALC) was established to drive the Action Agenda's implementation. This led to the release of *The National Strategy for the Transport and Logistics Freight Industry: Enhancing Australia's Supply Chains 08-15* (ALC, 2008). The Strategy required the transport and logistics sector, worth an estimated US$150 billion per year, to be capable, sustainable and productive through action in seven areas: safety, investment, regulatory reform, people, energy and environment, innovation and technology, and leadership. Prior to its publication a review of the Australian Logistics Industry Strategy (ALIS) concluded that the Action Agenda had gone as far as it could in its current form and resulted in the Council being recast as a lobby group based in Canberra (DOTARS, 2007). Except for specific projects of interest such as Future Supply Chains 2020 (ALC, 2010), Commonwealth Government funding was withdrawn from the Council, which is now reliant entirely on member subscriptions.

Meanwhile queues of up to 50 ships anchored offshore awaiting berths at three major ports prompted a Commonwealth Government investigation entitled 'The Great Freight Task: Is Australia's Transport Network up to the Challenge?' This highlighted the need for integration across all modes and intermodal hubs in state capital cities (COA, 2007). Before the report could be followed up, a Commonwealth (Labor) Government was elected in 2007. The new government sought to distinguish itself from the previous (Liberal–National) Government by adopting a fresh approach to economic management in Australia to advise governments, investors and infrastructure owners on future infrastructure needs, financing mechanisms and pricing, regulation and a national transport policy.

In 2008 the Commonwealth Government created Infrastructure Australia, a 12-person statutory council supported by an Infrastructure Coordinator located with the Commonwealth Government's then Infrastructure, Transport, Regional Development and Local Government portfolio. The new body was charged with creating a blueprint for fixing and modernizing transport, water, energy and communications infrastructure to meet seven national strategic priorities, covering an expansion in productive capacity, an increase in productivity, diversification of economic capabilities, building upon competitive advantages, developing cities and regions, reducing greenhouse emissions, and improving social equity and quality of life (Figure 11.6). As part of a national approach to funding and implementing the country's infrastructure, submissions from Government, industry and the community, which meet these criteria, are

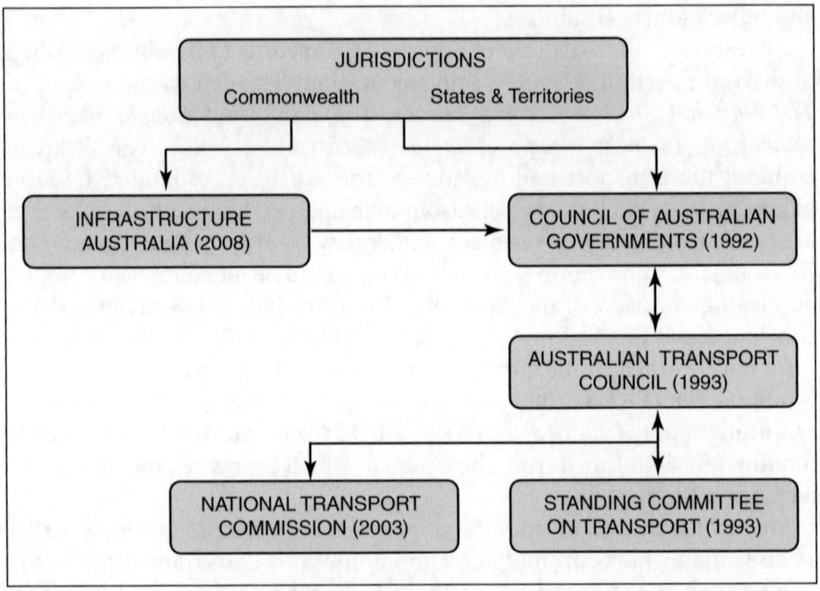

Note: In 2008 the Commonwealth Government inserted Infrastructure Australia into the national transport policy and regulatory reform agenda being driven by the Council of Australian Governments (COAG) and the ministers in the Australian Transport Council to develop the National Ports Strategy and National Freight Network Plan, and the National Transport Policy Framework. In 2011 the ministerial Standing Council on Transport and Infrastructure (SCOTI) replaced the Australian Transport Council (ATC). In turn, the Transport and Infrastructure Senior Officials' Committee (TISOC) replaced the Standing Committee on Transport (SCOT).

Figure 11.6 Infrastructure Australia's role, 2008

prioritized by Infrastructure Australia in terms of their strategic fit, net benefit and risk, and its findings are reported to the Council of Australian Governments. Infrastructure Australia has had to develop a national freight network strategy and to facilitate its implementation in partnership with state, territories and local government, and through public–private partnerships, by heeding the expressed need for observable government procurement procedures.

Consultations instituted by the National Transport Commission reveal strong support for the missing national freight network, although there are different ideas between stakeholders as to how it should be constituted to improve Australia's productivity and international competitiveness (Infrastructure Australia, 2010a). Concerns have been raised about places left off the network having no say in the process, city planning, the choice between road and rail, and ad hoc decision-making. Key concepts derived from the consultations suggest the need for a 20-year plan, which accommodates operations to meet social and economic aims, a national freight network, an infrastructure pipeline, customer involvement, and an access and improvement regime. Conceptually the resultant network should be seamless, intermodal, interconnected to major cities and ports with a positive impact on amenity, sustainability and safety, based on transparent data, with customers paying for rights and public reporting of progress. Of pivotal importance will be a shift from a preoccupation with freight corridors manifest in AusLink (renamed the Nation Building Program) to the broader development of competitive international gateways by establishing effective ports, and associated land and sea transport systems, to more efficiently cope with imports and exports.

The initial step by Infrastructure Australia and the National Transport Commission (Infrastructure Australia and NTC, 2010) has been to develop the first-ever 'national ports strategy' to coordinate long-term planning, reduce red tape in the execution of port plans and lower landside costs through increased efficiency, particularly as the country's container ports rank below the median of overseas ports on a series of benchmarks (BITRE, 2009b). As the port is the point of the supply chain where government involvement is greatest, this strategy takes into account regulatory and governance frameworks, land planning and corridor preservation, and future infrastructure requirements, including road and rail links. Given that Australia competes with other countries through its ports, a functional rather than a port authority or port precinct approach has been adopted to deal with all aspects of the logistics chain (NTC, 2013). Major port throughput is likely to triple between 2010 and 2030 (DTEI, 2007). Thus the resultant plan's priorities unveiled in 2011 were aimed at boosting productivity and eliminating bottlenecks and infrastructure gaps that impeded the energy boom of the late 1970s and early 1980s, particularly in steaming coal, oil and gas (Infrastructure Australia and NTC, 2012). Under this strategy nationally significant ports – bulk export (mainly single-commodity) ports and metropolitan (mainly container) ports – will be required to run as commercial businesses and publish 15–30-year master plans similar to those for airports. These plans will allow a panel of stakeholders to discuss future infrastructure requirements, including land-side issues, because the interfaces between port and hinterland affect organizations in the logistics chain. Distillation of these plans into a national framework will enable ports to plan with certainty when introducing additional capacity that meets trade forecasts and to develop buffer strategies to mitigate the environmental impacts of ports and their related transport corridors.

A 'national freight network strategy' has been derived from pursuing a seven-step audit process: goal definition, problem identification, problem assessment, problem analysis, option generation, solution assessment and solution prioritization. The strategy's defined goal is to derive better value for public expenditure and greater certainty for private sector investment, particularly in the road freight domain covering roads, bridges and tunnels (Infrastructure Australia, 2010b). This strategy is designed to identify key freight issues stemming from productivity being 'compromised by sub-optimality or lack of flexibility of transport (and storage) in national logistics chains' (Austen, 2009, 1). Assessments of various proposals put forward to Infrastructure Australia for augmenting transport networks to resolve these issues are based on the twin premises that: (1) government policies covering ownership and control, regulation, contracting, financing and planning determine network use; and (2) government freight plans decide network provision (roads, railways and terminals). If these policies and plans are distorted, the freight industry's response will result in inefficient and ineffective outcomes, as is evident in the absence of government involvement in the location of terminals in metropolitan areas that have a propensity for adverse community impacts.

An analysis of the key issues involved is discussed in the National Transport Commission's (NTC, 2008d) *National Transport Policy Framework: A New Beginning* and illustrated by reference to case studies of grain supply chains, the absence of a policy for inland ports, the livestock transport bottleneck, and skills shortages. The original ten priority areas highlighted in the Framework have been reduced to six – productivity and efficiency, environment, safety, maritime, network performance, and security – for consideration by the Australian Transport Commission. Rather than adopting a top-down approach, in which the Commonwealth dictates plans, or a purely market-driven approach to supersede the current unguided planning arrangement, Infrastructure Australia's preferred option for generating a consistent freight policy and plan involves national guidance and detailed jurisdictional plans through a partnership of the Commonwealth, state and territory, and local government requiring the establishment of a Transport Commission to act as a facilitator. Resolution of these issues should lead to a national plan for: improving outcomes for freight customers and the community; looking to the future by identifying likely determinants; being internally consistent; ranking issues in order of importance and urgency; and subjecting the plan to ongoing assessment and revision.

Progress on resolving key national cooperative reform on transport and logistics issues within Australia's federal system has been limited. Infrastructure Australia deemed it premature to prioritize solutions to the logistics challenges stemming from the country's decentralized port structure, high per capita cost of rail infrastructure by distance, a heavy reliance on road transport, and significant changes in local manufacturing profiles and import–export ratios. Instead Infrastructure Australia sought to progress the national freight strategy by completing four essential tasks: (1) definition of the network of gateways and corridors and identification of gaps on highly visible maps; (2) identification of inconsistencies in existing freight plans and governance stances of the Commonwealth, states and territories as they interact with the national network; (3) clarification of the Commonwealth's role in regard to the freight industry and other jurisdictions, including AusLink/Nation Building (roads) and the Australian Rail Track Corporation; and (4) case studies of city pairings, exemplified by the dominant Sydney–Melbourne axis, for government to address neglected interactions between cities with national freight movements to develop best practice for the planning of inland clearance depots (ICDs), access issues, community impact and funding.

Melbourne and Sydney

In considering the dominant Melbourne–Sydney pairing, attention is focused upon logistics activities at either end of the axis that have a marked impact on pollution, traffic congestion and productivity. Both Sydney and Melbourne experience difficulties in moving containers involved in the import–export system due to limited rail and road capacity, and constraints to intermodal terminals within their respective metropolitan areas. Reflecting these issues and the anticipated massive growth in container movements, the New South Wales Government has no less than five new terminals earmarked for Sydney, with Moorebank regarded as a priority, to augment the existing capacity provided by eight terminals, whereas

Melbourne's import–export system comprising three intermodal hubs is to be supplemented by three new terminals, including the Western Interstate Terminal (Figure 11.7). Both ports are serviced by rail, with road accounting for 80 per cent of the containers moved through Sydney's Port Botany compared with 85 per cent through the Port of Melbourne.

The Victorian Government's freight plan for Melbourne is designed to capitalize upon the city's claim to have the nation's strongest manufacturing base (SOV, 2008). Following channel dredging to accommodate larger ships, this plan is being used as a springboard to package the three existing terminals in Melbourne's western and north-eastern areas into a 'national logistics city' to foster global connectivity on a par with Dubai, Shanghai and Singapore (Nagel, 2007; Toh et al., 2009). Melbourne's key claim for national logistics city status is that it would be at the heart of a triangle encompassing four states, comprising 67 per cent of Australia's economic activity and 70 per cent of its population. By integrating seaport and

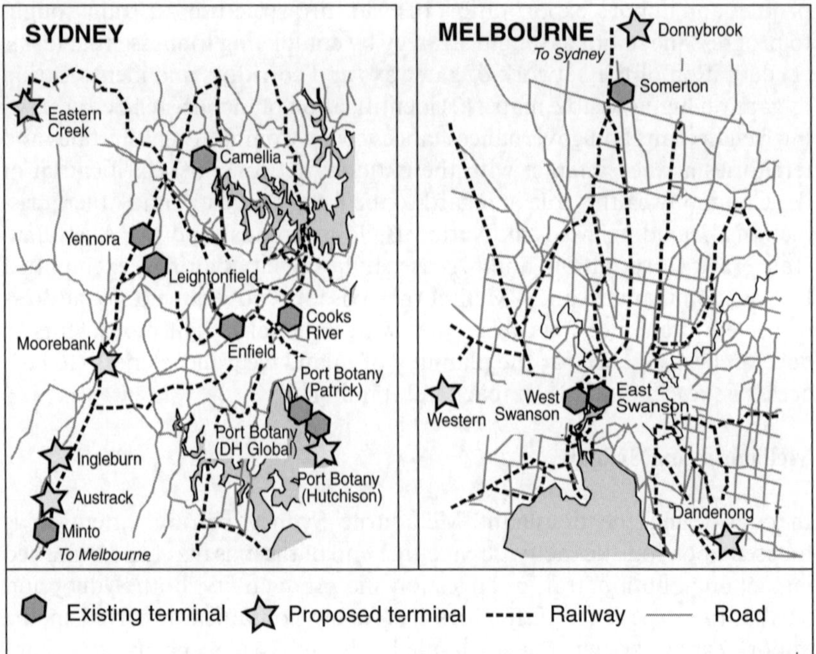

Source: Based on updating DOTARS (2006, vii–vii).

Figure 11.7 Intermodal terminals in metropolitan Sydney and Melbourne, 2011

airport freight terminals with inland clearance depot and their associated freight villages, Melbourne's logistics city concept promises to boost the effectiveness of managing materials and goods and the efficiencies of associated supply chains. Also the new entity could generate over an estimated US$2 billion per annum and provide additional metropolitan employment and reduce pollution. This bid falls short of a truly national strategy because the proposed 'four-state solution' fails to take into account the prospect of a direct inland rail connection with Brisbane, which is well located to serve Australia's dominant trade connections with Northeast Asia (ARTC, 2010).

The National Land Freight Strategy

In 2011 Infrastructure Australia's (2011, 2) discussion paper on the National Land Freight Strategy recognized that 'Rail and road infrastructure planning and investment can no longer be undertaken in isolation from each other, or worse, in competition with each other'. A new vision is required to overcome past policy segmented by mode and jurisdiction that inhibits productivity and international competitiveness. In response, a tightly defined land transport network, including both seaports and airports, is mapped out to overcome constraints to freight so that the best use of infrastructure can be made, freight and land use planning integrated, capacity for growth provided, any lack of responsiveness of infrastructure to meet economic demand overcome, and the opportunity for scenario testing and forecasting facilitated. Apart from improving economic, social and safety outcomes, and the establishment of infrastructure and operational performance indicators, the long-term goals of the national land freight network are the provision of high productive vehicle capability and access for long, double-stacked trains and B triple or super-double trucks, the incorporation of modern operating procedures and application of smart technologies, and the separation of passenger and freight transport. Rather than pursue issues of interfaces between gateways and corridors and the interim measures required to implement the proposed single national network, such as removing the impediments to high productivity vehicle use, a comparison is undertaken between its designated routes, precincts and terminals with the earlier AusLink map (see Figure 11.5).

Features of the indicative map of the single, new national land freight network highlight the development of: (1) existing seaports, notably Abbot Point, Bell Bay, Dampier, Port Kembla (Wollongong) and Portland, and prospective ports such as Oakajee and Hastings; (2) major airports and some regional airports with important freight tasks, such as Port Hedland, Rockhampton and Townsville; (3) intermodal terminals or freight cluster

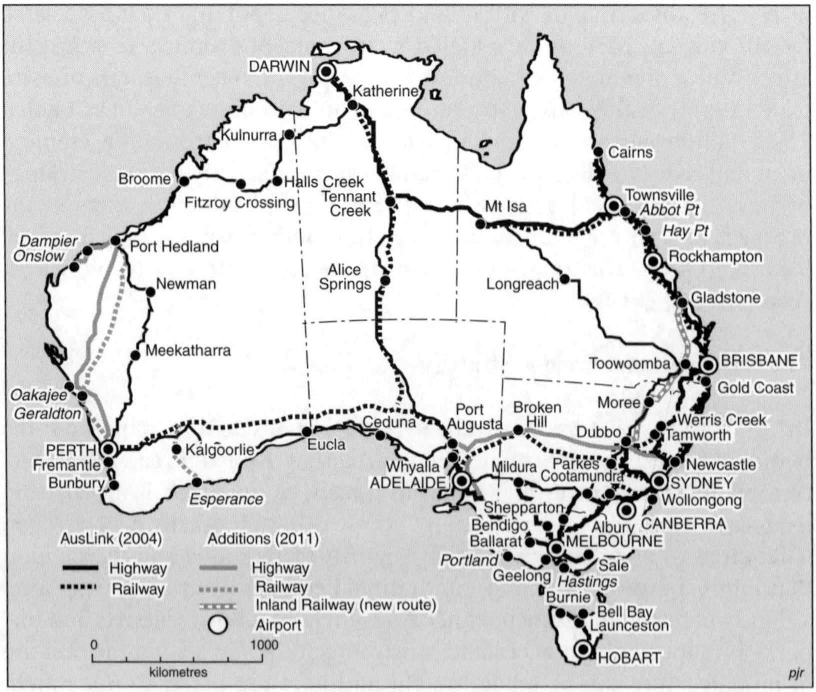

Note: The figure shows new or expanded ports (shown in italics), airports, road and rail links, including the re-routing of the proposed inland railway between Melbourne and Gladstone.

Source: DOTARS (2004), Infrastructure Australia (2011, 6).

Figure 11.8 A comparison of the National Land Freight Network with AusLink

sites in the state capital cities, Gold Coast and Canberra; and (4) a new inland rail line from Geraldton through the mineral rich Pilbara region to Port Hedland in Western Australia and a new version of the long-advocated inland Melbourne–Brisbane–Gladstone rail route (Figure 11.8). Also envisaged are additional roads to seaports, airports and intermodal or freight cluster sites; the completion of urban motorway networks to freight specifications or priorities; and the prospect of road pricing for heavier vehicles and congestion charging to encourage more efficient use of existing infrastructure and improvements paid for by freight to benefit freight. In working towards this desired long-term outcome, the prime emphasis is on interoperability with technical specifications included for rail, roads, communications, corridors and shipping. Stress is placed upon the development of priority standard gauge rail tracks between principal freight nodes; rail standardization in Queensland, Victoria and Western Australia; the incorporation of smart technology in infrastructure and operations; greater intermodal terminal capacity in state capital cities, major cities and interchange points such as Albury-Wodonga and Parkes; and dedicated freight infrastructures between state capital city ports and inland terminals.

What still seemed to be missing from any national freight strategy is its explicit setting within the wider Asian-Pacific Rim context. However, before this could be remedied the Commonwealth (Labor) Government was defeated. Since September 2013 the task of taking this wider view has reverted to the Commonwealth (Coalition) Government. The new government's Real Solutions Plan (Liberal Party, 2013) is committed to building projects under Infrastructure Australia's rolling 15-year national infrastructure plan that boost manufacturing competitiveness (for example, the world's largest coal port at Abbot Point). The challenge is to go further and position this plan within the wider Asian-Pacific Rim context.

CONCLUSIONS

Australia is the only nation that occupies an entire continent. Yet it still lacks a national spatial strategy to guide logistics development. An early attempt at national integration through the Inter-State Commission (1912–50) has long been forgotten. Since its abolition in 1950 there has been general agreement on the need for a national transport and logistics policy but little action. After the short-lived second coming of the Inter-State Commission (1983–89), the attention of the Council of Australian Governments during the 1990s was focused on the governance superstructure required to integrate Australia's transport and logistics system, which led to the introduction of competitive principles for all nationally significant infrastructure, except roads.

Since 2000 there has been a drift away from the earlier general logistics plans. They rarely rate a mention in the subsequent plethora of consultant reports, considered in this chapter, that are aimed at overcoming the short-term nature of political thinking in Australia's three-year election cycle and an estimated infrastructural backlog of $A700 billion, representing about half of the country's annual GDP (Dunn, 2013, S3). The cumbersome federal system and lack of consensus between the main political parties are not conducive to either national cooperative reform or bold visions for outlining and funding a seamless national freight transport system. Nevertheless the National Land Freight Strategy is an important first step, particularly with the establishment of a [ministerial] Standing Council on Transport and Infrastructure (SCOTI) in 2011 with designated priorities that include transport infrastructure and the strategic planning of state capital cities (Infrastructure Australia, 2012). Since January 2013 a national transport approach across borders has been made towards a seamless national economy with single regulators for heavy vehicles, rail safety and maritime safety replacing 23 different transport regulators (TISOC, 2012). This situation has prompted a review of the National Transport Commission's role with submissions for and against the continued separation of review and operations (e.g. ALC, 2012; NTC, 2012). Provided this matter is resolved and a political consensus is attainable, the creation of public–private partnerships and drawing upon Australian superannuation funds to buy or lease mature state assets such as ports promises to provide the necessary capital to expand the logistics infrastructure to support supply chain efficiency.

The 'national' in Australia's freight transport strategy may have been taken too literally, particularly as Singapore, for instance, plays a significant role as an offshore transport and communications hub for Australia (Haratsis, 2010). Greater consideration needs to be given to how Australia could be more closely integrated with the Asian-Pacific Rim, which does not rate a single mention in discussion papers. This task requires the adoption of a national spatial strategy that would better distribute economic activity by working with, rather than against, international pressures and taking into account the importance of offshore hubs and connections, and the need to remove artificial institutional barriers that increase the economic distance between Australia and Asia. While the Sydney–Melbourne axis will maintain its status as the dominant city pair in intermodal capacity and benefit from improved freight movements into and out of their ports, greater impetus could be given to the development of other gateways, notably Brisbane and Fremantle. The proposed direct north–south railway between Melbourne and Gladstone would enhance Brisbane's status, because it is well situated to take advantage of the country's strongest trading connection with Northeast Asia. Also Perth–Fremantle's position could be promoted through an improved east–west connection with Adelaide and stronger links with South Asia. In this way the proposed freight strategy would not only consolidate the national market but also provide a mechanism for closer integration with markets already being developed by Australia's manufacturers and retailers, and logistics service providers not only in the Asian-Pacific Rim but also in India.

12. India

The Indian Government is in a dilemma. Should India follow the People's Republic of China's transport and logistics strategy manifest in vertically integrated multinational supply chains, a large share of international trade in intermediate and unfinished goods, and openness to foreign domestic investment? Or, prompted by the Global Financial Crisis (2008–09), should India reduce its export dependence on Europe and North America and capitalize upon the prospect of increasing cross-border trade with the Asian-Pacific region, through a comparative advantage in the manufacture of motor vehicles, textiles and garments, information technology (IT) and IT-enabling services?

If India is to become a manufacturing powerhouse like China it will need investment in transport and communications infrastructure for just-in-time (JIT) delivery and opportunities to increase its participation in the global production and trading system. Should the Indian Government adopt the counter-strategy of reducing export dependence on Europe and North America to offset volatility, it will need to capitalize on its 1991 'Look East' policy and forge stronger links with the Asian-Pacific Rim to accommodate increasing trade, derive synergies from the fragmentation of production networks, and offer greater access to regional markets for seafood, fruit and vegetables, motor vehicles and apparel (Bhattacharyay, 2010).

Decoupling India from the global economy may not be a feasible proposition, but the sharp contrast between the two strategies focuses attention on infrastructural weaknesses between India and the Asian-Pacific Rim because they are affecting the country's entry into a broader economic community based on integrating and harmonizing transport and communications. Overcoming these weaknesses is essential for enhancing integration and improving productivity based on combining India's success in information technology and outsourcing with the Rim's advantage in manufacturing based on superior logistics and lower transport costs (ADB et al., 2005).

Existing low levels of connectivity between India and the Asian-Pacific Rim, stemming from the absence of key infrastructural linkages, results in trade with neighbouring countries being below its true potential (De, 2008;

Rahmatullah, 2010). Therefore the Indian Government and its counterparts in ASEAN+6 (Association of Southeast Asian Nations plus China, Japan, South Korea, Australia, India and New Zealand), spurred by the Japanese Government, are collaborating to improve connectivity through investment in world-class, environmentally friendly, soft and hard infrastructure networks (Matsushima, 2008; JETORO, 2009b; Kimura and Umezaki, 2011; ASEAN, 2010; ERIA, 2011; Sahoo, 2011; Umezaki, 2012). Apart from increasing the standard of living and reducing poverty, by connecting isolated places and people with economic centres, the aim in addressing the logistics needs of 1.8 billion people in both India and neighbouring ASEAN is to ensure economic growth is sustainable and inclusive. The free trade agreement signed between India and ASEAN on 1 January 2010 has already stimulated trade in car components. Ways still have to be found for financing the huge infrastructure investment needs and dealing with the negative externalities of increased connectivity.

Several key issues are involved in this strategy of efficiently and seamlessly linking India with the Asian-Pacific Rim to accelerate cooperation and produce a more competitive and integrated region. What is the present state of connectivity between the two areas? Where should infrastructure, including special economic zones, be located to enhance regional cooperation and integration? And how can the emerging spatial economy be defined and efficient transnational logistics networks be identified to reduce cost and time in transit, and increase reliability and flexibility? These issues in regional logistics systems not only involve physical bottlenecks but also traverse the entire range of policy and procedural issues in supply chains such as red tape and corruption in customs, bilateral highly restrictive protocols on cross-border movements, delays and pilferage in ports, and poor modal interfaces. These logistics systems are not only complex but also politically sensitive, because the Indian Government is using cross-border infrastructure as a major tool for economic diplomacy. India's 'soft power' inroads into the Rim, especially in Myanmar, are still modest compared with the growing presence of the People's Republic of China in commercial and infrastructure-oriented activities.

Initial attention in this chapter is centred on the levels of connectivity between India and the Asian-Pacific Rim by examining three transport long-distance routes that traverse the two areas – the Southern Ocean, Central Air and Northern Land Corridors – and scope for multimodal and logistics corridors that provide new perspectives for industrial development (Arnold, 2009). Then an evaluation is made of the economic corridor approach that seeks to overcome the infrastructure gap by enlivening and generating economic activities adjacent to major transport routes. As this approach is seen to be too narrow, there is an explicit need to introduce gateways into the equation to enable middle-income regions to become fully developed metropolitan regions. Once the full systems approach – gateways, corridors and non-corridor areas – is adopted for improving connectivity between India and the Rim, consideration can be given to developing a policy for transport and logistics services aimed at rebalancing development patterns to meet politically informed priorities.

CONNECTIVITY

The Southern Ocean Corridor is the principal trade route between industrial agglomerations in India and the Asian-Pacific Rim (Figure 12.1). As part of the east–west route that circumnavigates the world, the extended corridor provides the backbone of the global hub-and-spoke system that comprises mainline and feeder container shipping services interconnecting at transhipment hubs (Chapter 3). Within this system mainline shipping services connect India to Europe in 15–22 days, compared with 22–32 days for the Rim's ports. India's reliance upon feeder services dissipates much of this advantage because these add seven days to the journey time from Kolkata. Ports in India and the Rim are within 12–25 days' sailing time of each other. Most are within 14 days, which could be decreased to ten days if there was the inducement of an increased cargo mass. Chennai

Note: No port in India ranked among the world's top 25 in container throughput, but 17 ports in the Asian-Pacific Rim were in that tier. Jawarharial Nehru port (Mumbai) was the sole Indian representative within the second tier of top 50 ports that included Colombo and a further seven representatives from the Rim (CI, 2013).

Figure 12.1 The Southern Ocean Corridor, 2010

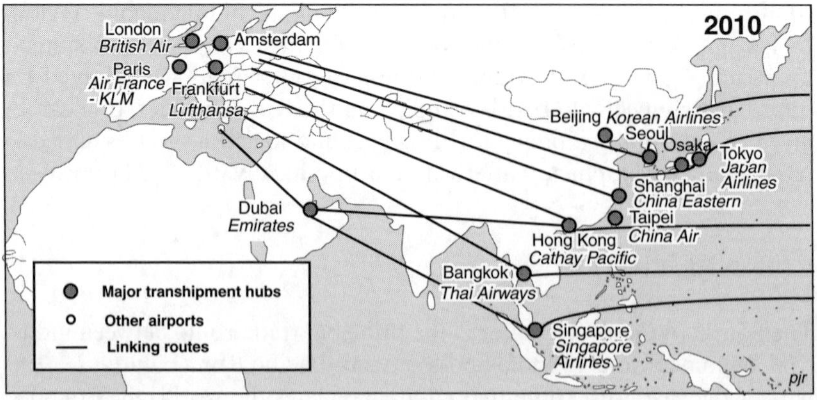

Note: No airport in India ranked among the top 25 in the world, whereas eight in the Asian-Pacific Rim were among the first tier; New Delhi was ranked 44th and Mumbai 45th (WATS, 2011).

Figure 12.2 The Central Air Corridor, 2010

(Madras), Kolkata (Calcutta) and Visakhapatnam in the Bay of Bengal are within 4–7 days of ports on the west coast of Thailand. Although port throughput could be enhanced with a new terminal costing US$250–200 million and a new port on a 'greenfield' site costing US$250–400 million, congested landside traffic outside seaports in India is still a major adverse issue (Arnold, 2009).

The Central Air Corridor, stretching from the Asian-Pacific Rim to Europe, offers India shorter transit times, but most national airlines, based at either end of the route, overfly India (Figure 12.2). Other than those from Bangkok, Hong Kong and Singapore, there are few direct flights between India and the Rim. Nevertheless airfreight is growing in importance, as the value of commodities traded has increased, but the market's expansion is limited by cost, and lags behind that served by ocean transport. Airfreight accounts for less than 1 per cent of cargo mass but 5 per cent of value. There is a pressing need to improve cargo handling within India, but a greenfield airport to handle 60 million passengers costs US$4–6 billion, a passenger terminal US$100–300 million and an air cargo facility US$10–20 million (Arnold, 2009).

The Northern Land Corridor, linking India and the Asian-Pacific Rim, comprises both road and rail transport. An increase in freight traffic is not anticipated by 2020 as existing trade flows by land transport are negligible and, except between northern India and western China, growth potential is so limited. Nevertheless this prospect has not stopped regional institutions and multilateral organizations anticipating that the Corridor will play an increasing role in bilateral trade as part of the Trans-Asian Railway (TAR) system and the Asian Highway (AH) initiatives. This prospect assumes that weak institutions and breakdowns in the rule of law can be overcome, and governments, the private sector and civil society can be galvanized to expand opportunities for participation in value-adding production networks.

The Trans-Asian Railway system offers a potential connection from Hanoi to New Delhi passing through Laos, Cambodia, Thailand and Myanmar (Figure 12.3). India has been involved in several cross-border rail projects in Myanmar that would contribute to this end. Nevertheless missing links would have to have to be bridged before this route can integrate India's northeast with the Mekong Delta and southern China. Even then there will be operational problems because the Indian broad gauge differs from both China's standard gauge and ASEAN's metre gauge.

The Asian Highway does not have these break-of-gauge issues (Figure 12.4). Roads are expected to link New Delhi with the ASEAN

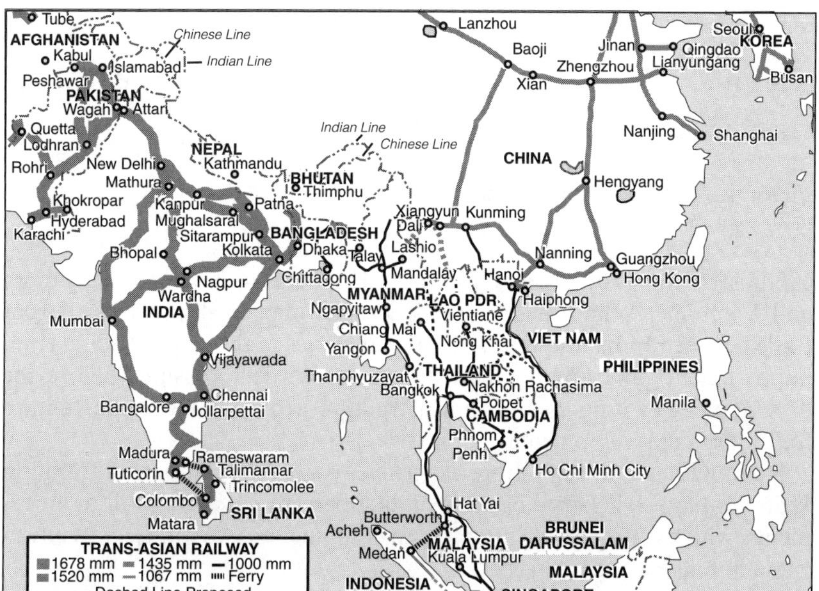

Note: The map is restricted to the section involving India and the Asian Pacific Rim.

Source: UNESCAP (2012a).

Figure 12.3 The Trans-Asian Railway (TAR) System, 2010

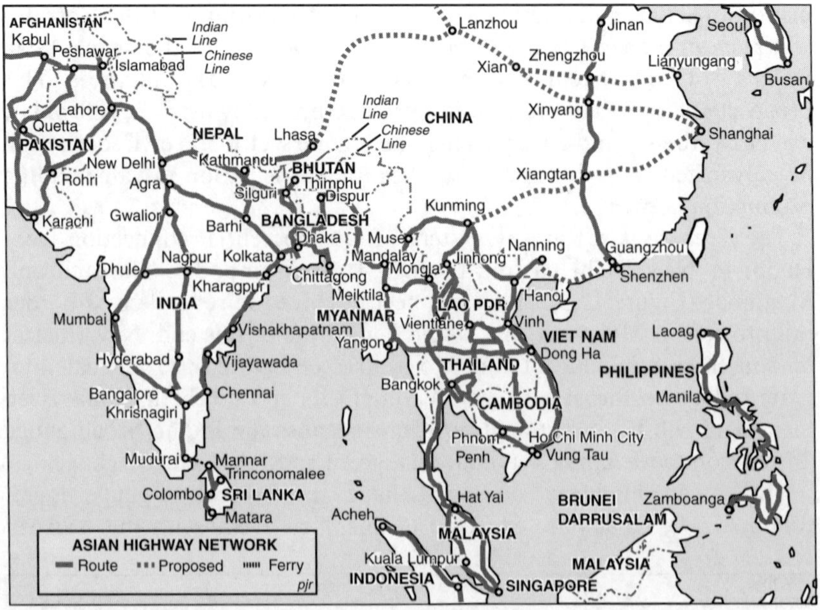

Note: The map is restricted to the section involving India and the Asian Pacific Rim.

Source: UNESCAP (2012b).

Figure 12.4 The Asian Highway (AH), 2010

capitals of Bangkok, Kuala Lumpur, Hanoi, Phnom Penh, Singapore and Vientiane. While these upgraded roads may facilitate cross-border trade between India and non-adjacent countries in the Asian-Pacific Rim, improvements are still required at remote border crossings before the development of long-distance infrastructure provides new opportunities for industrial development.

Road haulage, though more expensive, is generally preferred to rail in India (Table 12.1). This is because of its superiority in door-to-door movements, which is prompting attempts to combine the two modes not only in India but also in ASEAN.

Multimodal corridors are being contemplated to bridge the 'land gap' between the main corridors in India and Southeast Asia to enhance freight transport and intermodal facilities (Figure 12.5). As it straddles the gap, much effort is focused on Myanmar's government to unite the subcontinent and the Asian-Pacific Rim. Not only does Myanmar share a 1643 km boundary with India, but also it is rich in diamonds,

Table 12.1 Inland haulage charges from Delhi to selected ports, 2008

Port	State	Distance	Rail	Road
		km	Rupees/TEU	Rupees/TEU
Mundra	Gujarat	1295	16500	20000
Pipavav	Gujarat	1333	17000	25000
Jawaharlal Nehru Port (Mumbai)	Maharashtra	1388	18000	30600
Chennai	Tamil Nadu	2100	30000	70000

Note: TEU – twenty-foot equivalent unit.

Source: Vattamattathil and Rangayyan (2008).

hydropower, natural gas and timber. In 2001 the 160 km India–Myanmar Friendship Road link was completed connecting Tamu to Kalewa; Tamu is only 5 km from Moreh, the Indian border point linked to the country's highway and rail systems (Bhattacharyya and Chakraborty, 2010). Given that Myanmar is sandwiched between the two economic superpowers of China and India, its government's attitude has a vital role to play in helping to connect the subcontinent and the Rim (Caballero-Anthony et al., 2014).

Interest within India has been on domestic connections. Since 2006 India's Ministry of Railways has commissioned the Dedicated Freight Corridor Corporation of India (DFCCIL) to construct – with Japanese participation – two multimodal, high-axle-load freight corridors connecting the western and eastern hinterlands of northern India, and the major ports of Mumbai (Bombay) and Kolkata; the plan is to complete the Designated Economic Corridor between Mumbai, Delhi, Kolkata and Chennai (Government of India, 2006; JETORO, 2009b). This project matches the 5846 km 'Golden Quadrilateral' network of express highways between the four largest metropolitan areas that links the major ports. A north–south route between Srinigar and Kochi (Cochin) and an east–west route from Silchar in Assam to Porbandar complement the Golden Quadrilateral project. As shown by the logistics network map of India produced by the Japan External Trade Organization (JETORO, 2009b), these routes expand connectivity between India's largest cities and extend the prospect of fast road transport to other settlements within their vicinity.

An extension of this modern multimodal logistics infrastructure, in which road complements rail line haul for dedicated freight movements, can be used to bring India and ASEAN members states closer together. The Bay of Bengal Initiative Multi-Sectoral Technical and

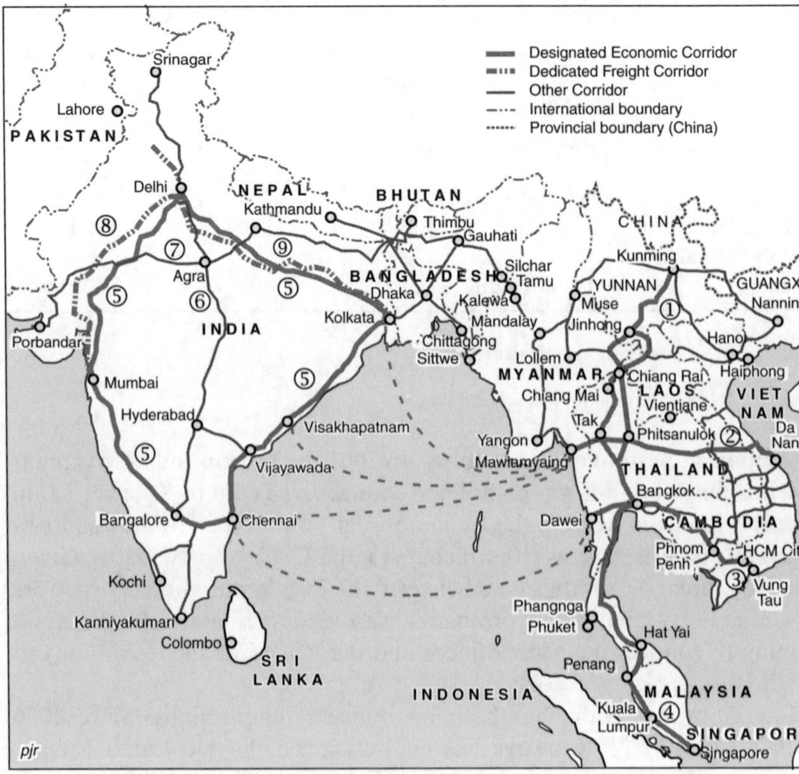

Note: 1. North–South Corridor; 2. East–West Corridor; 3. Southern Corridor; 4. Bangkok–Singapore Corridor; 5. India's Dedicated Economic Corridor (highway) known as the 'Golden Quadrilateral'; 6. Srinigar–Kochi; 7. Silchar (Assam)–Porbandar; 8. Western Dedicated Freight Corridor (rail); and 9. Eastern Dedicated Freight Corridor (rail) under construction.

Figure 12.5 The 'infrastructure gap' in connections between the key land corridors in India and the Asian-Pacific Rim

Economic Cooperation (BIMSTEC), which includes most of the members of the South Asian Association for Regional Cooperation (SAARC) – Bangladesh, India, Sri Lanka, Bhutan and Nepal – and Myanmar and Thailand, has endorsed this prospect of through-transport in the BIMSTEC 'Transport Infrastructure and Logistics Study' (ADB, 2008c). This study, covering road, rail, sea and air modes, has positive implications for bridging gaps in connectivity between member states, especially with financial and technical assistance on offer from Tokyo for multimodal transport initiatives to support local industries being incorporated in the multinational supply chains of Japanese firms (Palit, 2006; Wijayasiri and Mel, 2008; Rajkarnikar, 2010).

Also there is an opportunity to overcome security issues in India's landlocked northeast – linked to the rest of country by the 'chicken's neck' – by developing the area's cross-border transport agreements, so that the Siguri Corridor can serve as a bridge between Delhi and Hanoi (Subramanian and Arnold, 2001; Sarkar, 2010). In 2008 India signed an agreement with Myanmar to construct the Kaladan Multimodal Transport Corridor that bypasses Bangladesh and the port of Chittagong, and provides access to the northeast area from the upgraded port of Sittwe. A prime focus is on the completion of a new 5500 km Southern Silk Road route from Yangon in Myanmar to Kabul in Afghanistan (Bhattacharyay and De, 2009).

Logistics corridors do not exist between India and the Asian-Pacific Rim to harmonize the institutional framework, which facilitates the efficient flow of people, goods and related information by removing bottlenecks and developing logistics services providers. India's logistics industry is fragmented, with a large number of small fleet owners (5–10 trucks) offering transport services, rather than comprehensive logistics services designed to improve the quality, cost and scope of supply chain services. As multinational corporations are enhancing service levels by holding inventory closer to the point of delivery and adopting just-in-time deliveries, the pressure is growing in India to supplant import–export agents, national distributors and direct sales with more advanced logistics services (ADB, 2008c, xxv; ADB and ADBI, 2013). The logistics industry is expected to almost quadruple in value from US$100 billion in 2007 to US$385 billion in 2015, with the 'organized sector' increasing from 6 per cent to 12 per cent (Vattamattathil and Rangayyan, 2008).

There is still much reliance on fledgling third-party logistics companies in joint ventures with overseas firms, which are more geared to Europe and North America than services between India and the Asian-Pacific Rim (Vattamattathil and Rangayyan, 2008). Removal of the Central State Tax on the interstate transport of goods within India, coupled with the opening of free trade and warehousing zones, is encouraging the manufacturing sector to choose third-party logistics operators. The potential market for logistics service providers is expected to expand with the development of transport infrastructure, institutions and support services between India and the Rim.

ECONOMIC CORRIDORS

Economic corridors between India and the Asian-Pacific Rim are designed to attract investments in infrastructure and technology, and generate economic activity along the corridor's lesser-developed areas. International financial institutions support their construction as a means of facilitating cross-border trade (De, 2011). Logistics and infrastructure are seen as the keys for activating private sector dynamism. As the physical linkages and logistics facilities must be in place to increase private investment and develop supply chains, this opportunity to participate in production networks between India and the Rim is limited. Nevertheless the Master Plan on ASEAN Connectivity (ASEAN, 2010) provides the foundation for wider regional connectivity between India and ASEAN, with the Government of Thailand promoting Bangkok as the prime hub location (Srinarawat, 2009).

If the economic corridors stemming from industrial agglomerations are to participate in production networks there have to be reductions in: (1) network set-up costs, through improved institutional arrangements for hosting foreign direct investment; (2) service link costs, through the development of logistics infrastructure and services to improve cost, time and reliability and the promotion of trade liberalization; and (3) production costs, by initiating special economic zones, improving the investment climate and providing supportive infrastructure such as electricity supply (Kimura et al., 2009). The logistics infrastructure required to reduce these costs includes middle-distance roads, urban railways, container ports and upgraded airports. Also associated infrastructural investment is needed in energy and telecommunications within special economic zones in border areas and population centres, and in improved water and sanitary conditions in urban areas.

Four possible economic corridors between India and the Asian-Pacific Rim have been identified (Figure III.5). Already one of them – the Ho Chi Minh City–Phnom Penh–Bangkok–Dawei–Chennai Economic Corridor – has been the subject of detailed study by the Economic Research Institute for ASEAN and East Asia (ERIA) based in Jakarta which has considered the prospects of going beyond Chennai and linking Bangalore, Mumbai and Delhi. This possibility has been incorporated in ERIA's (2010) Comprehensive Asia Development Plan (CADP), which encourages the development of clusters in economic corridors and examines the critical issue of whether to locate economic activities in cities or border areas adjacent to neighbouring countries (Kimura et al., 2009).

GATEWAYS

Missing from the focus on economic corridors is any recognition that, for international sea and air movements, the gateway is also at the border and an integral part of supply chains. This omission in discussing economic corridors is now being compensated by studies that recognize the geographical distribution of international production networks is highly skewed (Kimura et al., 2009). These networks are concentrated on gateway areas in India and the Asian-Pacific Rim, notably Bangkok, Chennai, Hanoi, Ho Chi Minh City, Hong Kong, Jakarta, Kuala Lumpur, Manila and Singapore. In these instances agglomeration effects, incorporating the vertical interfirm production linkages and proximity to market, outweigh redispersion effects to avoid congestion manifest in traffic jams, pollution problems, land price surges and wage hikes (Chapter 1).

Policies to develop these gateways seek to expand their positive agglomeration effects and offset dispersion tendencies and the fragmentation of production by: (1) reducing fixed costs in the development of production and distribution networks by lowering investment changes and reducing establishment costs; (2) reducing the costs of logistics services connecting production blocks by overcoming border effects and developing an appropriate institutional environment; and (3) reducing the costs of production by strengthening locational advantages and the competitiveness of potential business partners (Kimura et al., 2009). In response the gateways have to invest in logistics infrastructure, comprising roads and bridges, railways, ports and airports; other economic infrastructure such as industrial estates, energy and power supplies and telecommunications; and urban and social infrastructure.

In establishing a Super Corridor between India and Viet Nam, for instance, investments will have to be made in the gateways of Ho Chi Minh City, Phnom Penh, Chennai and Mumbai and the hubs of Bangalore and Delhi; also a new deep seaport at Dawei in Myanmar will have to be envisaged (Htun et al., 2011; Banomyong et al., 2011; JIFFA, 2012b). Otherwise the full potential of the proposed Japanese-financed, multi-product Special Economic Zones dotting the Super Corridor's alignment, with provision for industrial estates or clusters to house motor vehicle manufacturing, textiles and garments, and information technology and IT enabled services, will not be fully realized (Figure 12.6). Plans are afoot to capitalize on Chennai's position as India's 'Eastern Gateway' and the potential of India and the Asian-Pacific Rim to outstrip world growth over the next decade.

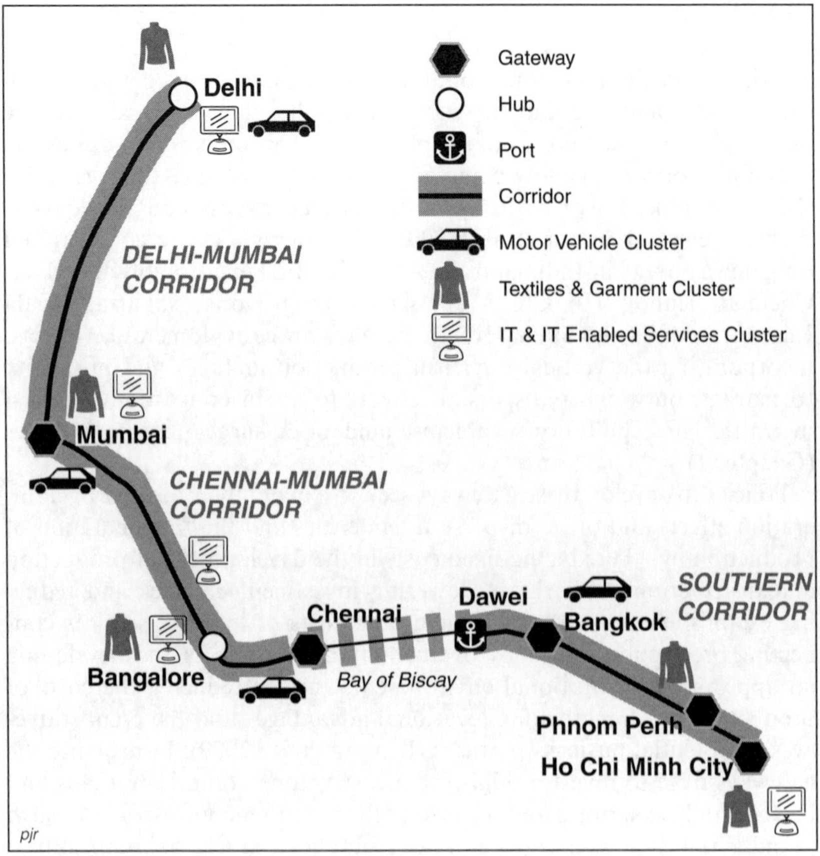

Sources: ERIA (2009), Kimura et al. (2009, 205).

Figure 12.6 Gateways and proposed industrial estates or clusters in the 'Super Corridor' between Delhi and Ho Chi Minh City

Chennai

Chennai is poised to benefit from the initiatives linking India and the Asian-Pacific Rim, and from its situation adjacent to the main shipping lane between them and Europe. The gateway is expected to be the pivot of Tamil Nadu's growth as India's second most industrialized state with key clusters in motor vehicles and textiles. With a network of almost 3000 engineering firms employing 250 000 skilled workers, the gateway has emerged as a major export base for motor vehicles. The growth in imports and export is expected to increase from almost US$28 billion in 2008 to over US$254 billion in 2020 (Zaidi, 2010).

Realization of this growth forecast hinges on removing a series of transport blockages hindering industrial growth. A pressing need exists for investment in Chennai metropolitan region's port and logistics facilities to meet an urgent demand for additional capacity in container facilities at both Port Chennai and Ennore Port, especially to overcome costly delays at the former (Figure 12.7). These delays are aggravated by severe road congestion on the existing highway linking the two ports. The railways are not in a position to relieve this situation, because the Ennore Port has no rail connection, and multimodal facilities integrating rail and road are absent. There are also capacity constraints at Chennai's airport where current annual demand exceeds 9 million passengers.

A high-capacity, semi-circular multimodal transport corridor is being provided within a 30 km radius of Chennai, linking Ennore Port and the Sriperumbudur and Irungattukottai Industrial Park to facilitate the speedy movement of goods between port, airport and the clusters that house an array of economic activities (for example, logistics, manufacturing and warehousing). Several projects are planned between 2014 and 2035 to enhance the Chennai–Ennore Economic Industrial Corridor's secondary hinterland and market connectivity to attract private sector investments into transport and industrial infrastructures (Kimura et al., 2009; De, 2011). These include the proposed Southern Dedicated Freight Corridor connecting Goa with Gudur that bifurcates at Vijayawada, leading to both Delhi and Kolkata, and the Peninsular Region Industrial Development (PRIDe) Corridor connecting Chennai with Bangalore, 'India's Silicon Valley', by high-speed rail (Heitzman, 2008; Goyal, 2009). A Chennai–Bangalore–Mumbai Dedicated Freight Corridor is also envisaged.

Once gateways and corridors are connected between India and the Asian-Pacific Rim, the only areas not covered are those remote from urban centres (for example, mountainous regions) that sometimes, but not always, have a small population size. These 'non-corridor' areas are reliant upon primary production, provided the necessary logistics infrastructure is in place. Although they do not attract high-frequency production networks in the short run, the argument is that the development of long-distance infrastructure promises new perspectives for industrial development within these areas in the longer term.

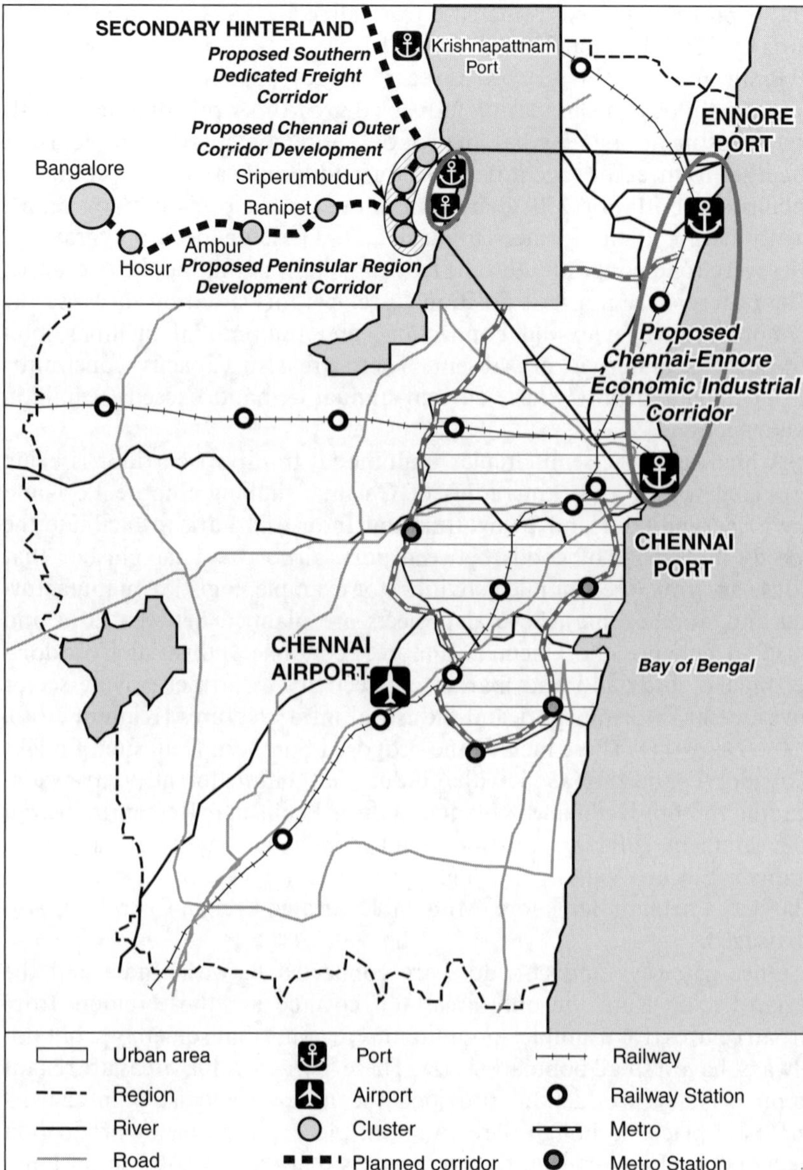

Sources: Kimura et al. (2009: 206), Zaidi (2010), De (2011, 122–5).

Figure 12.7 Plans for developing Chennai as a gateway, with inset showing connections to the region's secondary hinterland

CONCLUSION

The concepts of economic corridors, gateways and non-corridor areas provide the tools for planning a comprehensive spatial structure that connects India and the Asian-Pacific Rim. In pursuing this door-to-door logistics approach, overriding any distinctions between international and domestic connections, there must be an emphasis on the need to: (1) check the cost of removing at-border and behind-the-border obstacles; (2) recognize that not all sides will benefit equally from seamless development (for example, the Indian Government will have to bear the cost of connections with Bangladesh and Nepal); and (3) appreciate that the highest returns will be derived from overcoming negative externalities and bottlenecks in gateways.

Before this visionary seamless Pan-Asian connectivity structure can be realized, there is also a need for both an institutional framework and a range of funding mechanisms. Overlapping and fragmented subregional institutions covering India and the Rim have been ineffective and devoid of a clear and binding system of rules and policies in providing Pan-Asian connectivity.

In response to this dilemma, Biswanath Battacharyay (2010) has proposed a new overarching framework, the Pan-Asia Infrastructure Forum (PAIF), to coordinate cooperation and partnerships. Reflecting European and Latin American institutions for regional connectivity and integration (Chapter 10), the Forum's objective is to support enhanced connectivity through appropriate policies, reforms, systems and procedures, and by promoting effective cooperation and coordination. The new institution would be complemented by an Asian Infrastructure Fund (AIF) with the task of mobilizing international funds from public and private sources for 'bankable' regional connectivity projects.

If this institutional framework is to be successful, attention needs to focus on the proposed rebalancing of regional demand and trade-driven growth through increased regional productivity. Any comprehensive logistics action plan must redress the higher weighting given to overland cross-border economic corridors and relative neglect of the importance of gateways. This issue demands resolution before any 'Indo-Asian-Pacific Rim' concept can take hold.

Epilogue

Having established a wider Asian-Pacific Rim, with the addition of Australasia, and gone beyond its confines to add links with India, the next logical step is to discuss connections with the rest of Asia (Figure E.1). Major transit trade directions link the Rim with Northern Europe and Southern Europe, the Middle East and South Asia; those linking the Russian Federation and Europe with the Middle East and South Asia traverse these. While a detailed study of these Trans-Asian linkages is beyond this book's compass, it is appropriate to consider how integration could occur. This prospect provides an opportunity not only to revamp the global hub-and-spoke system by adding the Eurasian Landbridge, but also to examine studies contemplating the state of global and local logistics in 2050, before considering how aspects of the conceptual framework underpinning this study can be reformulated and enhanced.

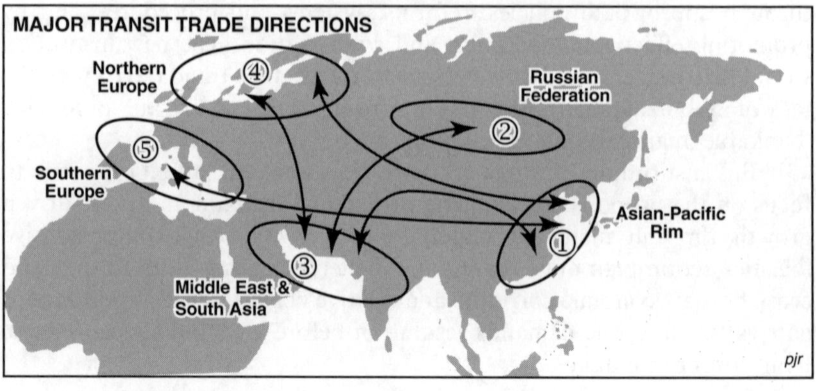

Source: ADB (2008d, 16).

Figure E.1 Major transit trade directions in Eurasia

EURASIAN LANDBRIDGE

There has been much emphasis on revitalizing historic links served by the Silk Road, which once comprised a series of caravan routes from China across the deserts and mountains of Central Asia, and by sea through the Black Sea and the Mediterranean to link with Rome (RIS, 2007; Bhattacharyay and De, 2009; Park et al., 2009; Rimmer and Dick, 2013). Booming cross-border trade involving Central Asia has generated interest from multinational industrial corporations headquartered in China, India, Japan, Korea and the Association of Southeast Asian Nations (ASEAN) and, in the process, is reviving the once famed land-based and maritime silk trading routes. The 'New Silk Road' is now a metaphor for a set of corridors accommodating rail, road, water, and gas and oil pipelines connecting China to Europe and the Middle East. These corridors promise to increase trade and assist the economic integration of Central Asia, and have been incorporated in China's vision of a New Silk Road Economic Belt outlined by President Xi Jinping in 2013.

The United Nations Economic Commission for Asia and the Pacific (ESCAP) has provided a long-term vision for an integrated logistics system across Eurasia (Ha, 2008). This system is designed to incorporate this historically least economically integrated area into the world economy by enhancing the capacities for international trade (Figure E.2). The Commission's vision of intermodal integration hinges on developing the 141 000 km Asian Highway and the 81 000 km Trans Asian Railway to extend the reach of seaports and the maritime networks inland.

A key element of the Commission's plan, based on the Busan Declaration on Transport Development in Asia and the Pacific (ESCAP, 2006), involves the establishment of logistics clusters at the intersection of highway and railway networks to accommodate the move of multinational manufacturers and retailers from coastal to inland locations. These clusters can serve as dry ports at inland locations, and are seen as providing the basis for establishing 'growth centres' to attract manufacturing, agricultural processing and associated services (Hanaoka and Regmi, 2012). This pattern is not without its shortcomings. All clusters in the Commission's vision have an equal weighting; there is no hierarchy. No mention is made of airports or telecommunications. Yet integrated infrastructure development, centred on multilevel gateways and corridors, depends upon thresholds being derived from analyses of goods, people and information flows (see Chapter 5).

The Central Asia Regional Economic Cooperation (CAREC) programme operated by the Asian Development Bank is addressing these subregional shortcomings (Koide, 2008). Investment by the Bank in

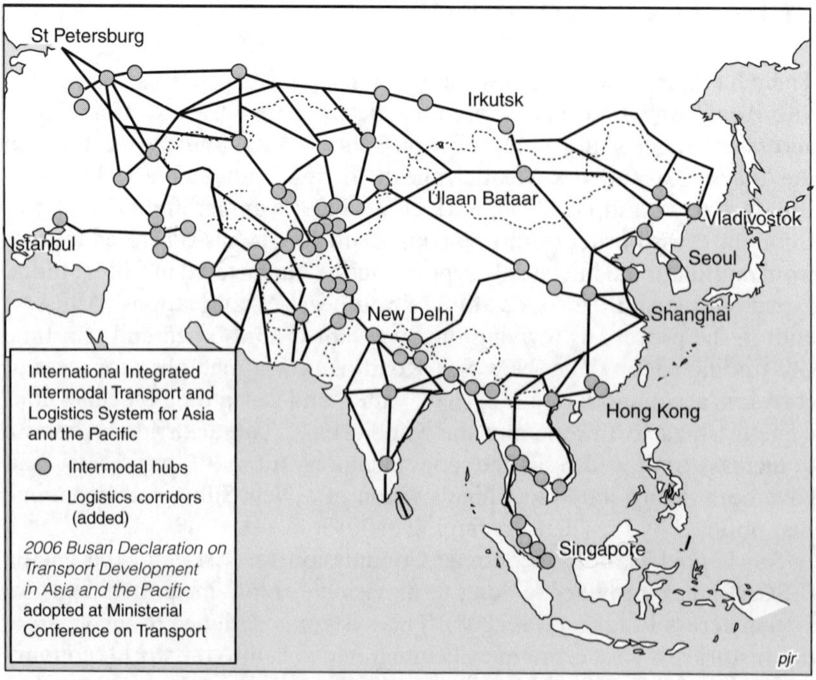

Source: Data from Ha (2008), Rimmer and Dick (2010).

Figure E.2 Linking intermodal hubs identified by United Nations Economic Commission for Asia and the Pacific (UN ESCAP) with a system of logistics corridors

cross-border infrastructure – airports, pipelines, railways, roads, bridges and tunnels, seaports and telecommunications – is designed to accommodate multinational supply chains and facilitate regional economic integration. This enhanced physical connectivity is complemented by the promotion of trade liberalization, including the reduction of non-trade barriers, improvements to legal and regulatory frameworks, and more efficient border clearances, to further reduce logistics costs and accelerate the flow of goods, people and information through Eurasia.

When critical thresholds are reached and Eurasia becomes better integrated, falling transport costs from the Landbridge may trigger an abrupt change in economic geography, disrupting any temporary equilibrium that may have been attained. Shifts in regional specialization would be prompted, leading to the coalescence of new economic regions. Also, should logistics costs fall, the progressive movement of regional economies into more complex and high-value computer-integrated manufacturing may transform the distribution of industry.

GLOBAL + LOCAL LOGISTICS 2050

Having inserted the Eurasian Landbridge into the global hub-and-spoke system, the next task is to discuss how the revamped network will be positioned by the middle of the twenty-first century (Figure E.3). Simple linear forecasts suggest that the Asian-Pacific Rim will be confirmed as the pivot of the world economy (Kohli et al., 2011; Franklin and Andrews, 2012). Greater urbanization will lead to more condensed transport flows within and between the region's gateways and other Main Street gateways. Also freight flows will strengthen along the diagonals from Asian-Pacific Rim gateways to both Africa and South America, subject to their necessary logistics infrastructure of gateways and corridors being provided in both regions (O'Neill and Stupnytak, 2012). Shifting from motor transport to ship and air for long-distance freight movements to save energy consumption will still be a challenge for proponents of multimodal transport. Nevertheless there is scope for reorganizing supply chains to increase efficiency by reducing empty cargo space in ships and aircraft.

As it is impracticable in a volatile and highly interconnected world to be satisfied with such a simple linear forecast, five different scenarios of trade, business and society in 2050 have been envisaged in a study commissioned by Deutsche Post (DP, 2012): untamed economy and impending collapse, mega-efficiency in megacities, customized lifestyles, paralyzing

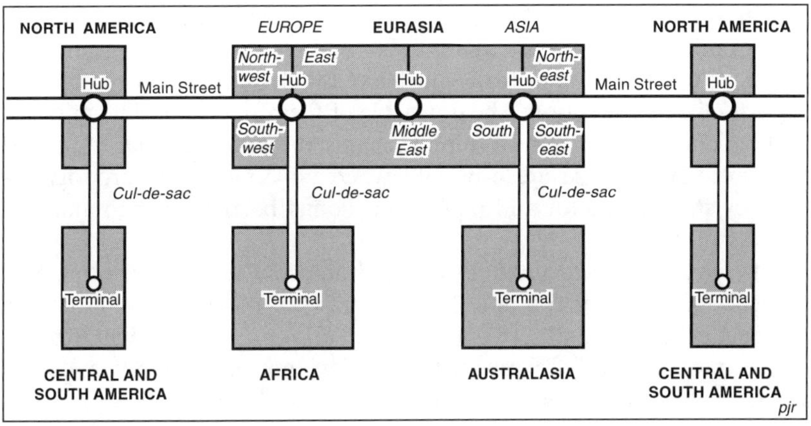

Figure E.3 The revamped global hub-and-spoke system

protectionism, and global resistance and local adaptation. These scenarios differ not only in the degree of globalization, extent of economic and social development, dominant technological standards and environmental conditions, but also in their likely impact upon the logistics sector. Rather than deal with five different scenarios, they are distilled below into the global, local and 'global + local' logistics frameworks that have permeated this book (Chapter 1).

The smooth running of the global logistics system is likely to be affected by increasing disruptions of multinational supply chains within a mass-consumption market arising from the relentless exploitation of resources and, notwithstanding the prospects of ice-free Arctic routes between Asia and Europe, the adverse impact of climate change on ports and landside areas (Smith, 2010; Ward, 2010; Bookbinder and Prentice, 2013). As these issues concern 'green consumers', analysts in the Deutsche Post study do not see this global system's reliance upon centralized and highly efficient operations using jumbo-transporters – larger than 18 000 TEU (twenty-foot equivalent unit) Triple E container ships and A380 aircraft – as the inevitable end state for long-distance trade in the hinterworld between the gateways. Nevertheless global logistics corporations located in the gateways will still be entrusted with city logistics, utilities, and services for airports, hospitals, seaports and shopping malls. The downside will be that the mega-efficiency of the metropolitan gateways will be achieved at the expense of rural areas and require infrastructural investments in the corridors to link hinterlands.

A plausible alternative is to switch from the long-distance movement of goods to the development of local logistics capabilities where consumption is closer to production. This switch to 'local–local' production (that is, near-sourcing) and centralized inventory and logistics management will enable multinational supply chains to be recast so that global logistics corporations can adjust their reach and serve the decentralized organization of customized production. The downside of the resultant decline in world trade and regionalization of supply chains for multinational industrial corporations will be severe, especially where governments regard logistics as a key strategic sector and raise protectionist barriers in the pursuit of techno-nationalism.

Perhaps the ultimate outcome will be a compromise offering both global resilience and local adaptation that makes use of the mobile Internet, the 'Internet of Things' and three-dimensional (3D) printing. Global logistics corporations will still orchestrate the physical movement of raw materials and the digital movement of blueprints for customized products produced by their customers on 3D printers. The top priority will involve strengthening regional logistics capabilities to ensure their security by providing relief and delivery systems by having strong backup infrastructures (for example, huge warehouses located close to industrial corporations). This will involve shifting the emphasis away from just-in-time delivery processes, to the last kilometre, so that the final leg of the supply chain is accommodated. In this 'ideal world' the battle against the relentless exploitation of resources and climate change in an increasingly urbanized world will be accomplished, sustainable business practices will have taken hold, and economic, social and cultural development will not be handicapped by protectionism and techno-nationalism.

THE CONCEPTUAL FRAMEWORK REVISITED

This book began by tracing the historical evolution of logistics and supply chain management that led to the formulation of the 'global + local' analytical framework featuring multinational industrial corporations, global logistics corporations and local state institutions (Chapter 1). Attention in discussing multinational manufacturers and retailers was focused initially upon the experiences of Wal-Mart Stores and Dell Inc. and on how they developed their dynamic capability in an evolutionary process (Chapter 2). Interest has been centred on how their supply chain strategies have been moulded by changes in principles – systems thinking, lean thinking, agility and dynamic flexibility – and how over time these principles have been combined into the just-in-time, postponement and structural flexibility concepts that have also shaped the experiences of multinational manufacturers and retailers headquartered within the Asian-Pacific Rim (Figure E.4).

The entire process has been cast in terms of a shift from a linear 'push' to a demand-driven 'pull' supply chain model, which has been used to identify and rank supply chain innovators among multinational manufacturers and retailers (see Figure 2.6 in Chapter 2). This self-renewing model sufficed because the study's prime emphasis has been on exploring interactions between multinational industrial corporations and global logistics corporations rather than on ranking supply chains across or within industry groups – a process always open to challenge because of the ranking's reliance on the variable weighting of public financial information, in-house and peer opinion, and innovation excellence such as time-to-value.

There is now scope for reformulating the self-renewing model to elaborate the scope, span, scale, skill and structure of the supply chains of multinational industrial corporations (Sengupta, 2008). Although the five pillars of supply chain excellence that drive economic profit and shareholder value – right talent; appropriate technology (that is, data

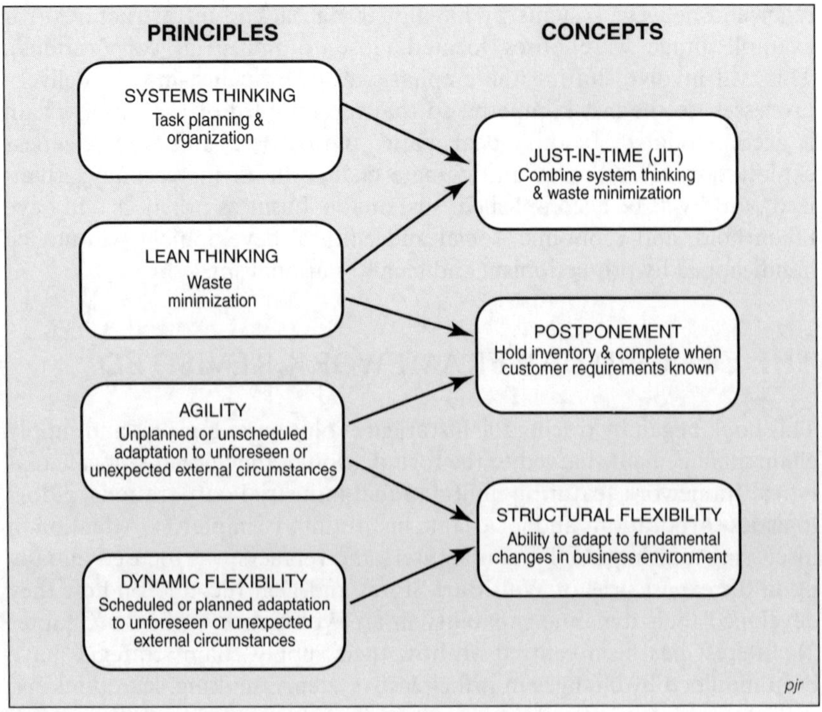

Sources: Christopher and Holweg (2011), Gattorna (2006, 2009)

Figure E.4 Key principles and concepts in supply chain management

processing capability); internal collaboration of sales, marketing and operations; external collaboration with suppliers and customers; and change management – are not novel, their resurrection in a proposed new supply chain agenda provides the basis for broadening the approach to analysing multinational industrial corporations (Slone et al., 2010). A brief review of supply chain configurations in Chapter 1 – continuous replenishment, lean, agile and fully flexible – shows that there is an opportunity for the nimbler multinational corporation to switch configurations to match 'strategies, internal corporate cultures and leadership styles with consumers, suppliers and third-party providers in the marketplace' (Gattorna, 2009, 127). The basic ingredients of this new mental framework for designing and supply chain configurations that prioritizes flexibility over efficiency to remain competitive in the new era have already been outlined (Christopher and Holweg, 2011). All that remains is to inject Joseph

Schumpeter's (1954) concept of 'creative destruction' to drive changes in the system (McCraw, 2007).

These reflections have led to a more detailed double circular model being developed that goes beyond the focus on the service elements where separate supply, demand and product circles overlap. Key players – supplier, customer and producer – in the reformulated model are identified in the inner core and linked by a circular distribution system (Figure E.5). These players are connected to an outer circular system in which supply responds to consumer behaviour (that is, the market), then in turn, consumer behaviour shapes production technology and sequentially

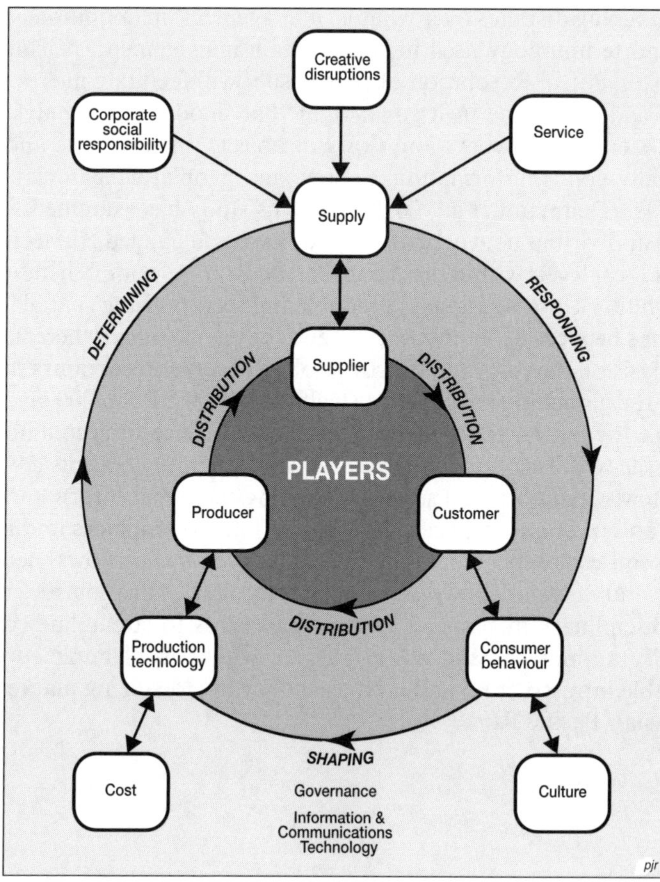

Source: Rimmer and Kam (2013, pers. comm.).

Figure E.5 The reformulated self-reinforcing model

production technology determines supply. Each of these key elements respond to other factors: consumer behaviour to culture, production to cost, and supply to the level of service and corporate social responsibility. An additional supply input is the insertion of Schumpeterian 'creative disruptions' or innovations that keep the self-renewing circular process in motion by injecting new sources of supply, new consumer goods, new production or transport technologies, new markets, new routes and new forms of organization. Suffusing the entire system are considerations of governance and the pervasiveness of information and communications technology.

Reformulating the conceptual framework coincides with attempts to resolve ongoing disputes over what is 'management' in definitions, frameworks and terminology used in supply chain management (Naslund and Williamson, 2010). Resolution of these issues will facilitate moves to cast logistics as a discipline in its own right that 'models and analyses economic systems as networks and flows of objects through time and space (specifically goods, information, money, and people) which create value for people' (Delfmann et al., 2010, 58). This study has examined flows in material and virtual networks at a global level and gauged connectivity at different local levels within the Asian-Pacific Rim. As comprehending hinterland–hinterworld relations is fundamental to appraising spatial interrelationships between economy, society and the environment, there has been an emphasis on the roles and functions of gateways and corridors that add value in the global logistics system (Delfmann, 2007; Pain, 2007a, 2007b). Although the nation-state has lost some significance in accommodating shifts in the world economy, the gateway and corridor concepts governing inter-gateway relations still serve as planning tools that inform territorial policies and meet governance challenges. While the emphasis in this book has been on economic geography and its concerns with flows, networks, nodes, hierarchies and land use surfaces, it recognizes that logistics inquiry is interdisciplinary in scope. The ongoing task is to streamline concepts that unify approaches and address issues with critical implications for sustainable infrastructure and land use policy in globalizing markets such as the Asian-Pacific Rim.

References

AASHTO (2002), *Transportation: Invest in America – Freight-Rail Bottom Line Report*, Washington, DC, USA: American Association of State Highways and Transportation Officials, available at http://www.rail.transportation.org/Documents/FreightRailReport.pdf (accessed 3 October 2012).

Abe, Masato (2013), 'Expansion of global value chains in Asian developing countries: automotive case study in Mekong Subregion', in Deborah L. Elms and Patrick Low (eds), *Global Value Chains in a Changing World*, Geneva, CH: WTO Publications, pp. 385–409, available at www.wto.org/english/res_e/...e/aid4tradeglobalvalue13_intro_e.pdf (accessed 5 November 2013).

ACCC (2008), *Report of the ACCC [Australian Competition and Consumer Commission] Inquiry into the Competitiveness of Retail Prices for Standard Groceries, July 2008*, Canberra, AU: Australian Competition and Consumer Commission, Government of Australia, available at www.accc.gov.au/content/index.phtml/itemId/838251 (accessed 13 January 2011).

ACCC (2013), *Qantas Airways Limited & Emirates – Authorisations – A91332 & A91333*, Melbourne, AU: Australian Competition & Consumer Commission, Government of Australia, available at http://transition.accc.gov.au/content/index.phtml/itemId/1078153/fromItemId/278039 (accessed 18 April 2013).

Acer (2013), *Acer Incorporated 2012 Annual Report*, Taipei, TW: Acer Inc., available at http://www.acer-group.com/public/Investor_Relations/presentations.htm (accessed 19 November 2013).

ACI (1995–2010), *Annual Traffic Data*, Montreal, CA: Data Center, Airports Council International, available at http://www.aci.aero/Data-Centre (accessed 11 November 2011).

ACI (2011), *Annual Traffic Data* 2010, Montreal, CA: Data Center, Airports Council International, available at http://www.aci.aero/Data-Centre (accessed 21 August 2013).

Action 2030 Institute (2009), *IIRSA: The Initiative for the Integration of Regional Infrastructure in South America: Policy Brief*, Buenos Aires, AR: Technical Coordination Committee, available at www.action2030.

org/publications/policybriefs/PolicyBriefIIRSA.pdf (accessed 24 October 2012).

ADB (2005), *The Mekong Region: Economic Corridors*, Metro Manila, PH: Asian Development Bank, available at www.adb.org/Documents/Others/GMS/Sector-Activities/gms-eco-corridors.pdf (accessed 11 February 2008).

ADB (2008a), *Logistics Development Study of the Greater Mekong Subregion North South Economic Corridor: Summary*, Metro Manila, PH: Asian Development Bank, available at www.adb.org/GMS/Economic.../NSEC-Logistics-Devt-Study-Summary.pdf (accessed 22 February 2010).

ADB (2008b), *People's Republic of China: Transport Efficiency through Logistics Development Policy Study*, Technical Assistance Report, Project Number 41112, Policy and Advisory Technical Assistance (PATA) November, Metro Manila, PH: Asian Development Bank, available at http://www.adb.org/Projects/project.asp?id=41112 (accessed 15 March 2013).

ADB (2008c), *Bay of Bengal Initiative for Multisectoral, Technical and Economic Cooperation (BIMSTEC) Transport Infrastructure and Logistics Study (BTILS), Consultant's Report*, TA 6335-REG, Metro Manila, PH: Asian Development Bank, available at www.bimstec.org/downloads/BTILS/BTILS%20Study.pdf (accessed 6 April 2011).

ADB (2008d), *REG: Central Asia Regional Economic Cooperation Transport Sector Strategy Study: Technical Assistance Consultant's Report*, December, prepared by TERA International Group Inc., Metro Manila PH: Asian Development Bank, available at http://www.carecprogram.org/uploads/corridors/Major%20Transit%20Trade%20Directions.pdf (accessed 7 September 2007).

ADB (2009), *Toward Sustainable and Balanced Development: A Strategy and Action Plan for the GMS North–South Economic Corridor*, draft, Metro Manila, PH: Asian Development Bank, available at www.adb.org/GMS/Economic-Corridors/NSEC-SAP.pdf (accessed 22 February 2010).

ADB (2012a), *Overview: Greater Mekong Subregion: Economic Cooperation*, Metro Manila, PH: Asian Development Bank, available at http://www.gmseoc.org/uploads/resources/61/attachment/GMS%20Economic%20Cooperation%20Program%20Overview.pdf (accessed 4 April 2013).

ADB (2012b), *Initial Assessments of Road Transport Infrastructure and Transport and Logistic Services for Trade Facilitation in the GMS Countries Draft Final Report*, Technical Assistance Consultant's Report Project Number: TA-7851(REG) Number: 26194, 4 May, Metro Manila PH: Asian Development Bank, available at http://www.adb.org/sites/default/files/ECF-4-Draft-Initial-Assessments-Road-Transport-Infrastructure-4-May-2012.pdf (accessed 17 October 2013).

ADB (2012c), *Transport Efficiency Through Logistics Development: Policy Study*, Mandaluyong City, Metro Manila, PH: Asian Development Bank.

ADB and ADBI (2009), *Infrastructure for a Seamless Asia*, Metro Manila, PH and Tokyo, JP: Asian Development Bank and Asian Development Bank Institute, available at http://www.adbi.org/book/2009/09/15/3322.infrastructure.seamless.asia/ (accessed 13 October 2013).

ADB and ADBI (2013), *Connecting South Asia and Southeast Asia: Interim Report*, Metro Manila, PH and Tokyo, JP: Asian Development Bank and Asian Development Bank Institute, available at http://www.adbi.org/files/2013.05.05.book.connecting.south.asia.southeast.asia.interim.report.pdf (accessed 16 September 2013).

ADB, JBIC and WB (2005), *Connecting East Asia: New Framework for Infrastructure*, Metro Manila, PH; Washington, DC, USA and Tokyo, JP: Asian Development Bank, International Bank for Reconstruction and Development/World Bank and Japan Bank for International Cooperation, available at http://www.dieselebooks.com/item/9780821361627/Bank-World/Connecting-East-Asia-A-New-Framework-for-Infrastructure/1.html (accessed 2 April 2011).

Agnew, John (2012), 'Is US security policy "pivoting" from the Atlantic to Asia-Pacific? A critical geopolitical perspective', Friedrich Ebert Stiftung Tiergarten Conference, Berlin, Germany, 12 September, available at library.fes.de/pdf-files/iez/global/09318.pdf (accessed 4 February 2014).

AL (2013), 'Quick to grow, slow to change', Sixth Annual Automotive Logistics Conference, Hyatt Regency, Mumbai, India, 5–7 December, available at http://www.automotivelogisticsmagazine.com/events/india-conference/archive/2012-conference/report (accessed 29 August 2013).

ALC (2008), *The National Strategy for the Transport and Logistics Industry: Enhancing Australia's Supply Chains 08-15*, Canberra, AU: Australia Logistics Council, available at www.qmfc.com.au/national-tandl-strategy (accessed 6 January 2011).

ALC (2010), *Future Supply Chains 2020: The First Iteration, September 2010*, Canberra, AU: Australian Logistics Council (Sponsor Group), available at www.austlogistics.com.au/index.php?option=com_docman&task... (accessed 16 March 2011).

ALC (2012), *Transport and Infrastructure Senior Officials' Committee 2012 Review of the National Transport Commission and other Relevant Transport Bodies Scoping Paper – ALC Response*, Canberra, AU: Australia Logistics Council, available at http://www.infrastructure.gov.au/transport/australia/ntc/files/alc.pdf (accessed 12 December 2013).

Alpha (2004), *Characteristics, Strategies and Trends for 3PL/4PL in Australia*, Sydney, AU: Alpha Research Consortium, available at www.laa.asn.au/pdf/3PL4PL_Report.PD (accessed 14 October 2012).

Alpha (2011), *Thailand in Figures 15th Edition 2010–2011: Volume I Whole Kingdom*, Bangkok, TH: Alpha Research Co. Ltd.

Anji (2013), *Anji Automotive Logistics: Network*, available at ppt.anji-logistics.com/jsp/us/advantage/network-advantage.jsp (accessed 12 March 2013).

Anji-CEVA (2013), *China Presence*, Shanghai, CN: Anji-CEVA Automobile Logistics Co. Ltd, available at http://www.anji-ceva.com/en/cmpn_ckfb.html (accessed 16 November 2013).

APEC PSU (2013a), *Improving Connectivity in the Asia Pacific Region: Perspectives of the APEC Policy Support Unit, September 2013*, Singapore, SG: Asia-Pacific Economic Cooperation Policy Support Unit, Asia-Pacific Economic Cooperation Secretariat, available at http://www.publications.apec.org/publication-detail.php?pub_id=1461 (accessed 8 October 2013).

APEC PSU (2013b), *The 2013 Interim Assessment for Supply Chain Connectivity Framework Action Plan*, Singapore, SG: Asia-Pacific Economic Cooperation Policy Support Unit, Asia-Pacific Economic Cooperation Secretariat, available at http://www.publications.apec.org/publication-detail.php?pub_id=1411 (accessed 21 September 2013).

APMT (2012), *APM Terminals: Lifting Global Trade*, The Hague, NL: APM Terminals Management B.V., available at http://www.apmterminals.com/aboutus.aspx?id=5123&image=8419 (accessed 11 November 2013).

Appel, Frank (2012), 'Deutsche-Post DHL: CEO Presentation, capital markets day – simply growing', London, 24 May, available at www.dp-dhl.com/.../Presentations/.../DPDHL_CMD_2012_CEO.pdf (accessed 27 February 2013).

Arai, Hirofumi (2013), 'Transportation corridors in Northeast Asia – to make a vision become a reality', Seminar on the Development of a Comprehensive Transport and Logistics Network in the Northeast Asia Subregion, UNESCAP, Seoul, Republic of Korea, 21–22 March, available at http://www.unescap.org/ttdw/common/Meetings/TIS/Logistics-in-NEA-2013/Presentations/7.2.ERINA-Mr.Arai.pdf (accessed 12 August 2013).

ARH (2010), *International Ports and Freight Policies, Strategies and Action Plans: Discussion Paper, June 2010*, Auckland, NZ: Auckland Regional Holdings, available at http://www.poal.co.nz/news_media/publications/International%20Ports%20and%20Freight%20Policies%20Strategies%20and%20Action%20Plans.pdf (accessed 13 November 2013).

ARM (2012), *FedEx.Gif*, Airline Route Maps.Com, available at airlinerroutemaps.com (accessed 1 October 2012).

Armstrong & Associates (2004), *Buyers of 3PL Services*, previously available at http://www.3plogistics.com/PR_3PL_Customers–2004.html (accessed 17 February 2005).

Armstrong & Associates (2008), 'Top 50 global logistics providers – May 2008', pers. comm., 30 May.

Armstrong & Associates (2009), *Who's Who in Logistics and Supply Chain Management – International, 17th Edition*, Stoughton, WI, USA: Armstrong & Associates Inc.

Armstrong & Associates (2010), *Current State of Third-Party Logistics*, available at http://www.3PLogistics.com (accessed 15 March 2014).

Armstrong & Associates (2012), *Top 25 Global Forwarders: Largest Providers by 2010 Gross Revenues and Freight Forwarding Volumes*, available at http://www.3plogistics.com/Top_25_Global_FF.htm (accessed 14 October 2012).

Armstrong & Associates (2013a), *Global 3PL Market Size Estimates*, available at http://www.3plogistics.com/3PLmarketGlobal.htm (accessed 3 February 2014).

Armstrong & Associates (2013b), *A&A's Top 50 Global 3PL List*, available at http://www.3plog0istics.com/Top_50_Global_3PLs.htm (accessed 3 February 2014).

Armstrong & Associates (2013c), *3PL Mergers & Acquisitions Tracking List: A&A's Historical List of 3PL Mergers and Acquisitions*, available at http://www.3plogistics.com/3PL_M&A_List_5-2013.pdf (accessed 3 February 2014).

Armstrong & Associates (2013d), *Top 25 Global Forwarders: Largest Providers by 2012 Gross Revenues and Freight Forwarding Volumes*, available at http://www.3plogistics.com/Top_25_Global_FF.htm (accessed 3 February 2014).

Armstrong & Associates (2013e), *Global Third-Party Logistics Market Information Report, 2013: Appendix VI*, Stoughton, WI, USA: Armstrong & Associates Inc., available at www.hkgem.com/reports/prelist/Documents/EKERRYL-20131122-22.pdf (accessed 11 February 2014).

Armstrong, Evan (2008), 'Continuing to add ever more to their offerings, 3PLs are-at your service', *Supply Chain Brain*, available at http://www.supplychainbrain.com/content/index.php?id=7098&type=98&tx_ttnews[tt_news]=3195&cHash=da03e20e36 (accessed 15 March 2014).

Armstrong, Richard (2005), 'The top 25 companies in North America', *LQ: The Official Magazine of the Logistics Institute*, 2 (1), 9–23, available at www.logisticsquarterly.com/issues/11-4/LQ_11-4.pdf (accessed 15 March 2014).

Armstrong, Richard (2012), 'Prediction and major trends for third-party logistics – 2012', *Journal of Commerce Webcast*, 24 January, available at http://event.on24.com/event/39/06/48/rt/1/documents/slidepdf/390648_1242012_joc_aro_3pl_v1_final.pdf (accessed 15 March 2014).

Arnold, John (2009), 'Regional integration in Asia: the role of infrastructure', in Joseph Francois, Padumna B. Rana and Ganesan Wignaraja (eds), *Pan-Asian Integration: Linking East and South Asia*, London, UK: Palgrave Macmillan, pp. 351–437.

ARTC (2010), *The Melbourne–Brisbane Inland Rail Alignment Study*, July, Canberra, AU: Australian Rail Track Corporation, available at http://www.artc.com.au/Content.aspx?p=175 (accessed 17 March 2011).

Arvis, Jean-François, Monica Alina Mustra, Lauri Ojala, Ben Shepherd and Daniel Saslavsky (2010), *Connecting to Compete 2010: Trade Logistics in the Global Economy*, Washington, DC, USA: International Bank for Reconstruction and Development / World Bank, available at siteresources.worldbank.org/INTTLF/Resources/LPI2010_for_web.pdf (accessed 17 January 2010).

Arvis, Jean-François, Monica Alina Mustra, Lauri Ojala, Ben Shepherd and Daniel Saslavsky (2012), *Connecting to Compete 2012: Trade Logistics in the Global Economy*, Washington, DC, USA: International Bank for Reconstruction and Development / World Bank, available at siteresources.worldbank.org/TRADE/Resources/.../LPI_2012_final.p... (accessed 5 December 2012).

Arvis, Jean-François, Monica Alina Mustra, John Panzer, Lauri Ojala and Tapio Naula (2007), *Logistics in the Global Economy: The Logistics Performance Index and Its Indicators*, Washington, DC, USA: International Bank for Reconstruction and Development / World Bank, available at www.siteresources.worldbank.org/INTTLF/Resources/lpireport.pdf (accessed 30 June 2009).

ASEAN (2007), *Appendix 1: Roadmap for the Integration of Logistics Services*, Jakarta, ID: ASEAN Secretariat, available at www.aseansec.org/20883.pdf (accessed 22 February 2010).

ASEAN (2010), *Master Plan on ASEAN Connectivity*, Jakarta, ID: ASEAN Secretariat, available at www.aseansec.org/documents/MPAC.pdf (accessed 13 August 2013).

ATC (2009), *Review of the National Transport Commission: Report to the Australian Transport Council (ATC) by the National Transport Review Steering Committee, June 2009*, Canberra, AU: Australian Government Department of Infrastructure and Transport, available at http://www.infrastructure.gov.au/transport/australia/ntc/index.aspx (accessed 3 March 2011).

Athukorala, Prem-Chandra (2007). *Multinational Enterprises in Asian Development*, Cheltenham, UK and Northampton, MA, USA: Edward Elgar Publishing.

ATK (2011), *2010 Global Cities Index*, Chicago, IL, USA: A.T. Kearney, available at http://www.atkearney.com/documents/10192/30bebf01-9591-46ef-8d06-a44b4e5ab364 (accessed 4 July 2013).

Austen, John (2009), *National Freight Network Strategy, July 2009*, Canberra, AU: Infrastructure Australia, Australian Government, available at www.infrastructureaustralia.gov.au/.../National_Freight_Network_Strategy_WEB.pdf (accessed 20 February 2011).

Australian Government (2012a), *Regional Comprehensive Economic Partnership Negotiations*, Canberra, AU: Department of Foreign Affairs and Trade, Australian Government, available at www.dfat.gov.au/fta/rcep (accessed 21 September 2013).

Australian Government (2012b), *Australia in the Asian Century: White Paper October 2012*, Australia in the Asian Century Implementation Task Force (AACITF), Department of Prime Minister and Cabinet, Canberra AU: Commonwealth of Australia, available at http://www.asiancentury.dpmc.gov.au/ (accessed 29 October 2012).

Backhouse, Peter (2006), 'Global logistics industry overview', The Logistics Event 06, Hilton Metropole, Birmingham, UK: Chartered Institute of Transport and Logistics UK, available at www.europe.ryder.com/.../$file/Ryder%20Plc%20at%20the%20CILT%20Convention%20June%202006.pdf (accessed 11 March 2008).

Bakker, Peter (2007), 'Analysts meeting: grow and build value', TNT N.V. Press Release, 6 December, Hoofddoorp, NL, available at TNTwww.afm.nl/.../20071206000000020_20071206_tnt_analysts_meet... (accessed 28 September 2012).

Bain, Joe Staten (1959), *Industrial Organization*, New York, USA: Wiley.

Baldwin, Richard (2006), *Globalisation: The Great Unbundling(s)*, Helsinki, FI: Prime Minister's Office, Economic Council of Finland, 20 September, available at graduateinstitute.ch/webdav/site/.../Globalization/Baldwin_06-09-20.pdf (accessed 11 February 2014).

Baldwin, Richard (2011), 'Trade and industrialisation after globalisation's 2nd unbundling: how building and joining a supply chain are different and why it matters', NBER Working Paper No. 17716, December, available at http://siteresources.worldbank.org/INTRANETTRADE/Resources/Baldwin_NBER_Working_Paper_17716.pdf (accessed 11 February 2014).

Baldwin, Richard (2013), 'Global supply chains: why they emerged, why they matter, and where they are going', in Deborah L. Elms and Patrick Low (eds), *Global Value Chains in a Changing World*, Geneva, CH: WTO Publications, pp. 13–59, available at www.wto.org/english/res_e/...e/aid-4tradeglobalvalue13_intro_e.pdf (accessed 5 November 2013).

Banomyong, Ruth (2007a), *Greater Mekong Subregion North South*

Economic Corridor, Metro Manila, PH: Asian Development Bank, available at www.adb.org/...Corridors/NSEC-Logistics-Devt-Study-Summary.pdf (accessed 23 May 2010).

Banomyong, Ruth (2007b), *Logistics Development Study of the Greater Mekong Subregion North South Economic Corridor*, Metro Manila, PH: Asian Development Bank, available at www.adb.org/GMS/Publications/NSEC-logistics-final.pdf (accessed 24 March 2008).

Banomyong, Ruth (2008), *Logistics Development Study of the Indonesia–Malaysia–Thailand Growth Triangle (IMT-GT) [Draft]*, Bangkok, TH: Centre for Logistics Research Faculty of Commerce and Accountancy, Thammasat University, Thailand, available at www.imtgt.org/Documents/Studies/Logistics-Development-Study.pdf (accessed 22 February 2010).

Banomyong, Ruth (2013), 'The Greater Mekong Sub-region of Southeast Asia', in James H. Bookbinder (ed.), *Handbook of Global Logistics: Transportation in International Supply Chains*, New York, NY, USA: Springer, pp. 69–96.

Banomyong, R., P. Cook and P. Kent (2008), 'Formulating regional logistics development policy: the case of ASEAN', *International Journal of Logistics Research and Applications*, 11 (5), 339–79.

Banomyong, Ruth, Paitoons Varadejsatitwong and Nuannalin Phanjan (2011), 'ASEAN–India connectivity: a Thai perspective', in Fukunari Kimura and So Umezaki (eds), *ASEAN–India Connectivity: The Comprehensive Asia Development Plan, Phase II*, ERIA Research Project Report 2010-7, Jakarta, ID: Economic Research Institute for *ASEAN* and East Asia (*ERIA*), pp. 205–42, available at www.eria.org/publications/research_project_reports/asean---india-connectivity-the-comprehensive-asia-development-plan-phase-ii.html (accessed 8 October 2013).

Barboza, David (2011), 'Exports perch on uncertain truck system', *New York Times*, 28 April.

Batson, A. (2008), 'China bets highways will drive its growth', *Wall Street Journal*, 11 November, available at http://online.wsj.com/article/SB122635482375915243.html (accessed 15 March 2013).

Batterby, Bryn (2006), 'Does distance matter? The effect of geographic isolation on productivity levels', Treasury Working Paper 2006-03, April, Canberra, AU: Treasury, Australian Government, available at http://www.treasury.gov.au/documents/1113/HTML/docshell.asp?URL=TWP_03_2006.htm (accessed 10 January 2011).

Baudin, Michel (2004), *Lean Logistics: The Nuts and Bolts of Delivering Materials and Goods*, New York, NY, USA: Productivity Press / Krauss Productivity Organization Ltd.

BBSR (2011), *Metropolitan Areas in Europe*, BBSR Online Publication, No.

01/2011, Bonn, DE: Federal Institute for Research on Building, Urban Affairs and Spatial Development (BBSR) within the Federal Office for Building and Research Planning (BBR), available at www.bbsr.bund.de/nn_23582/BBSR/EN/.../DL_ON012011.pdf (accessed 6 July 2011).

Beresford, Anthony, Stephen Pettit, Qing Xu and Sharon Williams (2012), 'A study of dry port development in China', *Maritime Economics and Logistics*, 14 (1), 73–98.

BESTUFS (2007), *Good Practice Guide on Urban Freight*, Rijswik, NL: REA Transport and Training, available at www.bestufs.net/gp_guide.html (accessed 27 June 2012).

Bhattacharyay, Biswanath (2010), 'Institutions for Asian connectivity', ADBI Working Paper Series, No. 220, Tokyo, JP: Asian Development Bank Institute, available at http://ideas.repec.org/p/ris/adbiwp/0220.html (accessed 8 April 2011).

Bhattacharyay, Biswanath and Prabir De (2009), 'Restoring the Silk Route: toward an integrated Asia', ADBI Working Paper Series, No. 140, Tokyo, JP: Asian Development Bank Institute, available at http://ideas.repec.org/p/ess/wpaper/id2165.html (accessed 8 April 2011).

Bhattacharyya, Anushree and Debashis Chakraborty (2010), *India's Recent Infrastructure Development Initiatives: A Comparative Analysis of South and Southeast Asia*, MPRA Munich Personal RePEc Archive, Munich, DE, University of Munich, available at http://mpra.ub.uni-muenchen.de/23030/ (accessed 5 April 2010).

BITRE (2009a), *Australian Transport Statistics Yearbook 2009*, Canberra: Bureau of Infrastructure, Transport and Regional Economy, Australian Government, available at www.btre.gov.au › ... › New release publications (accessed 20 January 2011).

BITRE (2009b), *Australian Container Ports in an International Context*, Information Paper 65, Canberra, AU: Bureau of Infrastructure, Transport and Regional Economy, Australian Government, available at http://www.btre.gov.au/Info.aspx?ResourceId=729&NodeId=60 (accessed 17 March 2011).

Blanchard, Benjamin S. (2004), *Logistics Engineering and Management*, 6th edn, Upper Saddle River, NJ, USA: Pearson/Prentice-Hall.

Bliss, Christoph and Ronald Haddock (2008), *Integrating China into Your Global Supply Chain – Lessons Learned from Global Supply Chain Integrators*, McLean, VA, USA: Booz Allen Hamilton, available at www.boozallen.com/media/file/Integrating_China_into_Your_Global_Supply_Chain.pdf (accessed 15 March 2013).

Bloch, Mark and Deborah Hofman (2011), *Supply Chain Top 25: Asia-Pacific, 1 September 2011*, Boston, MA, USA: Gartner Inc., available at http://www.gartner.com/id=1781414 (accessed 13 July 2012).

BMI (2012), *Japan Freight Transport Report Q2 2012*, London, UK: Business Monitor International, available at http://www.marketresearch.com/Business-Monitor-International-v304/Japan-Freight-Transport-Q2-7011431/ (accessed 26 November 2012).

Böhm, Anthony, Marcello Follan, Andrew Hewett, Sarah Jones, Neil Kemp, Denis Meares, David Pearce and Kevin Van Cauter (2004), *Vision 2020: Forecasting International Student Mobility: A UK Perspective*, London, UK and Sydney, AU: British Council, Universities UK, Sydney and IDP Education Australia.

Bookbinder, James H. (2005), 'Editorial: global logistics', *Transportation Research E: Logistics and Transportation Review*, 41 (6), 461–6.

Bookbinder, James H. (ed.) (2013), *Handbook of Global Logistics: Transportation in International Supply Chains*, New York, NY, USA; Heidelberg, DE; Dordrecht, DE and London, UK: Springer.

Bookbinder, James H. and Tiffany A. Matuk (2009), 'Logistics and transportation in global supply chains: review, critique and prospects', in Mohammed R. Oskooruchi (ed.), *Tutorials in Operations Research: Decision Technologies and Applications*, Presented at the INFORMS Annual Meeting, 11–14 October, Catonsville, MD, USA: Institute for Operations Research and the Management Sciences (INFORMS), pp. 182–211, available at http://www.mansci.uwaterloo.ca/~jbookbinder/publications.html (accessed 22 October 2013).

Bookbinder, James H. and Barry E. Prentice (ed.) (2013), 'The future', in James H. Bookbinder (ed.), *Handbook of Global Logistics: Transportation in International Supply Chains*, New York, NY, USA; Heidelberg, DE; Dordrecht, DE and London, UK: Springer, pp. 331–46.

Bowersox, Donald J., David J. Closs and M. Bixby Cooper (2002), *Supply Chain Logistics Management*, Boston, MA, USA: McGraw-Hill.

BPS (2009), *Produk Domestik Regional Bruto: Kabupaten/Kota di Indonesia, 2006–2010* [Gross regional domestic product regencies/municipalities in Indonesia], Jakarta, ID: Badan Pusan Statistics – Statisiks Indonesia, available at http://www.bps.go.id/eng/publications/publikasi2011.php?pg=27&key= (accessed 31 October 2012).

Brekelmans, Michel and Stephen Sunderland (2012a), 'China express logistics growing rapidly, creating opportunities', *Chaina*, November, available at http://www.chainamag.com/1211/cover#-/1211/articles/china-express-logistics-growing-rapidly-creating-opportunities (accessed 1 March 2013).

Brekelmans, Michel and Stephen Sunderland (2012b), 'Kuaidi touzi yu binggou jinxinggu' [Courier investment and merger and acquisition process], *Wuliu zazhi* [Logistics Magazine], October, available at http://

www.lek.com/sites/default/files/L.E.K._Express_Logistics_Investment_Logistics_Oct_20... (accessed 19 November 2013).

Brewster, David (2012), *India as an Asia Pacific Power*, Abingdon, UK and New York, NY, USA: Routledge.

Broeze, Frank (2002), *The Globalisation of the Oceans: Containerisation from the 1950s to the Present*, St John's Newfoundland, CA: Maritime Economic Association.

Brooks, Mary R. (2008), *North American Freight Transportation: The Road to Security and Prosperity*, Cheltenham, UK and Northampton, MA, USA: Edward Elgar Publishing.

Brown, Kerry, Justin Hempson-Jones and Jessica Pennisi (2010), *Investment Across the Taiwan Strait: How Taiwan's Relationship with China Affects its Position in the Global Economy*, London, UK: Chatham House (Royal Institute of International Affairs), available at www.chathamhouse.org/sites/default/files/public/.../1110pp_taiwan.pdf (accessed 19 November 2013).

BTE (2001), *Working Paper 49 – Logistics in Australia: A Preliminary Analysis*, Canberra, AU: Bureau of Transport Economics, available at www.btre.gov.au/info.aspx?NodeId=19&ResourceId=26 (accessed 16 February 2011).

BTM (2005), 'Kerry EAS brings us together', *Beijing This Month*, October, available at www.btmbeijing.com/contents/en/business/2005-10/investbeijing/kerryeasbringsustogether (accessed 19 March 2013).

Burnson, Patrick (2012), 'Will mergers and acquisitions alter the landscape?' *3PLS, Supplement to Logistics Management*, available at http://logisticsmgmt.com/images/site/LM1206_3PL_MergersSUP/pdf (accessed 15 March 2014).

Button, Kenneth, Kingsley Haynes and Roger Stough (1998), *Flying into the Future: Air Transport Policy in the European Union*, Cheltenham, UK and Northampton, MA, USA: Edward Elgar Publishing.

Buytenen van, Pieter M., Martin Christopher and C.S. Gordon Wills (eds) (1976), *Business Logistics*, The Hague, NL: Martinus Nijhoff.

Caballero-Anthony, Mely, Priscilla Clapp, Catharin Dalpiono, Abraham M. Denmark, Meredith Miller and Morten B. Pedersen (2014), *Myanmar's Growing Role*, NBBR Special Report #45, Seattle, WA and Washington, DC, USA: National Bureau of Asian Research.

CAGI (2007), *Asian Gateway Initiative: May 16 2007*, Tokyo, JP: Council for the Asian Gateway Initiative, available at www.kantei.go.jp/foreign/gateway/kettei/070516doc.pdf (accessed 6 March 2008).

CAGTC (2012), *Coalition for America's Gateways and Trade Corridors*, Washington, DC, USA: Coalition for America's Gateways and Trade

Corridors, available at www.tradecorridors.org/ (accessed 20 October 2012).

Calder, Kent and Ye Min (2010), *The Making of North East Asia*, Stanford, CA, USA: Stanford University Press.

CAPA (2009), *Global LCC Outlook Report*, Sydney, AU: Centre for Asia Pacific Aviation.

Carruthers, Robin, Jitendra N. Bajpai and David Hummels (2003), 'Trade and logistics in East Asia; a development agenda', World Bank EASTR Working Paper, No. 3, Washington, DC, USA: World Bank, available at www.lpcb.org/.../11295-2003-wb-trade-and-logistics-in-east-asia-a-devel (accessed 22 August 2013).

Cattaneo, Olivier, Gary Gereffi, Sebastien Miroudot and Darien Taglioni (2013), *Joining, Upgrading and Being Competitive in Global Value Chains: A Strategic Framework*, Washington, DC, USA: World Bank Poverty Reduction and Economic Management Network International Trade Department, available at http://econ.worldbank.org › Data & Research › Research › Document Search (accessed 4 February 2014).

CBO (2006), *The Economic Costs of Disruptions in Container Shipments*, Washington, DC, USA: Congressional Budget Office, US Congress, available at http://www.cbo.gov/sites/default/files/cbofiles/ftpdocs/71xx/doc7106/03-29-container_shipments.pdf (accessed18 September 2013).

CCTA (1986–2012), *Zhongguo jiao tong nian jian (Jing hua ben)* [Yearbook of China Transportation and Communications (Prime Edition)], Beijing, CN: Zhongguo Jiaotong Nianjian She [China Transport and Communications Association].

CDC (2006), *The Industrial Map of the Yangtze River Delta, 2005*, compiled by China Industrial Map Editorial Committee, China Economic Monitoring & Analysis Center and National Bureau of Statistics of China, Shanghai, CN: Shanghai ChinaDatabar Co.

CDC (2007), *Changjiang Sanjiaozhou chan ye di tu, 2006–2007* [The industrial map of the Yangtse River Delta, 2006–2007], Zhongguo chan ye di tu bian wei hui, Zhongguo jing ji jing qi jian ce zhong xin bian, Shanghai Shi, CN: Fu dan da xue chu ban she.

Cen, Xuepin (2005), *The Dynamics of the China Logistics Industry*, Master of Engineering in Logistics thesis, Massachusetts Institute of Technology, May, available at http://dspace.mit.edu/handle/1721.1/33311?show=full (accessed 15 February 2009).

CFLP (2004–13a), *Zhongguo wu liu nian jian* [China logistics yearbook], Zhongguo wu liu yu cai gou lian he hui [China Federation of Logistics and Purchasing], Beijing, CN: Zhongguo wu zi chu ban she.

CFLP (2004–13b), *Zhongguo wu liu fa zhan bao gao* [China logistics development report], Zhongguo wu liu yu cai gou lian he hui [China

Federation of Logistics and Purchasing], Beijing, CN: Zhongguo wu zi chu ban she.

CFLP (2005–13c), *Zhongguo wu liu yu cai gou ye fen xi bao gao* [Analysis report on China's logistics industry], annual report since 2005, Beijing, CN: Zhongguo wu iiu yu cai gou lian he hui, available at http://www.chinawuliu.com.cn (accessed 21 January 2014).

Chen, Feng and Chung-Yen Lee (2013), 'Logistics in China', in James H. Bookbinder (ed.), *Handbook of Global Logistics: Transportation in International Supply Chains*, New York, NY, USA: Springer, pp. 3–26.

Chen, Jason C.H., Binshan Lin, Lingil Li and Patty S. Chen (2004), 'Logistics management in China: a case study of Haier', *Human Systems Management*, 23 (1), 15–27.

Cheung, Anthony B.L. (2013), *Promoting the International Flow of People and Goods: The Hong Kong Experience*, 8th APEC Transportation Ministerial Meeting 2013, Tokyo, available at http://www.apec-tmm8.org/english/pdf/outline/Session1-1-3.pdf (accessed 9 October 2013).

Chin, Fu Chin, Jung-Han Bae and Gwi Ok Kim (2007), *A Survey on the Logistics Service Providers in Shanghai*, available at www.faculty.washington.edu/karyiu/confer/busan07/.../chin-bae-kim.pdf (accessed 29 November 2012).

China Briefing (2013), *Shanghai's New Free Trade Zone – General Plan and Regulation*, available at http://www.china-briefing.com/news/2013/09/28/china-releases-general-plan-and-regulations-for-the-shanghai-free-trade-zone.html (accessed 1 October 2013).

Choi, Wonsik, Richard Dobbs, Dongrok Syn, Jan Mischke, Eunjo Chon, Hangjip Cho, Boyoung Kim and Hyunmin Kim (2013), *Beyond Korean Style: Shaping a New Growth Formula*, Seoul, KR and San Francisco, CA, USA: McKinsey Global Institute.

Chongvilaivan, Aekapol (2012), 'Thailand's 2011 flooding: its impact on direct exports and global supply chains', ARTNeT Working Paper Series, No. 113, Bangkok, TH: Asia-Pacific Research and Training Network on Trade, United Nations ESCAP, available at http://www.unescap.org/tid/artnet/ (accessed 25 February 2014).

Chopra, Sunil and Peter Meindl (2013), *Supply Chain Management; Strategy, Planning and Operation*, 5th edn, Boston, MA, USA: Pearson.

Chow, Garland (2007), *Collateral Benefits of Security and Supply Chain Improvements at International Gateways*, Canada's Asia-Pacific Gateway and Corridor Initiative: Calgary Round Table, 28–29 March, available at http://www.gateway-corridor.com/calgaryroundtable/papers.htm (accessed 1 June 2011).

Christopher, Martin (1974), 'Logistics systems engineering – solving the distribution problem', *Long Range Planning*, 7 (6), 74–80.

Christopher, Martin (1992), *Logistics and Supply Chain Management: Creating Value-Added Networks*, London, UK: Pitman Publishing.
Christopher, Martin (2005), *Logistics and Supply Chain Management: Creating Value-Added Networks*, 3rd edn, Harlow, UK: Pearson Education.
Christopher, Martin (2011), *Logistics and Supply Chain Management: Creating Value-Adding Networks*, 4th edn, Harlow, UK: Financial Times / Prentice Hall.
Christopher, Martin and Matthias Holweg (2011), '"Supply Chain 2.0", managing supply chains in the era of turbulence', *International Journal of Physical and Logistics Management*, 41 (1), 63–82.
CI (1970–2013), *Containerisation International Yearbook*, London, UK: Informa.
CI (2001), *Containerisation International Yearbook*, London, UK: Informa.
CI (2011), *Containerisation International Yearbook, 2010*, London, UK: Informa Ltd.
CI (2013), *Containerisation International Yearbook, 2012*, London, UK: Informa Ltd.
CIFA (2013), *Zhongguo guo ji huo yun dai li xie hui* [China International Freight Forwarders Association], Bejing, CN: China International Freight Forwarders Association, available at www.cifa.org.cn/index.asp (accessed 20 March 2013).
CIMEC (2006), *The Industrial Map of the Yangtze River Delta*, China Industrial Map Editorial Committee (CIMEC), Shanghai, CN: Shanghai ChinaDatabar Co. Ltd.
CL (2013), *CEVA: Making Business Flow*, Hoofddorp, NL: CEVA Logistics, available at http://www.CEVA (accessed 27 February 2013).
CL and GSCC (2012), *State of Logistics China Survey 2012*, Hoofddorp, NL and Shanghai, CN: CEVA Logistics and Global Supply Chain Council (GSCC), available at http://www.cevalogistics.com/en-CN/Documents/2012%20state%20of%20logistics%20china%20survey.pdf (accessed 19 March 2013).
Clark, Tim (2007), *Re-defining Long Haul Travel – the Emergence of the Trans Global Hub*, China Civil Aviation Forum 2007, Beijing, 10 May, available at www.caac.gov.cn/.../P020080521577623873459.pdf (accessed 17 July 2013).
Clarke, Ian M. (1985), *The Spatial Organisation of Multinational Corporations*, London, UK: Croom Helm.
Clarkson (2011a), *Oil and Tanker Trades Outlook*, 16 (12), London: Clarkson Research Services Limited.
Clarkson (2011b), *Dry Bulk Trades Outlook*, 17 (12), London: Clarkson Research Services Limited.

CNN Money (2011), *Fortune Global 500, 2011*, available at http://www.money.cnn.com/magazines/fortune/global500/2011/ (accessed 4 June 2012).

COA (2007), *The Great Freight Task: Is Australia's Transport Network up to the Challenge?* House of Representatives Standing Committee on Transport and Regional Services (The Neville Report), Canberra, AU: Parliament of the Commonwealth of Australia, available at www.aph.gov.au/house/committee/trs/networks/.../fullreport.pdf (accessed 14 March 2011).

COAG (2007), *Australia's Infrastructure: National Overview Report, April 2007*, Canberra, AU: Council of Australian Governments, available at www.coag.gov.au/coag_meeting.../infrastructure_reports_nat.pdf (accessed 17 February 2011).

COSCO (2013a), *COSCO Logistics Co. Ltd (China Ocean Shipping Agency Co. Ltd)*, Beijing, CN: China COSCO Holdings Ltd, available at http://www.cosco-logistics.com.cb/about/4_e.htm (accessed 12 March 2013).

COSCO (2013b), '*Wu biao ti wen dang*' [Untitled document], available at www.cosco-logistics.com/e_lxwm/lxwm1_gz.html (accessed 15 April 2013).

Coyle, John J., Edward J. Bardi and C. John Langley Jr (2003), *The Management of Business Logistics*, 7th edn, Mason, OH, USA: South-Western/Thomson Learning.

Coyle, John J., Robert A. Novack, Brian J. Gibson and Edward Bardi (2011), *Transportation: A Supply Chain Perspective*, 7th edn, Mason, OH, USA: South-Western Cengage Learning, McGraw Hill.

CPrompt (2010), *Visualizing the Internet*, available at www.c-prompt-dev.com/the_internet.asp (accessed 16 April 2013).

CSCI (2012), *China Supply Chain Intelligence – Kerry EAS Logistics Limited*, Hong Kong, HK: Kerry Logistics, available at http://www.chinascintell.com/providers/provider_details.php?... (accessed 2 February 2012).

CSCMP (2012), *CSCMP Supply Chain Definitions*, Lombard, IL, USA: Council of Supply Chain Management Professionals, available at http://cscmp.org/aboutcscmp/definitions.asp (accessed 24 September 2012).

Dablanc, Laetitia (2013), 'City logistics', in Jean-Paul Rodrigue, Theo Notteboom and Jon Shaw (eds) (2013), *The Sage Handbook of Transport Studies*, London, UK; Thousand Oaks, CA, USA; New Delhi, IN and Singapore, SG: SAGE Publications Ltd, pp. 119–39.

DAFF (2012), *Resilience in the Australian Food Supply Chain, February 2012*, Canberra, AU: Department of Agriculture, Fisheries and Forestry, Australian Government.

Daft, Richard L. (2008), *Management*, 8th edn, Mason, OH, USA: Thomson South-Western.

Dai, Jiangang and Chen Zhou (2008), *Beer Distribution in China*, Centre of Excellence: Logistics in China, Atlanta, GA, USA: Supply Chain Logistics Institute, School of Industrial and Systems Engineering, Georgia Institute of Technology, available at http://www.scl.gatech.edu/research/china/beerreport2008.pdf (accessed 13 February 2009).

Damas, Philip (2010), 'The opportunities and challenges for international freight forwarders', presented at JIFFA Silver Jubilee Symposium 2010, Tokyo, JP: Japan International Freight Forwarding Association, available at www.jiffa.or.jp/notice/image/101125_Simposium_b.pdf (accessed 7 February 2014).

Data Monitor (2011), *Japan Logistics and Express Outlook: Trends Driving the Japanese Logistics Sector*, London, UK: Data Monitor, available at www.datamonitor.com/store (accessed 26 November 2012).

Davies, Ronald E.G. (1997), *Airlines of Asia since 1920*, London, UK: Putnam.

Dayal, Raghu (2013), 'SAARC: a story of missing opportunities', Regional Forum of Freight Forwarders, Multinational Transport Operators and Logistics Service Providers, Negombo, Sri Lanka, 6 June, available at http://www.unescap.org/ttdw/common/FFForum2013.asp (accessed 16 October 2013).

De, Prabir (2008), 'Comments on Dr M. Rahmatullah's Paper Session VI: Transport Issues and Integration in South Asia', 1st South Asia Economic Summit: Economic Integration in South Asia and Beyond, Colombo, 8–30 August, available at www.ips.lk/saes/conference_material/downloads/discussant_prabir_de.pdf (accessed 8 April 2011).

De, Prabir (2011), 'ASEAN–India connectivity: an Indian perspective', in Fukunari Kimura and So Umezaki (eds), *ASEAN – India Connectivity: The Comprehensive Asia Development Plan, Phase II, ERIA Research Project Report 2010-7*, Jakarta, ID: Economic Research Institute for ASEAN and East Asia (*ERIA*), pp. 95–150, available at www.eria.org/ (accessed 12 October 2012).

De Langen, Peter W., Jan C. Fransoo and Ben van Rooy (2013), 'Business models and network design in hinterland transport', in James H. Bookbinder (ed.), *Handbook of Global Logistics: Transportation in International Supply Chains*, New York, NY, USA; Heidelberg, DE; Dordrecht, DE and London, UK: Springer, pp. 367–89.

Delfmann, Werner (2007), 'Gateways and corridors: adding value in global logistics systems', ITLS Research Seminar, University of Sydney, 18 September, Sydney, AU: Institute of Transport and Logistics Studies, University of Sydney, available at www.itls.usyd.edu.au/seminars/presentations/Wernerd.pdf (accessed 29 January 2008).

Delfmann, Werner, Wilhelm Dangelmaier, Willibald Gunthner, Peter Klaus, Ludger Overmeyer, Werner Rothengatter, Jurgen Weber, Joachim Zentes and Working Group of the Scientific Advisory Board of German Logistics Association (BVL) (2010), 'Towards a science of logistics: cornerstones of a framework of understanding of logistics as an academic discipline', *Logistics Research*, 2 (2), 57–63.

Dell, Inc. (2010), *Annual Report for the fiscal year ended: January 29, 2010*, Washington, DC, USA: United States Securities and Exchange Commission, available at i.dell.com/sites/content/corporate/secure/.../FY10_Form10K_Final.pd... (accessed 29 September 2012).

Derudder, Ben, Michael Hoyler and Peter J. Taylor (2013), 'The network dimension', in Michele Acuto and Wendy Steele (eds), *Global City Challenges: Debating a Concept, Improving a Practice*, Basingstoke UK and New York, NY, USA: Palgrave Macmillan, pp. 33–46.

Desevedavy, Franck and Pascal Thien-Ah-Koon (2003), 'Logistics: Taiwan's take off for international presence', Paris, FR: UGGC & Associés Société d'Avocats, available at uggc.com/download_pdf.php?f=doc_200810131030.pdf&n...pdf (accessed 4 November 2013).

DHL (2012), *DHL's Business Strategy in China*, available at www.authorstream.com/Presentation/tanu123_zaq-1339622-final-ppt (accessed 27 February 2013).

Dick, Howard (2007), 'The TNT Group', in Howard Dick and David Merrett (eds), *The Internationalisation Strategy of Small Firms: The Australian Experience of Globalisation*, Cheltenham, UK and Northampton, MA, USA: Edward Elgar Publishing, pp. 300–307.

Dick, Howard and Peter J. Rimmer (2003), *Cities, Transport and Communications: The Integration of Southeast Asia since 1850*, Basingstoke, UK and New York, NY, USA: Palgrave Macmillan.

Dick, Howard and Peter J. Rimmer (2013), 'South East Asia and Australia', in Peter Clark (ed.), *The Oxford Handbook of Cities in World History*, Oxford, UK: Oxford University Press, pp. 581–602.

Dicken, Peter (2007), *Global Shift: Mapping the Changing Contours of the World Economy*, 5th edn, London, UK: Sage.

DITRDLG (2008), *Review of Australian Freight Council Performance and Australian Government Funding of Freight Council 2005–06 to 2007–08*, prepared by John Bowdler & Associates Pty Ltd, Canberra, AU: Department of Infrastructure, Transport, Regional Development and Local Government, Australian Government, available at www.infrastructure.gov.au/.../freight/pdf/ind_review_freight_execsumm.pdf (accessed 25 January 2011).

DMR (2013), *The 3P Alliance. How Will Ports Be Affected?* London, Archive Edition 2013–26, 30 June, London, UK: Drewry Maritime

Research, available at http://ciw.drewry.co.uk/port-developments/the-p3-alliance-how-will-ports-be-affected/#.UkDPBLxJMZI (accessed 24 September 2013).

DOSM (2011), *Gross Domestic Product (GDP) by State, 2008*, Kuala Lumpur, MY: Department of Statistics, Malaysia, available at http://www.statistics.gov.my/portal/index.php?option=com_content&view=article&id=861%3Agross-domestic-product-gdp-by-state-2008-updated-17052010&catid=98%3Agross-domestic-product-by-state&lang=en (accessed 27 July 2011).

DOTARS (2002), *Freight Logistics in Australia – An Agenda for Action*, prepared by the Industry Steering Committee of the Freight Transport Logistics Industry Action Agenda, Canberra, AU: Department of Transport and Regional Services, Australian Government, available at http://www.dotars.gov.au/transinfra/pdf/Action_Agenda_Final_Report.pdf (accessed 17 March 2011).

DOTARS (2004), *AusLink White Paper*, Canberra, AU: Australian Government Department of Transport and Regional Services, Australian Government.

DOTARS (2006), *National Intermodal Terminal Study Prepared for Final Report, February 2006*, prepared by Meyrick & Associates with ARUP, Canberra, AU: Department of Transport and Regional Services, Australian Government, available at www.infrastructure.gov.au/.../10781_MA_DOTARS_NIMTS_Final_report_13020_Final.pdf (accessed 13 October 2012).

DOTARS (2007), *Executive Summary: Evaluation of the Australian Logistics Industry Strategy*, prepared by John Bowdler and Associates Pty Ltd, Canberra, AU: Department of Transport and Regional Services, Australian Government, available at www.austlogistics.com.au/.../final_exec_summary%20of%20alis%20review.08022007.pdf (accessed 25 January 2011).

DP (2012), *Delivering Tomorrow: Logistics 2050 A Scenario Study*, Bonn, DE: Deutsche Post AG, available at www.dp dhl.com/en/.../delivering_tomorrow_logistics_2050.html (accessed 23 August 2013).

DPDHL (2011), *Deutsche Port DHL Annual Report 2010*, Bonn, DE: Deutsche DHL, available at www.dp-dhl.com/reports/2010/annual-report/ (accessed 3 October 2012).

DPDHL (2012a), *Deutsche Post DHL – Annual Report 2011*, Bonn, DE: Deutsche DHL, available at www.dp-dhl.com/reports/2011/annual report/indx.html (accessed 19 July 2011).

DPDHL (2012b), *The DHL Capabilities World Map: Network*, available at http://www.dhl.com/worldmap/intro.html#/GLOBAL/networkglobal (accessed 8 October 2012).

DPDHL Global (2012), *Worldwide Mail Network*, available at http://us.dhlglobalmail.com/worldwide-shipping-and-mailing-network.aspx (accessed 7 October 2012).

DPW (2013), *DP World*, available at http://webapps.dpworld.com/portal/page/portal/DP_WORLD_WEBSITE (accessed 5 June 2013).

Drucker, Peter F. (1962), 'The economy's dark continent', *Fortune*, 45 (4), 265–70.

DSC (2006), *Annual Review of Global Container Terminal Operators – 2006*, London, UK: Drewry Shipping Consultants Ltd.

DSC (2011a), *Container Market: 2011–12*, London, UK: Drewry Shipping Consultants Ltd.

DSC (2011b), *Global Container Terminal Operators 2010: Annual Review and Forecast*, London, UK: Drewry Shipping Consultants Ltd.

DTEI (2007), *International and Domestic Shipping and Ports Study*, prepared by Meyrick and Associates for the Australian Maritime Group, Adelaide, AU: Department of Transport, Energy and Infrastructure, Government of South Australia.

Dunn, James (2013), 'Building up the economy requires investment', Australia 2.0 Symposium Special Report, *Australian Financial Review*, 22 October, S3, available at www.afr.com/australia2-0 (accessed 22 October 2013).

EC/EPoSS (2008), *Internet of Things in 2020; Roadmap for the Future*, Joint European Commission /European Technology Platform on Smart Systems Integration Expert Workshop, Brussels, BE: European Commission, available at www.iot-visitthefuture.eu/.../270808_IoT_in_2020_Workshop_Repo... (accessed 3 August 2012).

The Economist (2011), 'Samsung: the next big bet', October, available at http://www.economist.com/node/21530976 (accessed 4 April 2013).

Edmonds, Christopher and Manabu Fujimura (2006), *Impact of Cross-Border Road Infrastructure on Trade and Investment in the Greater Mekong Sub-region*, Discussion Paper Series No. 48, Tokyo, JP: Asian Development Bank Institute, available at www.adbi.org/files/cpp.road.infrastructure.paper.pdf (accessed 6 March 2008).

Edmonds, Christopher and Manabu Fujimura (2008), 'Impact of cross-border road infrastructure on trade and investment in the Greater Mekong Subregion, *Integration and Trade*, 28 (January–June), pp. 267–96, available at http://www.iadb.org/intal/intalcdi/PE/2012/11144a04.pdf (accessed 21 August 2013).

EFT (2009), 'TNT launches domestic day-definite road service in China', 16 February, London, UK: FC Group eyefortransport, available at http://www.eyefortransport.com/content/tnt-launches-domestic-day-definite-road-service-china (accessed 20 March 2013).

EI Euroinfrastructure.eu (2010), *30 Priority Projects under the Trans-European Transport Network TEN-T*, Brussels, BE and Luxembourg, LU: Office of Infrastructure and Logistics, European Union, available at http://www.euroinfrastructure.eu/en/maps/30-priorytetowych-projektow-w-ramach-transeuropejskich-sieci-transportowych-ten-t/ (accessed 17 October 2012).

EIU (2012), *Supersized Cities: China's 13 Megalopolises: A Report from the Economist Intelligence Unit*, London, UK: Economist Intelligence Unit, available at http:www.eiu.com/public/topical_report.aspx?campaignid=Megalopolis2012 (accessed 11 June 2013).

Ellinger, Alexander, Hyunju Shin, William Magnus Northington, Frank G. Adams, Debra Hofman and Kevin O'Marah (2012), 'The influence of supply chain management competency on customer satisfaction and shareholder value', *Supply Chain Management: An International Journal*, 71 (3), 249–62.

Elms, Deborah L. and Patrick Low (eds) (2013), *Global Value Chains in a Changing World*, Geneva, CH: WTO Publications, available at www.wto.org/english/res_e/...e/aid4tradeglobalvalue13_intro_e.pdf (accessed 5 November 2013).

Emerson, Michael and Evgeny Vinokurov (2009), 'Optimisation of Central Asian and Eurasian inter-continental land transport corridors', MPRA Paper No. 20916, available at http://mpra.ub.uni-muenchen.de/20916/ (accessed 28 July 2010).

ERIA (2009), *Mekong–India Economic Corridor Development*, ERIA Research Project Report 2008, No. 4-2, Jakarta, ID: Economic Research Institute for ASEAN and East Asia, available at http://www.eria.org (accessed 12 October 2012).

ERIA (2010), *The Comprehensive Asia Development Plan*, ERIA Research Project Report 2009-7-1, Jakarta, ID: Economic Research Institute for ASEAN and East Asia (ERIA), available at www.eria.org/publications/research_project...1/Appendix2.pdf (accessed 10 October 2012).

ERIA (2011), *ASEAN Strategic Transport Plan, 2011–2015: Final Report, October 2010*, Jakarta ID: Economic Research Institute for *ASEAN* and East Asia (ERIA), available at http://www.eria.org/publications/key_reports/asean-strategic-transport-plan-astp-2011-2015.html (accessed 8 October 2013).

ERINA (2013), 'Vision for Northeast Asia transportation corridors', Economic Research Institute for Northeast Asia, Seminar on Development of a Comprehensive Transport and Logistics Network in North-East Asian Subregion, 22 March, Seoul, KR and Bangkok, TH: United Nations Economic and Social Commission for Asia and the Pacific, available at http://www.unescap.org/ttdw/common/Meetings/

TIS/Logistics-in-NEA-2013/Logistics-in-NEA.asp (accessed 9 October 2013).

Ernst & Young and JETRO (2009), *Japan Attractiveness Survey*, Tokyo, JP: Japan External Trade Organization for Ministry of Trade, Economy and Industry, Government of Japan, available at www.jetro.go.jp/en/reports/survey/pdf/2008_04_2_fdi.pdf (accessed 11 July 2012).

ESCAP (2004), *Manual on Modernization of Inland Water Transport for Integration within a Multimodal Transport System*, New York, NY, USA: United Nations Economic and Social Commission for Asia and the Pacific, available at http://www.unescap.org/ttdw/Publications/TFS_pubs/pub_2285/pub_2285_fulltext.pdf (accessed 30 October 2013).

ESCAP (2006), *Busan Declaration on Transport Development in Asia and the Pacific*, adopted at the Ministerial Conference on Transport, Busan, Republic of Korea, Press Release No. G/56/MCT/26/2006, 11 November, Bangkok, TH: United Nations Economic and Social Commission for Asia and the Pacific, available at http://www.unescap.org/ttdw/common/TIS/TAR/text/busan_declaration_11nov06.pdf (accessed 22 October 2013).

ESCAP and KMI (2007), *Logistics Sector Development: Planning Models for Enterprises and Logistics Clusters*, ST/ESCAP/2457, Bangkok, TH: United Nations Economic and Social Commission for Asia and the Pacific and and Korea Maritime Institute, available at www.unescap.org/ttdw/Publications/TFS.../pub.../pub_2457_ch6.pdf (accessed 30 October 2012).

European Commission (1999), *ESDP – European Spatial Development Perspective Towards Balanced and Sustainable Development of the Territory of the European Union*, Luxembourg, LU: Office for Official Publications of the European Communities, available at ec.europa.eu/regional policy/sources/docoffic/.../pdf/sum_en.pdf (accessed 16 October 2012).

Ewing, Robert and Bryn Batterby (2003), 'Measuring recent trends in Australia's remoteness', Treasury Working Paper, Canberra, AU: Treasury, Australian Government, available at www.treasury.gov.au/documents/958/pdf/03_remoteness.pdf (accessed 10 January 2011).

Faure, Guy (2010), 'The Asian Development Bank and Chinese and Japanese power plays', in Guy Faure (ed.), *New Dynamics Between China and Japan in Asia: How to Build the Future from the Past*, Singapore, SG: World Scientific, pp. 163–86.

FBIC (2013a), *China Logistics Prosperity Index*, Hong Kong, HK: Fung Business Intelligence Centre, available at http://www.funggroup.com/eng/knowledge/research.php?report=lpi_monthly (accessed 12 August 2013).

FBIC (2013b), 'Logistics industry in China', *China Distribution and Trading*, Issue 113, August, Hong Kong, HK: Fung Business Intelligence Centre, available at http://www.funggroup.com/eng/knowledge/research/china_dis_issue113.pdf (accessed 26 November 2013).

FBIC (2013c), 'Transport infrastructure development in China', *China Distribution and Trading*, 116 (October), Hong Kong, HK: Fung Business Intelligence Centre, available at http://www.funggroup.com/eng/knowledge/research/china_dis_issue116.pdf (accessed 26 November 2013).

FedEx (2012), *FedEx Annual Report 2011*, Memphis, TN, USA: FedEx, available at http://www.annualreport.ir.fedex.com/files/FedEx_Annual_Report_2011.pdf (accessed 19 July 2012).

FedEx (2013), *FedEx Locations*, Memphis, TN, USA: FedEx, available at http://www.fedex.com/cn_english/dropoff/ (accessed 15 March 2013).

Feng, Bang-yan (2007), *100 Years of Li & Fung: Rise from Family Business to Multinational*, Singapore, SG: Thomson Learning.

Ferrari, Bob (2009), 'Sony's supply chain challenges', *Supply Chain Matters*, available at www.theferrarigroup.com/supply.../sonys-supply-chain-challenges/ (accessed 14 January 2013).

Ferrari, Bob (2011), 'Sony's supply chain remains in turmoil', *Supply Chain Matters*, available at www.theferrarigroup.com/.../sonys-supply-chain-remains-in-turmoil/ (accessed 14 January 2013).

FHWA (2008), *Freight Mobility and Intermodal Connectivity in China: International Technology Scanning Program*, Reports No. FHWA-PL-08-020, Washington, DC, USA: Federal Highway Administration, US Department of Transportation, available at http://international.fhwa.dot.gov/links/pub_details.cfm?id=561 (accessed 21 March 2013).

Findlay, Christopher C., Lin Sien Chia and Karmjit Singh (eds) (1997), *Asia Pacific Air Transport: Challenges and Policy Reform*, Singapore, SG: Institute of Southeast Asian Studies.

Flath, David (2001), 'Japanese regulation of truck transport', *Journal of the Japanese and International Economies*, 15 (1), 1–28.

FLCWA (2009), *Freight Strategic Grain Network Report*, prepared by Sd+D Consult, Perth, AU: Freight and Logistics Council of Western Australia (on behalf of Strategic Grain Network Committee), available at www.transport.wa.gov.au/.../freight_Strategic_Grain_Network_Repo... (accessed 15 October 2012).

Flextronics (2013), *Flextronics Platform 2013: Annual Report*, Singapore, SG: Flextronics International Ltd, available at http://investors.flextronics.com/annuals.cfm (accessed 25 November 2013).

Florida, Richard L. (2002), *The Rise of the Creative Class*, New York, NY, USA: Basic Books.

Fossey, John (2007), 'Global and seamless', in *Containerisation International: 40 Years Supplement, 1967–2007*, London, UK: Informa, pp. 7–12.

Foster, Thomas A. and Richard Armstrong (2004), 'Top 25 third-party logistics providers extend their global reach', *Supply Chain Brain*, available at http://www.supplychainbrain.com/content/sponsored-channels/kenco-logistic-services-third-party-logistics/single-article-page/article/top-25-third-party-logistics-providers-extend-their-global-reach/ (accessed 15 March 2014).

Foster, Thomas A. and Richard Armstrong (2005), 'Top 25 third-party logistics providers: bigger and broader', *Supply Chain Brain*, available at http://www.supplychainbrain.com/content/logisticstransportation/third-party-logistics/single-article-page/article/top-25-third-party-logistics-providers-bigger-and-broader/ (accessed 15 March 2014).

Foster, Thomas A. and Richard Armstrong (2006), 'The top 25 global 3PLs: is bigger really better?' *Supply Chain Brain*, available at http://www.supplychainbrain.com/content/sponsored-channels/kenco-logistic-services-third-party-logistics/single-article-page/article/the-top-25-global-3pls-is-bigger-really-better/ (accessed 15 March 2014).

Francois, Joseph and Ganesan Wignaraja (2008), 'Pan-Asian integration: economic implications and integration scenarios', in Joseph Francois, Padumna B. Rana and Ganesan Wignaraja (eds), *Pan-Asian Integration: Linking East and South Asia*, London, UK: Palgrave Macmillan, pp. 487–536.

Franklin, Daniel and John Andrews (2012), *The World in 2050*, London, UK: The Economist.

Frémont, Antoine (2007), 'Global maritime networks: the case of Maersk', *Journal of Transport Geography*, 15 (6), 431–42.

Friedman, Thomas L. (2008), *The World is Flat: The Globalized World in the Twenty-First Century*, Melbourne, AU: Penguin Books.

Friscia, Tony, Kevin O'Marah, Debra Hofman and Joe Souza (2008), *The AMR Research Supply Chain Top 25 for 2007*, Boston, MA, USA: AMR Research Inc., available at http://www.supplychainstandard.com/assets/getAsset.aspx?liAssetID=324 (accessed 10 January 2014).

Friscia, Tony, Kevin O'Marah, Debra Hofman and Joe Souza (2010), *The AMR Research Supply Chain Top 25 for 2009*, Boston, MA, USA: AMR Research, available at http://www.slideshare.net/MarjoleinLondon/the-amr-research-supply-chain-top-25-for-2009 (accessed 10 January 2014).

Friscia, Tony, Kevin O'Marah and Joe Souza (2004), 'The AMR Research Supply Chain Top 25 and the New Trillion Dollar Opportunity', AMR Research Report, November, Boston, MA, USA: AMR Research Inc.

Frost & Sullivan (2007), *Shanghai Lingang Industrial Zone*, Mountain

Virew, CA, USA: Frost & Sullivan, available at www.frost.com/sublib/display-market-insight-top.do?id=93822116 (accessed 1 November 2012).

Fujihashi, Kenji (2010), 'Korea–Japan under sea tunnel: basic plan and development strategy', presented at the 2010 PCRD International Conference; Growing Together Across the Sea, Shilla Hotel, Jeju, 7–9 July, Seoul, KR: Presidential Committee on Regional Development, Ministry of Land Transportation and Marine Affairs and Ministry of Knowledge Economy.

Fujimura, Manabu (2006), 'Impact of cross border road infrastructure in GMS', presentation prepared for 17th ECMT/OECD Symposium, Benefiting from Globalization: Transport Sector Contribution and Policy Challenges, 25–27 October, Berlin, Germany.

Fujita, Masahisa (1999), 'Personal communication: commentary on Peter J. Rimmer and Howard Dick, "To plan or not to plan: Southeast Asian cities, communications and land use"', *Entering the 21st Century: World Development Report 1999/2000*, Singapore Workshop, 12–13 January, Co-hosted by World Bank and the Institute of Southeast Asian Studies, Singapore.

Fujita, Masahisa (ed.) (2008), *Economic Integration in Asia and India*, Basingstoke, UK and New York, NY, USA: Palgrave Macmillan.

Fujita, Masahisa (2012), 'Mainstreaming disaster risk management in developing countries: the lessons from the Great East Japan Earthquake', World Bank Seminar, 14 October, Tokyo, JP: World Bank, available at http://siteresources.worldbank.org/JAPANINJAPANESEEXT/Resources/515497-1196389582361/4451844-1331081087023/MasahisaFujita.pdf (accessed 24 February 2014).

Fung, Victor K., William K. Fung and Yoram (Jerry) Wind (2008), *Competing in a Flat World: Building Enterprises for a Borderless World*, Upper Saddle River, NJ, USA: Pearson Education / Wharton School Publishing.

Gartner (2013a), *Gartner Supply Chain Top 25*, Stamford, CT, USA: Gartner, Inc., available at http://www.gartner.com/technology/supply-chain/top25.jsp (accessed 13 August 2013).

Gartner (2013b), *Worldwide PC vendor Unit Shipment Estimates*, Stamford, CT, USA: Gartner, Inc., available at www.gartner.com (accessed 6 September 2013).

Gattorna, John L. (2006), *Living Supply Chains: How to Mobilize the Enterprises Around Delivering What Your Customers Want*, Harlow, UK: Pearson Education Limited.

Gattorna, John L. (2009), 'Revisiting and refining Lee's "Triple-A" supply chain", in John L. Gattorna and Friends (eds), *Dynamic Supply Chain Alignment: A New Business Model for Peak Performance in Enterprise*

Supply Chains Across All Geographies, Farnham, UK and Burlington, VT, USA: Gower Publishing and Ashgate Publishing Company, pp. 123–31.

Gattorna, John L. (2010), *Dynamic Supply Chains: Delivering Value Through People*, 2nd edn, Harlow, UK: Financial Times / Prentice Hall.

GaWC (2008), *The World According to GaWC 2008*, Loughborough, UK: Globalization and World Cities Study Group (GaWC), Geography Department, Loughborough University, available at http://www.lboro.ac.uk/gawc/world2008t.html (accessed 16 October 2012).

GaWC (2011), *GaWC 2010 [Globalization and World Cities (GaWC) Research Network 2010]*, Loughborough, UK: Globalization and World Cities Study Group (GaWC Geography Department, Loughborough University), available at www.lboro.ac.uk/gawc/world2010t.html (accessed 5 July 2012).

Gereffi, Gary and Michelle Christian (2009), 'The impacts of Wal-Mart: the rise and consequences of the world's dominant retailer', *Annual Review of Sociology*, 35, 573–91.

Gereffi, Gary and Joonkoo Lee (2012), 'Why the world suddenly cares about global supply chains', *Journal of Supply Chain Management*, 48 (3), 24–32.

Ghemawat, Pankaj (2007), *Redefining Global Strategy: Crossing Borders in a World Where Differences Still Matter*, Boston, MA, USA: Harvard Business School Press.

Ghemawat, Pankaj and Steven L. Altman (2011), *DHL Global Connectedness Index, 2011*, Bonn, DE: Deutsche Post DHL, available at www.dp-dhl.com/en/media.../global_connectedness_index_2011.htm (accessed 23 August 2013).

Gillen, David, Graham Parsons, Barry Prentice and Peter Wallis (2008), 'The dimensions of value added in gateways and corridors: adding value to national and international logistics system', Canada's Asia-Pacific Gateway and Corridor Initiative Workshop, Vancouver, CA, 13 June, available at http://www.gateway-corridor.com/cgreenworkshop/presentations.htm (accessed 26 April 2011).

Gilmour, Peter (1974), *Physical Distribution Management in Australia*, Sydney, AU: Cheshire.

Glencowets, George A. (1979), 'Physical distribution management', *Defense Transportation Journal*, 35 (4), 5–8, 10–12.

Goh, Mark (2013), 'Supply chains and connectivity Asia', in Deborah L. Elms and Patrick Low (eds), *Global Value Chains in a Changing World*, Geneva, CH: WTO Publications, pp. 245–59, available at www.wto.org/english/res_e/...e/aid4tradeglobalvalue13_intro_e.pdf (accessed 5 November 2013).

Gourdin, K.N. (2001), *Global Logistics Management: A Competitive Advantage for the New Millennium*, Malden, MA, USA: Blackwell.

Government of Canada (2007), 'Canada's Asia-Pacific Gateway and Corridor Initiative and future gateway strategies', International Conference on Gateways and Corridors Vancouver, 2–4 May, Government of Canada, available at www.gateway-corridor.com/.../Bohunicky%20Session%20I.pdf (accessed 19 June 2010).

Government of Canada (2010), *National Policy Framework for Strategic Gateways and Trade Corridors*, Ottawa, CA; Government of Canada, available at http://www.canadasgateways.gc.ca/NationalPolicyFramework/nationalpolicy.html (accessed 20 October 2012).

Government of India (2006), *Report of the Task Force: The Delhi–Mumbai and Delhi–Howrah Freight Corridors*, New Delhi, IN: Secretariat for the Committee on Infrastructure Planning Commission, Government of India, available at www.infrastructure.gov.in/pdf/Freight_Corridor.pdf (accessed 8 April 2011).

Government of Japan (1997), 'Comprehensive program of logistics policies', *Cabinet Decision*, 4 April, Tokyo, JP: Government of Japan.

Government of Japan (2001), 'New comprehensive program of logistics policies', *Cabinet Decision*, July, Tokyo, JP: Government of Japan.

Government of Japan (2005), *Shiryō: sōgō butsuryū shisaku taikō (2005–2009)* [Comprehensive Logistics Policy Outline (2005–2009)], *Cabinet Decision*, 15 November, Tokyo, JP: Government of Japan.

Government of Japan (2007a), *Sōgō butsuryū shisaku taikō (2005–2009) dai 2-kai forōappu (Heisei 19-nen 12-gatsu 18-nichi sōgō butsuryū shisaku suishin kaigi* [Second follow-up to the Comprehensive Logistics Policy Initiative (2005–2009)]. Tokyo, JP: Comprehensive Logistics Policy Promotion Council, 18 December.

Government of Japan (2007b), *Development of Logistics Policies in Japan and Regional Development in the Area*, Seoul, KR: Japanese Embassy in Republic of Korea, December, available at www.fki.or.kr/Common/Download.aspx?id=80557116-01af-4152-bedc-41b7598fa811 (accessed 6 March 2008).

Government of Japan (2009a), *Anzen katsu kōritsutekina* butsuryū *shisaku suishin kyōgikai ni tsuite* [Concerning the Committee for an Efficient and Safe International Logistics Policy], Tokyo, JP: Kokudo kōtsūshō [Ministry of Land, Infrastructure, Transport and Tourism], available at http://www.mlit.go.jp/report/press/tokatsu01_hh_000032.html (accessed 23 November 2012).

Government of Japan (2009b), *Sōgō butsuryū shisaku taikō: sankō shiryō* [Outline of the Comprehensive Logistics Policy: reference materials], Tokyo, JP: Kokudō kōtsūshō [Ministry of Land, Infrastructure,

Transport and Tourism], available at http://www.mlit.gov.jp/seisakutokatsu/freight/seisakutokatsu_freight_tk1_00024.html (accessed 23 November 2012).

Government of Japan (2013a), *Sōgō butsuryū shisaku taikō (2013–2017)* ni tsuite, Heisei 25-nen 6-gatsu 25-nichi kakugi kettei [Comprehensive Logistics Policy (2013–2017) 25 June 2013], Tokyo, JP: Keizai sangyōshō [Ministry of Economy, Trade and Industry], http://www.meti.go.jp/press/2013/06/20130625003/20130625003-2.pdf (accessed 11 September 2013).

Government of Japan (2013b), *Sōgō butsuryū shisaku taikō (2013–2017) ni tsuite* [Outline of comprehensive logistics measures (2013–2017)], Tokyo, JP: Keizai sangōshō [Ministry of Economy, Trade and Industry], http://www.meti.go.jp/press/2013/06/20130625003/20130625003-3.pdf (accessed 11 September 2013).

Government of New Zealand (2010), *National Infrastructure Plan, March 2010*, Wellington, NZ, Government of New Zealand, available at http://www.infrastructure.govt.nz/plan/mar2010/nip-mar10.pdf (accessed 18 November 2013).

Goyal, Anjali (2009), 'Dedicated freight corridors and high speed rail: India's ultra low carbon mega rail projects', paper delivered at the World Bank Transport Forum, Washington DC, USA, 30 March–1 April 2009, available at siteresources.worldbank.org/INTTRANSPORT/.../Goyal_India.pdf (accessed 8 April 2011).

Grubesic, Tony H. and Timothy C. Matisziw (2008), 'Prospects for assessing and managing vulnerable infrastructures: policy and practice', *Growth and Change*, 39 (4), 543–47.

Grubesic, Tony H. and Alan T. Murray (2006), 'Vital nodes, interconnected infrastructures, and the geographies of network survivability', *Annals of the Association of American Geographers*, 96 (1), 64–83.

GTA (2013), *Management of Grain Within the Australian Grain Supply Chain: Australian Grain Industry Code of Practice*, Melbourne, AU: Grain Trade Australia Ltd, available at http://www.graintrade.org.au/sites/default/files/file/Codes/Grain%20Industry%20Code%20of%20Practice/Code%20of%20Practice%20-%20July%202013%20final.pdf (accessed 31 October 2013).

Guo, Xichun (2012), 'Analysis for the third-party logistics enterprises of Chengdu', International Conference on Education Technology and Management Engineering, *Lecture Notes in Information Technology*, 16/17, 54–8, available at www.ier-institute.org/2070-1918/lnit16/v16/054.pdf (accessed 18 August 2013).

Gupta, Prashant, Rajat Gupta and Thomas Netzer (2009), *Building India: Accelerating Infrastructure Projects*, Mumbai and Gurgaon, IN:

McKinsey India, available at www.mckinsey.com/~/.../Infrastructure/.../01%20Building%20India.ashx \ (accessed 5 November 2013).

Gupta, Rajat, Hemang Mehta and Thomas Netzer (2010), *Building India: Transforming the Nation's Logistics Infrastructure*, Mumbai, IN: McKinsey India, available at http://www.mckinsey.com/global_locations/asia/india/en (access 5 November 2013).

Ha, Dongwoo (2008), 'Prospects and challenges of Pan-Asian transport network: Asian Highway and Trans-Asian Railway', delivered at the Inception Workshop of the ADBI's Flagship Study on 'Infrastructure and Regional Cooperation', 18–20 February, Tokyo, JP: Asian Development Bank Institute.

HACIS (2012), *HACIS [Hong Kong Air Cargo Industry Services Ltd] – Home*, Hong Kong, HK: Hong Kong Air Cargo Industry Services Ltd. available at www.hacis.com (accessed 1 November 2012).

Haier (2011), *Haier Electronics Group Co. Ltd: Annual Report 2010*, Qingdao, CN: Haier Group, available at http://www.haier.net/en/investor_relations/1169/finance_reports/201109/P020110909027161821250.pdf (accessed 14 March 2013).

Halifax Gateway (2012), *The Halifax Gateway*, Halifax, CA: Halifax Gateway Council, available at http://www.halifaxgateway.com/site-ghp2/media/HalifaxGateway/transportation%20profile_web.pdf (accessed 7 November 2013).

Hall, Peter, Robert J. McCalla, Claude Comtois and Brian Slack (2011), *Integrating Seaports and Trade Corridors*, Farnham, UK and Burlington, VT, USA: Ashgate Publishing Ltd.

Hamilton, Mary Krome (2005), 'A framework for studying global value networks: expanding the supply chain management paradigm', JRI International Seminar: Three Invited Lectures on Global Logistics and Supply Chain Management, 18 May, Incheon KR: Jungseok Research Institute of International Logistics and Trade.

Hanaoka, Shinya and Madan B. Regmi (2012), 'Promoting intermodal freight transport through the development of dry ports in Asia: an environmental perspective', *IATSS [International Association of Traffic and Safety Sciences] Research*, 35 (1), 16–23.

Handfield, Robert and Kevin McCormack (2008), *Supply Chain Risk Management: Minimizing Disruption in Global Supply Chains*, Boca Raton, FL, USA: Auerbach Publications.

Hanjin Group (2005), *The Hanjin Group*, Seoul, KR: Hanjin Group, available at www.hanjin.co.kr/english/aboutus/group.htm (accessed 26 August 2006).

Haratsis, Brian (2010), *Australia 2050: Big Australia? Volume 1*, Adelaide, AU: Digital Print.

Harbison, Peter (2011), 'Reality hits as Qantas settles for the long haul', *Sydney Morning Herald*, 19 August, available at http://www.smh.com.au/opinion/reality-hits-as-qantas-settles-in-for-long-haul-20110818-1j012.html (accessed 29 April 2013).

Hawkins, Jeff and Richard Gray (2000), *Strategies for Asia Pacific Shipping*, Aldershot, UK and Burlington, VT, USA: Ashgate Publishing Ltd.

HC (2007), *M&A Analysis and Research on Express Industry of PRC, 2006–2007*, Beijing, CN: Hearing Century, available at http://info.research.hc360.com/2007/06/06152437551.shtml (accessed 15 February 2009).

Heitzman, James (2008), *The City in South Asia*, London, UK and New York, NY, USA: Routledge.

Hejazi, Michael (2006), 'UPS and China: your ticket to growing market', Eye for Transport 2nd China Summit, Shanghai, 18 April, available at http://eyefortransport.com (accessed 20 November 2007).

Henshu, Iin-kai (1986), *Senshu toneru monogatari* [An account of the Seikan Tunnel], Tokyo, JP: Yoshie Shoten.

Higginson, James K. (2013), 'Cross-border issues and research', in James H. Bookbinder (ed.), *Handbook of Global Logistics: Transportation in International Supply Chains*, New York, NY, USA: Springer, pp. 391–416.

HIST (2012), *Hanjin Information Systems & Telecommunication Co. Ltd*, Seoul, KR: Hanjin Group, available at www.hist.co.kr/ENG/aboutus/about_02.aspx (accessed 12 November 2012).

HJS (1995), *1995 (Annual Report)*, Seoul, KR: Hanjin Shipping.

HJS (2009), *IR [Investor Relations] Presentation, May 2009*, Seoul KR: Hanjin Shipping, available at https://www.hanjin.com/hanjin/CUP_HOM_1779.do?sessLocale=en (accessed 5 June 2013).

HJS (2010), *Hanjin haeun 60-yŏn sa 1949–2009* [Hanjin Shipping: history of 60 years, 1949–2009], Seoul, KR: Hanjin Haeun.

HJS (2011), *2010 Business Report 2010.1.1–2010.12.31: Beyond the Ocean*, Seoul, KR: Hanjin Shipping, available at www.hanjin.com/hanjin/CUP_HOM_1110.do?sessLocale=en (accessed 12 November 2012).

HKIA (2012), *Hong Kong International Airport*, Hong Kong, HK: Airport Authority, Hong Kong, available at http://www.hongkongairport.com/eng/business/about-the-airport/air-cargo/air-cargo-intro.html (accessed 19 December 2012).

Ho, Mei Yueh (2003), *The Global Logistics Center: Challenges and Development*, Taipei, TW: Council for Economic Planning and Development.

Hofman, Debra, Kevin O'Marah and Carla Ehry (2011), *The Gartner Supply Chain Top 25 for 2011*, Boston, MA, USA: Gartner Inc., available at http://www.gartner.com/id=1709016 (accessed 2 October 2012).

Hoshino, Tatsuya (2012), 'Series: The Mekong Region and Japan Part 4: Vietnam (1): The Vietnamese economy today and Japan's economic cooperation', *IIST e-Magazine*, Institute for International Studies and Training, 31 July, available at www.iist.or.jp/en-m/2012/0214-0874/ (accessed 15 October 2013).

Hou, Quan and Si-Ming Li (2011), 'Transport infrastructure development and changing spatial accessibility in the Greater Pearl River Delta, China, 1990–2020', *Journal of Transport Geography*, 19 (6), 1350–60.

Howard, Elizabeth (ed.) (2010), *The Changing Face of Retailing in the Asia Pacific*, Abingdon, UK and New York, NY, USA: Routledge.

Hribernik, Karl A., Tobias Warden, Klaus-Dieter Thoben and Otthein Herzog (2010), 'An Internet of Things for transport logistics – an approach to connecting the information and material flows in autonomous cooperating logistics processes', *Proceedings MITIP 2010 – 12th International MITIP Conference on Information Technology & Innovation Processes of the Enterprises, 29–31 August 2010*, Centre for Logistics, Aalborg University, Denmark, pp. 54–67, available at www.sfb637.uni-bremen.de/pubdb/.../SFB637-C2-10-004-IC.pdf (accessed 3 August 2012).

Htun, Kyaw Min, Nu Nu Lwin, Htoo Naing Tin and Khine Tun (2011), 'ASEAN–India connectivity: a Myanmar perspective', in Fukunari Kimura and So Umezaki (eds), *ASEAN–India Connectivity: The Comprehensive Asia Development Plan, Phase II, ERIA Research Project Report 2010-7*, Jakarta, ID: Economic Research Institute for *ASEAN* and East Asia (*ERIA*), pp. 151–203, available at www.eria.org/ (accessed 12 October 2012).

Huang, Diana and Mark Kadar (2002–03), 'Third-party logistics in China: still a tough market', *Mercer on Travel and Transport*, 9 (2), 3–10, available at http://www.inderscience.com/filter.php?aid=5970 (accessed 16 February 2009).

Huang, Yasheng (2013), 'China's great rebalancing: promise and peril', *McKinsey Quarterly*, June, available at http://www.mckinsey.com/insights/asia-pacific/chinas_great_rebalancing_promise_and_peril?cid=other-eml-nsl-mip-mck-oth-1306 (accessed 8 June 2013).

Hummels, David (2001), *Time as a Trade Barrier*, West Lafayette, IN, USA: Department of Economics, Purdue University, available at www.krannert.purdue.edu/faculty/hummelsd/.../time3b.... - United States (accessed 16 October 2012).

Huntley, Stephen (2006), 'The Australian grocery supply chain: a study into the changes and associated implications', paper presented at AIP (Australian Institute of Packaging) National Conference held at Conrad Jupiters on the Gold Coast, Queensland, 15–16 June, available at www.

aipack.com.au/Content/Attachment/Stephen_Huntley.pdf (accessed 14 October 2012).

HWL (2011), *Annual Report 2010*, Hong Kong: Hutchison Whampoa Ltd, available at http://www.hutchison-whampoa.com/en/ir/annual.php (accessed 9 September 2013).

Hyundai (2011), *Hyundai Motor Company Annual Report 2010*, Seoul, KR: Hyundai Motor Company, available at http://worldwide.hyundai.com/WW/Corporate/InvestorRelations/FinancialInformation/Financial Statements/index.html (accessed 18 November 2012).

Hyundai Glovis (2012), *2011 Annual Report*, Seoul, KR: Hyundai Glovis Co. Ltd, available at ir.glovis.net/Common/FileDownload.aspx?... GLOVIS.., (accessed 18 November 2012).

IATA (2011), *WATS: World Air Transport Statistics: Digest and Key Performance Indicators CD-ROM*, 55th edn, Montreal, CA: International Air Transport Association.

IBISWorld (2010), *Road Freight Transport in Australia*, Melbourne, AU: IBISWorld, available at http://www.ibisworld.com.au/industry/default.aspx?indid=456 (accessed 1 March 2010).

ICAO (2013), 'Liberalization of cargo services', Worldwide Air Transport Conference Sixth Meeting, Montréal, 18–22 March, Montréal, CA: International Civil Aviation Organization.

Ichikawa, Hiroo and Yasyuki Miwa (2011), 'Business and travel linkages among world cities', in Won Bae Kim, Yue-man Yeung and Sang-Chuel Choe (eds), *Collaborative Regional Development in Northeast Asia: Towards a Sustainable Regional and Sub-Regional Future*, Hong Kong, HK: Hong Kong University Press, pp. 151–75.

ICL (2013), *Institute for City Logistics*, Kyoto JP: Kyoto University, available at http://www.citylogistics.org/index.html (accessed 30 August 2013).

ICS and ISF (2012), *Overview of the International Shipping Industry*, London, UK: International Chamber of Shipping and International Shipping Federation, available at http://www.marisec.org/shippingfacts/home/ (accessed 28 February 2012).

IEAT (2014), *Industrial Estate Authority Thailand*, available at http://www.ieat.go.th/ieat/index.php/en/ (accessed 24 February 2014).

IIRSA (2012), *The Initiative for the Integration of Regional Infrastructure in South America*, Buenos Aires, AR: Technical Coordination Committee, available at http://www.iirsa.org/Areas_ENG.asp?CodIdioma=ENG (accessed 24 October 2012).

IIST (2007), 'Action plan of partnership on international logistics competitiveness', IIST (Institute for International Studies and Training) World Forum, Tokyo, JP: Ministry of Economy, Trade and Industry, Distribution and Logistics Policy Office, Commerce and Distribution

Policy Group, Government of Japan, available at http://www.iist.or.jp/wf/magazine/0508/0508_E.html (accessed 15 October 2013).

Imamura, Yuji (2012), 'Series: The Mekong Region and Japan Part 9: Cambodia (3) Cambodia's investment environment and the current status of and challenges facing Japanese Companies in Cambodia', *IIST e-Magazine*, Institute for International Studies and Training, 27 December, available at www.iist.or.jp/en-m/2012/0214-0874/ (accessed 15 October 2013).

Infrastructure Australia (2010a), *Developing a National Freight Network Strategy: Perspectives of Freight Network Customers, May 2010*, prepared by the Allen Consulting Group, Canberra, AU: Infrastructure Australia, Australian Government, available at www.infrastructureaustralia.gov.au/.../National_Freight_Network_Strategy_WEB.pdf (accessed 23 February 2011).

Infrastructure Australia (2010b), *Road Access Improvement Regime: Issues Paper, September 2010*, prepared by the Allen Consulting Group, Canberra, AU: Infrastructure Australian, Australian Government, available at www.infrastructureaustralia.gov.au/.../Road_Access_Improvement_Regime Final_Issues_Paper_06092010.pdf (accessed 24 February 2011).

Infrastructure Australia (2011), *National Land Freight Strategy: Discussion Paper February 2011*, Canberra, AU: Infrastructure Australia, Australian Government, available at www.infrastructureaustralia.gov.au/national_freight/files/NLFS_220211.pdf (accessed 23 February 2011).

Infrastructure Australia (2012), *National Land Freight Strategy Update, June 2012*, Canberra, AU: Infrastructure Australia, Australian Government, available at http://www.infrastructureaustralia.gov.au/publications/files/National_Land_Freight_Strategy_Update_2012.pdf (accessed 1 November 2013).

Infrastructure Australia and NTC (2010), *National Ports Strategy: Background Paper 2010*, Canberra, AU: Infrastructure Australia and National Transport Commission, available at http://www.infrastructureaustralia.gov.au/national_ports/ (accessed 20 January 2011).

Infrastructure Australia and NTC (2012), *National Ports Strategy: Infrastructure for an Economically, Socially and Environmentally Sustainable Future 2011*, Canberra, AU: Infrastructure Australia and National Transport Commission available at http://www.ntc.gov.au/viewpage.aspx?documentid=1967 (accessed 1 November 2013).

INRETS (2009), *The French National Institute for Transport and Safety Research: INNOFRET Project –Visit to Tokyo on Freight Transport*, report, 19–25 January, Paris FR: Institut national du recherce sur les transport et leur sécurité.

Irawady, Edy Putra (2010), 'Strengthening Indonesian logistics', UNESCAP Regional Forum of Freight Forwarders, Multimodal Transport Operators and Logistics Service Providers, Bali, Indonesia, 15 July, available at http://www.unescap.org/ttdw/FFmeeting/FFForum_2010/2.pdf (accessed 17 October 2013).

ISC (2002), *Freight Logistics in Australia: An Agenda for Action, May 2002*, Canberra, AU: Industry Steering Committee of the Freight Transport Industry Action Agenda, available at www.ozlogistics.org/pdf/Action_Agenda_Final_Report.pdf (accessed 28 February 2011).

Ishida, Masami (2010), 'Evaluating effectiveness of GMS economic corridors: why more focus on Bangkok–Hanoi Road than East–West Corridor?' in Guy Faure (ed.), *New Dynamics Between China and Japan in Asia: How to Build the Future from the Past*, Singapore, SG: World Scientific, pp. 233–48.

ISNMS (2007), *General Survey Report on Logistics Industry in Japan: July 2007*, Tokyo, JP: Institute of Supply Network Management and Strategy, Tama University.

Isono, Ikumo (2011), 'Economic integration and the expansion of trade and transport networks', in Masahisa Fujita, Ikuo Kuroiwa and Satoru Kumagai (eds), *The Economics of East Asian Integration: A Comprehensive Introduction to Regional Issues*, Cheltenham, UK and Northampton MA: Edward Elgar Publishing, pp. 340–64.

ITU (2005), *ITU Internet Reports 2005: The Internet of Things*, Geneva, CH: International Telecommunications Union.

IUILC (2012), *Mullyuhak wollon* [The principles of logistics], *Inha Taehakkyo Mullyu Sanhak Hyomnyok Sento* [Inha University Industrial Logistics Center], 2nd edn, Seoul, KR: Kyongje Kyongyong Chulpansa.

Jeong, Seung Ju and Hong Seung Roh (2010), 'A long-range strategy to restructure the national logistics system', in Korea Transport Institute (ed.), *Towards a Green Transportation Logistics System in Korea (II)*, Seoul, KR: Korea Institute of Transport, pp. 181–6, available at english.koti.re.kr/board/special/index.asp?mode=view... (accessed 18 November 2012).

JETORO (2009a), *ASEAN butsuryū nettowāku mappu* [ASEAN logistics network map], 2nd edn, Tokyo, JP: JETORO (Nihon Bōeki Shinkō Kikō) [Japan External Trade Organization].

JETORO (2009b), *Indo butsuryū nettowāku mappu* [India logistics network map], Tokyo, JP: JETORO (Nihon Bōeki Shinkō Kikō) [Japan External Trade Organization].

JETRO (2008), *ASEAN Logistics Network Map*, Tokyo, JP: Japan External Trade Organization.

JETRO (2013), *Survey of Japanese-Affiliated Companies in Asia and Oceania*

(FY 2012 Survey) December, 2012, Tokyo, JP: Japan External Trade Organization, available at http://www.jetro.go.jp/en/reports/survey/pdf/2013_01_01_biz.pdf (accessed 8 January 2014).

Jetstar (2013), *Jetstar*, Melbourne, AU, Jetstar Airways, available at http://www.jetstar.com/mediacentre/facts-and-stats/jetstar-group (accessed 18 April 2013).

JFTC (2006), *Issues Concerning Postal Services and Competition Policy Coinciding with the Enactment of the Law of the Privatization of the Postal Services – Countering Anticompetitive Acts Using the Monopoly Area – (tentative translation version)*, Tokyo, JP: Japan Fair Trade Commission, available at www.jftc.go.jp/en/pressreleases/uploads/2006-July-21.pdf (accessed 10 December 2012).

Jiang, Xiao-mei (2013), 'Development status of China's logistics market', in Bing-lian Liu, Shao-ju Lee, Jian-hua Xiao, Ling Wang, Zhi-lun Jiao (eds), *Contemporary Logistics in China: Transformation and Revitalization*, Berlin and Heidelberg, DE: Springer-Verlag, pp. 17–31.

Jiao, Zhi-lun, Jian-hua Xiao and Qin Fan (2013), 'Logistics development in some key industrial segments', in Bing-lian Liu, Shao-ju Lee, Jian-hua Xiao, Ling Wang and Zhi-lun Jiao (eds), *Contemporary Logistics in China: Transformation and Revitalization*, Berlin and Heidelberg, DE: Springer Verlag, pp. 101–45.

JICA (2007), *The Research on the Cross-border Transportation Infrastructure: Phase 2: Final Report*, Tokyo, JP: Japan International Cooperation Agency and ALMEC Corporation, available at www.jica.go.jp/infosite/issues/transport/pdf/SDcbti_eng01.pdf (accessed 25 March 2008).

JIFFA (2012a), *Wagakuni fowādā no kaigai shinshutsu jōkyō to gaikoku fowādā no Nihon shinshutsu jōkyō*. [Japanese forwarders making inroads into other countries and foreign forwarders making inroads into Japan], Tokyo, JP: Japan International Freight Forwarders Association Inc.

JIFFA (2012b), *ASEAN Logistics Survey: Volume 5 Myanmar*, Tokyo, JP: Japan International Freight Forwarders Association Inc.

JILS (2010), *Makuro butsuryū kosuto no suii (1991–2007-nendo)* [Trends in logistics costs, 1991–2007], Tokyo, JP: Japan Logistics Industry Systems, available at http://www.logistics.or.jp/soken2/category.html (accessed 19 November 2012).

JLL (2008), *Post-earthquake Chengdu Logistics Infrastructure Facilities Report*, Chengdu, CN: Jones Lang La Salle, available at http://www.all-roadsleadtochina.com/reports/Chengdu_Logistics_Report.pdf (accessed 16 August 2013).

Jones, Ronald W. and Henryk Kierzkowski (1990), 'The role of services in international trade: a theoretical framework', in Ronald W. Jones and Anne O. Krueger (eds), *The Political Economy of International Trade*,

Oxford, UK: Basil Blackwell, pp. 31–48, available at http://www.econ.rochester.edu/people/jones/Role_of_Services.pdf (accessed 11 February 2014).

JRF-RC (2009), *Gekidōsuru Nihon keizai to butsuryū*: [Turbulent Japanese economy and logistics], JR Freight Author Research Center Co. Ltd, Tokyo, JP: Seizandō Publishing Company.

Jung, Ha-Young (2008), 'Korean logistics policy of Roh Moo-Hyun government', unpublished paper presented at the 2008 International Conference on Shipping, Port and Logistics Management, Kainan University, Taiwan, 28–29 March, available at www.dbpia.co.kr/view/ar_view.asp?arid=1783509 (accessed 12 March 2012).

KAL (1994), *1994 Annual Report*, Seoul, KR: Korean Air.

KAL (2010), *Korean Air: Morning Calm Magazine*, June, Seoul, KR: Korean Air.

KAL (2011), *Investor Relations: Korean Airlines 2010 4Q Results 2011 Business Plan, 27 February 2011*, Seoul, KR: Korean Air Line Co. Ltd, available at http://www.koreanair.com/local/na/gd/eng/au/ir/eng_au_ir.jsp (accessed 18 November 2012).

KAL (2012), *Investor Relations*, Seoul, KR: Korean Air, available at http://www.koreanair.com/(accessed 12 November 2012).

Kam, Booi and Peter J. Rimmer (2011), 'China's logistics enterprise structure: institutional impediment to multimodalism', in Theo Notteboom (ed.), *Current Issues in Shipping, Ports and Logistics*, Antwerp, BE: Utgeverij UPA University Press Antwerp, pp. 447–63.

Kapuscinski, Roman, Rachel Q. Zhang, Paul Carbonneau, Robert Moore and Bill Reeves (2004), 'Inventory decisions in Dell's supply chain', *Interfaces*, 34 (3), 191–205.

Kareem, Mohamed Shahabar Abdul (2010), 'Logistics and supply chain development in Malaysia', UNESCAP Regional Forum of Freight Forwarders, Multimodal Transport Operators and Logistics Service Providers, Bali, Indonesia, 15 July, http://www.unescap.org/ttdw/FFmeeting/FFForum_2010/3.pdf (accessed 17 October 2013).

Kasarda, John D. (2000–2001), 'Logistics and the rise of the Aerotropolis', *Real Estate Issues*, 25 (4), 43–8.

Kasarda, John D. (2010), 'The way forward', *Global Airport Cities*, London, UK: Insight Media, pp. 15–35, available at http://www.aerotropolis.com/files/GlobalAirportCities.pdf (accessed 12 February 2014).

Kasarda, John D. (2011), *List of Airport Cities and Aerotropolises*, available at http://www.aerotropolis.com/files (accessed 28 April 2013).

Kasarda, John D. (2013a), *Aerotropolis: Publications*, available at www.aerotropolis.com/airportCities/publications (accessed 28 April 2013).

Kasarda, John D. (2013b), 'Aerotropolis: business mobility and urban competitiveness in the 21st Century', in Klaus Benesch (ed.), *Cultures of Mobility*, Heidelberg, DE: Heidelberg University Press, pp. 9–20.

Kasarda, John and Greg Lindsay (2011), *Aerotropolis: The Way We'll Live Next*, London, UK: Allen Lane.

Katz, Rachel (2011), *Long-haul China*, available at http://www.Longhaulchina.com (accessed 3 August 2013).

Kayahara, Hideo (2004), 'The meanings of the Northeast Asia transportation corridors: economic growth and transportation infrastructures', 13th Northeast Asia Economic Form (NEAF), Inter-Continental Hotel, Seoul, 17–18 September, available at http://www.neaef.org/public/neaef/files/documents/publications_pdf/annual_meeting/13th-2004/3-3_Kayahara%20Paper.pdf (accessed 22 August 2013).

KCCG, SDAG and SCAG (2005), *The Southern California Mega-region – A Case Study of Global Gateway Regions: America's Third Century Strategy*, Los Angeles, CA, USA: Kent County Council of Governments, San Diego Association of Governments and Southern California Association of Governments, available at www.cqgrd.gatech.edu/sites/files/.../southern_california_2005.pdf (accessed 16 October 2012).

KCCI (2013), *Survey of Corporate Opinion about the New Government's Industrial Policy Directions*, Seoul, KR: Korea Chamber of Commerce and Industry, available at http://english.korcham.net/sub02/report_view.asp?nKey=1566 (accessed 4 April 2013).

KFEZ (2012), *Korean Free Economic Zones*, available at http://www.fez.go.kr/en/incheon-fez.jsp (accessed 12 November 2012).

Khanna, Tarun and Khrishna C. Palepu (2010), *Winning in Emerging Markets: A Road Map for Strategy and Execution*, Boston, MA, USA: Harvard Business Books.

Kim, Chin-Bang (2005), *Chaebŏl ŭi soyu kujo* [The ownership structure of Korean *Chaebol*], accompanying disk with *Hanguk ui Chaebol* five-volume series, Seoul, KR: Nanam Chulpan.

Kim, Hee-Jong (2012), 'Hyundai Glovis aims to expand business beyond Hyundai Motor', *Forbes*, 29 August, available at http://www.forbes.com/sites/heejoungkim/2012/08/29/hyundai-glovis-aims-to-expand-business-beyond-hyundai-motor/ (accessed 15 November 2012).

Kim, Soo Yeob (2009), 'Workshop on the China–Korea–Japan Intra Logistics Research, 30 March, 2009', Seoul, KR: Korea Maritime Institute, available at www.kmi.re.kr/data/gongi/(20090329-0401)%20일본-김수엽,이호 춘.pdf (accessed 8 May 2010).

Kim, Won Bae, Sung-Wook Hong and Kyung-Min Nam (2003), *Building Infrastructure for the Facilitation of Economic Cooperation in Northeast Asia in the 21st Century: Focusing on Land Transport Linkages between*

Korea and China, KRIHS Special Reports No. 3, Seoul KR: Korea Research Institute for Human Settlements.

Kimura, Fukunari (2013), 'Supply chain connectivity; genesis and concept', Symposium on Building APEC and ASEAN Connectivity; Areas of Mutual Interest and Prospects of Cooperation, 3 April, Singapore, SG: Institute for Southeast Asian Studies (ISEAS), available at www.iseas.edu.sg/ISEAS/upload/files/Kimura.pdf (accessed 15 January 2014).

Kimura, Fukunari, Ponciano S. Intal Jr, So Umezaki and Misa Okabe (2009), *The Comprehensive Asia Development Plan [CADP]*, ERIA Research Project 2009 No 7-1, Jakarta, ID: Economic Research Institute for ASEAN and East Asia, available at http://www.eria.org/research/y2009-no7-1.html (accessed 4 April 2011).

Kimura, Fukunari and So Umezaki (eds) (2011), *ASEAN–India connectivity: The Comprehensive Asia Development Plan, Phase II*, ERIA Research Project Report 2010-7, Jakarta, ID: Economic Research Institute for *ASEAN* and East Asia, available at www.eria.org/ (accessed 12 October 2012).

King, Rodney (2008), *The Singapore Miracle, Myth and Reality*, Inglewood, AU: Insight Press.

KKW (2012), *Kungnae chaegye sunwi 2012-yon, 4-wol* [The financial position as at 4 April 2012], Seoul, KR: Kongjong Korae Wiwonhoe [Korean Fair Trade Commission], available at http://201480.tistory.com/17 (accessed 29 May 2013).

KL (2013), *Kerry Logistics. Hong Kong, HK: Kerry Properties Ltd*, available at www.kerrylogistics.com (accessed 28 February 2013).

Klaus, Peter and Stefanie Müller (2012), 'Towards a science of logistics: milestones along converging paths', in Peter Klaus and Stefanie Müller (eds), *The Roots of Logistics: A Reader of Classical Contributions to the History and Conceptual Foundations of the Science of Logistics*, Berlin, DE and Heidelberg, DE: Springer-Verlag, pp. 3–26, available at http://www.springer.com/cda/content/.../cda.../9783642279218-c1.pdf?...0... (accessed 30 August 2012).

Kledal, Robert (2005), 'A foreign perspective on China's ports and shipping', *China Business Review*, available at https://www.chinabusinessreview.com/public/0507/interview-maersk.html (accessed 13 March 2013).

Kohli, Harinder S., Ashok Sharma and Anil Sood (2011), *Asia 2050: Realizing the Asian Century*, Metro Manila, PH: Asian Development Bank.

Koide, Haruya (2008), 'Strategic transport and trade development in Central and West Asia', paper delivered at the Inception Workshop of the ADBI's Flagship Study, on Infrastructure and Regional Cooperation, 18–20 February, Tokyo, JP: Asian Development Bank Institute.

Kono, Tatsuo and Tadashi Okutani (2006), 'VIII-3 Evaluation of freight transport network', unpublished paper, available at www.nilim.go.jp/english/conference/asia2006/8-3.pdf (accessed 23 November 2009).

KOTI (2009), 'Integrated international transport and logistics system for North-East Asia', paper delivered at Seminar on Overcoming Border Crossing Obstacles, 5–9 March, Paris, FR: UN ESCAP, available at www.unescap.org/ttdw/common/TIS/Corridor Study/.../16-KOTI-pdf (accessed 8 May 2010).

KOTI-KSP (2012), 'Logistics policy in Korea', unpublished presentation, May, Seoul, KR: Korea Transport Institute Knowledge Sharing Program.

Kotler, Philip, Michael Alan Hamlin, Irving Rein and Donald H. Haider (2002), *Marketing Asian Places: Attracting Investment, Industry and Tourism to Cities, States and Nations*, Singapore, SG and New York, NY, USA: Wiley.

KPMG (2011), *On the Move in China*, Beijing, CN: KPMG, available at www.kpmg.de/27847.htm (accessed 19 March 2013).

KRIHS (2013), *2012 Modularization of Korea's Development Experience: National Territorial and Regional Development Policy: Focusing on Comprehensive National Territorial Plan, 2013*, Seoul, KR: Korea Research Institute for Human Settlement (KRIHS), Ministry of Strategy and Finance, Government of South Korea, available at https://www.kdevelopedia.org/.../2013/.../04201306170126738076499.... (accessed 5 November 2013).

Kuhn, Robert L. (2004), *The Man Who Changed China: The Life and Legacy of Jiang Zemin*, New York, NY, USA: Crown Publishers.

Kunaka, Charles (2010), *Making Corridors Work*, Washington, DC, USA: World Bank, available at www.siteresources.worldbank.org/.../Resources/.../Charles_Kunaka.pdf (accessed 1 November 2011).

Kunaka, Charles, Robin Carruthers and Johnathan Stevens (2012), *Trade Corridor Management Toolkit: Overview*, Washington, DC, USA: World Bank, available at http://siteresources.worldbank.org/EXTTLF/Resources/515433-1274994820828/Trade_Corridor_Management_Toolkit.pdf (accessed 21 August 2013).

Kuroiwa, Ikuo and Satoru Kumagai (2011), 'A history of de facto economic integration in East Asia', in Masahisa Fujita, Ikuo Kuroiwa and Satoru Kumagai (eds), *The Economics of East Asian Integration*, Cheltenham, UK and Northampton, MA, UK: Edward Elgar Publishing, pp. 15–50.

KW (2012), 'Myriad bottlenecks: tackling logistics in China', *Knowledge Wharton: Strategic Management*, available at www.knowledgeatwharton.com.cn/index.cfm?fa=viewfeature (accessed 7 March 2013).

La Fortune, Sandra (2010), 'Canada's gateway update: connecting Canada

to global opportunities', Asia-Pacific Gateway and Corridor Initiative Workshop, Toronto, CA, 18 June, available at http://www.gateway-corridor.com/torontoworkshop/presentations.htm (accessed 20 October 2012).
LaLonde, Bemard J. and Leslie M. Dawson (1969), 'Early development of physical distribution thought', in Donald J. Bowersox, Bemard J. LaLonde and Edward W. Smykay (eds), *Readings in Physical Distribution: Logistics of Marketing*, New York, NY, USA: Macmillan, pp. 9–18.
LaLonde, Bemard J. and Paul H. Zinszer (1976), *Customer Service: Meaning and Measurement*, Chicago, IL, USA: National Council of Physical Distribution Management.
Lam, Wop-Lap Willy (1995), *China after Deng Xiaoping: The Power Struggle in Beijing since Tiananmen*, Singapore, SG and New York, NY, USA: J. Wiley & Sons.
Lam, Wop-Lap Willy (1999), *The Era of Jiang Zemin*, Singapore, SG and New York, NY, USA: Prentice Hall.
Lam, Wop-Lap Willy (2006), *Chinese Politics in the Hu Jintao Era: New Leaders, New Challenges*, Armonk, NY, USA: M.E. Sharpe.
Lambert, Douglas, M. (ed.) (2008), *Supply Chain Management: Processes, Partnerships, Performance*, 3rd edn, Sarasota, FL, USA: Supply Chain Management Institute.
Lambert, Douglas M., Martha C. Cooper and Janus D. Pagh (1998), 'Supply chain management: implementation issues and research opportunities', *International Journal of Logistics Management*, 9, (2), 1–19.
Larson, Paul D. and Arni Haldorsson (2004), 'Logistics versus supply chain management: an international survey', *International Journal of Logistics: Research and Applications*, 7 (1), 17–31.
LCG (2005), *China Logistics Sector Review*, Hong Kong, HK: Latitude Capital Group, available at http://www.latitudecapitalgroup.com/document/2005/0505_china_logistics.pdf (accessed 14 March 2013).
Lee, Chang Jae, Kyung Bang Ho, Kwon Na Seoung and Boram Lee (2013), 'Trilateral Economic Cooperation (TEC): proposal for enhancing economic cooperation dialogue channels among China, Japan and Korea', *World Economy Update*, 3 (20), 1–8, available at www.kiep.go.kr/include/filedown.jsp?fname=WEU-13-20.pdf (accessed 11 June 2013).
Lee, Hau L. (2004), 'The Triple-A Supply Chain', *Harvard Business Review*, 82 (10), 102–12.
Lee, Jae-ho and Sangyeong Mun (2008), 'Direction for Korean logistics industry', excerpted from Ju-hun Kim and Mun-jung Cha, *Policy Tasks for the Advancement of Service Sectors*, KDI Research Report 2008-4, Seoul, KR: Korea Development Institute, available at http://www.koreafocus.or.kr/design2/layout/contenet_print.asp (accessed 15 June 2009).
Lee, Sang Keun (2009), 'The changes of logistics environment and the

strategies of enterprises', 1st International Logistics Forum of Northeast Asia, Seoul, KR, available at http://www.sylogis.co.kr/jboard/download.php?file_name...pdf&file (accessed 28 September 2012).

Lee, Taihyeong (2013), 'Directions for sea-land intermodal transport in Northeast Asia', Seminar on Development of a Comprehensive Transport and Logistics Network in North-East Asian Subregion, 22 March, Seoul, Bangkok, TH: United Nations Economic and Social Commission for Asia and the Pacific, available at http://www.unescap.org/ttdw/common/Meetings/TIS/Logistics-in-NEA-2013/Logistics-in-NEA.asp (accessed 9 October 2013).

Lee, You-Il and Michael Hobday (2003), 'Korea's new globalization strategy: can Korea become a business hub in Northeast Asia?' *Management Decision*, 41 (5), 498–510.

Le Heron, Richard and Sam Ock Park (1995), *The Asian Pacific Rim and Globalization: Enterprises, Governance and Territoriality*, Aldershot, UK and Brookfield, VT, USA: Avebury.

Lenovo (2012), *2011/2012 Annual Report of Lenovo Group Limited*, Hong Kong, HK: Lenovo Group Ltd, available at www.lenovo.com/.../lenovo/.../report/E_0992201... - United States (accessed 11 March 2013).

Levinson, Marc (2006), *The Box: How the Shipping Container Made the World Smaller and the World Economy Larger*, Princeton, NJ, USA: Princeton University Press.

LFRC (2003), 'Potential of third-party logistics in China', *China Update*, Hong Kong, HK: Li & Fung Research Centre, 21 March 2003, available at http://www.idsgroup.com/profile/pdf/china_update/030321_log_market_potential.pdf (accessed 25 March 2009).

LFRC (2004), 'An overview of the logistics development in China', *China Distribution and Trading*, 12 (February), Hong Kong, HK: Li & Fung Research Centre, available at http://www.lifunggroup.com/research/china_did02.htm (accessed 12 February 2009).

LFRC (2006a), 'China's logistics industry update (2005–06)', *China Distribution and Trading*, 34 (July), Hong Kong, HK: Li & Fung Research Centre, available at http://www.funggroup.com/eng/knowledge/research/china_dis_issue34.pdf (accessed 13 March 2013).

LFRC (2006b), *Overview of the Industrial Clusters in China*, Industrial Cluster Series, No. 1, Hong Kong, HK: Li & Fung Research Centre, available at http://www.lifung.com/eng/global/home.php (accessed 27 March 2013).

LFRC (2007), 'China's logistics industry update (2006–07)', *China Distribution and Trading*, 39 (May), Hong Kong: Li & Fung Research Centre, available at http://www.funggroup.com/eng/knowledge/research/china_dis_issue39.pdf (accessed 13 March 2013).

LFRC (2008), 'China's logistics industry update (2007–08)', *China Distribution and Trading*, 53 (July), Hong Kong, HK: Li & Fung Research Centre, available at http://www.funggroup.com/eng/knowledge/research/china_dis_issue53.pdf (accessed 13 March 2013).

LFRC (2009), 'China's logistics industry update (2009)', *China Distribution and Trading*, 64 (July), Hong Kong, HK: Li & Fung Research Centre, available at http://www.funggroup.com/eng/knowledge/research/china_dis_issue64.pdf (accessed 13 March 2013).

LFRC (2010a), 'Analysis of the Economic Cooperation Agreement (ECFA) between China Mainland and Taiwan', *China Distribution and Trading*, 67 (July), Hong Kong, HK: Li & Fung Research Centre.

LFRC (2010b), *Update on Industrial Clusters in China (2010)*, Hong Kong, HK: Li & Fung Research Centre, available at http://www.funggroup.com/eng/knowledge/research/LFIndustrial6.pdf (accessed 27 March 2010).

LFRC (2011a), 'Consumption in Guangdong', *China Distribution and Trading*, 83 (May), Hong Kong, HK: Li & Fung Research Centre.

LFRC (2011b), 'China's logistics industry update 2011', *China Distribution and Trading*, 82 (May), Hong Kong, HK: Li & Fung Research Centre, available at http://www.funggroup.com/eng/knowledge/research/china_dis_issue82.pdf (accessed 13 March 2013).

LFRC (2012a), 'China's logistics industry update 2012', *China Distribution and Trading*, 96 (June), Hong Kong, HK: Li & Fung Research Centre, available at http://www.funggroup.com/eng/knowledge/research/china_dis_issue96.pdf (accessed 13 March 2013).

LFRC (2012b), 'China's logistics industry update 2012', *China Distribution and Trading*, 100 (September), Hong Kong, HK: Li & Fung Research Centre, Fung Group, available at http://www.funggroup.com/eng/knowledge/research/china_dis_issue100.pdf (accessed 13 March 2013).

LFRC (2012c), 'An update on the transport infrastructure development in China (2012)', *China Distribution and Trading*, 104 (September), Hong Kong, HK: Li & Fung Research Centre, Fung Group, available at http://www.funggroup.com/eng/knowledge/research/china_dis_issue104.pdf (accessed 25 March 2013).

LG (2009), *The People Company: 50 Years of LG Electronics*, Seoul: Young Nam, available at www.lg.com/au/corporate-information/overview/history (accessed 19 November 2012).

LG (2011), *LG Annual Report 2010*, Seoul, KR: LG Life's Good, available at www.lg.com/global/investor.../reports/annual-reports – United States (accessed 25 October 2012).

Liang, Haishan (2004), *Haier Supply Chain Management*, available at http://www.ceibs.edu/barcelona_c/images/20110329/31019.pdf (accessed 14 September 2013).

Libelium (2012), *50 Sensor Applications for a Smarter World*, Zaragoza, ES: Libelium Comunicaciones Distribuidas S.L., available at http://www.libelium.com/top_50_iot_sensor_applications_ranking/ (accessed 2 August 2012).

Liberal Party (2013), *Tony Abbott – the Coalition's Policy to Boost Manufacturing*, Canberra, AU, Liberal Party, available at http://www.liberal.org.au/latest-news/2013/08/21/tony-abbott-coalitions-policy-boost-manufacturing (accessed 16 September 2013).

Lim, Wonhyuk (2003), 'The emergence of the *chaebol* and the origins of the *chaebol* problem', in Stephan Haggard, Wonhyuk Lim and Euysung Kim (eds), *Economic Crisis and Corporate Restructuring in Korea: Reforming the Chaebol*, Cambridge, UK: Cambridge University Press, pp. 35–52.

Linfox (2011), 'Linfox home', Melbourne, AU: Linfox Logistics, available at http://www.linfox.com (accessed 28 February 2011).

Liu, Bing-lian, Shao-ju Lee, Zhilun Liao and Ling Wang (eds) (2011), *Contemporary Logistics in China: An Introduction*, Singapore, SG: World Scientific Publishing.

Liu, Bing-lian, Shao-ju Lee, Jian-hua Xiao, Ling Wang and Zhi-lun Jiao (eds) (2013), *Contemporary Logistics in China: Transformation and Revitalization*, Berlin and Heidelberg, DE: Springer Verlag.

Liu, Jianxin (2009), *Zhongguo bao quo kuai di shi chang qi pan jiao tong yun shu huan jing yi bu* [Parcel delivery market in China: looking forward to further improvements in the transportation environment], Beijing, CN: SINOTRANS Group.

Liu, Wei-lin, Lan-bing Li and Xiang Li (2013), 'Hot issues in China's logistics development', in Bing-lian Liu, Shao-ju Lee, Jian-hua Xiao, Ling Wang and Zhi-lun Jiao (eds), *Contemporary Logistics in China: Transformation and Revitalization*, Berlin, DE and Heidelberg, DE: Springer, pp. 147–90.

LM and WSJ (2013), 'Japanese car manufacturers tweak strategies to suit India', *Live Mint and Wall Street Journal*, 29 March, available at http://www.livemint.com/Industry/7AsDcOlKeFItehuxwFQZmK/Japanese-car-manufacturers-tweak-strategies-to-suit-India.html (accessed 14 October 2013).

Lombard, Marie-Christine (2006), *TNT: Growth in Europe and Emerging Markets*, Analysis Meeting, London, UK, 4 December, available at http://www.20061204_tnt_2006_analysts_meeting_presentation_marie_christine_lombard_english_tcm177-398327.pdf (accessed 21 March 2013).

Lufthansa (2012), *Traffic Rights: Certainty for Fair and Balanced Market Access*, Policy Brief 03/12, Lufthansa. October, available at http://www.lufthansagroup.com/fileadmin/downloads/en/policy-brief/10_2012/

LH-PolicyBrief-October-2012-Traffic-rights.png (accessed 24 April 2013).

Ma, Ji (2010), 'The logistics industry in China: development review and policies', presentation at the UN Economic and Social Commission for Asia and the Pacific Freight Forwarders, Multimodal Transport Operators and Logistics Service Providers Regional Forum, 15–16 July, Bali, Indonesia, Bangkok, TH: United Nations Economic Commissions for Asia and the Pacific, available at http://www.unescap.org/ttdw/FFmeeting/FFForum_2010/4.pdf (accessed 15 February 2012).

Maersk Line (2011), *The Maersk Line Service Network*, available at http://www.maerskline.com/link (accessed 6 March 2012).

Magill, Drew (2007), 'Aviation outlook 2030', paper delivered at Conference on Civil Aviation Futures, Incheon Airport, Incheon, Republic of Korea, 29 March.

Malecki, Edward J. and Hu Wei (2009), 'A wired world: the evolving geography of submarine cables and the shift to Asia,' *Annals of the Association of American Geographers*, 99 (2), 360–82.

Maltz, Arnold (2012), 'Global supply chains: other voices', *Journal of Supply Chain Management*, 48 (3), 3–6.

Mangan, John, Chandra Lalwani and Tim Butcher (2008 [2012]), *Global Logistics and Supply Chain Management*, 2nd edn 2012, Chichester, UK and New York, NY, USA: John Wiley & Sons.

Maring, Gary (2001), 'Freight issues and policy options', paper delivered at the Memphis Freight Planning Conference, 2 October, Washington, DC: FHWA Office of Freight Management and Operations, US Department of Transportation, available at http://www.ops.fhwa.dot.gov/freight/Memphis/appendix.../maring.ppt (accessed 5 June 2013).

Maritime Administration (2008), *National Port Gateway and Freight Corridor Strategy*, Washington, DC, USA: Maritime Administration United States of America available at https://www.nrf.com/modules.php?name=Documents&op...sp_id... (accessed 12 November 2013).

Matsushima, Daisuke (2008), 'Indo-ASEAN logistics network', in Nagesh Kumar (ed.), *International Infrastructure Development in East Asia – Towards Balanced Regional Development and Integration, ERIA Research Project Report 2007, No. 2*, Jakarta, ID: Economic Research Institute for ASEAN and East Asia, available at www.eria.our (accessed 26 February 2010).

McArthur, John B. and Ziming Rao (2009), 'Strategic cost structure choice in the transportation industry and its implications for organization growth and development in the People's Republic of China', *Journal of Business and Accounting*, 2 (1), 4–16.

McCormack, Gavan (2001), *The Emptiness of Japanese Affluence*, 2nd rev. edn, New York: MS Sharpe.

McCraw, Thomas (2007), *Prophet of Innovation – Joseph Schumpeter and Creative Destruction*, Cambridge, MA, USA: Belknap Press of Harvard University Press.

McIntire, Jonah and Chin Chye Lim (2010), 'A general model of supply chain visibility', *Supply Chain Council*, available at http://www.supply-chain.org/.../5- (accessed 12 March 2013).

McLaughlin, Heather and Colm Fearon (2013), 'Understanding the development of port and regional relationships: a new cooperation/competition matrix', *Maritime Policy and Management*, 40 (3), 278–94.

McMillan, Charles (2006), *Embracing the Future: The Atlantic Gateway and Canada's Trade Corridor*, prepared for the Asia Pacific Foundation of Canada, Moncton, New Brunswick, CA: Atlantic Canada Opportunity Agency (ACOA).

McMillan, Charles (2009), 'Global logistics and international supply chain management', in Hossein Bidgoli (ed.), *The Handbook of Technology Management, Volume 2: Supply Chain Management, Marketing and Advertising, and Global Management*, New York, NY, USA: Wiley, pp. 68–88.

Mentzer, John T., William De Witt, James S. Keebler, Soonhong Min, Nancy N. Nix, Carlo D. Smith and Zach G. Zacharia (2001), 'Defining supply chain management', *Journal of Business Logistics*, 22 (2), 1–25.

METI (2005), *Fiscal 2004 Pilot Demonstration Project for Construction of an Advanced Trade and Investment Environment: Report on the Demonstrative Project Relative to the Development of the Land Transportation Network in the Greater Mekong Economic Sub-region (Summary Version)*, undertaken by Sumitomo Corporation, Tokyo, JP: Ministry of Economy, Trade and Industry of Japan (administered by Japan Economic Trade Organization), Government of Japan, available at www.jetro.go.jp/thailand/e_activity/pdf/landtransportation.pdf (accessed 14 October 2013).

METI (2011), *White Paper on International Economy and Trade 2011*, Tokyo, JP: Policy Planning and Research Office, Trade Policy Bureau, Ministry of Economy, Trade and Industry, Government of Japan.

METI (2012), *White Paper on International Economy and Trade 2012: Extending the Frontiers of Growth Through Global Linkages*, Tokyo: Policy Planning and Research Office, Trade Policy Bureau, Ministry of Economy, Trade and Industry, Government of Japan.

METI (2013), *Joint Press Release with the Ministry of Land, Infrastructure, Transport and Tourism Announcement of the Fundamental Principles of General Logistics Policy (2013–2017)*, Tokyo, JP: Ministry of Economy, Trade and Industry, Government of Japan, available at http://www.meti.

go.jp/english/press/2013/0625_01.html (accessed 11 September 2013).
MGI (2009), *Preparing for China's Urban Billion*, San Francisco, CA: McKinsey Global Institute, available at www.mckinsey.com/.../urbanization/preparing_for_urban_billion_in_chi.. (accessed 11 June 2013).
MGI (2012), *Manufacturing the Future: The Next Era of Growth and Innovation*, San Francisco, CA, USA: McKinsey Global Institute, available at www.mckinsey.com/.../McKinsey/.../The%20Future%20of%20Manufacturi.. (accessed 25 September 2013).
MH&L (2004), 'Council of Logistics Management to become Council of Supply Chain Management Professionals', *Material Handling and Logistics*, available at http://mhlnews.com/global/outlog_story_5987/ (accessed 21 September 2012).
Millar, Mark (2007), 'China supply chain challenges', in Kerry Nelson (ed.), *Standard Chartered – Global Perspectives: The World Supply Chain Management and Logistics, 2007/2008*, 2nd edn, Hong Kong, HK: PPP Company Ltd, pp. 72–9.
Mitchell, Brian R. (2007), *International Historical Statistics: Africa, Asia & Oceania, 1750–2005*, 5th edn, Basingstoke, UK and New York, USA: Palgrave Macmillan.
Mitsuhashi, Ikuo (2000), 'Some issues and future direction of trade corridor in Northeast Asia', paper delivered at Northeast Asia Economic Conference, 26–27 January, Niigata, Japan, available at www.erina.or.jp/en/Ec/Forum2000/Sengen/sengen_e.pdf (accessed 28 October 2012).
MLIT (2006), *Recent Topics in Japanese Ports and Harbors*, Tokyo, JP: Ports and Harbor Bureau, Ministry of Land, Infrastructure and Transport, Government of Japan, available at www.mlit.go.jp/english/2006/k_port_and.../17.../ph_2_6_1.pdf (accessed 13 December 2012).
MLTM (2009), *Statistical Yearbook of MLTM*, Seoul, KR: Ministry of Land, Transport and Maritime Affairs, Government of South Korea.
MLTM, KITA and KOTRA (2009), *Logistics in Korea: Emerging Investment Opportunities*, Seoul, KR: Ministry of Land Transport and Maritime Affairs, Korea International Trade Association and Korea Trade-Investment Promotion Agency.
MMF (2010), *Global City Power Index 2010*, Tokyo, JP: Institute for Urban Studies, Mori Memorial Foundation.
Montague, Lord (2007), *The North–South Economic Corridor: Progress Towards a Full-Fledged Economic Corridor (July 2007): RETA-6310 Development Study of the North-South Economic Corridor Greater Mekong Subregion*, Metro Manila, PH, Asian Development Bank, available at www.adb.org/GMS/Economic-Corridors/NSEC-Stocktaking-Initiatives.pdf (accessed 25 February 2010).
MOT, MLIT, MLTM (2008), *Joint Statement of the Second China–Japan–*

Korea Ministerial Conference on Maritime Transport and Logistics: Okayama Declaration for Cooperation in Logistics in Northeast Asia, Ministry of Transport, China, Ministry of Land, Infrastructure, Transport & Tourism (MLIT), Japan, Ministry of Land Transport and Maritime Affairs (MLTM), Korea, Tokyo: Ministry of Land, Infrastructure, Transport & Tourism, available at http://www.mlit.go.jp/common/000015410.pdf (accessed 22 August 2013).

MQ (2013), 'Three snapshots from China's next chapter', *McKinsey Quarterly*, San Francisco, CA, USA: McKinsey, available at http://www.mckinsey.com/insights/economic_studies/three_snapshots_from_chinas_next_chaptee (accessed 11 June 2013).

MSC (2012), *Mediterranean Shipping Company*, Geneva: MSC, available at http://www.mscgva.ch/about_us/agents.html (accessed 15 March 2012).

Mustafa, Monica A. and Charles Kunaka (2012), *Developing a Trade Corridor Management Toolkit*, Washington, DC: World Bank, International Trade Department, available at http://www.comcec.org/UserFiles/File/ulastirma/sunumlar/Corridor%20Toolkit%20%28by%20C.%20Kunaka-A.Mustra%29.pdf (accessed 21 August 2013).

NAFI (2008), *The North American Trade Corridors*, Montreal, CA: North American Forum on Integration, available at http://www.finanafi.org/eng/integ/corridors.asp?langue=eng&menu=integ (accessed 16 October 2012).

Nagel, Pieter (2007), *A National Logistics City: Securing Australia's Global Competitiveness*, Melbourne, AU: Institute for Logistics and Supply Chain Management, Victoria University, available at www.supply-chainvictoria.com.au/resources/NationalLogisticsCity.pdf (accessed 20 December 2010).

Nakagawa, Ryoji (2005), 'The revival of "Northeast Asia": why have Japanese opinion leaders begun to speak of "Northeast Asia"?' *Ritsumeikan International Affairs*, 3, 81–104, available at http://www.ritsumei.ac.jp/acd/re/k-rsc/ras/04_publications/ria.../03_6.pdf (accessed 16 October 2013).

Naslund, Dag and Steven Williamson (2010), 'What is management in supply chain management: definitions, frameworks and terminology', *Journal of Management Policy and Practice*, 11 (4), 12–28, available at www.na-businesspress.com/JMPP/NaslundWeb.pdf (accessed 22 December 2013).

NBSC (2010), *2010 China Statistical Yearbook 2010*, compiled by National Bureau of Statistics of China, Beijing, CN: China Statistics Press.

NBSC (2011), *2011 China Statistical Yearbook*, compiled by National Bureau of Statistics of China, Beijing, CN: China Statistics Press.

NBSC (2013), *2012 China Statistical Yearbook*, compiled by National Bureau of Statistics of China, Beijing, CN: China Statistics Press.

NC (2005–12), *BizReport: Non-Consolidated Financial Highlights*, Yokohama, JP: Nissin Corporation, available at www.nissin-tw.co.jp/nissine/ir/biz... (accessed 12 December 2012).
NCA 2050 (2005), *America 2050; A Prospectus*, National Committee for America 2050, New York, NY, USA: Regional Plan Association, available at www.America2050.org (accessed 17 October 2012).
NDRC (2012), *'Shi er wu' zong he jiao tong yun shu ti xi gui hua* [12th Five-Year Development Plan for an Integrated Transportation System], Beijing, CN: National Development and Reform Commission, available at http://www.ndrc.gov.cn/zjgx/t20120723_493203.htm (accessed 26 February 2013).
NDRC and CFLP (2009), *Di er ci quan wu liu yuan gu ji diao cha bao gao* [Second National Logistics Park Survey Report], Beijing, CN: National Development and Reform Center and China Federation of Logistics & Purchasing.
NE (2005–12), *Annual Report*, Tokyo, JP: Nippon Express, available at http://www.nipponexpress.com/hq/ir/annual/index.html (accessed 10 September 2013).
NE (2006), *PowerPoint Presentation: Aiming to be No 1 Logistics Provider: Nippon Express*, Tokyo, JP: Nippon Express, available at www.nipponexpress.com/.../Aiming-to-be-the-No-1-Logistics-Provider.pdf (accessed 15 February 2010).
NE (2007), *Annual Report*, Tokyo, JP: Nippon Express, available at http://www.nipponexpress.com/hq/ir/annual/index.html (accessed 10 September 2013).
NE (2008), *Annual Report*, Tokyo, JP: Nippon Express, available at http://www.nipponexpress.com/hq/ir/annual/index.html (accessed 10 September 2013).
NE (2009), *Fact Book 2009: Year Ended March 31 2009*, Tokyo, JP: Nippon Express, available at www.nipponexpress.com/hq/ir/fact/index.html (accessed 15 February 2010).
NE (2010), *Annual Report*, Tokyo, JP: Nippon Express, available at http://www.nipponexpress.com/hq/ir/annual/index.html (accessed 10 September 2013).
NE (2012), *Annual Report*, Tokyo, JP: Nippon Express, available at http://www.nipponexpress.com/hq/ir/annual/index.html (accessed 10 September 2013).
NEAL-NET (2012), 'A [*sic*] introduction to NEAL-NET [Northeast Asia Logistics Information Service Network]', UNESCAP Regional Forum of Freight Forwarders, Mulitimodal Operators and Logistics Service Providers, Bangkok, 13 June 2012, Bangkok, TH: United Nations Economic and Social Commission (UNESCAP), available at http://

www.unescap.org/ttdw/ffmeeting/ffforum-2012/8.intro-of-neal-net.pdf (accessed 16 October 2013).

Nettsträter, Andreas, Jan R. Nopper, Christian Prasse, Michael ten Hompe (2010), 'The Internet of Things', in *Proceedings 2010 European Conference on Smart Objects: Systems, Technologies and Applications, Ciudad Spain*, Berlin, GE: VDE Verlag GMBH.

Ng, Adolf K.Y. and Gordon Wilmsmeier (2012), 'The geography of maritime transportation: space as a perspective in maritime transport research', *Maritime Policy and Management*, 39 (2), 127–32.

Niehues, Alexander, Justin Zubrod and Edward Tse (2007), *Express Opportunities in China – Packaging a Strategy for the International and Domestic Express Delivery Market*, McLean, VA, USA: Booz Allen Hamilton, available at http://www.boozallen.com/capabilities/Industries/industries_article/32222948?lpid=658822 (accessed 15 February 2009).

NIRA (2006), *A Grand Design for Northeast Asia: 2005 – national land planning and sectoral development strategies – (Volume 2)*, NIRA Research Output 2006 No. 0602, Tokyo: National Institute for Research Advancement, available at http://www.nira.or.jp/past/publ/routp/html/no0602.html (accessed 28 October 2012).

NIRA (2007), *Proposal for Promotion of the Realization of the BESETO Corridor – Towards Sustained Development in the Northeast Asia Region, March 2007*, Tokyo, JP: National Institute for Research Advancement, available at www.nira.or.jp/past/newse/paper/beseto/proposal.pdf (accessed 28 October 2012).

Nogales, Alberto (2004), *China: Transport Brief*, East Asia and Pacific Region Transport Sector Unit, Washington: World Bank, 1 March, available at web.worldbank.org (accessed 8 March 2013).

Nor, T.N. Linda (2011), 'Hong Kong's role in Mainland China's logistics industry: from physical gateway to differentiated logistics provider', *Asian Survey*, 51 (4), 659–82, available at http://www.jstor.org/stable/10.1525/as.2011.51.4.659 (accessed 4 October 2011).

Notteboom, Theo E. (2004), 'Container shipping and ports: an overview', *Review of Network Economies*, 3 (2), 86–106.

Notteboom, Theo (2011), 'In search of routing flexibility in container shipping: the Cape Route as an alternative to the Suez Canal', in Theo Notteboom (ed.), *Current Issues in Shipping, Ports and Logistics*, Antwerp, BE: University Press Antwerp, pp. 271–95.

Notteboom, Theo E. and Jean-Paul Rodrigue (2012), 'The corporate geography of global container terminal operators', *Maritime Policy and Management*, 39 (3), 249–79.

NPU (2011), *Strategy for Rebirth of Japan: Cabinet Decision December 24, 2011*, Tokyo, JP: National Policy Unit, Cabinet Secretariat, available at www.npu.go.jp/policy/pdf/20120127/20120127_en1.pdf (accessed 23 November 2012).

NPU (2012), *Rebirth of Japan: A Comprehensive Strategy: Cabinet Decision – July 31, 2012*, Tokyo, JP: National Policy Unit, Cabinet Secretariat, available at www.npu.go.jp/policy/pdf/20120821/20120821_en.pdf (accessed 23 November 2012).

NS (2013), *2012–2013 nendo no keizai to kamotsu yusō no mitōshi (kaitei) (2012-nen 3-gatsu 28-nichi kōhyō)* [Revised economic and freight prospects in FY 2012], Tokyo, JP: Nittsū Sōken, available at http://www.nittsu.soken.co.jp/report/index.html (accessed 22 January 2012).

NSCB (2011), *Regional Accounts*, Manila, PH: National Statistical Coordination Board, available at http://www.nscb.gov.ph/grdp/2009/2009conper.asp (accessed 27 July 2011).

NTC (2006), '*Twice the Task; A Review of Australia's Freight Transport Tasks, February 2006*, prepared by Meyrick and Associates and Sinclair Knight and Merz Pty Ltd, Melbourne, AU: National Transport Commission, available at www.ntc.gov.au/DocView.aspx?documentid=01257 (accessed 10 March 2011).

NTC (2008a), 'Capacity constraints and supply chain performance – intermodal: Working Paper #1 – Understanding the international supply chain', prepared by Booz & Co., Melbourne, AU: National Transport Commission, available at www.ntc.gov.au/filemedia/.../BoozCoInterSCWkgPap1App1Mar09.pdf (accessed 1 March 2011).

NTC (2008b), 'Capacity constraints and supply chain performance – intermodal: Working Paper #2 – Options for enhancing supply chain performance', prepared by Booz & Co., Melbourne, AU: National Transport Commission, available at www.ntc.gov.au/filemedia/Reports/IntermodalSupChainWorkingPaper2.pdf (accessed 1 March 2011).

NTC (2008c), *Livestock and Meat Supply Chain Pilot Study Stage One Final Report National Transport Commission*, prepared by SD+D, Melbourne, AU: National Transport Commission, available at http://www.ntc.gov.au/filemedia/Reports/LivestockMeatSupChainStage1Rep.pdf (accessed 1 March 2011).

NTC (2008d), *National Transport Policy Framework: A New Beginning, February 2008*, advice to the Commonwealth Minister for Infrastructure, Transport, Regional Development and Local Government, 2 vols, Melbourne, AU: National Transport Commission, available at www.ntc.gov.au/filemedia/.../NationalTransportPlanVol1Mar2008.pdf (accessed 3 February 2011).

NTC (2009a), *Supply Chain Pilots: Draft Position Paper, March 2009*, Melbourne, AU: National Transport Commission, available at www.ntc.gov.au/DocView.aspx?DocumentId=01830 (accessed 10 March 2011).

NTC (2009b), *Capacity Constraints & Supply Chain Performance – Intermodal: Final Report – Toward Co-modalism*, prepared by Booz & Co., Melbourne, AU: National Transport Commission, available at www.ntc.gov.au/filemedia/Reports/IntermodalSupplyChainFinMar09.pdf (accessed 31 October 2013).

NTC (2009c), *Review of Coal Supply Chains: Final Report March 2009*, prepared by Synergies Economic Consultants, Melbourne, AU, National Transport Commission, available at http://www.ntc.gov.au/filemedia/Reports/ReviewofCoalSupplyChFinMar09.pdf (accessed 31 October 2013).

NTC (2009d), *Pilot Supply Chain Studies – Grain and Livestock Stage 2 – Final Report, National Transport Commission February 2009*, prepared by SD+D, Melbourne, AU: National Transport Commission, available at www.ntc.gov.au/.../Reports/GrainLivestockSupChainFinalFeb09.pdf (accessed 31 October 2013).

NTC (2012), *Working Together on Transport Reform: Submission to the Review of the NTC and Other Bodies*, Melbourne, AU: National Transport Commission, available at www.ntc.gov.au/filemedia/Reports/WorkingTogetherNTCsubmission (accessed 12 December 2013).

NTC (2013), *International Ports and Supply Chain Observations: Information Paper June 2013*, Melbourne, AU: National Transport Commission, available at www.ntc.gov.au/filemedia/Reports/InternationalPortsObserv2013.pdf (accessed 1 November 2013).

NTS (2013), *NTS Logistics Management Co. Ltd*, Shanghai, CN: NTS, available at http://www.ntslog.com (accessed 25 March 2013).

NWMA Spatial Vision Group (2000), *North West Metropolitan Area 'Spatial Vision'*, Bristol, UK: University of the West of England, available at http://3b.nweurope.eu/upload/documents/spatial_vision/1069.Spatial_Vision_eng.pdf (accessed 18 February 2014).

NYK (2005–12), *Annual Report*, Tokyo: JP: Nihon Yūsen Kabushiki Kaisha, available at www.nyk.com/english/ir/library/nyk (accessed 11 September 2013).

NYK (2007), *Nihon Yûsen shashi: sôritsu 100-shûnen kara no 20-nen / (henshû, seisaku Nihon Yûsen Kabushiki Kaisha Shashi Hensanshitsu)*, [NYK Company History; 20 years after the centenary – Produced by the company's editorial staff], Tokyo, JP: Nihon Yūsen Kabushiki Kaisha.

NYK (2009a), *Annual Report*, Tokyo, JP: Nihon Yusen Kabushiki Kaisha, available at http://www.nyk.com/english/ir/library/annual/index.htm (accessed 14 Febuary 2010).

NYK (2009b), *Medium-term NYK Group Management Plan: Revision of New Horizon 2010, October 27, 2009*, Tokyo, JP: Nihon Yusen Kabushiki

Kaisha, available at www.nyk.com/english/profile/plan/ (accessed 20 February 2010).

NYK (2009c), *Commencement of Discussion for Reorganization and Integration of Logistics Businesses of NYK and YAS November 2, 2009*, Tokyo, JP: Nihon Yusen Kabushiki Kaisha, available at www.yusen.co.jp/eng/ir/news/2009/pdf/091102_2.pdf (accessed 20 February 2010).

NYK (2009d), *Fact Book 2009*, Tokyo, JP: Nihon Yusen Kabushiki Kaisha, available at http://www.nyk.com/english/ir/library/factbook/ (accessed 20 February 2010).

NYK (2012), *Annual Report*, Tokyo, JP: Nihon Yusen Kabushiki Kaisha, available at http://www.nyk.com/english/ir/library/annual/index.htm (accessed 11 September 2013).

OAG (2010), *Overseas Airline Guide, February 2010*, Dunstable, UK: UBM Aviation Worldwide Ltd.

Oakden, Roger and Katia Leonaite (2011), *A Framework for Supply Chains: Logistics Operations in the Asia-Pacific Region*, Sydney, AU: McGraw Hill Australia Pty Ltd.

OECD (2004), *OECD Territorial Review: Busan Korea*, Paris, FR: Organisation for Economic Development and Co-operation, available at www.oecd.org/korea/oecdterritorialreviewsbusankorea.htm (accessed 19 November 2012).

Ohashi Hiroshi, Tae-Seung Kim, Tae Hoon Oum and Chunyan Yu (2005), 'Choice of air cargo transshipment airport: an application to air cargo traffic to/from Northeast Asia', *Journal of Air Transport Management*, 11 (3), 149–59.

Olivier, Daniel (2005), 'Private entry and emerging partnerships in container terminal operations: evidence from Asia', *Maritime Economics and Logistics*, 7 (2), 87–115.

O'Neill, Jim and Anna Stupnytak (2012), *The Long-Term Outlook for the BRICs and N-11 Post Crisis*, Global Economic Papers, No. 192, Goldman Sachs Global Economics, Commodities and Strategy Report, New York, NY, USA: Goldman Sachs, available at http://www.goldmansachs.com/our-thinking/archive/brics-at-8/brics-the-long-term-outlook.pdf (accessed 23 August 2013).

Oneworld (2011), *Oneworld at a Glance*, New York, NY, USA: Oneworld, available at http://www.oneworld.com (accessed 29 December 2011).

Ono, Keiichi (2009), *A New Partnership between Japan and the Mekong Region – Today and Tomorrow of the Relations between Cambodia, Lao PDR, Myanmar, Thailand and Viet Nam*, Tokyo: JP: Ministry of Foreign Affairs, First Southeast Asia Division, available at http://r-cube.ritsumei.ac.jp/bitstream/10367/922/1/RCAPS20091202.pdf (accessed 17 October 2013).

Oum, Tae Hoon (2008), 'Keynote presentation: air transport liberalization, market expansion and preparation of the key players', Hong Kong, HK: Hong Kong Polytechnic University, available at www.lgt.polyu.edu.hk/Event/IFSPA2008/.../Tae%20Hoon%20Oum.pdf (accessed 1 June 2010).

Oum, Tae Hoon and Jong-Hun Park (2004), 'Multinational firms' location preferences for regional distribution centers: focus on the Northeast Asian region', *Transport Research-E*, 40 (2), 101–21.

Oum, Tae Hoon and Katsuhiro Yamaguchi (2006), 'Asia's tangled skies', *Far Eastern Economic Review*, Jan.–Feb., 31–33.

Oum, Tae Hoon and Chunyun Yu (1999), *Shaping Air Transport in Asia Pacific*, Aldershot, UK and Burlington, VT, USA: Ashgate Publishing Ltd.

P&H (2014), 'Winners and losers: P3 alliance', *Ports and Harbors: Official Journal of International Association of Ports and Harbors*, 59 (1), 6.

Pain, Kathy (2007a), 'Global cities, gateways and corridors: hierarchies, roles and functions', International Conference on Gateways and Corridors, Winnipeg, Canada, 27–29 February, available at http://www.gateway-corridor.com/roundconfpapers/papers.htm (accessed 1 June 2011).

Pain, Kathy (2007b), 'Gateways and corridors in globalization: planning sustainable infrastructures for transcontinental "spaces of flows"', Round Table and Conference Papers, Canada's Asia-Pacific Gateway and Corridor Initiative, Vancouver, Canada, 2–4 May, available at http://www.gateway-corridor.com/calgaryroundtable/papers.htm (accessed 1 June 2011).

Palit, Amitendu (2006), 'Technology upgradation through global value chains: challenges before BIMSTEC nations', CSIRD Discussion Paper 13/2006, Kolkata, IN: Centre for Studies in International Relations and Development (CSIRD), available at www.csird.org.in/pdf/DP%2013.pdf (accessed 7 April 2011).

Pan, Ting (2008), 'Improving Huawei international supply chain', Master's thesis, Faculty of Business Administration, University of Twente, NL, available at essay.utwente.nl/58672/1/scriptie_T_Pan.pdf (accessed 8 April 2013).

Pang, Fushing (2005), 'Developing government relations to benefit the industry: TNT China', Eye for Transport China Summit, Shanghai, 12–13 July, London, UK: Eyefortransport, available at http://eyefortransport.com (accessed 20 November 2007).

Park, Yong An, Yungsook Choe, Jung Hyun Kim, Dong-woo Ha and Madan B. Regmi (2009), *Operationalization of International Intermodal Transport Corridors in North-East and Central Asia*, Seoul, KR: Korean Maritime Institute.

Parliament of the Commonwealth of Australia (1968), *Report from the Senate Select Committee on the Container Method of Handling Cargoes*, Canberra, AU: Government Printer.

PCNABH (2003), *Presidential Committee on the Northeast Asia Business Hub*, October, available at www.nabh.go.kr (accessed 11 November, 2012).

PCNACI (2004), *Towards a Peaceful and Prosperous Northeast Asia*, Seoul, KR: Presidential Committee on Northeast Asia Cooperation Initiative (previously Presidential Committee on the Northeast Asia Business Hub), available at www.nabh.go.kr/english/about/greeting.html (accessed 21 August 2013).

PCRD (2011), *Presidential Committee on Regional Development*, available at http://eng.region.go.kr/index.jsp?mid1=00000003&mid2=00000010 (accessed 8 November 2011).

Petersen, Jon (2007), *Air Freight Industry – White Paper*, Atlanta, GA, UDA: Supply Chain and Logistics Institute, H. Milton Stewart School of Industrial and Systems Engineering, Georgia Institute of Technology.

Pettis, Michael (2013), 'Winners and losers in China's next decade: moving from investment to consumption, will drive some industries forward by hampering others', *McKinsey Quarterly*, 3, 37–9, available at http://www.mckinsey.com/insights/asia-pacific/winners_and_losers_in_chinas_next_decade (accessed 8 June 2013).

Pisano, Mark (2006), *Global Gateways: Being Competitive Participants in the Global Economy*, Los Angeles, CA, USA: Southern California Association of Governments (SCAG), available at www.iedconline.org/EDASymposia/Presentations/Pisano.pdf (accessed 16 October 2012).

Plowman, E. Grosvenor (1964), *Lectures on Elements of Business Logistics*, Stanford, CA, USA: Stanford University Graduate School of Business.

Popescu, Andreea, Pinar Keskinocak and Issam al Mutawaly (2010), 'The air cargo industry', reprinted from Lester A. Hoel, Genevieve Giulano and Michael D. Meyer (eds), *Intermodal Transportation: Moving Freight in a Global Economy*, Washington, DC, USA: Eno Foundation, pp. 209–37, available at www2.isye.gatech.edu/~pinar/Chapter7Eno.pdf (accessed 15 March 2014).

PR Newswire (2006), *AMR Research Releases Second Annual Supply Chain Top 25 [2005]*, New York, NY, USA: PR Newswire available at http://www.prnewswire.co.uk/news-releases/amr-research-releases-second-annual-supply-chain-top-25-153993785.html (accessed 10 January 2014).

PR Newswire (2009), *AMR Research Releases its 2008 Supply Chain Top 25*, New York, NY, USA: PR Newswire, available at www.prnewswire.com/.../amr-research-releases-its-2008-supply-chain-to (accessed 10 January 2014).

PRC (2005), *Zhong hua ren min gong he guo jia biao zhun GB/T 19680–2005, Wu liu qi ye fen lei yu ping qu zhi biao* [The People's Republic of China National Standards, GB/T19680-2005 Classification and Evaluation Indicators for Logistics Enterprises], available at www.whjtwl.com/u/cms/www/.../14162334pgkn (accessed 30 March 2013).

Proffitt, Michael (2006), 'A quantum leap for global supply chain efficiency', Air Cargo China / Transport Logistics China Conference, Shanghai, China, 21 September, available at http://media.nmm.de/23/proffitt_16390223.pdf (accessed 28 April 2013).

PSA (2011), *PSA Annual Report 2010*, Singapore, SG: Port of Singapore Authority, available at http://www.internationalpsa.com/about/annual-report.html (accessed 25 January 2011).

PwC (2006), *Retail and Consumer Outlook – Australia 2006: The Path Continues*, Sydney, AU: PricewaterhouseCoopers, available at www.pwc.com.au/industry/retail-consumer/.../rcoutlook_may06.pdf (accessed 14 October 2012).

PwC (2012), 'APEC's evolving supply chain', 2012 APEC CEO Summit, Vladivostok, Russia, 7–8 September, available at www.pwc.com.au/about-us/apec-ceo.../APEC-Supply-Chain-Sep12.pdf (accessed 21 September 2012).

Qantas (2013), *Qantas Annual Report 2013*, Sydney, AU: Qantas Airways Ltd, available at http://www.qantas2013.reportonline.com.au/ (accessed 18 February 2014).

Quelch, John A. (2005), *The Global Market: Developing a Strategy to Market Across Borders*, San Francisco, CA, USA: Jossey Bass.

Quelch, John A. and Katherine E. Jocz (2012), *All Business is Local: Why Place Matters More Than Ever in a Global Virtual World*, New York, NY, USA: Portfolio/Penguin.

Rahmatullah, M. (2010), 'Transport issues and integration in South Asia', in Sadiq Ahmad, Saman Kelegama and Ejaz Ghani (eds), *Promoting Economic Cooperation in South Asia: Beyond SAFTA*, New Delhi, IN: Sage, pp. 174–94, available at siteresources.worldbank.org/SOUTHASIAEXT/.../BeyondSAFTAFeb2010FullText.pdf (accessed 8 April 2011).

Rajkarnikar, Pushpa Raj (2010), 'Adequacy and effectiveness of logistics services in Nepal: implications for export performance', Asia-Pacific Research and Training Network (ARTNet) on Trade, Working Paper Series, No. 79, Bangkok, TH: United Nations Economic and Social Commission for Asia and the Pacific, available at http://www.unescap.org/tid/artnet/pub/wp.asp (accessed 7 April 2011).

RCL (2013), *Service Pattern*, Bangkok, TH: Regional Container Lines, available at http://www.rclgroup.com/SvcPtrn_02.asp (accessed 5 June 2013).

Regmi, Madan B. (2012), 'Review of transport and logistics development in Asia and Pacific', Seminar on the Development of an Integrated Transport and Logistics System in ASEAN and Pacific Region, Bangkok, 21–23 November, available at http://www.unescap.org/ttdw/common/Meetings/TIS/IntegratedTx-2012/Presentations/2.ESCAP-Mr.Regmi.pdf (accessed 1 October 2013).

Reich, Robert B. (1991), *The Work of Nations: Preparing Ourselves for 21st Century Capitalism*, New York, NY, USA: A. Knopf.

Reveley, James and Malcolm Tull (eds) (2008), *Port Privatisation: the Asia-Pacific Experience*, Cheltenham, UK and Northampton, MA, USA: Edward Elgar Publishing.

Reynolds-Feighan, Aisling (2013), 'Comparative analysis of air freight networks in regional markets around the globe', in James H. Bookbinder (ed.), *Handbook of Global Logistics: Transportation in International Supply Chains*, New York, NY, USA; Heidelberg, DE; Dordrecht, DE and London, UK: Springer, pp. 325–66.

Rickards, Jane (2012a), 'Shipping in a slump', *Taiwan Business Topics*, 42 (9), 13–22.

Rickards, Jane (2012b), 'Modernizing the airport', *Taiwan Business Topics*, 42 (4), 15–23.

Rimmer, Peter J. (1970), *Freight Forwarding in Australia*, Department of Human Geography Publication HG/4(1970), Canberra, AU: Research School of Pacific Studies, Australian National University.

Rimmer, Peter J. (1977), 'Freight forwarding: changes in structure, conduct and performance', in K.A. Tucker (ed.), *Economics of the Australian Service Sector*, London, UK: Croom Helm, pp. 167–207.

Rimmer, Peter J. (1986), *Rikisha to Rapid Transit: Urban Public Transport Systems and Policy in Southeast Asia*, Sydney AU: Pergamon Press.

Rimmer, Peter J. (1991), 'Internationalisation of the Japanese freight forwarding industry', *Asian Geographer*, 10 (1), 17–38.

Rimmer, Peter J. (1994), 'Regional integration in Pacific Asia', *Environment and Planning A*, 26 (11), 1731–59.

Rimmer, Peter J. (1995), 'The political geography of transport infrastructure development in Korea', in J. Cotton (ed.), *Politics and Policy in the New Korean State: From Roh Tae-woo to Kim Young-sam*, New York, NY, USA: St Martin's Press, pp. 199–225.

Rimmer, Peter J. (1996a), 'Airlines as information networks: Qantas and Singapore Airlines', in H.W. Dick (ed.), *Airline Deregulation in the Asia-Pacific: Towards Open Skies?* Sydney: Institute of Transport Studies, pp. 63–94.

Rimmer, Peter J. (1996b), 'Taiwan's prospects as an Asian Pacific regional operations center', in David Hensher, Jenny King and Tae Hoon Oum (eds), *World Transport Research Proceedings of the 7th World Conference on Transport Research Sydney, Australia*, Volume 3: Transport Policy, Sydney, AU: Pergamon, pp. 587–601.

Rimmer, Peter J. (1996c), 'Australian freight forwarding revisited: Brambles Mayne Nickless and TNT since the mid-1980s', in D. Hensher, J. King and T.H. Oum (eds), *World Transport Research, Volume 4 Transport Management*, Oxford, UK: Pergamon, pp. 73–86.

Rimmer, Peter J. (1997a), 'Global network firms in transport and communications: Japan's NYK, KDD and JAL?', in Peter J. Rimmer (ed.) *Pacific Rim Development: Integration and Globalisation in East Asia*, Sydney, AU: Allen & Unwin, pp. 83–113.

Rimmer, Peter J. (1997b), 'China's infrastructure and economic development in the 21st Century', *Futures*, 29 (4–5), 435–65.

Rimmer, Peter J. (1998a), 'Ocean liner shipping services: corporate restructuring and port selection/competition', *Asia-Pacific Viewpoint*, 39 (2), 193–208.

Rimmer, Peter J. (1998b), 'Urban and regional development', in Patrick Heenan (ed.), *Japan Handbook*, Chicago, IL, USA: Francis Dearborn Publishers, pp. 155–81.

Rimmer, Peter J. (1999), 'The Asia-Pacific Rim's transport and telecommunications systems: spatial structure and corporate control since the mid-1980s', *GeoJournal*, 48 (1), 43–65.

Rimmer, Peter J. (2001), 'A cul-de-sac off Main Street: transport', in Christopher Sheil (ed.), *Globalisation: Australian Impacts*, Sydney, AU: UNSW Press, pp. 35–57.

Rimmer, Peter J. (2003), 'The spatial restructuring of Northeast Asia in the new millennium', *Korea Observer*, 34 (3), 559–88.

Rimmer, Peter J. (2004a), 'Global flows, local hubs, platforms and corridors: regional and economic integration in Northeast Asia', *Journal of International Trade and Logistics*, 1 (2), 1–24.

Rimmer, Peter J. (2004b), 'Marketing Incheon: gateway for Seoul, Northeast Asia and the world', *Journal of International Trade and Logistics*, 2 (2), 99–121.

Rimmer, Peter J. (2005a), 'Australia through the prism of Qantas', *Bulletin of Australian Studies, Otemon Gakuin University*, 31, 135–57.

Rimmer, Peter J. (2005b), 'Towards a more integrated transportation market in Northeast Asia: considering a proposal for regional coordinating committee', in Kang Jae-Hong and Sungwon Lee (eds), *Policymaking for an Integrated Transport Market for China, Japan and Korea*, Seoul, KR and Honolulu, HI, USA: Korea Transport Institute and The East-West Center, pp. 198–258.

Rimmer, Peter J. (2006a), 'Asian-Pacific Rim: developmental state and regional integration: Volume One The Japanese ascendancy, Volume Two Integrating the Asian-Pacific Rim', unpublished DLitt. thesis, Australian National University, Canberra, Australia.

Rimmer, Peter J. (2006b), 'Engineer Kondoh's collection lives on', National Library of Australia, *NLA News*, 16 (5), 15–18.

Rimmer, Peter J. (2007), 'Port dynamics since 1965: past patterns, current conditions and future directions', *Journal of International Trade and Logistics*, 5 (1), 75–97.

Rimmer, Peter J. (2008), 'Modelling the Port of Gunsan's potential: echoes of the Japanese "Construction State"', *Korea Review of International Studies (KRIS)*, 11 (1), 3–15.

Rimmer, Peter J. (2011), 'Evolving transport and logistics networks', in Won Bae Kim, Yue-man Yeung and Sang-Chuel Cho (eds), *Collaborative Regional Development in Northeast Asia: Towards a Sustainable Regional and Sub-Regional Future*, Hong Kong, HK: Chinese University Press, pp. 117–50.

Rimmer, Peter J. and Claude Comtois (2002), 'China's transport and communications firms: transforming national champions into global players', *Asia Pacific Viewpoint*, 43 (1), 93–114.

Rimmer, Peter J. and Claude Comtois (2005), 'China's extra- and intra-Asian liner shipping connections, 1990–2000', *Journal of International Logistics and Trade*, 3 (1), 75–98.

Rimmer, Peter J. and Claude Comtois (2009), 'China's container related dynamics, 1995–2005', *GeoJournal*, 74 (1), 35–50.

Rimmer, Peter J. and Howard Dick (2009), *The City in Southeast Asia: Patterns, Processes and Policy*, Singapore, SG: NUS Press.

Rimmer, Peter J. and Howard Dick (2010), *Appropriate Economic Space for Transnational Infrastructural Projects: Gateways, Multimodal Corridors, and Special Economic Zones*, ADBI Working Paper Series, No. 237, Tokyo, JP: Asian Development Bank Institute, available at http://www.adbi.org/files/2010.08.06.wp237.asia.transnational.infrastructural.projects.pdf (accessed 7 September 2013).

Rimmer, Peter J. and Howard Dick (2012), 'Economic space for transnational infrastructure: gateways, multimodal corridors and special economic zones', in Bhattacharyay Biswa Nath, Masahiro Kawai and Rajat M. Nag (eds), *Infrastructure for Asian Connectivity*, Cheltenham, UK and Northampton, MA, USA: Edward Elgar Publishing, pp. 217–53.

Rimmer, Peter and Howard Dick (2013), 'The historical dimension', in Michele Acuto and Wendy Steele (eds), *Global City Challenges: Debating a Concept, Improving the Practice*, Basingstoke, UK and New York, NY, USA: Palgrave Macmillan, pp. 63–87.

Rimmer, Peter J. and Mary Krome Hamilton (2005), 'Personal communication', Incheon, KR, 19 May.

Rimmer, Peter J. and Mary Krome Hamilton (2008), 'Integrating the supply chain management system operated by multinational corporations within global logistics', *Journal of International Logistics and Trade*, 6 (1), 47–55.

Rimmer, Peter J. and Il-Soo Jun (2000), 'A vision for an integrated transportation system in Northeast Asia', in Il-Soo Jun (ed.), *Creating A Regional Transportation System in Northeast Asia*, Seoul, KR and Honolulu, HI, USA: Korea Transport Institute and East–West Center, pp. 363–415.

Rimmer, Peter J. and Booi Kam (2013), 'Personal communication', Melbourne, AU, 27 August.

Rimmer, Peter J., Minsung Kim and Sang-Yoon Lee (2007), *Student Handbook 2007: Graduate School of Logistics – Master of Global Logistics Management*, Incheon, KR: Inha University.

Rimmer, Peter J. and Paul T.W. Lee (2007), 'Repercussions of impeding shipping in the Malacca and Singapore Straits', *Journal of International Trade and Logistics*, 5 (1), 7–26.

Rimmer, Peter J. and Michael J. Taylor (1987), 'Freight forwarding', in Peter J. Rimmer (ed.), *The ASEAN Australian Transport Interchange: Proceedings of the 1985 Australian Workshop for Senior ASEAN Transport Officials*, Canberra, AU: National Centre for Development Studies, pp. 283–301.

RIS (2007), *Restoring the Afghanistan–Pakistan–India–Bangladesh–Myanmar (APBIM) Corridor: Towards a New Silk Road*, RIS Policy Briefs, No 30, New Delhi, IN: Research and Information Systems for Developing Countries, http://www.ris.org.in/ (accessed 7 April 2011).

Robinson, Ross (2002), 'Ports as elements in value-driven chain systems: the new paradigm', *Maritime Policy and Management*, 29 (3), 241–55.

Rodrigue, Jean-Paul (1996), 'Transportation corridors in Pacific Asian urban regions', in David A. Hensher and Jennifer King (eds), *Proceedings of the 7th World Conference on Transport Research, Volume 3: Transport Policy*, Sydney, AU: Pergamon, pp. 571–86, available at http://people.hofstra.edu/Jean-paul_Rodrigue/downloads/transport%20corridors%20in%20pacific%20asia.pdf (accessed 21 August 2013).

Rodrigue, Jean-Paul (2012), 'The geography of global supply chains: evidence from third-party logistics', *Journal of Supply Chain Management*, 48 (3), 15–23.

Rodrigue, Jean-Paul, Claude Comtois and Brian Slack (2013), 'The evolution of a port (The Anyport Model)', *The Geography of Transport Systems*, 3rd edn, available at http://people.hofstra.edu/geotrans/eng/ch4en/conc4en/portdev.html (accessed 20 May 2013).

Rodrigue, Jean-Paul and Theo Notteboom (2013), 'Containerized freight distribution in North America and Europe', in James H. Bookbinder (ed.), *Handbook of Global Logistics: Transportation in International Supply Chains*, New York, NY, USA; Heidelberg, DE; Dordrecht, DE and London, UK: Springer, pp. 219–46.

Roh, Hong-Seung (2012), 'Sustainable transport and green logistics in Korea', UNESCAP Regional Forum of Freight Forwarders, Mulitimodal Operators and Logistics Service Providers, Bangkok, 13 June, Bangkok, TH: United Nations Economic and Social Commission (UNESCAP), available at http://www.unescap.org/ttdw/ffmeeting/ffforum-2012/8.intro-of-neal-net.pdf (accessed 16 October 2013).

ROK (2001), *The Fourth Comprehensive National Territorial Plan in Korea (2000–2020): Government of the Republic of Korea*, Seoul, KR: Ministry of Construction and Transport and Korea Institute for Human Settlements, available at www.mltm.go.kr/...//N...//20031008145200_국토4차계획_영문.pdf (accessed 19 November 2012).

ROK (2002), *Jae-4-cha Kuk to Jung-hab Gae-wheok, 2000–2020* [The Fourth Comprehensive National Territorial Plan, 2000–2020]. Seoul, KR: Dae Han Min Kuk Jung Pan (Republic of Korea).

Rosenberg, D. (2005), 'Managing the resources of the China Seas: China's bilateral fisheries agreement with Japan, South Korea and Vietnam', *Asia-Pacific Journal: Japan Focus*, ID 1789, available at http://japanfocus.org/article.asp?id-319 (accessed 10 June 2010).

Rozman, Gilbert (2004), *Northeast Asia's Stunted Regionalism: Bilateral Distrust in the Shadow of Globalization*, Cambridge, UK: Cambridge University Press.

RWBL (2007), *Transport and Logistics: Third Party Logistics – Industrial Research, July 2007*, Milwaukee, WI, USA: Robert W. Baird Ltd, available at www.werc.org/publications/publication.aspx?PublicationId=217 (accessed 8 October 2012).

Sahoo, Pravakar (2011), *Transport Infrastructure in India: Developments, Challenges and Lessons from Japan*, V.R.F. [Visiting Research Fellow] Series, No. 467 (March), Tokyo, JP: Institute for Developing Economies and Japan External Trade Organization, available at www.ide.go.jp/English/Publish/Download/Vrf/pdf/465.pdf (accessed 8 January 2014).

Samsung (2011), *Samsung Electronics Annual Report 2010*, Seoul KR: Samsung Electronics, available at www.samsung.com ›... › Financial information (accessed 9 September 2012).

Sandberg, E. (2007), 'The role of top management in supply chain management practices', unpublished PhD dissertation, Linköping University, Linköping, available at http://liu.divaportal.org/smash/record.jsf?pid=diva2:16980 (accessed 6 June 2011).

Sarkar, Jayanta (2010), *North East and BIMSTEC: Made for Each Other?*, CSIRD Policy Brief, 30 June, Kolkata, IN: Centre for Studies in International Relations and Development (CSIRD), available at http://www.csird.org.in/ (accessed 7 April 2011).

Sawai, Yasuo (2004), 'New evolution of research on a grand design for Northeast Asia', 13th Northeast Asia Economic Forum (NEAF), Inter-Continental Hotel, Seoul, 17–18 September, available at www.neaef.org/.../1-1_Yasuo%20Sawai%20Full%20paper.pdf (accessed 24 October 2012).

SB (2010), *Japan Statistical Yearbook 2011*, Tokyo, JP: Statistics Bureau, Ministry of Internal Affairs and Communications.

SB (2013), *Japan Statistical Yearbook 2014*, Tokyo, JP: Statistics Bureau, Ministry of Internal Affairs and Communications and Statistical Research and Training Institute, Ministry of Internal Affairs and Communications.

Scherer, Frederic M. and David Ross (1990 [1970]), *Industrial Market Structure and Economic Performance*, 3rd edn, Boston, MA, USA: Houghton Miffin.

Schiller Institute (2012), *Maps of Great Infrastructure Projects around the World: Infrastructure Development Corridor – Magnetically Levitated Trains*, available at http://www.schillerinstitute.org/economy/maps/maps2.html#maglev (accessed 16 October 2012).

Schmitt, Bernard (2011), 'Hyundai 4th largest automaker, overtakes Ford', *Truth About Cars*, available at http://www.thetruthaboutcars.com/2011/01/hyundai-4th-largest-automaker-overtakes-ford/ (accessed 12 November 2012).

Schumpeter, Joseph A. (1954), *History of Economic Analysis*, ed. Elizabeth Boody Schumpeter, New York, NY, USA: Oxford University Press.

Sd+D (2004), *The Integrated Transport Network: Market Power and Logistics Chains – An Integrated Logistics Network Discussion Paper*, September, Sydney, AU: Strategic Design + Development Pty Ltd, available at www.infrastructure.gov.au/transport/.../Freight_Consolidation.pdf (accessed 15 January 2011).

SE (2012), 'S.F. Express seeks e-commerce boost', *Sina English*, 23 May, available at http://www.english.sina.com/business/p/2012/0523/469935.html (accessed 1 March 2013).

SEJ (2013), *Number of Stores in each Administrative Division*, Tokyo, JP: Seven-Eleven Japan Co. Ltd, available at http://www.sej.co.jp/company/en/n_stores.html (accessed 20 November 2013).

Self, Will (2011), 'The frowniest spot on earth', *London Review of Books*, 23 (8), 1–5.

Sengupta, Sumantra (2008), 'A plan for building a new supply chain', *Supply Chain Management Review*, 12 (1), 46–52.

Seo, Sang-beom (2009), 'Korean global logistics company promotion', *Incheon International Logistics Forum, 2009*, 471–87 [Korean and English].

Seo, Sang-beom (2011), *National Logistics Plan in Korea*, Seoul, KR: Korea Transport Institute, available at http://www.elogistica.economia.gob.mx/swb/work/models/elogistica/Resource/23/1/images/Corea.pdf (accessed 2 April 2013).

SFE (2003–04), *Just-In-time (JIT) Manufacturing*, available at http://www.siliconfareast.com/jit.htm (accessed 3 February 2010).

SF Express (2013), *S.F. Express*, Shenzhen, CN, S.F, Express Co. Ltd, available at http://www.sf-express.com/cn/sc/ (accessed 28 February 2013).

Shambaugh, David (2012), 'Are China's multinational corporations really multinational?', *East Asia Quarterly*, 4 (2), 7–9.

Sheffi, Yossi (2005), *Resilient Enterprise: Overcoming Vulnerability for Competitive Advantage*, Cambridge, MA, USA: MIT Press.

Sheffi, Yossi (2012), *Logistics Clusters: Delivering Value and Growth*, Cambridge, MA, USA: MIT Press.

Shinohara, M. (2006), *European and Japanese Logistics Paradigms: An Explorative and Comparative Study of the Dynamics of Logistics Management*, Tokyo, JP: Maruzen Planet Co. Ltd, available at www.publishing.eur.nl/ir/repub/asset/7547/M.%20Shinohara%20Dissertation%202006-1.pdf (accessed 5 March 2008).

Shiraishi, Masaya (2010), 'Japan and the reconstruction of Indo-China', in Guy Faure (ed.), *New Dynamics Between China and Japan in Asia: How to Build the Future from the Past*, Singapore, SG: World Scientific, pp. 125–62.

SIA (2013), *Annual Report FY2012–13*, Singapore, SG: Singapore Airlines, available at http://www.singaporeair.com/jsp/cms/en_UK/global_header/annualreport.jsp (accessed 18 February 2013).

Simchi-Levi, David, Philip Kaminsky and Edith Simchi-Levi (2007), *Designing and Managing the Supply Chain: Concepts, Strategies and Case Studies*, 3rd edn, New York, NY, USA: McGraw Hill.

SK (2011), *Regional Income (2010) Preliminary*, Seoul, KR: Statistics Korea, available at http://kostat.go.kr/portal/english/news/1/8/index.board?bmode=read&bSeq=&aSeq=253494&pageNo=1&rowNum=10&navCount=10&currPg=&sTarget=title&sTxt= (accessed 31 October 2012).

SK (2013), *Korea Statistical Yearbook 2012*, Seoul, KR: Statistics Korea.

Skjøtt-Larsen, Tage, Philip B. Schary, Juliana H. Mikkola and Herbert Kotzab (2007), *Managing the Global Supply Chain*, Copenhagen, DK: Copenhagen Business School Press.

Sky Team (2011), *Sky Team*, available at http://www.skyteam.com (accessed 29 December 2011).

Slone, Reuben, J., Paul Dittmann and Tom Mentzer (2010), *The New Supply Chain Agenda, The Five Steps That Drive Real Value*, Boston, MA, USA: Harvard Business Publishing Corporation.

Smith, Laurence C. (2010), *The World in 2050: Four Forces Shaping Civilization's Northern Future*, London, UK: Dutton.

Smykay, Edward, W., Donald J. Bowersox and Frank H. Mossman (1961), *Physical Distribution Management: Logistics Problems of the Firm*, New York, NY, USA: Macmillan.

So, Gary (2005), 'Pan-China logistics – challenges & future strategies', Eye for Transport China Summit, Shanghai, 12–13 July, London: Eyefortransport, available at http://eyefortransport.com (accessed 20 November 2007).

Sony Corporation (2008–12), *Annual Report*, Tokyo, JP: Sony Corporation, available at http://www.sony.net (accessed 13 January 2013).

Sony Global (2012), *Press Room, Sony Global Headquarters*, Tokyo, JP: Sony Corporation, available at http://www.sony.net/pressroom/operat/index.html (accessed 17 January 2012).

Sorensen, Clark (2003), 'Cultural dimensions of quality of life for expatriate business talent in Korea', *Korea Observer*, 34 (3), 461–83.

SOV (2008), *Freight Futures: Victorian Freight Network Strategy for a More Prosperous and Liveable Victoria*, Melbourne, AU: State of Victoria, available at www.doi.vic.gov.au/doi/doielect.nsf/.../$FILE/freightfutures.pdf (accessed 28 February 2011).

Srinarawat, Maitree (2009), 'Panel discussion: regional logistics and supply chain development', ASEAN and GMS, 30 September, Grand Millennium Sukhumvit, Bangkok, available at www.linkpdf.com/download/.../microsoft-powerpoint-dr-maitree-.pdf (accessed 7 April 2011).

STAL (2009), *Shenzhen ST-Anda Logistics*, available at http://www.st-anda.com/en/about.asp (accessed 2 March 2009).

Stalk, George and Charles McMillan (2013), *Seizing the Continent: Opportunities for a North American Gateway*, Vancouver, CA: Asia Pacific Foundation of Canada.

Star Alliance (2011), *The Way the World Connects*, available at http://www.staralliance.com (accessed 29 December 2011).

Stone, Susan, Anna Strutt and Thomas Hertel (2012), 'Socio-economic impact of regional transport infrastructure in the Greater Mekong Subregion', in Biswa Nath Bhattacharyay, Kawai Masahiro and Rajat

M. Nag (eds), *Infrastructure for Asian Connectivity*, Cheltenham, UK and Northampton, MA, USA: Edward Elgar Publishing, pp. 95–131.

Subramanian, Uma and John Arnold (2001), *Forging Subregional Links in Transportation and Logistics in South Asia*, Washington, DC, USA: World Bank.

Suenaga, Satoshi (2004), *Japan's Technical Cooperation in Logistics*, Tokyo, JP: Technical Cooperation Division, Ministry of Economy, Trade and Industry (administered by Japan Economic Trade Organization), Government of Japan.

Sun, Yat-sen (1928 [1922]), *The International Development of China*, London, UK: Hutchison.

Supatn, Nucharee (2011), 'Industrial estates, ports, airports and city transport in the Greater Bangkok Area for promoting connectivity in the Mekong Region', in Masami Ishida (ed.), *Intra- and Inter-City Connectivity in the Mekong Region*, BRC Research Report No. 6, Bangkok, TH: Bangkok Research Center, IDE-JETRO (Institute of Developing Economies-Japan External Trade Organization), pp. 32–97, available at http://www.ide.go.jp/English/Publish/Download/Brc/pdf/06_chapter2.pdf (accessed 24 February 2014).

SYCG (2013), *Shanghai Yuan Cheng Logistics*, available at www.ycgwl.com (accessed 28 February 2013) [in Chinese].

Sys, Christa (2007), 'Measuring the degree of concentration in the container shipping industry', in A. Costa (ed.), *Proceedings of the NECTAR Conference*, Porto: Universidade do Porto – Engineer Faculty, available at http://www.feb.ugent.be/soceco/sherppa/members/christa/documents/paper1.pdf (accessed 27 May 2013).

Taillard, Christian (2010), 'Corridor linkages in the GMS', in Guy Faure (ed.), *New Dynamics Between China and Japan in Asia: How to Build the Future from the Past*, Singapore, SG: World Scientific, pp. 187–233.

Takeda, Toshio (2008), *Kansai Economy and its Challenges in the Global Era*, Osaka, JP: Institute for Social and Economic Research, available at www.apir.or.jp/ja/others/pdf/268_Pdf01.ppt (accessed 11 July 2012).

Takeuchi, Hiroshi (2007), 'The research on the cross-border transportation infrastructure; progressive development of regionalization', *JICA*, Tokyo, JP: Social Development Study Department, Japan International Cooperation Agency, available at www.jica.go.jp/infosite/issues/transport/pdf/cbti_eng04.pdf (accessed 25 March 2008).

Taniguchi, Eiichi and Toshinori Nemoto (2001), *Shitirojisutikusu – kōritsu teki de kankyō ni yasashii toshi butsuryū keikaku ron* [City logistics – efficient and environment friendly urban freight transport planning], Tokyo, JP: Morikita Publishing Co.

Tanimoto, Taniichi (2000), *Butsuryū: rojisutikusu no riron to jittai* [Theory and reality of transport and logistics], Tokyo: Hakutō Shobō.

Tanner, Travis, Yochiro Stao, Ren Xiao and Sung-Yoon Lee (2013), 'Northeast Asia's new leaders and the challenges ahead', *Asia Policy*, 15 (January), 45–68, available at http://asiapolicy.nbr.org (accessed 28 May 2012).

Tata (2012), *Tata Motors: 67th Annual Report, 2011–12*, Mumbai: Tata Motors, available at tatamotors.com/investors/financials/67-ar-html/downloads.html (accessed 7 September 2012).

Taylor, Peter J. (2001), 'Urban hinterworlds: geographies of corporate service provision under conditions of contemporary globalization', *Geography*, 86 (1), 51–60.

Taylor, Peter J. and David R.F. Walker (2004), 'Urban hinterworlds revisited', *Geography*, 89 (2), 145–51.

TDTW (2007), *Tianjin Datian Wuliu [DTW]*, available at http://www.dtw.com.cn/eng/about/dtls.htm (accessed 19 November 2007 [in Chinese]). Since removed from web.

TDTW (2013), *Tianjin Datian W. Group Ltd: DTW Logistics*, Beijing, CN: Tianjin Datian W. Group Ltd, available at http://www.dtw.com.cn/eng/about/jrdt.htm (accessed 14 March 2013).

TG (2011), *TeleGeography 2010*, Washington, DC, USA: PriMetrica, Inc.

Tiger Airways (2011), *Annual Report for the Year Ended 31 March 2011*, Singapore, SG: Tiger Airways http://www.tigerairways.com/au/en/ (accessed 18 April 2013).

Tinseth, Randy (2012), *Boeing: Current Market Outlook 2012*, Chicago, IL, USA: Boeing Commercial Airplanes, available at http://www.boeing.com/commercial/cmo/pdf/CMO_2012_Presentation.pdf (accessed 16 April 2013).

TISOC (2012), *2012 Review of the National Transport Commission and other Relevant Transport Bodies: Scoping Paper*, Transport and Infrastructure Senior Officials' Committee, Canberra AU: Commonwealth Department of Infrastructure and Transport, available at www.infrastructure.gov.au/transport/.../pg2_key_documents_scoping_pa... (accessed 10 December 2013).

TNT (2011), *TNT Annual Report 2010*, Hoofddoorp, NL. TNT N.V., available at www.postnl.com/.../TNT-Annual-Report-2010_tcm216-5... - Netherlands (accessed 19 July 2010).

TNT (2012), *TNT Express Annual Report 2011*, Hoofddoorp, NL. TNT N.V., available at www.tnt.com/.../Quarterly%20reports/.../AR2011/tnt-express-annual- (accessed 19 July 2012).

TNT (2013a), *Corporate Information, October 2013*, Hoofddorp, NL: TNT Express, N.V.

TNT (2013b), *TNT Express: China Locations*, Hoofddoorp, NL: TNT N.V., available at http://www.tnt.com/express/en_cn/site/home/about_us/tnt_locations_in_china.html (accessed 15 March 2013).

Toal, Gerard (2009), 'Movie geopolitics: response to Robert Kaplan's the Revenge of Geography essay', *Human Geography*, 2 (2), 48–51.

Toh, Keith T.K., Pieter Nagel and Roger Oakden (2009), 'A business and ICT architecture for a logistics city', *International Journal of Production Economics*, 122 (1), 216–28.

Toh, Mun-Heng (2012), 'Internationalization of tertiary education services in Singapore', ADBI Working Paper Series No. 388, October, Tokyo, JP: Asian Development Bank Institute, available at www.adbi.org/.../2012.10.12.wp388.internationalization.tertiary.edu. (accessed 9 April 2013).

Toll (2011), *About Toll: Milestones/Acquisitions*, Melbourne, AU: Toll Group, available at http://www.toll.com.au/milestones1.html (accessed 3 March 2011).

Toll (2012), *Annual Financial Report For the Year Ended 30 June 2012*, Melbourne, AU: Toll Group, available at www.tollgroup.com/reports (accessed 2 March 2014).

Toyota (2005–11), *Annual Report: Year Ended March 31*, Toyota City, JP: Toyota Motor Corporation, available at www.toyota-global.com/investors/ir_library/annual/ (accessed 21 August 2013).

Toyota (2012a), *Annual Report: Year Ended March 31*, Toyota City, JP: Toyota Motor Corporation, available at www.toyota-global.com/investors/ir_library/annual/ (accessed 21 August 2013).

Toyota (2012b), *Worldwide Operations: Toyota Motor Corporation – Global Website*, Tokyo, JP: Toyota Motor Corporation, available at http://www.toyota-global.com/company/profile/facilities/worldwide_operations.html (accessed 26 November 2012).

TPRI (2012), *Transport Efficiency through Logistics Development: Policy Study – Main Report*, Beijing, CN: Transport Planning and Research Institute.

Tranos, Emmanouil (2011), 'The topology and emerging urban geographies of the Internet backbone and aviation networks in Europe', *Environment and Planning A*, 43 (2), 378–92.

Tranos, Emmanouil (2013), *The Geography of the Internet: Cities, Regions and Internet Infrastructure in Europe*, Cheltenham, UK and Northampton, MA, USA: Edward Elgar Publishing.

Travelmath (2010), *Travelmath – Trip Calculator*, available at http://www.travelmath.com/ (accessed 8 July 2012).

Tretheway, Michael W. (1991), 'The characteristics of modern post deregulation air transport', Working Paper, University of British Columbia,

Faculty of Commerce and Business Administration, Vancouver, CA: University of British Columbia.

TUDB (2006), *'Sōgō butsuryū bijon' no kōhyō ni tsuite* [Vision of comprehensive logistics], Tokyo, JP: Tōkyōto toshi seibi kyoku [Tokyo Urban Development Bureau], available at http://www.toshiseibi.metro.tokyo.jp/topics/h17/topi037.htm (accessed 27 June 2012).

TURBLOG (2011a), *Deliverable 3: Urban Logistics Practices – Synthesis of Selected Case Studies: Joint Delivery Systems*, Transferability of Urban Logistics Concepts and Practices from a Worldwide Perspective (TURBLOG_WW), Brussels, BE: Directorate-General for Research, European Commission, available at http://www.transport-research.info/Upload/Documents/201307/20130703_153411_40208_D3_UrbanLogisticsPracticesSynthesisSelectedCaseStudies.pdf (accessed 21 August 2013).

TURBLOG (2011b), *Deliverable 3.6: Urban Logistics Practices – Case Study: Joint Delivery Systems in Tokyo*, Transferability of Urban Logistics Concepts and Practices from a World Wide Perspective (TURBLOG_WW), Brussels, BE: Directorate-General for Research, European Commission, available at http://www.transport-research.info/Upload/Documents/201307/20130703_154723_64123_D3.6_casestudy-TokyoJapan.pdf (accessed 21 August 2013).

Umezaki, So (2012), 'ASEAN–India connectivity: Comprehensive Asia Development Plan (CADAP), Phase 2', INCRIER Seminar on India–Japan Relations: Trends and Prospects, 29 February 2012, Claridges Hotel, New Delhi, India, available at www.eria.org/.../asean---india-connectivity-the-comprehensive-asia (accessed 10 October 2012).

UN (2010), *World Urbanization Prospects: The 2009 Revision*, New York, NY, USA: Population Division of the Department of Economic and Social Affairs of the United Nations Secretariat, available at http://www.esa.un.og/wup2009/unup/ (accessed 28 October 2010).

UNCTAD (2012), *Review of Maritime Transport 2011*, New York, NY, USA: United Nations Conference on Trade and Development, available at http://unctad.org/en/Docs/rmt2011_en.pdf (accessed 24 August, 2013).

UNESCAP (2012a), *Trans-Asian Railway (TAR)*, Bangkok, TH: United Nations Economic and Social Commission for Asia and the Pacific, available at www.unescap.org/ttdw/index.asp?...TheTrans-AsianRailway (accessed 9 October 2012).

UNESCAP (2012b), *Asian Highway*, Bangkok, TH: United Nations Economic and Social Commission for Asia and the Pacific, available at www.unescap.org/ttdw/index.asp?menuname=asianhighway (accessed 9 October 2012).

UNI-LC Japan (2012), 'Revised Postal Privatization Reform Law established: New Japan Post starts from October 2012', *Japan Post and Logistics Bulletin*, 14, Tokyo, JP: UNI (Union Network International) Liaison Council Japan, available at UNI LC Japan Post&Logistics BulletinU14.pdf (accessed 10 December 2012).

UPS (2006), 'UPS', Eye for Transport 2nd China Summit, Shanghai, 18–19 April, London, UK: Eyefortransport, available at http://eyefortransport.com (accessed 20 November 2007).

UPS (2012), *Annual Report*, Atlanta, GA, USA: United Parcel Service, available at http://www.investors.ups.com/phoenix.zhtml?c=62900&p=irol-reportsannual (accessed 17 February 2014).

UPS (2013), *Contact UPS: China*, Shanghai, CN: UPS Corporate, available at http://www.ups.com/content/cn/en/contact/index.html (accessed 1 February 2013).

USDA (2003), *China, Peoples [sic] Republic of: Market Development Reports – China Logistics Profile 2003*, GAIN Report No. CH3833, Washington DC, USA: United States Department of Agriculture Foreign Agricultural Service, available at http://www.fas.usda.gov/gainfiles/200312/146085452.doc (accessed 15 February 2009).

USDOT (2009), *Top 15 Global Third-party Logistics Providers: 2008*, Washington, DC: US Department of Transportation, Research and Innovative Technology Administration, Bureau of Transportation Statistics, available at http://www.rita.dot.gov/bts/sites/rita.dot.gov.bts/files/publications/freight_transportation/html/table_18.html (accessed 15 March 2014).

USDOT (2012), *Moving Ahead for Progress in the 21st Century (MAP-21)*, Washington, DC: Federal Highway Administration, US Department of Transportation, available at http://www.dot.gov/map21 (accessed 20 October 2012).

US GAO (2004a), *Transatlantic Aviation: Effects of Easing Restrictions on US–European Markets*, Report to Congressional Requesters, Washington DC, USA: United States Government Accountability Office, available at http://www.gao.gov/new.items/d04835.pdf (accessed 24 April 2013).

US GAO (2004b), *Commercial Aviation: Legacy Airlines Must Further Reduce Costs to Restore Profitability*, Report to Congressional Committees, Washington, DC, USA: US Government Accountability Office, available at www.gao.gov/products/GAO-04-836 (accessed 29 June 2013).

US News and World Report (2013), *Best Business Schools Specialty Rankings: Supply Chain /Logistics*, available at http://grad-schools.usnews.rankingsandreviews.com/best-graduate-schools/top-business-schools/logistics (accessed 23 April 2013).

Valentine, Vincent F., Hassiba Benamara and Jan Hoffmann (2013),

'Maritime transport and international seaborne trade', *Maritime Policy and Management*, 40 (3), 226–42.

Vattamattathil, Sreenivasan and Deepak Rangayyan (c. 2008), *Business Opportunities in Rail Logistics Parks in India: Study of the Indian Context with Focus on Vapi, Gujurat*, London, UK: Commonwealth Business Council, available at www.cbcglobal.org/CBCG_Library/Report%20for%20CBC.PDF (accessed 8 April 2011).

Vitali, Stefania, James B. Glattfelder and Stefano Battison (2011), 'The network of corporate control', *PLOS ONE*, 6 (1), 1–6.

Vollman, Thomas E., William Lee Berry, Clay Whybark and F. Robert Jacobs (2004), *Manufacturing Planning and Control Systems for Supply Chain Management*, 5th edn, Boston, MA, USA and London, UK: McGraw Hill Professional.

Voortman, Craig (2004), *Global Logistics: Management*, Landsdowne, Cape Town, ZA: Juta & Co. Ltd.

Walker, Andrew (1999), *The Legend of the Golden Boat: Regulation, Trade and Traders in the Borderlands of Laos, Thailand, China and Burma*, Richmond, UK: Curzon.

Walmart (2011), *Annual Report*, Bentonville, AR, USA: Walmart Corporate, available at www.walmartstores.com/sites/annualreport/2010/ (accessed 8 October 2012).

Walmart (2013), *Annual Report*, Bentonville, AR, USA: Walmart Corporate, available at http://stock.walmart.com/microsites/annual-report-2013/ourPerformance.aspx (accessed 4 February 2014).

Wang, Charles G. (2006), *China: CSCMP Global Perspective*, Oak Brook, IL, USA: Council of Supply Chain Management Professionals.

Wang, James (2007), 'Logistics in China', in Donald Waters (ed.), *Global Logistics: New Directions in Supply Chain Management*, 5th edn, London, UK: Kogan Page Publishers, pp. 391–402.

Wang, James, Daniel Olivier, Theo Notteboom and Brian Slack (2007), *Ports, Cities and Global Supply Chains*, Aldershot, UK and Burlington, VT, USA: Ashgate Publishing Ltd.

Wang, James J. and Michael C. Cheng (2010), 'From a hub port city to a global supply chain management centre: a case study of Hong Kong', *Journal of Transport Geography*, 18 (1), 104–15.

Wang, Ling (2013), 'Development of China's logistics', in Bing-lian Liu, Lee Shao-ju Lee, Jian-hua Xiao, Ling Wang and Zhi-lun Jiao (eds), *Contemporary Logistics in China: Transformation and Revitalization*, Berlin and Heidelberg, DE: Springer Verlag, pp. 1–15.

Wang, Qingyun (ed.) (2006), *Jiao tong yun shu fa zhan li lun yu shi jian* [China's transportation studies strategy, planning and policies], Beijing, CN: Zhongguo ke xue ji shu chu ban she.

Wang, Wei (2003), 'Retrospect and prospect of logistics development in China', paper presented at Tokyo Club for Global Studies, 20–21 February, available at http://www.tcf.or.jp/materials/asian_me.html (accessed 20 March 2013).

Wang, Yang (2005), *China Logistics: Past Present And Future*, Logistics Institute-Asia Pacific, National University of Singapore, Singapore, available at http://www.authorstream.com/Presentation/Flemel-18556-DHL-presentation-China-LogisticsPast-Present-Future-Survey-distribution-infrastructure-goods-service-effici-as-Entertainment-ppt-powerpoint/ (accessed 15 February 2009).

Ward, Peter D. (2010), *The Flooded Earth*, New York: Basic Books.

Waters, C. Donald J. (ed.) (1988 [2003]), *Global Logistics and Distribution Planning, Strategies for Management*, 4th edn 2003, London, UK: Kogan Page.

Waters, C. Donald J. (ed.) (2007), *Global Logistics: New Directions in Supply Chain Management*, 5th edn, 2007, 6th ed., 2010, London, UK and Philadelphia, PA, USA: Kogan Page Limited.

WATS (1995–2010), *WATS: World Air Transport Statistics*, 45th–54th edns, Geneva, CH: IATA Centre.

WATS (2011), *WATS: World Air Transport Statistics*, 55th edn, Geneva, CH: IATA Centre.

WEF (2012), *New Models for Addressing Supply Chain and Transport Risk*, Geneva, CH: World Economic Forum, available at www3.weforum.org/.../WEF_SCT_RRN_ (accessed 5 October 2012).

Weinberg, Bill (2010), *Will Android Drive Mobile Commodization [sic]?*, available at http://linuxpundit.wordpress.com/2010/05/26/will-android-drive-mobile-commodization/ (accessed 20 November 2013).

WG (2012), 'World metropolitan areas', *World Gazetteer*, available at http://worldgazetteer.com/wg.php?x=&men=gcis&lng=en&dat=32&srt=npan&col=aohdq&pt=a&va=&srt=pnan (accessed 27 October 2012).

WGL (2002), *Developing Singapore into a Global Integrated Logistics Hub, Report of the Working Group on Logistics (WGL)*, Singapore, SG: International Enterprise Singapore, available at www.mti.gov.sg/.../app.mti.../ERC_SVS_LOG_MainReport.pdf (accessed 31 October 2012).

Wijayasiri, Janaka and Deshal De Mel (2008), 'BIMSTEC–Japan cooperation in trade and investment: a Sri Lankan perspective', CSRID Discussion Paper No. 38, May, Kolkata: Centre for Studies in International Relations and Development (CSIRD), available at www.ips.lk/research/highlights/highlight_archive/2008/.../bimstec.pdf (accessed 7 April 2011).

Wilding, Richard (2013), *Supply Chain Management and Logistics:*

An Introduction to Principles and Concepts, Bedford, UK: Cranfield School of Management, Cranfield University, available at http://itunes.apple.com/gb/course/supply-chain-management-logistics/id500143911 (accessed 19 August 2013).

Wilding, Richard D. and Alan Braithwaite (2004), 'Laws of logistics and supply chain management', in Ed. Crainer and Des Dearlove (eds), *The Financial Times Handbook of Management*, London, UK: Pearson, pp. 249–59.

Williams, Alan (2006), *Developing Strategies for the Modern International Airport: East Asia and Beyond*, Aldershot, UK: Ashgate Publishing.

Wisner, Joel D., Keah-Choon Tan and G. Keong Leong (2008), *Principles of Supply Chain Management: A Balanced Approach*, 2nd edn, Mason, OH, USA: South-Western Cengage Learning.

World Bank (2005), *Best Practices in Corridor Management*, Trade Logistics Group, Washington, DC: World Bank, available at www4.worldbank.org/afr/ssatp/Open.aspx?id=539 (accessed 21 August 2013).

World Bank (2011a), *Gross Domestic Product, 2010, PPP*, available at http://siteresources.worldbank.org/DATASTATISTICS/Resources/GDP_PPP.pdf (accessed 28 July 2011).

World Bank (2011b), *World Development Indicators 2011 Database*, available at http://data.worldbank.org (accessed 21 August 2013).

World Bank (2011c), *The Recent Earthquake and Tsunami in Japan: Implications for East Asia*, Washington, DC, USA: World Bank, available at siteresources.worldbank.org/.../EAP_Update_March2011_japan.pdf (accessed 12 December 2012).

World Bank (2012a), *Data: Country Profiles*, World Bank, Washington, DC, USA: International Bank for Reconstruction and Development /World Bank, available at http://data.worldbank.org/data-catalog/country-profiles (accessed 17 December 2012).

World Bank (2012b), *World Development Indicators and Global Development Finance*, Washington, DC, USA: World Bank, available at http://data.worldbank.org/ (accessed 8 November 2012).

World Bank and DRCSC (2012), *China 2030: Building a Modern, Harmonious, and Creative High-Income Society*, Washington DC, USA and Beijing CN: World Bank and Development Research Center of the State Council, available at www.worldbank.org/content/dam/.../China-2030-complete.pdf (accessed 20 March 2013).

WOW (2010a), *Woolworths Limited Annual Report 2010*, Sydney, AU: Woolworths Ltd, available at http://www.woolworthslimited.com.au/phoenix.zhtml?c=144044&p=ww-working (accessed 6 March 2011).

WOW (2010b), *Woolworths Supply Link: Supply Chain*, Sydney, AU:

Woolworths Ltd, available at http://www.wowlink.com.au (accessed 6 March 2011).

WOW (2011), *Woolworths National Distribution Centre Directory*, Sydney, AU: Woolworths Ltd, available at www.wowlink.com.au/.../topic_centre?.../Topic%20Centre/... (accessed 6 March 2011).

Wynne, Michael (2001), *The Collusion and Price Fixing Scandal: Mayne Nickless*, available at http://www.uow.edu.au/~/bmartin/dissent/documents/health/mayne_collusion.html (accessed 4 January 2011).

Yamada, Hideo (1997), 'Supply-side economics and its mechanism: the reality of the ocean shipping economy', paper presented at the International Symposium on Liner Shipping, Hamburg, 21–23 April.

Yeh, Kuang-Shih (2013), 'The future development of Taoyuan Aerotropolis: promoting the international flow of people and goods', 8th APEC Transportation Ministerial Meeting 2013, Tokyo, available at http://www.apec-tmm8.org/english/pdf/outline/Session1-1-2.pdf (accessed 9 October 2013).

Yew, Lui Tuck (2013), 'Enhancing Singapore's transport infrastructure', 8th APEC Transportation Ministerial Meeting 2013, Tokyo, available at http://www.apec-tmm8.org/english/pdf/outline/Session2-1-3.pdf (accessed 9 October 2013).

YHCL (2005–10), *Annual Report: Year Ended March 31*, Tokyo, JP: Yamato Holdings Co. Ltd, available at www.yamato-hd.co.jp/english/investors/.../annualreport/index.html (accessed 1 July 2013).

YHCL (2011), *Annual Report: Year Ended March 31*, Tokyo, JP: Yamato Holdings Co. Ltd, available at www.yamato-hd.co.jp/english/investors/.../annualreport/index.html (accessed 1 July 2013).

YHCL (2012), *Annual Report: Year Ended March 31*, Tokyo, JP: Yamato Holdings Co. Ltd, available at www.yamato-hd.co.jp/english/investors/.../annualreport/index.html (accessed 1 July 2013).

Yoshida, Yu (2006), *The ASEAN Logistics Network Map: Brief Introduction of our Study in 2006 and Hereafter*, Tokyo, JP: Asian Cooperation Division, Trade and Economic Cooperation Department, Japan External Trade Organization (PowerPoint presentation), available at www.jetro.go.jp/malaysia/activities/aseanlogistics/index.../aseanlogmap.pdf (accessed 24 February 2010).

YRCW (2008), *Annual Report*, YRC Worldwide Inc: Kansas City, KS, USA, available at www.yrcw.com (accessed 27 February 2013).

YRCW (2009), *Annual Report*, YRC Worldwide Inc: Kansas City, KS, USA, available at www.yrcw.com (accessed 27 February 2013).

YRCW (2010), *Annual Report*, YRC Worldwide Inc: Kansas City, KS, USA, available at www.yrcw.com (accessed 27 February 2013).

YRCW (2011), *Annual Report*, YRC Worldwide Inc: Kansas City, KS, USA, available at www.yrcw.com (accessed 27 February 2013).

Yuen, Andrew, Leonardi J. Basso and Anming Zhang (2008), 'Effects of gateway congestion pricing on optimal road pricing and hinterland', *Journal of Transport Economics and Policy*, 42 (3), 496–526.

Zaidi, Adil (2010), 'Role of industrial corridors for regional integration and development – a Chennai–Ennore Economic (CEEIC) Initiative', New Delhi, IN: Ernst & Young, presentation at the Conference on India–East Asia Economic Integration: The Role of Economic Corridors and the Emerging Architecture sponsored by RIS (Research and Information Systems to Developing Countries), 10 September, available at www.ris.org.in/index.php?option=com_content&view...32 (accessed 7 April 2011).

Zapko, John (2009), 'World sourcing the supply chain', 94th Annual International Supply Management Conference, May, Charlotte, NC, USA, available at www.ism.ws/files/Pubs/Proceedings/09ProcBB-Zapko.pdf (accessed 15 January 2013).

Zapko, John (2012), *Inside Lenovo's Hybrid Supply Chain*, Supply Chain Council, Cypress, TX, USA: Supply Chain Council, available at http://www.supply-chain.org/.../Zapko-Inside_Lenovo's_Hybrid_Supply_Chain (accessed 15 January 2013).

Zhang, Anming (2007), 'Congestion pricing and capacity investment in a gateway-hinterland intermodal system', International Conference on Corridors and Gateways, Vancouver, Canada, 2–4 May, available at www.gateway-corridor.com/.../Zhang_Anming_Vancouver.pdf (accessed 1 September 2009).

Zhang, Anming, Yimin Zhang and Joseph A. Clogherty (2011), 'Competition and regulation in air transport', in Andre de Palme, Emile Quinet and Roger Vickerman (eds), *Handbook of Transport Economics*, Cheltenham, UK and Northampton, MA, USA: Edward Elgar Publishing, pp. 797–821.

Zhang, Chrystal B. (2009), *Analysis of China's Liberalization Policy with Respect to International Air Transport*, Bedford, UK: Cranfield University, available at http://www.garsonline.de/Downloads/100701/Chrysal_Zhang_Cranfield%20University_GARS_Paper.pdf (accessed 16 April 2013).

Zhang, Lily, Gary Liu and Peter Lorange (2010), 'Case 8: COSCO', in Bob De Wit and Ron Meyer (eds), *Strategy, Process, Content, Context: An International Perspective*, Andover, UK: South-Western Cengage Learning, pp. 748–9.

Index